Panel Data Econometrics

Panel Data Econometrics

Theory

Edited By

Mike Tsionas

ELSEVIER

ACADEMIC PRESS

An imprint of Elsevier

Academic Press is an imprint of Elsevier
125 London Wall, London EC2Y 5AS, United Kingdom
525 B Street, Suite 1650, San Diego, CA 92101, United States
50 Hampshire Street, 5th Floor, Cambridge, MA 02139, United States
The Boulevard, Langford Lane, Kidlington, Oxford OX5 1GB, United Kingdom

Library of Congress Cataloging-in-Publication Data

A catalog record for this book is available from the Library of Congress

British Library Cataloguing-in-Publication Data

A catalogue record for this book is available from the British Library

ISBN 978-0-12-814367-4

For information on all Academic Press publications
visit our website at https://www.elsevier.com/books-and-journals

Publisher: Candice Janco
Acquisition Editor: Scott Bentley
Editorial Project Manager: Susan Ikeda
Production Project Manager: Maria Bernard
Cover Designer: Miles Hitchen

Typeset by SPi Global, India

Dedication

Dedicated to John F. Geweke.

Contents

Contributors

Numbers in paraentheses indicate the pages on which the authors' contrbutions begin.

I-Lok Chang (289), Department of Mathematics (Retired), American University, Washington, DC, United States

Stefanos Dimitrakopoulos (147), Economics Division, Leeds University Business School, University of Leeds, Leeds, United Kingdom

William Greene (45), Department of Economics, Stern School of Business, New York University, New York, NY, United States

Stephen G. Hall (1), Leicester University, Leicester, United Kingdom, Bank of Greece, Athens, Greece, University of Pretoria, Pretoria, South Africa

Arne Henningsen (345), Department of Food and Resource Economics, University of Copenhagen, Frederiksberg C, Denmark

Géraldine Henningsen (345), Department of Management Engineering, Technical University of Denmark, Kgs. Lyngby, Denmark

Bo E. Honoré (197), Department of Economics, Princeton University, Princeton, NJ, United States

Chihwa Kao (175), Department of Economics, University of Connecticut, Storrs, CT, United States

Subal C. Kumbhakar (225), Department of Economics, State University of New York at Binghamton, Binghamton, NY, United States

Levent Kutlu (131), University of Texas at Arlington, Arlington, TX, United States; Istinye University, İstanbul, Turkey

Ekaterini Kyriazidou (197), Department of Economics, Athens University of Economics and Business, Athens, Greece

Wei Lin (21), Institute for Economic and Social Research, Jinan University, Guangzhou, People's Republic of China

Jatinder S. Mehta (289), Department of Mathematics (Retired), Temple University, Philadelphia, PA, United States

Christopher F. Parmeter (97,225), Department of Economics, University of Miami, Coral Gables, Department of Economics, University of Miami, Miami, FL, United States

Peter Pedroni (251), Williams College, Williamstown, MA, United States

Jeffrey S. Racine (97), Department of Economics and Graduate Program in Statistics, McMaster University, Hamilton, ON, Canada; Department of Economics and Finance, La Trobe University, Melbourne, VIC, Australia; Info-Metrics Institute, American University, Washington, DC, United States

P.A.V.B. Swamy (289), Federal Reserve Board (Retired), Washington, DC, United States

Kien C. Tran (131), University of Lethbridge, Lethbridge, AB, Canada

Peter von zur Muehlen (289), Federal Reserve Board (Retired), Washington, DC, United States

Fa Wang (175), Faculty of Finance, Cass Business School, London, United Kingdom

Jeffrey M. Wooldridge (21), Department of Economics, Michigan State University, East Lansing, MI, United States

Qiushi Zhang (45), Department of Economics, Duke University, Durham, NC, United States

Foreword

This book consists of two volumes, edited by E.G. Tsionas, that provide a broad and deep coverage of the literature about panel data. The first volume covers theory, and the second volume covers various categories of empirical applications.

This is not a textbook. There are some very good texts about panel data, including Arellano, *Panel Data Econometrics,* 2003; Hsiao, *Analysis of Panel Data*, 2003; and Baltagi, *Econometric Analysis of Panel Data*, 2013. A lot of material about panel data can be found in Wooldridge, *Econometric Analysis of Cross-Section and Panel Data*, 2010. These textbook treatments assume some knowledge of statistics and econometrics, but do not assume any prior knowledge about panel data techniques. This book is a collection of chapters that require some background in panel data econometrics and attempt to take the reader to the research frontier in the specific topic covered in the chapter. Compared to the texts listed above, this book will appeal to more advanced readers and will be extremely useful as a reference.

Some other edited books about panel data have the same general intent as this one, including Mátyás and Sevestre, *The Econometrics of Panel Data*, 2008, and Baltagi, *The Oxford Handbook of Panel Data*, 2015. The field of panel data is advancing quickly enough that being more up-to-date by even a few years is a significant advantage. Compared to the two other edited books cited, this book's chapters are narrower, but deeper, in scope. That is, they cover more specifically defined topics in more detail. In addition, many chapters contain a significant amount of new material. Although there is naturally some overlap in topics with the other edited books, there is less than might be expected. As a result this book will be interesting and useful even for people who already have access to all of the existing the panel data books.

Volume 1 (Theory) covers standard panel data topics such as dynamic models, nonlinear models, nonparametric methods, Bayesian methods, and panel cointegration. It also covers some important but less well-known topics, such as endogeneity in stochastic frontier models, panel VARs with binary data and implementation of estimation procedures for complicated panel data models. Each of the chapters is written by a leading expert about the topic.

Volume 2 (Empirical Applications) discusses a wide array of empirical applications in which panel data techniques have been or could be used. Some of these chapters also contain useful theoretical material, about topics such as spatial panels and factor models. A partial listing of fields of application that are covered includes education, banking, energy, transportation, health, and international trade. As in Volume 1, each of the chapters is written by a leading expert in the field.

The breadth and depth of the coverage of this book is impressive. It is an important reference work for anyone interested in research in or application of panel data.

General Introduction

Panel data always have been at the center of econometric research and have been used extensively in applied economic research to refute a variety of hypotheses. The chapters in these two volumes represent, to a large extent, much of what has been accomplished in the profession during the last few years. Naturally, this is a selective presentation and many important topics have been left out because of space limitations. The books cited at the end of this Introduction, however, are well known and provide more details about specific topics. The coverage extends from fixed and random effect formulations to nonlinear models and cointegration. Such themes have been instrumental in the development of modern theoretical and applied econometrics.

Panel data are used quite often in applications, as we see in Volume 2 of this book. The range of applications is vast, extending from industrial organization and labor economics to growth, development, health, banking, and the measurement of productivity. Although panel data provide more degrees of freedom, their proper use is challenging. The modeling of heterogeneity cannot be exhausted to fixed and random effect formulations, and slope heterogeneity has to be considered. Dynamic formulations are highly desirable, but they are challenging both because of estimation issues and because unit roots and cointegration cannot be ignored. Moreover, causality issues figure prominently, although they seem to have received less attention relative to time-series econometrics. Relative to time-series or cross-sections, the development of specification tests for panel data seems to have been slower than usual.

The chapters in these two volumes show the great potential of panel data for both theoretical and applied research. There are more opportunities as more problems arise, particularly when practitioners and economic theorists get together to discuss the empirical refutation of their theories or conjectures. In my view, opportunities are likely to arise from three different areas: the interaction of econometrics with game theory and industrial organization; the prominence of both nonparametric and Bayesian techniques in econometrics; and structural models that explain heterogeneity beyond the familiar paradigm of fixed/random effects.

1. Detailed Presentation

In Chapter 1, Stephen Hall provides background material about econometric methods that is useful in making this volume self-contained.

In Chapter 2, Jeffrey M. Wooldridge and Wei Lin study testing and estimation in panel data models with two potential sources of endogeneity: that because of correlation of covariates with time-constant, unobserved heterogeneity and that because of correlation of covariates with time-varying idiosyncratic errors. In the linear case, they show that two control function approaches allow us to test exogeneity with respect to the idiosyncratic errors while being silent on exogeneity with respect to heterogeneity. The linear case suggests a general approach for nonlinear models. The authors consider two leading cases of nonlinear models: an exponential conditional mean function for nonnegative responses and a probit conditional mean function for binary or fractional responses. In the former case, they exploit the full robustness of the fixed effects Poisson quasi-MLE; for the probit case, they propose correlated random effects.

In Chapter 3, William H. Greene and Qiushi Zhang point out that the panel data linear regression model has been studied exhaustively in a vast body of literature that originates with Nerlove (1966) and spans the entire range of empirical research in economics. This chapter describes the application of panel data methods to some nonlinear models such as binary choice and nonlinear regression, where the treatment has been more limited. Some of the methodology of linear panel data modeling can be carried over directly to nonlinear cases, while other aspects must be reconsidered. The ubiquitous fixed effects linear model is the most prominent case of this latter point. Familiar general issues, including dealing with unobserved heterogeneity, fixed and random effects, initial conditions, and dynamic models, are examined. Practical considerations, such as incidental parameters, latent class and random parameters models, robust covariance matrix estimation, attrition, and maximum simulated likelihood estimation, are considered. The authors review several practical specifications that have been developed around a variety of specific nonlinear models, including binary and ordered choice, models for counts, nonlinear regressions, stochastic frontier, and multinomial choice models.

In Chapter 4, Jeffrey S. Racine and Christopher F. Parmeter provide a survey of nonparametric methods for estimation and inference in a panel data setting. Methods surveyed include profile likelihood, kernel smoothers, and series and sieve estimators. The practical application of nonparametric panel-based techniques is less prevalent than nonparametric density and regression techniques. The material covered in this chapter will prove useful and facilitate their adoption by practitioners.

In Chapter 5, Kien Tran and Levent Kutlu provide a recent development in panel stochastic frontier models that allows for heterogeneity, endogeneity, or both. Specifically, consistent estimation of the models' parameters as well as observation-specific technical inefficiency is discussed.

In Chapter 6, Stefanos Dimitrakopoulos and Michalis Kolossiatis discuss how Bayesian techniques can be used to estimate the Poisson model, a well-known panel count data model, with exponential conditional mean. In particular, they focus on the implementation of Markov Chain Monte Carlo methods to various specifications of this model that allow for dynamics, latent heterogeneity and/or serial error correlation. The latent heterogeneity distribution is assigned a nonparametric structure, which is based on the Dirichlet process prior. The initial conditions problem also is addressed. For each resulting model specification, they provide the associated inferential algorithm for conducting posterior simulation. Relevant computer codes are posted as an online supplement.

In Chapter 7, Chih-Hwa Kao and Fa Wang review and explain the techniques used in Hahn and Newey (2004) and Fernandez-Val and Weidner (2016) to derive the limit distribution of the fixed effects estimator of semiparametric panels when the time dimension tends to infinity jointly with the cross-section dimension. The techniques of these two papers are representative and understanding their working mechanism is a good starting point. Under a unified framework, this paper explicitly points out the difficulties in extending from models with fixed dimensional parameter space to panels with individual effects and from panel with individual effects to panel with both individual and time effects, and how Hahn and Newey (2004) and Fernandez-Val and Weidner (2016) solve them.

In Chapter 8, Bo Honore and Ekaterini Kyriazidou study the identification of multivariate dynamic panel data logit models with unobserved fixed effects. They show that in the pure VAR(1) case (without exogenous covariates) the parameters are identified with as few as four waves of observations and can be estimated consistently at rate square-root-n with an asymptotic normal distribution. Furthermore, they show that the identification strategy of Honore and Kyriazidou (2000) carries over in the multivariate logit case when exogenous variables are included in the model. The authors also present an extension of the bivariate simultaneous logit model of Schmidt and Strauss (1975) to the panel case, allowing for contemporaneous cross-equation dependence both in static and dynamic frameworks. The results of this chapter are of particular interest for short panels, that is, for small T.

In Chapter 9, Subal Kumbhakar and Christopher F. Parmeter notice that, in the last 5 years, we have seen a marked increase in panel data methods that can handle unobserved heterogeneity, persistent inefficiency, and time-varying inefficiency. Although this advancement has opened up the range of questions and topics for applied researchers, practitioners, and regulators, there are various estimation proposals for these models and, to date, no comprehensive discussion about how these estimators work or compare to one another. This chapter lays out in detail the various estimators and how they can be applied. Several recent applications of these methods are discussed, drawing connections from the econometric framework to real applications.

In Chapter 10, Peter Pedroni discusses the challenges that shape panel cointegration techniques, with an emphasis on the challenge of maintaining the robustness of cointegration methods when temporal dependencies interact with both cross-sectional heterogeneities and dependencies. It also discusses some of the open challenges that lie ahead, including the challenge of generalizing to nonlinear and time varying cointegrating relationships. The chapter is written in a nontechnical style that is intended to make the information accessible to non-specialists, with an emphasis on conveying the underlying concepts and intuition.

In Chapter 11, by P.A.V.B. Swamy, Peter von zur Muehlen, Jatinder S. Mehta, and I-Lok Chang show that estimators of the coefficients of econometric models are inconsistent if their coefficients and error terms are not unique. They present models having unique coefficients and error terms, with specific applicability to the analyses of panel data sets. They show that the coefficient on an included nonconstant regressor of a model with unique coefficients and error term is the sum of bias-free and omitted-regressor bias components. This sum, when multiplied by the negative ratio of the measurement error to the observed regressor, provides a measurement-error bias component of the coefficient. This result is important because one needs the bias-free component of the coefficient on the regressor to measure the causal effect of an included nonconstant regressor of a model on its dependent variable.

In Chapter 12, Arne Heggingsen and Geraldine Henningsen give practical guidelines for the analysis of panel data with the statistical software R. They start by suggesting procedures for exploring and rearranging panel data sets and for preparing them for further analyses. A large part of this chapter demonstrates the application of various traditional panel data estimators that frequently are used in scientific and applied analyses. They also explain the estimation of several modern panel data models such as panel time series models and dynamic panel data models. Finally, this chapter shows how to use statistical tests to test critical hypotheses under different assumptions and how the results of these tests can be used to select the panel data estimator that is most suitable for a specific empirical panel data analysis.

In Chapter 13, Robin Sickles and Dong Ding empirically assess the impact of capital regulations on capital adequacy ratios, portfolio risk levels and cost efficiency for banks in the United States. Using a large panel data of US banks from 2001 to 2016, they first estimate the model using two-step generalized method of moments (GMM) estimators. After obtaining residuals from the regressions, they propose a method to construct the network based on clustering of these residuals. The residuals capture the unobserved heterogeneity that goes beyond systematic factors and banks' business decisions that affect its level of capital, risk, and cost efficiency, and thus represent unobserved network heterogeneity across banks. They then reestimate the model in a spatial error framework. The comparisons of Fixed Effects, GMM Fixed Effect models with spatial fixed effects models provide clear evidence of the existence of unobserved spatial effects in the interbank network. The authors find a stricter capital requirement causes banks to reduce investments in risk-weighted assets, but at the same time, increase holdings of nonperforming loans, suggesting the unintended effects of higher capital requirements on credit risks. They also find the amount of capital buffers has an important impact on banks' management practices even when regulatory capital requirements are not binding.

In Chapter 14, Gerraint Johnes and Jill Johnes survey applications of panel data methods in the economics of education. They focus first on studies that have applied a difference-in-difference approach (using both individual and organization level data). Then they explore the way in which panel data can be used to disentangle age and cohort effects in the context of investigating the impact of education on subsequent earnings. The survey next examines the role of panel data in assessing education peer effects and intergenerational socioeconomic mobility. The review ends by looking at adaptations of methods to assess efficiency in a panel data context, and dynamic discrete choice models and their importance in the context of evaluating the likely effects of policy interventions. The survey is intended to highlight studies that are representative of the main areas in which the literature has been developed, rather than to be encyclopedic.

In Chapter 15, corresponding author Scott Atkinson analyzes panel data studies of the most widely examined energy consumption industries—electric power, railroads, and airlines. For electric power, the choices between utility level versus plant-level data, cross-sectional versus panel data, and pooled-data analysis versus fixed-effects (FE) estimation generally makes little difference. A consensus also exists across estimates of cost, profit, and distance functions, the systems including these functions. Generally, studies reject homogeneous functional forms and find nearly constant returns to scale (RTS) for the largest firms. Residual productivity growth declines over time to small, positive levels, and substantial economies of vertical integration exist. Cost saving can accrue from a competitive generating sector. Controversy remains regarding the Averch-Johnson effect and the relative efficiency of publicly owned versus privately owned utilities. Railroads exhibit increasing RTS, substantial inefficiencies, and low productivity growth. Airlines operate close to constant RTS and enjoy modest productivity growth. Substantial inefficiencies decrease with deregulation. A valuable alternative to FE estimation is a control function approach to model unobserved productivity.

In Chapter 16, Georgia Kosmopoulou, Daniel Nedelescu, and Fletcher Rehbein survey commonly used methods and provide some representative examples in the auction literature in an effort to highlight the value of panel data techniques in the analysis of experimental data obtained in the laboratory.

In Chapter 17, Paul D. Allison, Richard Williams, and Enrique Moral-Benito point out that panel data make it possible both to control for unobserved confounders and to allow for lagged, reciprocal causation. Trying to do both at the same time, however, leads to serious estimation difficulties. In the econometric literature, these problems have been solved by using lagged instrumental variables together with the generalized method of moments (GMM). In this chapter, the authors show that the same problems can be solved by maximum likelihood estimation implemented with standard software packages for structural equation modeling (SEM). Monte Carlo simulations show that the ML-SEM method is less biased and more efficient than the GMM method under a wide range of conditions. ML-SEM also makes it possible to test and relax many of the constraints that typically are embodied in dynamic panel models.

In Chapter 18, Rico Merkert and Corinne Mulley notice that panel data have been widely used for analyzing both the demand and supply sides of transport operations. Obtaining true panels at the international level, however, appears to be difficult for various reasons. For the demand side, their peer review of the transport literature has demonstrated that pseudo panel data can be treated as if it is true panel data. For the supply side, this approach results in many studies using unbalanced panels instead. In terms of methods, they find that the DEA approach overcomes the problems of conflicting KPIs when considering overall cost efficiency while providing a robust tool for implementing change through the understanding of the key determinants of efficiency. Their case study about determinants of urban and regional train operator efficiency has evidenced, that the spatial context matters for the sample composition of DEA panel analysis in transport and that separating the panel into context specific subsamples can produce more robust results.

In Chapter 19, David Humphrey outlines the problems encountered when using banking panel data. Workarounds and solutions to these problems are noted. Although many of these problems occur when selecting and obtaining a panel data set, others are specific to the topics investigated, such as bank scale and scope economies, technical change, frontier efficiency, competition, and productivity. Illustrative results from published studies on these topics also are reported.

In Chapter 20, Christoph Siebenbrunner and Michael Sigmund point out that financial contagion describes the cascading effects that an initially idiosyncratic shock to a small part of a financial system can have on the entire system. They use two types of quantile panel estimators to imply that if certain bank-specific drivers used by leading regulatory authorities are good predictors of such extreme events, where small shocks to some part of the system can cause the collapse of the entire system. Comparing the results of the quantile estimation to a standard fixed-effects estimator they conclude that quantile estimators are better suited for describing the distribution of systemic contagion losses. Comparing the results to the aforementioned regulations, they find several recommendations for improvement.

In Chapter 21, Keshab Bhattarai reviews applications of panel data models. The process of substitution of labor by capital as discussed in Karabarbounis and Neiman (2014) and Picketty (2014) has increased the capital share, causing a reduction in labor share of about 10% magnitude. They also studied the impacts of trade and aid on economic growth. Fixed and random effect estimates show that investment rather than aid was a factor contributing to growth. Exports tied to aid are always harmful for growth of recipient countries. Although the evidence is mixed for the individual economies, there appear to be trade-offs between unemployment and inflation in the panel of Organisation for Economic Co-operation and Development (OECD) countries as shown by the random and fixed effect models in which the Hausman test is in favor of random effect model. A simple VAR model with two lags on inflation and unemployment shows persistence of inflation and unemployment rates among the OECD economies. The ratio of investment to GDP (gross domestic product) is a significant determinant of growth rates across OECD countries, and FDI contributes positively to growth. Regression results are robust on the grounds of stationarity and cointegration criteria. Threshold panel models developed by Hansen (1997) and Caner and Hansen (2004) show how to study regime changes occurring in the real world.

In Chapter 22, Andrew Jones, Apostolos Davillas, and Michaela Benzeval add to the literature about the income-health gradient by exploring the association of short-term and long-term income with a wide set of self-reported health measures and objective nurse-administered and blood-based biomarkers, as well as employing estimation techniques that allow for analysis beyond the mean. The income-health gradients are greater in magnitude in cases of long-run rather than cross-sectional income measures. Unconditional quantile regressions reveal that the differences between the long-run and the short-run income gradients are more evident toward the right tails of the distributions, where both higher risk of illnesses and steeper income gradients are observed.

In Chapter 23, Steve Ongena, Andrada Bilan, Hans Degryse, and Kuchulain O'Flynn review the data, econometric techniques, and estimates with respect to two recent and salient developments in the banking industry, i.e., securitization and globalization. The traditional banking market has become wider in its business models, through securitization, and in its geographical dispersion, through global operations. Both developments have brought new challenges for the understanding of basic questions in banking. Questions such as what determines credit flows or what are the channels of transmission for monetary policy recently have been addressed through this new optic. This review establishes that access to micro data has enabled researchers to arrive at increasingly better identified and more reliable estimates.

In Chapter 24, Claire Economidou, Kyriakos Drivas, and Mike Tsionas develop a methodology for stochastic frontier models of count data allowing for technological and inefficiency induced heterogeneity in the data and endogenous regressors. They derive the corresponding log-likelihood function and conditional mean of inefficiency to estimate technology regime-specific inefficiency. They apply our proposed methodology for the states in the United States to assess efficiency and growth patterns in producing new knowledge in the United States. The findings support the existence of two distinct innovation classes with different implications for their members' innovation growth.

In Chapter 25, Emmanuel Mamatzakis and Mike Tsionas propose a novel approach to identify life satisfaction and thereby happiness within a latent variables model for British Household Panel Survey longitudinal data. By doing so, they overcome issues related to the measurement of happiness. To observe happiness, they employ a Bayesian inference procedure organized around

Sequential Monte Carlo (SMC)/particle filtering techniques. Happiness efficiency captures individuals' optimal happiness to be achieved should they use their resource endowment efficiently. In addition, they propose to take into account individual-specific characteristics by estimating happiness efficiency models with individual-specific thresholds to happiness. This is the first study that departs from restrictions that happiness efficiency, and thereby inefficiency, would be time-invariant. Key to happiness is to have certain personality traits; being agreeable and being an extrovert assist efforts to enhance happiness efficiency. On the other hand, being neurotic would impair happiness efficiency.

In Chapter 26, Vasso Ioannidou and Jan de Dreu study how the introduction of an explicit deposit insurance scheme in Bolivia in 2001 affected depositors' incentives to monitor and discipline their banks for risk-taking. They find that after the introduction of the explicit deposit insurance scheme, the sensitivity of deposit interest rates and volumes to bank risk is reduced significantly, consistent with a reduction in depositor discipline. This effect operates mainly though large depositors—the class of depositors who were sensitive to their banks' risk in the first place. The authors also find that the larger the decrease in depositor discipline is, the larger the insurance coverage rate is. Deposit interest rates and volumes become almost completely insensitive to bank risk when the insurance coverage is higher than 60%. The results provide support for deposit insurance schemes with explicit deposit insurance limits per depositor.

In Chapter 27, Sarantis Kalyvitis, Sofia Anyfantaki, Margarita Katsimi, and Eirini Thomaidou review the growing empirical literature that explores the determinants of export prices at the firm level. They first present evidence from empirical studies that link firm export pricing to destination characteristics (gravity-type models). The main implications of channels that can generate price differentiation, such as quality customization, variable markups, and exchange rate pass-through, and financial frictions then are explored. A newly compiled panel data set from Greek exporting firms is used to present evidence from regressions with export price as the dependent variable and show how the main economic hypotheses derived in theoretical models are nested in empirical specifications.

In Chapter 28, Almas Hermati and Nam Seok Kim investigate the relationship between economic growth and democracy by estimating a nation's production function specified as static and dynamic models using panel data. In estimating the production function, they use a single time trend, multiple time trends, and the general index formulations to the translog production function to capture time effects representing technological changes of unknown forms. In addition to the unknown forms, implementing the technology shifters model enabled this study to find possible known channels between economic growth and democracy. Empirical results based on a panel data of 144 countries observed from 1980 to 2014 show that democracy had a robust positive impact on economic growth. Credit guarantee is one of the most significant positive links between economic growth and democracy. In order to check the robustness of these results, a dynamic model constructed with a flexible adjustment speed and a target level of GDP also is tested.

In Chapter 29, Almas Hesmati, Esfandiar Maasoumi, and Biwei Su examine the evolution of well-being (household income) of Chinese households over time, and its determinants. They study (stochastic) dominance relations based on Chinese Household Nutrition Survey (CHNS) data. They reveal a profile of general mobility/inequality and relative welfare in China over time and among population subgroups. The authors report that from 2000 to 2009, welfare has improved steadily along with Chinese economic development and growth. Pairwise comparison of subgroups reveals that there is no uniform ranking by household type, gender of household head, or age cohort. Married group and nonchild rearing group second order dominate single/divorced group and child rearing group. Inequality in subgroups with different educational levels and household sizes suggests groups with higher education and smaller household size tend to be better off than their counterparts. Longitudinal data allow estimation of permanent incomes, which smooth out short-term fluctuations. Treating the data as a time series of cross sections also avoids imposition of constant partial effects over time and across groups. This is appropriate given the observed heterogeneity in this population. Individual/group specific components are allowed and subsumed in conditional dominance rankings, rather than identified by panel data estimation methods.

In Chapter 30, Mike G. Tsionas, Konstantinos N. Konstantakis, and Panayotis G. Michaelides present a production function, which is based on a family of semi-parametric artificial neural networks that are rich in parameters, in order to impose all the properties that modern production theory dictates. Based on this approach, this specification is a universal approximator to any arbitrary production function. All measures of interest, such as elasticities of substitution, technical efficiency, returns to scale, and total factor productivity, also are derived easily. Authors illustrate our proposed specification using data for sectors of the US economy. The proposed specification performs very well and the US economy is characterized by approximately constant RTS and moderate TFP, a finding that is consistent with previous empirical work.

General References

Baltagi, B.H., 2001. Econometric analysis of panel data, second ed. John Wiley & Sons.

Cameron, A.C., Trivedi, P.K., 2010. Microeconometrics using Stata, Rev. ed. Stata Press Publ.

Greene, W.H., 2012. Econometric analysis, seventh ed. Prentice Hall, Upper Saddle River, NJ. 740 p.

Hsiao, C., 2002. Analysis of panel data, second ed. Cambridge University Press.

Wooldridge, J.M., 2010. Econometric analysis of cross section and panel data, second ed. MIT Press, Cambridge, MA.

Chapter 1

A Synopsis of Econometrics

Stephen G. Hall
Leicester University, Leicester, United Kingdom, Bank of Greece, Athens, Greece, University of Pretoria, Pretoria, South Africa

Chapter Outline

1 Introduction

In this chapter, we provide a broad synopsis and background to standard econometric techniques. The aim of this chapter is to act as a foundation for the rest of this book and to make it a self-contained reference book. Inevitably, this will mean a brief account of many of the issues we discuss, and we aim to provide references that will give more complete and comprehensive accounts of each section we address.

We begin by outlining some fundamental concepts that lie behind much of what goes on in econometrics: the idea of a population, random variables, random sampling, the sampling distribution, and the central limit theorem. We then explore two of the basic approaches to constructing an econometric estimator: the maximum likelihood principal and the general method of moments. We then go through the standard linear model, the basic workhorse of econometrics, and

Panel Data Econometrics. https://doi.org/10.1016/B978-0-12-814367-4.00001-0

the various problems that can arise in this familiar case. We then explore the issue of nonstationarity, which has dominated many of the developments in econometrics during the last 30 years.

2 Some Basic Concepts

At its heart, econometrics is about quantifying effects in the real world and assessing these effects to gain some notion of their reliability. Economic theory often can suggest the direction of a causal effect, but it rarely suggests the exact magnitude of such an effect nor what the correct functional form should be. To make the realm of econometrics operational, we need a statistical framework that allows us to operate in a wide range of situations, at least to a good approximation of the real world. This framework begins with the concept of the population. We assume that there is an infinitely large population of events or outcomes that are of interest to us. We cannot know or observe all of these outcomes, but we wish to make some inference about the population as a whole. We then assume that this population is made up of individual events that are random but drawn from the population that has some given distribution. This distribution can be described by a set of moments (mean, variance, skewness, kurtosis, and higher moments), so the mean is simply the average of the population distribution $E(y) = \mu_y$ where y is some random variable, and μ_y is the mean of the population distribution, the variance of the population distribution is $E(y - \mu_y)^2 = {\sigma_y}^2$ and so on for the higher moments. We cannot observe these population moments, of course, because we cannot observe the whole population. Instead, we try to make some inference about the population by drawing a sample from this population. Our statistical framework then rests on some key assumptions about this sample; the first of which is that the sample is drawn at random; y is a random variable that is part of a population with a population distribution. When we draw a sample from this population of size n $(y_1 \dots y_n)$, these observations about y cease to be random variables and become simple numbers. The basic notion of random sampling then has some important implications. First, as we draw each y_i at random from the sample, they should be independent of each other. That is to say, for example knowing y_3 will not help us in any way to know what value y_4 will take, so the observations about y are independent. Also, as each observation is drawn at random from the same population, they will have an identical distribution. Hence, the observations have an independent identical distribution (IID) regardless of the shape or form of the population distribution.

The next step is to begin to think about the properties of the sample we have drawn. The sample $(y_1 \dots y_n)$ can be used to make inference about the population in a wide variety of ways, some of which might be sensible and some might be highly misleading. For example, we could use the first observation as an estimate of the population mean, although this might not be the best thing to do. We also could take the average of the sample and use this as an estimate of the population mean. The important question is which would be better and how do we make an objective judgment. The answer to this question lies in another important concept: the sampling distribution. Let's suppose we derive some measure from our sample, say $\tau = f(y_1 \ldots y_n)$. If we then pick another sample, we can derive another estimate of this measure, $\tau' = f(y_1' \ldots y_n')$. If we pick yet another sample, we can derive another estimate, and so on. This then allows us to define the sampling distribution of τ and this sampling distribution will have a mean and a variance. We then would like to see this distribution being related to the population distribution in a way we can clearly understand. If we are trying to estimate the mean of the population distribution, we would like to find that $E(\tau) = \mu_y$, in which case we would say that τ is an unbiased estimate of the population mean, which means that even in a small sample the expected value of τ equals the true population mean. In some circumstances, this is not possible and then a weaker but desirable property is $\lim_{n \to \infty}(\tau) = \mu_y$, which says that, in the limit, as the sample size grows to infinity τ equals the true population mean. This is termed consistency. Of course, there might be more than one unbiased estimation technique, and we need some way to judge between them. A natural way to judge between two consistent procedures is to ask which of the two makes smaller errors on average, that is, to ask which of the two has a sampling distribution with a smaller variance. So, if we have another procedure, $\upsilon = h(y_1 \ldots y_n)$, and both are unbiased, then we would prefer τ if $\text{var}(\tau) < \text{var}(\upsilon)$.

This gives us a basic approach to estimation: We want to find unbiased and efficient estimators. The other main part of econometric methodology is to draw inferences about our estimated effects, that is, to be able to draw a confidence interval around our central estimate and formally test the hypothesis. In order to do this, we need to know the shape of the sampling distribution. At first sight, this seems quite challenging. We have a population distribution that might have any shaped distribution, then we draw a sample from this and derive an indicative measure about that sample. To be able to conduct inference, we need to know the shape of the sampling distribution. This seems to be a challenging requirement, but a core theorem that underlies much of econometrics allows us to do exactly that. This is the central limit theorem. There are actually many versions of the central limit theorem (Davidson, 1994), but the result is that if we have a sample of n observations from a population and we derive a statistic which has a sampling distribution, then as n goes to infinity, the sampling distribution will converge on a normal distribution. The following multivariate version of the central limit theorem is given by Greenberg and Webster (1983).

If $(y_1 \ldots y_n)$ are independently distributed random vectors with mean vector μ and covariance matrices $V_1 \ldots V_n$ and the third moment of y exists, then

$$n^{-1/2} \sum_{i=1}^{n} (y_i - \mu) \rightarrow N(0, \Sigma) \tag{1}$$

where

$$\Sigma = \lim n^{-1} \sum_{i=1}^{n} V_i \tag{2}$$

The key thing here, common to the many extensions of the central limit theorem, is that, without making any assumption about the distribution of the population distribution, the sampling distribution is normally distributed. This then allows us to conduct standard classical inference, which can typically be done in one of three equivalent ways: the classic student t test, the P-value, or a confidence interval. In the case of a set of single values discussed previously, if we had derived a particular value for y, say y^* the t test would be given by

$$t = \frac{y^* - \mu}{\sqrt{\Sigma}} \tag{3}$$

showing the point on the t distribution where the value y^* is located. As n grows large, this converges on the normal distribution. The point on the normal distribution beyond which there is only 2.5% of the distribution is 1.96; so a t value greater than 1.96 would allow us to reject the null hypothesis that the true value of y is actually μ at a 5% critical value on a two-tailed test. In a convenient but broadly equivalent way, this often is expressed as a P-value; that is the probability under the null that y^* is a correct value.

$$P - \text{value} = \Pr_{H_0}(|y^* - \mu| > |y^{act} - \mu|) \tag{4}$$

If the t value is exactly 1.96, the P-value will equal 0.05; as the t value rises above 1.96, the P-value falls below 0.05. P-values are particularly useful when the relevant distribution is not a normal one, and it is not easy to remember the correct critical value.

The final largely equivalent way of presenting inference is in terms of a confidence interval, which shows the range of values within which the true value should lie with a particular degree of certainty. The formula for a 95% confidence interval is

$$CI_{95\%} = \left\{ y^* + 1.96\sqrt{\Sigma}, y^* - 1.96\sqrt{\Sigma} \right\} \tag{5}$$

These three methods of presenting basic inference are well known, but the key point is that their existence is based on the central limit theorem, which underlies the normality assumption that is being made in each of these calculations.

The final point to emphasize in this section is that we were rather vague regarding exactly what the function is when we previously stated $\tau = f(y_1 \ldots y_n)$. This vagueness was deliberate because this function can go well beyond simple descriptive statistics. Therefore, we could think of τ as simply being the mean of y, but it also could be a regression coefficient or a wide range of other statistics that are derived from a sample and therefore have a sampling distribution.

3 Two Basic Approaches to Estimation

In many basic textbooks, estimation is presented in a rather ad hoc way. It can be argued, for example, that a model will generate errors and it is sensible to minimize the squared error as a natural way to motivate ordinary least squares (OLS) estimation. This is both simple and appealing, but a little extra thought raises a number of questions: Why not minimize the absolute error? Why not a higher power of the absolute error? Why not some other nonlinear transformation of the error, such as the absolute log? Historically, OLS has been preferred because it has an easy analytical solution that makes it feasible in the absence of a modern computer, whereas most of the alternatives would be infeasible. This is no longer an acceptable answer because computers can do any of the previous calculations quite easily. The correct justification for OLS and other techniques is that some underlying principles of estimation make it possible under certain circumstances to justify OLS or other estimation strategies. These principals are maximum likelihood (ML) and the Generalized Method of Moments (GMM).

4 Maximum Likelihood (ML)

The basic approach of maximum likelihood is both very general and powerful: If we assume some specific model, this model generally will have some unknown parameters to be estimated. Given this model structure and a specific set of parameters, we then are generally able to calculate the probability that a real-world event (or sample) actually would have occurred. We then choose the unknown parameters of the model to maximize the probability (or likelihood) that the real-world event would have occurred. This gives the maximum likelihood estimates of the unknown parameters, which then are generally consistent and fully efficient. When it is possible to do maximum likelihood, it is generally the best estimator. Hendry (1976) has shown that many other estimation techniques, such as two-stage least squares, three-stage least squares, and other instrumental variable estimation techniques can be interpreted as approximations to the ML estimator.

Suppose we have a sample $(y_1 \ldots y_n)$ that is drawn from a population probability distribution $P(y|A)$, where A is a set of unknown parameters to be estimated. We assume that the y_i are independent each with probability distribution of $P(y_i|A)$. The joint probability distribution then is given by $\Pi_{i=1}^{n} P(y_i|A)$, because the y_i are a sample that are also fixed. We then can restate the joint probability distribution as the likelihood function.

$$L(A) = \Pi_{i=1}^{n} P(y_i|A) \tag{6}$$

It is generally more convenient to work with the log of the likelihood function.

$$\log(L(A)] = \sum_{i=1}^{n} P(y_i | A) \tag{7}$$

This can then be maximized with respect to the parameters A to yield the maximum likelihood estimates. The advantage of this approach is that it can be applied to any situation in which we can define the probability of a particular event, and therefore it can be applied to many nonstandard situations.

If we consider as a starting point a general nonlinear model $e = Y - f(X, \beta)$, where Y is a vector of n endogenous variables, X is a matrix of exogenous variables that would be $n \times k$, e is a vector of n error terms and β is a vector of k parameters, if we also assume that $e \sim N(0, \Sigma)$, that is, the error terms are normally distributed, then the likelihood function for one period is proportional to,

$$\log(L(A)) \approx -n\log(\Sigma) - e'\Sigma^{-1}e \tag{8}$$

That is to say, under the assumption of normally distributed errors, the likelihood function is a function of the squared errors scaled by the covariance matrix. This is very close to standard OLS, although it includes a term in the variance of the residuals. Another useful concept, concentrating the likelihood function, allows us to transform this into the standard OLS result, making this function useful in much more complex situations. The idea of concentrating the likelihood function starts from the idea that without loss of generality we can always split the parameter vector A into two subvectors (A_1, A_2). If we know A_1, it is possible to derive an analytical expression for A_2, such as $A_2 = g(A_1)$. Then it is possible to substitute A_2 out of the likelihood function and state a concentrated likelihood function just in terms of A_1. This often is used to simplify ML procedures. If we take the model given previously and assume the variance matrix is a single constant scaler, then, over a sample of n observations, the likelihood function becomes.

$$\log(L(A)) \approx -n\log\left(\sigma^2\right) - e'e/\sigma^2 \tag{9}$$

If we know the parameters A, we can then take the first-order conditions with respect to σ^2 to give

$$\delta\log(L(A))/\delta\sigma^2 = -n/\sigma^2 + e'e/\left(\sigma^2\right)^2 \tag{10}$$

Solving this for the variance gives

$$\sigma^2 = e'e/n \tag{11}$$

We can use this expression to eliminate the variance from the standard likelihood function to get the concentrated likelihood function

$$\log(L^*(A)) = -n - n\log(e'e/n) \tag{12}$$

which is now simply a function of the squared errors. This is the maximum likelihood justification for OLS, under the assumption of independent normal residuals with a constant variance OLS is the maximum likelihood estimator. After we have estimated the parameters of the model, we can recover the maximum likelihood estimate of the variance from Eq. (11).

Maximum likelihood is generally a consistent and efficient estimation technique on the assumption that the model being estimated is correctly specified. Two important matrices that are derived from the likelihood function provide the bases for most standard inference: the efficient score matrix and the information matrix. The efficient score matrix usually is defined as

$$\frac{\delta \log(L(A))}{\delta A} = S(A) \tag{13}$$

This needs some explanation $S(A)$ is actually a $k \times n$ matrix, where k is the number of parameters; for each observation, $1 \ldots n$, it contains the derivative of the likelihood function with respect to each of the parameters at that observation. At the maximum, the sum down each column will be zero, because at the maximum this will effectively be the first-order conditions. This matrix is telling us how far the maximum at each observation is away from the sample average.

The information matrix is given by the second derivative of the likelihood function with respect to the parameters.

$$E\left[-\frac{\delta^2 \log(L(A))}{\delta A \delta A'}\right] = I(A) \tag{14}$$

An important result is that the variance of the ML parameters is asymptotically given by the inverse of the information matrix, and this is asymptotically equivalent to the outer product of the score matrix.

$$\text{Var}(A_{\text{ML}}) = (I(A_{\text{ML}}))^{-1} = S(A_{\text{ML}})' S(A_{\text{ML}}) \tag{15}$$

The Cramer-Rao lower bound theorem states that any other estimation technique must yield a variance that is equal to or greater than the ML variance. For example, if A^* is a set of parameters generated by any other estimation technique, then the lower bound theorem states that $\text{Var}(A^*) \geq (I(A_{\text{ML}}))^{-1}$. This is truly remarkable because it states that ML is better than any other technique, even one we have not invented yet.

ML also forms the bases of most of the ways we construct hypothesis tests. In any classic hypothesis test, we set up a null hypothesis (H_0), and we see if we can reject this against an alternative (H_1). This typically involves deciding if an unrestricted model (H_1) is significantly different from a set of theoretical restrictions (H_0). ML provides a natural framework to formalize this idea, so all we need to do is to compare the value of the likelihood function at the unrestricted point and the restricted point and to find a way to judge if this difference is significant. This is exactly what the fundamental likelihood ratio test does. It also can be shown that in a testing context, twice the difference between the value of the log likelihood function at the maximum point and the restricted point has a χ^2 distribution. The likelihood ratio test is given by

$$\mathrm{LRT} = 2\left(\log\left(L(A_{\mathrm{ML}})\right) - \log\left(L(A_r)\right) \sim \chi^2(m)\right. \tag{16}$$

where A_r is a set of restricted parameters and m is the number of restrictions.

This formulation is the fundamental of testing, but it is not always convenient to employ because, in some circumstances, it can be difficult to estimate either the restricted or unrestricted models. For this reason, two other basic testing procedures allow us to approximate the likelihood ratio test without estimating either the restricted or unrestricted model. If we estimate only the unrestricted model and approximate the likelihood ratio test from this point, we are conducting a Wald test. If we estimate only the restricted model, then we are performing a LaGrange Multiplier (LM) test.

The Wald (1943) test is given by

$$W = [g(A_{\mathrm{ML}})]'\left\{G(I(A_{\mathrm{ML}}))^{-1}G'\right\}[g(A_{\mathrm{ML}})] \sim \chi^2(k) \tag{17}$$

where G is a set of k restrictions on A, and g is the derivative of the restrictions ($\delta G(A)/\delta A$). This test requires us only to estimate the model at the unrestricted point. The most common example of a Wald test is the student t test, in which we estimate an unrestricted model and then test individual coefficients for a restricted value (typically zero), but without estimating the model subject to this restriction.

The LaGrange Multiplier (LM) test estimates the model only at the restricted point and then approximates the LR test from that point. The test is defined as

$$\mathrm{LM} = [S(A_r)]'[I(A_r)]^{-1}[S(A_r)] \sim \chi^2(k) \tag{18}$$

where A_r is the restricted set of parameters. Common examples of the LM tests are tests for ARCH or serial correlation in which we estimate the model without these features (the restricted model) and then calculate a test against these features as the alternative. A particularly common and convenient version of the LM test under linear OLS estimation is to take the residuals from an OLS model and regress them on the exogenous variable and the restrictions (lagged errors in the case of serial correlation). The LM test then is given by nR^2 from this auxiliary regression.

Both the LM and Wald tests make a quadratic approximation to the likelihood ratio test. If the likelihood function were quadratic (which it usually is not), then all three would give the same answer. In general, however, we expect that W > LR > LM, that it the Wald test overestimates the LR test, and the LM test underestimates it (Berndt & Savin, 1977).

One limiting assumption given previously is that so far we have assumed that the observations on y are independent. This will be true under that assumption of random sampling, but, in many cases, this is not valid. The most obvious case is time series data in which an observation at period t is not generally independent of the observation at $t-1$. There is, however, an important extension to ML that allows us to deal with this case—the prediction error decomposition (Harvey, 1981). This rests on a basic definition of conditional probability, $\Pr(\alpha,\beta) = \Pr(a|\beta)\Pr(\beta)$. Because likelihood functions are essentially statements about probability, this can be applied directly to a likelihood function. Suppose we have a general joint log likelihood function for a set of time series observations $y_1 \ldots y_T$. This can be factorized to turn it into a sequence of likelihood functions, each of which condition on the past variables as if they were fixed.

$$\log(L(y_1\ldots y_T)) = \sum_{i=0}^{T-k} \log(y_{T-i}|\, y_1\ldots y_{T-1-i}) + \log(y_1\ldots y_k) \tag{19}$$

where k is the number of lags in the relationship between y and its past values. The last term in Eq. (19) is essentially initial conditions that can be dropped from the maximization.

It often has been said that a weakness of maximum likelihood is that we assume that we have the correct model and, if this assumption is false, then the whole procedure collapses. A much simpler process, such as OLS, might be more robust. This argument was effectively countered by White (1982), who introduced the notion of quasi maximum likelihood (QML). This states that under a wide range of misspecifications, ML still will be a consistent estimator although it will no longer be fully efficient because it will not be the correct ML estimator. White, however, showed that what goes seriously wrong is the inference we draw under maximum likelihood, neither the inverse information matrix nor the outer product of the score matrix are consistent estimators for the correct covariance matrix of the parameters. Instead, he derives a generic robust covariance matrix, which is consistent under full ML assumptions and when QML is only a consistent estimator but not efficient. The formula for this robust covariance matrix is

$$C(A_{QML}) = I(A_{QML})^{-1}\left[S(A_{QML})'S(A_{QML})\right]I(A_{QML})^{-1} \tag{20}$$

where $C(A_{QML})$ is the QML robust covariance matrix, given as a combination of the information matrix and the outer product of the score matrix. Under full ML assumptions, these two are equivalent, so the last two terms would cancel, giving us the standard information matrix. Under QML assumptions, these two matrices are no longer even asymptotically equivalent, and we get this more general formula. This is the basis of all the robust covariance matrices that have been later developed in econometrics. In general, we can use this robust covariance matrix in the construction of either Wald or LM tests to give robust test statistics. The LR test, however, is no longer valid because it runs directly from the likelihood function, which in the case of QML, is incorrect.

5 Generalized Method of Moments (GMM)

GMM was introduced into econometrics by Hansen (1982), and an excellent survey of the approach can be found in Hall (2005). Although ML is always the best option when it is feasible, there are many circumstances in which it is not a practical option: Theory rarely tells us exactly from which distribution a set of errors should be drawn, a crucial factor in formulating the correct ML estimator; it might not always be possible to fully specify the probability distribution; and the computational burden might be extreme or the likelihood function might be relatively flat and therefore hard to maximize. In these circumstances, GMM provides a computationally convenient alternative to ML, which, although inevitably less efficient, is feasible and computationally tractable.

As the name suggests, GMM is a generalization of a much earlier technique, method of moments, which has been part of the statistical toolkit since the late 19th century. At its most basic level, method of moments is a technique that allows us to estimate the moments of a population distribution based on the estimated moments from a particular sample. The key distinguishing feature of method of moments is that if we have K moment conditions that we wish to satisfy, then we also will have K parameters to estimate. This implies that generally we will be able to make each of the moment conditions hold exactly. In GMM estimation, we typically will have $L > K$ moment conditions, where K is the number of parameters being estimated. Because we will not be able to make all the moment conditions hold at the same time, there must be a tradeoff between competing moment conditions.

Method of moments estimation typically was used to estimate the form of a particular population distribution. In the late 19th century, Karl Pearson developed what is now known as the Pearson family of distributions, which are defined by a vector of four parameters that describe the form of a particular distribution. These four parameters can capture a wide variety of different standard distributions. For example, suppose we want to know the first moment of the population distribution of a random variable y, the moment condition we want to satisfy is $E(y) - \mu = 0$ where μ is the population mean. The sample analogue to this moment condition, for a sample of n is then $n^{-1}\sum_{i=1}^{n} y_i - \hat{\mu} = 0$. Here we have one moment condition and one parameter to estimate, so we can solve this condition exactly to give $\hat{\mu} = n^{-1}\sum_{i=1}^{n} y_i$. This basic idea of method of moments can be extended to produce a range of standard instrumental variable estimators (see Hall, 2005) in which the moment conditions involve orthogonality between the instruments and the error terms. Instrumental variable estimation first entered mainstream econometrics in the 1940s as a solution to the error in variables problem (although strictly speaking, the first example of this technique was in Wright (1925), which had little impact at the time). Consider a simple case:

$$y_t = \alpha x_t^0 + u_{1t} \tag{21}$$

But the independent variable is observed with error such that

$$x_t = x_t^0 + u_{2t} \tag{22}$$

Because the true regressor is unobservable in estimation, we replace this with the observed variable

$$y_t = \alpha x_t + u_t \tag{23}$$

If we estimate this using OLS, we will have a biased coefficient because of the correlation between the observed regressor and the error term. Reiersol (1941) and Geary (1948) both suggested the instrumental variable approach as a solution to this problem. This suggestion was to propose the existence of another variable z, which is correlated with x but uncorrelated with the error in Eq. (23). This then gives the following moment condition

$$Cov(z_t, y_t) - \alpha Cov(z_t, x_t) = 0 \tag{24}$$

This method of moments estimator gives rise to the instrumental variable estimator for α. Sagan (1958) then gave a full statistical underpinning for instrumental variable estimation.

To set up the GMM estimator in its most general form, we first have to define a set of population moment conditions, following Hall (2005). If we let φ be a vector of unknown parameters to be estimated, ν a vector of random variables, and g a vector of functions, then the population moment conditions can be stated in a general form as

$$E[g(\nu_t, \varphi)] = 0 \tag{25}$$

The example in Eq. (24) is a special case of this; when there are k moments and k parameters, it gives rise to a method of moments estimator and each moment can hold exactly in a sample. In general, however, there can be more moment conditions than parameters to be estimated, and all the moments generally cannot be met simultaneously. Therefore, there must be a tradeoff between the moments as to how close each is to zero. It is this tradeoff that gives rise to the GMM technique. Therefore, the GMM estimator is given by the value of φ, which for a given sample of T observations minimizes

$$Q(\varphi) = T^{-1} g(\nu_t, \phi)' W_t T^{-1} g(\nu_t, \varphi) \tag{26}$$

where W_t is a positive semi definite matrix that converges in probability to a matrix of constants. GMM generally is consistent for any matrix W_t that obeys this restriction. Clearly different matrices could give very different results, so we need some way to choose between these alternatives. The question then arises as to how we should choose the optimal weighting matrix and exactly what we mean by optimal in this context. This is resolved by defining the optimal weighting matrix W^* to be the matrix that minimizes the asymptotic variance of φ. Similar to the argument that the Cramer Roa lower bound justifies the use of ML over other estimation techniques, we choose the estimator within the class of GMM estimators that is the most efficient.

It is possible to use the central limit theorem to show that

$$T^{-1}\sum_{t=1}^{T} g(\nu_t, \varphi) \sim N(0, S) \tag{27}$$

where S is the covariance matrix of the moment conditions; Hansen (1982) demonstrated that $W^* = S^{-1}$. This then has an apparent circularity, to estimate W^* we must first know φ and to estimate φ we must first knowW^*. This circularity can be resolved by implementing Hansen's two-step procedure. First, we obtain a consistent estimate of φ by using any admissible matrix W, often just the identity matrix. Based on this set of parameters, we estimate W^*, and given this estimate, we estimate φ in a second estimation step. It would be possible to iterate this procedure to convergence, but this is not often done because, theoretically at least, there is no advantage in further steps.

6 Some Examples of Moment Conditions

It helps understanding to give some simple examples of moment conditions. Consider the case of a standard linear model:

$$y_i = x_i \phi + u_i \tag{28}$$

where y is the dependent variable, x is a vector of n exogenous variables, ϕ is a suitably dimensioned vector of parameters, and u is an error term. The moment conditions that will generate exactly the same result as OLS will be

$$E\left(x_i' u_i\right) = E\left(x_i'(y_i - x_i\phi)\right) = 0 \tag{29}$$

which reflects that fact that OLS produces parameter estimates that make the exogenous variables orthogonal to the error term. This is a method of moment's estimator because there will be exactly as many moment conditions as parameters to estimate. We can generalize this to be an instrumental variable estimator or generalized methods of moment estimator by introducing a vector of variables z_i of p suitable instruments, in which there are more instruments in the z vector than x's ($p > n$). The moment conditions then become

$$E\left(z_i' u_i\right) = E\left(z_i'(y_i - x_i\phi)\right) = 0 \tag{30}$$

7 The Standard Linear Model and Least Squares

In this section, we consider the basic properties of least squares estimation of the standard linear model, which has for years been the workhorse of econometrics. Consider

$$y_t = x_t\phi + u_t \tag{31}$$

as defined previously and let the least squares estimate of the parameters be $\hat{\phi}$. Now let us assume that following;

1. The vector x_t is nonstochastic
2. The error term u_t is a normal random error with mean zero and covariance matrix $E(uu') = \sigma^2 I$

It is easy to show that we can write the least squares estimator as

$$\hat{\phi} = \phi + (x'x)^{-1}x'u \tag{32}$$

In order to make statements about the behavior of $\hat{\phi}$, we need to know about the behavior of$(x'x)^{-1}$ and $x'e$. The strongest and usual assumption is that[1]

$$\lim_{t\to\infty}\left(\frac{x'x}{T}\right) = \Omega \text{ and } \lim_{t\to\infty}\left(\frac{x'u}{T}\right) = 0 \tag{33}$$

where Ω is a finite nonsingular matrix. The x's are not linearly dependent in the limit, they settle down to a constant matrix on average and in the limit there is no relationship between the x's and the error term. Under these assumptions, the least squares is the maximum likelihood estimator, and it is consistent and efficient and often is described as the best linear unbiased estimator (BLUE). Given these assumptions, it is easy to demonstrate the consistency of LS estimation. We can restate Eq. (32) as

$$\hat{\phi} = \phi + p\lim\left[\left(\frac{x'x}{T}\right)^{-1}\frac{x'u}{T}\right] \tag{34}$$

$$\hat{\phi} = \phi + p\lim\left[\left(\frac{x'x}{T}\right)^{-1}\right]p\lim\left[\frac{x'u}{T}\right] \tag{35}$$

$$\hat{\phi} = \phi + \lim_{T\to\infty}\left[\left(\frac{x'x}{T}\right)^{-1}\right]p\lim\left[\frac{x'u}{T}\right] \tag{36}$$

$$\hat{\phi} = \phi + \Omega^{-1}0 \tag{37}$$

$$\hat{\phi} = \phi \tag{38}$$

1. We define orders of magnitude and convergence in the appendix to this chapter.

Therefore, LS estimation gives a consistent estimate of the true parameters.

The failures of OLS can be summarized in terms of failures of the two sets of the previous assumptions in one way or another. Consider the following cases.

8 Failure of $E(uu') = \sigma^2 I$

This can occur in two principal ways: the identity matrix might have constant diagonal elements but its off-diagonal elements might be non-zero. In the case of a time series regression, this would be interpreted as a serially correlated error term. In the case of a cross-section or panel regression model, this would be interpreted as a spillover in the errors from one individual to another, giving rise to spatial econometrics literature. It also is possible that the off-diagonal elements might be non-zero, but the diagonal elements have different values. This would give rise to the case of heteroskedasticity.

In both of these cases, LS remains a consistent estimation technique, although it is no longer the maximum likelihood estimator and so it is not fully efficient. Inference regarding the parameter estimates, however, is no longer correct using the standard formulas, and inference then must be based on some version of the quasi maximum likelihood covariance matrix (Eq. 20). In practice, when using LS, it is not generally possible to apply Eq. (20) directly. Therefore, some specific form of the QML covariance matrix must be used; typically for serial correlation in a time series regression, this would be the Newey and West (1987) covariance matrix and for heteroscedasticity, it would be a version of the White (1980) covariance matrix.

9 The Vector x_t is Stochastic

Relaxing the assumption that x is nonstochastic has only minor consequences as long as the second assumption in Eq. (33) still holds. LS will no longer be unbiased in small samples, but it remains consistent and efficient.

10 Failure of $\lim_{t \to \infty} \left(\frac{x'u}{T}\right) = 0$

This can arise for a variety of reasons, but principally because either x is not weakly exogenous or that u is not random, perhaps because it contains some element of measurement error in the $x's$.

There are various definitions of exogeneity, but in terms of obtaining consistent parameter estimates, the key definition is weak exogeneity. Engle, Hendry, and Richard (1983) found that this requires a weakly exogenous variable to be independent of the current relevant endogenous variables and that the parameters that generate the endogenous variable and the weakly exogenous variable are variation free. The most obvious way in which this can be violated is if x is a function of the current endogenous variable, giving rise to the standard case of simultaneous equation bias.

The other main cause of the failure of this condition is when the error terms are contaminated by something other than a purely random component. The principal way in which this can happen is when we measure the x variables with error. Therefore, if $x = x^* + \upsilon$ where x^* is the true value of the variable, υ is a measurement error, and x is the observed value of the variable including the measurement error. In this case, Eq. (31) becomes $y_t = x_t\phi + (u_t - \phi\upsilon_t)$ where the term in brackets is the total error term. Now there is a clear correlation between the error term and x because both contain υ and the condition will be violated.

In both of these cases, LS estimation will give biased estimates of the parameters, and it is no longer consistent. The most efficient way forward would be to specify an appropriate structural model and estimate it using maximum likelihood. This is not always feasible, however, because it might not be possible to specify a complete model nor to estimate it in a practical way. The usual alternative is to resort to an instrumental variable estimator or GMM, and then the challenge is to find some appropriate set of instruments that are both properly exogenous and not weak.

11 Failure of $\lim_{t\to\infty}\left(\frac{x'x}{T}\right)=\Omega$

This assumption might be violated for a number of trivial reasons and for one very important reason. The most obvious of the trivial reasons is where perfect multicollinearity exists between the x's. In this case, $x'x/T$ becomes singular and this assumption is violated. The multicollinearity needs to be removed by reducing the size of the x vector.

Another trivial reason would be if one of the x variables contains a deterministic linear trend, although in this case the properties of LS estimation might be recovered by a slightly more complex analysis.

The important reason why this condition might fail is simply that implicitly behind this statement is the assumption that the x variables are weakly stationary. A stochastic process x_t is weakly (second-order or covariance) stationary if the first two moments of the process do not change over time. A stationary process will obey the following conditions:

$$E(x_t) = \mu < \infty \quad \text{for all } t \tag{39}$$

$$E\left[(x_t - \mu)^2\right] < \infty \quad \text{for all } t \tag{40}$$

$$E[(x_t - \mu)(x_{t+k} - \mu)] = \gamma_k \quad \text{for all } t, k \tag{41}$$

If any of these conditions is violated, then the variable is not weakly stationary. One of the simplest forms of nonstationary process is the random walk

$$x_t = x_{t-1} + \varepsilon_t \tag{42}$$

where ε_t is a white noise error process with constant variance σ^2. We can alternatively write this as

$$x_t = x_0 + \sum_{i=1}^{t} \varepsilon_i \tag{43}$$

In this case, the expected value of x_t is x_{t-1} and therefore it changes at each point in time violating Eq. (39). Also, the variance of x_t is easily shown to be $\text{var}(x_t) = \text{var}(\varepsilon_1 + \varepsilon_2 + \cdots + \varepsilon_t) = t\sigma^2$, which goes to ∞ as $t \to \infty$, thus violating Eq. (40). This also means that

$$\lim_{t \to \infty} \left(\frac{x'x}{T} \right) \neq \Omega \tag{44}$$

as the variance of x will go to infinity. A process such as Eq. (42) can be rendered stationary by taking the first difference $x_t - x_{t-1} = w_t = \varepsilon_t$, in which case x is referred to as an integrated process. Because it needs only to be differenced once to make it stationary, it is integrated of order 1, or $I(1)$. A random walk series such as Eq. (42) is of smaller order in magnitude than T, that is $T^{-1}\sum_{t=1}^{T} x_t^2 \sim o_p(T)$.

The nonstationarity of the x variables raises another important issue. If both x and y are stationary in the standard linear model $y_t = x_t\phi + u_t$, then the error term u_t also will be stationary. If either x or y is nonstationary, however, then there is no guarantee of the stationarity of the error term, and it is again possible that we have a failure in the assumption that $\lim_{t \to \infty} \left(\frac{x'u}{T}\right) = 0$. This is the classic case of a spurious regression defined by Granger and Newbold (1974), which comes about essentially when the last term in Eq. (34) is undefined and the LS estimator does not converge to anything well defined.

12 Cointegration

Although it generally is true that if x and y are nonstationary then the error term also will be nonstationary, this does not always have to be the case. When this happens, it gives rise to the important special case of cointegration. Following Engle and Granger (1987), we can define cointegration. Let w_t be a $k \times$ I vector of variables, then the components of w_t are said to be cointegrated of order (d,b) if

(1) All the components of w_t are $I\ (d)$
(2) There is at least on vector of coefficients α such that $\alpha w_t \sim I(d-b)$

In other words, there is a combination of the w_t variables that is integrated at a lower order than the variables themselves.

This gives rise to the important Granger Representation Theorem.

Let w_t be a vector of $k \times I(1)$ components and assume that there exists $r > 0$ cointegrating combinations of w_t. Then there exists a valid error correction model of the form

$$\varphi(L)(1-L)w_t = -\pi w_{t-k} + \upsilon + \varepsilon_t \tag{45}$$

where π has rank $r < n$.

A moving average representation also exists.

$$\begin{aligned}(1-L)w_t &= C(L)(\varepsilon_t + \upsilon) \\ &= C(1)(\varepsilon_t + \upsilon) + C^*(L)\Delta(\varepsilon_t + \upsilon)\end{aligned} \tag{46}$$

where $C(1)$ has rank $n - r$.

This theorem demonstrates several things. First, in the presence of nonstationary variables, cointegration is required for a model to be valid. Second, if there are r cointegrating vectors, there are $n - r$ common stochastic trends (represented by the rank of the C(1) matrix). Third, in the absence of cointegration, the regression will be spurious. Fourth, the existence of cointegration implies the existence of Granger causality in at least one direction. Finally, that the time dating of the levels terms is unimportant.

Given these concepts, we now can define the property of an LS regression in the presence of cointegration. We start with the formula for the LS estimator:

$$\hat{\phi} = \phi + p\lim\left[\left(\frac{x'x}{T}\right)^{-1}\frac{x'u}{T}\right] \tag{47}$$

We already have seen that $\frac{x'x}{T} \sim o_p(T)$ that is, the x variables explode proportionally to the sample size T. Because the model is cointegrated and the error is stationary, we also can show that $\frac{x'u}{T} \sim o_p(1)$, therefore

$$T(\hat{\phi} - \phi) \sim O_p(1) \tag{48}$$

$$(\hat{\phi} - \phi) \sim O_p(T^{-1}) \tag{49}$$

which means that the bias in the LS estimator disappears in proportion to the inverse of the sample size T. This is in contrast to the standard case of LS with stationary variables, in which $(\hat{\phi} - \phi) \sim O_p(T^{-0.5})$, where the bias disappears in proportion to the inverse of the square root of the sample size. This is known as the super consistency of LS estimation with cointegrated nonstationary variables.

13 Conclusion

In this chapter, we have reviewed some of the basic concepts that lie behind standard estimation and regression work. This began with the simple ideas of sampling, the population, and the sample distribution. We discussed the central limit theorem and the law of large numbers. We then outlined the two basic approaches to classical estimation: the maximum likelihood approach and instrumental variables/Generalized Methods of Moments. We then discussed the basic linear regression model and the problems that can arise in LS estimation when the underlying assumptions prove to be false. Finally, we outlined the problem of nonstationarity and cointegration and showed how under cointegration estimation actually can be more effective based on the super consistency proof.

Appendix Order of Magnitude and Convergence

In this appendix, we summarize the important concept of orders of magnitude and convergence, which is fundamental to understanding the analysis of statements such as Eq. (33). More detail about these fundamental concepts are found in Judge, Griffiths, Carter Hill, Lutkepohl, and Lee (1985).

Order of magnitude of a sequence: A sequence a_T is at most of order T^k if there exists a real number N such that

$$T^{-k}|a_T| \leq N \tag{A.1}$$

This is written as $a_T = O(T^k)$.

Smaller order of magnitude: A sequence a_T is of smaller order of magnitude than T^k if

$$\lim_{T\to\infty} T^{-k} a_T = 0 \tag{A.2}$$

This is written as $a_T = o(T^k)$.

These definitions can be extended to vectors and matrices by applying the definitions to every element of the matrix under consideration.

There are also some useful algebraic results in this area. Let $a_T = O(T^k)$ and $b_T = O(T^j)$, then

$$\begin{aligned} a_T b_T &= O\left(T^{k+j}\right) \\ |a_T|^s &= O\left(T^{ks}\right) \\ a_T + b_T &= O\left(\max\left\{T^k, T^j\right\}\right) \end{aligned} \tag{A.3}$$

Convergence in probability: A sequence of random variables $x_1, x_2, \dots, x_T$ converges in probability to the random variable x if, for all $\varepsilon > 0$

$$\lim_{t\to\infty} = P[| x_T - x| > \varepsilon] = 0 \tag{A.4}$$

That is, the probability that $|x_T - x|$ is greater than some small positive number is zero. Then, x is called the probability limit of x_T, which is written as $p \lim x_T = x$ or alternatively $x_T \xrightarrow{p} x$.

Almost sure convergence: This is a stronger concept of convergence than convergence in probability, the basic idea here for $T > T_0$. The probability that any two $x_t's$ differ from x by more than an arbitrarily small amount is vanishingly small. The random variable x_T converges almost surely to the random variable x if

$$P(\lim_{T\to\infty} x_T - x > \varepsilon) = 0 \tag{A.5}$$

We write this as $x_T \xrightarrow{a.s.} x$

Slutsky's theorem is important when working with probability limits. It states that, for any continuous function g then$p$ lim $(g(x_T)) = g(p \lim (x_T))$. This is in contrast to Siegel's paradox, which states that for standard expectations $E(g(x_T)) \neq g(E(x_T))$.

Order in Probability: We can combine the ideas of probability limits and order in magnitude to give a weaker version of orders in magnitude. A sequence of random variables x_T is at most of order in probability T^k if for every $\varepsilon > 0$ there exists a real number N such that

$$P\left[T^{-k}|x_T| \geq N\right] \leq \varepsilon \text{ for all } T \tag{A.6}$$

This is expressed as $x_T = O_p(T^k)$.

Similarly to orders in magnitude, we can say that x_T is of smaller order in probability than T^kif

$$p\lim T^{-k} x_T = 0 \tag{A.7}$$

Which again is expressed as $x_T = o_p(T^k)$.

A final useful relationship in this area of econometric theory is Chebyshev's inequality, which states that if x is a random variable with mean $\overline{x}$, then for every$\delta > 0$

$$P[|x - \overline{x}| \geq \delta] \leq \frac{E\left[(x-\overline{x})^2\right]}{\delta^2} \tag{A.8}$$

References

Berndt, E.R., Savin, N.E., 1977. Conflict among criteria for testing hypotheses in the multivariate linear regression model. Econometrics 45, 1263–1278.

Davidson, J., 1994. Stochastic limit theory. Oxford University Press, Oxford.

Engle, R.F., Granger, C.W.J., 1987. Cointegration and error correction: Representation, estimation and testing. Econometrica 55, 251–276.

Engle, R.F., Hendry, D.F., Richard, J.-F., 1983. Exogeneity. Econometrica 51, 277–304.

Geary, R.C., 1948. Studies in the relations between economic time series. Journal of the Royal Statistical Society B 10, 140–158.

Granger, C., Newbold, P., 1974. Spurious regression in econometrics. Journal of Econometrics 2, 111–120.

Greenberg, E., Webster, C.E., 1983. Advanced econometrics; A bridge to the literature. Wiley, New York.

Hall, A.R., 2005. Generalized method of moments. Oxford University Press, Oxford. advanced texts in econometrics.

Hansen, L.P., 1982. Large sample properties of generalised method of moments estimators. Econometrica 50, 1029–1054.

Harvey, A.C., 1981. The econometric analysis of time series. Phillip Allen, Hemel Hempstead.

Hendry, D.F., 1976. The structure of simultaneous equation estimators. Journal of Econometrics 4, 51–85.

Judge, G.G., Griffiths, W.E.M., Carter Hill, R., Lutkepohl, H., Lee, T.-C., 1985. The theory and practise of econometrics, second ed. John Wiley, Chichester.

Newey, W.K., West, K.D., 1987. A simple positive definite heteroskedasticity and autocorrelation-consistent covariance matrix. Econometrica 55, 703–708.

Reiersol, O., 1941. Confluence analysis by means of lag moments and other methods of confluence analysis. Econometrica 9, 1–24.

Sagan, J.D., 1958. The estimation of economic relationships using instrumental variables. Econometrica 26, 393–415.

White, H., 1980. A heteroskedasticity-consistent covariance matrix estimator and a direct test of heteroscedasticity. Econometrica 48, 817–838.

White, H., 1982. Maximum likelihood estimation of misspecified models. Econometrica 50 (1), 1–25.

Wright, S., 1925. Corn and Hog correlations. US Department of Agriculture Bulletin 1300, Washington, DC.

Chapter 2

Testing and Correcting for Endogeneity in Nonlinear Unobserved Effects Models

Wei Lin* and Jeffrey M. Wooldridge†

**Institute for Economic and Social Research, Jinan University, Guangzhou, People's Republic of China,* †*Department of Economics, Michigan State University, East Lansing, MI, United States*

Chapter Outline

1 Introduction

The availability of panel data can greatly facilitate the estimation of causal effects from nonexperimental data. For example, for studying policy interventions using linear models, the methods of fixed effects (FE) estimation and first differencing (FD) estimation are used routinely. The primary attractiveness of the FE and FD methods is because of their eliminating additive, unobserved heterogeneity that is thought to be correlated with the policy variable or variables of interest. Fixed effects-type approaches are available in special cases for nonlinear models, although in such cases they are best viewed as conditional maximum likelihood or conditional quasimaximum likelihood estimators, in which a conditioning argument essentially removes the dependence of an objective function on unobserved heterogeneity. The leading cases are the FE logit and

Panel Data Econometrics. https://doi.org/10.1016/B978-0-12-814367-4.00002-2

FE Poisson estimators. To handle heterogeneity more generally in a microeconometric setting, in which the number of available time periods, T, is typically small, the correlated random effects (CRE) approach can be effective. Wooldridge (2010) shows how the CRE approach can be used for a variety of nonlinear panel data models used in practice. See also Wooldridge (2018) for some developments using unbalanced panels.

One drawback to FE, FD, and CRE approaches is that they allow for only one kind of endogeneity: correlation between the time-varying explanatory variables, often through sometime like the time average of these variables, and time-constant heterogeneity. But in many contexts we might be worried about correlation between at least some of the covariates and unobserved shocks—often called idiosyncratic errors. In the case of a linear model, combining instrumental variables (IV) approaches with the FE and FD transformations can be quite powerful. For example, Levitt (1996, 1997) uses IV approaches after eliminating heterogeneity at either the state or city level.

Fixed effects IV approaches explicitly recognize two potential sources of endogeneity: "heterogeneity endogeneity," which arises when one or more explanatory variables is correlated with time-constant heterogeneity, and "idiosyncratic endogeneity," which arises when one or more explanatory variables is correlated with time-varying unobservables. Both kinds of endogeneity also can be present in nonlinear models. Papke and Wooldridge (2008) [hereafter, PW (2008)], in the context of a probit fractional response model, show how to combine the CRE and control function approaches to allow for heterogeneity endogeneity and idiosyncratic endogeneity. [More recently, Murtazashvili & Wooldridge, 2016 use a similar approach for panel data switching regression models with lots of heterogeneity.] The approach is largely parametric, although it is robust to distributional misspecification other than the conditional mean, and it allows unrestricted serial dependence over time—a feature not allowed, for example, by random effects probit or fixed effects logit approaches. The PW (2008) approach is attractive because it leads to simple estimation methods, robust inference, and easy calculation of average partial effects. It does, however, have a couple of potential drawbacks. The first is that the method does not allow one to tell whether a rejection of the null hypothesis of exogeneity of the covariates is because of heterogeneity or idiosyncratic endogeneity. Second, the explanatory variables that are potentially endogenous in the structural equation are not rendered *strictly* exogenous in the estimating equation. Rather, they are only contemporaneously exogenous, which means that only pooled methods, or method of moments versions of them, produce consistent estimators. This leaves out the possibility of applying quasigeneralized least squares approaches, such as the generalized estimating equations (GEE) approach that is popular in fields outside economics.

In this paper, we show how to modify, in a straightforward way, the CRE/CF approach of PW (2008) so that we can easily separate the two kinds of endogeneity. One benefit is that we can test the null hypothesis of idiosyncratic exogeneity while allowing for heterogeneity exogeneity, which effectively allows us to determine whether an IV approach is needed. Section 2 covers the linear case, in which we show that our new control function approach leads to a test statistic that is identical to the variable addition Hausman test discussed in Wooldridge (2010, Chapter 11). This sets the stage for two leading cases of nonlinear models, an exponential mean function and a probit mean function. The exponential mean case, treated in Section 3, is interesting because the robustness properties of the Poisson FE estimator can be combined with the control function approach to obtain a test for idiosyncratic exogeneity that is fully robust to distributional misspecification, as well as to serial dependence of arbitrary form. We also cover the issue of estimating average partial effects, and discuss the merits of a CRE/CF approach. In Section 4 we turn to a probit response function—as in PW (2008)—and show how to modify PW's CRE approach to separately analyze the two kinds of endogeneity. Section 5 discusses how the approach applied to general nonlinear unobserved effects models, and provides a discussion of the pros and cons of using a joint MLE—such as random effects probit or random effects Tobit—in the second stage. Two empirical applications in Section 6 show how the methods are easily applied, and Section 7 contains concluding remarks.

2 Models Linear in Parameters

We start with a "structural" equation

$$y_{it1} = \mathbf{x}_{it1}\boldsymbol{\beta}_1 + c_{i1} + u_{it1} \tag{1}$$

where, for now, the explanatory variables are

$$\mathbf{x}_{it1} = (\mathbf{y}_{it2}, \mathbf{z}_{it1}).$$

The vector $\mathbf{z}_{it1}$ typically would include a full set of time effects to allow for secular changes over time. We suspect the vector $\mathbf{y}_{it2}$ is endogenous in that it might be correlated with the unobserved effect (or heterogeneity), c_{i1}, and possibly with the idiosyncratic error, u_{it1}. In what follows, we allow all exogenous variables, which include the vector $\mathbf{z}_{it1}$ and variables excluded, $\mathbf{z}_{it2}$, to be correlated with the heterogeneity. Therefore, we proceed as if all explanatory variables can be correlated with the unobserved heterogeneity, c_{i1}. In other words, we are not taking a traditional random effects approach.

The difference between $\mathbf{y}_{it2}$ and $\mathbf{z}_{it}$ is that we take the latter to be strictly exogenous with respect to $\{u_{it1}\}$:

$$Cov(\mathbf{z}_{it}, u_{ir1}) = 0, \text{all } t, \quad r = 1, \ldots, T.$$

By contrast, $\{\mathbf{y}_{it2}\}$ can be correlated with $\{u_{it1}\}$, either contemporaneously or across time periods.

Given a suitable rank condition, which is discussed in Wooldridge (2010, Chapter 11), β_1 can be estimated by fixed effects 2SLS (FE2SLS), sometimes called FEIV. To describe the estimator, define the deviations from time averages as

$$\ddot{y}_{it1} = y_{it1} - T^{-1}\sum_{r=1}^{T} y_{ir1}, \quad \ddot{\mathbf{y}}_{it2} = \mathbf{y}_{it2} - T^{-1}\sum_{r=1}^{T} \mathbf{y}_{ir2}, \quad \ddot{\mathbf{z}}_{it} = \mathbf{z}_{it} - T^{-1}\sum_{r=1}^{T} \mathbf{z}_{ir}.$$

Given a random sample (in the cross section) of size N, one characterization of FE2SLS estimator is that it is pooled 2SLS applied to the equation

$$\ddot{y}_{it1} = \ddot{\mathbf{x}}_{it1}\beta_1 + \ddot{u}_{it1}, \quad t = 1, \ldots, T$$

using IVs $\ddot{\mathbf{z}}_{it}$. With fixed T and $N \to \infty$, the estimator is generally consistent and $\sqrt{N}$-asymptotically normal. Fully robust inference that allows arbitrary serial correlation and heteroskedasticity in $\{u_{it1}\}$ is straightforward.

In terms of precision, the FE2SLS estimator can have large standard errors. We first remove much of the variation in the data by removing the time averages, and then we apply 2SLS. At a minimum, we require sufficient variation in the excluded exogenous variables that serve as instruments for $\mathbf{y}_{it2}$. Therefore, it is of some interest to test the null hypothesis that $\{\mathbf{y}_{it2}\}$ is exogenous with respect to $\{u_{it1}\}$.

A common approach is to apply the Hausman (1978) principle, where the two estimators being compared are the usual FE estimator and the FE2SLS estimator. The usual FE estimator is consistent if we add the assumption

$$Cov(\mathbf{y}_{it2}, u_{ir1}) = 0, \text{all } t, \quad r = 1, \ldots, T.$$

The FE2SLS estimator does not require this stronger form of exogeneity of $\mathbf{y}_{it2}$.

There are a couple of drawbacks to the traditional Hausman test. Most importantly, because it assumes that one estimator is relatively efficient—in this case, the FE estimator plays the role of the efficient estimator—it is not robust to serial correlation or heteroskedasticity in $\{u_{it1}\}$. If we make our inference concerning $\beta 1$ robust to departures from the standard, usually unrealistic, assumptions, then it is logically inconsistent to use nonrobust specification tests. Wooldridge (1990) makes this point in the context of a variety of specification tests. The second problem with the traditional Hausman test is the asymptotic variance required is singular, and this can lead to computational problems as well as incorrect calculation of degrees of freedom.

A simpler approach is to obtain a variation addition test (VAT), which is based on the control function approach. Wooldridge (2010, Chapter 11) describes the procedure:

Procedure 1 (FE Variable Addition Test):

1. Estimate the reduced form of $\mathbf{y}_{it2}$,

$$\mathbf{y}_{it2} = \mathbf{z}_{it}\Pi_2 + \mathbf{c}_{i2} + \mathbf{u}_{it2},$$

by fixed effects, and obtain the FE residuals,

$$\hat{\ddot{\mathbf{u}}}_{it2} = \ddot{\mathbf{y}}_{it2} - \ddot{\mathbf{z}}_{it}\hat{\Pi}_2$$

$$\ddot{\mathbf{y}}_{it2} = \mathbf{y}_{it2} - T^{-1}\sum_{r=1}^{T} \mathbf{y}_{ir2}$$

2. Estimate the equation

$$y_{it1} = \mathbf{x}_{it1}\beta_1 + \hat{\hat{\mathbf{u}}}_{it2}\boldsymbol{\rho}_1 + c_{i1} + error_{it1}$$

by *usual* FE and compute a robust Wald test of H_0: $\boldsymbol{\rho}_1 = \mathbf{0}$. □

The VAT version of the Hausman test has a simple interpretation, because the $\hat{\boldsymbol{\beta}}_1$ obtained in the second step is actually the FEIV estimate. If we set $\boldsymbol{\rho}_1$ to zero, we are using the usual FE estimator. If we estimate $\boldsymbol{\rho}_1$, we obtain the FEIV estimator. Importantly, it is very easy to make the test robust to arbitrary serial correlation and heteroskedasticity. As a practical matter, it is important to understand that the nature of $\mathbf{y}_{it2}$ is unrestricted. It can be continuous, discrete (including binary), or some mixture. Later, we will discuss what happens if we allow more general functional forms.

In motivating our general approach for nonlinear models, it is useful to obtain a test based on Mundlak's (1978) CRE approach. We must use some care to obtain a test that rejects only in the presence of idiosyncratic endogeneity. We start with a linear reduced form for $\mathbf{y}_{it2}$, but we emphasize that, for linear models, this equation is not restrictive. A linear unobserved effects reduced form is

$$\mathbf{y}_{it2} = \mathbf{z}_{it}\boldsymbol{\Pi}_2 + \mathbf{c}_{i2} + \mathbf{u}_{it2}$$

where $\boldsymbol{\Pi}_2$ is dimension $L \times G_1$ where G_1 is the dimension of $\mathbf{y}_{it2}$. Now we apply the Mundlak (1978) to the vector of unobserved heterogeneity, $\mathbf{c}_{i2}$:

$$\mathbf{c}_{i2} = \psi_2 + \bar{\mathbf{z}}_i\boldsymbol{\Xi}_2 + \mathbf{a}_{i2},$$

where $\bar{\mathbf{z}}_{ii} = T^{-1}\sum_{t=1}^{T}\mathbf{z}_{it}$ is the row vector of time averages of all exogenous variables and $\boldsymbol{\Xi}_2$ is $L \times G_1$. Plugging into the previous equation gives

$$\mathbf{y}_{it2} = \psi_2 + \mathbf{z}_{it}\boldsymbol{\Pi}_2 + \bar{\mathbf{z}}_i\boldsymbol{\Xi}_2 + \mathbf{a}_{i2} + \mathbf{u}_{it2}, \quad t = 1, \ldots, T.$$

In what follows, we operate *as if*

$$Cov(\mathbf{z}_{it}, \mathbf{u}_{is2}) = 0, \text{ all } t, s$$

$$Cov(\mathbf{z}_{it}, \mathbf{a}_{i2}) = 0, \text{ all } t,$$

but, as we will see, even these mild assumptions need not actually hold.

The key now in obtaining a test of idiosyncratic endogeneity is how we apply the Mundlak device to c_{i1} in the structural equation

$$y_{it1} = \mathbf{x}_{it1}\boldsymbol{\beta}_1 + c_{i1} + u_{it1}.$$

One possibility is to project c_{i1} only onto $\bar{\mathbf{z}}_i$. It turns out that this approach is fine for estimating $\beta 1$ but, for testing endogeneity of $\mathbf{y}_{it2}$, it does not distinguish between

$$Cov(\mathbf{y}_{it2}, c_{i1}) \neq 0$$

and

$$Cov(\mathbf{y}_{it2}, u_{is1}) \neq 0.$$

Instead, it is better to project c_{i1} onto $(\bar{\mathbf{z}}_i, \bar{\mathbf{v}}_{i2})$ where

$$\mathbf{v}_{it2} = \mathbf{a}_{i2} + \mathbf{u}_{it2}.$$

Then we have

$$c_{i1} = \eta_1 + \bar{\mathbf{z}}_i \lambda_1 + \bar{\mathbf{v}}_{i2} \boldsymbol{\pi}_1 + a_{i1}$$
$$Cov(\mathbf{z}_i, a_{i1}) = 0$$
$$Cov(\mathbf{y}_{i2}, a_{i1}) = 0$$

Importantly, the remaining heterogeneity, a_{i1}, is uncorrelated not only with $\mathbf{z}_i = \{\mathbf{z}_{it}\text{: } t = 1, \ldots, T\}$ but also with $\mathbf{y}_{i2} = \{\mathbf{y}_{it2}\text{: } t = 1, \ldots,\}$. Plugging into the structure equation produces the following estimating equation:

$$\begin{aligned} y_{it1} &= \mathbf{x}_{it1}\boldsymbol{\beta}_1 + \eta_1 + \bar{\mathbf{z}}_i \boldsymbol{\lambda}_1 + \bar{\mathbf{v}}_{i2}\boldsymbol{\pi}_1 + a_{i1} + u_{it1} \\ &= \mathbf{x}_{it1}\boldsymbol{\beta}_1 + \eta_1 + \bar{\mathbf{z}}_i \boldsymbol{\lambda}_1 + (\bar{\mathbf{y}}_{i2} - \psi_2 - \bar{\mathbf{z}}_i \boldsymbol{\Lambda}_2)\boldsymbol{\pi}_1 + a_{i1} + u_{it1} \\ &\equiv \mathbf{x}_{it1}\boldsymbol{\beta}_1 + \psi_1 + \bar{\mathbf{y}}_{i2}\boldsymbol{\pi}_1 + \bar{\mathbf{z}}_i \boldsymbol{\xi}_1 + a_{i1} + u_{it1}. \end{aligned}$$

Now, by the Mundlak device, a_{i1} is uncorrelated with *all* RHS observables, that is, $(\mathbf{y}_{it2}, \mathbf{z}_{it1}, \bar{\mathbf{y}}_{i2}, \bar{\mathbf{z}}_i)$. By the strict exogeneity assumption on $\{\mathbf{z}_{it}\text{: } t = 1, \ldots, T\}$, u_{it1} is uncorrelated with $(\mathbf{z}_{it1}, \bar{\mathbf{z}}_i)$. Therefore, we can now test whether $\mathbf{y}_{it2}$, is uncorrelated with u_{it1} by testing whether $\mathbf{v}_{it2}$ is uncorrelated with u_{it1}.

Procedure 2 (CRE/CF Variable Addition Test):

1. Run a pooled OLS regression

$$\mathbf{y}_{it2} = \psi_2 + \mathbf{z}_{it}\boldsymbol{\Pi}_2 + \bar{\mathbf{z}}_i \boldsymbol{\Xi}_2 + \mathbf{v}_{it2},$$

   and obtain the residuals, $\hat{\mathbf{v}}_{it2}$.

2. Estimate

$$y_{it1} = \mathbf{x}_{it1}\boldsymbol{\beta}_1 + \psi_1 + \bar{\mathbf{y}}_{i2}\boldsymbol{\pi}_1 + \bar{\mathbf{z}}_i \boldsymbol{\xi}_1 + \hat{\mathbf{v}}_{it2}\boldsymbol{\rho}_1 + error_{it1} \tag{2}$$

   by POLS or RE and use a robust Wald test of H_0: $\boldsymbol{\rho}_1 = \mathbf{0}$. □

Because the derivation of the estimating equation in Procedure 2 uses the Mundlak device, it nominally appears that it is less robust than that based on fixed effects in Procedure 1. This turns out not to be the case; in fact, the two approaches yield identical estimates of $\beta 1$ and $\boldsymbol{\rho}_1$. The estimate of $\beta 1$ is still the FEIV estimate. Therefore, we can use either the FE approach or the Mundlak CRE approach, and it does not matter whether the residuals we add to the equation are the FE residuals, $\hat{\ddot{\mathbf{u}}}_{it2}$, or the Mundlak residuals, $\hat{\mathbf{v}}_{it2}$. These residuals are not the same, but in the appendix it is shown that

$$\hat{\mathbf{v}}_{it2} = \hat{\ddot{\mathbf{u}}}_{it2} + \hat{\mathbf{r}}_{i2}$$

where

$$\hat{\mathbf{r}}_{i2} = \overline{\mathbf{y}}_{i2} - \hat{\kappa}_2 - \overline{\mathbf{z}}_i \hat{\mathbf{\Lambda}}_2$$

are the between residuals from regressing $\overline{\mathbf{y}}_{i2}$ on $1, \overline{\mathbf{z}}_i$. In particular, $\hat{\mathbf{r}}_{i2}$ is a linear combination of $(\overline{\mathbf{y}}_{i2}, 1, \overline{\mathbf{z}}_i)$. It follows immediately that replacing $\hat{\mathbf{v}}_{it2}$ in Eq. (2) does not change $\beta 1$ and $\hat{\rho}_1$. Only $\hat{\psi}_1$, $\hat{\boldsymbol{\pi}}_1$ and $\hat{\boldsymbol{\xi}}_1$ would change.

Interestingly, if we drop $\overline{\mathbf{y}}_{i2}$ from step (2) in Procedure 2, the resulting estimate of $\beta 1$ is still the FEIV estimate. But we obtain a different estimate of $\boldsymbol{\rho}_1$, and basing a test of endogeneity on the equation without including $\overline{\mathbf{y}}_{i2}$ conflates heterogeneity endogeneity and idiosyncratic endogeneity. Evidently, this point has gone unnoticed, probably because Procedure 1 is the usual VAT in testing for idiosyncratic endogeneity. Neverthless, this observation is very important when we must use the Mundlak CRE approach in nonlinear models (because an FE approach is not available).

The conclusion from this section is that, for using the CRE/CF approach for testing

$$H_0 : Cov(\mathbf{y}_{it2}, u_{is1}) = 0,$$

we should use the equations

$$\begin{aligned}
\mathbf{y}_{it2} &= \hat{\psi}_2 + \ddot{\mathbf{z}}_{it}\hat{\Pi}_2 + \overline{\mathbf{z}}_i\hat{\Xi}_2 - \hat{\mathbf{v}}_{it2} \\
y_{it1} &= \mathbf{x}_{it1}\beta_1 + \psi_1 + \overline{\mathbf{y}}_{i2}\boldsymbol{\pi}_1 + \overline{\mathbf{z}}_i\boldsymbol{\xi}_1 + \hat{\mathbf{v}}_{it2}\boldsymbol{\rho}_1 + error_{it1},
\end{aligned}$$

being sure to include $\overline{\mathbf{y}}_{i2}$.

As an aside, one might want to know what happens if the seemingly less restrictive Chamberlain (1982) version of the CRE approach is used in place of Mundlak. The answer is: nothing. At least not if we use the basic estimation methods that do not attempt to exploit serial correlation or heteroskedasticity in the $\{u_{it1}\}$. To be clear, letting

$$\mathbf{z}_i = (\mathbf{z}_{i1}, \ldots, \mathbf{z}_{iT}), \quad \mathbf{y}_{i2} = (\mathbf{y}_{i12}, \ldots, \mathbf{y}_{iT2}),$$

the equations

$$\begin{aligned}
\mathbf{y}_{it2} &= \hat{\psi}_2 + \mathbf{z}_{it}\hat{\Pi}_2 + \mathbf{z}_i\hat{\Xi}_2 - \hat{\mathbf{v}}_{it2} \\
y_{it1} &= \mathbf{x}_{it1}\beta_1 + \psi_1 + \mathbf{z}_i\boldsymbol{\xi}_1 + \mathbf{y}_{i2}\boldsymbol{\pi}_1 + \hat{\mathbf{v}}_{it2}\boldsymbol{\rho}_1 + error_{it1}
\end{aligned}$$

result in the same estimates of $\boldsymbol{\beta}_1$ and $\boldsymbol{\rho}_1$ as the Mundlak approach, provided we use either pooled OLS or RE in the second equation.

How can one use the test of idiosyncratic endogeneity? Guggenberger (2010) shows that the pretesting problem that exists from using the Hausman test to determine an appropriate estimation strategy can be severe. Nevertheless, such practice is common in empirical work. If the VAT rejects at, say, the 5% significance level, one typically uses the FEIV estimator. If one fails to reject, it provides some justification for dropping the IV approach and instead using the usual FE estimator.

3 Exponential Model

If $\mathbf{y}_{it1}$ is nonnegative, and especially if it can take the value zero, an exponential conditional mean function is attractive. (The common alternative when $\mathbf{y}_{it1} > 0$ is to use $\log(\mathbf{y}_{it1})$ in a linear model, but some researchers prefer to model $\mathbf{y}_{it1}$ directly.) An unobserved effects model that allows for heterogeneity endogeneity and idiosyncratic endogeneity is

$$E(\mathbf{y}_{it1} | \mathbf{y}_{i2}, \mathbf{z}_i, c_{i1}, r_{it1}) = E(\mathbf{y}_{it1} | \mathbf{y}_{it2}, \mathbf{z}_{it1}, c_{i1}, r_{it1}) = c_{i1} \exp(\mathbf{x}_{it1}\beta_1 + r_{it1}), \quad (3)$$

where, again, $\mathbf{x}_{it1} = (\mathbf{y}_{it2}, \mathbf{z}_{it1})$. Now the heterogeneity, c_{i1}, is nonnegative and multiplicative. We use r_{it1} to denote time-varying omitted factors that we suspect are correlated with $\mathbf{y}_{it2}$. We could make r_{it1} multiplicative but it is slightly more convenient to have it appear inside the exponential function.

3.1 An FE Poisson/CF Approach

As discussed in Wooldridge (1999) and Wooldridge (2010, Chapter 18), without r_{it1} an appealing estimator is what is typically called the fixed effects Poisson estimator. In Hausman, Hall, and Griliches (1984), the FE Poisson estimator was obtained as a conditional MLE, in which the Poisson assumption was assumed to hold along with conditional independence. Wooldridge (1999) showed that the neither assumption is needed to ensure consistency and asymptotic normality of the FE Poisson estimator. Viewed as a quasiMLE, the estimator is fully robust in the sense that it only requires, in the current notation (with idiosyncratic endogeneity),

$$E(\mathbf{y}_{it1} | \mathbf{x}_{i1}, c_{i1}) = E(\mathbf{y}_{it1} | \mathbf{x}_{it1}, c_{i1}) = c_{i1} \exp(\mathbf{x}_{it1}\beta_1).$$

The first equality imposes a strict exogeneity requirement with respect to idiosyncratic shocks. It will be violated if r_{it1} is present and correlated with $\mathbf{y}_{is2}$ for any time period s, including, of course, $s = t$.

To obtain a test of the null hypothesis that there is no idiosyncratic endogeneity, we again need time-varying, strictly exogenous instruments that are excluded from $\mathbf{z}_{it1}$. Formally, the null hypothesis is

$$E(y_{it1} | \mathbf{y}_{i2}, \mathbf{z}_i, c_{i1}) = E(\mathbf{y}_{it1} | \mathbf{y}_{it2}, \mathbf{z}_{it1}, c_{i1}) = c_{i1} \exp(\mathbf{x}_{it1}\beta_1),$$

where the key is that $\mathbf{z}_{it2}$ is exclused from the mean function. Also, all variables are strictly exogenous conditional on c_{i1}. In order to obtain a test, we need to specify an alternative, and this is where explicitly introducing a time-varying unobservables into the structural model, and a reduced form for $\mathbf{y}_{it2}$, come into play. But we emphasize that these do not play a role under the null hypothesis. They are used only to obtain a test. In addition to Eq. (3), we write

$$\mathbf{y}_{it2} = \mathbf{z}_{it}\mathbf{\Pi}_2 + \mathbf{c}_{i2} + \mathbf{u}_{it2}, \quad t = 1, \ldots, T,$$

and, because the $\{\mathbf{z}_{it}\}$ is strictly exogenous, we test for correlation between $\{r_{it1}\}$ and functions of $\{\mathbf{u}_{it2}\}$. We use the analog of the test from Procedure 1.

Procedure 3 (Poisson FE/VAT):

1. Estimate the reduced form for $\mathbf{y}_{it2}$ by fixed effects and obtain the FE residuals,

$$\hat{\ddot{\mathbf{u}}}_{it2} = \ddot{\mathbf{y}}_{it2} - \ddot{\mathbf{z}}_{it}\hat{\Pi}_2$$

2. Use FE Poisson on the mean function

$$E\left(\mathbf{y}_{it1} \mid \mathbf{z}_{it1}, \mathbf{y}_{it2}, \hat{\ddot{\mathbf{u}}}_{it2}, c_{i1}\right) = c_{i1}\exp\left(\mathbf{x}_{it1}\beta_1 + \hat{\ddot{\mathbf{u}}}_{it2}\boldsymbol{\rho}_1\right)$$

and use a robust Wald test of $H_0 : \boldsymbol{\rho}1 = 0$. □

It turns out that, as in the linear case, the fixed effects residuals can be replaced with the Mundlak residuals. Again let $\hat{\mathbf{v}}_{it2}$ be the OLS residuals from estimating

$$\mathbf{y}_{it2} = \psi_2 + \mathbf{z}_{it}\mathbf{\Pi}_2 + \bar{\mathbf{z}}_i\mathbf{\Xi}_2 + \mathbf{v}_{it2}.$$

Then, as shown in the appendix, step (2) in Procedure 3 produces the same estimates of $(\boldsymbol{\beta}_1, \boldsymbol{\rho}_1)$. This follows from the form of the FE Poisson quasilog-likelihood function and the fact that $\hat{\mathbf{v}}_{it2} = \hat{\ddot{\mathbf{u}}}_{it2} + \hat{\mathbf{r}}_{i2}$, and so removing the time averages of $\hat{\mathbf{v}}_{it2}$ produces the FE residuals $\hat{\ddot{\mathbf{u}}}_{it2}$.

As in the linear case, it is useful to remember that, under the null hypothesis, no restrictions are placed on $\mathbf{y}_{it2}$. In fact, the EEVs could include binary variables, in which case the reduced forms are linear probability models estimated by FE or the CRE approach. Under the null hypothesis that $\{\mathbf{y}_{it2}\}$ is exogenous, we can use any way of generating residuals that we want. More power might be obtained by using different models for the elements of $\mathbf{y}_{it2}$, but that is a power issue.

The equivalance between the between using the FE residuals $\hat{\ddot{\mathbf{u}}}_{it2}$ and the Mundlak residuals $\hat{\mathbf{v}}_{it2}$ means that we can obtain sufficient conditions for Procedure 3 to correct for idiosyncratic endogeneity when it is present. But now we need to make assumptions on the reduced form of $\mathbf{y}_{it2}$. We can get by with somewhat less, but a convenient assumption is

$$(\mathbf{r}_{i1}, \mathbf{u}_{i2}) \text{ is independent of } (c_{i1}, \mathbf{c}_{i2}, \mathbf{z}_i),$$

where $\mathbf{r}_{i1}$ is the vector of omitted variables in Eq. (3) and $\mathbf{u}_{i2}$ is the reduced form error. This assumption that v_{it2} is independent of means that the Mundlak equation is in fact a conditional expectation. Moreover, there cannot be heteroskedasticity.

Now, if we make a functional form assumption,

$$E[\exp(r_{it1}) \mid \mathbf{u}_{i2}] = \exp(\theta_1 + \mathbf{u}_{it2}\boldsymbol{\rho}_1) = \exp[\theta_1 + (\mathbf{v}_{it2} - \mathbf{a}_{i1})\boldsymbol{\rho}_1],$$

which follows under joint normality of $(\mathbf{r}_{i1}, \mathbf{u}_{i2})$ but can hold more generally. The structural expectation is in Eq. (3), where now we also assume this is the expectation when we add $\mathbf{c}_{i2}$ to the conditioning set. Then

$$\begin{aligned} E(y_{it1} \mid \mathbf{y}_{i2}, \mathbf{z}_i, c_{i1}, \mathbf{c}_{i2}, \mathbf{v}_{i2}) &= c_{i1}\exp[\mathbf{x}_{it1}\beta_1 + \theta_1 + (\mathbf{v}_{it2} - \mathbf{a}_{i1})\boldsymbol{\rho}_1] \\ &= g_{i1}\exp(\mathbf{x}_{it1}\beta_1 + \mathbf{v}_{it2}\boldsymbol{\rho}_1) \end{aligned}$$

where $g_{i1} = c_{i1} \exp(-\mathbf{a}_{i1}\boldsymbol{\rho}_1)$. Now we can use Procedure 3, with either the FE residuals or the Mundlak residuals, to consistently estimate β_1, along with $\boldsymbol{\rho}_1$, using the Poisson FE estimator. We require nothing more about the Poisson distribution to be correctly specified, and serial independence is entirely unrestricted. However, because we now allow $\boldsymbol{\rho}_1 \neq 0$, the standard errors need to be adjusted for the two-step estimation. One can use the delta method, or use a panel bootstrap, where both estimating steps are done with each bootstrap sample.

3.2 Estimating Average Partial Effects

In addition to consistently estimating $\beta 1$, we might want to obtain partial effects on the conditional expectation itself. One possibility is to estimate the average structural function (Blundell & Powell, 2004), which averages out the unobservables for fixed $\mathbf{x}_{t1}$:

$$\begin{aligned} ASF_t(\mathbf{x}_{t1}) &= E_{(c_{i1}, r_{it1})}[c_{i1} \exp(\mathbf{x}_{t1}\beta_1 + r_{it1})] \\ &= E_{(c_{i1}, r_{it1})}[c_{i1} \exp(r_{it1})] \exp(\mathbf{x}_{t1}\beta_1). \end{aligned}$$

Let

$$\begin{aligned} v_{it1} &= c_{i1} \exp(r_{it1}) \\ \theta_{t1} &\equiv E(v_{it1}). \end{aligned}$$

Because we have a consistent estimate of $\beta 1$—which typically would include time effects—we just need to estimate θ_{t1} for each t (or, we might assume these are constant across t). Write

$$\begin{aligned} y_{it1} &= v_{it1} \exp(\mathbf{x}_{it1}\beta_1) e_{it1} \\ E(e_{it1} | \mathbf{x}_{i1}, c_{i1}, \mathbf{r}_{i1}) &= 1. \end{aligned}$$

In particular,

$$E(v_{it1}e_{it1}) = E[v_{it1}E(e_{it1} | v_{it1})] = E(v_{it1}) = \theta_{t1}.$$

Therefore,

$$\theta_{t1} = E\left[\frac{y_{it}}{\exp(\mathbf{x}_{it1}\beta_1)}\right]$$

and so a consistent estimator of θ_{t1} is

$$\hat{\theta}_{t1} = N^{-1} \sum_{i=1}^{N} \left[\frac{y_{it}}{\exp(\mathbf{x}_{it1}\hat{\beta}_1)}\right].$$

Therefore, a consistent and $\sqrt{N}$-asymptotically normal estimator of $ASF_t(\mathbf{x}_{t1})$.

is

$$\widehat{ASF}_t(\mathbf{x}_{t1}) = \hat{\theta}_{t1} \exp\left(\mathbf{x}_{t1}\hat{\beta}_1\right).$$

One can compute derivatives or changes with respect to the elements of $\mathbf{x}_{t1}$ and insert interesting values. A valid standard error for the resulting partial effects can be obtained via the delta method or bootstrapping.

Sometimes one wishes to have a single measure of partial effects, averaged across both the unobservables and observables. If x_{t1j} is continuous—for example, an element of $\mathbf{y}_{t2}$—we usually obtain the derivative and then average. The average partial effect (*APE*) is

$$APE_{tj} = \beta_{1j} E_{(\mathbf{x}_{it1},\, c_{i1},\, r_{it1})}\left[c_{i1} \exp\left(\mathbf{x}_{it1}\beta_1 + r_{it1}\right)\right]$$

and this is particularly easy to estimate because, by iterated expectations,

$$E_{(\mathbf{x}_{it1},\, c_{i1},\, r_{it1})}\left[c_{i1} \exp\left(\mathbf{x}_{it1}\beta_1 + r_{it1}\right)\right] = E(y_{it}).$$

(This simplification comes because of the exponential mean function.) Therefore, for each t,

$$APE_{tj} = \beta_{1j} E(y_{it}),$$

and a simple, consistent estimator is $\hat{\beta}_{1j}\left(N^{-1}\sum_{i=1}^{N} y_{it}\right)$. In many cases one would average across t as well to obtain a single partial effect.

3.3 A CRE/Control Function Approach

A CRE/CF approach can be used, although it requires more assumptions. Let

$$\begin{aligned} E(y_{it1} \mid \mathbf{y}_{it2}, \mathbf{z}_{it1}, c_{i1}, r_{it1}) &= c_{i1} \exp\left(\mathbf{x}_{it1}\beta_1 + r_{it1}\right) \\ v_{it1} &= c_{i1} \exp\left(r_{it1}\right) \\ \mathbf{y}_{it2} &= \psi_2 + \mathbf{z}_{it}\mathbf{\Pi}_2 + \bar{\mathbf{z}}_i \Xi_2 + \mathbf{v}_{it2}. \end{aligned}$$

Then there are two possibilities. Papke and Wooldridge (2008) suggest modeling the conditional distribution

$$D(v_{it1} \mid \mathbf{z}_i, \mathbf{v}_{it2}),$$

where and assuming that this depends only on $(\bar{\mathbf{z}}_i, \mathbf{v}_{it2})$. Although this approach leads to consistent estimation under maintained parametric assumptions, it does not lead to a straightforward test of idiosyncratic endogeneity: $\mathbf{v}_{it1}$ might be related to $\mathbf{v}_{it2}$ because of heterogeneity or idiosyncratic endogeneity. In addition. because we obtain an equation for $E(y_{it1} \mid \mathbf{x}_{it1}, \mathbf{z}_i, \mathbf{v}_{it2})$, only contemporaneous exogeneity holds because we are only conditioning on $\mathbf{v}_{it2}$ at time t. Therefore, only pooled methods can be used for consistent estimation.

Drawing on the linear case, a second possibility is attractive: Model the distribution

$$D(v_{it1}|\mathbf{z}_i, \mathbf{v}_{i2}).$$

Here, we use a Mundlak assumption:

$$\begin{aligned} D(v_{it1}|\mathbf{z}_i, \mathbf{v}_{i2}) &= D(v_{it1}|\overline{\mathbf{z}}_i, \overline{\mathbf{v}}_{i2}, \mathbf{v}_{it2}) \\ &= D(v_{it1}|\overline{\mathbf{z}}_i, \overline{\mathbf{y}}_{i2}, \mathbf{v}_{it2}). \end{aligned}$$

By construction, strict exogeneity holds for the conditioning variables, and so GLS-type procedures can be used. Moreover, even before we use a parametric model, this approach endogeneity of $\{\mathbf{y}_{it2}\}$ with respect to c_{i1} and $\{u_{it1}\}$.

If we use a linear index structure, the estimating equation is

$$E(y_{it1}|\mathbf{z}_i, \mathbf{y}_{i2}) = \exp(\psi_1 + \mathbf{x}_{it1}\beta_1 + \overline{\mathbf{y}}_{i2}\boldsymbol{\pi}_1 + \overline{\mathbf{z}}_i\boldsymbol{\xi}_1 + \mathbf{v}_{it2}\boldsymbol{\rho}_1).$$

Identification of the parameters follows because the time-varying exogenous variables $\mathbf{z}_{it2}$ are excluded from $\mathbf{x}_{it1}$, and therefore generate variation in $\mathbf{v}_{it2}$. The presence of $\overline{\mathbf{y}}_{i2}$ and $\overline{\mathbf{z}}_i$ allows the unobserved heterogeneity to be correlated with all explanatory variables and the excluded exogenous variables. The test of H_0: $\boldsymbol{\rho}_1 = \mathbf{0}$ is a clean test of idiosyncratic endogeneity, provided we assume our instruments are strictly exogenous and that the Mundlak device holds.

There are several approaches to estimating. The simplest is to use the pooled Poisson QMLE; naturally, we need to use fully robust inference to allow serial correlation and violations of the Poisson assumption. But we also can use a generalized least squares approach, where a working variance-covariance matrix is used to potentially increase efficiency over pooled estimation. Typically, one would use the Poisson variance, up to a scaling factor, as the working variances, and then choose a simple working correlation matrix—such as an exchangeable one, or at least one with constant pairwise correlations. Wooldridge (2010, Chapter 12) shows how the GEE approach is essentially multivariate weighted nonlinear least squares with a particular weighting matrix.

Because of the properties of the exponential function, it is possible to estimate the parameters $\beta 1$ using a generalized method of moments approach on a particular set of nonlinear moment conditions. The GMM approach does not restrict that nature of $\mathbf{y}_{it2}$. (See Wooldridge (1997) and Windmeijer (2000).) At a minimum, one can use the test for idiosyncratic endogeneity based on the Poisson FE estimator before proceeding to a more complicated GMM procedure.

4 Probit Response Function

With a probit conditional mean function, there are no versions of a fixed effects estimator that have attractive statistical properties, at least when T is not fairly large. Therefore, we consider only CRE/CF approaches to testing and correcting for endogeneity.

A probit conditional mean for $y_{it1} \in [0, 1]$, which we consider the structural equation, is

$$E(y_{it1} | \mathbf{z}_i, \mathbf{y}_{i2}, c_{i1}, u_{it1}) = E(y_{it1} | \mathbf{z}_{it1}, \mathbf{y}_{it2}, c_{i1}, u_{it1}) = \Phi(\mathbf{x}_{it1}\beta_1 + c_{i1} + u_{it1}), \quad (4)$$

and this can hold when y_{it1} is binary or when it is a fractional response. We assume that $\mathbf{y}_{it2}$ continuous and write a Mundlak reduced form, as before:

$$\mathbf{y}_{it2} = \psi_2 + \mathbf{z}_{it}\mathbf{\Pi}_2 + \bar{\mathbf{z}}_i\Xi_2 + \mathbf{v}_{it2}.$$

The important restriction (which can be relaxed to some degree) is

$$\mathbf{v}_{it2} \text{ is independent of } \mathbf{z}_i.$$

Define

$$r_{it1} = c_{i1} + u_{it1}.$$

Now we assume

$$D(r_{it1} | \mathbf{z}_i, \mathbf{v}_{i2}) = D(r_{it1} | \bar{\mathbf{z}}_i, \bar{\mathbf{v}}_{i2}, \mathbf{v}_{it2}) = D(r_{it1} | \bar{\mathbf{z}}_i, \bar{\mathbf{y}}_{i2}, \mathbf{v}_{it2}),$$

where the second equality holds because of the relationships among $\bar{\mathbf{z}}_i$, $\bar{\mathbf{y}}_{i2}$, and $\bar{\mathbf{v}}_{i2}$. In the leading case, we use a homoskedastic normal with linear mean:

$$r_{it1} | \bar{\mathbf{z}}_i, \bar{\mathbf{y}}_{i2}, \mathbf{v}_{it2} \sim Normal(\psi_1 + \bar{\mathbf{y}}_{i2}\boldsymbol{\pi}_1 + \bar{\mathbf{z}}_i\boldsymbol{\xi}_1 + \mathbf{v}_{it2}\boldsymbol{\rho}_1, 1).$$

We set the variance to unity because we cannot identify a separate variance, and it has no effect on estimating the average partial effects—see Papke and Wooldridge (2008) for further discussion. Then, an argument similar to that in Papke and Wooldridge (2008) gives the estimating equation

$$E(y_{it1} | \mathbf{z}_i, \mathbf{y}_{i2}) = \Phi(\psi_1 + \mathbf{x}_{it1}\beta_1 + \bar{\mathbf{y}}_{i2}\boldsymbol{\pi}_1 + \bar{\mathbf{z}}_i\boldsymbol{\xi}_1 + \mathbf{v}_{it2}\boldsymbol{\rho}_1),$$

which is clearly similar to the estimating equation in the exponential case.

Procedure 4 (CRE/CF Probit):

1. Obtain the Mundlak residuals, $\hat{\mathbf{v}}_{it2}$, by pooled OLS.
2. Insert $\hat{\mathbf{v}}_{it2}$ in place of $\mathbf{v}_{it2}$, use pooled (fractional) probit of
$$\mathrm{y_{it1} \text{ on } 1, x_{it1}, \bar{y}_{i2}, \bar{z}_i, \hat{v}_{it2}, \quad t = 1, \ldots, T; \; i = 1, \ldots, N.} \quad \square$$

As in the linear case, Procedure 2, because $\hat{\mathbf{v}}_{it2} = \hat{\ddot{\mathbf{u}}}_{it2} + \hat{\mathbf{r}}_{i2}$ we can replace $\hat{\mathbf{v}}_{it2}$ with $\hat{\ddot{\mathbf{u}}}_{it2}$ and not change $\hat{\boldsymbol{\beta}}_1$ or $\hat{\boldsymbol{\rho}}_1$; only $\hat{\psi}_1$, $\hat{\boldsymbol{\pi}}_1$ and $\hat{\boldsymbol{\xi}}_1$ would change.

As before, we can use a cluster-robust Wald test of H_0: $\boldsymbol{\rho}1 = \mathbf{0}$ as a test of idiosyncratic exogeneity. Compared with Papke and Wooldridge (2008), $\bar{\mathbf{y}}_{i2}$ has been added to the equation, and doing so allows one to separate the two sources of endogeneity. Further, because the conditional mean satisfies a strict exogeneity assumption, we can use a GEE (quasiGLS) procedure, although bootstrapping should be used to obtain valid standard errors. Technically, the assumptions under which Procedure 4 is consistent are different from those for the PW procedure, but in practice the difference is unlikely to be important.

Procedure 4 leads to a cleaner test and also has the potential to produce more efficient estimators. Namely, GEE approaches can be used in place of the pooled probit estimation.

Consistent estimation of the APEs is also straightforward. Using the same arguments in Papke and Wooldridge (2008),

$$APE_{tj} = \beta_{1j} E_{(\mathbf{x}_{it1}, \bar{\mathbf{z}}_i, \bar{\mathbf{y}}_{i2}, \mathbf{v}_{it2})}[\phi(\mathbf{x}_{it1}\beta_1 + \psi_1 + \bar{\mathbf{z}}_i\boldsymbol{\xi}_1 + \bar{\mathbf{y}}_{i2}\boldsymbol{\pi}_1 + \mathbf{v}_{it2}\boldsymbol{\rho}_1)]$$

$$\widehat{APE}_{t_j} = \hat{\beta}_{1j}\left[N^{-1}\sum_{i=1}^{N}\phi\left(\mathbf{x}_{it1}\hat{\beta}_1 + \hat{\psi}_1 + \bar{\mathbf{z}}_i\hat{\boldsymbol{\xi}}_1 + \bar{\mathbf{y}}_{i2}\hat{\boldsymbol{\pi}}_1 + \hat{\mathbf{v}}_{it2}\hat{\boldsymbol{\rho}}_1\right)\right].$$

To obtain a single value, $\widehat{APE}_{t_j}$ can be averaged across t, too, and this is what would be produced by applying the Stata margins command after pooled estimation or GEE estimation. The standard error of the APE is complicated because of the two-step estimation and the averaging. Bootstrapping the entire procedure is practically sensible and not difficult computationally.

It can be shown that, just like the parameters, estimation of the APEs does not depend on whether $\hat{\mathbf{v}}_{it2}$ or $\hat{\ddot{\mathbf{u}}}_{it2}$ is used as the control function.

It is easy to make Procedure 4 more flexible. For example, rather than just entering each variable linearly, any nonlinear functions of

$$(\mathbf{x}_{it1}, \bar{\mathbf{z}}_i, \bar{\mathbf{y}}_{i2}, \hat{\mathbf{v}}_{it2})$$

can be included. These would typically include squares and cross products, but maybe higher order terms, too. One still can obtain the APEs by differentiating or differencing with respect to the elements of $\mathbf{x}_{t1}$ and then averaging across everything. For example, if we extend the estimating equation to

$$E(y_{it1}|\mathbf{z}_i, \mathbf{y}_{i2}) = \Phi(\psi_1 + \mathbf{x}_{it1}\beta_1 + \bar{\mathbf{y}}_{i2}\boldsymbol{\pi}_1 + \bar{\mathbf{z}}_i\boldsymbol{\xi}_1 + \mathbf{v}_{it2}\boldsymbol{\rho}_1 + (\mathbf{x}_{it1}\otimes\bar{\mathbf{x}}_{i1})\psi_1 + (\mathbf{x}_{it1}\otimes\mathbf{v}_{it2})\delta_1),$$

then we simply add the terms $\mathbf{x}_{it1}\otimes\bar{\mathbf{x}}_{i1}$ and $\mathbf{x}_{it1}\otimes\hat{\mathbf{v}}_{it2}$ to the probit or fractional probit estimation. We then have to account for the interactions when taking derivatives, and then average the resulting function.

Another possibility is to allow the variance in the probit equation, whether fractional or not, to depend on

$$(\bar{\mathbf{z}}_i, \bar{\mathbf{y}}_{i2}, \mathbf{v}_{it2}).$$

Then, one uses heteroskedastic probit or fractional heteroskedastict probit to allow c_{i1} to have nonconstant variance.

5 Other Nonlinear Models

5.1 Pooled Methods

The approach taken in the previous section applies to other nonlinear models, including the unobserved effects Tobit model. The approach is unchanged from the model with a probit response function. First, model the heterogeneity as a function of the history of the exogenous and endogenous variables, $(\mathbf{z}_i, \mathbf{y}_{i2})$, typically (but not necessarily) through simple functions, such as the time averages, $(\bar{\mathbf{z}}_i, \bar{\mathbf{y}}_{i2})$. Then add reduced-form Mundlak residuals, $\hat{\mathbf{v}}_{it2}$, in a pooled Tobit estimation. The key assumption is that for each t, y_{it1} conditional on $(\mathbf{z}_i, \mathbf{y}_{i2})$ follows a Tobit model with linear index $\psi_1 + \mathbf{x}_{it1}\beta_1 + \bar{\mathbf{y}}_{i2}\boldsymbol{\pi}_1 + \bar{\mathbf{z}}_i\boldsymbol{\xi}_1 + \mathbf{v}_{it2}\boldsymbol{\rho}_1$ and constant variance. If we use a pooled estimation method, then abitrary serial dependence is allowed. As usual, we must account for two-step estimation in calculating standard errors, and we must cluster to account for the serial dependence.

If y_{it1} is a count variable, and we prefer to use, say, a negative binomial model, then we can simple assume that, conditional on $(\mathbf{z}_{it1}, \mathbf{y}_{it2}, \bar{\mathbf{z}}_i, \bar{\mathbf{y}}_{i2}, \mathbf{v}_{it2})$, y_{it1} follows the appropriate model. Notice that we would not be able to derive such a model if we start with the assumption that the structural model for y_{it1}—conditional unobservables (c_{i1}, u_{it1}) as in the previous section—follow a negative binomial model. Therefore, purists might be reluctant to adopt such a strategy even though it would perhaps provide a good approximation that accounts for the count nature of y_{it1}.

One can even apply the approach to less obvious situations, such as two-part models. For example, suppose the Tobit model is replaced by the Cragg (1971) truncated normal hurdle model—see also Wooldridge (2010, Section 17.6). Then one can model the two parts both as functions of $(\mathbf{z}_{it1}, \mathbf{y}_{it2}, \bar{\mathbf{z}}_i, \bar{\mathbf{y}}_{i2}, \mathbf{v}_{it2})$, and then separately test for endogeneity of $\mathbf{y}_{it2}$ in each part by testing coefficients on $\hat{\mathbf{v}}_{it2}$. Average partial effects are obtained easily by averaging out $(\bar{\mathbf{z}}_i, \bar{\mathbf{y}}_{i2}, \hat{\mathbf{v}}_{it2})$, across i or across (i, t), in the partial derivatives with respect to $\mathbf{x}_{t1}$. The form of the partial effects is given in, for example, Wooldridge (2010, Eq. (17.48)).

5.2 Joint Estimation Methods

So far our discussion has centered on pooled estimation methods. There are two reasons for this. First, pooled two-step methods are computationally simple, and panel bootstrap methods run quickly in most cases for obtaining valid standard errors. Second, and just as important, pooled methods are robust to any kind of serial dependence.

It is possible to apply the CRE/CF approach to joint MLE estimation in the second stage. For example, rather than using pooled probit, as in Section 5, one might want to estimate a so-called random effects probit in the second stage. The explanatory variables would be

$$(\mathbf{x}_{it1}, \bar{\mathbf{z}}_i, \bar{\mathbf{y}}_{i2}, \hat{\mathbf{v}}_{it2}),$$

where recall $\mathbf{x}_{it1}$ is a function of $(\mathbf{z}_{it1}, \mathbf{y}_{it2})$. Or, we could use more flexible functions of the histories $(\mathbf{z}_i, \mathbf{y}_{i2})$. Although joint MLEs can be used in the second stage, one should be aware of the costs of doing so. First, computationally joint MLEs are usually significantly more difficult to obtain than pooled MLEs.

Although the difference in computational times often is irrelevant for one pass through the data, adding $\hat{\mathbf{v}}_{it2}$ to account for idiosyncratic endogeneity of $\mathbf{y}_{it2}$ requires some sort of adjustment for inference, although testing the null hypothesis that $\hat{\mathbf{v}}_{it2}$ has zero coefficients does not require an adjustment. If one uses the bootstrap, then the increased computational burden can be nontrivial.

The second cost to use joint MLE in the second step is lack of robustness to distributional misspecification and serial dependence. Standard joint MLEs used for nonlinear random effects models maintain that innovations—what we would call $\{u_{it1}\}$ in Eqs. (1) and (4)—are independent over time, as well as being independent of c_{i1} and $\mathbf{z}_i$. None of random effects probit, RE logit, RE Tobit, RE Poisson, and so on has robustness properties in the presence of serial correlation of the innovations. Moreover, even if the innovations in Eq. (4) are serially independent, the RE probit joint MLE is not known to be consistent.

When we apply a joint MLE in the second step, there is another subtle point. Suppose we express the relationship between innovations in, say, Eq. (4) and those in the reduced form of $\mathbf{y}_{it2}$, $\mathbf{v}_{it2}$, as

$$u_{it1} = \mathbf{v}_{it2}\boldsymbol{\rho}_1 + e_{it1}.$$

The relevant innovations underlying the joint MLE in the second step are $\{e_{it1}\}$, not $\{u_{it1}\}$—unless $\boldsymbol{\rho}_1 = \mathbf{0}$. Consequently, serial correlation in the reduced form of $\mathbf{y}_{it2}$ can cause serial correlation in the second stage MLE, even though there was none in the original innovations.

For robustness and computational reasons, the pooled methods generally are preferred. Future research could focus on how to improve in terms of efficiency over the pooled methods without adding assumptions.

6 Empirical Example

Papke and Wooldridge (2008) estimate the effect of spending on fourth-grade mathematics test using data from Michigan. The years straddle the Michigan School Reform, which was passed in 1995. The response variable, *math4*, is a pass rate, and so we use a fractional probit model response in addition to a linear model estimated by fixed effects IV. The variable of interest is the natural log of real per-pupil spending, averaged over the current and previous 3 years. The instrumental variable is the foundation allowance. Which is the amount given by the state to each school district—after the spending reform. A kinked relationship between the allowance and prereform per-pupil revenue means that, after controlling for a district effect, the foundation allowance is exogenous. Not surprisingly, its log is a very strong instrument for the log of average real spending. Other controls include the proportion of students eligible for free and reduced lunch and the log of district enrollment. A full set of year effects also is included. There are $N = 501$ school districts over the 7 years 1995 to 2001.

TABLE 1 **Effects of Spending on Test Pass Rates**

Model:	Linear	Linear	FProbit		FProbit	
Estimation:	*FE*	*FEIV*	*PQMLE*		*PQMLE*	
	Coef	*Coef*	*Coef*	*APE*	*Coef*	*APE*
lavgrexp	0.377 (0.071)	0.420 (0.115)	0.821 (0.334)	0.277 (0.112)	0.797 (0.338)	0.269 (0.114)
$\hat{u}_{it2}$	–	−0.060 (0.146)	–	–	–	–
$\hat{v}_2$	–	–	0.076 (0.145)	–	−0.666 (0.396)	–
$\overline{lavgrexp}$?	–	–	Yes		No	

The results of the test are given in Table 1 for the spending variable. The linear fixed effects estimate, 0.377, implies that a 10% increase in average spending increases the pass rate by about 3.8 percentage points, and the effect is very statistically significant. The FEIV estimate actually increases to 0.420, and remains strongly significant. The fully robust test of idiosyncratic endogeneity, where the null is exogeneity, gives $t = -0.41$, which is not close to being statistically significant. Therefore, the evidence is that, once spending is allowed to be correlated with the district heterogeneity, spending is not endogenous with respect to idiosyncratic shocks.

Columns (3) and (4) in Table 1 apply the fractional probit CRE/CF approaches. In column (3) we apply Procedure 4, which includes the time average of *lavgrexp* along with the time average of all exogenous variables, including *lfound*, the log of the foundation allowance. The coefficient is 0.821 and it is strongly statistically significant. The APE, which is comparable to the FEIV estimate, is quite a bit lower: 0.277, but with $t = 2.47$ is still pretty significant. The test for idiosyncratic endogeneity fails to reject the null of exogeneity, with $t = 0.52$. This is entirely consistent with the linear model estimates and test. By contrast, when we apply the Papke-Wooldridge approach in column (4), the t statistic for the coefficient on the reduced form residual $\hat{\mathbf{v}}_2$ is $t = -1.68$, which is significant at the 10% level. This is not a strong rejection of exogeneity, but it is much stronger than when the time average of *lavgrexp*. The outcomes in columns (3) and (4) are consistent with the conclusion that spending is correlated with district-level heterogeneity but not district-level shocks, which is why the test in column (3) marginally rejected exogeneity and that in column (4) does not come close to rejecting. In the end, the new approach in column (3) and the PW approach in column (4) give similar estimates of the APE of spending: 0.277 versus 0.269, and the standard errors are similar.

7 Extensions and Future Directions

The main message in this chapter is that, when combining the CRE and control function approaches in nonlinear panel data models, there is a good case to separately model—even if only implicitly—the distribution of the heterogeneity conditional on all explanatory variables and outside exogenous variables. In this way, adding the control functions to account for idiosyncratic endogeneity leads to a pure test of the null hypothesis of exogeneity. In linear models, a common variable addition test after fixed effects estimation achieves this goal. We have shown how the same goal can be achieved for two popular nonlinear models.

We have used parametric assumptions in our discussion and applications. Nevertheless, when the EEVs $\mathbf{y}_{it2}$ are continuous, there is a more general message when semiparametric, or even purely nonparametric, approaches are taken. For example, when applying the insights of Blundell and Powell (2004), it makes sense to separately include functions of the entire history, $(\mathbf{y}_{i2}, \mathbf{z}_i)$, and the control functions, $\hat{\mathbf{v}}_{it2}$. We touched on this at the end of Section 5, where we showed a model with interactions between the variables of interests, the time averages, and the control functions can be added for flexibility. The general point is that by adding, say, $\overline{\mathbf{y}}_{i2}$ along with $\overline{\mathbf{z}}_i$ we then obtain an estimating equation in which $\hat{\mathbf{v}}_{it2}$ is added to account for possible idiosyncratic endogeneity.

In nonlinear models, the assumptions imposed on the reduced form of $\mathbf{y}_{it2}$ will not be met when $\mathbf{y}_{it2}$ has discreteness. Even allowing for a single binary EEV, y_{it2} poses challenges for nonlinear unobserved effects panel data models. In particular, the parametric assumptions that can be viewed as convenient approximations when $\mathbf{y}_{it2}$ now have real bite when it comes to identifying the average partial effects. If one is willing to make distributional assumptions—such as normality in the probit case—the methods in Wooldridge (2014) and Lin and Wooldridge (2016) can be extended to allow CRE. As a simple example, if y_{it2} is assumed to follow a reduced form probit, one can use as a control function the generalized residuals,

$$\widehat{gr}_{it2} = y_{it2}\lambda\left(\mathbf{w}_{it}\hat{\boldsymbol{\theta}}_2\right) - (1 - y_{it2})\lambda\left(-\mathbf{w}_{it}\hat{\boldsymbol{\theta}}_2\right),$$

where $\mathbf{w}_{it} = (1, \mathbf{z}_{it}, \overline{\mathbf{z}}_i)$. But then the issue of how to best model the relationship between heterogeneity and $(\mathbf{y}_{i2}, \mathbf{z}_i)$ arises. The Munklak device, or Chamberlain's version of it, might work reasonably well, but neither might be flexible enough. We leave investigations into the quality of CF approximations in discrete cases to future research.

As discussed in Wooldridge (2018), unbalanced panels pose challenges for the CRE approach, although the challenges are not insurmountable. In the context of heterogeneity endogeneity only, Wooldridge suggests a modeling strategy in which unobserved heterogeneity is a function of $\{(s_{it}, s_{it}\mathbf{x}_{it}): t = 1, \ldots, T\}$, where s_{it} is a binary selection indicator that is unity when a complete set of data is observed for unit i in time t. This approach can be extended to the current setting, but the details remain to be worked out.

Appendix

This appendix verifies some of the algebraic claims made in Sections 2 and 3.

A.1 Relationship Between the FE and Mundlak Residuals

We first find a relationship between the FE residuals and the Mundlak residuals. Let $\mathbf{w}_i$ be any collection of time-constant variables. The FE and Mundlak residuals are, respectively,

$$\hat{\ddot{u}}_{it} = \ddot{y}_{it} - \ddot{\mathbf{x}}_{it}\hat{\boldsymbol{\beta}}_{FE}$$

$$\hat{v}_{it} = y_{it} - \mathbf{x}_{it}\hat{\boldsymbol{\beta}}_{FE} - \hat{\psi} - \overline{\mathbf{x}}_{ii}\hat{\boldsymbol{\xi}} - \mathbf{w}_i\hat{\boldsymbol{\lambda}},$$

where we use the fact that the estimates $\mathbf{x}_{it}$ are identical using FE and the Mundlak approaches. Further, because $\ddot{\mathbf{x}}_{it}$ is a nonsingular linear combination of $\mathbf{x}_{it}$ and $\overline{\mathbf{x}}_{ii}$, we obtain the same Mundlak residuals if instead we run the pooled regression

$$y_{it} \text{ on } \ddot{\mathbf{x}}_{it}, 1, \overline{\mathbf{x}}_i, \mathbf{w}_i.$$

In fact, we can add $\overline{\mathbf{x}}_i\hat{\boldsymbol{\beta}}_{FE}$ and subtract it off:

$$\begin{aligned}
\hat{v}_{it} &= y_{it} - (\mathbf{x}_{it} - \overline{\mathbf{x}}_i)\hat{\boldsymbol{\beta}}_{FE} - \hat{\psi} - \overline{\mathbf{x}}_i\left(\boldsymbol{\xi} + \hat{\boldsymbol{\beta}}_{FE}\right) - \mathbf{w}_i\hat{\boldsymbol{\lambda}} \\
&= y_{it} - \ddot{\mathbf{x}}_{it}\hat{\boldsymbol{\beta}}_{FE} - \hat{\psi} - \overline{\mathbf{x}}_i\left(\boldsymbol{\xi} + \hat{\boldsymbol{\beta}}_{FE}\right) - \mathbf{w}_i\hat{\boldsymbol{\lambda}} \\
&\equiv y_{it} - \ddot{\mathbf{x}}_{it}\hat{\boldsymbol{\beta}}_{FE} - \hat{\psi} - \overline{\mathbf{x}}_i\hat{\delta} - \mathbf{w}_i\hat{\boldsymbol{\lambda}}
\end{aligned}$$

From Mundlak (1978), it is known that $\left(\hat{\psi}, \hat{\delta}, \hat{\boldsymbol{\lambda}}\right)$ are the between estimates, that is, from the cross-section OLS regression $\overline{y}_i$ on $1, \overline{\mathbf{x}}_i, \mathbf{w}_i$.

This is easy to see directly in our setup. Define $\mathbf{z}_i = (1, \overline{\mathbf{x}}_i, \mathbf{w}_i)$ and let $\hat{\theta}$ be the set of coefficients: $\left(\hat{\psi}, \hat{\delta}, \hat{\boldsymbol{\lambda}}\right)$. Then

$$\sum_{t=1}^{T} \mathbf{z}_i'\ddot{\mathbf{x}}_{it} = \mathbf{z}_i'\sum_{t=1}^{T}\ddot{\mathbf{x}}_{it} = 0$$

so that the regressors are orthogonal in sample. By Frisch-Waugh, $\hat{\theta}$ also is obtained by dropping $\ddot{\mathbf{x}}_{it}$, that is, from

$$y_{it} \text{ on } \mathbf{z}_i, t = 1, \ldots, T; i = 1, \ldots, N.$$

But

$$\begin{aligned}
\hat{\theta} &= \left(\sum_{i=1}^{N}\sum_{t=1}^{T}\mathbf{z}_i'\mathbf{z}_i\right)^{-1}\sum_{i=1}^{N}\sum_{t=1}^{T}\mathbf{z}_i'y_{it} \\
&= \left(T\sum_{i=1}^{N}\mathbf{z}_i'\mathbf{z}_i\right)^{-1}\sum_{i=1}^{N}\mathbf{z}_i'\sum_{t=1}^{T}y_{it} = \left(\sum_{i=1}^{N}\mathbf{z}_i'\mathbf{z}_i\right)^{-1}\sum_{i=1}^{N}\mathbf{z}_i'\left(T^{-1}\sum_{t=1}^{T}y_{it}\right) \\
&= \left(\sum_{i=1}^{N}\mathbf{z}_i'\mathbf{z}_i\right)^{-1}\sum_{i=1}^{N}\mathbf{z}_i'\overline{y}_i = \hat{\theta}_B.
\end{aligned}$$

Now we can write

$$\begin{aligned}\hat{v}_{it} &\equiv y_{it} - \bar{y}_i - \ddot{\mathbf{x}}_{it}\hat{\boldsymbol{\beta}}_{FE} + \bar{y}_i - \hat{\psi}_B - \bar{\mathbf{x}}_i\hat{\delta}_B - \mathbf{w}_i\hat{\boldsymbol{\lambda}}_B \\ &= \ddot{y}_{it} - \ddot{\mathbf{x}}_{it}\hat{\boldsymbol{\beta}}_{FE} + \left(\bar{y}_i - \hat{\psi}_B - \bar{\mathbf{x}}_i\hat{\delta}_B - \mathbf{w}_i\hat{\boldsymbol{\lambda}}_B\right) \quad + \hat{r}_i, \\ &= \hat{\ddot{u}}_{it}\end{aligned}$$

where $\hat{r}_i$ is the between residual. One important feature of this relationship is that $\hat{r}_i$ does not change over time. Therefore,

$$\sum_{t=1}^{T} \hat{r}_i \hat{\ddot{u}}_{it} = 0.$$

More importantly, for demeaned variables $\ddot{\mathbf{x}}_{it}$,

$$\sum_{t=1}^{T} \ddot{\mathbf{x}}_{it}' \hat{v}_{it} = \sum_{t=1}^{T} \ddot{\mathbf{x}}_{it} \hat{\ddot{u}}_{it}$$

because $\sum_{t=1}^{T} \ddot{\mathbf{x}}_{it}' \hat{r}_i = 0$.

A.2 Equivalence in Using the FE and Mundlak Residuals in FE Poisson Estimation

Now we obtain a general result that shows that adding time-constant variables to the explanatory variables does not affect $\hat{\boldsymbol{\beta}}$ in the Poisson FE case. For a cross-section observation i, the quasilog likelihood is

$$\ell_i(\boldsymbol{\beta}) = \sum_{t=1}^{T} y_{it} \left\{ \mathbf{x}_{it}\boldsymbol{\beta} - \log\left[\sum_{r=1}^{T} \exp\left(\mathbf{x}_{it}\boldsymbol{\beta}\right)\right]\right\},$$

and the score is

$$\mathbf{s}_i(\boldsymbol{\beta}) = \sum_{t=1}^{T} y_{it} \left\{ \mathbf{x}_{it}' - \frac{\sum_{r=1}^{T} \mathbf{x}_{it} \exp\left(\mathbf{x}_{it}\boldsymbol{\beta}\right)}{\sum_{r=1}^{T} \exp\left(\mathbf{x}_{it}\boldsymbol{\beta}\right)} \right\}$$

Therefore, the FOC is

$$\sum_{i=1}^{N} \mathbf{s}_i\left(\hat{\boldsymbol{\beta}}\right) = 0$$

Now suppose

$$\mathbf{x}_{it} = \mathbf{g}_{it} + \mathbf{h}_i,$$

which allows for the case that some $\mathbf{h}_i$ are identically zero for all i. Then for any i,

$$
\begin{aligned}
s_i\left(\hat{\boldsymbol{\beta}}\right) &= \sum_{t=1}^{T} y_{it}\left\{\mathbf{x}_{it}' - \frac{\sum_{r=1}^{T}\mathbf{x}_{ir}'\exp\left(\mathbf{g}_{ir}\hat{\boldsymbol{\beta}} + h_i\hat{\boldsymbol{\beta}}\right)}{\sum_{r=1}^{T}\exp\left(\mathbf{g}_{ir}\hat{\boldsymbol{\beta}} + h_i\hat{\boldsymbol{\beta}}\right)}\right\} = \sum_{t=1}^{T} y_{it}\left\{\mathbf{x}_{it}' - \frac{\exp\left(h_i\hat{\boldsymbol{\beta}}\right)\sum_{r=1}^{T}\mathbf{x}_{ir}'\exp\left(\mathbf{g}_{ir}\hat{\boldsymbol{\beta}}\right)}{\exp\left(h_i\hat{\boldsymbol{\beta}}\right)\sum_{r=1}^{T}\exp\left(\mathbf{g}_{ir}\hat{\boldsymbol{\beta}}\right)}\right\} \\
&= \sum_{t=1}^{T} y_{it}\left\{\mathbf{x}_{it}' - \frac{\sum_{r=1}^{T}\mathbf{x}_{ir}'\exp\left(\mathbf{g}_{ir}\hat{\boldsymbol{\beta}}\right)}{\sum_{r=1}^{T}\exp\left(\mathbf{g}_{ir}\hat{\boldsymbol{\beta}}\right)}\right\} = \sum_{t=1}^{T} y_{it}\left\{\left(\mathbf{g}_{it}' + \mathbf{h}_i'\right) - \frac{\sum_{r=1}^{T}\left(\mathbf{g}_{ir}' + \mathbf{h}_i'\right)\exp\left(\mathbf{g}_{ir}\hat{\boldsymbol{\beta}}\right)}{\sum_{r=1}^{T}\exp\left(\mathbf{g}_{ir}\hat{\boldsymbol{\beta}}\right)}\right\} \\
&= \sum_{t=1}^{T} y_{it}\left\{\mathbf{g}_{it}' - \frac{\sum_{r=1}^{T}\mathbf{g}_{ir}'\exp\left(\mathbf{g}_{ir}\hat{\boldsymbol{\beta}}\right)}{\sum_{r=1}^{T}\exp\left(\mathbf{g}_{ir}\hat{\boldsymbol{\beta}}\right)} + \mathbf{h}_i' - \mathbf{h}_i'\frac{\sum_{r=1}^{T}\exp\left(\mathbf{g}_{ir}\hat{\boldsymbol{\beta}}\right)}{\sum_{r=1}^{T}\exp\left(\mathbf{g}_{ir}\hat{\boldsymbol{\beta}}\right)}\right\} \\
&= \sum_{t=1}^{T} y_{it}\left\{\mathbf{g}_{it}' - \frac{\sum_{r=1}^{T}\mathbf{g}_{ir}'\exp\left(\mathbf{g}_{ir}\hat{\boldsymbol{\beta}}\right)}{\sum_{r=1}^{T}\exp\left(\mathbf{g}_{ir}\hat{\boldsymbol{\beta}}\right)}\right\}.
\end{aligned}
$$

Note that the final expression is the score with explanatory variables $\mathbf{g}_{it}$, and so we have shown $\hat{\boldsymbol{\beta}}$ is the same whether we use $\mathbf{x}_{it}$ or $\mathbf{g}_{it}$.

The previous result applies to the control function estimation in Section 3 because, as shown in Appendix A.1,

$$\hat{\mathbf{v}}_{it2} = \hat{\ddot{\mathbf{u}}}_{it2} + \hat{\mathbf{r}}_{i2},$$

where $\hat{\mathbf{r}}_{i2}$ are the between residuals and do not vary over time. The other explanatory variables are unchanged. Therefore, we obtain the same estimates whether we obtain the FE residuals in the first stage or the Mundlak residuals.

References

Blundell, R., Powell, J.L., 2004. Endogeneity in semiparametric binary response models. Review of Economic Studies 71, 655–679.

Guggenberger, P., 2010. The impact of a Hausman pretest on the size of a hypothesis test: The panel data case. Journal of Econometrics 156, 337–343.

Chamberlain, G., 1982. Multivariate regression models for panel data. Journal of Econometrics 1, 5–46.

Hausman, J.A., 1978. Specification tests in econometrics. Econometrica 46, 1251–1271.

Hausman, J.A., Hall, B.H., Griliches, Z., 1984. Econometric models for count data with an application to the patents-R&D relationship. Econometrica 52, 909–938.

Levitt, S.D., 1996. The effect of prison population size on crime rates: evidence from prison overcrowding litigation. Quarterly Journal of Economics 111, 319–351.

Levitt, S.D., 1997. Using electoral cycles in police hiring to estimate the effect of police on crime. American Economic Review 87, 270–290.

Lin, W., Wooldridge, J.M., 2016. Binary and fractional response models with continuous and binary endogenous explanatory variables, working paper. Michigan State University Department of Economics.

Mundlak, Y., 1978. On the pooling of time series and cross section data. Econometrica 46, 69–85.

Murtazashvili, I., Wooldridge, J.M., 2016. A control function approach to estimating switching regression models with endogenous explanatory variables and endogenous switching. Journal of Econometrics 190, 252–266.

Papke, L.E., Wooldridge, J.M., 2008. Panel data methods for fractional response variables with an application to test pass rates. Journal of Econometrics 145, 121–133.

Windmeijer, F., 2000. Moment conditions for fixed effects count data models with endogenous regressors. Economics Letters 68, 21–24.

Wooldridge, J.M., 1990. A unified approach to robust, regression-based specification tests. Econometric Theory 6, 17–43.

Wooldridge, J.M., 1997. Multiplicative panel data models without the strict Exogeneity assumption. Econometric Theory 13, 667–678.

Wooldridge, J.M., 1999. Distribution-free estimation of some nonlinear panel data models. Journal of Econometrics 90, 77–97.

Wooldridge, J.M., 2010. Econometric analysis of cross section and panel data, 2nd ed. MIT Press, Cambridge, MA.

Wooldridge, J.M., 2014. Quasi-maximum likelihood estimation and testing for nonlinear models with endogenous explanatory variables. Journal of Econometrics 182, 226–234.

Wooldridge, J.M., 2018. Correlated random effects models with unbalanced panels. forthcoming-Journal of Econometrics. .

Further Reading

Altonji, J.G., Matzkin, R.L., 2005. Cross section and panel data estimators for nonseparable models with endogenous regressors. Econometrica 73, 1053–1102.

Chapter 3

Nonlinear and Related Panel Data Models

William Greene* **and Qiushi Zhang**[†]
*Department of Economics, Stern School of Business, New York University, New York, NY, United States, [†]Department of Economics, Duke University, Durham, NC, United States

Chapter Outline

1 Introduction

This chapter explores the intersection of two topics: nonlinear modeling and the treatment of panel data. Superficially, nonlinearity merely compels parameter estimation to use methods more involved than linear least squares. But, in many ways, nonlinear models are qualitatively different from linear ones; it is more

Panel Data Econometrics. https://doi.org/10.1016/B978-0-12-814367-4.00003-4

than a simple matter of functional form, i.e., nonlinearity is more than the simple difference between [$y = \boldsymbol{\beta}'\mathbf{x} + \varepsilon$] and [$y = h(\boldsymbol{\beta},\mathbf{x}) + \varepsilon$]. Analysis often involves reinterpreting the objects of estimation. Most of the received analysis of panel data models focuses on the treatment of unobserved heterogeneity. The full set of issues that appear in the (fixed or random effects) linear panel data regression appear in more complicated forms in nonlinear contexts.

The application of panel data methods to nonlinear models is a subarea of microeconometrics (see Cameron & Trivedi, 2005). The analyst is interested in the behavior of individual units, such as people, households, firms, etc., in which the typical model examines the outcome of an individual decision. We are interested in nonlinear models, using methods and models defined for panel data. To cite a template example, many researchers have analyzed health outcomes data, including health satisfaction (a discrete, ordered, categorical outcome), retirement (a discrete, binary outcome), and health system utilization (usually a discrete count of events), in the context of the German Socioeconomic Panel data set or the European Community Household Panel data set. These are repeated surveys of a large number of households gathered over a number of years. We are interested in models and methods that extend beyond linear regression.

Many of the longitudinal data sets that are used in contemporary microeconometric research provide researchers with rich studies of outcomes such as fertility, health decisions and outcomes, income, wealth and labor market experiences, subjective health, and well-being and consumption decisions. Most of these variables are discrete or discontinuous and not amenable to conventional linear regression modeling. The literature provides a wide variety of theoretical and empirical frameworks for nonlinear modeling, such as binary, ordered and multinomial choice, censoring, truncation, attrition, and sample selection. These nonlinear models have adapted econometric methods to more complicated settings than linear regression and simple instrumental variable (IV) techniques. This chapter will provide an overview of these applications. Some theoretical developments are presented to give context to the practical implementations. The particular interest is in the extension of panel data methods to these nonlinear models that have long provided the econometric platforms. This includes development of treatments of fixed and random effects models and random parameter forms for unobserved heterogeneity, models that involve dynamic effects and sample attrition. We also are interested in the theoretical issues and complications that define this area of analysis and in a number of specific kinds of applications, such as random utility based discrete choice models, random parameter, and latent class models and applications of the stochastic frontier model.

Overall, we are interested in a general arena of models that have appeared in empirical applications. The treatment leans more toward the parametric treatments than some recent treatments, such as Honoré (2002) and Arellano and Hahn (2006). Some essential theory is presented, as well as a variety of applications. The selection of topics in this survey is wider than in some others (e.g., Honoré, 2002, 2013, Honoré and Kesina, 2017), but not exhaustive. A large literature about deeper theory (see Wooldridge, 2010) and results that advance the fundamental methodology, such as set vs. point identification in discrete choice models (e.g., Chesher, 2013) is left for more advanced treatments. Many additional practical results appear in Cameron and Trivedi (2005). One of the important features of the analysis described here is that familiar results for the linear model cannot be carried over to nonlinear ones. We begin in Section 2 by examining the interpretation of parameters and partial effects in nonlinear models. Specific aspects of panel data modeling, notably heterogeneity under different assumptions, the incidental parameters problem, and dynamic effects are treated in Section 3. Section 4 describes features that are common to most nonlinear panel data models. Applications, including the essential layout of longitudinal data sets are treated in Sections 5 and 6. The last two sections also consider the problem of attrition and issues related to robust estimation and inference.

The following notation is used throughout the survey:

Panel data set dimensions:

i = index for observations (individuals),

t = index for periods, or replications,

n = sample size; $i = 1,\ldots,n$,

T_i = number of observations in group i, not assumed constant,

$N = \Sigma_{i=1}^{n} T_i$;

Panel data:

$y_{i,t}$ = variable of interest in the model, might be one or more than one outcome,

$\mathbf{x}_{i,t}$ = exogenous variables = $(1,\mathbf{z}_{i,t}{}')'$, column vectors,

$\mathbf{y}_i = (y_{i,1},\ldots,y_{i,Ti})'$ = sequence of realizations of $y_{i,t}$,

$\mathbf{X}_i$ = sequence of observations on exogenous variables, $T_i \times K$; $\mathbf{x}_{i,t}{}'$ = row t of $\mathbf{X}_i$,

$\mathbf{d}(i) = \mathbf{d}(i)_{j,t} = \mathbf{d}_i = \mathbf{1}[j = i, t = 1,\ldots,T_i]$ = sample length dummy variable for i,

$\mathbf{i}$ = constant term = column of ones.

Functions:

$\phi(t)$, $\Phi(t)$ = standard normal pdf, cdf,

$\Lambda(t)$ = logistic cdf,

$N[\mu,\sigma^2]$ = normal distribution,

$N^+[\mu,\sigma^2]$ = truncated at zero normal distribution = $|u|$ where $u \sim N[0,\sigma^2]$,

$f(c|\mathbf{X})$ = conditional density of c given $\mathbf{X}$,

$f(c{:}\sigma)$ or $f(c|\mathbf{X}{:}\sigma)$ = density of variable that involves parameter σ,

$f(y_{i,t}|\ldots)$ = density for $y_{i,t}$, used generally for the model for $y_{i,t}$,

$\mathbf{1}$[condition] = 1 if condition is true, 0 if false,

$E[c]$ = expected value,

$E_c[g(x,c)] = h(x)$ = expected value over c.

Model components:
$\varepsilon_{i,t}$ = general idiosyncratic disturbance in model,
c_i = unobserved heterogeneity, usually univariate,
α_i = fixed effects version of c_i, $\boldsymbol{\alpha} = (\alpha_1,\ldots,\alpha_n)'$,
$\eta_i = \exp(\alpha_i)$,
u_i = random effects version of c_i,
$\boldsymbol{\beta}$ = slope vector in index function model, appears as $\boldsymbol{\beta}'\mathbf{x}_{i,t} = \pi + \boldsymbol{\gamma}'\mathbf{z}_{i,t}$,
$\boldsymbol{\gamma}$ = subvector of $\boldsymbol{\beta}$ omitting the constant,
π = constant term, $\boldsymbol{\beta} = (\pi,\boldsymbol{\gamma}')'$,
$\phi_{i,t} = \exp(\boldsymbol{\gamma}'\mathbf{z}_{i,t})$,
$\lambda_{i,t} = \exp(\boldsymbol{\beta}'\mathbf{x}_{i,t} + c_i) = \eta_i\phi_{i,t}$, $c_i = \alpha_i$ or u_i,
$\boldsymbol{\theta}$ = one or more ancillary parameters in parametric model,
σ_u^2 = variance of u_i in random effects model,
σ_ε^2 = variance of $\varepsilon_{i,t}$ in random index function model.

2 Nonlinear Models

The *linear panel data regression model* is

$$y_{i,t} = \boldsymbol{\beta}'\mathbf{x}_{i,t} + c_i + \varepsilon_{i,t}, \quad i = 1,\ldots,n, t = 1,\ldots,T_i,$$

where $y_{i,t}$ is the outcome variable of interest, $\mathbf{x}_{i,t}$ is a vector of time varying and possibly time invariant variables, also possibly including $y_{i,t-1}$, c_i is unobserved time invariant heterogeneity that is independent of $\varepsilon_{i,t}$ and $\varepsilon_{i,t}$ is a classical disturbance. Since c_i is unobserved, no coefficient or scale is attached to it. The linearity of the model relates (1) to the way that the natural estimator of the parameter vector of interest, $\boldsymbol{\beta}$, is computed, that is, by using some variant of linear least squares or instrumental variables (IV) to solve a set of linear equations, and (2) to the way that the unobserved heterogeneity, c_i enters the function of interest, here the conditional mean function.

We are interested in models in which the function of interest, such as a conditional mean, is intrinsically nonlinear. This would include, for example, the Poisson regression model (see Cameron & Trivedi, 2005; Greene, 2018):

$$\begin{array}{ll}\text{(Data generating process)} & \text{Prob}(y_{i,t} = j \mid \mathbf{x}_{i,t}, c_i) = \left[\exp(-\lambda_{i,t})\lambda_{i,t}^j\right]/j!;\\ \text{(Function of interest)} & E[y_{i,t} \mid \mathbf{x}_{i,t}, c_i] = \lambda_{i,t} = \exp(\boldsymbol{\beta}'\mathbf{x}_{i,t} + c_i).\end{array}$$

Most models of interest in this area involve missing data in which $y_{i,t}$, the outcome of some underlying process involving $\boldsymbol{\beta}$ as well as c_i, passes through a filter between the data generating process (DGP) and the observed outcome.[1] The most common example is the familiar (semiparametric) random effects binary choice model:

1. Nearly all of the models listed above in Section 6 are of this type.

$$(\text{Random utility DGP})\quad y_{i,t}{}^* = \boldsymbol{\beta}'\mathbf{x}_{i,t} + c_i + \varepsilon_{i,t},$$
$$y_{i,t}{}^* = \text{unobserved random utility};$$
$$(\text{Revealed preference})\quad y_{i,t} = \mathbf{1}[y_{i,t}{}^* > 0].$$

(The model becomes parametric when distributions are specified for c_i and $\varepsilon_{i,t}$.) In this case, the nonlinear function of interest is

$$F[(\boldsymbol{\beta}'\mathbf{x}_{i,t} + c_i)/\sigma_\varepsilon],$$

where $F[.]$ is the cdf of $\varepsilon_{i,t}$. This example also fits into category (1).[2] It will not be possible to use least squares or IV for parameter estimation; (2) Some alternative to group mean deviations or first differences is needed to proceed with estimation in the presence of the unobserved, heterogeneity. In the most familiar cases, the issues center on persuasive forms of the model and practicalities of estimation, such as how to handle heterogeneity in the form of fixed or random effects. The linear form of the model involving the unobserved heterogeneity is a considerable advantage that will be absent from all of the extensions we consider here. A panel data version of the stochastic frontier model (Aigner, Lovell, & Schmidt, 1977) is

$$\begin{aligned} y_{i,t} &= \boldsymbol{\beta}'\mathbf{x}_{i,t} + c_i + v_{i,t} - u_{i,t} \\ &= \boldsymbol{\beta}'\mathbf{x}_{i,t} + c_i + \varepsilon_{i,t}, \end{aligned}$$

where $v_{i,t} \sim N[0,\sigma_v{}^2]$ and $u_{i,t} \sim N^+(0,\sigma_u{}^2)$ (see Greene, 2004a, 2004c). Superficially, this is a linear regression model with a disturbance that has a skew normal distribution,

$$\begin{aligned} f(\varepsilon_{i,t}) &= \frac{2}{\sigma}\phi\left(\frac{\varepsilon_{i,t}}{\sigma}\right)\Phi\left(\frac{-\lambda\varepsilon_{i,t}}{\sigma}\right), \\ \lambda &= \frac{\sigma_u}{\sigma_v}, \\ \sigma^2 &= \sigma_v^2 + \sigma_u^2. \end{aligned}$$

In spite of the apparent linearity, the preferred estimator is (nonlinear) maximum likelihood. A second, similar case is Graham, Hahn, Poirier, and Powell's (2015) quantile regression model, $y_{i,t}(\tau) = \boldsymbol{\beta}(\tau, c_i)'\mathbf{x}_{i,t} + \varepsilon(\tau)_{i,t}$ (see Geraci & Bottai, 2007). The model appears to be intrinsically linear. The preferred estimator, however, is, again, not linear least squares; it usually is based on a linear programming approach. For current purposes, in spite of appearances, this model is intrinsically nonlinear.

2. In cases in which the function of interest is a nonlinear conditional mean function, it is sometimes suggested that a linear approximation to quantities of intrinsic interest, such as partial effects, be obtained by simply using linear least squares. See, e.g., Angrist and Pischke (2009) for discussion of the canonical example, the binary probit model.

2.1 Coefficients and Partial Effects

The feature of interest usually will be a nonlinear function, $g(\mathbf{x}_{i,t},c_i)$ derived from the probability distribution, $f(y_{i,t}|\mathbf{x}_{i,t},c_i)$, such as the conditional mean function, $E[y_{i,t}|\mathbf{x}_{i,t},c_i]$ or some derivative function such as a probability in a discrete choice model, $\text{Prob}(y_{i,t} = j|\mathbf{x}_{i,t},c_i) = F(\mathbf{x}_{i,t},c_i)$. In general, the function will involve structural parameters that are not, themselves, of primary interest; $g(\mathbf{x}_{i,t},c_i) = g(\mathbf{x}_{i,t},c_i\text{: }\boldsymbol{\theta})$ for some vector of parameters, $\boldsymbol{\theta}$. The partial effects will then be $\text{PE}(\mathbf{x},c) = \boldsymbol{\delta}(\mathbf{x},c\text{: }\boldsymbol{\theta}) = \partial g(\mathbf{x},c:\theta)/\partial\mathbf{x}$. In the probit model, the function of interest is the probability, and the relevant quantity is a partial effect,

$$\text{PE}(\mathbf{x},c) = \partial\text{Prob}(y_{i,t} = 1|\,\mathbf{x},c)/\partial\mathbf{x}.$$

Estimation of partial effects is likely to be the main focus of the analysis. Computation of partial effects will be problematic even if $\boldsymbol{\theta}$ is estimable in the presence of c, because c is unobserved and the distribution of c remains to be specified. If enough is known about the distribution of c, computation at a specific value, such as the mean, might be feasible. The partial effect at the average (of c) would be

$$\text{PEA}(\mathbf{x}) = \boldsymbol{\delta}(\mathbf{x},E[c]:\boldsymbol{\theta}) = \partial\text{Prob}(y_{i,t} = 1|\,\mathbf{x}_{i,t},E[c_i])/\partial\mathbf{x},$$

while the average (over c) partial effect would be

$$\text{APE}(\mathbf{x}) = E_c[\boldsymbol{\delta}(\mathbf{x},c:\boldsymbol{\theta})] = E_c[\partial\text{Prob}(y_{i,t} = 1|\,\mathbf{x},c)/\partial\mathbf{x}].$$

One might have sufficient information to characterize $f(c_i|\mathbf{x}_{i,t})$ or $f(c_i|\mathbf{X}_i)$. In this case, the PEA could be based on $E[c_i|\mathbf{X}_i]$ or the APE might be based on the conditional distribution, rather than the marginal. Altonji and Matzkin (2005) identify this as a local average response (LAR, i.e., local to the subpopulation associated with the specific realization of $\mathbf{X}_i$). If c_i and $\mathbf{X}_i$ are independent, then the conditional and marginal distributions will be the same, and the LAR and APE also will be the same.

In single index function models, in which the covariates enter the model in a linear index function, $\boldsymbol{\beta}'\mathbf{x}_{i,t}$, the partial effects usually simplify to a multiple of $\boldsymbol{\beta}$;

$$\text{PEA}(\mathbf{x}) = \boldsymbol{\beta}\,h(\boldsymbol{\beta}'\mathbf{x}E[c]) \quad\text{where}\quad h(\boldsymbol{\beta}'\mathbf{x}E[c]) = \frac{\partial g(tE[c])}{\partial t}\Big|_{t=\boldsymbol{\beta}'\mathbf{x}},$$

$$\text{APE}(\mathbf{x}) = \boldsymbol{\beta}\,E_c[h(\boldsymbol{\beta}'\mathbf{x},c)].$$

For the normalized ($\sigma_\varepsilon = 1$) probit model, $\text{Prob}(y_{i,t} = 1|\mathbf{x}_{i,t},c_i) = \boldsymbol{\Phi}(\boldsymbol{\beta}'\mathbf{x}_{i,t}+c_i)$. Then, $g(\boldsymbol{\beta}'\mathbf{x},c) = \boldsymbol{\Phi}(\boldsymbol{\beta}'\mathbf{x} + c)$ and $h(\boldsymbol{\beta}'\mathbf{x},c) = \boldsymbol{\beta}\boldsymbol{\phi}(\boldsymbol{\beta}'\mathbf{x} + c)$. The coefficients have the same signs as partial effects, but their magnitude might be uninformative;

$$\text{APE}(\mathbf{x}) = \boldsymbol{\beta}\int_c \phi(\boldsymbol{\beta}'\mathbf{x} + c)dF(c|\,\mathbf{x}).$$

To complete this example, if $c \sim N[0,\sigma^2]$ and $\varepsilon \sim N[0,1^2]$. Then, $y^* = \boldsymbol{\beta}'\mathbf{x} + c + \varepsilon = \boldsymbol{\beta}'\mathbf{x} + w$, where $w \sim N[0,1+\sigma^2]$. It follows that

$$\text{Prob}[y=1|\,\mathbf{x},c] = \text{Prob}(\varepsilon < \boldsymbol{\beta}'\mathbf{x}+c) = \Phi(\boldsymbol{\beta}'\mathbf{x}+c),$$

$$\text{Prob}(y=1|\,\mathbf{x}) = \text{Prob}(w < \boldsymbol{\beta}'\mathbf{x}) = \Phi(\boldsymbol{\beta}'\mathbf{x}/\sigma_w) = \Phi\left[\boldsymbol{\beta}'\mathbf{x}/\left(1+\sigma^2\right)^{1/2}\right].$$

Then $\text{PEA}(\mathbf{x}) = \boldsymbol{\beta}\,\phi(\boldsymbol{\beta}'\mathbf{x}+0) = \boldsymbol{\beta}\,\phi(\boldsymbol{\beta}'\mathbf{x})$ while

$$\begin{aligned}\text{APE}(\mathbf{x}) &= \boldsymbol{\beta}\int_c \phi(\boldsymbol{\beta}'\mathbf{x}+c)(1/\sigma)\phi(c/\sigma)dc \\ &= \left(\boldsymbol{\beta}/\left(1+\sigma^2\right)^{1/2}\right)\times\phi\left[\boldsymbol{\beta}'\mathbf{x}/\left(1+\sigma^2\right)^{1/2}\right] = \boldsymbol{\delta}\phi(\boldsymbol{\delta}'\mathbf{x}).\end{aligned}$$

2.2 Interaction Effects

Interaction effects arise from second-order terms; $y_{i,t} = \beta x_{i,t} + \gamma z_{i,t} + \delta x_{i,t}z_{i,t} + c_i + \varepsilon_{i,t}$, so that

$$\begin{aligned}\text{APE}(x|\,z) &= E_c\{\partial E[y|\,x,z,c]/\partial x\} = E_c[\partial(\beta x_{i,t}+\gamma z_{i,t}+\delta x_{i,t}z_{i,t}+c_i)/\partial x] \\ &= \beta+\delta z_{i,t}.\end{aligned}$$

The interaction effect is $\partial\text{APE}(x|z)/\partial z = \delta$. What appear to be interaction effects will arise unintentionally in nonlinear index function models. Consider the nonlinear model, $E[y_{i,t}|x_{i,t},z_{i,t},c_i] = \exp(\beta x_{i,t}+\gamma z_{i,t}+c_i)$. The average partial effect of $x|z$ is $\text{APE}(x|z) = E_c\{\partial E[y|x,z,c]/\partial x\} = \beta\exp(\beta x+\gamma z)E[\exp(c)]$. The second-order (interaction) effect of z on the partial effect of x is $\beta\gamma\exp(\beta x+\gamma z)E[\exp(c)]$, which generally will be nonzero even in the absence of a second-order term. The situation is worsened if an interaction effect is built into the model. Consider $E[y|x,z,c] = \exp(\beta x + \gamma z + \delta xz + c)$. The average partial effect is

$$\text{APE}(x|\,z) = E_c\{\partial E[y|\,x,z,c]/\partial x\} = E[\exp(c)](\beta+\delta z)\exp(\beta x+\gamma z+\delta xz)].$$

The interaction effect is, now,

$$\partial APE(x|\,z)/\partial z = E[\exp(c)]\exp(\beta x+\gamma z+\delta xz)]\{\delta+(\beta+\delta z)(\gamma+\delta x)\}.$$

The effect contains what seems to be the anticipated part plus an effect that clearly results from the nonlinearity of the conditional mean. Once again, the result generally will be nonzero even if δ equals zero. This creates a considerable amount of ambiguity about how to model and interpret interactions in a nonlinear model (see Mandic, Norton, & Dowd, 2012; Ai & Norton, 2003; Greene, 2010a for discussion).

2.3 Identification Through Functional Form

Results in nonlinear models can be identified through the form of the model rather than through covariation of variables. This is usually an unappealing result. Consider the triangular model of health satisfaction and SNAP (food stamp) program participation by Gregory and Deb (2015):

$$SNAP = \boldsymbol{\beta}_S{}'\mathbf{x} + \boldsymbol{\delta}'\mathbf{z} + \varepsilon$$

$$HSAT = \boldsymbol{\beta}_H{}'\mathbf{x} + \gamma SNAP + w.$$

Note that $\mathbf{x}$ is the same in both equations. If $\boldsymbol{\delta}$ is nonzero, then this linear simultaneous equations model is identified by the usual rank and order conditions. Two stage least squares likely would be the preferred estimator of the parameters in the *HSAT* equation (assuming that *SNAP* is endogenous, that is, if ε and w are correlated). However, if $\boldsymbol{\delta}$ equals $\mathbf{0}$, the *HSAT* equation will fail the order condition for identification and be inestimable. The model in the application, however, is not linear—*SNAP* is binary and *HSAT* is ordered and categorical—both outcome variables are discrete. In this case, the parameters are fully identified, even if $\boldsymbol{\delta}$ equals $\mathbf{0}$. Maximum likelihood estimation of the full set of parameters is routine in spite of the fact that the regressors in the two equations are identical. The parameters are identified by the likelihood equations under mild assumptions (essentially that the Hessian of the full information log likelihood with respect to $(\boldsymbol{\beta}_S,\boldsymbol{\delta},\boldsymbol{\beta}_H,\gamma)$ is nonsingular at $\boldsymbol{\delta} = \mathbf{0}$). This is identification by functional form. The causal effect, γ is identified when $\boldsymbol{\delta} = \mathbf{0}$, even though there is no instrument ($\mathbf{z}$) that drives *SNAP* participation independently of the exogenous influences on *HSAT*. The authors note this, and suggest that the nonzero $\boldsymbol{\delta}$ (exclusion of $\mathbf{z}$ from the *HSAT* equations) is a good idea to improve identification, in spite of result.[3]

2.4 Endogeneity

In the linear regression model, $y_{i,t} = \alpha + \beta x_{i,t} + \delta z_{i,t} + \varepsilon_{i,t}$, there is little ambiguity about the meaning of endogeneity of x. Various theories might motivate it, such as omitted variables or heterogeneity, reverse causality, nonrandom sampling, and so on. In any of these events, however, the ultimate issue is tied to some form of covariation between $x_{i,t}$ (the observable) and $\varepsilon_{i,t}$ (the unobservable). Consider, instead, the Poisson regression model described earlier, where now, $\lambda_{i,t} = \exp(\alpha + \beta x_{i,t} + \delta z_{i,t})$. For example, suppose $y_{i,t}$ equals hospital or doctor visits (a health outcome) and $x_{i,t}$ equals income. This should be a natural application of reverse causality. No mechanism within this Poisson regression model, however, supports this notion of endogeneity. The model leaves open the question of what (in the context of the model) is correlated with $x_{i,t}$ that induces the endogeneity (see Cameron & Trivedi, 2005, p. 687). For this

3. Scott, Schurer, Jensen, and Sivey (2009) make the same observation. Rhine and Greene (2013) is a similar application. See also Filippini, Greene, Kumar, and Martinez-Cruz (2018), Wilde (2000) and Mourifie and Meango (2014) for discussion of some special cases.

particular application, a common approach is to include the otherwise absent unobserved heterogeneity in the conditional mean function, as

$$\lambda_{i,t}|w_{i,t} = \exp\left(\beta x_{i,t} + \delta z_{i,t} + w_{i,t}\right).$$

As a regression framework, the Poisson model has a shortcoming: It specifies the model for observed heterogeneity, but lacks a coherent specification for unobserved heterogeneity (a disturbance). The model suggested above is a mixture model. For the simpler case of exogenous x, the feasible empirical specification is obtained by analyzing

$$\text{Prob}(y_{i,t} = j|\, x_{i,t}, z_{i,t}) = \int_{w_{i,t}} \text{Prob}(y_{it} = j|\, x_{i,t}, z_{i,t}, w_{i,t}) dF(w_{i,t}).$$

This parametric approach would require a specification for $F(w)$. The traditional approach is a log-gamma that produces a closed form, the negative binomial model, for the unconditional probability. Recent applications use the normal distribution. A semiparametric approach could be taken as well if less is known about the distribution of w. This might seem less ad hoc than the parametric model, but the assumption of the Poisson distribution is not innocent at the outset. To return to the earlier question, a parametric approach to the endogeneity of $x_{i,t}$ would mandate a specification of the joint distribution of w and x, $F(w_{i,t}, x_{i,t})$. For example, it might be assumed that $x_{i,t} = \boldsymbol{\theta}'\mathbf{f}_{i,t} + v_{i,t}$ where w and v are bivariate normally distributed with correlation ρ. This completes a mechanism for explaining how $x_{i,t}$ is endogenous in the Poisson model. This is precisely the approach taken in Gregory and Deb's *SNAP/HSAT* model.

3 Panel Data Models

The objective of analysis is some feature of the joint conditional distribution of a sequence of outcomes for individual i;

$$f(y_{i,1}, y_{i,2}, \ldots, y_{i,T_i}|\, \mathbf{x}_{i,1}, \mathbf{x}_{i,2}, \ldots, \mathbf{x}_{i,T_i}, c_{i,1}, \ldots, c_{i,M}) = f(\mathbf{y}_i|\, \mathbf{X}_i, \mathbf{c}_i). \quad (1)$$

The sequence of random variables, $y_{i,t}$ is the outcome of interest. Each will typically be univariate, but need not be. In Riphahn, Wambach, and Million's (2003) study, $\mathbf{y}_{i,t}$ consists of two count variables that jointly record health care system use, counts of doctor visits, and counts of hospital visits. In order to have a compact notation, in Eq. (1), $\mathbf{y}_i$ denotes a column vector in which the observed outcome $y_{i,t}$ is either univariate or multivariate—the appropriate form will be clear in context. The observed conditioning effects are a set of time varying and time invariant variables, $\mathbf{x}_{i,t}$ (see, e.g., *EDUC* and *FEMALE*, respectively in Table 2). The matrix $\mathbf{X}_i$ is $T_i \times K$ containing the K observed variables $\mathbf{x}_{i,t}$ in each row. To accommodate a constant term, $\mathbf{X}_i = [\mathbf{i}, \mathbf{Z}_i]$.

For now, $\mathbf{x}_{i,t}$ is assumed to be strictly exogenous. The scalars, $c_{i,m}$ are unobserved, time invariant heterogeneity. The presence of the time invariant, unobserved heterogeneity is the signature feature of a panel data model. For current purposes, with an occasional exception noted later, it will be sufficient to work with a single unobserved variate, c_i.

Most cases of practical interest depart from an initial assumption of strict exogeneity. That is, for the marginal distribution of $y_{i,t}$, we have

$$f(y_{i,t}|\,\mathbf{x}_{i,1},\mathbf{x}_{i,2},\ldots,\mathbf{x}_{i,T_i},c_i)=f(y_{i,t}|\,\mathbf{x}_{i,t},c_i). \tag{2}$$

That is, after conditioning on $(\mathbf{x}_{i,t},c_i)$, $\mathbf{x}_{i,r}$ for $r \neq t$ contains no additional information for the determination of outcome $y_{i,t}$.[4] Assumption (2) will suffice for nearly all of the applications to be considered here. The exception that will be of interest will be dynamic models, in which, perhaps, sequential exogeneity,

$$f(y_{i,t}|\,\mathbf{x}_{i,1},\mathbf{x}_{i,2},\ldots,\mathbf{x}_{i,T_i},c_i)=f(y_{i,t}|\,\mathbf{x}_{i,1},\mathbf{x}_{i,2},\ldots,\mathbf{x}_{i,t},c_i), \tag{3}$$

is sufficient.

Given Eq. (2), the natural next step is to characterize $f(\mathbf{y}_i|\mathbf{X}_i,c_i)$. The conditional independence assumption adds that $y_{i,t}|\mathbf{x}_{i,t},c_i$ are independent within the cross section group, $t = 1,\ldots,T_i$. It follows that

$$f(y_{i,1},y_{i,2},\ldots,y_{i,T_i}|\,\mathbf{X}_i,c_i)=\prod_{t=1}^{T_i} f(y_{i,t}|\,\mathbf{x}_{i,t},c_i). \tag{4}$$

The large majority of received applications of nonlinear panel data modeling are based on fully parametric specifications. With respect to the previous model, this adds a sufficient description of the DGP for c_i that estimation can proceed.

3.1 Objects of Estimation

In most cases, the platform for the analysis is the distribution for the observed outcome variable in Eq. (1). The desired target of estimation is some derivative of that platform, such as a conditional mean or variance, a probability function defined for an event, a median, or some other conditional quantile, a hazard rate or a prediction of some outcome related to the variable of interest. For convenience, we restrict attention to a univariate case. In many applications, interest will center on some feature of the distribution of y_{it}, $f(y_{it}|\mathbf{x}_{i,t}, c_i)$, such as the conditional mean function, $g(\mathbf{x}, c) = E[y|\mathbf{x}, c]$. The main object of estimation often will be partial effects, $\boldsymbol{\delta}(\mathbf{x}, c) = \partial g(\mathbf{x}, c)/\partial\mathbf{x}$, for some specific value of $\mathbf{x}$ such as $E[\mathbf{x}]$ if $\mathbf{x}$ is continuous, or $\Delta(\mathbf{x},d,c) = g(\mathbf{x},1, c) - g(\mathbf{x},0, c)$ if the margin of interest relates to a binary variable.

4. For some purposes, only the restriction on the derived function of interest, such as the conditional mean, $E[y_{i,t}|\mathbf{X}_i, c_i] = E[y_{i,t}|\mathbf{x}_{i,t},c_i]$ is necessary (see Wooldridge, 1995). Save for the linear model, where this is likely to follow by simple construction, obtaining this result without (2) is likely to be difficult. That is, asserting the mean independence assumption while retaining the more general (1) is likely to be difficult.

A strictly nonparametric approach to $\boldsymbol{\delta}(\mathbf{x},c)$ offers little promise outside the narrow case in which no other variables confound the measurement.[5] Without at least some additional detail about distribution of c, there is no obvious way to isolate the effect of c from the impact of the observable $\mathbf{x}$. Because c is unobserved, as it stands, $\boldsymbol{\delta}$ is inestimable without some further assumptions. For example, if it can be assumed that c has mean μ_c (zero, for example) and is independent of $\mathbf{x}$, then a partial effect at this mean, PEA($\mathbf{x}$, μ) = $\boldsymbol{\delta}(\mathbf{x}, \mu)$ might be estimable. If the distribution of c can be more completely specified, then it might be feasible to obtain an average partial effect,

$$\text{APE}(\mathbf{x}) = E_c[\boldsymbol{\delta}(\mathbf{x}, c)].$$

Panel data modeling is complicated by the presence of unobserved heterogeneity in estimation of parameters and functions of interest. This situation is made worse because of the nonlinearity of the target feature. In most cases, the results gained from the linear model are not transportable. Consider the linear model with strict exogeneity and conditional independence, $E[y_{it}|\mathbf{x}_{it},c_i] = \boldsymbol{\beta}'\mathbf{x}_{it} + c_i + \varepsilon_{it}$. Regardless of the specification of $f(c)$, the desired partial effect is $\boldsymbol{\beta}$. Now consider the (nonlinear) probit model,

$$\text{(DGP)}\ \ y_{i,t}{}^* = \boldsymbol{\beta}'\mathbf{x}_{i,t} + c_i + \varepsilon_{i,t}, \varepsilon_{i,t}|\mathbf{x}_{i,t}, c_i \sim N\left[0, 1^2\right],$$

$$\text{(Observation)}\ \ y_{i,t} = \mathbf{1}[y_{i,t}{}^* > 0],$$

$$\text{(Function of interest)}\ \ \text{Prob}(y_{i,t} = 1|\,\mathbf{x}_{i,t}, c_i) = \Phi(\boldsymbol{\beta}'\mathbf{x}_{i,t} + c_i).$$

With sufficient assumptions about the generation of c_i, such as $c_i \sim N[0,\sigma^2]$, estimation of $\boldsymbol{\beta}$ will be feasible. The relevant partial effect is now

$$\boldsymbol{\delta}(\mathbf{x}, c) = \partial\Phi(\boldsymbol{\beta}'\mathbf{x} + c)/\partial\mathbf{x} = \boldsymbol{\beta}\phi(\boldsymbol{\beta}'\mathbf{x} + c).$$

If $f(c)$ is sufficiently parameterized, then an estimator of PE($\mathbf{x}\,|\hat{c}$) = $\boldsymbol{\beta}\phi(\boldsymbol{\beta}'\mathbf{x} + \hat{c})$ such as

$$\text{PEA}(\mathbf{x}|\,\hat{c}) = \boldsymbol{\beta}\phi\left[\boldsymbol{\beta}'\mathbf{x} + \hat{E}(c)\right]$$

might be feasible. If c can be assumed to have a fixed conditional mean, $\mu_c = E[c\,|\mathbf{x}] = 0$, and if $\mathbf{x}$ contains a constant term, then the estimator might be PEA($\mathbf{x}$,0) = $\boldsymbol{\beta}\phi(\boldsymbol{\beta}'\mathbf{x})$. This is not sufficient to identify the average partial effect. If it is further assumed that c is normally distributed (and independent of $\mathbf{x}$) with variance σ^2, then,

$$\begin{aligned}\text{APE}(\mathbf{x}) &= \boldsymbol{\beta}/\left(1+\sigma^2\right)^{1/2}\phi\left[\boldsymbol{\beta}'/\left(1+\sigma^2\right)^{1/2}\mathbf{x}\right] = \boldsymbol{\beta}\,(1-\rho)^{1/2}\phi\left[\boldsymbol{\beta}'(1-\rho)^{1/2}\mathbf{x}\right] \\ &= \boldsymbol{\gamma}\phi(\boldsymbol{\gamma}'\mathbf{x}),\end{aligned}$$

5. If there are no $\mathbf{x}$ variables in $E[y\,|\mathbf{x}, c]$, then with independence of d and c and binary y, there might be scope for nonparametric identification.

where ρ is the intragroup correlation, $\text{Corr}[(\varepsilon_{i,t} + c_i),(\varepsilon_{i,s} + c_i)] = \sigma^2/(1 + \sigma^2)$. In the context of this model, what will be estimated with a random sample (of panel data)? Will APE and PEA be substantively different? In the linear case, $\text{PEA}(\mathbf{x}|\hat{c})$ and $\text{APE}(\mathbf{x})$ will be the same $\boldsymbol{\beta}$. It is the nonlinearity of the function that implies that they might be different.

If c_i were observed data, then fitting a probit model for $y_{i,t}$ on $(\mathbf{x}_{i,t},c_i)$ would estimate $(\boldsymbol{\beta}, 1)$. We have not scaled c_i, but because we are treating c_i as observed data (and uncorrelated with $\mathbf{x}_{i,t}$), we can use $c^* = c_i/s_c$ as the variable, and attach the parameter σ_c to c_i^*. Therefore, a fully specified parametric model might estimate $(\boldsymbol{\beta}, \sigma_c)$. If c_i were simply ignored, we would fit a pooled probit model. The true underlying structure is $y_{i,t} = \mathbf{1}\{\boldsymbol{\beta}'\mathbf{x}_{i,t} + c_i + \varepsilon_{i,t} > 0 | \varepsilon_{i,t} \sim N[0,1^2]\}$. The estimates, shown before, would reveal $\boldsymbol{\gamma} = \boldsymbol{\beta}(1 - \rho)^{1/2}$. Each element of $\boldsymbol{\gamma}$ is an attenuated (biased toward zero) version of its counterpart in $\boldsymbol{\beta}$. If the model were linear, then omitting a variable that is uncorrelated with the included $\mathbf{x}$, would not induce this sort of omitted variable bias. Conclude that the pooled estimator estimates $\boldsymbol{\gamma}$ while the MLE estimates $(\boldsymbol{\beta}, \sigma_c)$, and the attenuation occurs even if $\mathbf{x}$ and c are independent.

An experiment based on real data will be suggestive. The data in Table 1 are a small subsample from the data used in Riphahn et al. (2003).[6] The sample contains 27,326 household/year observations in 7293 groups ranging in size from one to seven. We have fit simple pooled and panel probit models based on

$$Doctor_{i,t}^* = \beta_1 + \beta_2 Age_{i,t} + c_i + \varepsilon_{i,t};\;\; Doctor = \mathbf{1}[Doctor_{i,t}^* > 0]$$

where $Doctor = \mathbf{1}[Doctor\ Visits > 0]$. The results are

$$\text{(Pooled)}\;\; Doctor_{i,t}^* = -0.37176 + 0.01625 Age_{i,t}$$

$$\text{(Panel)}\;\; Doctor_{i,t}^* = -0.53689 + 0.02338 Age_{i,t} + 0.90999 c_i^*,$$

where c_i^* is normalized to have variance 1.[7] The estimated value of $\rho = \sigma^2/(1 + \sigma^2)$ is 0.45298, so the estimated value of σ is 0.90999. The estimator of the attenuation factor, $(1 - \rho)^{1/2}$, is 0.73961. Based on the previous results,

6. The original data set is found at the Journal of Applied Econometrics data archive, **http://qed.econ.queensu.ca/jae/2003-v18.4/riphahn-wambach-million/**. The raw data set contains variables INCOME and HSAT (self-reported health satisfaction) that contain a few anomalous values. In the 27,326 observations, three values of income were reported as zero. The minimum of the remainder was 0.005. These three values were recoded to 0.0015. The health satisfaction variable is an integer, 0,..,10. In the raw data, 40 observations were recorded between 6.5 and 7.0. These 40 values were rounded up to 7.0. The data set used here, with these substitutions is at **http://people.stern.nyu.edu/wgreene/text/healthcare.csv**. Differences between estimators computed with the uncorrected and corrected values are trivial.

7. The model was estimated as a standard random effects probit model using the Butler and Moffitt (1982) method. The estimate of σ was 0.90999. With this in hand, the implied model is as shown. When the model is estimated in precisely that form ($\boldsymbol{\beta}'\mathbf{x} + \sigma c^*$) using maximum simulated likelihood, the estimates are 0.90949 for σ and (–0.53688,0.02338) for $\boldsymbol{\beta}$. Quadrature and simulation give nearly identical results, as expected.

TABLE 1 Bias of Unconditional Fixed Effects Estimators in Limited Dependent Models

		$T=2$		$T=8$		$T=20$	
		Parameter	*APE*	*Parameter*	*APE*	*Parameter*	*APE*
Logit	β	+102.00	+67.60	+21.70	+ 19.10	+06.90	+ 3.40
	δ	+103.00	+ 66.00	+19.10	+12.80	+06.20	+5.20
Probit	β	+108.30	+47.40	+32.80	+24.10	+10.80	+8.80
	δ	+93.80	+38.80	+24.30	+15.20	+6.80	+4.70
Ordered probit	β	+132.80	–	+16.60	–	+5.80	–
	δ	+160.50	–	+12.20	–	+6.80	–
Tobit	β	+0.67	+15.33	+0.29	+1.30	+0.05	+0.08
	δ	+0.33	+19.67	+0.54	+2.16	+0.14	+0.27
	σ	−36.14	–	−8.40	–	−3.30	–
Truncated regression	β	−17.13	−7.52	−4.92	−1.72	−2.11	− 0.67
	δ	−22.81	−11.64	−7.51	−3.64	−3.27	−1.53
	σ	−35.36	–	−9.12	–	−3.75	–

then, we obtain the estimate of γ based on the panel model, $0.02338 \times 0.73961 = 0.01729$. The finite sample discrepancy is about 6%. The average value of *Age* is 43.5 years. The average partial effects based on the pooled model and the panel model, respectively, would be

$$\text{(Pooled)}\ \ \text{APE}(Age:\boldsymbol{\gamma}) = 0.01625 \times \phi(-0.37176 + 0.01625 \times 43.5) \\ = 0.00613$$

$$\text{(Panel)}\ \ \text{APE}(Age:\boldsymbol{\beta},\sigma) = 0.02338(1-0.45298)^{1/2} \\ \times \phi\left[(1-0.45298)^{1/2}(-0.53689 + 0.02338 \times 43.5)\right] \\ = 0.00648.$$

The estimate of APE(Age:$\boldsymbol{\gamma}$) should not be viewed as PEA(Age,$E[c]$) = PEA (Age,0). That estimator would be PEA(Age,0:$\boldsymbol{\beta}$,σ) = $0.02338 \times \phi(-0.53689 + 0.02338 \times 43.5) = 0.008312$.[8] This estimator seems to be misleading. Finally, simple least squares estimation produces

8. The slope in the OLS regression of *Doctor* on (1,*Age*) is 0.00601. This suggests, as observed elsewhere, that to the extent OLS estimates any defined quantity in this model, it likely will resemble APE(**x**).

$$\text{(Linear PM)}\quad Doctor_{i,t} = 0.36758 + 0.00601 Age_{i,t} + e_{i,t}.$$

This appears to be a reasonable approximation.[9]

Most situations to be considered in the subject of this chapter focus on nonlinear models such as the probit or Poisson regression and pursue estimates of appropriate partial effects (or causal effects) in many cases. As we will see in Section 6, there are a variety of situations in which something other than partial effects is of interest. In the stochastic frontier model,

$$\begin{aligned} y_{i,t} &= \alpha + \boldsymbol{\gamma}'\mathbf{z}_{i,t} + c_i + v_{i,t} - u_{i,t}, \\ &= \alpha + \boldsymbol{\gamma}'\mathbf{z}_{i,t} + c_i + \varepsilon_{i,t}, \end{aligned}$$

the object of interest is an estimator of the inefficiency term, $u_{i,t}$. The estimator used is $\hat{u}_{i,t} = E_c[E[u_{i,t}|\,\varepsilon_{i,t}]]$. The various panel data formulations focus on the role of heterogeneity in the specification and estimation of the inefficiency term.

In the analysis of individual data on multinomial choice, the counterpart to panel data modeling in many studies is the stated choice experiment. The random utility based multinomial logit model with heterogeneity takes the form

$$\text{Prob}[Choice_{i,t} = j] = \frac{\exp\left(\alpha_{i,j} + \boldsymbol{\gamma}'\mathbf{z}_{i,t,j}\right)}{1 + \sum_{j=1}^{J} \exp\left(\alpha_{i,j} + \boldsymbol{\gamma}'\mathbf{z}_{i,t,j}\right)}, \quad j = 1, \ldots, J.$$

Some applications involve mixed logit modeling, in which not only the alternative specific constants, $\alpha_{i,j}$ but also the marginal utility values, $\boldsymbol{\gamma}_i = \boldsymbol{\gamma} + \mathbf{u}_i$ are heterogeneous. Quantities of interest include willingness to pay for specific attributes (such as trip time), WTP $= E_c[E[\gamma_{i,k}/\gamma_{i,income}]]$ and elasticities of substitution, $\eta_{j,l|k} = E_c[-\gamma_i P_{i,j} P_{i,l}]$, and entire conditional distributions of random coefficients.

3.2 General Frameworks

Three general frameworks are employed in empirical applications of panel data methods. Except for the cases we will note below, they depart from strict exogeneity and conditional independence.

3.2.1 Fixed Effects

If no restriction is imposed on the relationship between c and $\mathbf{X}$, then the conditional density $f(c\,|\,\mathbf{x}_1,\ldots,\mathbf{x}_T)$ depends on $\mathbf{X}$ in some unspecified fashion. The assumption that $E[c\,|\,\mathbf{X}]$ is not independent of $\mathbf{X}$ is sufficient to invoke the fixed

---

9. There is no econometric framework available within which it can be suggested that the OLS slope is a consistent estimator of an average partial effect (at the means, for example). It just works much of the time.

effects setting. With strict exogeneity and conditional independence, the application takes the form

$$f(y_{it}|\,\mathbf{x}_{i,t},c_i)=f_y(y_{i,t},\boldsymbol{\beta}'\mathbf{x}_{i,t}+c_i),$$

such as in the linear panel data regression.[10] In most cases, the models are estimated by treating the effects as parameters to be estimated, using a set of dummy variables, $\mathbf{d}(j)$. The model is thus

$$f(y_{it}|\,\mathbf{x}_{i,t},c_i)=f_y\left(y_{i,t},\boldsymbol{\beta}'\mathbf{x}_{i,t}+\Sigma_j\alpha_j\mathbf{d}(j)_{i,t}\right).$$

The dummy variable approach presents two obstacles. First, in practical terms, estimation involves at least $K + n$ parameters. Many modern panels involve tens or hundreds of thousands of units, which might make the physical estimation of $(\boldsymbol{\beta},\boldsymbol{\alpha})$ impractical. Some considerations follow. The more important problem arises in models estimated by M estimators; that is, by optimizing a criterion function such as a log likelihood function. The incidental parameters problem (IP) arises when the number of parameters in the model (α_i) increases with the number of observation units. In particular, in almost all cases, it appears that the maximum likelihood estimator of $\boldsymbol{\beta}$ in the fixed effects model is inconsistent when T is small or fixed, even if the sample is large (in n), and the model is correctly specified.

3.2.2 Random Effects

The random effects model specifies that $\mathbf{X}$ and c are independent so $f(c\,|\,\mathbf{X}) = f(c)$. With strict independence between $\mathbf{X}$ and c, the model takes the form $f(y_{it}\,|\,\mathbf{x}_{i,t},c_i) = f(y_{i,t},\boldsymbol{\beta}'\mathbf{x}_{i,t} + u_i)$. Estimation of parameters still can be problematic. But, pooled estimation (ignoring u_i) can reveal useful quantities such as average partial effects. More detailed assumptions, such as a full specification of $u_i \sim N[0,\sigma^2]$ will allow full estimation of $(\boldsymbol{\beta}',\sigma)'$. It still will be necessary to contend with the fact that u_i remains unobserved. The Butler and Moffitt (1982) and maximum simulated likelihood approaches are based on the assumption that

$$E_{c_i}[f(y_{i,1},\ldots,y_{i,t}|\,\mathbf{X}_i,c_i)]=\int_{c_i}\prod\nolimits_{t=1}^{T_i}f(y_{i,t}|\,\boldsymbol{\beta}'\mathbf{x}_{i,t}+c_i:\boldsymbol{\theta})dF(c_i:\sigma)$$

depends on $(\boldsymbol{\beta}',\boldsymbol{\theta}',\sigma)'$ in a way that the expected likelihood can be the framework for the parameters of interest.

10. Greene (2004c) labels index function models in this form true fixed effects and true random effects models. There has been some speculation as to what the author meant by effects models that were not true. The use of the term was specifically meant only to indicate linear index function models in contrast to models that introduced the effects by some other means. The distinction was used to highlight certain other models, such as the fixed effects negative binomial regression model in Hausman, Hall, and Griliches (1984). In that specification, there were fixed effects defined as in the text in terms of $f(c\,|\,\mathbf{x})$, but the effects were not built into a linear index function.

3.2.3 Correlated Random Effects

The fixed effects model is appealing for its weak restrictions on $f(c_i|\mathbf{X}_i)$. But, as noted, practical and theoretical shortcomings follow. The random effects approach remedies these shortcomings, but rests on an assumption that might be unreasonable: that the heterogeneity is uncorrelated with the included variables. The correlated random effects model places some structure on $f(c_i|\mathbf{X}_i)$. Chamberlain (1980) suggested that the unstructured $f(c_i|\mathbf{X}_i)$ be replaced with

$$c_i|\mathbf{Z}_i = \pi + \boldsymbol{\theta}_1{}'\mathbf{z}_{i,1} + \boldsymbol{\theta}_2{}'\mathbf{z}_{i,2} + \cdots + \boldsymbol{\theta}_{Ti}{}'\mathbf{z}_{i,Ti} + u_i.$$

with $f(u_i)$ to be specified—u_i would be independent of $\mathbf{z}_{i,t}$. A practical problem with the Chamberlain approach is the ambiguity of unbalanced panels. Substituting $\mathbf{z}_i = 0$ for missing observations or deleting incomplete groups from the data set, are likely to be unproductive. The amount of detail in this specification might be excessive; in a modern application with moderate T and large K (say 30 or more), this implies a potentially enormous number of parameters. Mundlak (1978) and Wooldridge (2005, 2010) suggest a useful simplification,

$$c|\mathbf{X}_i = \pi + \boldsymbol{\theta}'\bar{\mathbf{z}}_i + u_i.$$

Among other features, it provides a convenient device to distinguish fixed effects ($\boldsymbol{\theta} \neq \mathbf{0}$) from random effects ($\boldsymbol{\theta} = \mathbf{0}$).

3.3 Dynamic Models

Dynamic models are useful for their ability (at least in principle) to distinguish between state dependence such as the dominance of initial outcomes and dependence induced by the stickiness of unobserved heterogeneity. In some cases, such as in stated choice experiments, the dynamic effects might themselves be an object of estimation (see Contoyannis, Jones, & Rice, 2004).

A general form of dynamic model would specify $f(y_{i,t}|\mathbf{X}_i, c_i, y_{i,t-1}, y_{i,t-2}, \ldots y_{i,0})$. Because the time series is short, the dependence on the initial condition, $y_{i,0}$, is likely to be substantive. Strict exogeneity is not feasible, because $y_{i,t}$ depends on $y_{i,t-1}$ in addition to $\mathbf{x}_{i,t}$, it also must depend on $\mathbf{x}_{i,t-1}$. A minor simplification in terms of the lagged values produces the density $f(y_{i,t}|\mathbf{X}_i, c_i, y_{i,t-1}, y_{i,0})$. The joint density of the sequence of outcomes is then

$$f(y_{i,1}, y_{i,2}, \ldots, y_{i,Ti}|\,\mathbf{X}_i, y_{i,t-1}, c_i, y_{i,0}) = \prod_{t=1}^{T_i} f(y_{i,t}|\,\mathbf{X}_i, y_{i,t-1}, c_i, y_{i,0}).$$

It remains to complete the specification for c_i and y_{i0}. A pure fixed effects approach that treats $y_{i,0}$ as predetermined (or exogenous) would specify

$$f(y_{i,t}|\,\mathbf{X}_i, y_{i,t-1}, c_i, y_{i,0}) = f\left(y_{i,t}|\,\boldsymbol{\gamma}'\mathbf{z}_{i,t} + \theta y_{i,t-1} + \gamma y_{i,0} + \alpha_i\right),$$

with $\mathbf{Z}_i$ implicitly embedded in α_i. This model cannot distinguish between the time invariant heterogeneity and the persistent initial conditions effect.

Moreover, as several authors (e.g., Carro, 2007) have examined, the incidental parameters problem is made worse than otherwise in dynamic fixed effects models. Wooldridge (2005) suggests an extension of the correlated random effects model,

$$c_i|\mathbf{X}_i, y_{i,0} = \pi + \boldsymbol{\pi}'\bar{\mathbf{z}}_i + \theta y_{i,0} + u_i.$$

This approach overcomes the two shortcomings noted earlier. At the cost of the restrictions on $f(c\,|\,\mathbf{X},y_0)$, this model can distinguish the effect of the initial conditions from the effect of state persistence because of the heterogeneity. Cameron and Trivedi (2005) raise a final practical question: How should a lagged dependent variable appear in a nonlinear model? They propose, for example, a Poisson regression that would appear

$$\begin{aligned}\text{Prob}[y_{i,t} = j|\,\mathbf{X}_i, y_{i,0}, c_i] &= \frac{\exp(-\lambda_{i,t})\lambda_{i,t}^j}{j!}, \lambda_{i,t}\\ &= \exp(\boldsymbol{\eta}'\mathbf{z}_{i,t} + \rho y_{i,t-1} + \theta_0 y_{i,0} + \pi + \boldsymbol{\theta}'\bar{\mathbf{z}}_i + u_i)\end{aligned}$$

Contoyannis et al. (2004) proposed a similar form for their ordered probit model.

4 Nonlinear Panel Data Modeling

Some of the methodological issues in nonlinear panel data modeling have been considered in Sections 2 and 3. We examine some of the practical aspects of common effects models.

4.1 Fixed Effects

The fixed effects model is semiparametric. The model framework, such as the probit or Tobit model is fully parameterized (see Ai, Li, Lin, & Ment, 2015). But the conditional distribution of the fixed effect, $f(c\,|\,\mathbf{X})$ is unrestricted. We can treat the common effects as parameters to be estimated with the rest of the model. Assuming strict exogeneity and conditional independence, the model is

$$f(y_{i,1}, y_{i,2}, \ldots, y_{i,T_i}|\,\mathbf{X}_i, c_i) = \prod\nolimits_{t=1}^{T_i} f(y_{i,t}|\,\mathbf{x}_{i,t}, c_i) = \prod\nolimits_{t=1}^{T_i} f(y_{i,t}|\,\boldsymbol{\gamma}'\mathbf{z}_{i,t} + \alpha_i : \boldsymbol{\theta}),$$

where $\boldsymbol{\theta}$ is any ancillary parameters such as σ_ε in a Tobit model. Denote the number of parameters in $(\boldsymbol{\gamma},\boldsymbol{\theta})$ as $K^* = K + M$. A full maximum likelihood estimator would optimize the criterion function,

$$\ln L(\boldsymbol{\gamma}, \boldsymbol{\alpha}, \boldsymbol{\theta}) = \sum_{i=1}^{n}\sum_{t=1}^{T_i} \ln f(y_{i,t}|\,\mathbf{z}_{i,t} : \boldsymbol{\gamma}, \alpha_i, \boldsymbol{\theta}) = \sum_{i=1}^{n}\sum_{t=1}^{T_i} \ln f(y_{i,t}, \boldsymbol{\gamma}'\mathbf{z}_{i,t} + \alpha_i : \boldsymbol{\theta}), \quad (5)$$

where $\boldsymbol{\alpha}$ is the $n \times 1$ vector of fixed effects. The unconditional estimator produces all $K^* + n$ parameters of the model directly using conventional means.[11] The conditional approach operates on a criterion function constructed from the joint density of ($y_{i,t}$, $t = 1,\ldots,T_i$) conditioned on a sufficient statistic, such that the resulting criterion function is free of the fixed effects.

4.1.1 Unconditional Estimation

The general log likelihood in Eq. (5) is not separable in $\boldsymbol{\gamma}$ and $\boldsymbol{\alpha}$. (For current purposes, $\boldsymbol{\theta}$ can be treated the same as $\boldsymbol{\gamma}$, so it is omitted for convenience.) Unconditional maximum likelihood estimation requires the dummy variable coefficients to be estimated along with the other structural parameters. For example, for the Poisson regression,

$$\text{Prob}(y_{i,t} = j | \mathbf{z}_{i,t} : \boldsymbol{\gamma}, \alpha_i) = \frac{\exp(-\lambda_{i,t})\lambda_{i,t}^j}{j!}, \lambda_{i,t} = \exp(\alpha_i + \boldsymbol{\gamma}'\mathbf{z}_{i,t}).$$

The within transformation or first differences of the data does not eliminate the fixed effects. The same problem will arise in any other nonlinear model in which the index function is transformed or the criterion function is not based on deviations from means to begin with.[12]

For most cases, full estimation of the fixed effects model requires simultaneous estimation of $\boldsymbol{\beta}$ and α_i. The likelihood equations are

$$\frac{\partial \ln L}{\partial \boldsymbol{\gamma}} = \sum_{i=1}^{n} \sum_{t=}^{T_i} \frac{\partial \ln f(y_{i,t} | \mathbf{z}_{i,t} : \boldsymbol{\gamma}, \alpha_i)}{\partial \boldsymbol{\gamma}} = \mathbf{0},$$

$$\frac{\partial \ln L}{\partial \boldsymbol{\alpha}} = \sum_{t=1}^{T_i} \frac{\partial \ln f(y_{i,t} | \mathbf{z}_{i,t} : \boldsymbol{\gamma}, \alpha_i)}{\partial \alpha_i} = 0, \quad i = 1, \ldots, n. \tag{6}$$

Maximum likelihood estimation can involve matrix computations involving vastly more memory than would be available on a computer. Greene (2005) noted that this assessment overlooks a compelling advantage of the fixed effects model. The large submatrix of the Hessian, $\partial^2 \ln L / \partial \boldsymbol{\alpha} \partial \boldsymbol{\alpha}'$ is diagonal, which allows a great simplification of the computations. The resulting algorithm

11. If the model is linear, the full unconditional estimator is the within groups least squares estimator. If $\mathbf{z}_{i,t}$ contains any time invariant variables (TIVs), it will not be possible to compute the within estimator. The regressors will be collinear; the TIV will lie within the column space of the individual effects, $\mathbf{D} = (\mathbf{d}_1,\ldots,\mathbf{d}_n)$. The same problem arises for other true fixed effects nonlinear models. The collinearity problem arises in the column space of the first derivatives of the log likelihood. The Hessian for the log likelihood will be singular, as will the OPG matrix. A widely observed exception is the negative binomial model proposed in Hausman et al. (1984) which is not a true fixed effects model.

12. If the model is a nonlinear regression of the form $y_{i,t} = \eta_i h(\boldsymbol{\gamma}'\mathbf{z}_{i,t}) + \varepsilon_{i,t}$, then, $E[y_{i,t}/\bar{y}_i] \approx h_{i,t}/\bar{h}_i$, does eliminate the fixed effect (see Cameron & Trivedi, 2005, p. 782).

reduces the order of the computations from $(K+n) \times (K+n)$ to $K \times K + n$. Fernandez-Val (2009) used the method to fit a fixed effects probit model with 500,000 fixed effects coefficients.[13] The method can easily be used for most of these models considered.

Unconditional fixed effects estimation, in fact, is straightforward in principle, however, it is still often an unattractive way to proceed. The disadvantage is not the practical difficulty of the computation. In most cases—the linear regression and Poisson regression are exceptions—the unconditional estimator encounters the incidental parameters problem. Even with a large sample (n) and a correctly specified likelihood function, the estimator is inconsistent when T is small, as assumed here.

4.1.2 Concentrated Log Likelihood and Uninformative Observations

For some models, it is possible to form a concentrated log likelihood for $(\boldsymbol{\gamma},\alpha_1,\ldots,\alpha_n)$. The strategy is to solve each element of Eq. (6) for $\alpha_i(\boldsymbol{\gamma}\,|\,\mathbf{y}_i,\mathbf{X}_i)$, then insert the solution into Eq. (5) and maximize the resulting log likelihood for $\boldsymbol{\gamma}$. The implied estimator of α_i then can be computed. For the Poisson model, define

$$\lambda_{i,t} = \exp\left(\alpha_i + \boldsymbol{\gamma}'\mathbf{z}_{i,t}\right) = \eta_i \exp\left(\boldsymbol{\gamma}'\mathbf{z}_{i,t}\right) = \eta_i \phi_{i,t}.$$

The log likelihood function is[14]

$$\ln L(\boldsymbol{\gamma}, \boldsymbol{\alpha}) = \sum_{i=1}^{n}\sum_{t=1}^{T_i}\left[-\eta_i\phi_{i,t} + y_{i,t}\ \ln\eta_i + y_{i,t}\ \ln\phi_{i,t} - \ \ln y_{i,t}!\right].$$

The likelihood equation for η_i is $\partial \ln L/\partial \eta_i = -\Sigma_t\, \phi_{i,t} + \Sigma_t\, y_{i,t}/\eta_i$. Equating this to zero produces

$$\hat{\eta}_i = \frac{\Sigma_{t=1}^{T_i} y_{i,t}}{\Sigma_{t=1}^{T_i}\phi_{i,t}} = \frac{\overline{y}_i}{\overline{\phi}_i}. \tag{7}$$

Inserting this solution into the full log likelihood produces the concentrated log likelihood,

$$\ln L_{conc} = \sum\nolimits_{i=1}^{n}\left[-\frac{\overline{y}_i}{\overline{\phi}_i}\sum\nolimits_{t=1}^{T_i}\phi_{i,t} + \ \ln\left(\frac{\overline{y}_i}{\overline{\phi}_i}\right)\sum\nolimits_{t=1}^{T_i} y_{i,t} + \sum\nolimits_{t=1}^{T_i}\left(y_{i,t}\ \ln\phi_{i,t} - \ \ln\left(y_{i,t}!\right)\right)\right]$$

---

13. The Hessian for a model with $n = 500{,}000$ will, by itself, occupy about 950gb of memory if the symmetry of the matrix is used to store only the lower triangle. Exploiting the special form of the Hessian reduces this to less than 4mb.

14. The log likelihood in terms of $\eta_i = \exp(\alpha_i)$ relies on the invariance of the MLE to 1:1 transformations (see Greene, 2018).

The concentrated log likelihood now can be maximized to estimate $\boldsymbol{\gamma}$. The solution for $\boldsymbol{\gamma}$ then can be used in Eq. (7) to obtain each estimate of η_i and $\alpha_i = \ln(\eta_i)$.

Groups of observations in which $\Sigma_t\, y_{i,t} = 0$ contribute zero to the concentrated log likelihood. In the full log likelihood, if $y_{i,t} = 0$ for all t, then $\partial \ln L/\partial \eta_i = \Sigma_t \phi_{i,t}$ which cannot equal zero. The implication is that there is no estimate of α_i if $\Sigma_t\, y_{i,t} = 0$. Surprisingly, for the Poisson model, estimation of a nonzero constant does not require within group variation of $y_{i,t}$ but it does require that there be at least one nonzero value. Notwithstanding the preceding issue, this strategy will not be available for most models, including the one of most interest, the fixed effects probit model.

4.1.3 Conditional Estimation

For a few cases, the joint density of the T_i outcomes conditioned on a sufficient statistic, A_i, is free of the fixed effects;

$$f(y_{i,1}, \ldots, y_{i,T_i} | \mathbf{X}_i, c_i, A_i) = g(y_{i,1}, \ldots, y_{i,T_i} | \mathbf{X}_i, A_i).$$

The most familiar example is the linear regression with normally distributed disturbances, in which, after the transformation,

$$f(y_{i,1}, \ldots, y_{i,Ti} | \mathbf{X}_i, c_i, \overline{y}_i) = N\left[\boldsymbol{\gamma}'(\mathbf{z}_{i,t} - \overline{\mathbf{z}}_i), \sigma_\varepsilon^2\right).$$

The within groups estimator is the conditional maximum likelihood estimator, then the estimator of c_i is $\overline{y}_i - \hat{\boldsymbol{\gamma}}'\overline{\mathbf{z}}_i$. The Poisson regression model is another.[15] For the sequence of outcomes, with $\lambda_{i,t} = \exp(\alpha_i)\exp(\boldsymbol{\gamma}'\mathbf{z}_{i,t}) = \eta_i \phi_{i,t}$ (see Cameron & Trivedi, 2005, p. 807),

$$f\left(y_{i,1}, \ldots, y_{i,T_i} | \mathbf{X}_i, \Sigma_{t=1}^{T_i} y_{i,t}\right) = \frac{\left(\Sigma_{t=1}^{T_i} y_{i,t}\right)!}{\Pi_{t=1}^{T_i}(y_{i,t}!)} \times \Pi_{t=1}^{T_i}\left(\frac{\phi_{i,t}}{\Sigma_s \phi_{i,s}}\right)^{y_{i,t}}.$$

Maximization of the conditional log likelihood produces a consistent estimator of $\boldsymbol{\gamma}$, but none of the fixed effects. Computation of a partial effect, or some other feature of the distribution of $y_{i,t}$, will require an estimate of α_i or $E[\alpha_i]$ or a particular value. The conditional estimator provides no information about the distribution of α_i. For index function models, it might be possible to compute ratios of partial effects, but these are generally of limited usefulness. With a consistent estimator of $\boldsymbol{\gamma}$ in hand, one might reverse the concentrated log likelihood approach. Taking $\boldsymbol{\gamma}$ as known, the term of the log likelihood relevant to estimating α_i is

15. The exponential regression model, $f(y_{i,t} | \mathbf{x}_{i,t}) = \lambda_{i,t}\exp(-y_{i,t}\lambda_{i,t})$, $y_{i,t} > 0$, is a third. This model appears in studies of duration, as a base case specification, unique for its feature that its constant hazard function, $h(y_{i,t} | \mathbf{x}_{i,t}) = f(y_{i,t} | \mathbf{x}_{i,t})/[1 - F(y_{i,t} | \mathbf{x}_{i,t})] = \lambda_{i,t}$, is independent of $y_{i,t}$.

$$\frac{\partial \ln L}{\partial \boldsymbol{\alpha}}|\hat{\boldsymbol{\gamma}} = \sum_{t=1}^{T_i} \frac{\partial \ln f(y_{i,t}|\, \mathbf{x}_{i,t}, \hat{\boldsymbol{\gamma}} : \alpha_i)}{\partial \alpha_i} = 0, \quad i = 1, \ldots, n.$$

In principle, one could solve each of these in turn to provide an estimator of α_i that would be consistent in T. Because T is small (and fixed), estimation of the individual elements is still dubious. However, by this solution, $\hat{\alpha}_i = \alpha_i + w_i$ where $\text{Var}(w_i) = O(1/T)$. Then $\bar{\hat{\alpha}} = \frac{1}{n}\sum_{i=1}^{n} \hat{\alpha}_i$ could be considered the mean of a sample of observations from the population generating α_i. (Each term could be considered an estimator of $E[\alpha_i | \mathbf{y}_i]$.) Based on the law of iterated expectations, $\bar{\hat{\alpha}}$ should estimate $E_{\mathbf{y}}[E[\alpha | \mathbf{y}_i]] = E[\alpha]$. The terms in the mean are all based on common $\hat{\boldsymbol{\gamma}}$. But by assumption, $\text{Plim}_n\, \hat{\boldsymbol{\gamma}} = \boldsymbol{\gamma}$. Then, $\text{plim}\, \bar{\hat{\alpha}}(\hat{\boldsymbol{\gamma}}) = \text{plim}\, \bar{\hat{\alpha}}(\boldsymbol{\gamma}) = E[\alpha]$, which is what will be needed to estimated partial effects for fixed effects model.[16]

4.1.4 The Incidental Parameters Problem and Bias Reduction

The disadvantage of the unconditional fixed effects estimator is the incidental parameters (IP) problem (see Lancaster, 2000). The unconditional maximum likelihood estimator is generally inconsistent in the presence of a set of incidental (secondary) parameters whose number grows with the dimension of the sample (n) while the number of cross-sections (T) is fixed. The phenomenon was first identified by Neyman and Scott (1948), who noticed that the unconditional maximum likelihood estimators of $\boldsymbol{\beta}$ and σ^2 in the linear fixed effects model are the within groups estimator for $\boldsymbol{\gamma}$ and $\hat{\sigma}^2 = \mathbf{e}'\mathbf{e}/(nT)$, with no degrees of freedom correction. The latter estimator is inconsistent; $\text{plim}\ \hat{\sigma}^2 = [(T-1)/T]\ \sigma^2 < \sigma^2$. The downward bias does not diminish as n increases, though it does decrease to zero as T increases. In this particular case, $\text{plim}\ \hat{\boldsymbol{\gamma}} = \boldsymbol{\gamma}$. No bias is imparted to $\hat{\boldsymbol{\gamma}}$. Moreover, the estimators of the fixed effects, $\hat{\alpha}_i = \Sigma_t(y_{i,t} - \hat{\boldsymbol{\gamma}}'\mathbf{x}_{i,t})$, are unbiased, albeit inconsistent because $\text{Asy.Var}[\hat{\alpha}_i]$ is $O(1/T)$

There is some misconception about the IP problem. The bias usually is assumed to be transmitted to the entire parameter vector and away from zero. The inconsistency of the estimators of α_i taints the estimation of the common parameters, $\boldsymbol{\gamma}$, but this does not follow automatically. The nature of the inconsistencies of $\hat{\alpha}_i$ and $\hat{\boldsymbol{\gamma}}(\hat{\boldsymbol{\alpha}})$are different. The FE estimator, $\hat{\alpha}_i$, is inconsistent because its asymptotic variance does not converge to zero as the sample (n) grows. There is no obvious sense in which the fixed effects estimators are systematically biased away from the true values. (In the linear model, the fixed

---

16. Wooldridge (2010, p. 309) makes this argument for the linear model. There is a remaining complication about this strategy for nonlinear models that will be pursued again in Section 6. Broadly, $\bar{\hat{\alpha}}$ estimates α_i for the subsample for which there is a solution for $\hat{\alpha}_i$. For example, for the Poisson model, the likelihood equation for α_i has no solution if $\Sigma_t y_{it} = 0$. These observations have been dropped for purposes of estimation. The average of the feasible estimators would estimate $E[\alpha_i | \Sigma_t y_{i,t} \neq 0]$. This might represent a nontrivial truncation of the distribution. Whether this differs from $E[\alpha_i]$ remains to be explored.

effects estimators are actually unbiased.) In many nonlinear settings, however, the common parameters, γ, are estimated with a systematic bias that does not diminish as n increases. No internally consistent theory implies this result. It varies by model. In the linear regression case, there is no systematic bias. In the binary logit case, the bias in the common parameter vector is proportional for the entire vector, away from zero. The result appears to be the same for the probit model, though this remains to be proven analytically. Monte Carlo evidence (Greene, 2005) for the Tobit model suggests, again, that the estimator of the scale parameter, σ_ε is biased, but the common slope estimators are not. In the true fixed effects stochastic frontier model, which has common parameters γ and two variance parameters, σ_u and σ_v, the IP problem appears to reside only in σ_v, which resembles the Neyman and Scott case.

As suggested by the Neyman and Scott application, it does seem that the force of the result is actually exerted on some explicit or embedded scaling parameters in index models. For example, the linear regression, Tobit, stochastic frontier, and even in binary choice models, where the bias appears equally in the entire vector. The only theoretically verified case is the binary logit model, for which it has been shown that plim $\hat{\gamma} = 2\gamma$ when $T = 2$ (see Abrevaya, 1997). It also can be shown that plim $\hat{\gamma} = \gamma$ as $(n,T) \rightarrow \infty$. What applies between 2 and ∞, and what occurs in other models has been suggested experimentally (see e.g., Greene, 2004a). A general result that does seem widespread is suggested by Abrevaya's result, that the IP bias is away from zero. But, in fact, this seems not to be the case, either. In the Tobit case, for example, and in the stochastic frontier, the effect seems to reside in the variance term estimators. In the truncated regression, it appears that both slopes and standard deviation parameters are biased downward. Table 1 shows some suggestive Monte Carlo simulations from Greene (2004a, 2005). All simulations are based on a latent single index model $y_{i,t}{}^* = \alpha_i + \beta x_{i,t} + \delta d_{i,t} + \sigma \varepsilon_{i,t}$ where $\varepsilon_{i,t}$ is either a standardized logistic variate or standard normal, $\beta = \delta = 1$, $x_{i,t}$ is continuous, $d_{i,t}$ is a dummy variable, and α_i is a correlated random effect (i.e., the DGP is actually a true fixed effects model). Table entries in each case are percentage biases of the unconditional estimators, computed as $100\%[(b - \beta)/\beta]$ where β is the quantity being estimated (1.0) and b is the unconditional FE estimator. The simulation also estimates the scale factor for the partial effects. The broad patterns that emerge are, first, when there is discrete variation in $y_{i,t}$, the slopes are biased away from zero. When there is continuous variation, the bias, if there is any, in the slopes, is toward zero. The bias in $\hat{\sigma}_\varepsilon$ in the censored and truncated regression models is toward zero. Estimates of partial effects seem to be more accurate than estimates of coefficients. Finally, the IP problem obviously diminishes with increases in T. Fig. 1 shows the results of a small experimental study for a stochastic frontier model, $y_{i,t} = \alpha_i + \beta x_{i,t} + \sigma_v v_{i,t} - \sigma_u |u_{i,t}|$ where, again, this is a true fixed effects model, and $v_{i,t}$ and $u_{i,t}$ are both standard normally distributed. The true values of the parameters β, σ_u and σ_v are 0.2, 0.18, and 0.10, respectively. For β and σ_u, the deviation of the estimator from the true value is

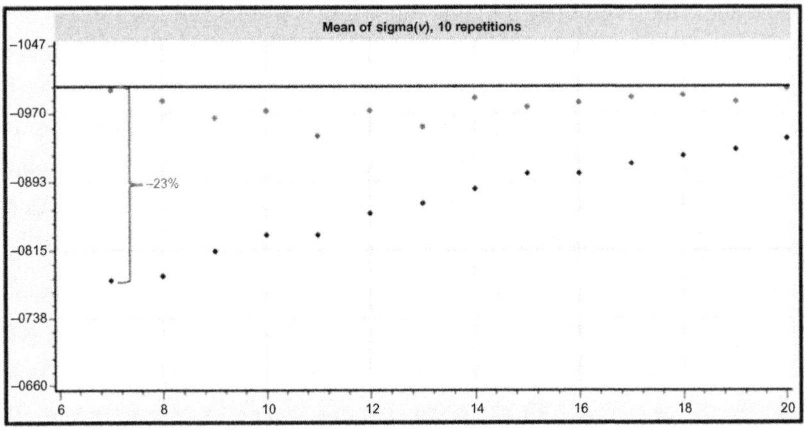

FIG. 1 Unconditional fixed effects stochastic frontier estimator.

persistently only 2%–3%. Fig. 1 compares the behavior of a consistent method of moments estimator of σ_v to the maximum likelihood estimator. The results strongly suggest that the bias of the true fixed effects estimator is relatively small compared to the models in Table 1, and it resides in the estimator of σ_v.

Proposals to correct the unconditional fixed effects estimator have focused on the probit model. Several approaches involving operating directly on the estimates, maximizing a penalized log likelihood, or modifying the likelihood equations, have been suggested. Hahn and Newey's (2004) jackknife procedure provides a starting point. The central result for an unconditional estimator based on n observations and T periods is

$$\text{plim}_{n\to\infty}\hat{\boldsymbol{\gamma}} = \boldsymbol{\gamma} + \frac{1}{T}\mathbf{b}_1 + \frac{1}{T^2}\mathbf{b}_2 + O\left(\frac{1}{T^3}\right),$$

where $\hat{\boldsymbol{\gamma}}$ is the unconditional MLE, $\mathbf{b}_1$ and $\mathbf{b}_2$ are vectors and the final term is a vector of order $(1/T^3)$.[17] For any t, a leave one period out estimator without that t, has

$$\text{plim}_{n\to\infty}\hat{\boldsymbol{\gamma}}_{(t)} = \boldsymbol{\gamma} + \frac{1}{T-1}\mathbf{b}_1 + \frac{1}{(T-1)^2}\mathbf{b}_2 + O\left(\frac{1}{T^3}\right).$$

It follows that

$$\text{plim}_{n\to\infty} T\hat{\boldsymbol{\gamma}}_T - (T-1)\hat{\boldsymbol{\gamma}}_{(t)} = \boldsymbol{\gamma} - \frac{1}{T(T-1)}\mathbf{b}_2 + O\left(\frac{1}{T^3}\right) = \boldsymbol{\gamma} + O\left(\frac{1}{T^2}\right).$$

17. For the probit and logit models, it appears that the relationship could be $\text{plim}\hat{\boldsymbol{\gamma}} = \boldsymbol{\gamma}\, g(T)$ where $g(2) = 2$, $g'(T) < 0$ and $\lim_{T\to\infty} g(T) = 1$. This simpler alternative approach remains to be explored.

This reduces the bias to $O(1/T^2)$. In order to take advantage of the full sample, the jackknife estimator would be

$$\hat{\hat{\boldsymbol{\gamma}}} = T\hat{\boldsymbol{\gamma}}_T - (T-1)\overline{\hat{\boldsymbol{\gamma}}} \text{ where } \overline{\hat{\boldsymbol{\gamma}}} = \frac{1}{T}\Sigma_{t=1}^{T}\hat{\boldsymbol{\gamma}}_{(t)}.$$

Based on these simulation results, one might expect the bias in this estimator to be trivial if T is in the range of many contemporary panels (about 15). Imbens and Wooldridge (2012) raise a number of theoretical objections that together might limit this estimator, including a problem with $\hat{\boldsymbol{\gamma}}_{(t)}$ in dynamic models and the assumption that $\mathbf{b}_1$ and $\mathbf{b}_2$ will be the same in all periods. Several other authors, including Fernandez-Val (2009), Carro (2007), and Carro and Browning (2014), have provided refinements on this estimator.

4.2 Random Effects Estimation and Correlated Random Effects

The random effects model specifies that c_i is independent of the entire sequence $\mathbf{x}_{i,t}$. Then, $f(c_i|\mathbf{X}_i) = f(c)$. Some progress can be made analyzing functions of interest, such as $E[y|\mathbf{x},c]$ with reasonably minimal assumptions. For example, if only the conditional mean, $E[c]$ is assumed known (typically zero), then estimation sometimes can proceed semiparametrically, by relying on the law of iterated expectations and averaging out the effects of heterogeneity. Thus, if sufficient detail is known about $E[y|\mathbf{x},c]$, then partial effects such as $\text{APE} = E_c\,[\partial E[y|\mathbf{x},c]/\partial \mathbf{x}]$ can be studied by averaging away the heterogeneity. However, most applications are based on parametric specifications of c_i.

4.2.1 Parametric Models

With strict exogeneity and conditional independence,

$$f(y_{i,1}, \ldots, y_{i,T_i}|\,\mathbf{X}_i, c_i) = \prod_{t=1}^{T_i} f(y_{i,t}|\,\mathbf{x}_{i,t}, c_i).$$

The conditional log likelihood for a random effects model is, then,

$$\ln L(\boldsymbol{\beta}, \boldsymbol{\theta}, \sigma) = \sum_{i=1}^{n} \ln\left(\prod_{t=1}^{T_i} f(y_{i,t}|\,\boldsymbol{\beta}'\mathbf{x}_{i,t} + c_i : \theta, \sigma)\right).$$

It is not possible to maximize the log likelihood with the unobserved c_i present. The unconditional density will be

$$\int_{c_i} \left(\prod_{t=1}^{T_i} f(y_{i,t}|\,\boldsymbol{\beta}'\mathbf{x}_{i,t} + c_i : \theta)\right) f(c_i : \sigma)\,dc_i.$$

The unconditional log likelihood is

$$\ln L_{unconditional}(\boldsymbol{\beta}, \boldsymbol{\theta}, \sigma) = \sum_{i=1}^{n} \ln \int_{c_i} \left(\prod_{t=1}^{T_i} f(y_{i,t}|\,\boldsymbol{\beta}'\mathbf{x}_{i,t} + c_i : \theta)\right) f(c_i : \sigma)\,dc_i.$$

The maximum likelihood estimator now is computed by maximizing the unconditional log likelihood. The remaining obstacle is computing the integral. Save for the two now familiar cases, the linear regression with normally distributed disturbances and normal heterogeneity and the Poisson regression with log-gamma distributed heterogeneity, integrals of this type do not have known closed forms, and must be approximated.[18] Two approaches are typically used, Gauss-Hermite quadrature and Monte Carlo simulation.

If c_i normally is distributed with mean zero and variance σ^2, the unconditional log likelihood can be written

$$\ln_{unconditional} L(\boldsymbol{\beta}, \boldsymbol{\theta}, \sigma) = \sum_{i=1}^{n} \ln \int_{-\infty}^{\infty} \left[\prod_{t=1}^{T_i} f(y_{i,t} | \mathbf{x}_{i,t}, c_i : \boldsymbol{\beta}, \boldsymbol{\theta})\right] \frac{1}{\sigma} \phi\left(\frac{c_i}{\sigma}\right) dc_i$$

With a change of variable and some manipulation, this can be transformed to

$$\ln L_{unconditional}(\boldsymbol{\beta}, \boldsymbol{\theta}, \sigma) = \sum_{i=1}^{n} \ln \int_{-\infty}^{\infty} g(h_i) e^{-h_i^2} dh_i,$$

which is in the form needed to use Gauss-Hermite quadrature. The approximation to the unconditional log likelihood is

$$\ln L_{quadrature}(\boldsymbol{\beta}, \boldsymbol{\theta}, \sigma) = \sum_{i=1}^{n} \ln \sum_{h=1}^{H} \left[\prod_{t=1}^{T_i} f(y_{i,t} | \mathbf{x}_{i,t}, a_h : \boldsymbol{\beta}, \boldsymbol{\theta})\right] w_h,$$

where a_h and w_h are the nodes and weights for the quadrature. The method is fast and remarkably accurate, even with small numbers (H) of quadrature points. Butler and Moffitt (1982) proposed the approach for the random effects probit model. It has since been used in many different applications.[19]

Monte Carlo simulation is an alternative method. The unconditional log likelihood is,

$$\begin{aligned}\ln L(\boldsymbol{\beta}, \boldsymbol{\theta}, \sigma) &= \sum_{i=1}^{n} \ln \int_{-\infty}^{\infty} \left[\prod_{t=1}^{T_i} f(y_{i,t} | \mathbf{x}_{i,t}, c_i : \boldsymbol{\beta}, \boldsymbol{\theta})\right] \frac{1}{\sigma} \phi\left(\frac{c_i}{\sigma}\right) dc_i \\ &= \sum_{i=1}^{n} \ln E_c \left[\prod_{t=1}^{T_i} f(y_{i,t} | \mathbf{x}_{i,t}, c_i : \boldsymbol{\beta}, \boldsymbol{\theta})\right].\end{aligned}$$

By relying on a law of large numbers, it is possible to approximate this expectation with an average over a random sample of observations on c_i. The sample can be created with a pseudo-random number generator. The simulated log likelihood is

$$\ln L_{simulation}(\boldsymbol{\beta}, \boldsymbol{\theta}, \sigma) = \sum_{i=1}^{n} \ln \frac{1}{R} \sum_{r=1}^{R} \left[\prod_{t=1}^{T_i} f(y_{i,t} | \mathbf{x}_{i,t}, \widetilde{c}_{i,r} : \boldsymbol{\beta}, \boldsymbol{\theta}, \sigma)\right]$$

18. See Greene (2018).

19. See, e.g., Stata (2018) and Econometric Software Inc. (2017).

where $\widetilde{c}_{i,r}$ is the rth pseudo random draw.[20] Maximum simulated likelihood has been used in a large and growing number of applications. Two advantages of the simulation method are, first, if integration must be done over more than one dimension, the speed advantage of simulation over quadrature becomes overwhelming and, second, the simulation method is not tied to the normal distribution—it can be applied with any type of population that can be simulated.

In most applications, the parameters of interest are partial effect of some sort, or some other derivative function of the model parameters. In random effects models, these functions likely will involve c_i. For example, for the random effects probit model, the central feature is $\text{Prob}(y_{i,t}=1\,|\,\mathbf{x}_{i,t}c_i)=\Phi(\boldsymbol{\beta}'\mathbf{x}_{i,t}+\sigma v_i)$ where $c_i = \sigma v_i$ with $v_i \sim N[0,1]$. As we have seen earlier, the average partial effect is

$$\text{APE}=E_v\left[\boldsymbol{\beta}\phi(\boldsymbol{\beta}'\mathbf{x}+\sigma v)\right]=\boldsymbol{\beta}(1-\rho)^{1/2}\phi\left(\boldsymbol{\beta}'\mathbf{x}(1-\rho)^{1/2}\right).$$

The function also could be approximated using either of the previously noted methods. In more involved cases that do not have closed forms, it would be a natural way to proceed.

4.2.2 Correlated Random Effects

The fixed effects approach, with its completely unrestricted specification of $f(c\,|\,\mathbf{X})$ is appealing, but difficult to implement empirically. The random effects approach, in contrast, imposes a possibly unpalatable restriction. The payoff is the detail it affords as seen in the previous section. The correlated random effects approach suggested by Mundlak (1978), Chamberlain (1980), and Wooldridge (2010) is a useful middle ground. The specification is $c_i = \pi + \boldsymbol{\theta}'\overline{\mathbf{z}}_i + u_i$. This augments the random effects model shown earlier.

$$\ln L(\boldsymbol{\gamma},\pi,\boldsymbol{\theta},\sigma)=\sum_{i=1}^{n}\ln\left(\prod\nolimits_{t=1}^{T_i} f\left(y_{i,t}\,|\,\pi+\boldsymbol{\gamma}'\mathbf{z}_{i,t}+\boldsymbol{\theta}'\overline{\mathbf{z}}_i+u_i\right)\right)$$

For example, if $u_i \sim N[0,\sigma^2]$, as is common, the log likelihood for the correlated random effects probit model would be

$$\ln L(\boldsymbol{\gamma},\pi,\boldsymbol{\theta},\sigma)=\sum_{i=1}^{n}\ln\int_{-\infty}^{\infty}\left(\prod\nolimits_{t=1}^{T_i}\Phi[(2y_{i,t}-1)(\pi+\boldsymbol{\gamma}'\mathbf{z}_{i,t}+\boldsymbol{\theta}'\overline{\mathbf{z}}_i+\sigma v_i)]\right)\phi(v_i)dv_i$$

After estimation, the partial effects for this model would be based on[21]

$$PE=\frac{\partial\Phi(\pi+\boldsymbol{\gamma}'\mathbf{z}+\boldsymbol{\theta}'\overline{\mathbf{z}}+\sigma v)}{\partial\mathbf{z}}=\boldsymbol{\gamma}\phi(\pi+\boldsymbol{\gamma}'\mathbf{z}+\boldsymbol{\theta}'\overline{\mathbf{z}}+\sigma v)=\boldsymbol{\delta}(\mathbf{z},\overline{\mathbf{z}},v).$$

20. See Cameron and Trivedi (2005, p. 394) for some useful results about properties of this estimator.
21. We note, in application, $\partial\Phi(\pi+\boldsymbol{\gamma}'\mathbf{z}+\boldsymbol{\theta}'\overline{\mathbf{z}}+\sigma v)/\partial\mathbf{z}$ should include a term $\frac{1}{T_i}\boldsymbol{\theta}$. For purpose of the partial effect, the variation of z is not taken to be variation of a component of $\overline{\mathbf{z}}$.

Empirically, this can be estimated by simulation or, as before, with

$$\hat{PE} = \boldsymbol{\gamma}(1-\rho)^{1/2}\phi\left[(1-\rho)^{1/2}(\pi+\boldsymbol{\gamma}'\mathbf{z}+\boldsymbol{\theta}'\overline{\mathbf{z}})\right]$$

The CRE model relaxes the restrictive independence assumption of the random effects specification, while overcoming the complications of the unrestricted fixed effects approach.

4.2.3 Random Parameters Models

The random effects model can be written $f(y_{i,t}|\mathbf{x}_{i,t},c_i) = f[y_{i,t}|\boldsymbol{\gamma}'\mathbf{z}_{i,t} + (\pi + u_i):\theta]$; that is, as a nonlinear model with a randomly distributed constant term. We could extend the idea of heterogeneous parameters to the other parameters. A random utility based multinomial choice model might naturally accommodate heterogeneity in marginal utilities over the attributes of the choices with a random specification $\boldsymbol{\gamma}_i = \boldsymbol{\gamma} + \mathbf{u}_i$ where $E[\mathbf{u}_i] = \mathbf{0}$, $\text{Var}[\mathbf{u}_i] = \boldsymbol{\Sigma} = \boldsymbol{\Gamma\Gamma}'$ and $\boldsymbol{\Gamma}$ is a lower triangular Cholesky factor for $\boldsymbol{\Sigma}$. The log likelihood function for this random parameters model is

$$\ln L(\boldsymbol{\beta},\boldsymbol{\theta},\boldsymbol{\Sigma}) = \sum_{i=1}^{n} \ln \int_{\mathbf{v}_i} \left[\prod\nolimits_{t=1}^{T_i} f\left(y_{i,t}|\,(\boldsymbol{\beta}+\boldsymbol{\Gamma}\mathbf{v}_i)'\mathbf{x}_{i,t}:\boldsymbol{\theta}\right)\right] f(\mathbf{v}_i)d\mathbf{v}_i.$$

The integral is over K (or fewer) dimensions, which makes quadrature unappealing—the amount of computation is $O(H^K)$, and the amount of computation needed to use simulation is roughly linear in K.

4.2.4 A Semiparametric Random Effects Model

The preceding approach is based on a fully parametric specification for the random effect. Heckman and Singer (1984) argued (in the context of a duration model), that the specification was unnecessarily detailed. They proposed a semiparametric approach using a finite discrete support over c_i, c_q, $q = 1,\ldots, Q$, with associated probabilities, τ_q. The approach is equivalent to a latent class, or finite mixture model. The log likelihood, would be

$$\ln L(\boldsymbol{\beta},\boldsymbol{\theta},\mathbf{c},\boldsymbol{\tau}) = \sum_{i=1}^{n} \ln \frac{1}{Q}\sum\nolimits_{q=1}^{Q}\tau_q\left[\prod\nolimits_{t=1}^{T_i} f\left(y_{i,t}|\,\mathbf{x}_{i,t}:c_q,\boldsymbol{\beta},\boldsymbol{\theta}\right)\right],$$
$$0<\tau_q<1,\ \Sigma_q\tau_q=1.$$

Willis (2006) applied this approach to the fixed effects binary logit model proposed by Cecchetti (1986). The logic of the discrete random effects variation could be applied to more than one, or all of the elements of $\boldsymbol{\beta}$. The resulting latent class model has been used in many recent applications.

4.3 Robust Estimation and Inference

In nonlinear (or linear) panel data modeling, robust estimation arises in two forms. First, the difference between fixed or correlated random effects and pure random effects arises from the assumption about restrictions on $f(c_i|\mathbf{X}_i)$. In the correlated random effects case, $f(c_i|\mathbf{X}_i)=f(c_i|\pi+\boldsymbol{\theta}'\overline{\mathbf{z}}_i)$, and in the pure random effects, case, $f(c_i|\mathbf{X}_i) = f(c_i)$. A consistent fixed effects estimator should be robust to the other two specifications. This proposition underlies much of the treatment of the linear model. The issue is much less clear for most nonlinear models because, at least in the small T case, there is no sharply consistent fixed effects estimator because of the incidental parameters problem. This forces the analyst to choose between the inconsistent fixed effects estimator and a possibly nonrobust random effects estimator. In principle, at the cost of a set of probably mild, reasonable assumptions, the correlated random effects approach offers an appealing approach.

The second appearance of the idea of robustness in nonlinear panel data modeling will be the appropriate covariance matrix for the ML estimator. The panel data setting is the most natural place to think about clustering and robust covariance matrix estimation (see Abadie et al., 2017; Cameron & Miller, 2015; Wooldridge, 2003). In the linear case, where the preferred estimator is OLS,

$$\mathbf{b}-\boldsymbol{\beta}=\left[\Sigma_{i=1}^{n}\left(\Sigma_{t=1}^{T_i}\mathbf{x}_{i,t}\mathbf{x}_{i,t}'\right)\right]^{-1}\left[\Sigma_{i=1}^{n}\left(\Sigma_{t=1}^{T_i}\mathbf{x}_{i,t}\varepsilon_{i,t}\right)\right].$$

The variance estimator would be

$$\text{Est.Var}[\mathbf{b}\mid\mathbf{X}]=\left[\Sigma_{i=1}^{n}\left(\Sigma_{t=1}^{T_i}\mathbf{x}_{i,t}\mathbf{x}_{i,t}'\right)\right]^{-1}\left[\Sigma_{i=1}^{n}\left(\Sigma_{t=1}^{T_i}\mathbf{x}_{i,t}e_{i,t}\right)\left(\Sigma_{t=1}^{T_i}\mathbf{x}_{i,t}'e_{i,t}\right)\right]$$
$$\left[\Sigma_{i=1}^{n}\left(\Sigma_{t=1}^{T_i}\mathbf{x}_{i,t}\mathbf{x}_{i,t}'\right)\right]^{-1}.$$

The correlation accommodated by the cluster correction in the linear model arises through the within group correlation of $(\mathbf{x}_{i,t}e_{i,t})$. Abadie et al. (2017) discuss the issue of when clustering is important. For the linear model with normally distributed disturbances, the first and second derivatives of the log likelihood function are $\mathbf{g}_{i,t}=\mathbf{x}_{i,t}\varepsilon_{i,t}/\sigma^2$ and $\mathbf{H}_{i,t}=-\mathbf{x}_{i,t}\mathbf{x}_{i,t}'/\sigma^2$. In this case, whether clustering is important would turn on whether $(-\Sigma_{t=1}^{T_i}\hat{\mathbf{H}}_{i,t})=\mathbf{X}_i'\mathbf{X}_i/\hat{\sigma}^2$ differs substantially from

$$\left(\Sigma_{t=1}^{T_i}\hat{\mathbf{g}}_{i,t}\right)\left(\Sigma_{t=1}^{T_i}\hat{\mathbf{g}}'_{i,t}\right)=\Sigma_{t=1}^{T_i}\Sigma_{s=1}^{T_i}e_{i,t}e_{i,s}\mathbf{x}_{i,t}\mathbf{x}_{i,s}'/\hat{\sigma}^4=\Sigma_{t=1}^{T_i}\Sigma_{s=1}^{T_i}\hat{\mathbf{g}}_{i,t}\hat{\mathbf{g}}_{i,t}'$$

(apart from the scaling $\hat{\sigma}^2$). This, in turn, depends on the within group correlation of $(\mathbf{x}_{i,t}e_{i,t})$, not necessarily on that between $e_{i,t}$ or $\mathbf{x}_{i,t}$ separately.

For a maximum likelihood estimator, the appropriate estimator is built up from the Hessian and first derivatives of the log likelihood. By expanding the likelihood equations for the MLE $\hat{\boldsymbol{\gamma}}$ around $\boldsymbol{\gamma}$,

$$\hat{\boldsymbol{\gamma}}-\boldsymbol{\gamma}\approx\left[\Sigma_{i=1}^{n}\left(\Sigma_{t=1}^{T_i}\mathbf{H}_{i,t}\right)\right]^{-1}\left[\Sigma_{i=1}^{n}\left(\Sigma_{t=1}^{T_i}\mathbf{g}_{i,t}\right)\right]$$

The estimator for the variance of $\hat{\boldsymbol{\gamma}}$ is then

$$\text{Est.Var}[\hat{\boldsymbol{\gamma}}]=\left[\Sigma_{i=1}^{n}\left(\Sigma_{t=1}^{T_i}\hat{\mathbf{H}}_{i,t}\right)\right]^{-1}\left[\Sigma_{i=1}^{n}\left(\Sigma_{t=1}^{T_i}\hat{\mathbf{g}}_{i,t}\right)\left(\Sigma_{t=1}^{T_i}\hat{\mathbf{g}}'_{i,t}\right)\right]\left[\Sigma_{i=1}^{n}\left(\Sigma_{t=1}^{T_i}\hat{\mathbf{H}}_{i,t}\right)\right]^{-1}$$

where the terms are evaluated at $\hat{\gamma}$. The result for the nonlinear model mimics that for the linear model. In general, clustering is important with respect to the within group correlation of the scores of the log likelihood. It might be difficult to interpret this in natural terms, such as membership in a group. Abadie et al. also take issue with the idea that clustering is harmless, arguing it should be substantive. We agree with this, especially given the almost reflexive (even in cross-section studies) desire to secure credibility by finding something to cluster on. The necessary and sufficient condition is that some form of unobservable be autocorrelated within the model. For example, the mere existence of some base similarity within defined groups in a population is not alone sufficient to motivate this correction.

Clustering appears universally to be viewed as conservative. The desire is to protect against being too optimistic in reporting standard errors that are too small. It seems less than universally appreciated that the algebra of the cluster correction (and robust covariance matrix correction more generally) does not guarantee that the resulting estimated standard errors will be larger than the uncorrected version.

4.4 Attrition

When the panel data set is unbalanced, the question of ignorability is considered. The methodological framework for thinking about attrition is similar to sample selection. If attrition from the panel is related systematically to the unobserved effects in the model, then the observed sample might be nonrandom. (In Contoyannis et al.'s (2004) study of self-assessed health, the attrition appeared to be most pronounced among those whose initial health was rated poor or fair.) It is unclear what the implications are for data sets affected by nonrandom attrition. Verbeek and Nijman (1992) suggested some variable addition tests for the presence of attrition bias. The authors examined the issue in a linear regression setting. The application of Contoyannis et al. (2004) to an ordered probit model is more relevant here. The Verbeek and Nijman tests add (one at a time) three variables to the main model: NEXT WAVE is a dummy variable added at observed wave t that indicates if the individual is observed in the next wave; ALL WAVES is a dummy variable that indicates whether the individual is present for all waves; NUMWAVES is the total number of waves for which individual i is present in the sample. (Note that all of these variables are time invariant, so they cannot appear in a fixed effects model.) The authors note these tests might have low power against some alternatives and are nonconstructive—they do not indicate what response should follow a finding of attrition bias. A Hausman style test might work. The comparison would be between the estimator based only on the full balanced panel and the full, larger, unbalanced panel. Contoyannis et al. (CRJ) note that this approach likely would not work because of the internal structure of the ordered probit model. The problem, however, is worse than that. The more efficient estimator of the pair is only more efficient because it uses more observations, not because of some aspect of the model specification, as is generally required for the Hausman (1978) test. It is not clear, therefore, how the right asymptotic covariance matrix for the test should be constructed. This would apply in any modeling framework. The outcome of the VN test suggests whether the analyst should restrict the sample to the balanced panel that is present for all waves, or they can gain the additional efficiency afforded by the full, larger, unbalanced sample.

Wooldridge (2002) proposed an inverse probability weighting scheme to account for nonrandom attrition. For each individual in the sample, $d_{i,t} = 1$[individual i is present in wave t, $t = 1,\ldots,T$]. A probit model is estimated for each wave based on characteristics $\mathbf{z}_{i,1}$ that are observed for everyone at wave 1. For Contoyannis et al. (2004), these included variables such as initial health status and initial values of several characteristics of health. At each period, the fitted probability $\hat{p}_{i,t}$ is computed for each individual. The weighted pooled log likelihood is

$$\ln L = \sum_{i=1}^{n}\sum_{t=1}^{T_i}\left(d_{i,t}/\hat{p}_{i,t}\right)\log L_{i,t}.$$

CRJ suggested some refinements to allow $\mathbf{z}$ to evolve. The application of the set of procedures suggested the presence of attrition bias for men in the sample, but not for women. Surprisingly, the difference between the estimates based on the full sample and the balanced panel were negligible.

4.5 Specification Tests

The random effects and fixed effects models each encompass the pooled model (linear or not) via some restriction on $f(c_i|\mathbf{X}_i)$. The tests are uncomplicated for the linear case. For the fixed effects model, the linear restriction, $H_0{:}\alpha_i = \alpha_1$, $i = 2,\ldots,n$ can be tested with an F statistic with $(n–1)$ and $N–n–K$ degrees of freedom. Under the normality assumption, a likelihood ratio statistic, $-2\ln(\mathbf{e}_{LSDV}'\mathbf{e}_{LSDV}/\mathbf{e}_{POOLED}'\mathbf{e}_{POOLED})$ would have a limiting chi-squared distribution with $n–1$ degrees of freedom under H_0. There is no counterpart to the F statistic for nonlinear models. The likelihood ratio test might seem to be a candidate, but this strategy requires the unconditional fixed effects estimator to be consistent under H_0. The Poisson model is the only clear candidate. Cecchetti (1986) proposed a Hausman (1978) test for the binary logit model based on a comparison of the efficient pooled estimator to the inefficient conditional ML estimator.[22] This option will not be available for many other models; it requires the conditional estimator or some other consistent (but inefficient under H_0) estimator. The logit and Poisson are the only available candidates. The strategy certainly

22. The validity of Cecchetti's test depends on using the same sample for both estimators. The observations with $\Sigma_t y_{i,t} = 0$ or T_i should be omitted from the pooled sample even though they are useable.

is not available for the probit model. A generic likelihood ratio test will not be available because of the incidental parameters problem, and, for some cases, the fixed effects estimator must be based on a smaller sample.

A useful middle ground is provided by the correlated random effects (CRE) strategy. The CRE model restricts the generic fixed effects model by assuming $c_i = \pi_0 + \theta'\overline{\mathbf{z}} + u_i$. If we embed this in the generic fixed effects model,

$$f(y_{i,1}, \ldots, y_{i,Ti} | \mathbf{X}_i, c_i) = \Pi_t f(\pi + \boldsymbol{\gamma}'\mathbf{z}_{i,t} + \boldsymbol{\theta}'\overline{\mathbf{z}}_i + u_i).$$

This model can be estimated as a random effects model if a distribution (such as normal) is assumed for u_i. The Wald statistic for testing H_0:$\boldsymbol{\theta} = \mathbf{0}$ would have a limiting chi-squared distribution with K degrees of freedom. (The test should be carried out using a robust covariance matrix because of the loose definition of c_i.[23])

The test for random effects likewise has some subtle complications. For the linear model, with normally distributed random effects, the standard approach is Breusch and Pagan's LM test based on the pooled OLS residuals:

$$LM = \frac{\left(\Sigma_{i=1}^{n} T_i\right)^2}{2\Sigma_{i=1}^{n} T_i(T_i - 1)} \left[\frac{\Sigma_{i=1}^{n} (T_i \overline{e}_i)^2}{\Sigma_{i=1}^{n} \Sigma_{t=1}^{T_i} e_{i,t}^2} - 1\right]^2 \rightarrow \chi^2[1].$$

Wooldridge (2010) proposes a method of moments based test statistic that uses $\text{Cov}(\varepsilon_{i,t}, \varepsilon_{i,s}) = \text{Var}(\varepsilon_{i,t}) = \sigma^2$,

$$Z = \frac{\frac{1}{n}\Sigma_{i=1}^{n}\left(\Sigma_{t=1}^{T_i-1}\Sigma_{s=T_i+1}^{T_i} e_{i,t}e_{i,s}\right)}{\sqrt{\frac{1}{n}\Sigma_{i=1}^{n}\left(\Sigma_{t=1}^{T_i-1}\Sigma_{s=T_i+1}^{T_i} e_{i,t}e_{i,s}\right)^2}} \rightarrow N[0, 1]$$

Some manipulation of this reveals that $Z = \sqrt{n\overline{r}}/s_r$ where $r_i = \left[(T_i\overline{e}_i)^2 - \mathbf{e}_i'\mathbf{e}_i\right]$. The difference between the two is that the *LM* statistic relies on variances (and underlying normality) while Wooldridge's relies on the covariance between $e_{i,t}$ and $e_{i,s}$ and the central limit theorem.

There is no direct counterpart to either of these statistics for nonlinear models, generally because nonlinear models do not produce residuals to provide a basis for the test.[24] There is a subtle problem with tests of H_0:$\sigma_c^2 = 0$ based on the likelihood function. The regularity conditions required to derive the limiting chi-squared distribution of the statistic require the parameter to be in the interior

23. The same test in the linear regression presents a direct approach. Linear regression of $y_{i,t}$ on $(\mathbf{z}_{i,t}, \overline{\mathbf{z}}_i)$ is algebraically identical to the within estimator. A Wald test of the hypothesis that the coefficients on $\overline{\mathbf{z}}_i$ equal zero (using a robust covariance matrix) is loosely equivalent to the test described here for nonlinear models. This is the Wu (1973) test, but the underlying logic parallels the Hausman test.

24. Greene and McKenzie (2015) develop an *LM* test for H_0 for the random effects probit model using generalized residuals (see Chesher & Irish, 1987). For a single index nonlinear (or linear) model, the generalized residual is $u_{i,t} = \partial \ln f(y_{i,t}|\bullet)/\partial(\boldsymbol{\beta}'\mathbf{x})$, i.e., the derivative with respect to the constant term. For the linear model, this is $\varepsilon_{i,t}/\sigma_\varepsilon^2$.

of the parameter space, not on its boundary, as it would be here. (Greene and McKenzie 2015) examine this issue for the random effects probit model.)

Under the fairly strong assumptions that underlie the Butler and Moffitt or random constants model, a simpler Wald test is available. For example, for the random effects probit model, maximization of the simulated log likelihood,

$$\ln L(\boldsymbol{\beta}, \sigma) = \sum_{i=1}^{n} \ln \frac{1}{R} \sum\nolimits_{r=1}^{R} \left[\prod\nolimits_{t=1}^{T_i} \Phi[(2y_{i,t} - 1)(\boldsymbol{\beta}' \mathbf{x}_{i,t} + \sigma v_{i,r})] \right]$$

produces estimates of $\boldsymbol{\beta}$ and σ. The latter can form the basis of a Wald or likelihood ratio test. The Butler and Moffitt estimator produces an estimate of $\rho = \sigma^2/(1 + \sigma^2)$ that can be treated similarly.

The random and fixed effects models are not nested without some restrictions; H_0: $f(c \mid \mathbf{X}) = f(c)$ requires some formal structure to provide a basis for statistical inference. Once again, the correlated random effects model provides a convenient approach. The log likelihood function under a suitable definition of $f(c \mid \mathbf{X}_i)$ would be

$$\ln L(\boldsymbol{\beta}, \theta, \sigma) = \sum_{i=1}^{n} \ln \int_{-\infty}^{\infty} \left[\prod\nolimits_{t=1}^{T_i} f(y_{i,t} \mid (\pi + \boldsymbol{\gamma}' \mathbf{z}_{i,t} + \boldsymbol{\theta}' \overline{\mathbf{z}}_i + \sigma u_i)) \right] f(u_i) du_i$$

A Wald test of H_0:$\boldsymbol{\theta} = \mathbf{0}$ tests the difference between fixed and random effects under this specification.

5 Panel Data

Panel data are found in several forms. Broadly, n observational units each are observed T times in sequence. One useful distinction can be made by delineating the sampling frame that generates n and T. In the longitudinal data settings of interest here, we treat T as fixed, though not necessarily very small. The Panel Survey of Income Dynamics (PSID) contains more than 50 years of data; the German Socioeconomic Panel (GSOEP) is near 20 years. The European Community Household Panel (ECHP) data set was ended after eight waves. Econometric considerations in such data generally are based on n multivariate (T-variate) observations. The statistical theory for longitudinal analysis is labeled fixed T. In particular, although some of these data sets might be long enough to be considered otherwise, the time series properties of the data (e.g., stationarity) are not of interest. The Penn World Tables (http://www.rug.nl/ggdc/productivity/pwt/) consist of $T = 65$ years of data on $n = 182$ countries (as of version 9.0 in 2017). In analyzing these aggregate time series data, the time series properties are of paramount importance. These could be regarded as fixed n, though the number of countries in any particular analysis is typically not an important feature of the analysis. Asymptotic properties of estimators in this context, for example, hinge on T, not n. A style of analysis rather different from longitudinal modeling is called for in this setting. In contrast, the Center for Research in Security Prices (CRSP) data (http://www.crsp.com) provide financial analysts with extremely wide (large n) data on some very long time series (large T), such as stock and bond data for corporations. Each of these settings calls for its own classes of models and methods. In this (now, admittedly parochial) survey, we are interested in longitudinal analysis (small or fixed T and large n). Some examples of these national (or international) data sets are as follows:

- European Community: SHARE (Survey of Health, Ageing and Retirement in Europe);
- European Community: ECHP (European Community Household Panel);
- Australia: HILDA (Household Income and Labor Dynamics in Australia);
- UK: *BHPS* (now, Understanding Society, previously the British Household Panel Survey);
- Germany: GSOEP (German Socioeconomic Panel);
- Mexico: ENEU (Encuesta Nacional de Empleo Urbano, Urban Employment Survey)
- China: CFPS (China Family Panel Study);
- Italy: WHIP (Work Histories Italian Panel);
- USA: PSID (Panel Survey of Income Dynamics);
- USA: MEPS (Medical Expenditure Panel Survey);
- USA: NLS (National Longitudinal Survey);
- USA: SIPP (Survey of Income and Program Participation).

We note an immediate complication in the previous description. In practice, most longitudinal data sets do not actually involve a fixed T observation on n units. Rather, units come and go from the sample for various reasons. This could be by design. In a rotating panel, such as the SIPP and ENEU data, units enter the panel for a fixed number of waves, and the entry of specific units is staggered. In a particular wave of the panel, the number of appearances of any unit could be any of $1,\ldots,T$. (T varies from two to four years for the SIPP data and is five for the ENEU data) The reasons for exit and possible reentry by any unit, however, might be unexplainable in the context of the study. Full generality would require us to specify that the $i=1,\ldots,n$ observations each is observed T_i times. In nearly all received cases, this sort of variation merely presents a notational inconvenience for the econometrician and a practical, accounting complication for the model builder. It is necessary, however, to distinguish randomly missing observations from attrition. For purpose of the analysis, attrition will have two features: (1) It is an absorbing state; the unit that attrites from the sample does not return later. (There is churn in some of the data sets listed above.); (2) In the context of whatever model is under consideration, the unobservable features that explain attrition will be correlated with the unobservables that enter the model for the interesting variable under analysis. These two results produce a complication because of nonrandom sampling. For example, it is not simply association of attrition with the dependent variable that creates an attrition problem. The association is with the unobservable effects in the model. In a model for *Income*, if attrition is explainable completely in terms of *Income*—individuals whose income reaches a certain level are asked to exit the panel—then the phenomenon can be modeled straightforwardly in terms of truncation. But if the attrition is associated with the disturbance in the *Income* equation, matters become much more complicated. To continue the example, in an *Income* model, attrition that is related to *Health* might well be nonrandom with respect to *Income*. We will examine a subsequent application.

A panel data set that consists precisely of T observations on N units is said to be a balanced panel. In contrast, if the number of observations T_i varies with i, then the panel is unbalanced. Attrition is a potential problem in unbalanced panels. Table 2 displays an extract from an unbalanced panel data set. The analysis in the remainder of this survey is concerned with data such as these. (The data are extracted from the GSOEP sample that was used in Riphahn et al. 2003.) For our purposes, the interesting variables in this data set are *HSAT*, health satisfaction, and *DOCVIS*, number of doctor visits.

6 Modeling Frameworks and Applications

We illustrate the applications of the panel data methods in several different nonlinear settings. We begin with the binary choice model that dominates the received literature, and then examine several others. A few relatively uncommon applications such as duration models (Lee 2008) are left for more extensive treatments.

6.1 Binary Choice

The probit and logit models for binary choice are the standard settings for examining nonlinear modeling, in general, and panel data modeling, in particular. The canonical origin of the topic would be Chamberlain's (1980) development of the fixed effects model and Butler and Moffitt's (1982) treatment of the random effects model.[25] The unconditional fixed effects estimators for the panel probit and logit models (see Greene 2004a, 2004b, 2018) exemplify the incidental parameters problem and therefore are unappealing approaches. The literature about extensions and less parameterized alternatives to the two models includes Hahn and Kuersteiner (2011), Hahn and Newey (2004), Carro (2007), Fernandez-Val (2009), Honoré and Lewbel (2002), Honoré and Kesina (2017), Manski (1975), Aguirrebiria and Mira (2007), and Lewbel and Dong (2015).

6.1.1 *Random and Unconditional Fixed Effects Probit Models*

The log likelihood function for a panel probit model[26] is

$$\ln L(\boldsymbol{\beta},\sigma)=\sum_{i=1}^{n}\sum_{t=1}^{T_i}\ln\Phi[q_{i,t}(\pi+\boldsymbol{\gamma}'\mathbf{z}_{i,t}+c_i)],q_{i,t}=(2y_{i,t}-1).$$

25. Rasch (1960) is a precursor to the fixed effects logit model.

26. We distinguish this from the panel probit model described in Bertschuk and Lechner (1998), which was essentially a constrained seemingly unrelated regressions model for a set of T binary choices;

$y_{i,t}=\mathbf{1}[\boldsymbol{\beta}'\mathbf{x}_{i,t}+\varepsilon_{i,t}>0]$ with $\text{Cov}(\varepsilon_{i,t},\varepsilon_{j,s})=\mathbf{1}[i=j]\rho_{t,s}$ with $\rho_{t,t}=1$. Their formulation describes cross period correlation, not individual heterogeneity.

TABLE 2 Unbalanced Panel Data

ID	Female	Year	Age	Educ	Married	Docvis	Hsat	Income	Children
1	0	1984	54	15	1	1	8	0.305	0
1	0	1985	55	15	1	0	8	0.451005	0
1	0	1986	56	15	1	0	7	0.35	0
2	1	1984	44	9	1	0	7	0.305	0
2	1	1985	45	9	1	1	8	0.318278	0
2	1	1986	46	9	1	2	7	0.35	0
2	1	1988	48	9	1	1	8	0.35305	0
3	1	1984	58	11	0	0	10	0.1434	0
3	1	1986	60	11	0	0	9	0.3	0
3	1	1987	61	11	0	10	10	0.11	0
3	1	1988	62	11	0	3	10	0.1	0
4	1	1985	29	18	0	4	10	0.13	0
5	0	1987	27	11.8182	0	1	9	0.065	0
5	0	1988	28	11.8182	0	2	10	0.06	0
5	0	1981	31	11.8182	0	0	10	0.155	0
6	0	1985	25	9	0	2	10	0.16	1
6	0	1986	26	9	1	3	9	0.3	1
6	0	1987	27	9	1	0	8	0.3	1
6	0	1988	28	9	1	1	10	0.2	1
6	0	1991	31	9	1	18	2	0.18	1
7	1	1987	26	10	1	0	9	0.3	1
7	1	1988	27	10	1	0	7	0.2	1
7	1	1991	30	10	1	2	9	0.18	1
8	0	1984	64	10.5	0	7	0	0.15	0
9	0	1984	30	13	0	6	9	0.24	0
9	0	1987	33	13	0	7	8	0.265	0
9	0	1988	34	13	1	0	8	0.6	1
9	0	1991	37	18	1	4	7	0.7	1
9	0	1994	40	18	1	0	9	0.75	1
10	1	1988	30	18	0	0	6	0.36	0
10	1	1994	36	18	1	0	6	0.92	1

The pooled estimator was examined earlier. The random effects estimator would be based either on simulation or Hermite quadrature. There is no conditional likelihood estimator for the fixed effects form of this model. To illustrate the model, we will compare the various estimators using the GSOEP health data described earlier. The data are an unbalanced panel with 7293 groups, 27,326 household/year observations. We have used the 877 households that were observed in all seven waves (so there are no issues of attrition embedded in the data). For purposes of computing the dynamic models, the last six years of data were used in all cases. The outcome variable is $Doctor_{i,t} = \mathbf{1}[DocVis_{i,t} > 0]$. Groups for which $\Sigma_t\, Doctor_{i,t}$ equals 0 or 6 were omitted from the sample, leaving $n^* = 597$ observations.

Estimates for random and unconditional fixed effects for a small specification are shown in Table 3. (Standard errors are not shown, because the discussion of the various models is not concerned with efficiency of different estimators.) Overall, the pooled and fixed effects (FE) estimators seem distinctly removed from the random effects (RE) counterparts. The correlated random effects model seems likewise to have substantial effect on the estimated partial effects. Based on the *LM* test, the pooled approach is rejected for any static or dynamic form. The simple RE form also is rejected in favor of the CRE form for both cases, which would argue in favor of the FE model. A direct test for the FEM soundly rejects all other forms of the model, static or dynamic. It is not clear whether this is a valid test, however, because the FE log likelihood is not based on a consistent estimator of the parameters estimated by any other form. Still using the LR test, the dynamic CRE rejects the static one, so the preferred model is the dynamic CRE. Comparing to the static pooled model, the extensions substantially change the partial effects.

6.1.2 Logit Model and Conditional Fixed Effects Estimation

The binary logit model is the most familiar of the few models that provide a conditional estimator (see Lancaster, 2000). The probability with fixed effects is

$$\text{Prob}(y_{i,t} = 1 | \mathbf{x}_{i,t}, \alpha_i) = \Lambda(\alpha_i + \boldsymbol{\gamma}'\mathbf{z}_{i,t}) = e^{\alpha_i + \boldsymbol{\gamma}'\mathbf{z}_{i,t}} / \left[1 + e^{\alpha_i + \boldsymbol{\gamma}'\mathbf{z}_{i,t}}\right].$$

The unconditional logit log likelihood is

$$\ln L(\boldsymbol{\gamma}, \boldsymbol{\alpha}) = \sum_{i=1}^{n^*} \sum_{t=1}^{T_i} \ln \Lambda[q_{i,t}(\boldsymbol{\gamma}'\mathbf{z}_{i,t} + \alpha_i)], q_{i,t} = (2y_{i,t} - 1).$$

Groups for which $\Sigma_t\, y_{i,t}$ equals 0 or T_i do not contribute to this log likelihood, so the sum is over the n^* observations for which $0 < \Sigma_t y_{i,t} < T_i$. The unconditional log likelihood is straightforward to maximize over $(\boldsymbol{\gamma},\boldsymbol{\alpha})$ using the remaining observations. The conditional log likelihood is the sum of the logs of the probabilities conditioned on $S_i = \sum_{t=1}^{T_i} y_{i,t}$,

TABLE 3 Estimated Probit Models (Estimated Partial Effects in Parentheses)

	Static				Dynamic		
Pooled	*Pooled*	*RE*	*CRE*	*FE*	*Pooled*	*RE*	*CRE*
Constant	1.603	1.612	2.668		0.648	0.880	1.449
Age	0.007	0.015	0.033	0.040	0.005	0.010	0.030
	(0.002)	(0.004)	(0.009)	(0.008)	(0.002)	(0.003)	(0.008)
Education	−0.042	−0.052	0.178	0.109	−0.026	−0.035	0.165
	(−0.014)	(−0.014)	(0.046)	(0.019)	(−0.008)	(−0.009)	(0.044)
Income	0.051	0.046	−0.119	−0.177	0.005	0.054	−0.116
	(0.018)	(0.012)	(−0.031)	(−0.315)	(0.001)	(−0.014)	(−0.031)
Health	−0.180	−0.197	−0.144	−0.180	−0.141	−0.171	−0.143
	(−0.062)	(−0.052)	(−0.037)	(−0.032)	(−0.044)	(−0.046)	(−0.038)
Married	0.119	0.105	−0.007	0.016	0.099	0.099	−0.146
	(0.041)	(0.028)	(−0.019)	(0.003)	(0.031)	(0.027)	(−0.004)
$\overline{Age}$			−0.029				−0.027
$\overline{Educ}$			−0.221				−0.198
$\overline{Income}$			0.220				0.105
$\overline{Health}$			−0.175				−0.079
$\overline{Married}$			0.250				0.220
$Doctor_{t-1}$					0.667	0.230	0.207
$Doctor_0$					0.475	0.799	0.774
ρ	0.436		0.430			0.300	0.305
Ln *L*	−3212.59	−2923.37	−2898.88	−1965.63	−2898.18	−2826.68	−2815.87
LM		215.754	212.28			112.64	121.03

$$\text{Prob}(y_{i,1}, y_{i,2}, \ldots, y_{i,T_i}|S_i) = \frac{\exp\left(\sum_{t=1}^{T_i} y_{i,t}\boldsymbol{\gamma}'\mathbf{z}_{i,t}\right)}{\sum_{\Sigma_t d_{i,t}=S_i} \exp\left(\sum_{t=1}^{T_i} d_{i,t}\boldsymbol{\gamma}'\mathbf{z}_{i,t}\right)}$$

$$= \frac{\exp\left(\sum_{t=1}^{T_i} y_{i,t}\boldsymbol{\gamma}'\mathbf{z}_{i,t}\right)}{\sum_{\text{that } \Sigma_t d_{i,t} \text{can equal } S_i}^{\binom{T_i}{S_i} \text{ different ways}} \exp\left(\sum_{t=1}^{T_i} d_{i,t}\boldsymbol{\gamma}'\mathbf{z}_{i,t}\right)}.$$

The denominator is summed over all the different combinations of T_i values of $y_{i,t}$ that sum to the same total as the observed data. There are $\binom{T_i}{S_i}$ terms. This might be large. With $T = 6$ (as in our example), it reaches 30 at $S = 3$. With $T = 50$, it reaches 10^{14} at $S = 25$.[27] The algorithm by Krailo and Pike (1984) makes the computation extremely fast and simple. The estimators of α_i are not individually consistent, but one might expect $(1/n^*)\Sigma_i\hat{\alpha}_i$ to be a consistent estimator of $E[\alpha_i]$. A remaining question to be considered is whether $E[\alpha_i|0 < S_i < T_i]$ differs from $E[\alpha_i]$. Assuming not, partial effects for the fixed effects logit model can be estimated with

$$A\hat{P}E = \hat{\gamma}\left\{\frac{1}{n^*}\Sigma_{i=1}^{n*}\Sigma_{t=1}^{T_i}\left[\Lambda\left(\bar{\hat{\alpha}} + \hat{\gamma}'\mathbf{z}_{i,t}\right)\right]\left[1 - \Lambda\left(\bar{\hat{\alpha}} + \hat{\gamma}'\mathbf{z}_{i,t}\right)\right]\right\}.$$

(The average could be over n^* alone using $\bar{\mathbf{z}}_i$.) Table 4 shows the estimates. They are quite close even though n^* is moderate and $T_i = 6$ for all i, which is small by modern standards. The unconditional estimates are uniformly slightly larger. The percentage differences between the two estimates are shown in parentheses in the table. The results are consistent with the results for $T = 8$ in Table 1. This does suggest that the effect diminishes from the benchmark of 100% at $T = 2$ rather rapidly. We also examined the estimated fixed effects. The unconditional estimates are estimated with $\boldsymbol{\gamma}$. The conditional estimates are computed by solving the unconditional likelihood equation for α_i using the consistent conditional estimator of $\boldsymbol{\gamma}$. The means of the conditional and unconditional estimators are –2.4 for the unconditional and –2.1 for the conditional. Fig. 2 compares the two sets of estimates.

TABLE 4 Estimated Fixed Effects Logit Models (Percentage Excess in Parentheses)

	Unconditional		Conditional	
	Estimate	*PEA*	*Estimate*	*PEA*
Age	0.065 (14)	0.017 (21)	0.057	0.014
Educ	0.168 (17)	0.041 (14)	0.144	0.036
Income	–0.284 (21)	–0.070 (21)	–0.234	–0.058
Health	–0.304 (21)	–0.074 (19)	–0.251	–0.062
Married	0.041 (24)	0.010 (25)	0.033	0.008

27. Estimation of a model with $n = 1000$ and $T = 50$ required about 0.5 seconds. Of course, if $T = 50$, the incidental parameters problem would be a moot point.

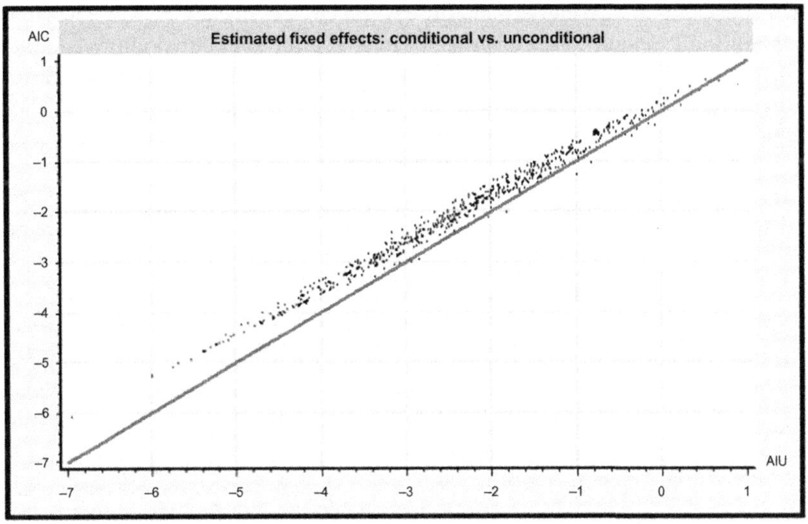

FIG. 2 Plot of estimates of α_i conditional vs. unconditional.

Chamberlain (1980) also proposed a conditional estimator for a multinomial logit model with fixed effects. The model is defined for a sequence of choices from $J+1$ alternatives by individual i in repetition t, J choices and an opt-out or none choice that is taken a substantive number of times. The choice probabilities are then

$$\text{Prob}\left(y_{i,t,j}=1 \mid \mathbf{z}_{i,t,j}\right)=\frac{e^{\alpha_{i,j}+\gamma' z_{i,t,j}}}{1+\Sigma_{m=1}^{J} e^{\alpha_{i,m}+\gamma' z_{i,t,m}}};\ \text{Prob}\left(y_{i,t,0}=1 \mid \mathbf{z}_{i,t,0}\right)$$
$$=\frac{1}{1+\Sigma_{m=1}^{J} e^{\alpha_{i,m}+\gamma' z_{i,t,m}}},\quad j=1,\ldots,J,$$

where the outcome is $d_{i,t,j}=\mathbf{1}$[individual i makes choice j in choice task t] and $\mathbf{z}_{i,t,j}$ = a set of alternative specific attributes of choice j. Individual specific, choice invariant characteristics, such as age or income, could be introduced into the model by interacting them with J alternative specific constants. The probability attached to the sequence of choices is constructed similarly, but the summing in the denominator of the conditional probability is for the sum of $d_{i,t,j}$ over $(J+1)T$ terms for individual i. The summing for the conditional probability itemizes terms for which the denominator $\Sigma_{j,t} d_{i,j,t}$ equals S_i, subject to the constraint that the terms in each block of $(J+1)$ sum to 1 (only one choice is made) and the sum in the T blocks equals the sum for the observed blocks. The counterpart to the uninformative observations in the binomial case are individuals who make the same choice, j, in every period, t. There is an enormous amount of computation (see Pforr 2011, 2014), but there is a much simpler way to proceed. For each of the J alternatives, there is a set of T blocks of two alternatives, each consisting of alternative j and the opt-out choice. In each $n(2T)$ set, there is a binary logit model to be constructed, in which the individual chooses either alternative j or the opt-out choice. Each of these binary choice models produces a consistent estimator of $\boldsymbol{\gamma}$, say $\hat{\boldsymbol{\gamma}}(j)$, $j=1,\dots,J$. Because there are J such estimators, they can be reconciled with a minimum distance estimator,

$$\hat{\boldsymbol{\gamma}}_{MD} = \left[\Sigma_{j=1}^{J}\left\{\hat{\boldsymbol{\Omega}}(j)\right\}^{-1}\right]^{-1}\left[\Sigma_{j=1}^{J}\left\{\hat{\boldsymbol{\Omega}}(j)\right\}^{-1}\hat{\boldsymbol{\gamma}}(j)\right] = \Sigma_{j=1}^{J}\mathbf{W}(j)\hat{\boldsymbol{\gamma}}(j),$$

$$\mathbf{W}(j) = \left[\Sigma_{j=1}^{J}\left\{\hat{\boldsymbol{\Omega}}(j)\right\}^{-1}\right]^{-1}\left\{\hat{\boldsymbol{\Omega}}(j)\right\}^{-1} \text{ such that } \Sigma_{j=1}^{J}\mathbf{W}(j) = \mathbf{I},$$

where $\hat{\boldsymbol{\Omega}}(j)$ is the estimated asymptotic covariance matrix for the jth estimator. The amount of computation involved is a very small fraction of that developed in Pforr (2011, 2014). The reduction in the amount of computation is enormous at the possible cost of some efficiency. For Pforr's example, which involves 26,200 individual/period choices and $J+1=2$ alternatives, the author reports the full Chamberlain computation requires 101.58 seconds. Partitioning the problem and using the minimum distance estimator produces the numerically identical result in 0.297 seconds.[28]

6.2 Bivariate and Recursive Binary Choice

The bivariate probit model (there is no logit counterpart), and recursive bivariate probit (probit model with an endogenous binary variable) has attracted some recent attention.[29] The two-equation model with common effects would be

$$y_{1,i,t} = \mathbf{1}\left[\boldsymbol{\beta}_1{}'\mathbf{x}_{1,i,t} + \boldsymbol{\gamma}'\mathbf{z}_{i,t} + c_{1,i} + \varepsilon_{1,i,t} > 0\right]$$

$$y_{2,i,t} = \mathbf{1}\left[\boldsymbol{\beta}_2{}'\mathbf{x}_{2,i,t} + \boldsymbol{\delta}y_{1,i,t} + c_{2,i} + \varepsilon_{2,i,t} > 0\right].$$

A full fixed effects treatment would require two sets of fixed effects and would be affected by the IP problem; no conditional estimator is available. The random effects model, or the correlated random effects model would be a natural choice. A dynamic model would proceed along the lines developed earlier for the single equation case. (Rhine and Greene (2013) treated y_1 as the initial value and y_2 as the second value in a two-period RBP.)

28. Pforr's data for this application are obtained from Stata at http://www.stata-press.com/data/r11/r.html under the CLOGIT heading. The data are reconfigured for NLOGIT (Econometric Software Inc., 2017). The data can be downloaded from the author's website at http://people.stern.nyu.edu/wgreene/DiscreteChoice/Data/felogit.csv. A second example involving $J=3$, $T=8$ and $n=400$ required 0.229 seconds using the MDE.

29. Wilde (2000), Han and Vytlacil (2017), Mourifie and Meango (2014), Filippini et al. (2018), Rhine and Greene (2013), Scott et al. (2009), Gregory and Deb (2015).

6.3 Ordered Choice

Contoyannis et al. (2004) used the dynamic CRE model in their analysis of health satisfaction in the BHPS. One of the complications in their case is the treatment of lagged effects for an ordered choice outcome that takes $J+1$ values, $0,\ldots,J$. The solution is a set of J endogenous lagged dummy variables, one for each category. A fixed effects treatment of the ordered probit (logit) model presents the same complications as the binary probit or logit model. Ferrer-i-Carbonell and Frijters (2004) note that the ordered choice model can be broken up into a set of binary choice models. If

$$\text{Prob}(y_{i,t}=j)=\Lambda\left(\mu_j-\alpha_i-\boldsymbol{\gamma}'\mathbf{z}_{i,t}\right)-\Lambda\left(\mu_{j-1}-\alpha_i-\boldsymbol{\gamma}'\mathbf{z}_{i,t}\right)$$

then

$$\text{Prob}(y_{i,t}>j)=\Lambda\left(\alpha_i+\gamma' z_{i,t}-\mu_j\right).$$

The transformed model can be treated with Chamberlain's conditional fixed effects approach. The time invariant threshold becomes an outcome-specific constant and will be lost in the fixed effects. Like the multinomial logit model considered earlier, this produces multiple estimates of $\boldsymbol{\gamma}$, which can be reconciled with a minimum distance estimator. Bias corrections for the fixed effects ordered probit and logit models are developed by Bester and Hansen (2009), Carro (2007), Carro and Trafferri (2014), Muris (2017), and others.

6.4 Censored or Truncated Regression

Much less is known (or studied) about the censored (Tobit) and truncated regression models. Greene's (2005) results (in Table 1) suggest that the incidental parameters problem appears, but in a fashion different from discrete choice models, and the censored and truncated models behave differently from each other. Honoré and Kesina (2017) examine a number of issues in this setting and a semiparametric specification. A serious complication will arise in a dynamic Tobit models; it is unclear how a lagged effect that is either zero or continuous should be built into the model.

6.5 Stochastic Frontier: Panel Models

Panel data considerations in the stochastic frontier model focus on both inefficiency and heterogeneity. The model framework is built from the canonical model

$$y_{i,t}=\boldsymbol{\beta}'\mathbf{x}_{i,t}+v_{i,t}\ -\ u_{i,t}$$

where $u_{i,t}<0$ and typically $v_{i,t}$ is $N[0,\sigma_v^2]$. Aigner et al.'s (1977) base case specifies $u_{i,t}$ as $N^+(0,\sigma_u^2)$. The early developments for panel data treatments focused on $u_{i,t}$, not on heterogeneity. Pitt and Lee (1981) specified u_i as a time invariant, random one-sided term that represented inefficiency. Schmidt and Sickles (1984) and Cornwell et al. (1990) developed a fixed effects approach that respecified $u_{i,t}$ as a fixed value, a_i or time varying, $a_i(t)$. Subsequent developments as given by Kumbhakar et al. (2014) and Battese and Coelli (1995) and Cuesta (2000) extended the time variation of $u_{i,t}$ by various specifications of $\sigma_u(t)$. These developments oriented the focus on inefficiency measurement while leaving unobserved heterogeneity ambiguous or assumed to be time varying and embedded in $v_{i,t}$. Greene (2005) proposed the true random effects and true fixed effects models

$$y_{i,t} = (\alpha + w_i) + \boldsymbol{\gamma}'\mathbf{z}_{i,t} + v_{i,t} - u_{i,t}$$

where $u_{i,t}$ is as originally specified in Aigner et al. and w_i is treated as either a true fixed or random effect. The latter model, with its combination of normal w_i and skew normal $(v_{i,t} - u_{i,t})$ is estimated by maximum simulated likelihood. Kumbhakar et al. (2014) completed the development with the generalized true random effects model,

$$y_{i,t} = (\alpha + w_i - f_i) + \boldsymbol{\gamma}'\mathbf{z}_{i,t} + v_{i,t} - u_{i,t}$$

where f_i now has a truncated normal distribution like $u_{i,t}$, and the full model is based on the sum of two skew normal variables, which has a closed skew normal distribution. The authors developed a full maximum likelihood estimator. Greene and Filippini (2015) showed how the estimation could be simplified by simulation.

6.6 Count Data

With the binary probit and logit models, the Poisson regression model for count data has been the proving ground for methods of nonlinear panel data modeling. A comprehensive early reference is Hausman et al. (1984).[30] The fixed effects conditional estimator is identical to the unconditional estimator, so the latter is consistent. The random effects model (or correlated random effects) is a straightforward application of Butler and Moffitt's method. As a nonlinear regression, the specification provides a convenient framework for modeling multiple equations. Riphahn et al. (2003) specified a two equation random effects Poisson model,

$y_{i,t,j} \sim$ Poisson with $\lambda_{i,t,j} = \exp(\pi_j + \boldsymbol{\gamma}_j'\mathbf{z}_{i,t,j} + \varepsilon_{i,t,j} + u_{i,j})$, $j = 1,2$, $i = 1,\ldots,n$, $t = 1,\ldots,T_i$.

The two equations are correlated through the means, $\rho = \text{Cov}(\varepsilon_{i,t,1},\varepsilon_{i,t,2})$. (A natural extension would be to allow correlation between the random effects

30. Hausman et al.'s (1984) formulation of the fixed effects NB model embedded the fixed effects in a variance parameter, not as an offset in the conditional mean as is familiar in other models. As a consequence, their FE model permits time invariant variables in the mean function, a result that continues to surprise researchers who are not warned about this (see Greene, 2018, p. 901).

as well, or instead of.) In the univariate, cross-section case, the heterogeneous Poisson regression is specified with conditional mean $\lambda_{i,t} = \exp(\pi + \boldsymbol{\gamma}'\mathbf{z}_{i,t} + u_i)$. If $u_i \sim$ log-gamma with mean 1, the unconditional distribution after integrating out u_i is the negative binomial (NB). This convenience has motivated use of the NB form. The usually convenient log-gamma is extremely inconvenient (intractable) in a model such as RWM's. Recent applications of mixed models have used the normal distribution, and computed the necessary integrals by Monte Carlo simulation.

The Poisson and negative binomial models also have been frequently the setting for latent class models. Jones and Schurer (2011) examined the frequency of doctor visits in a two-class negative binomial latent class model. Their methodology provides a useful example for using latent class modeling. Two questions that attend this type of modeling are: Is it possible to characterize the latent classes (other than by number)? and Is it possible to assign individuals to their respective classes? Strictly, the answer to both classes is no. Otherwise, the classes would not be latent. It is possible, however, to do both probabilistically. The latent class Poisson model is

$$\text{Prob}[y_{i,t} = j | \, class = q] = \frac{\exp(-\lambda_{i,t} | \, class = q)(\lambda_{i,t} | \, class = q)^j}{j!},$$

$$(\lambda_{i,t} | \, class = q) = \exp\left(\boldsymbol{\beta}_q'\mathbf{x}_{i,t}\right) \quad \ln L$$

$$= \sum\nolimits_{i=1}^{n} \log \sum\nolimits_{q=1}^{Q} \tau_q \prod\nolimits_{t=1}^{T_i} \frac{\exp(-\lambda_{i,t} | \, q)(\lambda_{i,t} | \, q)^j}{j!}$$

$$= \sum\nolimits_{i=1}^{n} \ln \sum\nolimits_{q=1}^{Q} \tau_q (H_i | \, q)$$

Maximization of the log likelihood produces estimates of $(\boldsymbol{\beta}_1,\ldots,\boldsymbol{\beta}_Q)$ and $(\tau_1,\ldots,\tau_q)$. (A more elaborate specification that bears some similarity to the correlated random effects model would make τ_q a function of exogenous factors, $\mathbf{z}_i$ and/or the group means of $\mathbf{x}_{i,t}$ (see Greene, 2018, Section 18.4). With the estimates of $(\boldsymbol{\beta}_q,\tau_q)$ in hand, the posterior class probabilities for each individual can be computed;

$$\hat{\tau}_{i,q} = \frac{\hat{\tau}_q\left(\hat{H}_i | \, q\right)}{\Sigma_{s=1}^{Q} \hat{\tau}_s\left(\hat{H}_i | \, s\right)}$$

Individuals then can be assigned to the class with the highest posterior probability. Jones and Schurer (2011) then characterized the two classes as light users and heavy users by the average frequency of doctor visits within the classes. They also computed characteristics such as average partial effects by the two groups to characterize the system. Table 5 repeats this exercise with the GSOEP data used earlier. The three classes do appear to be separating individuals by the intensity of usage. The pattern of the partial effects suggests

TABLE 5 Latent Class Model for Doctor Visits

	Class 1		Class 2		Class 3	
	Parameter	*APE*	*Parameter*	*APE*	*Parameter*	*APE*
Constant	3.253	–	1.524	–	0.116	–
Age	0.015	0.132	0.024	0.102	0.038	0.048
Educ	− 0.061	− 0.535	− 0.035	− 0.137	− 0.040	− 0.050
Income	− 0.178	−0.156	− 0.274	−0.107	0.301	0.038
HSAT	− 0.220	−1.929	− 0.178	−0.696	−0.275	−0.347
Married	0.134	1.175	0.080	0.313	0.005	0.006
$\overline{DocVis}\mid\hat{q}_i$	10.423		4.174		1.642	
$Mean\,\hat{E}[\bullet]\mid\hat{q}_i$	8.771		3.914		1.262	
$\hat{\tau}_q$	0.158		0.474		0.368	

6.7 A General Nonlinear Regression

Papke and Wooldridge (1996, 2008) proposed a model for aggregates of binary responses. The resulting outcome is a fractional variable. Minimum chi-squared methods for fractional variables have long provided a useful consistent approach. The model developed here builds from a common effects binary choice model. The resulting treatment is a heteroscedastic nonlinear regression that lends itself well to the correlated random effects treatment (see, also Wooldridge (2010), pp. 748–755 and 759–764). No obvious likelihood-based approach emerges, so the preferred estimator is nonlinear (possibly weighted) least squares.

6.8 Sample Selection Models

Most treatments of sample selection have layered the fixed and/or random effects treatments over Heckman's (1979) sample selection model. Verbeek (1990) and Verbeek and Nijman (1992) proposed a hybrid fixed and random effects specification,

$$d_{i,t} = \mathbf{1}\left[\boldsymbol{\gamma}'\mathbf{z}_{i,t} + u_i + \eta_{i,t} > 0\right] \quad \text{(random effects probit)}$$
$$y_{i,t}|(d_{i,t}=1) = \boldsymbol{\beta}'\mathbf{x}_{i,t} + \alpha_i + \varepsilon_{i,t}; \quad \text{(Fixed effects regression)}$$

Zabel (1992) argued that the FE model should have appeared in both equations. He then proposed the CRE form for the usual reasons. The system that results is two CRE models with correlation of the idiosyncratic disturbances. A natural extension would be correlation of u_i and v_i.

$$d_{i,t} = \mathbf{1}\left[\pi + \boldsymbol{\gamma}'\mathbf{z}_{i,t} + \boldsymbol{\theta}'\overline{\mathbf{z}}_i + u_i + \eta_{i,t} > 0\right] \text{ (correlated random effects probit)}$$
$$y_{i,t}|(d_{i,t} = 1) = \psi + \boldsymbol{\kappa}'\mathbf{z}_{i,t} + \boldsymbol{\lambda}'\overline{\mathbf{z}}_i + v_i + \varepsilon_{i,t}; \text{ (correlated random effects regression)}$$

Vella (1998) provides some details about this strand of development. Fernandez-Val and Vella (2009) continue the analysis with bias corrections based on the fixed effects specification. Kyriazidou (1997) suggested a semiparametric approach based on a fixed effects logit selection and weighted least squares with kernel estimators for the weights. Refinements are considered by Vella and Verbeek (1999), Barrachina (1999), Dustman and Rochina-Barrachina (2007), and Semykina and Wooldridge (2010).

In all of these treatments, the selection process is run at the beginning of each period—the selection equation is repeated, without autocorrelation, for every t. Bravo-Ureta et al. (2012) applied the selection model in a setting in which the selection occurs at the baseline, and is unchanged for all T periods. The selection effect becomes a correlated random effect. In their application, the main outcome equation is a stochastic frontier model. Greene (2010a, b) shows how the model can be estimated either by full information maximum likelihood or by Monte Carlo simulation.

6.9 Individual Choice and Stated Choice Experiments

The choice probability in the multinomial choice model we examined in Section 6.1 is

$$\text{Prob}(choice = j) = \frac{\exp\left(\boldsymbol{\beta}'\mathbf{x}_{i,j}\right)}{\Sigma_{s=1}^{J}\exp\left(\boldsymbol{\beta}'\mathbf{x}_{i,s}\right)}.$$

More than any other model examined in this survey, the coefficients in this model are not of direct use. After the parameters have been estimated, the model will be used to compute probabilities, simulate market shares under policy scenarios, estimate willingness to pay and distributions of willingness to pay, and compute elasticities of probabilities. Because all of these require a full set of components for the probabilities, the fixed effects model that bypasses computation of the fixed effects does not seem helpful. A random effects approach is considered in Hensher et al. (2007)

The counterpart of a panel in recent applications of choice modeling is the stated choice experiment (see Hensher et al., 2015). The individual being interviewed is offered a choice task involving J alternatives with a variety of attributes, $\mathbf{x}_{i,t,j}$. In the typical experiment, this scenario will be repeated T times with widely varying attribute sets in order to elicit the characteristics of the respondent's preferences. The common fixed or random effect that is persistent across choice settings serves to accommodate the feature that this is the same individual with the same latent attributes making the choices with short intervals between tasks. It is unlikely that the random utility formulation of the model could be so complete that the choice tasks would be independent conditioned on the information that appears in the utility functions. The mixed logit is the current standard in the modeling of choice experiments. The model is

$$\text{Prob}(Choice_{i,t}=j|\, \mathbf{X}_i) = \frac{\exp\left(V_{i,t,j}\right)}{\sum_{s=1}^{J} \exp\left(V_{i,t,s}\right)}, \quad V_{i,t,j} = \alpha_j + \boldsymbol{\beta}_i'\mathbf{x}_{i,t,j} + \varepsilon_{i,t,j}$$

$$\boldsymbol{\beta}_i = \boldsymbol{\beta} + \boldsymbol{\Delta}\mathbf{z}_i + \boldsymbol{\Gamma}\mathbf{u}_i$$

Revelt and Train (1998) modeled results of a survey of California electric utility customers. Train (2009) summarizes the theory and relevant practical aspects of discrete choice modeling with random parameters.

6.10 Multilevel Models Hierarchical (Nonlinear) Models

The general methodology of multilevel modeling (often linear modeling) builds a random parameters specification that bears some resemblance to the correlated random effects model (see Raudebush and Bryk, 2002). A generic form would be

$$f(y_{i,t}|\, \mathbf{x}_{i,t}, \mathbf{u}_i : \boldsymbol{\beta}, \boldsymbol{\Sigma}) = f\left(y_{i,t}, (\boldsymbol{\beta} + \boldsymbol{\Gamma}\mathbf{u}_i)'\mathbf{x}_{i,t} : \boldsymbol{\theta}\right) = f\left(y_{i,t}, \boldsymbol{\beta}_i'\mathbf{x}_{i,t} : \boldsymbol{\theta}\right).$$

A useful extension is $\boldsymbol{\beta}_i = \boldsymbol{\beta} + \boldsymbol{\Delta}\mathbf{z}_i + \boldsymbol{\Gamma}\mathbf{u}_i$, where $\mathbf{z}_i$ indicates exogenous factors; $\mathbf{z}_i$ also could include the correlated random effects treatment with the group means of $\mathbf{x}_{i,t}$. For a linear model, estimation often is based on manipulation of feasible generalized least squares. For a nonlinear model, this will require multivariate integration to deal with the unobserved random effects. This can be done with Monte Carlo simulation.

6.11 Fixed Effects With Large *N* and Large *T*

The gravity model is a standard approach to analyzing trade flows between countries. A typical application, with fixed effects might begin with

$$y_{i,j}^* = \alpha_i + \gamma_j + \boldsymbol{\beta}'\mathbf{x}_{i,j} + \varepsilon_{i,j}, \quad i,j = 1,\ldots,n.$$

The model involves two sets of incidental parameters. Charbonneau (2017) examined the case in which $y_{i,j} = 1[y_{i,j}^* > 0]$ indicates whether or not trade takes place, a binary response. The conditional logit approach will eliminate either α_i or γ_j, but will retain the other. By applying the conditioning recursively, the author arrives at the conditional log likelihood,

$$\ln L = \sum_{i=1}^{n}\sum_{j=1}^{n}\sum_{l,k\in Z_{i,j}} \ln\left(\frac{\exp\left(\boldsymbol{\beta}'\left((\mathbf{x}_{l,j} - \mathbf{x}_{l,k}) - (\mathbf{x}_{i,j} - \mathbf{x}_{i,k})\right)\right)}{1 + \exp\left(\boldsymbol{\beta}'\left((\mathbf{x}_{l,j} - \mathbf{x}_{l,k}) - (\mathbf{x}_{i,j} - \mathbf{x}_{i,k})\right)\right)}\right)$$

where $Z_{i,j}$ is the set of all potential l,k that satisfy $y_{l,j} + y_{l,k} = 1$, $y_{i,j} + y_{i,k} = 1$ and $y_{i,j} + y_{l,j} = 1$ for the pair i,j. As the author notes, because the fixed effects have been eliminated, it is not possible to compute partial effects. To explore the effects of covariates, e.g., the log of distance, on the probability of trade, the unconditional probabilities are computed at the means of $\mathbf{x}_{i,j}$ and with the fixed effects all set to zero.

The gravity model contains two sets of fixed effects that grow equally with the sample size. The incidental parameters problem, if there is one, is accommodated by using a conditional estimator. Fernandez-Val and Weidner (2016) consider a similar case with more general data observation mechanism—two cases considered are a probit binary response model and a Poisson regression. Both begin with an index function model,

$$y_{i,t}{}^* = \alpha_i + \gamma_t + \boldsymbol{\beta}'\mathbf{x}_{i,t}, \quad i = 1,\ldots,n;\ t = 1,\ldots,T,$$

where for the probit model, $y_{i,t} = 1[y_{i,t}{}^* + \varepsilon_{i,t} > 0]$ while in the Poisson model, $E[y_{i,t} | \mathbf{x}_{i,t}] = \exp(y_{i,t}{}^*)$. The model extension allows both i and t to grow, such that N/T converges to a constant. The authors focus on bias-corrected unconditional estimators. This enables estimation of partial effects as well as coefficients. Consistent with Greene's (2004a, 2005) results, they find that the bias of estimators of APEs is much smaller than that of the coefficients themselves. For their case, with biases diminishing in both n and T simultaneously, they find the biases in the partial effects to be negligible.

Interactive effects of the form

$$y_{i,t}{}^* = \alpha_i\gamma_t + \boldsymbol{\beta}'\mathbf{x}_{i,t} + \varepsilon_{i,t}$$

were examined by Bai (2009). Chen et al. (2014) treat this as a fixed effects model, and derived a two-step maximum likelihood estimator for probit and Poisson regression models. Boneva and Linton (2017) extend the model to allow multiple common latent factors.

References

Abadie, A., Athey, S., Imbens, G., Wooldridge, J., 2017. When should you adjust standard errors for clustering? MIT Department of Economics Working Paper 13927. https://economics.mit.edu/files/13927. (Accessed 18 January 2018).

Abrevaya, J., 1997. The equivalence of two estimators of the fixed effects logit model. Economics Letters 55, 41–43.

Aguirrebiria, V., Mira, P., 2007. Sequential estimation of dynamic discrete games. Econometrics 75 (1), 1–53.

Ai, C., Li, H., Lin, Z., Ment, M., 2015. Estimation of panel data partly specified tobit regression with fixed effects. Journal of Econometrics 188 (2), 316–326.

Ai, C., Norton, E., 2003. Interaction terms in logit and probit models. Economics Letters 80, 123–129.

Aigner, D., Lovell, K., Schmidt, P., 1977. Formulation and estimation of stochastic frontier production models. Journal of Econometrics 6, 21–37.

Altonji, J., Matzkin, R., 2005. Cross section and panel data for nonseparable models with endogenous regressors. Econometrica 73 (4), 1053–1102.

Angrist, J., Pischke, J., 2009. Mostly harmless econometrics. Princeton University Press, Princeton, NJ.

Arellano, M., Hahn, J., 2006. Understanding bias in nonlinear panel models: some recent developments. In: Advances in Economics and Econometrics Ninth World Congress. Cambridge University Press, New York.

Bai, J., 2009. Panel data models with interactive fixed effects. Econometrica 77, 1229–1279.

Barrachina, M., 1999. A new estimator for panel data sample selection models. Annales d'Economie et Statistique (55/56), 153–181.

Battese, G., Coelli, T., 1995. A model for technical inefficiency effects in a stochastic frontier production for panel data. Empirical Economics 20, 325–332.

Bertschuk, I., Lechner, M., 1998. Convenient estimators for the panel Probit Model. Journal of Econometrics 87 (2), 329–372.

Bester, C., Hansen, A., 2009. A penalty function approach to bias reduction in nonlinear panel models with fixed effects. Journal of Business and Economic Statistics 27 (2), 131–148.

Boneva, L., Linton, O., 2017. A discrete choice model for large heterogeneous panels with interactive fixed effects with an application to the determinants of corporate bond issuance. Journal of Applied Econometrics 32, 1226–1243.

Bravo-Ureta, B., Greene, W., Solis, D., 2012. Technical efficiency analysis correcting for biases from observed and unobserved variables: an application to a natural resource management project. Empirical Economics 43 (1), 55–72.

Butler, J., Moffitt, R., 1982. A computationally efficient quadrature procedure for the one factor multinomial probit model. Econometrica 50, 761–764.

Cameron, C., Miller, D., 2015. A practitioner's guide to cluster robust inference. Journal of Human Resources 50 (2), 317–373.

Cameron, C., Trivedi, P., 2005. Microeconometrics: Methods and applications. Cambridge University Press, New York, NY.

Carro, J., 2007. Estimating dynamic panel data discrete choice models with fixed effects. Journal of Econometrics 140, 503–528.

Carro, J., Browning, M., 2014. Dynamic binary outcome models with maximal heterogeneity. Journal of Econometrics 178 (2), 805–823.

Carro, J., Trafferri, A., 2014. State dependence and heterogeneity in health using a bias corrected fixed effects estimator. Journal of Econometrics 29, 181–207.

Cecchetti, S., 1986. The frequency of price adjustment: a study of newsstand prices of magazines. Journal of Econometrics 31 (3), 255–274.

Chamberlain, G., 1980. Analysis of covariance with qualitative data. Review of Economic Studies 47, 225–238.

Charbonneau, K., 2017. Multiple fixed effects in binary response panel data models. The Econometrics Journal 20, S1–S13.

Chen, M., Fernandez-Val, I., Weidner, M., 2014. Nonlinear panel models with interactive effects. arXiv:1412.5647v1.

Chesher, A., 2013. Semiparametric structural models of binary response: shape restrictions and partial identification. Econometric Theory 29, 231–266.

Chesher, A., Irish, M., 1987. Residual analysis in the grouped data and censored normal linear model. Journal of Econometrics 34, 33–62.

Contoyannis, C., Jones, A., Rice, N., 2004. The dynamics of health in the British household panel survey. Journal of Applied Econometrics 19 (4), 473–503.

Cornwell, C., Schmidt, P., Sickles, R., 1990. Production frontiers with cross-section and time-series variation in efficiency levels. Journal of Econometrics 46, 185–200.

Cuesta, R., 2000. A production model with firm-specific temporal variation in technical inefficiency: with application to Spanish dairy farms. Journal of Productivity Analysis 13 (2), 139–158.

Dustman, C., Rochina-Barrachina, M.E., 2007. Selection correction in panel data models: an application to the estimation of females' wage equations. The Econometrics Journal 10, 263–293.
Econometric Software Inc., 2017. NLOGIT. ESI Inc., Plainview, NY.
Fernandez-Val, I., 2009. Fixed effects estimation of structural parameters and marginal effects in panel probit models. Journal of Econometrics 150 (1), 71–75.
Fernandez-Val, I., Vella, F., 2009. Bias corrections for two-step fixed effects panel data estimators. Journal of Econometrics 163 (2), 144–162.
Fernandez-Val, I., Weidner, M., 2016. Individual and time effects in nonlinear panel models with large N, T. Journal of Econometrics 192, 291–312.
Ferrer-i-Carbonell, A., Frijters, P., 2004. The effect of methodology on the determinants of happiness. Economic Journal 1114, 641–659.
Filippini, M., Greene, W., Kumar, N., Martinez-Cruz, A., 2018. A note on the different interpretation of the correlation parameters in the bivariate probit and the recursive bivariate probit. Economics Letters. 2018, forthcoming.
Geraci, M., Bottai, M., 2007. Quantile regression for longitudinal data using the asymmetric Laplace distribution. Biostatistics 8 (1), 140–151.
Graham, B., Hahn, J., Poirier, A., Powell, J., 2015. Quantile regression with panel data. NBER Working Paper 21034. NBER, Cambridge, MA.
Greene, W., 2004a. The behaviour of the maximum likelihood estimator of limited dependent variable models in the presence of fixed effects. The Econometrics Journal 7, 98–119.
Greene, W., 2004b. Convenient estimators for the panel probit model. Empirical Economics 29 (1), 21–47.
Greene, W., 2004c. Distinguishing between heterogeneity and inefficiency: stochastic frontier analysis of the world health organization's panel data on national health care systems. Health Economics 13, 959–980.
Greene, W., 2005. Fixed effects and bias due to the incidental parameters problem in the tobit model. Econometric Reviews 23 (2), 125–147.
Greene, 2010a. Testing hypotheses about interaction terms in nonlinear models. Economics Letters 107 (2010), 291–296.
Greene, W., 2010b. A sample selection corrected stochastic frontier model. Journal of Productivity Analysis 41, 15–24.
Greene, W., 2018. Econometric Analysis. Pearson, New York, NY.
Greene, W., Filippini, M., 2015. Persistent and transient productive inefficiency: a maximum simulated likelihood approach. Journal of Productivity Analysis 45 (2), 187–196.
Greene, W., McKenzie, C., 2015. An LM test for random effects based on generalized residuals. Economics Letters 127 (1), 47–50.
Gregory, C., Deb, P., 2015. Does SNAP improve your health? Food Policy 50, 11–19.
Hahn, J., Kuersteiner, G., 2011. Bias reduction for dynamic nonlinear panel models with fixed effects. Econometric Theory 27 (6), 1152–1191.
Hahn, J., Newey, W., 2004. Jackknife and analytical bias reduction for nonlinear panel models. Econometrica 77, 1295–1313.
Han, S., Vytlacil, E., 2017. Identification in a generalization of bivariate probit models with dummy endogenous regressors. Journal of Econometrics 199, 63–73.
Hausman, J., 1978. Specification tests in econometrics. Econometrica 46, 1251–1271.
Hausman, J., Hall, B., Griliches, Z., 1984. Economic models for count data with an application to the patents-R&D relationship. Econometrica 52, 909–938.
Heckman, J., 1979. Sample selection as a specification error. Econometrica 47, 153–161.

Heckman, J., Singer, B., 1984. A method for minimizing the impact of distributional assumptions in econometric models for duration data. Econometrica 52, 748–755.

Hensher, D., Jones, S., Greene, W., 2007. An error component logit analysis of corporate bankruptcy and insolvency risk in Australia. The Economic Recort 63 (260), 86–103.

Hensher, D., Rose, J., Greene, W., 2015. Applied Choice Analysis, second ed. Cambridge University Press, New York.

Honoré, B., 2002. Nonlinear models with panel data. Portuguese Economic Journal 2002 (1), 163–179.

Honoré, B., 2013. Non-linear models with panel data. CEMMAP working paper 13/02. IFS, Department of Economics, UCL, London.

Honoré, B., Kesina, M., 2017. Estimation of some nonlinear panel data models with both time-varying and time-invariant explanatory variables. Journal of Business and Economic Statistics 35 (4), 543–558.

Honoré, B., Lewbel, A., 2002. Semiparametric binary choice panel data models without strictly exogenous regressors. Econometrica 70 (5), 2053–2063.

Imbens, G., Wooldridge, J., 2012. Nonlinear Panel Data Models, Notes 4. National Bureau of Economic Research, Cambridge, MA. http://www.nber.org/WNE/lect_4_nlpanel.pdf (Accessed 18.01.18).

Jones, A., Schurer, S., 2011. How does heterogeneity shape the socioeconomic gradient in health satisfaction. Journal of Applied Econometrics 26 (4), 549–579.

Krailo, M., Pike, M., 1984. Conditional multivariate logistic analysis of stratified case control studies. Applied Statistics 44 (1), 95–103.

Kumbhakar, S., Colombi, M., Martini, A., Vittadini, S., 2014. Closed skew normality in stochastic frontiers with individual effects and long/short-run efficiency. Journal of Productivity Analysis 42, 123–136.

Kyriazidou, E., 1997. Estimation of a panel data sample selection model. Econometrica 65 (6), 1335–1364.

Lancaster, T., 2000. The incidental parameters problem since 1948. Journal of Econometrics 95 (2), 391–414.

Lee, S., 2008. Estimating panel data duration models with censored data. Econometric Theory 24 (5), 1254–1276.

Lewbel, A., Dong, Y., 2015. A simple estimator for binary choice models with endogenous regressors. Econometric Reviews 34, 82–105.

Mandic, P., Norton, E., Dowd, B., 2012. Interaction terms in nonlinear models. Health Services Research 47 (1), 255–274.

Manski, C., 1975. The maximum score estimator of the stochastic utility model of choice. Journal of Econometrics 3, 205–228.

Mourifie, I., Meango, R., 2014. A note on the identification in two equations probit model with dummy endogenous regressor. Economics Letters 125, 360–363.

Mundlak, Y., 1978. On the pooling of time series and cross sectional data. Econometrica 56, 342–365.

Muris, C., 2017. Estimation in the fixed-effects ordered logit model. Review of Economics and Statistics 99 (3), 465–477.

Nerlove, M., 1966. Pooling cross section and time series data in the estimation of a dynamic model: the demand for natural gas. Econometrica 34 (3), 585–612.

Neyman, J., Scott, E., 1948. Consistent estimates based on partially consistent observations. Econometrica 16, 1–32.

Papke, L., Wooldridge, J., 1996. Econometric methods for fractional response variables with an application to 401(k) panel participation rates. Journal of Applied Econometrics 11 (6), 619–632.

Papke, L., Wooldridge, J., 2008. Panel data methods for fractional response variables with an application to test pass rates. Journal of Econometrics 145 (1-2), 121–133.

Pforr, K., 2011. Implementation of a multinomial logit model with fixed effects. In: Presented at ninth german stata users group meeting. University of Mannheim, Bamberg https://core.ac.uk/download/pdf/6278780.pdf (accessed 18.01.19).

Pforr, K., 2014. Femlogit—implementation of the multinomial logit model with fixed effects. Stata Journal 14 (4), 847–862.

Pitt, M., Lee, L., 1981. The measurement and sources of technical inefficiency in the Indonesian weaving industry. Journal of Development Economics 9, 43–64.

Rasch, G., 1960. Probabilistic models for some intelligence and attainment tests. Paedogiska, Copenhagen, Denmark.

Raudebush, S., Bryk, A., 2002. Hierarchical linear models: Applications and data analysis methods, second ed. Sage, Thousand Oaks, CA.

Revelt, D., Train, K., 1998. Mixed logit with repeated choices: households' choices of appliance efficiency level. Review of Economics and Statistics 80, 647–658.

Rhine, S., Greene, W., 2013. Factors that contribute to becoming unbanked. Journal of Consumer Affairs 47 (1), 27–45.

Riphahn, R., Wambach, A., Million, A., 2003. Incentive effects in the demand for health care: a bivariate panel count data estimation. Journal of Applied Econometrics 18 (4), 387–405.

Schmidt, P., Sickles, R., 1984. Production frontiers and panel data. Journal of Business and Economic Statistics 2, 367–374.

Scott, A., Schurer, S., Jensen, P., Sivey, P., 2009. The effects of an incentive program on quality of care in diabetes management. Health Economics 18 (9), 1091–1108.

Semykina, A., Wooldridge, J., 2010. Estimating panel data models in the presence of endogeneity and selection. Journal of Econometrics 157 (2), 375–380.

Stata, 2018. Stata manual. Stata Press, College Station, TX.

Train, K., 2009. Discrete choice methods with simulation. Cambridge University Press, New York.

Vella, F., 1998. Estimating models with sample selection bias: a survey. Journal of Human Resources 33, 439–454.

Vella, F., Verbeek, M., 1999. Two-step estimation of panel data models with censored endogenous variables and selection bias. Journal of Econometrics 90m, 239–263.

Verbeek, M., 1990. On the estimation of a fixed effects model with selectivity bias. Economics Letters 34, 267–270.

Verbeek, M., Nijman, T., 1992. Testing for selectivity bias in panel data models. International Economic Review 33 (3), 267–270.

Wilde, J., 2000. Identification of multiple equation probit models with endogenous dummy regressors. Economics Letters 69, 309–312.

Willis, J., 2006. Magazine prices revisited. Journal of Applied Econometrics 21 (3), 337–344.

Wooldridge, J., 1995. Selection corrections for panel data models under conditional mean independence assumptions. Journal of Econometrics 68 (1), 115–132.

Wooldridge, J., 2002. Inverse probability weighted M estimators for sample stratification, attrition and stratification. Portuguese Economic Journal 1, 117–139.

Wooldridge, J., 2003. Cluster sample methods in applied econometrics. American Economic Review 93, 133–138.

Wooldridge, J., 2005. Simple solutions to the initial conditions problem in dynamic nonlinear panel data models with unobserved heterogeneity. Journal of Applied Econometrics 20 (1), 39–54.

Wooldridge, J., 2010. Econometric analysis of cross section and panel data. MIT Press, Cambridge, MA.

Wu, D., 1973. Alternative tests of independence between stochastic regressors and disturbances. Econometrica 41, 733–750.

Zabel, J., 1992. Estimating fixed and random effects models with selectivity. Economics Letters 40, 269–272.

Chapter 4

Nonparametric Estimation and Inference for Panel Data Models

Christopher F. Parmeter* **and Jeffrey S. Racine**[†,‡,$]
*Department of Economics, University of Miami, Coral Gables, FL, United States, †Department of Economics and Graduate Program in Statistics, McMaster University, Hamilton, ON, Canada, ‡Department of Economics and Finance, La Trobe University, Melbourne, VIC, Australia, $Info-Metrics Institute, American University, Washington, DC, United States

Chapter Outline

1 Introduction

Although panel data models have proven particularly popular among applied econometricians, the most widely embraced approaches rely on parametric assumptions. When these assumptions are at odds with the data generating process (DGP), the corresponding estimators will be biased and worse, inconsistent. Practitioners who subject their parametric models to a battery of diagnostic tests often are disappointed to learn that their models are rejected

Panel Data Econometrics. https://doi.org/10.1016/B978-0-12-814367-4.00004-6

by the data. Consequently, they might find themselves in need of more flexible nonparametric alternatives.

Given the popularity of panel data methods in applied settings, and given how quickly the field of nonparametric panel methods is developing, this chapter presents a current survey of available nonparametric methods and outlines how practitioners can avail themselves of these recent developments. The existing literature that surveys semi- and nonparametric panel data methods includes Li and Racine (2007), Ai and Li (2008), Su and Ullah (2011), Chen, Li, and Gao (2013), Henderson and Parmeter (2015), Sun, Zhang, and Li (2015), and Rodriguez-Poo and Soberon (2017), among others. Our goal here is to unify and extend existing treatments and inject some additional insight that we hope is useful for practitioners trying to keep abreast of this rapidly growing field. By way of illustration, Rodriguez-Poo and Soberon (2017) provide a nice survey of available estimators, however, they do not address inference, which is a practical necessity. We attempt to provide a more comprehensive treatment than found elsewhere, keeping the needs of the practitioner first and foremost.

2 How Unobserved Heterogeneity Complicates Estimation

To begin, we start with the conventional, one-way nonparametric setup for panel data:

$$y_{it} = m(\mathbf{x}_{it}) + \alpha_i + \varepsilon_{it}, \quad i = 1, \ldots, n, \quad t = 1, \ldots, T, \tag{1}$$

where $\mathbf{x}_{it}$ is a $q \times 1$ vector, $m(\cdot)$ is an unknown smooth function, α_i captures individual specific heterogeneity, and ε_{it} is the random error term. The standard panel framework treats i as indexing the individual and t as indexing time, though in many applications t might not represent time. For example, in the metaanalysis field, i represents a given research study and t the individual estimates produced from the study. As in a fully parametric setting, the α_is need to be accounted for because of the incidental parameters problem under the fixed effects framework. Two common transformations to eliminate α_i prior to estimation are linear differencing or time-demeaning.

Consider time-demeaning: In this case we use the standard notation $\overline{z}_{i\cdot} = T^{-1}\sum_{t=1}^{T} z_{it}$ to represent the mean of variable z for individual i. Given that α_i is constant over time, time-demeaning will eliminate α_i from Eq. (1):

$$y_{it} - \overline{y}_{i\cdot} = m(\mathbf{x}_{it}) - T^{-1}\sum_{t=1}^{T} m(\mathbf{x}_{it}) + \varepsilon_{it} - \overline{\varepsilon}_{i\cdot}. \tag{2}$$

Unfortunately, we now have the function $m(\cdot)$ appearing $T+1$ times on the right side. Given that $m(\cdot)$ is unknown, this causes problems with standard estimation because we must ensure that the same $m(\cdot)$ is being used. Moreover, even if $m(\cdot)$ were known, if it is nonlinear in the parameter space, then the resulting nonlinear estimating equation might complicate optimization of the associated objective function. This is true in other settings as well, for example, in the estimation of conditional quantiles with panel data. As we will discuss, a variety of approaches have been proposed for tackling the presence of unobserved heterogeneity.

In the random effects framework, the incidental parameters problem no longer exists, however, a complicating factor for estimation is how to effectively capture the structure of the variance covariance matrix of $v_{it} = \alpha_i + \varepsilon_{it}$. In this case it is not clear how best to smooth the data, and a variety of estimators have been proposed. At issue is the best way to smooth the covariates while simultaneously accounting for the covariance structure. As we will discuss, several early estimators that were proposed were not able to achieve asymptotic gains because the smoothing procedure advocated did not adequately capture the covariance structure, asymptotically.

We also could discuss the two-way error component setting, but in this case if the fixed effects framework is assumed, then it is easier to treat time as a covariate and smooth it appropriately (using an ordered discrete kernel), although in the random effects framework it further complicates the variance matrix of the error term. In light of this, we will focus on the one-way error component model.

Prior to moving on to the discussion of estimation in either the fixed or random effects framework in a one-way error component model, some definitions are in order. Under the random effects framework, we assume that $E[\alpha_i | \mathbf{x}_{i1}, \ldots, \mathbf{x}_{iT}] = E[\alpha_i] = 0$, whereas under the fixed effects framework we assume that $E[\alpha_i | \mathbf{x}_{i1}, \ldots, \mathbf{x}_{iT}] = \alpha_i$. The difference between the two should be clear; under the random effects framework, α_i is assumed to be independent of $\mathbf{x}_{it}$ for any t, whereas under the fixed effects framework α_i and $\mathbf{x}_{it}$ are allowed to be dependent upon one another. No formal relationship on this dependence is specified under the fixed effects framework. One could relax this set of all or nothing assumptions by following the approach of Hausman and Taylor (1981), however, this is an unexplored area within the field of nonparametric estimation of panel data models. We now turn to a discussion of nonparametric estimation under both the fixed and random effects frameworks.

3 Estimation in the Random Effects Framework

3.1 Preliminaries

If we assume that α_i is uncorrelated with $\mathbf{x}_{it}$, then its presence in Eq. (1) can be dealt with in a more traditional manner as it relates to kernel smoothing. To begin, assume that $\text{Var}(\varepsilon_{it}) = \sigma_\varepsilon^2$ and $\text{Var}(\alpha_i) = \sigma_\alpha^2$. Then, for $v_{it} = \alpha_i + \varepsilon_{it}$ we set $v_i = [v_{i1}, v_{i2}, \ldots, v_{iT}]'$, a $T \times 1$ vector, and $V_i \equiv \text{E}(v_i v'_i)$ takes the form

$$V_i = \sigma_\varepsilon^2 \mathbf{I}_T + \sigma_\alpha^2 \mathrm{i}_T \mathrm{i}'_T, \tag{3}$$

where $\mathbf{I}_T$ is an identity matrix of dimension T and $\mathbf{i}_T$ is a $T \times 1$ column vector of ones. Because the observations are independent over i and j, the covariance matrix for the full $nT \times 1$ disturbance vector u, $\Omega = \mathrm{E}(vv')$ is a $nT \times nT$ block diagonal matrix where the blocks are equal to V_i, for $i = 1, 2, \ldots, n$. Note that this specification assumes a homoskedastic variance for all i and t.

Note that serial correlation over time is admitted, but only between the disturbances for the same individuals. In other words

$$\mathrm{Cov}\left(v_{it}, v_{js}\right) = \mathrm{Cov}\left(\alpha_i + \varepsilon_{it}, \alpha_j + \varepsilon_{js}\right) = \mathrm{E}\left(\alpha_i \alpha_j\right) + \mathrm{E}\left(\varepsilon_{it}\varepsilon_{js}\right),$$

given the independence assumption between α_j and ε_{js} and the independent and identically distributed (i.i.d.) nature of ε_{it}. The covariance between two error terms equals $\sigma_\alpha^2 + \sigma_\varepsilon^2$ when $i = j$ and $t = s$, it is equal to σ_α^2 when $i = j$ and $t \neq s$, and it is equal to zero when $i \neq j$. This is the common structure in parametric panel data models under the random effects framework as well. Estimation can ignore this structure at the expense of a loss in efficiency. For example, ignoring the correlation architecture in Ω, standard kernel regression methods, such as local-constant or local-linear least-squares could be deployed.

Parametric estimators under the random effects framework typically require the use of $\Omega^{-1/2}$ so that a generalized least squares estimator can be constructed. Inversion of the $nT \times nT$ matrix is computationally expensive but Baltagi (2013) provides a simple approach to inverting Ω based on the spectral decomposition. For any integer r,

$$\Omega^r = \left(T\sigma_\alpha^2 + \sigma_\varepsilon^2\right)^r P + \left(\sigma_\varepsilon^2\right)^r Q, \tag{4}$$

where $P = I_n \otimes \bar{J}_T$, $Q = I_n \otimes E_T$, $\bar{J}_T$ is a $T \times T$ dimensional matrix where each element is equal to $1/T$ and $E_T = (I_T - \bar{J}_T)$. Ω is infeasible as both σ_α^2 and σ_ε^2 are unknown; a variety of approaches exists to estimate the two unknown variance parameters, which we will discuss in the sequel. An important feature of Ω is that its structure is independent of $m(\mathbf{x}_{it})$. Thus, when we model the unknown conditional mean as either parametric or nonparametric it does not influence the manner in which we will account for the variance structure.

3.2 Local-Polynomial Weighted Least-Squares

Lin and Carroll (2000) and Henderson and Ullah (2005) were among the first attempts to properly capture the architecture of the covariance of the one-way error component model. To begin, take a pth order Taylor approximation of Eq. (1) around the point $\mathbf{x}$:

$$y_{it} = m(\mathbf{x}) + \alpha_i + \varepsilon_{it},$$

where

$$m(\mathbf{x}) = \sum_{0 \leq |\mathbf{j}| < p} \beta_{\mathbf{j}} (\mathbf{x}_{it} - \mathbf{x})^{\mathbf{j}}$$

where $\mathbf{j} = (j_1, \ldots, j_q)$, $|\mathbf{j}| = \sum_{i=1}^{q} j_i$, $\mathbf{x}^{\mathbf{j}} = \prod_{i=1}^{q} x_i^{j_i}$, $\mathbf{j}! = \prod_{i=1}^{q} j_i! = j_1! \times \cdots \times j_q!$ and

$$\sum_{0 \le |\mathbf{j}| < p} = \sum_{l=0}^{p} \sum_{j_1=0}^{l} \cdots \sum_{\substack{j_q=0 \\ j_1+\cdots+j_q=l}}^{l}$$

where we have used the notation of Masry (1996). $\mathbf{j}!\beta_{\mathbf{j}}(\mathbf{x})$ corresponds to $(D^{\mathbf{j}}m)(\mathbf{x})$, the partial derivative of $m(\mathbf{x})$, which is defined as:

$$\left(D^{\mathbf{j}}m\right)(\mathbf{x}) \equiv \frac{\partial^{\mathbf{j}} m(\mathbf{x})}{\partial(x_1)^{j_1} \cdots \partial\left(x_q\right)^{j_q}},$$

and β vertically concatenates $\beta_{\mathbf{j}}$ $(0 \le |\mathbf{j}| \le p)$ in lexicographical order, with highest priority to the last position so that $(0, \ldots, 0, i)$ is the first element in the sequence and $(i, 0, \ldots, 0)$ is the last element.

Thus, the pth-order local-polynomial estimator corresponds to the minimizer of the objection function

$$\min_{\beta} (NT)^{-1} \sum_{i=1}^{N} \sum_{t=1}^{T} \left(y_{it} - \sum_{0 \le |\mathbf{j}| < p} \beta_{\mathbf{j}} (\mathbf{x}_{it} - \mathbf{x})^{\mathbf{j}} \right)^2 K_{it\mathbf{x}h}, \tag{5}$$

where $K_{it\mathbf{x}h} = \prod_{s=1}^{q} h_s^{-1} k\left(\frac{x_{its} - x_s}{h_s}\right)$ is the standard product kernel where $k(\cdot)$ is any second-order univariate kernel (e.g., Epanechnikov, Gaussian) and h_s is the sth element of the bandwidth vector h and smooths the sth dimension of $\mathbf{x}$. Let $\mathcal{K}_{\mathbf{x}} = \text{diag}(K_{11\mathbf{x}}, K_{12\mathbf{x}}, \ldots, K_{1T\mathbf{x}}, K_{21\mathbf{x}}, \ldots, K_{nT\mathbf{x}})$. Finally, collecting y_{it} into the vector y and denoting the matrix $D_{it\mathbf{x}}$ which vertically concatenates $(\mathbf{x}_{it} - \mathbf{x})^{\mathbf{j}}$ for $0 \le |\mathbf{j}| \le p$, in lexicographical order, we use the notation $D_{\mathbf{x}} = [D_{11\mathbf{x}}, D_{12\mathbf{x}}, \ldots, D_{1T\mathbf{x}}, D_{21\mathbf{x}}, \ldots, D_{nT\mathbf{x}}]'$.

For example, $D_{it\mathbf{x}} = 1$ for $p = 0$ (the local-constant setting), and $D_{it\mathbf{x}} = [1, (\mathbf{x}_{it} - \mathbf{x})']'$ for $p = 1$ (the local-linear setting).

It can be shown that the local polynomial estimator for the minimization problem in Eq. (5) is

$$\hat{\beta}(\mathbf{x}) = \left(D_{\mathbf{x}}' \mathcal{K}_{\mathbf{x}} D_{\mathbf{x}}\right)^{-1} D_{\mathbf{x}}' \mathcal{K}_{\mathbf{x}} y. \tag{6}$$

The local-polynomial estimator in Eq. (6) ignores the covariance structure in the one-way error component model. Both Lin and Carroll (2000) and Henderson and Ullah (2005) proposed alternative weighting schemes to capture this covariance structure. Henderson and Ullah (2005) focused on the specific setting of $p = 1$, and thus used what they termed the local-linear weighted least-squares (LLWLS) estimator. This estimator is identical to that in Eq. (6) except that the diagonal kernel weighting matrix $\mathcal{K}_{\mathbf{x}}$ is replaced with a nondiagonal weighting matrix, designed to account for within individual correlation. This nondiagonal weighting matrix is designated as $\mathcal{W}_{\mathbf{x}}$ and can take an array of shapes.

Ullah and Roy (1998) propose

$$\mathcal{W}_{1\mathbf{x}} = \Omega^{-1/2}\mathcal{K}_{\mathbf{x}}\Omega^{-1/2}$$

while Lin and Carroll (2000) propose

$$\mathcal{W}_{2\mathbf{x}} = \Omega^{-1}\mathcal{K}_{\mathbf{x}}$$

and

$$\mathcal{W}_{3\mathbf{x}} = \sqrt{\mathcal{K}_{\mathbf{x}}}\Omega^{-1}\sqrt{\mathcal{K}_{\mathbf{x}}}$$

resulting in the LPWLS estimator

$$\hat{\beta}_r(\mathbf{x}) = \left(D_{\mathbf{x}}'\mathcal{W}_{r\mathbf{x}}D_{\mathbf{x}}\right)^{-1}D_{\mathbf{x}}'\mathcal{W}_{r\mathbf{x}}y, \; r=1,2,3. \tag{7}$$

When Ω is diagonal $\mathcal{W}_{1\mathbf{x}} = \mathcal{W}_{2\mathbf{x}} = \mathcal{W}_{3\mathbf{x}}$, both $\mathcal{W}_{1\mathbf{x}}$ and $\mathcal{W}_{3\mathbf{x}}$ are symmetric and amount to local-polynomial estimation of the transformed observations $\sqrt{\mathcal{K}_{\mathbf{x}}}\Omega^{-1/2}y$ on $\sqrt{\mathcal{K}_{\mathbf{x}}}\Omega^{-1/2}\mathbf{x}$ and $\Omega^{-1/2}\mathcal{K}_{\mathbf{x}}y$ on $\Omega^{-1/2}\mathcal{K}_{\mathbf{x}}\mathbf{x}$, respectively.[1] Given that Ω is unknown, because of the presence of σ_α^2 and σ_ε^2, a feasible matrix must be constructed. This can be accomplished most easily by deploying the local-polynomial least-squares estimator in Eq. (6) first, obtaining the residuals, and then using the best linear unbiased predictors for these variances as provided in Baltagi (2013):

$$\hat{\sigma}_1^2 = \frac{T}{N}\sum_{i=1}^{N}\overline{\hat{v}}_{i\cdot}^2,$$

$$\hat{\sigma}_\varepsilon^2 = \frac{1}{NT-N}\sum_{i=1}^{N}\sum_{t=1}^{T}\left(\hat{v}_{it}-\overline{\hat{v}}_{i\cdot}\right)^2,$$

where $\overline{\hat{v}}_{i\cdot} = T^{-1}\sum_{t=1}^{T}\hat{v}_{it}$ is the cross-sectional average of the residuals for cross-section i and $\hat{v}_{it} = y_{it} - \hat{m}(\mathbf{x}_{it})$ is the LPLS residual based on the first stage estimator of $\beta(\mathbf{x})$. Here $\sigma_1^2 = T\sigma_\alpha^2 + \sigma_\varepsilon^2$ in Eq. (4).

Lin and Carroll (2000) derive the bias and variance of $\beta(\mathrm{x})$ while Henderson and Ullah (2005) provide the rate of convergence of $\beta(\mathbf{x})$ for $p=1$ under the assumption of $N \to \infty$.

Most importantly, Lin and Carroll (2000) note that the asymptotic variance of the LPWLS estimator in Eq. (7) for $r = 1, 2, 3$, is actually larger than that of the LPLS estimator in Eq. (6). Although this result seems counterintuitive, Wang (2003) explains that this is natural when T is finite. By assumption, as $N \to \infty$, $h \to 0$, and the kernel matrix, evaluated at the point, $\mathbf{x}_{it}$, for example,

1. The most popular weighting scheme is $\mathcal{W}_{3\mathbf{x}}$ of Lin and Carroll (2000). See Henderson and Ullah (2014) for a Monte Carlo comparison of these alternative weighting schemes.

implies that the other points for individual i, $\mathbf{x}_{is}$, $s \neq t$, will not provide weight asymptotically. This is true because, as $N \to \infty$, we obtain information about more individuals, not more information about a given individual. Under the common assumption in the random effects framework that we have independence across individuals, this suggests that the most efficient estimator occurs when $\mathcal{W}_{r\mathbf{x}} = \mathcal{K}_{\mathbf{x}}$.

A more general approach for local-polynomial estimation in the presence of specific covariance structure is found in Rucksthul, Welsh, and Carroll (2000) and Martins-Filho and Yao (2009). While Martins-Filho and Yao (2009) consider a more general structure for Ω, both provide a two-step estimator which that achieve asymptotic efficiency gains relative to the LPLS estimator. The proposed estimator can be explained as follows. First, premultiply both sides of Eq. (1) by $\Omega^{-1/2}$ to obtain

$$\Omega^{-1/2}y_{it} = \Omega^{-1/2}m(\mathrm{x}_{it}) + \Omega^{-1/2}v_{it},$$

and then add and subtract $m(\mathbf{x}_{it})$ from the right side

$$\Omega^{-1/2}y_{it} = \Omega^{-1/2}m(\mathbf{x}_{it}) + m(\mathbf{x}_{it}) - m(\mathbf{x}_{it}) + \Omega^{-1/2}v_{it}.$$

This results in

$$\begin{aligned} \Omega^{-1/2}y_{it} - \Omega^{-1/2}m(\mathrm{x}_{it}) - m(\mathrm{x}_{it}) &= m(\mathrm{x}_{it}) + \Omega^{-1/2}v_{it} \\ \widetilde{y}_{it} &= m(\mathrm{x}_{it}) + \Omega^{-1/2}v_{it} \end{aligned}$$

where $\widetilde{y}_{it} = \Omega^{-1/2}y_{it} - \Omega^{-1/2}m(\mathbf{x}_{it}) + m(\mathbf{x}_{it}) = \Omega^{-1/2}y_{it} + (1 - \Omega^{-1/2})m(\mathbf{x}_{it})$. For given $\widetilde{y}_{it}$, $m(\mathbf{x}_{it})$ can be estimated using local-polynomial least-squares. Unfortunately $\widetilde{y}_{it}$ is unknown because of the presence of Ω and $m(\mathbf{x}_{it})$. Rucksthul et al. (2000) and Martins-Filho and Yao (2009) propose estimation of Ω in a first stage that ignores the error structure. The two-step estimator is

1. Estimate $m(\mathbf{x}_{it})$ using local-polynomial least-squares, and obtain the residuals to construct $\hat{\Omega}$.
2. Run the local-polynomial least-squares regression of $\hat{\widetilde{y}}_{it}$ on $\mathbf{x}_{it}$ where $\hat{\widetilde{y}}_{it} = \hat{\Omega}^{-1/2}y_{it} + \left(1 - \hat{\Omega}^{-1/2}\right)\hat{m}(\mathbf{x}_{it})$.

Both Su and Ullah (2007) and Martins-Filho and Yao (2009) discuss the large sample properties of this random effects estimator.

3.3 Spline-Based Estimation

Unlike Ullah and Roy (1998), who consider kernel-based procedures, Ma, Racine, and Yang (2015) consider a B-spline regression approach toward nonparametric modeling of a random effects (error component) model. Their focus is on the estimation of marginal effects in these models, something that perhaps has not received as much attention as it might otherwise. To describe their estimator, first, for the vector of covariates, $\mathbf{x}_{it} = (x_{it1}, \ldots, x_{itd})'$ assume for $1 \le s \le d$, each x_{its} is distributed on a compact interval $[a_s, b_s]$, and without loss of generality, Ma et al. (2015) take all intervals $[a_s, b_s] = [0, 1]$. Furthermore, they allow ε_{it} to follow the random effects specification, where $\varepsilon_i = (\varepsilon_{i1}, \ldots, \varepsilon_{iT})'$ be a $T \times 1$ vector. Then $\mathbf{V} \equiv E(\varepsilon_i \varepsilon_i')$ takes the form

$$\mathbf{V} = \sigma_v^2 \mathbf{I}_T + \sigma_\alpha^2 1_T 1_T',$$

where $\mathbf{I}_T$ is an identity matrix of dimension T and 1_T is a $T \times 1$ column vector of ones. The covariance matrix for $\varepsilon = \varepsilon_{1'}, \ldots, \varepsilon_{n'})'$ is

$$\boldsymbol{\Omega} = E(\varepsilon\varepsilon') = \mathbf{I}_N \otimes \mathbf{V}, \boldsymbol{\Omega}^{-1} = \mathbf{I}_N \otimes \mathbf{V}^{-1}$$

By simple linear algebra, $\mathbf{V}^{-1} = (V_{tt'})_{t,\, t'=1}^{T} = V_1 \mathbf{I}_T + V_2 1_T 1'_T$ with $V_1 = \sigma_v^{-2}$ and $V_2 = -(\sigma_v^2 + \sigma_\alpha^2 T)^{-1} \sigma_\alpha^2 \sigma_v^{-2}$.

Ma et al. (2015) use regression B-splines to estimate the mean function $m(\cdot)$ and its first derivative. Let $N = N_n$ be the number of interior knots and let q be the spline order. Divide [0, 1] into $(N + 1)$ subintervals $I_j = [r_j, r_{j+1}), j = 0, \ldots, N - 1, I_N = [r_N, 1]$, where $\{r_j\}_{j=1}^N$ is a sequence of interior knots, given as

$$r_{-(q-1)} = \cdots = r_0 = 0 < r_1 < \cdots < r_N < 1 = r_{N+1} = \cdots = r_{N+q}.$$

Define the q-th order B-spline basis as $B_{s,q} = \{B_j\ (x_s)\colon 1 - q \le j \le N\}'$ (de Boor, 2001, p. 89). Let $G_{s,q} = G_{s,q}^{(q-2)}$ be the space spanned by $B_{s,q}$, and let G_q be the tensor product of $G_{1,q}, \ldots, G_{d,q}$, which is the space of functions spanned by

$$\begin{aligned}
\mathcal{B}_q(\mathbf{x}) &= B_{1,q} \otimes \cdots \otimes B_{d,q} \\
&= \left[\left\{\prod_{s=1}^{d} B_{j_s,q}(x_s) : 1 - q \le j_s \le N, 1 \le s \le d\right\}'\right]_{\mathbf{K}_n \times 1} \\
&= \left[\left\{\mathcal{B}_{j_1,\ldots,j_d,q}(\mathbf{x}) : 1 - q \le j_s \le N, 1 \le s \le d\right\}'\right]_{\mathbf{K}_n \times 1},
\end{aligned}$$

where $\mathbf{x} = (x_1, \ldots, x_d)'$ and $\mathbf{K}_n = (N + q)^d$. Let $\mathbf{B}_q = [\{\mathcal{B}_q(\mathbf{x}_{11}), \ldots, \mathcal{B}_q(x_{nT})\}']_{nT \times \mathbf{K}_n}$, where $\mathbf{x}_{it} = (x_{it1}, \ldots, x_{itd})'$. Then m ($\mathbf{x}$) can be approximated by $\mathcal{B}_q(\mathbf{x})' \beta$, where β is a $\mathbf{K}_n \times 1$ vector. Letting $\mathbf{Y} = [\{(Y_{it})_{1 \le t \le T,\, 1 \le i \le n}\}']_{nT \times 1}$, they estimate β by minimizing the weighted least squares criterion,

$$\{\mathbf{Y} - \mathbf{B_q}\beta\}' \boldsymbol{\Omega}^{-1} \{\mathbf{Y} - \mathbf{B_q}\beta\}.$$

Then the estimator of β, $\hat{\beta}$, solves the estimating equations $\mathbf{B}_q' \Omega^{-1} \{\mathbf{Y} - \mathbf{B}_q \beta\} = 0$, which gives the GLS estimator

$$\hat{\beta} = \left(\mathbf{B}_q' \Omega^{-1} \mathbf{B}_q\right)^{-1} \mathbf{B}_q' \boldsymbol{\Omega}^{-1} \mathbf{Y}.$$

The estimator of m ($\mathbf{x}$) is then given by $\hat{m}(\mathbf{x}) = \mathcal{B}_q(\mathbf{x})' \hat{\beta}$. In de Boor (2001, page 116), it is shown that the first derivative of a spline function can be expressed in terms of a spline of one order lower. For any function

$s(\mathbf{x}) \in G_q$ that can be expressed by $s(\mathbf{x}) = \sum_{j_1, \ldots, j_d} B_{i_1, q}(x_1) \ldots B_{j_d, q}(x_d)$, the first derivative of $s(\mathbf{x})$ with respect to x_s is

$$\frac{\partial s}{\partial x_s}(\mathbf{x}) = \sum_{j_s=2-q}^{N} \sum_{1-q \le j_{s'} \le N, 1 \le s' \ne s \le d} a^{(1s)}_{j_1,\ldots,j_d} B_{j_s,q-1}(x_s) \prod_{s' \ne s} B_{j_{s'},q}(x_{s'}),$$

In which $a^{(1s)}_{j_1,\ldots,jd} = (q-1)(a_{j_1,\ldots,js,\ldots,jd} - a_{j_1,\ldots,js-1,\ldots,jd})/(t_{j_s+q-1} - t_{j_s})$, for $2 - q \le j_s \le N$ and $1 \le s' \ne s \le d$, $1 - q \le j_{s'} \le N$. Let $\mathbf{L}_n = (N+q)^{d-1}(N+q-1)$, and

$$\mathcal{B}_{s,q-1}(\mathbf{x}) = \left[\left\{B_{j_1,q}(x_1) \cdots B_{j_s,q-1}(x_s) \cdots B_{j_d,q}(x_d)\right\}'_{1-q \le j_{s'} \le N, s' \ne s, 2-q \le j_s \le N}\right]_{\mathbf{L}_n \times 1}.$$

For $1 \le s \le d$, $\frac{\partial m}{\partial x_s}(\mathbf{x})$, which is the first derivative of $m(\mathbf{x})$ with respect to x_s, the estimate is

$$\frac{\hat{\partial m}}{\partial x_s}(\mathbf{x}) = \mathcal{B}_{s,q-1}(\mathbf{x})' D_s \left(\mathbf{B}_q' \boldsymbol{\Omega}^{-1} \mathbf{B}_q\right)^{-1} \mathbf{B}_q' \boldsymbol{\Omega}^{-1} \mathbf{Y},$$

in which $K_n = \{\mathbf{I}_{(N+q)^{s-1}} \otimes M_1 \mathbf{I}_{(N+q)^{d-s}}\}_{\mathbf{L}_n \times \mathbf{K}n}$, and

$$M_1 = (q-1)\begin{pmatrix} \frac{-1}{t_1 - t_{2-q}} & \frac{1}{t_1 - t_{2-q}} & 0 & \cdots & 0 \\ 0 & \frac{-1}{t_2 - t_{3-q}} & \frac{1}{t_2 - t_{3-q}} & \cdots & 0 \\ \vdots & \vdots & \ddots & \frac{-1}{} & \vdots \\ 0 & 0 & \cdots & \frac{-1}{t_{N+q-1} - t_N} & \frac{1}{t_{N+q-1} - t_N} \end{pmatrix}_{(N+q-1)\times(N+q)}$$

Let $\nabla m(\mathbf{x})$ be the gradient vector of $m(\mathbf{x})$. The estimator of $\nabla m(\mathbf{x})$ is

$$\begin{aligned}\widehat{\nabla \mathrm{m}}(\mathbf{x}) &= \left\{\widehat{\frac{\partial m}{\partial x_1}}(\mathbf{x}), \ldots, \widehat{\frac{\partial m}{\partial x_d}}(\mathbf{x})\right\}' \\ &= \mathcal{B}^*_{q-1}(\mathbf{x})'\left(\mathbf{B}_q' \boldsymbol{\Omega}^{-1} \mathbf{B}_q\right)^{-1} \mathbf{B}_q' \boldsymbol{\Omega}^{-1} \mathrm{Y},\end{aligned}$$

in which $\mathcal{B}^*_{q-1}(\mathbf{x}) = [\{D_{1,1'} \mathcal{B}_{q-1,1}(\mathbf{x}), \ldots, D_{1,d'} \mathcal{B}_{q-1,d}(\mathbf{x})\}]_{\mathbf{K}_n \times d}$. For any $\mu \in (0, 1]$, we denote by $C^{0,\mu}[0, 1]^d$ the space of order μ-H{"o}lder continuous functions on $[0, 1]^d$, i.e.,

$$C^{0,\mu}[0,1]^d = \left\{\phi : \|\phi\|_{0,\mu} = \sup_{\mathbf{x} \ne \mathbf{x}', \mathbf{x}, \mathbf{x} \in [0,1]^d} \frac{|\phi(\mathbf{x}) - \phi(\mathbf{x}')|}{\|\mathbf{x} - \mathbf{x}'\|_2^{\mu}} < +\infty\right\}$$

in which $\|\mathbf{x}\|_2 = (\sum_{s=1}^{d} x_s^2)^{1/2}$ is the Euclidean norm of $\mathbf{x}$, and $\|\phi\|_{0,\mu}$ is the $C^{0,\mu}$-norm of φ.

Given a d-tuple $\alpha = (\alpha_1, \ldots, \alpha_d)$ of nonnegative integers, let $[\alpha] = \alpha_1 + \ldots + \alpha_d$ and let D^α denote the differential operator defined by $D^\alpha = \frac{\partial[\alpha]}{\partial x_1^{\alpha_1} \cdots \partial x_d^{\alpha_d}}$.

Ma et al. (2015) establish consistency and asymptotic normality for the estimator $\hat{m}(\mathbf{x})$ and $\nabla\hat{m}(\mathbf{x})$, i.e.,

$$\sigma_n^{-1}(\mathbf{x})\{\hat{m}(\mathbf{x})-m(\mathbf{x})\}\rightarrow \mathbf{N}(0,1)$$

and

$$\Phi_n^{-1/2}(\mathrm{x})\{\nabla\hat{m}(\mathbf{x})-\nabla m(\mathbf{x})\}\rightarrow \mathbf{N}(0_d,\mathbf{I}_d),$$

in which $\mathbf{0}_d$ is a $d\times 1$ vector of 0's, and where $\sigma_n^2(\mathbf{x})=\mathcal{B}_q(\mathbf{x})'\Sigma^{-1}\mathcal{B}_q(\mathbf{x})$ and where $\Phi_n(\mathbf{x})=\{\mathcal{B}_{q-1}^*(\mathbf{x})'\Sigma^{-1}\mathcal{B}_{q-1}^*(\mathbf{x})\}_{d\times d}$.

Ma et al. (2015) use cross-validation to determine the degree vector for their B-spline method, and the approach admits discrete covariates. (See Ma et al. 2015 for details.)

Although the previous description might be notationally cumbersome, the approach is in fact extremely simple and requires only a few lines of code for its implementation.

3.4 Profile Likelihood Estimation

Profile likelihood methods often are used when traditional maximum likelihood methods fail. This is common in nonparametric models where the unknown function is treated as an infinite dimensional parameter. These methods commonly require specifying a criterion function based around an assumption of Gaussianity of the error term.[2] In the current setting, we would have, for individual i, the criterion function

$$\mathcal{L}_i(\cdot)=\mathcal{L}(y_i,m(\mathbf{x}_i))=-\frac{1}{2}(y_i-m(\mathbf{x}_i))'V_i^{-1}(y_i-m(\mathbf{x}_i)),$$

where $y_i=(y_{i1},y_{i2},\ldots,y_{iT})'$ and $m\,(\mathbf{x}_i)=(m\,(\mathbf{x}_{i1}),m\,(\mathbf{x}_{i2}),\ldots,m\,(\mathbf{x}_{iT}))'$. Differentiating $\mathcal{L}_i(\cdot)$ with respect to $m(\mathbf{x})$ yields

$$\mathcal{L}_{itm}=\frac{\partial\mathcal{L}_i}{\partial m(\mathbf{x}_{it})}=e_t'V_i^{-1}(y_i-m(\mathbf{x}_i))=\sum_{s=1}^{T}\sigma^{ts}(y_{is}-m(\mathbf{x}_{is}))\tag{8}$$

where e_t is a T dimensional vector whose tth element is unity and all other elements are zero and where σ^{ts} is the (t,s) element of V_i^{-1}.[3]

Lin and Carroll (2006) show that $m\,(\mathbf{x})$ can be estimated in a local-linear fashion by solving the first-order condition

$$0=\sum_{i=1}^{N}\sum_{t=1}^{T}K_{it\mathbf{x}h}G_{it\mathbf{x}}\mathcal{L}_{itm}(y_i,\check{m}(\mathbf{x}_i)),$$

where $G_{it\mathbf{x}}$ vertically concatenates $(\mathbf{x}_{it}-\mathbf{x})^{\mathbf{j}}\oslash h^{\mathbf{j}}$ for $0\leq|\mathbf{j}|\leq p$ in lexicographical order, $\check{m}(\mathbf{x}_i)=\left(\hat{m}(\mathbf{x}_{i1}),\ldots,\hat{m}(\mathbf{x})+\check{\mathbf{x}}_{it}\hat{\beta}(\mathbf{x}),\ldots,\hat{m}(\mathbf{x}_{iT})\right)$, and $\check{\mathbf{x}}_{it}=\mathbf{x}_{it}=\mathbf{x}$.

2. Note that the assumption of Gaussianity is required only to construct a criterion function.

3. σ^{tt} and σ^{ts} will differ across cross-sectional units in the presence of an unbalanced panel.

Note that the argument for $\mathcal{L}_{itm}$ is $\hat{m}(\mathbf{x}_{it})$ for $s \neq t$ and $\hat{m}(\mathbf{x}) + \check{\mathbf{x}}_{it}\hat{\beta}(\mathbf{x})$ for $s = t$. Plugging in Eq. (8) and solving yields

$$\mathcal{L}_{itm}(y_i, \check{m}(\mathbf{x}_i)) = \sigma^{tt}\left(y_{it} - \hat{m}(\mathbf{x}) - \check{\mathbf{x}}_{it}\hat{\beta}(\mathbf{x})\right) + \sum_{\substack{s=1\\ s\neq t}}^{T} \sigma^{ts}(y_{is} - \hat{m}(\mathbf{x}_{is})).$$

Wang (2003) developed an iterative procedure to estimate $m(\mathbf{x})$. This estimator is shown to produce efficiency gains relative to the local-linear estimator of Lin and Carroll (2000). The iterative estimator is composed of two parts: one based off a standard local-linear (or polynomial) least-squares regression between y and $\mathbf{x}$, and a secondary component that uses the residuals.

The first-stage estimator is constructed using any consistent estimator of the conditional mean; the pooled LLLS estimator suffices in this setting. To highlight the fact that we have an iterative estimator, we will refer to our first-stage estimator as $\hat{m}_{[1]}(\mathbf{x})$ (the subscript [1] represents that we are at the $l = 1$ step); the residuals from this model are given by $\hat{v}_{[1]it} = y_{it} - \hat{m}_{[1]}(\mathbf{x}_{it})$. At the lth step, $\hat{m}_{[l]}(\mathbf{x})$, and the gradient, $\hat{\beta}_{[l]}(\mathbf{x})$, are shown by Wang (2003) to be

$$\begin{pmatrix} \hat{m}_{[l]}(\mathbf{x}) \\ \hat{\beta}_{[l]}(\mathbf{x}) \end{pmatrix} = J_1^{-1}(J_2 + J_3),$$

where

$$J_1 = \sum_{i=1}^{N}\sum_{t=1}^{T} \sigma^{tt} K_{it\mathbf{x}h} G_{it\mathbf{x}} G'_{it\mathbf{x}},$$

$$J_2 = \sum_{i=1}^{N}\sum_{t=1}^{T} \sigma^{tt} K_{it\mathbf{x}h} G_{it\mathbf{x}} y_{it},$$

$$J_3 = \sum_{i=1}^{N}\sum_{t=1}^{T}\sum_{\substack{s=1\\ s\neq t}}^{T} \sigma^{st} K_{it\mathbf{x}h} G_{it\mathbf{x}} \hat{v}_{[\ell-1]it}.$$

If one ignores the presence of J_3, then the estimator of Wang (2003) is nearly identical to the pooled LLLS estimator, outside of the presence of σ^{tt} (which has an impact only if there is an unbalanced panel). The contribution of J_3 is what provides asymptotic gains in efficiency. J_3 effectively contributes the covariance among the within cluster residuals to the overall smoothing. To see why this is the case, consider the LLWLS estimator in Eq. (7). Even though the within cluster covariance is included via $\mathcal{W}_{r\mathbf{x}}$, asymptotically this effect does not materialize since it appears in both the numerator and denominator in an identical fashion. For the estimator of Wang (2003), this effect materializes given that the within cluster covariance occurs only in the numerator (i.e., through J_3).

The Wang (2003) estimator is iterated until convergence is achieved; for example a useful convergence criterion is $\sum_{i=1}^{N}\sum_{t=1}^{T}\left\{\hat{m}_{[\ell]}(\mathbf{x}_{it}) - \hat{m}_{[\ell-1]}(\mathbf{x}_{it})\right\}^2 / \sum_{i=1}^{N}\sum_{t=1}^{T}\hat{m}_{[\ell-1]}(\mathbf{x}_{it})^2 < \omega$, where ω is some small number. Wang (2003) demonstrates that the estimator usually converges in only a few iterations and argues that the once-iterated ($\ell = 2$) estimator has the same asymptotic behavior as the fully iterated estimator.

Feasible estimation requires estimates of σ^{ts} that can be obtained using the residuals from $\hat{m}_{[1]}(\mathbf{x})$. The (t, s)th element is

$$\sigma^{ts} = \frac{\sigma_\varepsilon^2 - \sigma_1^2}{\sigma_1^2 \sigma_\varepsilon^2 T},$$

and the (t, t)th element is

$$\sigma^{tt} = \frac{\sigma_\varepsilon^2 + (T-1)\sigma_1^2}{\sigma_1^2 \sigma_\varepsilon^2 T}.$$

4 Estimation in the Fixed Effects Framework

4.1 Differencing/Transformation Methods

Consider first differencing Eq. (1), which leads to

$$y_{it} - y_{it-1} = m(\mathbf{x}_{it}) - m(\mathbf{x}_{it-1}) + \varepsilon_{it} - \varepsilon_{it-1}, \quad i = 1, \ldots, N, \;\; t = 2, \ldots, T.$$

By assuming a fixed number of derivatives of $m(\mathbf{x})$ to exist, Ullah and Roy (1998) posited that the derivatives of $m(\mathbf{x})$ would be identified and easily estimated using local-linear (polynomial) regression. For example, consider $q = 1$, and use the notation $\Delta z_{it} = z_{it} - z_{it-1}$ resulting in

$$\Delta y_{it} = m(x_{it}) - m(x_{it-1}) + \Delta \varepsilon_{it}.$$

Next, a first-order Taylor expansion of $m(x_{it})$ and $m(x_{it-1})$ around the point x results in

$$\begin{aligned} \Delta y_{it} &= m(x) + m'(x)(x_{it} - x) - (m(x) + m'(x)(x_{it-1} - x)) + \Delta \varepsilon_{it} \\ &= m(x) - m(x) + m'(x)((x_{it} - x) - (x_{it-1} - x)) + \Delta \varepsilon_{it} \\ &= \Delta x_{it} m'(x) + \Delta \varepsilon_{it} \end{aligned}$$

This same argument also could be done using the within transformation. The local-linear estimator of $m'(x)$ as proposed in Lee and Mukherjee (2014) is

$$\hat{m}'(x) = \frac{\sum_{i=1}^{N} \sum_{t=2}^{T} K_{it\mathbf{x}h} \Delta x_{it} \Delta y_{it}}{\sum_{i=1}^{N} \sum_{t=2}^{T} K_{it\mathbf{x}h} \Delta x_{it}^2}. \tag{9}$$

There are two main problems with this differencing estimator. First, the conditional mean is not identified in this setting. Second, as Lee and Mukherjee (2014) demonstrate, the local-linear estimator possesses a nonvanishing asymptotic bias even as $h \to 0$. Note that in the construction of Eq. (9), the linear expansion is around the point x_{it} (which is acceptable in a cross-sectional setting).

However, in the panel setting, information from the same individual (i.e., $x_{is}, s \neq t$) cannot be controlled as $h \to 0$. In particular, we took the Taylor expansion around both the points x_{it} and x_{it-1} in our first differencing, however, the kernel weights account only for the difference between x and x_{it}. This means that the Taylor approximation error will not decay to zero as the bandwidth decays.

Several approaches have been proposed to overcome the nonvanishing asymptotic bias. For example, Mundra (2005) considers local-linear estimation around the pair (x_{it}, x_{it-1}), which produces the estimator (termed the first-difference local-linear estimator, or FDLL)

$$\hat{m}'_{FDLL}(x) = \frac{\sum_{i=1}^{N}\sum_{t=2}^{T} K_{itxh}K_{it-1xh}\Delta x_{it}\Delta y_{it}}{\sum_{i=1}^{N}\sum_{t=2}^{T} K_{itxh}K_{it-1xh}\Delta x_{it}^2}.$$

Even with this simple fix, however, the issue remains that only the derivatives of the conditional mean are identified. In some settings this is acceptable. For example, in the hedonic price setting the gradients of the conditional mean are of interest because they can be used to recover preferences of individuals. Bishop and Timmins (2018) use this insight and follow the previous logic (albeit using the within transformation) to recover the gradients of a hedonic price function to value preferences for clean air in the San Francisco Bay area of California.

As an alternative to the first-difference transformation, the within transformation also could be applied, as in Eq. (2). Again, as noted in Lee and Mukherjee (2014), direct local-linear estimation in this framework ignores the application of the Taylor approximation and results in an asymptotic bias. To remedy this, Lee and Mukherjee (2014) propose the local within transformation. To see how this estimator works, consider that the standard within transformation calculates the individual specific mean of a variable z as $\overline{z}_{i\cdot} = T^{-1}\sum_{t=1}^{T} z_{it}$. Lee and Mukherjee (2014) replace the uniform $1/T$ weighting with kernel weights, producing the local individual specific means

$$\widetilde{\overline{z}}_{i\cdot} = \frac{\sum_{t=1}^{T} K_{itzh} z_{it}}{\sum_{s=1}^{T} K_{iszh}} = \sum_{t=1}^{T} w_{itzh} z_{it}.$$

Using the notation $z_{it}^* = z_{it} - \widetilde{\overline{z}}_{i\cdot}$, the locally within transformed local-constant estimator is

$$\hat{m}'_{LWTLC}(x) = \frac{\sum_{i=1}^{N}\sum_{t=2}^{T} K_{itxh}x_{it}^* y_{it}^*}{\sum_{i=1}^{N}\sum_{t=2}^{T} K_{itxh}x_{it}^{*2}}.$$

These local differencing and transformation methods are simple to implement. However, it is not clear if they can be used to recover the conditional mean, which would be important in applications where forecasting or prediction is desirable.

4.2 Profile Estimation

The obvious drawback of the differencing/transformation approaches proposed by Ullah and Roy (1998), Mundra (2005), and Lee and Mukherjee (2014) is that the conditional mean cannot be identified. To remedy this, Henderson, Carroll, and Li (2008) consider estimation of Eq. (1) under the fixed effects framework using the first difference transformation based off period 1:

$$\widetilde{y}_{it} \equiv y_{it} - y_{i1} = m(\mathbf{x}_{it}) - m(\mathbf{x}_{i1}) + \varepsilon_{it} - \varepsilon_{i1}. \tag{10}$$

Although this estimator could be implemented using period $t-1$, as is more common, we follow their approach here. The benefit of this transformation is that, the fixed effects are removed, and, under exogeneity of the covariates, E $[m(\mathbf{x}_{it})] = \mathrm{E}(y_{it})$. The problem as it stands with Eq. (10) is the presence of both $m(\mathbf{x}_{it})$ and $m(\mathbf{x}_{i1})$. The main idea of Henderson et al. (2008) is to exploit the variance structure of $\varepsilon_{it} - \varepsilon_{i1}$ when constructing the estimator, which is similar to Wang (2003)'s approach in the random effects setting.

Start by defining $\widetilde{\varepsilon}_{it} = \varepsilon_{it} - \varepsilon_{i1}$ and $\widetilde{\varepsilon}_i = (\widetilde{\varepsilon}_{i2}, \dots, \widetilde{\varepsilon}_{iT})'$. The variance-covariance matrix of $\widetilde{\varepsilon}_i, V_i = \mathrm{Cov}(\widetilde{\varepsilon}_i | \mathbf{x}_{i1}, \dots, \mathbf{x}_{iT})$, is defined as

$$V_i = \sigma_\varepsilon^2 \left(I_{T-1} + \mathbf{i}_{T-1}\mathbf{i}_{T-1}'\right),$$

where I_{T-1} is an identity matrix of dimension $T-1$, and $\mathbf{i}_{T-1}$ is a $(T-1) \times 1$ vector of ones (note that in the random effects case it was of dimension T). Further, $V_i^{-1} = \sigma_\varepsilon^{-2}(I_{T-1} - \mathbf{i}_{T-1}\mathbf{i}_{T-1}'/T)$. Following Wang (2003) and Lin and Carroll (2006), Henderson et al. (2008) deploy a profile likelihood approach to estimate $m(\cdot)$. The criterion function for individual i is

$$\begin{aligned} \mathcal{L}_i(\cdot) &= \mathcal{L}(y_i, m(\mathbf{x}_i)) \\ &= -\frac{1}{2}(\widetilde{y}_i - m(\mathbf{x}_i) + m(\mathbf{x}_{i1})\mathbf{i}_{T-1})' V_i^{-1} (\widetilde{y}_i - m(\mathbf{x}_i) + m(\mathbf{x}_{i1})\mathbf{i}_{T-1}), \end{aligned} \tag{11}$$

where $\widetilde{y}_i = (\widetilde{y}_{i2}, \dots, \widetilde{y}_{iT})'$ and $m(\mathbf{x}_i) = (m(\mathbf{x}_{i2}), m(\mathbf{x}_{i3}), \dots, m(\mathbf{x}_{iT}))'$.

As in the construction of Wang (2003)'s random effects estimator, define $\mathcal{L}_{itm} = \partial \mathcal{L}_i(\cdot)/\partial m(\mathbf{x}_{it})$. From Eq. (11) we have

$$\begin{aligned} \mathcal{L}_{i1m} &= -\mathrm{i}_{T-1}' V_i^{-1}(\widetilde{y}_i - m(\mathbf{x}_i) + m(\mathrm{x}_{i1})\mathrm{i}_{T-1}); \\ \mathcal{L}_{itm} &= c_{t-1}' V_i^{-1}(\widetilde{y}_i - m(\mathbf{x}_i) + m(\mathbf{x}_{i1})\mathrm{i}_{T-1}) \quad \text{for } T \geq 2, \end{aligned}$$

where c_{t-1} is a vector of dimension $(T-1) \times 1$ with the $(t-1)$ element being 1 and all other elements being 0.

We estimate the unknown function $m(\mathbf{x})$ by solving the first-order condition

$$0=\sum_{i=1}^{N}\sum_{t=1}^{T}K_{it\mathbf{x}h}G_{it\mathbf{x}}\mathcal{L}_{itm}\left[y_i,\hat{m}(\mathbf{x}_{i1}),\ldots,\hat{m}(\mathbf{x})+\check{\mathbf{x}}_{it}\hat{\beta}(\mathbf{x}),\ldots,\hat{m}(\mathbf{x}_{iT})\right],$$

where the argument of $\mathcal{L}_{itm}$ is $\hat{m}(\mathbf{x}_{is})$ for $s\neq t$ and $\hat{m}(\mathbf{x})+\check{\mathbf{x}}_{it}\hat{\beta}(\mathbf{x})$ when $s=t$.

As in Wang (2003), an iterative procedure is required. Denote the estimate of $m(\mathbf{x})$ at the $[\ell-1]$th step as $\hat{m}_{[\ell-1]}(\mathbf{x})$. Then the current estimate of $m(\mathbf{x})$, and its derivative, $\beta(\mathbf{x})$, are $\hat{m}_{[\ell]}(\mathbf{x})$ and $\hat{\beta}_{[\ell]}(\mathbf{x})$, which solve:

$$0=\sum_{i=1}^{N}\sum_{t=1}^{T}K_{it\mathbf{x}h}G_{it\mathbf{x}}\mathcal{L}_{itm}\left[y_i,\hat{m}_{[\ell-1]}(\mathbf{x}_{i1}),\ldots,\hat{m}_{[\ell]}+\check{\mathbf{x}}_{it}\hat{\beta}_{[\ell]}(\mathbf{x}),\ldots,\hat{m}_{[\ell-1]}(\mathbf{x}_{iT})\right].$$

Henderson et al. (2008) use the restriction $\sum_{i=1}^{N}\sum_{t=1}^{T}(y_{it}-\hat{m}(\mathbf{x}_{it}))=0$ so that $m(\cdot)$ is uniquely defined because $\mathrm{E}(y_{it})=\mathrm{E}\,[m(\mathbf{x}_{it})]$.

The next step estimator is

$$\left(\hat{m}_{[\ell]},\hat{\beta}_{[\ell]}\right)'=D_1^{-1}(D_2+D_3),$$

where

$$D_1=\frac{T-1}{T\sigma_\varepsilon^2}\sum_{i=1}^{N}\sum_{t=1}^{T}K_{it\mathbf{x}h}G_{it\mathbf{x}}G'_{it\mathbf{x}}$$

$$D_2=\frac{T-1}{T\sigma_\varepsilon^2}\sum_{i=1}^{N}\sum_{t=1}^{T}K_{it\mathbf{x}h}G_{it\mathbf{x}}\hat{m}_{[\ell-1]}(\mathbf{x}_{it});$$

$$D_3=\sum_{i=1}^{N}\sum_{t=2}^{T}\left(K_{it\mathbf{x}h}G_{it\mathbf{x}}c'_{t_i-1}-K_{i1\mathbf{x}h}G_{i1\mathbf{x}}\mathbf{i}'_{T-1}\right)V_i^{-1}H_{i,[\ell-1]},$$

and

$$H_{i,[\ell-1]}=\begin{pmatrix}\varepsilon_{i2}^{[\ell-1]}\\ \vdots\\ \varepsilon_{iT}^{[\ell-1]}\end{pmatrix}-\varepsilon_{i1}^{[\ell-1]}\mathbf{i}_{T-1}$$

where $\varepsilon_{is}^{[\ell-1]}=y_{is}-\hat{m}_{[\ell-1]}(\mathbf{x}_{is})$ are the differenced residuals. Henderson and Parmeter (2015) note that the derivative estimator of Henderson et al. (2008) is incorrect; $\hat{\beta}_{[\ell]}$ defined previously needs to be divided by h to produce the correct vector of first derivatives of $\hat{m}_{[\ell]}(\mathbf{x})$. Regarding the asymptotic properties of this profile likelihood estimator, Henderson et al. (2008) provide only a sketch of the form of the asymptotic bias, variance, and asymptotic normality, whereas Li and Liang (2015), using the theory of Mammen, Støve, and Tjøstheim (2009), provide a full derivation of asymptotic normality and also demonstrate the robustness of the estimator to which period is used for differencing.

Recall that the estimator proposed by Wang (2003) required a consistent initial estimator of V_i to be operational. There, setting V_i to be an identity matrix resulted in the pooled local-linear least-squares estimator as an ideal choice. The same is true here; if we replace V_i by an identity matrix, Eq. (10) is an additive model with the restriction that the two additive functions have the same functional form. Either a fourth order-polynomial or a series estimator can be used in this setting to construct an initial consistent estimator of $m(\cdot)$ and subsequently, of V_i. The variance parameter σ_ε^2 can be consistently estimated by

$$\hat{\sigma}_\varepsilon^2 = \frac{1}{(2NT-2N)} \sum_{i=1}^{N} \sum_{t=2}^{T} (y_{it} - y_{i1} - \{\hat{m}(\mathbf{x}_{it}) - \hat{m}(\mathbf{x}_{i1})\})^2.$$

However, note that $\hat{\sigma}_v^2$ is necessary only in order to estimate the covariance matrix of $\hat{m}(\mathbf{x})$. It is not necessary for the construction of $\left(\hat{m}_{[\ell]}, \hat{\beta}_{[\ell]}\right)$ given that $\hat{\sigma}_\varepsilon^2$ simply drops out of Eq. (10).

4.3 Marginal Integration

An alternative to the iterative procedure of Henderson et al. (2008) is to estimate the model in Eq. (10) using marginal integration. This was proposed by Qian and Wang (2012). To describe their estimator we first restate the first-differenced regression model as follows:

$$\Delta y_{it} \equiv y_{it} - y_{it-1} = m(\mathbf{x}_{it}) \quad m(\mathbf{x}_{it-1}) + \Delta\varepsilon_{it}. \tag{12}$$

Qian and Wang (2012) suggest estimating the model in Eq. (12) by estimating

$$\Delta y_{it} = m(\mathbf{x}_{it}, \mathbf{x}_{it-1}) + \Delta\varepsilon_{it}$$

and then integrating out $\mathbf{x}_{it-1}$ to obtain an estimator of $m(\mathbf{x}_{it})$. The benefit of this approach is that any standard nonparametric estimator can be used, such as local-polynomial least-squares. Consider our earlier discussion of local-polynomial least-squares estimation in which the estimator was defined in Eq. (6). Now, instead of estimation at the point $\mathbf{x}$, we have estimation at the pair $(\mathbf{x}, \mathbf{z})$, resulting in the estimator

$$\hat{\beta}(\mathbf{x}, \mathbf{z}) = \left(D'_{\mathbf{xz}} \mathcal{K}_{\mathbf{xz}} D_{\mathbf{xz}}\right)^{-1} D'_{\mathbf{xz}} \mathcal{K}_{\mathbf{xz}} \Delta y.$$

Here we have used the notation $\mathcal{K}_{\mathbf{xz}} = \mathcal{K}_{\mathbf{x}} \mathcal{K}_{\mathbf{z}}$ and $D_{\mathbf{xz}}$ is the same vertically concatenated matrix, but now combined over the points $\mathbf{x}$ and $\mathbf{z}$. Regardless of p, $\hat{m}(\mathbf{x}, \mathbf{z}) = e_1' \hat{\beta}(\mathbf{x}, \mathbf{z})$ where e_1 is a vector with 1 in the first position and zeros everywhere else. After this estimator has been constructed, we can estimate $m(\mathbf{x})$ from $\hat{m}(\mathbf{x}, \mathbf{z})$ by integrating out $\mathbf{z}$. The easiest way to do this is

$$\hat{m}(\mathbf{x}) = (NT)^{-1} \sum_{i=1}^{N} \sum_{t=1}^{T} \hat{m}(\mathbf{x}, \mathbf{x}_{it}). \tag{13}$$

There are two main issues with the marginal integration estimator of Qian and Wang (2012). First, given the well-known curse of dimensionality, estimation of $m(\mathbf{x}, \mathbf{z})$ is likely to be plagued by bias if q is large and/or NT is relatively small. Second, the marginal integration estimator in Eq. (13) requires counterfactual construction, which implies that to evaluate the estimator at a single point requires $N\,T$ function evaluations and so $(N\,T)^2$ evaluations are needed to estimate the function at all data points. Even for moderately sized N and T this could prove computationally expensive. In simulations, Gao and Li (2013) report that the marginal integration estimator takes substantial amounts of time to compute even for small N and T.

Even given these two drawbacks, the marginal integration estimator of Qian and Wang (2012) has much to offer. First, given that the only transformation that is required is first-differencing, this estimator can be implemented easily in any software that can conduct kernel smoothing and allow the construction of counterfactuals. Moreover, this estimator does not require iteration or an arbitrary initial consistent estimator. Both of these advantages might lead to the increasing adoption of this estimator in the future. Qian and Wang (2012) prove asymptotic normality of the estimator for the local-linear setting. They demonstrate that the estimator works well in Monte Carlo simulations, and they show that the marginal integration estimator outperforms the profile likelihood estimator of Henderson et al. (2008).

4.4 Profile Least Squares

Gao and Li (2013), Li, Peng, and Tong (2013), and Lin et al. (2014), following Su and Ullah (2006) and Sun, Carroll, and Li (2009), propose estimation of the model in Eq. (1) through profile least squares. Assuming the data are ordered so that t is the fast index, then the profile least-squares estimator of Li et al. (2013) and Lin, Li, and Sun (2014) begins by assuming that α_i is known. In the local-linear setting, $M(\mathbf{z}) = (m(\mathbf{z}), h \odot \dot{m}(\mathbf{z})')'$ (where $\odot$ represents Hadamard multiplication) is estimated from

$$M_\alpha(\mathbf{x}) = \arg \min_{M \in \mathbb{R}^{q+1}} (Y - D_\alpha - D_\mathbf{x} M)' \mathcal{K}_\mathbf{x} (Y - D_\alpha - D_\mathbf{x} M), \tag{14}$$

where $D = (I_n \otimes i_T) \cdot d_n$, $d_n = [-i_{n-1}, I_{n-1}]'$, and i_n is a $n \times 1$ vector of ones. D is introduced in such a way to ensure that $N^{-1}\sum_{i=1}^{N} \alpha_i = 0$, a necessary identification condition. Define the smoothing operator

$$S(\mathbf{x}) = \left(D_\mathbf{x}' \mathcal{K}_\mathbf{x} D_\mathbf{x}\right)^{-1} D_\mathbf{x}' \mathcal{K}_\mathbf{x},$$

and the estimator that solves the minimization problem in Eq. (13) is

$$\hat{M}_\alpha(\mathbf{x}) = S(\mathbf{x}) \ddot{\varepsilon}$$

where $\ddot{\varepsilon} = \ddot{Y} - D\alpha \ldots \hat{M}_\alpha(\mathbf{x})$ contains the estimator of the conditional mean, $\hat{m}_\alpha(\mathbf{x})$ as well as the $q \times 1$ vector of first derivatives, scaled by the appropriate bandwidth, $h \odot \hat{m}_\alpha(\mathbf{x})'$. Define $s(\mathbf{x})' = e' \ S(\mathbf{x})$ with $e = (1, \ 0, \ldots, 0)'$ the $(q+1) \times 1$ vector. Then $\hat{m}_\alpha(\mathbf{x}) = s(\mathbf{x})'\ddot{\varepsilon}$.

After the estimator of $m(\mathbf{x})$ is obtained, α is estimated through profile least squares from

$$\hat{\alpha} = \arg\min_{\alpha}(Y - D_\alpha - \hat{m}_\alpha(\mathbf{x}))'\mathcal{K}_\mathbf{x}(Y - D_\alpha - \hat{m}_\alpha(\mathbf{x})),$$

with $\hat{m}_\alpha(\mathbf{x}) = (\hat{m}_\alpha(\mathbf{x}_{11}), \hat{m}_\alpha(\mathbf{x}_{12}), \ldots, \hat{m}_\alpha(\mathbf{x}_{1T}), \hat{m}_\alpha(\mathbf{x}_{21}), \ldots, \hat{m}_\alpha(\mathbf{x}_{NT}))'$. Lin et al. (2014) show that the parametric estimator that solves the profile least-squares problem is

$$\hat{\alpha} = \left(\widetilde{D}'\widetilde{D}\right)^{-1}\widetilde{D}'\widetilde{Y},$$

with $\widetilde{D} = (1_{NT} - S)D$ and $\widetilde{Y} = (I_{NT} - S)Y$. Here $S = (s(\mathbf{x}_{11}), \ s(\mathbf{x}_{12}), \ \ldots, \ s(\mathbf{x}_{1T}), \ s(\mathbf{x}_{21}), \ \ldots, \ s(\mathbf{x}_{NT}))'$.

Finally, $\hat{\alpha}_1 = -\sum_{i=2}^{n}\hat{\alpha}_i$.

The profile least-squares estimator for $M(\mathbf{x})$ is given by

$$\hat{M}(\mathbf{x}) = \hat{M}_{\hat{\alpha}}(\mathbf{x}) = S(\mathbf{x})\hat{\ddot{\varepsilon}} \tag{15}$$

with $\hat{\ddot{\varepsilon}} = Y - D\hat{\alpha}$.

Su and Ullah (2006) discuss the asymptotic properties of the profile-least squares estimator in the context of the partially linear model, Sun et al. (2009) for the smooth coefficient model, and Gao and Li (2013), Li et al. (2013), and Lin et al. (2014) in the full nonparametric model setting. The elegance of the profile least-squares estimator is that neither marginal integration techniques nor iteration are required. This represents a computationally simple alternative to the other estimators previously discussed. To our knowledge only Qian and Wang (2012) and Gao and Li (2013) have compared the profile least-squares estimator in a fully nonparametric setting. Gao and Li (2013) run an extensive set of simulations, comparing the profile least-squares estimator, the profile likelihood estimator of Henderson et al. (2008), and the marginal integration estimation of Qian and Wang (2012), finding that the profile least squares estimator outperforms these other estimators in a majority of the settings considered. Lastly, we know of no application using the profile least-squares approach to estimate the conditional mean nonparametrically, which would be a true test of its applied appeal.

The practitioner might find the profile least-squares estimator to be the most accessible of all of the fixed effects estimators described herein. This is no doubt in part because iteration is not required, nor is counterfactual analysis necessary when performing marginal integration. Moreover, in the local-linear setting described here, both the conditional mean and the corresponding gradients are easily calculated (unlike the local within transformation). Lastly, the profile least-squares estimator can be adapted easily to any order local polynomial and readily modified to include other panel type settings. For example, both time and individual specific heterogeneity could be accounted for, or if three-way panel data were available, as in the gravity model of international trade, a range of heterogeneity types could be included, such as importer, exporter, and time-specific heterogeneity. This estimator offers a range of attractive features for the applied economist, and we anticipate it will become increasingly popular over time.

4.4.1 Estimation With Unbalanced Panel Data

Given the way in which the data are ordered and how the smoothing is conducted, if unbalanced panel data is present, the only modification to the estimator is the construction of the matrix D. Whereas in the balanced setting where D is an $nT \times (n-1)$ matrix, D becomes a $\check{T} \times (n-1)$ matrix where $\check{T} = \sum_{i=1}^{n} T_i$ is the total number of observations in the data set and T_i is the number of time periods that firm i appears in the data.

To understand how D changes when unbalanced panel data is present, define Δ_1 as the $T \times (n-1)$ matrix consisting of all -1 s and $\Delta_j, j \in (2, \ldots, n)$ as the $T \times (n-1)$ matrix that has all entries 0 except for the $j-1$ column, which contains 1 s. Then in the balanced case

$$D_{bal} = \begin{bmatrix} \Delta_1 \\ \Delta_2 \\ \vdots \\ \Delta_n \end{bmatrix}.$$

In the unbalanced setting let e_j be the vector of 1 s and 0 s representing in which of the T time periods individual j appears. Let Γ_j be the $T_j \times T$ matrix that contains 1 s along the main diagonal and 0 s everywhere else. Finally, Γ_1 be the matrix that vertically concatenates all of the e_js. If we assume that the first individual appears T times, then in the unbalanced case we have

$$D_{unbal} = \begin{bmatrix} \Gamma_1 \odot \Delta_1 \\ \Gamma_2 \Delta_2 \\ \vdots \\ r_n \Delta_n \end{bmatrix}.$$

Aside from this specification of D, no other changes are needed to implement the profile estimator of Li et al. (2013) or Lin et al. (2014) in the presence of panel data.

5 Dynamic Panel Estimation

Su and Lu (2013) consider kernel estimation of a dynamic nonparametric panel data model under the fixed effects framework that can be expressed as

$$y_{it} = m(y_{i,t-1}, \mathbf{x}_{it}) + \alpha_i + \varepsilon_{it}.$$

To construct a kernel estimator for this dynamic model, we first eliminate the fixed effect, obtaining

$$\Delta y_{it} = m(y_{i,t-1}, \mathbf{x}_{it}) - m(y_{i,t-2}, \mathbf{x}_{i,t-1}) + \Delta\varepsilon_{it}, \tag{16}$$

where $\Delta y_{it} = y_{it} - y_{i,t-1}$ and $\Delta \varepsilon_{it} = \varepsilon_{it} - \varepsilon_{i,t-1}$. The model in Eq. (16) is identified only up to location, and a further restriction is needed to ensure full identification. Because $\mathrm{E}\,(y_{it}) = \mathrm{E}\,[m(\mathbf{z}_{i,t-1})]$, recentering is a simple way to achieve full identification of the unknown conditional mean. This model can be estimated using additive methods, following the marginal integration approach of Qian and Wang (2012), however, as noted earlier, several complications arise. First, the fact that the two functions are identical is not used by the marginal integration estimator, most likely resulting in a loss of efficiency. Second, the marginal integration estimator requires counterfactual construction, which can be prohibitive for large $N\,T$. Third, the curse of dimensionality is likely to impede reliable estimation of the first-stage function. Given these hurdles, Su and Lu (2013)'s proposed estimator is a simplification of the profile likelihood estimator of Henderson et al. (2008), being computationally easier to implement.

To describe how Su and Lu (2013) construct a dynamic nonparametric panel data estimator, define $\mathbf{z}_{i,t-1} = (y_{i,t-1}, \mathbf{x}_{it})$ and assume that $\mathrm{E}\,[\Delta\varepsilon_{it} | \mathbf{z}_{i,t-2}] = 0$. Then

$$\mathrm{E}(\Delta y_{it} | \mathbf{z}_{i,t-2}) = \mathrm{E}[m(\mathbf{z}_{i,t-1}) | \mathbf{z}_{i,t-2}] - m(\mathbf{z}_{i,t-2}).$$

Setting $\mathbf{z}_{i,t-2} = \mathbf{z}$ and rearranging we have

$$\begin{aligned} m(\mathbf{z}) &= -\mathrm{E}(\Delta y_{it} | \mathbf{z}_{i,t-2} = \mathbf{z}) + \mathrm{E}[m(\mathbf{z}_{i,t-1}) | \mathbf{z}_{i,t-2} = \mathbf{z}] \\ &= -\mathrm{E}(\Delta y_{it} | \mathbf{z}_{i,t-2} = \mathbf{z}) + \int m(\mathbf{v}) f(\mathbf{v} | \mathbf{z}_{i,t-2} = \mathbf{z}) d\mathbf{v}. \end{aligned} \tag{17}$$

The last equality is known as a Fredholm integral equation of the second kind (Kress, 1999). Although a variety of avenues exists to solve integral equations of the second kind, perhaps the most straightforward is through iteration, which is the way Su and Lu (2013) constructed their estimator.

To see how an iterative approach works, assume that $m(\mathbf{z})$ is known. In this case the integral in Eq. (17) could be evaluated by setting $\mathbf{v} = \mathbf{z}_{i,t-1}$ and running local-polynomial least-squares regression with $\mathbf{z}_{i,t-2}$ as the covariates and $m(\mathbf{z}_{i,t-1})$ as the regressand. Obviously, $m(\mathbf{z})$ is unknown and thus an initial consistent estimator is required. (Su and Lu (2013) propose a two-stage least-squares sieve estimator.) The iterations are designed to mitigate the impact that the initial estimator has on the final estimates.

Su and Lu (2013)'s iterative estimation routine is implemented as follows:

1. For a given bandwidth, perform local-polynomial least-squares estimation of $-\Delta y_{it}$ on $\mathbf{z}_{i,t-2}$, evaluating this conditional mean at $\mathbf{z}_{i,t-1}$. Call these estimates $\hat{r}$.
2. Define $\hat{m}_{[0]} = (NT_2)^{-1}\sum_{i=1}^{N}\sum_{t=1}^{T} y_{it}$ where $NT_j = \sum_{i=1}^{N}(T-j)$. Using the same band- width as in Step 1, regress $\hat{m}_{[0]}$ on $\mathbf{z}_{i,t-2}$ using local-polynomial least-squares, evaluating this conditional mean at $\mathbf{z}_{i,t-1}$. Recentering our estimates of $\hat{m}_{[0]}$ by $(NT_1)^{-1}\sum_{i=1}^{N}\sum_{t=2}^{T}\left(y_{it} - \hat{m}_{[0]}(\mathbf{z}_{i,t-1})\right)$, the initial estimator of the unknown conditional mean is

$$\widetilde{m}_{[0]} = \hat{m}_{[0]} + (NT_1)^{-1}\sum_{i=1}^{N}\sum_{t=2}^{T}\left(y_{it} - \hat{m}_{[0]}(\mathbf{z}_{i,t-1})\right).$$

3. Our next step estimator of $m(\mathbf{z}_{i,t-1})$ is

$$\hat{m}_{[1]}(\mathbf{z}_{i,t-1}) = \widetilde{m}_{[1]}(\mathbf{z}_{i,t-1}) + \hat{r}.$$

   Again, for identification purposes, recenter $\hat{m}_{[1]}(z_{i,t-1})$ by $(NT_1)^{-1}\sum_{i=1}^{N}\sum_{t=2}^{T}\left(y_{it} - \hat{m}_{[1]}(\mathbf{z}_{i,t-1})\right)$ to produce $\widetilde{m}_{[1]}(\mathbf{z}_{i,t-1})$..
4. Repeat step 3, which at the ℓth step produces

$$\hat{m}_{[\ell]}(\mathbf{z}_{i,t-1}) = \widetilde{m}_{[\ell-1]}(\mathbf{z}_{i,t-1}) + \hat{r}$$

   Lastly, recenter $\hat{m}_{[\ell]}(\mathbf{z}_{i,t-1})$ to obtain the ℓth step estimator of the unknown conditional mean, $\widetilde{m}_{[\ell]}(\mathbf{z}_{i,t-1})$.

The estimator should be iterated as with the estimators of Wang (2003) and Henderson et al. (2008). Given that the evaluation of the unknown conditional mean does not change, there is no need to recalculate the kernel weights across iterations, potentially resulting in dramatic improvements in computational speed for even moderately sized panels. The previously listed steps are for the estimation of the conditional mean, through application of local-polynomial least-squares estimation. If higher order derivatives from the local-polynomial approach are desired, they can be taken from the corresponding higher order derivatives of the last stage estimator, along with the appropriate derivatives from $\hat{r}$, given that recentering amounts to a location shift. Su and Lu (2013) demonstrate that the limiting distribution of this estimator is normal.

5.1 The Static Setting

Nothing prevents application of the Su and Lu (2013) estimator in the static setting of Eq. (1). In comparison to Henderson et al. (2008)'s iterative estimator,

Su and Lu (2013)'s estimator is less computationally expensive given that it requires only successive local polynomial estimation of an updated quantity. This estimator also avoids performing marginal integration as required by Qian and Wang (2012) for their fixed effects nonparametric panel data estimator.

In the static setting Su and Lu (2013)'s iterative estimation routine is implemented as follows:

1. For a given bandwidth, perform local-polynomial least-squares estimation of $-\Delta y_{it}$ on $\mathbf{x}_{i,t-2}$, evaluating this conditional mean at $\mathbf{x}_{i,t-1}$. Call these estimates $\hat{r}$.
2. Define $\hat{m}_{[0]}=(NT_2)^{-1}\sum_{i=1}^{N}\sum_{t=1}^{T}y_{it}$ Using the same bandwidth as in Step 1, regress $\hat{m}_{[0]}$ on $\mathbf{x}_{i,t-2}$ using local-polynomial least-squares, evaluating this conditional mean at $\mathbf{x}_{i,t-1}$. Recentering our estimates of $\hat{m}_{[0]}$ by $(NT_1)^{-1}$ $\sum_{i=1}^{N}\sum_{t=2}^{T}(y_{it}-\hat{m}_{[0]}(\mathbf{x}_{i,t-1}))$, the initial estimator of the unknown conditional mean
$$\widetilde{m}_{[0]}=\hat{m}_{[0]}+(NT_1)^{-1}\sum_{i=1}^{N}\sum_{t=2}^{T}y_{it}-\hat{m}_{[0]}(\mathbf{x}_{i,t-1}).$$
3. Our next step estimator of $m(\mathbf{x}_{i,t-1})$ is
$$\hat{m}_{[1]}(\mathbf{x}_{i,t-1})=\widetilde{m}_{[1]}(\mathbf{x}_{i,t-1})+\hat{r}.$$
Again, for identification purposes, recenter $\hat{m}_{[1]}(\mathbf{x}_{i,t-1})$ by $(NT_1)^{-1}\sum_{i=1}^{N}$ $\sum_{t=2}^{T}(y_{it}-\hat{m}_{[1]}(\mathbf{x}_{i,t-1}))$ to produce $\widetilde{m}_{[1]}(\mathbf{x}_{i,t-1})$.
4. Repeat step 3, which at the ℓth step produces
$$\hat{m}_{[\ell]}(\mathbf{x}_{i,t-1})=\widetilde{m}_{[\ell-1]}(\mathbf{x}_{i,t-1})+\hat{r}.$$

Lastly, recenter $\hat{m}_{[\ell]}(\mathbf{x}_{i,t-1})$ to construct the ℓth step estimator of the unknown conditional mean, $\hat{m}_{[\ell]}(\mathbf{x}_{i,t-1})$.

Outside of Qian and Wang (2012) and Gao and Li (2013), there are no finite sample comparisons of the range of nonparametric estimators of the static nonparametric panel data model under the fixed effects framework. This would be an interesting avenue to explore for future research to help guide authors toward the most appropriate estimator for this model.

6 Inference

6.1 Poolability

Having access to panel data affords researchers the ability to examine the presence (or lack thereof) of heterogeneity in many interesting dimensions that do not exist when cross-sectional data are present. One of the main tests of homogeneity is that of poolability. Baltagi et al. (1996) proposed one of the first nonparametric tests of poolability. The importance of such a test is that the size and power of a parametric test of poolability (such as a Chow test) could be adversely affected by parametric misspecification of the conditional mean.

Baltagi, Hidalgo, and Li (1996) consider a test of poolability for the model

$$y_{it} = m_t(\mathbf{x}_{it}) + \varepsilon_{it}, \quad i = 1, \ldots, N, \ t = 1, \ldots, T, \tag{18}$$

where $m_t\,(\mathbf{x}_{it})$ is the unknown functional form that can vary over time, $\mathbf{x}_{it}$ is a $1 \times q$ vector of regressors, and ε_{it} is the error term. For the data to be poolable across time, $m_t\,(\mathbf{x}) = m\,(\mathbf{x})\ \forall t$ almost everywhere, with $m\,(\mathbf{x})$ representing the unknown functional form in the pooled model. More specifically, Baltagi et al. (1996) test

$$H_0 : m_t(\mathbf{x}) = m(\mathbf{x}) \forall t$$

almost everywhere versus the alternative that

$$H_1 : m_t(\mathbf{x}) \neq m(\mathbf{x})$$

for some t with positive probability.

Under H_0, E $(\varepsilon_{it}|\mathbf{x}_{it}) = 0$ almost everywhere, where $\varepsilon_{it} = y_{it} - m\,(\mathbf{x}_{it})$. Under H_1, $\hat{\varepsilon}_{it}$ from the pooled model will not converge to ε_{it} and hence E $(\varepsilon|\mathbf{x}) \neq 0$ almost everywhere. Hence, a consistent test for poolability based on E [ε E $(\varepsilon|\mathbf{x})$] is available.

Baltagi et al. (1996) construct the test statistics as

$$\hat{J}_{NT} = \frac{N|h|^2 \hat{I}_{NT}}{\hat{\sigma}_{NT}},$$

where

$$\hat{I}_{NT} = \frac{1}{NT(N-1)|h|} \sum_{i=1}^{N} \sum_{t=1}^{T} \sum_{\substack{j=1 \\ j \neq i}}^{N} K_{it\mathbf{x}_{js}h} \hat{\varepsilon}_{it} \hat{\varepsilon}_{jt} \hat{f}(\mathbf{x}_{it}) \hat{f}(\mathbf{x}_{jt}),$$

and

$$\hat{\sigma}^2_{NT} = \frac{2}{NT(N-1)|h|} \sum_{i=1}^{N} \sum_{t=1}^{T} \sum_{\substack{j=1 \\ j \neq i}}^{N} \hat{\varepsilon}^2_{it} \hat{\varepsilon}^2_{jt} \hat{f}(\mathbf{x}_{it})^2 \hat{f}(\mathbf{x}_{jt})^2 K^2_{it\mathbf{x}_{js}h}$$

with $|h| = h_1 \ldots h_q$. Baltagi et al. (1996) prove that $\hat{J}_{NT}$ has a standard normal distribution under H_0. Although the limiting distribution of $\hat{J}_{NT}$ is available, typically in nonparametric inference it is recommended to use resampling plans (bootstrapping or subsampling) to construct the finite sample distribution. The steps used to construct the wild bootstrap test statistic are as follows:

1. For $i = 1, 2, \ldots N$ and $t = 1, 2, \ldots T$ generate the two-point wild bootstrap error $\varepsilon^*_{it} = \frac{(1-\sqrt{5})}{2}\left(\hat{\varepsilon}_{it} - \bar{\hat{\varepsilon}}\right)$ with probability $p = \frac{(1+\sqrt{5})}{2\sqrt{5}}$ and $u^*_{it} = \frac{(1+\sqrt{5})}{2}$

$(\hat{\varepsilon}_{it} - \overline{\hat{\varepsilon}})$ with probability $1-p$ where $\hat{\varepsilon}_{it} = y_{it} - \hat{m}(\mathbf{x}_{it})$ is the residual from the pooled estimator. Here we are using the common wild bootstrap weights, but Rademacher weights could also be used.

2. Construct the bootstrap left side variable $y_{it}^* = \hat{m}(\mathbf{x}_{it}) + \varepsilon_{it}^*$ for $i = 1, 2, \ldots, N$ and $t = 1, 2, \ldots T$. The resulting sample $\{y_{it}^*, \mathbf{x}_{it}\}$ is the bootstrap sample. Note that these data are generated under the null of a pooled sample. Using the bootstrap sample, estimate $\hat{m}^*(\mathbf{x}_{it})$ via pooled LCLS where y_{it} is replaced by y_{it}^*.
3. Use the bootstrap residuals $\hat{\varepsilon}_{it}^*$ to construct the bootstrap test statistic $\hat{J}_{NT}^*$.
4. Repeat steps 1–3 a large number (B) of times and then construct the sampling distribution of the bootstrapped test statistics. The null of poolability is rejected if $\hat{J}_{NT}$ is greater than the upper α-percentile of the bootstrapped test statistics.

Lavergne (2001) is critical of this test partially because the smoothing parameter used in the pooled model is the same in each period. Further, he disagrees that the density of the regressors, $\hat{f}(\mathbf{x})$, should remain fixed across time. Lavergne (2001) argues that if $\hat{f}(\mathbf{x})$ varies over time it can lead to poor performance of Baltagi et al. (1996)'s test of poolability.

An alternative approach to test poolability is that of Jin and Su (2013). They consider the model

$$y_{it} = m_i(\mathbf{x}_{it}) + \varepsilon_{it}, \quad i = 1, \ldots, N, \ t = 1, \ldots, T,$$

where $m_i(\mathbf{x}_{it})$ is the unknown functional form that can vary over individuals with everything else defined as in Eq. (18). For the data to be poolable across individuals $m_i\ (\mathbf{x}) = m_j\ (\mathbf{x})\ \forall i, j$ almost everywhere, with $m(\mathbf{x})$ representing the unknown functional form in the pooled model. More specifically, the null hypothesis is

$$H_0 : m_i(\mathbf{x}) = m_j(\mathbf{x}) \forall i, j$$

almost everywhere versus the alternative that

$$H_1 : m_i(\mathbf{x}) \neq m_j(\mathbf{x})$$

for some $i \neq j$ with positive probability.

Jin and Su (2013) do not consider a conditional moment based test for poolability as do Baltagi et al. (1996), but rather a weighted integrated squared error statistic, defined as

$$\Gamma_{NT} = \sum_{i=1}^{N-1} \sum_{j=i+1}^{N} \int \left(m_i(\mathbf{x}) - m_j(\mathbf{x})\right)^2 w(\mathbf{x})\, d\mathbf{x}, \tag{19}$$

where $w(\mathbf{x})$ is a user-specified probability density function. Under H_0, $\Gamma_{NT} = 0$, otherwise $\Gamma_{NT} > 0$. Jin and Su (2013) point out that Γ_{NT} cannot distinguish all departures from H_0. Rather, Eq. (19) corresponds to testing

$$\overline{H}_0 : \Delta_m = 0 \text{ versus } \overline{H}_1 : \Delta_m > 0$$

where $\Delta_m = \lim_{N \to \infty} (N(N-1))^{-1} \Gamma_{NT}$. The difference between H_0 and $\overline{H}_0$ is that $\overline{H}_0$ allows for some $i \neq j$, $m_i(\mathbf{x}) \neq m_j(\mathbf{x})$ with probability greater than zero, but the count measure of such pair has to be of smaller order than $N(N-1)$. That is, it can happen that $m_i(\mathbf{x}) \neq m_j(\mathbf{x})$, but these occurrences cannot increase as N increases. This is intuitive because the test of poolability in this case is predicated on increasing the number of cross sections, and as more cross-sections become available, it would seem likely that it will be difficult to rule out that $m_i(\mathbf{x}) \neq m_j(\mathbf{x})$ for every pair (i, j). Jin and Su (2013) show theoretically that under $\overline{H}_1$, the poolability test is consistent as long as $(N(N-1))^{-1} \Gamma_{NT}$ does not shrink too fast to 0.

The statistic in Eq. (19) is calculated under H_1 and requires the user to estimate $m_i(\mathbf{x})$ across all individuals. For example, using local-polynomial least-squares, with $\hat{m}_j(\mathbf{x})$, the Γ_{NT} is estimated by

$$\hat{\Gamma}_{NT} = \sum_{i=1}^{N-1} \sum_{j=i+1}^{N} \int \left(\hat{m}_i(\mathbf{x}) - \hat{m}_j(\mathbf{x})\right)^2 w(\mathbf{x})\, d\mathbf{x}.$$

Jin and Su (2013) show that after appropriate normalization, $\hat{\Gamma}_{NT}$ is normally distributed under reasonable assumptions.[4] A bootstrap approach similar to that of Baltagi et al. (1996) can be deployed to construct the finite sample distribution of the test statistic.

6.1.1 Poolability Through Irrelevant Individual and Time Effects

An informal way to determine whether the data is poolable is to directly smooth over both individual and time and assess the size of the bandwidths on these two variables. It is well known that discrete variables whose bandwidths hit their upper bounds are removed from the smoothing operation. Thus, rather than splitting the data on time (Baltagi et al., 1996) or individual (Jin & Su, 2013), individual and time heterogeneity can be included directly in the set of covariates and the pooled regression model can be estimated. If the bandwidths on either of these variables are at their corresponding upper bounds, then this would signify the ability to pool in that dimension. This approach was advocated by Racine (2008) and would seem to hold promise, though further development of the theoretical properties as they pertain to the data-driven bandwidths is warranted.

We again note that this is informal, but it will reveal poolability in either the individual and/or time dimension. Further, there is no need to construct a test statistic or use resampling plans. The problem facing practitioners will occur

4. Jin and Su (2013)'s theory focuses on the setting where $mi(\mathbf{x})$ is estimated using sieves, but it can be adapted to the kernel setting.

when the estimated bandwidth is close, but not equal, to its upper bound. In that case, a more formal approach would need to be undertaken.

An alternative to the approach of Racine (2008) would be that of Lu and Su (2017), who develop a consistent model selection routine for the fixed effects panel data model. Although their test is developed and studied in a parametric setting, $m(\mathbf{x}) = x\beta$, it can be extended easily to the nonparametric setting that we have described here. Lu and Su (2017)'s selection device entails choosing the estimator from the model that has the lowest leave-one-out cross validation score. For example, if we compare the pooled model against the one-way, individual effects model, we estimate both models omitting a single observation, predict y_{it} for the omitted observation, and repeat this over all nT observations, to calculate the squared prediction error. The model with the lowest squared prediction error is then chosen as the best model. Lu and Su (2017) demonstrate that this approach works remarkably well even in the presence of serial correlation or cross-section dependence and substantially outperforms more common model selection approaches such as AIC or BIC.

6.2 Specification Testing

Lin et al. (2014) provide an integrated squared error statistic to test for correct specification of a panel data model under the fixed effects framework. The null hypothesis is

$$H_0 : \Pr\{m(\mathbf{x}) = \mathbf{x}\beta_0\} = 1,$$

for some $\beta_0 \in \mathbb{R}^q$ against the alternative hypothesis

$$H_0 : \Pr\{m(\mathbf{x}) = \mathbf{x}\beta_0\} < 1,$$

for any $\beta_0 \in \mathbb{R}^q$. Let $\hat{\beta}$ denote the parametric estimator of β_0 (perhaps using within estimation) and $\hat{m}(\mathbf{x})$ the profile least-squares estimator. Then a consistent test for H_0 is based off

$$\int \left(\hat{m}(\mathbf{x}) - \mathbf{x}\hat{\beta}\right)^2 d\mathbf{x}.$$

However, as noted in Lin et al. (2014), this test statistic would possess several nonzero centering terms that, if not removed, would lead to an asymptotic bias. To avoid this Lin et al. (2014) use the approach of Härdle and Mammen (1993) and smooth $\mathbf{x}_{it}\hat{\beta}$. More specifically, estimate $m(\mathbf{x})$ using local-constant least-squares (our earlier discussion focused on local-linear least-squares) as

$$\hat{m}(\mathbf{x}) = \left(i'_{NT} S(\mathbf{x}) i_{NT}\right)^{-1} i'_{NT} S(\mathbf{x}) y \tag{20}$$

where $S(\mathbf{x}) = Q(\mathbf{x})' \mathcal{K}_\mathbf{x} Q(\mathbf{x})$ and $Q(\mathbf{x}) = I_{NT} - D\ (D'\mathcal{K}_\mathbf{x} D)^{-1}\ D'\mathcal{K}_\mathbf{x}$ with $\imath_{NT}$ an $NT \times 1$ vector of ones. Note that we smooth over y in Eq. (20) as $Q(\mathbf{x})$

$D = 0$, which will eliminate the presence of the fixed effects as in Eq. (15). The same smoothing is applied to the parametric estimates to produce

$$\hat{m}_{para}(\mathbf{x}) = \left(i'_{NT}S(\mathbf{x})i_{NT}\right)^{-1} i'_{NT}S(\mathbf{x})\left(\mathbf{x}_{it}\hat{\beta}\right).$$

Let $\hat{\epsilon}_{it} = y_{it} - \mathbf{x}_{it}\hat{\beta}$ (the parametric residuals, free of the fixed effects). Then it holds that $\hat{m}(\mathbf{x}) - \hat{m}_{para}(\mathbf{x}) = \left(i'_{NT}S(\mathbf{x})i_{NT}\right)^{-1} i'_{NT}S(\mathbf{x})\hat{\epsilon}$. Lin et al. (2014) discuss the fact that the presence of the random denominator in $\hat{m}(\mathbf{x}) - \hat{m}_{para}(\mathbf{x})$ will complicate computation of the asymptotic distribution of the integrated squared error test statistic.

Instead, Lin et al. (2014) propose a simpler leave-one-out test-statistic (which omits center terms), given by

$$\hat{I}_{NT} = \frac{1}{N^2|h|}\sum_{i=1}^{N}\sum_{j\neq i}^{N}\sum_{t=1}^{T}\sum_{s=1}^{T}\hat{\tilde{\epsilon}}_{it}\hat{\tilde{\epsilon}}_{js}K_{itjsh}, \tag{21}$$

where $\hat{\tilde{\epsilon}}_{it} = \hat{\epsilon}_{it} - \hat{\epsilon}_{i\cdot}$. An alternative test statistic is proposed by Henderson et al. (2008), however, this test is less appealing because it involves iteration of the estimator of the unknown conditional mean. The test statistic of Lin et al. (2014) requires only kernel weighting of the within residuals from parametric estimation.[5] This simplicity allows Lin et al. (2014) to demonstrate that when $\hat{I}_{NT}$ is appropriately normalized it has an asymptotically normal distribution. They focus on the asymptotic behavior of $\hat{I}_{NT}$ for $N \to \infty$, but the theory can be established if both N and T are increasing.

Kernel-based nonparametric tests commonly display poor finite sample size and power. To remedy this Lin et al. (2014) propose a bootstrap procedure to approximate the distribution of the scaled test statistic $\hat{J}_{NT} = N\sqrt{|h|}I_{NT}/\sqrt{\hat{\sigma}_0^2}$ where

$$\hat{\sigma}_0^2 = \frac{2}{N^2|h|}\sum_{i=1}^{N}\sum_{j\neq i}^{N}\sum_{t=1}^{T}\sum_{s=1}^{T}\hat{\tilde{\epsilon}}_{it}^2\hat{\tilde{\epsilon}}_{js}^2K_{itjsh}^2. \tag{22}$$

Their bootstrap procedure is

1. Estimate the linear panel data model under the fixed effects framework using the within estimator and obtain the residuals $\hat{\epsilon}_{it} = y_{it} - \mathbf{x}_{it}\hat{\beta}$.
2. For $i = 1, 2, \ldots N$ and $t = 1, 2, \ldots, T$ generate the two-point wild bootstrap error $\epsilon_{it}^* = \frac{(1-\sqrt{5})}{2}\left(\hat{\epsilon}_{it} - \bar{\hat{\epsilon}}\right)$ with probability $p = \frac{(1+\sqrt{5})}{2\sqrt{5}}$ and $u_{it}^* = \frac{(1+\sqrt{5})}{2}$

5. This fact can be used to exploit existing software to implement the test. For example, the np package (Hayfield & Racine, 2008) offers a test of consistent model specification in the cross-sectional setting. However, the adept user could simply within transform their data and call npcmstest(), making implementation straightforward.

$(\hat{e}_{it} - \bar{\hat{e}})$ with probability $1 - p$. Then construct $y_{it}^* = \mathbf{x}_{it}\hat{\beta} + \varepsilon_{it}^*$. Call $(y_{it}^*, \mathbf{x}_{it})$ for $i = 1, 2, \ldots, N$ and $t = 1, 2, \ldots, T$ the bootstrap sample.

3. Use the bootstrap sample to estimate β based on the bootstrap sample using the within estimator. Calculate the residuals $\hat{\varepsilon}_{it}^* = y_{it}^* - \mathbf{x}_{it}\hat{\beta}^*$.
4. Compute J_{NT}^*, where J_{NT}^* is obtained from J_{NT} using the residuals $\hat{\tilde{\varepsilon}}_{it}^*$.
5. Repeat steps (2)–(4) a large number (B) of times and reject H_0 if the estimated test statistic $\hat{J}_{NT}$ is greater than the upper α-percentile of the bootstrapped test statistics.

Lin et al. (2014) demonstrate that this bootstrap approach provides an asymptotically valid approximation of the distribution of J_{NT}. Moreover, in the simulations that they conduct, the bootstrap test has correct size in both univariate and bivariate settings and also displays high power.

6.3 A Hausman Test

In addition to testing for poolability of the data, another interesting question that researchers can ask in the presence of panel data is whether the fixed or random effects framework is appropriate. As should be obvious from our earlier discussion, the estimators for Eq. (1) under the fixed or random effects framework take on different forms. Further, if the random effects estimator is applied erroneously, then it is inconsistent. The common approach to testing between these two frameworks is to use the Hausman test (Hausman, 1978). Even with the range of estimators that we have discussed for the fixed effects framework, to our knowledge, only Henderson et al. (2008) describe a nonparametric Hausman test. One of the benefits of using a random effects estimator (Martins-Filho & Yao, 2009, for example), when the random effects framework is true, is that the gains in efficiency relative to a fixed effects estimator, profile least-squares, say, can be substantial. In general, the larger T is or the larger that σ_α is relative to σ_v, the more efficient the random effects estimator is over the fixed effect estimator.

Recall that a Hausman test works by examining the difference between estimators in which one estimator is consistent under both the null and alternative hypotheses, while another estimator is consistent only under the null hypothesis. Formally, under the random effects framework, the null hypothesis is

$$H_0 : \mathrm{E}(\alpha_i | \, \mathbf{x}_{it}) = 0$$

almost everywhere. The alternative hypothesis is

$$H_1 : \mathrm{E}(\alpha_i | \, \mathbf{x}_{it}) \neq 0$$

on a set with positive measure. Henderson et al. (2008) test H_0 based on the sample analogue of $J = \mathrm{E}\,[v_{it}\, \mathrm{E}(v_{it} | \mathbf{x}_{it}) f(\mathbf{x}_{it})]$. Note that $J = 0$ under H_0 and is positive under H_1, which makes this a proper statistic for testing H_0.

Let $\hat{m}(\mathbf{x})$ denote a consistent estimator of $m(\mathbf{x})$ under the fixed effects assumption, profile least-squares for example. Then a consistent estimator of v_{it} is given by $\hat{v}_{it} = y_{it} - \hat{m}(\mathbf{x}_{it})$. A feasible test statistic is given by

$$\hat{J}_{NT} = \frac{1}{NT(NT-1)} \sum_{i=1}^{N} \sum_{t=1}^{T} \underset{\{j,s\} \neq \{i,t\}}{\sum_{j=1}^{N} \sum_{s=1}^{T}} \hat{v}_{it} \hat{v}_{js} K_{itjsh}.$$

It can be shown that $\hat{J}_{NT}$ is a consistent estimator of J. Hence, $\hat{J}_{NT} \xrightarrow{p} 0$ under the null hypothesis, and $\hat{J}_{NT} \xrightarrow{p} C$ if H_0 is false, where $C > 0$ is a positive constant. This test works by assessing if there is any dependence between the residuals and the covariates. Under H_0, the fixed effects estimator is consistent and so the residuals, $\hat{v}_{it}$, should be unrelated to the covariates, $\mathbf{x}_{it}$.

Henderson et al. (2008) suggest a bootstrap procedure to implement this test to approximate the finite sample null distribution of $\hat{J}$. The steps are as follows:

1. Let $\widetilde{v}_i = (\widetilde{v}_{i1}, \ldots, \widetilde{v}_{iT})'$, where $\widetilde{v}_{it} = y_{it} - \widetilde{m}(\mathbf{x}_{it})$ is the residual from a random effects model, and $\widetilde{m}(\mathbf{x})$ is a random effects estimator of $m(\mathbf{x})$. Compute the two-point wild bootstrap errors by $v_i^* = \left\{\left(1-\sqrt{5}\right)/2\right\}\widetilde{v}_i$ with probability $p = \left(1+\sqrt{5}\right)/\left(2\sqrt{5}\right)$ and $v_i^* = \left\{\left(1+\sqrt{5}\right)/2\right\}\widetilde{v}_i$ with probability $1-p$. Generate y_{it}^* via $y_{it}^* = \widetilde{m}(\mathbf{x}_{it}) + v_{it}^*$. Call $\{y_{it}^*, \mathbf{x}_{it}\}_{i=1,\, t=1}^{N,\, T}$ the bootstrap sample. Note here that all residuals for a given individual are scaled by the same point of the two-point wild bootstrap.
2. Use $\{y_{it}^*, \mathbf{x}_{it}\}_{i=1,\, t=1}^{N,\, T}$ to estimate $m(\mathbf{x})$ with a fixed effects estimator and denote the estimate by $\hat{m}^*(\mathbf{x})$. Obtain the bootstrap residuals as $\hat{v}_{it}^* = y_{it}^* - \hat{m}^*(\mathbf{x}_{it})$.[6]
3. The bootstrap test statistic $\hat{J}_{NT}^*$ is obtained as for $\hat{J}_{NT}$ except that $\hat{v}_{it}\left(\hat{v}_{js}\right)$ is replaced by $\hat{v}_{it}^*\left(\hat{v}_{js}^*\right)$ wherever it occurs.
4. Repeat steps (1)–(3) a large number (B) of times and reject if the estimated test statistic $\hat{J}$ is greater than the upper α-percentile of the bootstrapped test statistics.

6.4 Simultaneous Confidence Bounds

Li et al. (2013) provide the maximum absolute deviation between $\hat{m}(\mathbf{x})$ and $m(\mathbf{x})$, allowing for the construction of uniform confidence bounds on the profile least-squares estimator for Eq. (1) under the fixed effects framework. Their theoretical work focuses on the univariate case. Specifically, they establish that

6. Henderson et al. (2008) suggest using a random effects estimator. However, as pointed out in Amini et al. (2012), asymptotically the performance of the test is independent of the estimator used within the bootstrap, but in finite samples the use of the fixed effects estimator leads to improved size.

$$P\left\{(-2\log h)^{1/2}\left(\sup_{x\in[0,1]}\left|\frac{\hat{m}(\mathbf{x})-m(\mathbf{x})-\widehat{\text{Bias}}(\hat{m}(x))}{\sqrt{\hat{\text{Var}}(\hat{m}(x)|\,\mathcal{X})}}\right|-d_n\right)\right\}\rightarrow e^{-2e^{-z}}, \tag{23}$$

where $d_n=(-2\log h)^{1/2}+\frac{1}{(-2\log h)^{1/2}}\log\left(\frac{1}{4\pi v_0}R(K')\right)$, $\widehat{\text{Bias}}(\hat{m}(x))$ is a consistent estimator of the bias of the local-linear profile least-squares estimator, defined as

$$\text{Bias}(\hat{m}(x))=h^2k_2m''(x)/2,$$

$\hat{\text{Var}}(\hat{m}(x)|\,\mathcal{X})$ is a consistent estimator of the bias of the local-linear profile least-squares estimator, defined as

$$\text{Var}(\hat{m}(x)|\,\mathcal{X})=v_0\overline{\sigma}^2(x)/f^2(x)$$

where $k_j=\int u^j\ K(u)du$, $v_j=\int u^j\ K^2(u)du$, $\mathcal{X}=\{x_{it},\ 1\leq i\leq N,\ 1\leq t\leq T\}$, $f(x)=\sum_{t=1}^{T}f_t(x)$ where $f_t(x)$ denotes the density function of x for each time period t, $\overline{\sigma}^2(x)=\sum_{t=1}^{T}\sigma_t^2(x)f_t(x)$, with $\sigma_t^2(x)=\text{E}\left[\widetilde{\varepsilon}_{it}^2|\,x_{it}=x\right]$ with $\widetilde{\varepsilon}_{it}=\varepsilon_{it}-\overline{\varepsilon}_i$ and $R(K)=\int K^2(u)du$.

From Eq. (23), a $(1-\alpha)\times 100\%$ simultaneous confidence bound for $\hat{m}(x)$ is

$$\left(\hat{m}(x)-\widehat{\text{Bias}}(\hat{m}(x)\pm\Delta_{1,\alpha}(x)\right)$$

where

$$\Delta_{1,\alpha}(x)=\left(d_n+(\log 2-\log(-\log(1-\alpha)))(-2\log h)^{1/2}\right)\sqrt{\hat{\text{Var}}(\hat{m}(x)|\,\mathcal{X})}.$$

As with inference, it is expected that a bootstrap approach will perform well in finite samples. To describe the bootstrap proposed by Li et al. (2013) set

$$T=\sup_{x\in[0,1]}\frac{|\hat{m}(x)-m(x)|}{\sqrt{\hat{\text{Var}}(\hat{m}(x)|(\mathcal{X})}}.$$

Denote the upper α-quantile of T as c_α. When c_α and $\hat{\text{Var}}(\hat{m}(x)|\,\mathcal{X})$ are known, the simultaneous confidence bound of $\hat{m}(x)$ would be $\hat{m}(x)\pm c_\alpha\sqrt{\hat{\text{Var}}(\hat{m}(x)|\,\mathcal{X})}$. As these are unknown in practice, they need to be estimated. The bootstrap algorithm is

1. Obtain the residuals from the fixed effects framework model and denote them as $\hat{\varepsilon}_{it}$.
2. For each i and t, compute $\varepsilon_{it}^*=a_{it}\hat{\varepsilon}_{it}$ where a_i are i.i.d. $N(0, 1)$ across i. Generate the bootstrap observations as $y_{it}^*=\hat{m}(x_{it})+\varepsilon_{it}^*$. Call $\{y_{it}^*,x_{it}\}_{i=1,\ t=1}^{N,\ T}$ the bootstrap sample. Note here that all residuals for a given individual are scaled by the same factor.

3. With the bootstrap sample $\{y_{it}^{*}, x_{it}\}_{i=1,t=1}^{N,T}$, use local-linear profile least-squares to obtain the bootstrap estimator of $m(x)$, denoted as $\hat{m}^{*}(x)$.
4. Repeat steps 2 and 3 a large number (B) of times. The estimator $\hat{\text{Var}}^{*}(\hat{m}(x)|\mathcal{X})$ of $\text{Var}(\hat{m}(x)|\mathcal{X})$ is taken as the sample variance of the B estimates of $\hat{m}^{*}(x)$. Compute

$$T_b^{*} = \sup_{x\in[0,1]} \frac{|\hat{m}^{*}(x) - \hat{m}(x)|}{\sqrt{\hat{\text{Var}}(\hat{m}(x)|(\mathcal{X})\ \text{for} b = 1,\ldots,B.}}$$

5. Use the upper α-percentile of $\{T_b^{*}\}_{b=1,\ldots,B}$ to estimate the upper α-quantile c_α of T, call this $\hat{c}_\alpha$ construct the simultaneous confidence bound of $\hat{m}(x)$ as $\hat{m}(x) \pm \hat{c}_\alpha\sqrt{\hat{\text{Var}}^{*}(\hat{m}(x)|\mathcal{X})}$.

The simultaneous confidences bounds, in the univariate setting, can be used to provide a graphical depiction of when to reject a parametric functional form for $m(x)$, offering an alternative to the functional form test of Lin et al. (2014).

7 Conclusions

This chapter has reviewed the recent literature focusing on estimation and inference in nonparametric panel data models under both the random and fixed effects frameworks. A range of estimation techniques were covered. This area is ripe for application across a range of domains. Nonparametric estimation under both fixed and random effects allows the practitioner to explore a wide range of hypotheses of interest, while consistent model specification tests provide a robustness check on less than fully nonparametric approaches. Bandwidth selection remains less studied, but as these methods are more widely embraced, it is likely that a potentially wider range of data-driven approaches will become available. We are optimistic that the interested practitioner can keep abreast of this rapidly expanding field by digesting this chapter and the references herein.

Acknowledgments

Racine would like to gratefully acknowledge support from the Natural Sciences and Engineering Research Council of Canada (NSERC 312840:www.nserc.ca), the Social Sciences and Humanities Research Council of Canada (SSHRC 162544:www.sshrc.ca), and the Shared Hierarchical Academic Research Computing Network (SHARCNET:www.sharcnet.ca).

References

Ai, C., Li, Q., 2008. Semi-parametric and non-parametric methods in panel data models. In: Matyas, L., Sevestra, P. (Eds.), The econometrics of panel data: Fundamentals and recent developments in theory and practice. Springer, pp. 451–478.

Amini, S., Delgado, M.S., Henderson, D.J., Parmeter, C.F., 2012. Fixed vs. random: the Hausman test four decades later. In: Baltgi, B.H., Hill, R.C., Newey, W.K., White, H.L. (Eds.), Advances in econometrics: Essays in honor of Jerry Hausman. In: Vol. 29. Emerald, pp. 479–513.

Baltagi, B.H., 2013. Econometric analysis of panel data, 5th ed. John Wiley & Sons, West Sussex, United Kingdom.

Baltagi, B.H., Hidalgo, J., Li, Q., 1996. A nonparamtric test for poolabilty using panel data. Journal of Econometrics 75, 345–367.

Bishop, K.C., Timmins, C., 2018. Using panel data to easily estimate hedonic demand functions. Journal of the Association of Environmental and Resource Economists 5 (3), 517–543.

Chen, J., Li, D., Gao, J., 2013. Non-and semi-parametric panel data models: A selective review. Monash University Working Paper 18/13.

de Boor, C., 2001. A practical guide to splines. Springer.

Gao, Y., Li, K., 2013. Nonparametric estimation of fixed effects panel data models. Journal of Nonparametric Statistics 25 (3), 679–693.

Härdle, W., Mammen, E., 1993. Comparing nonparamtric versus parametric regression fits. The Annals of Statistics 21, 1926–1947.

Hausman, J.A., 1978. Specification tests in econometrics. Econometrica 46, 1251–1271.

Hausman, J.A., Taylor, W.E., 1981. Panel data and unobservable individual effects. Econometrica 49, 1377–1398.

Hayfield, T., Racine, J.S., 2008. Nonparametric econometrics: the np package. Journal of Statistical Software. 27(5). http://www.jstatsoft.org/v27/i05/.

Henderson, D.J., Carroll, R.J., Li, Q., 2008. Nonparametric estimation and testing of fixed effects panel data model. Journal of Econometrics 144 (2), 257–275.

Henderson, D.J., Parmeter, C.F., 2015. Applied nonparametric econometrics. Cambridge University Press.

Henderson, D.J., Ullah, A., 2005. A nonparametric random effects estimator. Economics Letters 88 (3), 403–407.

Henderson, D.J., Ullah, A., 2014. Nonparametric estimation in a one-way error component model: a Monte Carlo analysis. In: Sengupta, A., Samanta, T., Basu, A. (Eds.), Statistical paradigms: Recent advances and reconciliations. World Scientific Review, pp. 213–237. Chapter 12.

Jin, S., Su, L., 2013. A nonparametric poolability test for panel data models with cross section dependence. Econometric Reviews 32 (4), 469–512.

Kress, R., 1999. Linear integral equations, 2nd ed. Springer-Verlag, New York.

Lavergne, P., 2001. An equality test across nonparametric regressions. Journal of Econometrics 103, 307–344.

Lee, Y., Mukherjee, D., 2014. Nonparametric estimation of the marginal effect in fixed-effect panel data models: An application on the Environmental Kuznets Curve. Unpublished working paper.

Li, C., Liang, Z., 2015. Asymptotics for nonparametric and semiparametric fixed effects panel models. Journal of Econometrics 185 (3), 420–434.

Li, G., Peng, H., Tong, T., 2013. Simultaneous conifdence band for nonparametric fixed effects panel data models. Economics Letters 119 (2), 229–232.

Li, Q., Racine, J.S., 2007. Nonparametric econometrics: Theory and practice. Princeton University Press, Princeton, NJ.

Lin, X., Carroll, R.J., 2000. Nonparametric function estimation for clustered data when the predictor is measured without/with error. Journal of the American Statistical Association 95, 520–534.

Lin, X., Carroll, R.J., 2006. Semiparametric estimation in general repeated measures problems. Journal of the Royal Statistical Society: Series B 68, 68–88.

Lin, Z., Li, Q., Sun, Y., 2014. A consistent nonparametric test of parameteric regression functional form in fixed effects panel data models. Journal of Econometrics 178 (1), 167–179.

Lu, X., Su, L., 2017. Determining individual or time effects in panel data models. Unpublished working paper. .

Ma, S., Racine, J.S., Ullah, A., 2015. Nonparametric estimation of marginal effects in regression-spline random effects models. Technical report working paper 2015-10. McMaster University.

Ma, S., Racine, J.S., Yang, L., 2015. Spline regression in the presence of categorical predictors. Journal of Applied Econometrics 30, 703–717.

Mammen, E., Støve, B., Tjøstheim, D., 2009. Nonparametric additive models for panels of time series. Econometric Theory 25, 442–481.

Martins-Filho, C., Yao, F., 2009. Nonparametric regression estimation with general parametric error covariance. Journal of Multivariate Analysis 100, 309–333.

Masry, E., 1996. Multivariate local polynomial regression for time series: uniform strong consistency and rates. Journal of Time Series Analysis 17, 571–599.

Mundra, K., 2005. Nonparmetric slope estimation for the fixed-effect panel data model. Working paper. Department of Economics, San Diego State University.

Qian, J., Wang, L., 2012. Estimating semiparametric panel data models by marginal integration. Journal of Econometrics 167 (3), 483–493.

Racine, J.S., 2008. Nonparametric econometrics: a primer. Foundations and Trends in Econometrics 3 (1), 1–88.

Rodriguez-Poo, J.M., Soberon, A., 2017. Nonparametric and semiparametric panel data models: recent developments. Journal of Economic Surveys 31 (4), 923–960.

Rucksthul, A.F., Welsh, A.H., Carroll, R.J., 2000. Nonparametric function estimation of the relationship between two repeatedly measured variables. Statistica Sinica 10, 51–71.

Su, L., Ullah, A., 2011. Nonparametric and semiparametric panel econometric models: estimation and testing. In: Giles, D.E.A., Ullah, A. (Eds.), Handbook of empirical economics and finance. Chapman & Hall/CRC, Boca Raton, FL, pp. 455–497.

Su, L., Lu, X., 2013. Nonparametric dynamic panel data models: kernel estimation and specification testing. Journal of Econometrics 176 (1), 112–133.

Su, L., Ullah, A., 2006. Profile likelihood estimation of partially linear panel data models with fixed effects. Economics Letters 92 (1), 75–81.

Su, L., Ullah, A., 2007. More efficient esitmation of nonparametric panel data models with random effects. Economics Letters 96 (3), 375–380.

Sun, Y., Carroll, R.J., Li, D., 2009. Semiparametric estimation of fixed effects panel data varying coefficient models. In: Li, Q., Racine, J.S. (Eds.), Advances in econometrics: Nonparametric econometric methods. Vol. 25. Emerald, pp. 101–130. Chapter 3.

Sun, Y., Zhang, Y.Y., Li, Q., 2015. Nonparametric panel data regression models. In: Baltagi, B.H. (Ed.), The Oxford handbook of panel data. Oxford University Press, pp. 285–324.

Ullah, A., Roy, N., 1998. Nonparametric and semiparametric econometrics of panel data. In: Giles, D.E.A., Ullah, A. (Eds.), Handbook of applied economic statistics. Marcel Dekker, New York, pp. 579–604.

Wang, N., 2003. Marginal nonparametric kernel regression accounting for within-subject correlation. Biometrika 90 (1), 43–52.

Chapter 5

Heterogeneity and Endogeneity in Panel Stochastic Frontier Models

Levent Kutlu*,† and Kien C. Tran‡
*University of Texas at Arlington, Arlington, TX, United States, †Istinye University, İstanbul, Turkey, ‡University of Lethbridge, Lethbridge, AB, Canada

Chapter Outline

1 Introduction

Stochastic frontier literature originated with Aigner, Lovell, and Schmidt (1977) and Meeusen and van den Broeck (1977). Jondrow, Lovell, Materov, and Schmidt (1982) provided a way to estimate technical efficiency. These studies are framed in a cross-sectional framework, however, a panel contains more. As noted by Kumbhakar and Lovell (2003), an immediate implication is that, in a panel data model, we can relax some of the distributional assumptions that we make in cross-sectional models or get efficiency estimates that have more desirable statistical properties such as consistency of efficiency estimates.

Pitt and Lee (1981) and Schmidt and Sickles (1984) are among the first studies that applied fixed and random effects models in which the inefficiency is time-invariant. Panel data models that allow time-varying efficiency, such as Cornwell, Schmidt, and Sickles (1990), Kumbhakar (1990), Battese and Coelli (1992), and Lee and Schmidt (1993), followed those early models. More recently, papers that allow dynamic efficiency have been published, with authors including Ahn, Good, and Sickles (2000), Desli, Ray, and Kumbhakar (2003), Tsionas (2006), Huang and Chen (2009), Assaf, Gillen, and Tsionas (2014), Duygun, Kutlu, and Sickles (2016), and Kutlu (2017). A recent

Panel Data Econometrics. https://doi.org/10.1016/B978-0-12-814367-4.00005-8

development in panel data models is identifying heterogeneity and efficiency separately (Chen, Schmidt, & Wang, 2014; Greene, 2005a, 2005b; Wang and Ho, 2010). In sum, myriad studies about the panel data stochastic frontier concentrate on a variety of aspects of efficiency estimation.

Although the endogeneity issue has been a concern in production models in which the firms are assumed to be fully efficient, e.g., Olley and Pakes (1996), Levinsohn and Petrin (2003), Ackerberg, Caves, and Frazer (2015), the endogeneity issues have been ignored for long time in the stochastic frontier literature and haven't been studied in the papers cited earlier.[1] This is surprising, because it seems that the endogeneity is likely to be a more serious problem in the stochastic frontier models than in the standard production/cost function models as the presence of the one-sided (non-negative) inefficiency term introduces additional complications regarding endogeneity. The standard stochastic frontier models generally assumed this one-sided inefficiency term to be independent from the two-sided error term, but this assumption can be violated easily for a variety of reasons. For example, in the context of health care cost function estimation, Mutter, Greene, Spector, Rosko, and Mukamel (2013) argue that if quality is one of the relevant factors that affects costs, then endogeneity issues occur when the parameter and efficiency estimates obtained from a standard stochastic frontier model that ignores endogeneity are inconsistent. Moreover, omitting the quality variable from the frontier does not solve the inconsistency problem. Besides quality variables, there might be many other endogenous variables in a stochastic frontier model, including input prices and market concentration measures.

The purpose of this chapter is to provide a recent development in panel stochastic frontier models that allows for heterogeneity, endogeneity, or both. Specifically, consistent estimation of the models' parameters as well as observation-specific technical inefficiency is discussed. Section 2 presents the panel stochastic frontier models that allow for heterogeneity under the exogeneity assumptions of regressors. Section 3 discusses the panel stochastic frontier models that allow for endogeneity of regressors under homogeneity assumption. Models that allow for both heterogeneity and endogeneity are presented in Section 4. Section 5 concludes the chapter.

2 Panel Stochastic Frontier Models With Heterogeneity

In this section, we discuss a recent theoretical development of general panel stochastic frontier model that incorporates heterogeneity and time-varying technical inefficiency.[2] Most of the discussion in this section draws heavily on the

1. See Shee and Stefanou (2014) for a stochastic frontier study in the Levinsohn and Petrin (2003) context.

2. See Kutlu and McCarthy (2016) for an empirical study, in the context of airport cost efficiency, illustrating consequences of ignoring heterogeneity.

work of Wang and Ho (2010), Chen et al. (2014), and Kutlu, Tran, and Tsionas (2019). For exposition simplicity, we focus on production functions. The benchmark model for our discussion is given by Wang and Ho (2010):

$$y_{it} = \alpha_i + x_{1it}\beta - u_{it} + v_{it}, \tag{1}$$

$$u_{it} = h_{it}u_i^*, \tag{2}$$

$$h_{it} = f(x_{2it}\varphi_u), \tag{3}$$

$$u_i^* \sim N^+(\mu, \sigma_u^2), \tag{4}$$

$$v_{it} \sim N(0, \sigma_v^2), \tag{5}$$

where y_{it} is the logarithm of the output of the ith panel unit at time t; α_i is a time-invariant unit specific term that captures the firm heterogeneity; $u_{it} \geq 0$ is the one-sided inefficiency term; x_{1it} is a $(1 \times k_1)$ vector of input variables; x_{2it} is $(1 \times k_2)$ vector of environmental variables that effect the inefficiency term; and v_{it} is the conventional two-sided error. For identification purposes, we assume that neither x_{1it} nor x_{2it} contains constant terms (intercepts). This model is fundamentally different from earlier treatments of panel data, such as Pitt and Lee (1981) and Schmidt and Sickles (1984), in which the only source of heterogeneity was the normal error v_{it}, and the inefficiency was time invariant. A simpler and closely related model in which steps 2–5 are replaced by $u_{it} \sim N^+(0, \sigma_u^2)$ has been discussed by Greene (2005a, 2005b), Kumbhakar and Wang (2005), and Chen et al. (2014). In addition, by setting $\alpha_i = \alpha$ in Eq. (1) and the term u_{it} is modeled as in Eq. (2), this model also nests many of the earlier stochastic frontier models including Kumbhakar (1990), Reifschneider and Stevenson (1991), Battese and Coelli (1992), and Caudill and Ford (1993). The main motivation for the frontier in Eq. (1) is to allow for time invariant factors that affect the firm's output but that are beyond the firm's control. These factors are captured in the term α_i which are allowed to be freely correlated with x_{1it} and x_{2it}. Let $v_i = (v_{i1}, \ldots, v_{iT})'$, x_{1i} and x_{2i} are defined similarly. The following assumptions regarding the nature of x_{jit}, $j = 1, 2$ are essential to guarantee the consistency of the parameters and inefficiency estimates:

A.1: $E(v_i | x_{1i}, x_{2i}, \alpha_i) = 0$ for all i.
A.2: $E(u_i^* | x_{1i}, x_{2i}, \alpha_i) = E(u_i^*)$ for all i.
A.3: $E(v_i | u_i^*, \alpha_i) = E(v_i)$ for all i.

Assumption A.1 states that both set of regressors x_{1it} and x_{2it} are strictly exogenous with respect to the two-sided error v_{it}. Assumptions A.2 and A.3 require that u_i^* to be independent of x_{1it} and x_{2it} as well as v_i, respectively. Under A.3, u_{it} still can be correlated with v_{it} if x_{2it} is correlated with v_{it}. Under the above assumptions, Wang and Ho (2010) proposed two different approaches that are based on first difference and within transformations. They show that both approaches yield the same log-likelihood function and, therefore, they are numerically identical. To simplify our discussion, we present only the within transformation approach here. Let $w_{i.} = T^{-1}\sum_{t=1}^{T} w_{it}$, $\overline{w}_{it} = w_{it} - w_{i.}$ and $\widetilde{w}_i = (\overline{w}_{i1}, \ldots, \overline{w}_{iT})'$, then the model after transformation is given by:

$$\widetilde{y}_i = \widetilde{x}_{1i}\beta + \widetilde{v}_i - \widetilde{u}_i, \tag{6}$$

$$\widetilde{v}_i \sim MN(0, \Sigma), \tag{7}$$

$$\widetilde{u}_i = \widetilde{h}_i u_i^*, \tag{8}$$

$$u_i^* \sim N^+\left(\mu, \sigma_u^2\right), \quad i = 1, 2, \ldots, n \tag{9}$$

where $\Sigma = \sigma_v^2\left[I_T - \frac{\tau_T\tau_T'}{T}\right] = \sigma_v^2 M_T$ is a $(T \times T)$ variance-covariance matrix of $\widetilde{v}_i$, with I_T is an identity matrix of dimension T, τ_T is a $(T \times 1)$ vector of 1's, and the definition of M is apparent; $\widetilde{u}_i$ is a $(T \times 1)$ stacked vector of $\overline{u}_{it}$ where $\overline{u}_{it} = u_{it} - u_{i.} = \overline{h}_{it}u_i^*$. From Eqs. (8) and (9), we see that the distribution of u_i* is unaffected by the transformation, making the derivation of the likelihood function possible. Because Σ is an idempotent matrix, it is singular and, therefore, it is not invertible. To resolve this problem, Wang and Ho (2010) suggest using Khatri (1968) singular multivariate normal distribution, which is defined on a $(T - 1)$-dimensional subspace. Thus, the density of the vector $\widetilde{v}_i$ is

$$f(\widetilde{v}_i) = (2\pi)^{-(T-1)/2}\sigma_v^{-(T-1)} \exp\left(-\frac{1}{2}\widetilde{v}_i'\Sigma^-\widetilde{v}_i\right), \tag{10}$$

where Σ^- denotes the generalized inverse of Σ. Given Eq. (10), the marginal likelihood function of the ith panel can be derived based on the joint density of $\widetilde{v}_i$ and $\widetilde{u}_i$, and the marginal likelihood function of the model is given by:

$$\begin{aligned} \ln L = & -\frac{N(T-1)}{2}\left[\ln(2\pi) + \ln\left(\sigma_v^2\right)\right] - \frac{1}{2}\sum_{i=1}^{n}\widetilde{\varepsilon}_i'\Sigma^-\widetilde{\varepsilon}_i + \frac{1}{2}\sum_{i=1}^{n}\left(\frac{\mu_*^2}{\sigma_*^2} - \frac{\mu^2}{\sigma_u^2}\right) \\ & + \sum_{i=1}^{n}\ln\left(\sigma_*\Phi\left(\mu_*/\sigma_*\right)\right) - \sum_{i=1}^{n}\ln\left(\sigma_u\Phi(\mu/\sigma_u)\right), \end{aligned} \tag{11}$$

where $\Phi(.)$ is the cumulative density function of standard normal distribution, and

$$\widetilde{\varepsilon}_i = \widetilde{v}_i - \widetilde{u}_i = \widetilde{y}_i - \widetilde{x}_i\beta, \tag{12}$$

$$\mu_* = \left(\left(\mu/\sigma_u^2\right) - \widetilde{\varepsilon}_i'\Sigma^-\widetilde{h}_i\right) / \left(\widetilde{h}_i'\Sigma^-\widetilde{h}_i + \left(1/\sigma_u^2\right)\right), \tag{13}$$

$$\sigma_*^2 = 1 / \left(\widetilde{h}_i'\Sigma^-\widetilde{h}_i + \left(1/\sigma_u^2\right)\right). \tag{14}$$

Maximizing the marginal log-likelihood function in Eq. (11) with respect to $\theta = (\beta', \varphi_u', \sigma_v^2, \sigma_u^2)'$ provides the within MLE (WMLE). Under assumptions A.1–A.3 and subject to other regularity conditions (which we will not pursue here), the WMLE of θ is consistent and asymptotically normal when $n \to \infty$ with fixed T or $T \to \infty$. The asymptotic variance of the WMLE would be evaluated at the inverse of the information matrix based on ln$L$ in Eq. (11).

It is important to point out that the WMLE solves the incidental parameter problem as discussed in Greene (2005a), because α_i has been eliminated by the within transformation.

After the WMLE estimate of θ is obtained, the main objective of estimating the stochastic frontier model is to compute observational-specific technical inefficiency, $E(u_{it} | \varepsilon_{it})$ evaluated at point estimate $\varepsilon_{it} = \hat{\varepsilon}_{it}$. There are two ways to do this. One way is to adopt the conditional estimator proposed by Jondrow et al. (1982), but this estimator requires the estimation of $\hat{\alpha}_i$ which can be obtained as in Wang and Ho (2010, Eq. (31)). An alternative and simpler way that does not require the estimation of α_i is to compute the conditional estimator of $E(u_{it} | \tilde{\varepsilon}_i)$ evaluated at $\tilde{\varepsilon}_i = \hat{\tilde{\varepsilon}}_i = \tilde{y}_i - \tilde{x}_i \hat{\beta}_{\text{WMLE}}$. This conditional estimator is derived in Wang and Ho (2010) and it is given by:

$$E\left(u_{it} \middle| \hat{\tilde{\varepsilon}}_i\right) = \hat{h}_{it}\left[\hat{\mu}^* + \frac{\hat{\sigma}_* \phi\left(\hat{\mu}_* / \hat{\sigma}_*\right)}{\Phi\left(\hat{\mu}_* / \hat{\sigma}_*\right)}\right], \tag{15}$$

where ^denotes the WMLE and $\phi(.)$ is the probability density function of standard normal distribution.

Chen et al. (2014) consider a simpler model than Wang and Ho (2010) where Eqs. (2)–(5) are replaced by $u_{it} \sim N^+(0, \sigma_u^{\ 2})$, and propose a somewhat different but related approach to solve the heterogeneity and the incidental parameter problems. Their approach also is based on within transformation to eliminate the α_i as in Eq. (6), but the derivation of the log-likelihood function is based on the closed skew normal (CSN) results of Gonzalez-Farlas, Dominguez-Molina, and Gupta (2004). Specifically, they show that, with slightly abuse of notations,

$$\tilde{\varepsilon}_i = (\bar{\varepsilon}_{i1}, \ldots, \bar{\varepsilon}_{iT-1})' \sim CSN_{T-1,T}\left(0_{T-1}, \sigma^2 M_{T-1}, -\frac{\lambda}{\sigma}\begin{bmatrix} I_{T-1} \\ \tau'_{T-1} \end{bmatrix}, 0_T, I_T + \lambda^2 \frac{\tau_T \tau'_T}{T}\right), \tag{16}$$

and

$$\varepsilon_{i.} \sim CSN_{1,T}\left(0, \frac{\sigma^2}{T}, -\frac{\lambda}{T}\tau_T, (1+\lambda^2) I_T - \lambda^2 \frac{\tau_T \tau'_T}{T}\right), \tag{17}$$

where $\sigma^2 = \sigma_v^{\ 2} + \sigma_u^{\ 2}$ and $\lambda = \sigma_u / \sigma_v$. Based on Eqs. (16) and (17), Chen et al. (2014) derived the within and between log-likelihood function, respectively. In fact, under the specification of $u_{it} \sim N^+(0, \sigma_u^{\ 2})$, it is straightforward to show that the derived within log-likelihood function is the same as the within log-likelihood function of Wang and Ho (2010). The main advantage of

Chen et al. (2014) approach is that the between log-likelihood function can be used to obtain the consistent estimation of α_i.

Kutlu et al. (2019) generalize the Wang and Ho (2010) model to allow for time-varying heterogeneity and endogeneity problems (i.e., violation of assumptions A.1–A.3). In their model, they maintain the same specifications in Eqs. (2)–(5), but the specification of Eq. (1) is modified as:

$$y_{it} = x_{3it}\alpha_i + x_{1it}\beta - u_{it} + v_{it}, \tag{18}$$

where x_{3it} is a $(1 \times k_3)$ represents exogenous variables capturing the heterogeneity, variables that are allowed to be freely correlated with x_{1it} and x_{2it}; α_i is a productive unit specific coefficient vector, and other variables are defined as earlier. For identification purposes, it is assumed that x_{3it} and x_{1it} have no elements in common. For example, x_{1it} contains the usual input variables (in case of production) such as capital, labor, and materials; while a potential choice for x_{3it} might be the firms' research and development expenditures or $x_{3it} = (1, t, t^2)'$as in Cornwell et al. (1990). Another interesting choice for x_{3it} would be $x_{3it} = (1, d_{it}, d_{it}{}^2)'$ where d_{it} stands for spatial distance for panel unit i at time t, which might or might not refer to a physical distance. For example, in differentiated products setting, the distance might be an index representing the quality differences of a product relative to a benchmark. Therefore, the heterogeneity can be modeled in a variety of ways.

To solve the heterogeneity and incidental parameter problems, under the assumptions A.1–A.3, Kutlu et al. (2019) use the orthogonal projection transformation to eliminate α_i. To see this, let $y_i = (y_{i1}, y_{2i}, \dots, y_{iT})'$ is a $(T \times 1)$ vector, and other variables x_{1i}, x_{3i}, u_i and v_i are defined similarly. Also let $M_{x_{3i}} = I_T - x_{3i}(x_{3i}'x_{3i})^{-1}x_{3i}'$, $\widetilde{y}_{i.} = M_{x_{3i}}y_{i.}$, $\widetilde{x}_{1i.} = M_{x_{3i}}x_{1i.}$, $\widetilde{v}_{i.} = M_{x_{3i}}v_{i.}$, $\widetilde{u}_{i.} = M_{x_{3i}}u_{i.}$, and $\widetilde{h}_{i.} = M_{x_{3i}}h_{i.}$. By applying this transformation to Eq. (18), the transformed model becomes:

$$\widetilde{y}_i = \widetilde{x}_{1i}\beta - \widetilde{u}_i + \widetilde{v}_i, \tag{19}$$

then it is clear from Eq. (19) that α_i has been eliminated and the derivation of the marginal likelihood function of the ith panel follows similarly to Wang and Ho (2010) which is:

$$\ln L_i = -\frac{1}{2}(T - k_3)\ \ln\left(2\pi\sigma_v^2\right) - \frac{1}{2}\frac{\widetilde{e}_i'\widetilde{e}_i}{\sigma_v^2} + \frac{1}{2}\left(\frac{\widetilde{\mu}_{i*}^2}{\widetilde{\sigma}_{i*}^2} - \frac{\mu^2}{\sigma_u^2}\right) + \ln\left(\frac{\widetilde{\sigma}_{i*}\Phi\left(\frac{\widetilde{\mu}_{i*}}{\widetilde{\sigma}_{i*}}\right)}{\sigma_u\Phi\left(\frac{\mu}{\sigma_u}\right)}\right), \tag{20}$$

where $\widetilde{\mu}_{i*} = \frac{-\sigma_u^2\widetilde{e}_i'\widetilde{h}_i + \mu\sigma_v^2}{\sigma_u^2\widetilde{h}_i'\widetilde{h}_i + \sigma_v^2}$, $\widetilde{\sigma}_{i*}^2 = \frac{\sigma_v^2\sigma_u^2}{\sigma_u^2\widetilde{h}_i'\widetilde{h}_i + \sigma_v^2}$, and $\widetilde{e}_i = \widetilde{y}_i - \widetilde{x}_{1i}\beta$. By maximizing the total log-likelihood function $\mathcal{L} = \sum_{i=1}^n \ln L_i$, they obtain the ML estimates of all the parameters of the model. Under the standard regularity conditions, the ML estimator is consistent for $n \to \infty$ and T_i is fixed.

Another variation of the stochastic panel frontier model discussed previously is the four-component stochastic frontier model that was considered by Colombi, Kumbhakar, Martini, and Vittandini (2014), Kumbhakar, Lien, and Hardaker (2014), and Lai and Kumbhakar (2017, 2018). It is given by:

$$y_{it} = x_{it}'\beta + \alpha_i - \nu_i - u_{it} + v_{it} \tag{21}$$

where α_i is time-invariant heterogeneity, ν_i is time-invariant firm persistent inefficiency, u_{it} is time-varying transient inefficiency, and v_{it} is a symmetric two-sided random error. This is a reasonably general model that nests models of Schmidt and Sickles (1984), Greene (2005a, 2005b), Wang and Ho (2010), and Chen et al. (2014) as special cases.

Kumbhakar et al. (2014) use a three-step approach. In the first step, the standard random effect estimation procedure is used to obtain the estimates of β, and the estimates of the remaining parameters are obtained in the second and third steps using standard MLE. Colombi et al. (2014) take a different approach by applying CSN distributions results similar to Chen et al. (2014) to obtain the log-likelihood function and then maximize it directly to obtain the parameter estimates in one step. Lai and Kumbhakar (2017) extend the model in Eq. (5) to allow for the time-invariant and time-varying determinants of inefficiency to enter the variances of ν_i and u_{it}, respectively; while Lai and Kumbhakar (2018) also allow for x_{it} to be correlated with α_i and ν_i. The estimation procedures for both models use difference and within transformation to first remove the time-invariant components, and then applying CSN distribution results to construct the joint density and the log-likelihood function of the resulting transformation of the composed-error. Finally, the simulated MLE is used to obtain the consistent estimates of all the parameters in the model.

We conclude this section by noting that all the previous discussion assumed the distribution for either u_i* or u_{it} is half-normal or truncated normal; however, other distributions such as exponential (Meeusen & van den Broeck, 1977); the gamma (Greene, 1980a, 1980b, 2003), and the doubly truncated normal (Almanidis, Qian, & Sickles, 2014) also can be used. Therefore, it would be a good idea to test for normal-half-normal distributional assumption of the data in practice. Chen and Wang (2012) proposed one such test that is based on the moment generating function of the assumed distribution. It can be written as:

$$C = \begin{bmatrix} \cos\left(\omega_1 \varepsilon_{it}^*\right) - E\left(\cos\left(\omega_1 \varepsilon_{it}^*\right)\right) \\ \vdots \\ \cos\left(\omega_q \varepsilon_{it}^*\right) - E\left(\cos\left(\omega_q \varepsilon_{it}^*\right)\right) \end{bmatrix}, \tag{22}$$

where $\varepsilon_{it}^* = \varepsilon_{it} - E(\varepsilon_{it})$ is the centered composed error and ω_j is a predetermined constant for $j = 1, \ldots, q$. In practice, setting $q = 1$ would be sufficient for most of the application. The test statistics given in Eq. (22) have a limiting $\chi^2_{(q)}$ distribution.

3 Panel Stochastic Frontier Models With Endogeneity

In this section, we present some developments of standard panel data stochastic frontier models that allow for the regressors x_{1it} and x_{2it} to be correlated with either v_{it} or u_i* or both. Specifically, we focus mainly on the homogenous panel stochastic frontier models. To this end, the benchmark model is given by:

$$y_{it} = \alpha + x_{1it}\beta - u_{it} + v_{it}, \tag{23}$$

$$x_{it} = Z_{it}\gamma + \varepsilon_{it}, \tag{24}$$

$$u_{it} = h_{it}u_i^*, \tag{25}$$

$$h_{it} = f(x_{2it}\varphi_u), \tag{26}$$

$$u_i^* \sim N^+\left(\mu, \sigma_u^2\right), \tag{27}$$

$$v_{it} \sim N\left(0, \sigma_v^2\right), \tag{28}$$

where $x_{it} = (x_{1it}, x_{2it})'$, Z_{it} is a $((k_1 + k_2) \times l)$ matrix of exogeneous instruments $(l \geq k_1 + k_2)$, ε_{it} is a $((k_1 + k_2) \times 1)$ vector of reduced form errors and all other variables are defined in Section 2. Assume that $E(\varepsilon_{it}|Z_{it}, u_i^*) = 0$ and, to facilitate our discussion, it would useful to distinguish different type of endogeneity (i.e., violation of assumptions A.1–A.2 given in previous section). To this end, we provide the following definition.

Definition 1 In the Model (23)–(28), (a) x_{1it} is endogenous of Type I if $E(v_{it}|x_{1it}) \neq 0$, $E(v_{it}|x_{2it}) = 0$, and A.2–A.3 hold; (b) x_{1it} is endogenous of Type II if $E(v_{it}|x_{1it}, x_{2it}) \neq 0$, and A.2–A.3 hold; (c) x_{1it} is endogenous of Type III if $E(v_{it}|x_{1it}, x_{2it}) \neq 0$, and $E(u_{it}|x_{1it}, x_{2it}) \neq E(u_{it})$.

Given this definition, the most common endogeneities that arise in many practical applications are Type I and II. Type II endogeneity implies that v_{it} and u_{it} are correlated, but v_{it} and u_i* are independent. Type III endogeneity provides the most general case, in which x_{1it} and x_{2it} are allowed to be correlated with both v_{it} and u_{it}, and v_{it} and u_i* are not independent.[3]

The Type I endogeneity problem, in which there are no environmental variables, has been analyzed by Kutlu (2010) and Tran and Tsionas (2013). Kutlu (2010) consider the case with no environmental variables, $h_{it} = \exp(-\gamma(t - T))$, while Tran and Tsionas (2013) consider a special case where $u_{it} \sim N^+(0, \sigma_u^2)$. Karakaplan and Kutlu (2017a)[4] introduce endogenous environmental variables in the cross-sectional data framework; Karakaplan and Kutlu (2017b) extend the panel data model of Kutlu (2010) to allow for the endogenous environmental variables to solve Type II endogeneity problem. In the earlier model, Type I and II endogeneities are introduced via the

3. In cross-section context, all three types of endogeneity have been analyzed by Tran and Tsionas (2013) and Amsler, Prokhorov, and Schmidt (2016, 2017).

4. See Karakaplan and Kutlu (2018, 2019) for an application of Karakaplan and Kutlu (2017a).

correlation between v_{it} and e_{it}. For exposition simplicity, we focus on the Type I endogeneity problem because Type II endogeneity can be handled in similar manner.

Kutlu (2010) suggests a one-step control function approach, in which the estimation is done by the direct maximum likelihood method.[5] First, he assumes that:

$$\begin{bmatrix} \varepsilon_{it}^* \\ v_{it} \end{bmatrix} = \begin{bmatrix} \Omega_\varepsilon^{-1/2}\varepsilon_{it} \\ v_{it} \end{bmatrix} \sim \mathbf{N}\left(\begin{bmatrix} 0 \\ 0 \end{bmatrix}, \begin{bmatrix} \mathrm{I}_p & \rho\sigma_v \\ \rho'\sigma_v & \sigma_v^2 \end{bmatrix}\right) \tag{29}$$

where Ω_ε is the variance-covariance matrix of ε_{it}, and ρ is the vector representing the correlation between ε_{it}^* and v_{it}. Next, he applies a Cholesky's decomposition method to the variance-covariance matrix of $(\varepsilon_{it}^{*\prime}, v_{it})'$:

$$\begin{bmatrix} \varepsilon_{it}^* \\ v_{it} \end{bmatrix} = \begin{bmatrix} I_p & 0 \\ \rho'\sigma_v & \sigma_v\sqrt{1-\rho'\rho} \end{bmatrix} \begin{bmatrix} \varepsilon_{it}^* \\ r_{it}^* \end{bmatrix} \tag{30}$$

where $r_{it}^* \sim N(0,1)$, r_{it}^* and ε_{it}^* are independent. Therefore, we have:

$$\begin{aligned} y_{it} &= \alpha + x_{1it}\beta + \varepsilon_{it}\eta + e_{it} \\ \varepsilon_{it} &= x_{it} - Z_{it}\delta \\ e_{it} &= r_{it} - u_{it} \end{aligned} \tag{31}$$

where $\eta = \sigma_r\Omega_e^{-1/2}\rho/\sqrt{1-\rho'\rho}$, $\sigma_r = \sigma_v\sqrt{1-\rho'\rho}$, $r_{it} = \sigma_v(1-\rho'\rho)^{1/2}r_{it}^*$ and $\varepsilon_{it}\eta$ is the bias correction term. The log-likelihood of this model is:

$$\ln L = \ln L_1 + \ln L_2, \tag{32}$$

where

$$\begin{aligned} \ln L_1 \propto \frac{nT}{\sigma_r^2} + \sum_{i=1}^{n}\sum_{t=1}^{T} \ln\Phi\left(-\frac{\lambda}{\sigma_r}(y_{it} - \alpha - x_{it}\beta - \varepsilon_{it}\eta)\right) - \\ \frac{1}{2\sigma_r^2}\sum_{i=1}^{n}\sum_{t=1}^{T}(y_{it} - \alpha - x_{it}\beta - \varepsilon_{it}\eta)^2, \end{aligned} \tag{33}$$

$$\ln L_2 \propto -\frac{nT}{2}\ln(|\Omega_\varepsilon|) - \frac{1}{2}\sum_{i=1}^{n}\sum_{t=1}^{T}\varepsilon_{it}'\Omega_\varepsilon^{-1}\varepsilon_{it}, \tag{34}$$

where $\lambda = \sigma_u/\sigma_v(1-\rho'\rho)^{1/2}$ and $\varepsilon_{it} = x_{it} - Z_{it}\delta$. Under standard conditions, consistent estimation of all the unknown parameters can be obtained by maximizing the log-likelihood function (32). The observation-specific efficiency $E[\exp(-u_{it})|e_{it}, v_{it}]$ can be calculated using the corresponding conventional stochastic frontier formula of Jondrow et al. (1982).

5. The one-step or direct method of Kutlu (2010) is similar to the one used in Kutlu and Sickles (2012) in the Kalman filter setting. These two papers were written concurrently.

Maximizing Eq. (32) is equivalent to maximizing individual terms (33) and (34). Moreover, maximizing Eq. (34) is the same as conducting OLS regression of x_{it} on Z_{it}, so the two-step estimation is also discussed in Kutlu (2010). The main problems with the two-step approach, however, are that it is generally inefficient and, more importantly, the second step standard errors are not correct because the estimation errors from the first-step are not accounted for in the second-step estimation. Consequently, either analytical approaches, such as that of Murphy and Topel (1985), or proper bootstrapping methods need to be used to correct for the standard errors in the second-step.

Tran and Tsionas (2013) propose an alternative estimation strategy under the specification of $u_{it} \sim N^{+}(0, \sigma_u^2)$. Their approach is based on GMM estimation using the likelihood scores of Eqs. (33) and (34) to form the moment conditions. The GMM approach suggested by Tran and Tsionas (2013) is asymptotically similar to the one-step MLE but computationally simpler, and the asymptotic efficiency of the estimator can be obtained in just one iteration, so that the numerical searches can be minimized or avoided.

Karakaplan and Kutlu (2017b) extend the Kutlu (2010) model to also allow for endogenous environmental variables (i.e., Type II endogeneity). Estimation approaches can be carried out similarly as previously discussed with some minor modifications.

In Bayesian inference context, Griffiths and Hajargasht (2016) propose several different but related panel stochastic frontier models that handled all three types of endogeneity problems. First, they consider a model with time-invariant inefficiency, in which the endogeneity is modeled through the correlations between this time-invariant inefficiency and the regressors, using the correlated random effects formulation of Mundlak (1978). Next, they extended the model in two directions. The first extension is along the lines of Colombi et al. (2014), in which they introduce a time-varying inefficiency error into the original model, and the endogeneity is modeled as before. The second extension of the model looks similar to Eqs. (23)–(28), and they consider endogeneity problem of Type III. In all models, Bayesian inference was used to estimate the unknown parameters and inefficiency distributions. Finally, Kutlu (2018) generalizes the distribution-free model of Cornwell et al. (1990) to allow endogeneity in both frontier and environmental variables.

We conclude this section by pointing out that all the approaches discussed previously have the advantage that the endogeneity problem, regardless whether it is Type I or II, can be tested easily using standard F or Wald-type statistics on the joint significance of the coefficient vector η. Other instrumental variable approaches that do not use reduced form equations are possible but presumably more complex, and we have not seen any recent work with such approaches.

4 Panel Stochastic Frontier Models With Both Heterogeneity and Endogeneity

Our discussion in the previous two sections has been confined to panel stochastic frontier models that allow either for heterogeneity with exogenous regressors or endogeneity with homogenous panel. In this section, we consider models that allow for both heterogeneity and endogenous regressors, because these models have important implications in empirical applications.

Little work has been done on panel stochastic frontier models that allow for both heterogeneity and endogenous regressors. Guan, Kumbhakar, Myers, and Lansink (2009) employ an input requirement stochastic frontier model to measure excess capacity in agriculture production for the Dutch crop cash farms. They consider the following model:

$$
\begin{aligned}
k_{it} &= f(y_{it}, x_{it}, w_i; \beta) + e_{it}, \\
e_{it} &= \alpha_i + v_{it} - u_{it}, \\
v_{it} &\sim N\left(0, \sigma_v^2(\omega_{it})\right), \\
u_{it} &\sim N^+\left(0, \sigma_u^2(z_{it})\right),
\end{aligned}
\tag{35}
$$

where k_{it} is the log of capital input; y_{it} is log of output; x_{it} is a vector of log of other inputs; $f(.)$ is known input production function; w_i is a vector of logarithm of exogenous variables that are time-invariant; α_i, v_{it} and u_{it} are defined as before; ω_{it} and z_{it} are exogenous factors that affect the variance of v_{it} and u_{it}, respectively. They also allow for y_{it} and some of the x_{it} to be correlated with the composite error e_{it} (in essence, they consider the Type I endogeneity problem). To obtain consistent estimation of the unknown parameters in the model, Guan et al. (2009) propose a two-stage estimation method that can be described as follows. In the first stage, frontier parameter vector β is estimated using the GMM method based on the moment conditions $E(M_{it}\Delta e_{it}) = 0$, where M_{it} is a vector of exogenous instruments. In the second stage, using the residuals obtained from the first stage as a dependent variable, ML is used on the following auxiliary stochastic frontier equation:

$$
\hat{e}_{it} = w_i\gamma + v_{it} - u_{it}, \tag{36}
$$

to obtain the estimates of the remainder parameter. In a different framework, Orea and Steinbuks (2018) apply a similar methodology when estimating market powers of firms by modeling the distribution of firm conducts by the doubly truncated normal distribution.[6]

Kutlu et al. (2019) propose a general model that allows for time-varying heterogeneity as well as endogeneity of all three types. Their model has been considered in Section 2, which consists of Eqs. (2)–(5) and (18) under the

6. Other related applications of stochastic frontier models with endogenous variables in the market power measurement context include Kutlu and Wang (2018) and Karakaplan and Kutlu (2019).

exogeneity assumptions of all regressors. We revisit their model in this section to discuss the endogeneity problem. To this end, their model with endogenous regressors can be written as:

$$\begin{aligned} y_{it} &= x_{3it}\alpha_i + x_{1it}\beta - u_{it} + v_{it}, \\ x_{it} &= z_{it}\delta + \varepsilon_{it} \\ u_{it} &= h_{it}u_i^*, \\ h_{it} &= f(x_{2it}\varphi_u), \\ u_i^* &\sim N^+\left(\mu, \sigma_u^2\right), \\ v_{it} &\sim N\left(0, \sigma_v^2\right), \end{aligned} \tag{37}$$

where $x_{it} = (x_{1it}, x_{2it})'$, z_{it} is a matrix of exogenous instruments and ε_{it} is a vector of random errors. Generally speaking, this model can be considered to be an extension and a generalization of Greene (2005a, 2005b), Guan et al. (2009), Wang and Ho (2010), and Chen et al. (2014) to allow for various types of endogeneity.

To obtain consistent estimation of the model's parameters, using the same notations as discussed in Section 2, Kutlu et al.(2019) suggest first to eliminate α_i using orthogonal projection transformation matrix $M_{x_{3i}}$, and then apply a Cholesky's decomposition method to the variance-covariance matrix of $(\varepsilon_{it}^{*\prime}, v_{it})'$ where $\varepsilon_{it}^* = \Omega_\varepsilon^{-1/2}\varepsilon_{it}$ (see Eq. (29)) to obtain the bias correction term and the log-likelihood function:

$$\ln L = \ln L_1 + \ln L_2 \tag{38}$$

where

$$\ln L_1 = -\frac{n}{2}(T-k_3)\ln\left(2\pi\sigma_r^2\right) - \frac{1}{2}\sum_{i=1}^{n}\left(\frac{\widetilde{e}_i'\widetilde{e}_i}{\sigma_r^2}\right) + \frac{1}{2}\sum_{i=1}^{n}\left(\frac{\widetilde{\mu}_{i*}^2}{\widetilde{\sigma}_{i*}^2} - \frac{\mu^2}{\sigma_u^2}\right) + \sum_{i=1}^{n}\ln\left(\frac{\widetilde{\sigma}_{i*}\Phi\left(\frac{\widetilde{\mu}_{i*}}{\widetilde{\sigma}_{i*}}\right)}{\sigma_u\Phi\left(\frac{\mu}{\sigma_u}\right)}\right)$$

$$\ln L_2 = -\frac{n}{2}(T-k_3)\ln(|2\pi\Omega_\varepsilon|) + \frac{1}{2}\sum_{i=1}^{n} tr\left(\Omega_\varepsilon^{-1}\widetilde{\varepsilon}_i'\widetilde{\varepsilon}_i\right)$$

where $\sigma_r = \sigma_v\sqrt{1-\rho'\rho}$, $\widetilde{\mu}_i^* = \frac{-\sigma_u^2\widetilde{e}_i'\widetilde{h}_i + \mu\sigma_r^2}{\sigma_u^2\widetilde{h}_i'\widetilde{h}_i + \sigma_r^2}$, $\widetilde{\sigma}_{i*}^2 = \frac{\sigma_r^2\sigma_u^2}{\sigma_u^2\widetilde{h}_i'\widetilde{h}_i + \sigma_r^2}$, $\widetilde{e}_i = \widetilde{y}_i - \widetilde{x}_{1i}\beta - \widetilde{\varepsilon}_i\eta$, $\eta = \sigma_r\Omega_e^{-1/2}\rho/\sqrt{1-\rho'\rho}$ and $\widetilde{\varepsilon}_i = \widetilde{x}_i - \widetilde{z}_i\delta$. Estimates of model's parameters are obtained by maximizing the total log-likelihood of Eq. (38). Under standard regularity conditions, the ML estimator is consistent as $n \to \infty$ with either fixed T or $T \to \infty$.

Kutlu et al. (2019) also extend the model to allow for Type III endogeneity by allowing for x_{it} to be correlated with both v_{it} and u_{it}. To the best of our knowledge, they are the first to consider both heterogeneity and Type III endogeneity in panel stochastic frontier framework. Griffiths and Hajargasht (2016) also consider Type III endogeneity, but they do not allow for heterogeneity in their model. The consistent estimation for this case is more complex and quite involved. It requires a construction of the joint density of $(v_{it}, u_{it}, \varepsilon_{it}')$, which can be achieved using Copula function approach. Detailed discussion about how to use Copula function method to obtain consistent estimation for this case is given in Appendix A of Kutlu et al. (2019). Readers who want to learn more about the use of Copula function method in stochastic frontier models in cross-section context are referred to Tran and Tsionas (2015) and Amsler et al. (2017).

5 Concluding Remarks

This chapter provides discussion about developments of panel stochastic frontier models that allow for heterogeneity, endogeneity, or both. In particular, we focus on the consistent estimation of the parameters of the models as well as the estimation of observation-specific technical inefficiency. We hope that this chapter provides useful guidance for practitioners using panel data to conduct efficiency analyses.

References

Ackerberg, D. A., Caves, K., & Frazer, G., 2015. Identification properties of recent production function estimators. *Econometrica 83*, 2411–2451.

Ahn, S. C., Good, D. H., & Sickles, R. C., 2000. Estimation of long-run inefficiency levels: a dynamic frontier approach. *Econometric Reviews 19*, 461–492.

Aigner, D. J., Lovell, C. A. K., & Schmidt, P., 1977. Formulation and estimation of stochastic frontier production functions. *Journal of Econometrics 6*, 21–37.

Almanidis, P., Qian, J., & Sickles, R., 2014. *Stochastic frontiers with bounded inefficiency. Festschrift in honor of Peter Schmidt: Econometric methods and applications.* Springer Science and Business Media, Berlin.

Amsler, C., Prokhorov, A., & Schmidt, P., 2016. Endogeneity in stochastic frontier models. *Journal of Econometrics 190*, 280–288.

Amsler, C., Prokhorov, A., & Schmidt, P., 2017. Endogenous environmental variables in stochastic frontier models. *Journal of Econometrics 199*, 131–140.

Assaf, A. G., Gillen, D., & Tsionas, E. G., 2014. Understanding relative efficiency among airports: a general dynamic model for distinguishing technical and allocative efficiency. *Transportation Research Part B 70*, 18–34.

Battese, G. E., & Coelli, T. J., 1992. Frontier production functions, technical efficiency and panel data with application to paddy farmers in India. *Journal of Productivity Analysis 3*, 153–169.

Caudill, S. B., & Ford, J., 1993. Biases in frontier estimation due to heteroscedasticity. *Economic Letters 41*, 17–20.

Chen, Y. -Y., Schmidt, P., & Wang, H. -J., 2014. Consistent estimation of the fixed effects stochastic frontier model. *Journal of Econometrics 181*, 65–76.

Chen, Y. -T., & Wang, H. -J., 2012. Centered-residual based moment tests for stochastic frontier models. *Econometric Reviews 31*, 625–653.

Colombi, R., Kumbhakar, S., Martini, G., & Vittandini, G., 2014. Closed-skew normality in stochastic frontiers with individual effects and long/short-run efficiency. *Journal of Productivity Analysis 42*, 123–136.

Cornwell, C., Schmidt, P., & Sickles, R. C., 1990. Production frontiers with cross-sectional and time-series variation in efficiency levels. *Journal of Econometrics 46*, 185–200.

Desli, E., Ray, S. C., & Kumbhakar, S. C., 2003. A dynamic stochastic frontier production model with time-varying efficiency. *Applied Economics Letters 10*, 623–626.

Duygun, M., Kutlu, L., & Sickles, R. C., 2016. Measuring productivity and efficiency: a Kalman filter approach. *Journal of Productivity Analysis 46*, 155–167.

Gonzalez-Farlas, G., Dominguez-Molina, J. A., & Gupta, A. K., 2004. The closed skew normal distribution. In M. Genton (Ed.), *Skew elliptical distributions and their applications: A journey beyond normality*. Chapman and Hall/CRC, Boca Raton, FL (Chapter 2).

Greene, W. H., 1980a. Maximum likelihood estimation of econometric frontier functions. *Journal of Econometrics 3*, 27–56.

Greene, W. H., 1980b. On the estimation of a flexible frontier production model. *Journal of Econometrics 13*, 101–115.

Greene, W. H., 2003. Simulated likelihood estimation of the normal-gamma stochastic frontier function. *Journal of Productivity Analysis 19*, 179–190.

Greene, W. H., 2005a. Fixed and random effects in stochastic frontier models. *Journal of Productivity Analysis 23*, 7–32.

Greene, W. H., 2005b. Reconsidering heterogeneity in panel data estimators of the stochastic frontier model. *Journal of Econometrics 126*, 269–303.

Griffiths, W. E., & Hajargasht, G., 2016. Some models for stochastic frontiers with endogeneity. *Journal of Econometrics*, *190*, 341–348.

Guan, Z., Kumbhakar, S. C., Myers, R. J., & Lansink, A. O., 2009. Measuring excess capital capacity in agricultural production. *American Journal of Agricultural Economics 91*, 765–776.

Huang, T. H., & Chen, Y. H., 2009. A study on long-run inefficiency levels of a panel dynamic cost frontier under the framework of forwardlooking rational expectations. *Journal of Banking & Finance 33*, 842–849.

Jondrow, J., Lovell, C. A. K., Materov, I. S., & Schmidt, P., 1982. On the estimation of technical inefficiency in the stochastic frontier production function model. *Journal of Econometrics 19*, 233–238.

Karakaplan, M. U., & Kutlu, L., 2017a. Handling endogeneity in stochastic frontier analysis. *Economics Bulletin 37*, 889–901.

Karakaplan, M. U., & Kutlu, L., 2017b. Endogeneity in panel stochastic frontier models: an application to the Japanese Cotton Spinning Industry. *Applied Economics 49*, 5935–5939.

Karakaplan, M. U., & Kutlu, L., 2018. School district consolidation policies: endogenous cost inefficiency and saving reversals. forthcoming in *Empirical Economics 56*, 1729–1768.

Karakaplan, M. U., & Kutlu, L., 2019. Estimating market power using a composed error model. *Scottish Journal of Political Economy*, forthcoming.

Khatri, C. G., 1968. Some results for the singular normal multivariate regression models. *Sankhya*, *30*, 267–280.

Kumbhakar, S. C., 1990. Production frontiers, panel data, and timevarying technical inefficiency. *Journal of Econometrics 46*, 201–211.

Kumbhakar, S. C., Lien, G., & Hardaker, J. B., 2014. Technical efficiency in competing panel data models: a study of Norwegian grain farming. *Journal of Productivity Analysis 41*, 321–337.

Kumbhakar, S. C., & Lovell, C. A. K., 2003. *Stochastic frontier analysis*. Cambridge University Press, Cambridge.

Kumbhakar, S. C., & Wang, H. J., 2005. Estimation of growth convergence using a stochastic production frontier approach. *Economics Letters 88*, 300–305.

Kutlu, L., 2010. Battese-Coelli estimator with endogenous regressors. *Economics Letters 109*, 79–81.

Kutlu, L., 2017. A constrained state space approach for estimating firm efficiency. *Economics Letters 152*, 54–56.

Kutlu, L., 2018. A distribution-free stochastic frontier model with endogenous regressors. *Economics Letters 163*, 152–154.

Kutlu, L., & McCarthy, P., 2016. US Airport Governance and Efficiency. *Transportation Research Part E 89*, 117–132.

Kutlu, L., & Sickles, C. R., 2012. Estimation of market power in the presence of firm level inefficiencies. *Journal of Econometrics 168*, 141–155.

Kutlu, L., Tran, K. C., & Tsionas, M. G., 2019. A time-varying true individual effects model with endogenous regressors. *Journal of Econometrics* forthcoming.

Kutlu, L., & Wang, R., 2018. Estimation of cost efficiency without cost data. *Journal of Productivity Analysis 49*, 137–151.

Lai, H. -P., & Kumbhakar, S. C., 2017. *Panel data stochastic frontier model with determinants of persistent and transient inefficiency* Unpublished Manuscript.

Lai, H. -P., & Kumbhakar, S. C., 2018. Endogeneity in panel data stochastic frontier model with determinants of persistent and transient inefficiency. *Economics Letters 162*, 5–9.

Lee, Y. H., & Schmidt, P., 1993. A production frontier model with flexible temporal variation in technical efficiency. In H. Fried, K. Lovell, & S. Schmidt (Eds.), Measuring Productive Efficiency. Oxford, UK. Oxford University Press.

Levinsohn, J., & Petrin, A., 2003. Estimating production functions using inputs to control for unobservables. *Review of Economic Studies 70*, 317–342.

Meeusen, W., & van den Broeck, J., 1977. Efficiency estimation from Cobb–Douglas production functions with composed error. *International Economic Review* (2), 435–444.

Mundlak, Y., 1978. On the pooling of time series and cross-section data. *Econometrica 36*, 69–85.

Murphy, K. M., & Topel, R. H., 1985. Estimation and inference in two-step econometric models. *Journal of Business and Economic Statistics 3*, 370–379.

Mutter, R. L., Greene, W. H., Spector, W., Rosko, M. D., & Mukamel, D. B., 2013. Investigating the impact of endogeneity on inefficiency estimates in the application of stochastic frontier analysis to nursing homes. *Journal of Productivity Analysis 39*, 101–110.

Olley, S., & Pakes, A., 1996. The dynamics of productivity in the telecommunications equipment, industry. *Econometrica 64*, 1263–1295.

Orea, L., & Steinbuks, J., 2018. Estimating market power in homogenous product markets using a composed error model: application to the California electricity market. *Economic Inquiry 56*, 1296–1321.

Pitt, M. M., & Lee, L. F., 1981. The measurement and sources of technical inefficiency in the Indonesian weaving industry. *Journal of Development Economics 9*, 43–64.

Reifschneider, D., & Stevenson, R., 1991. Systematic departures from the frontier: a framework for the analysis of firm inefficiency. *International Economic Review 32*, 715–723.

Schmidt, P., & Sickles, R. C., 1984. Production frontiers and panel data. *Journal of Business and Economic Statistics, 2*, 367–374.

Shee, A., & Stefanou, S. E., 2014. Endogeneity corrected stochastic production frontier and technical efficiency. *American Journal of Agricultural Economics* aau083.

Tran, K. C., & Tsionas, E. G., 2013. GMM estimation of stochastic frontier model with endogenous regressors. *Economics Letters 118*, 233–236.
Tran, K. C., & Tsionas, E. G., 2015. Endogeneity in stochastic frontier models: Copula approach without external instruments. *Economics Letters 133*, 85–88.
Tsionas, E. G., 2006. Inference in dynamic stochastic frontier models. *Journal of Applied Econometrics 21*, 669–676.
Wang, H. J., & Ho, C. W., 2010. Estimating fixed-effect panel stochastic frontier models by model transformation. *Journal of Econometrics 157*, 286–296.

Chapter 6

Bayesian Estimation of Panel Count Data Models: Dynamics, Latent Heterogeneity, Serial Error Correlation, and Nonparametric Structures

Stefanos Dimitrakopoulos
Economics Division, Leeds University Business School, University of Leeds, Leeds, United Kingdom

Chapter Outline

1 Introduction

This chapter deals with short panel count data regression models. In other words, models for which the dependent variable takes nonnegative integer values (e.g., the number of doctor visits) and for which the time span is small but the number of cross-section units (e.g., patients) can be large. Throughout the chapter, we also assume that the panel data sets are balanced with no missing observations.

Panel Data Econometrics. https://doi.org/10.1016/B978-0-12-814367-4.00006-X

As is the case with many classes of models, the regression analysis of event counts constitutes a vast field in econometrics. For this reason, it is almost impossible and also out of the scope of this chapter to cover all the advances in panel count data models. Excellent textbooks that provide a detailed and thorough (but mainly frequentist) introduction to a variety of panel count data models are that of Winkelmann (2008) and Cameron and Trivedi (2013). For a review of such models, refer to Cameron and Trivedi (2014).

In this chapter, we take a Bayesian approach to the analysis of the Poisson model with exponential conditional mean, a well-known panel count data model. We consider various specifications of this model step by step, by first setting up its static version, which we then equip progressively with dynamics, latent heterogeneity, and serial error correlation. Dynamics are introduced in the Poisson model through the inclusion of a one-period lagged dependent variable as an additional explanatory variable in the latent regression. Serial correlation in the idiosyncratic disturbances is captured by a stationary first-order autoregressive process.

The motivation behind such model specifications is that, in many empirical applications of panel count data, a persistent behavior of counts across economic units (individuals or firms) has been observed. That persistence can be attributed to the past experience of economic units that induces a dependence of the current realizations of a count process from past outcomes or to their unobserved time-invariant heterogeneity. The first case is referred to as true state dependence and usually is captured through a lagged dependent variable, whereas the second one is known as spurious state dependence and is often accounted for by a latent random variable (Heckman, 1981a). A third potential source of persistence in panel counts can be attributed to the serial correlation in the idiosyncratic errors.

However, our models suffer from what is known in the panel data econometrics literature as the initial conditions problem. This problem states that in dynamic nonlinear panel data models with latent heterogeneity, the initial observation of the dependent variable for each cross-sectional unit might be endogenous and correlated with latent heterogeneity.

Treating the initial observations as exogenous tends to overestimate the dynamic effects (true state dependence) and leads to biased and inconsistent estimates (Fotouhi, 2005). Econometrics literature provides two main approaches for tackling the initial values problem, both of which model the relationship between unobserved heterogeneity and initial values. The first approach, proposed by Heckman (1981b), approximates the conditional distribution of the endogenous initial observation given the latent heterogeneity and the covariates. However, Heckman's estimation procedure entails a computation burden for obtaining the parameter estimates and estimates of the average effects.[1] Alternatively, Wooldridge (2005) adopts a computationally simpler

1. Arulampalam and Stewart (2009) have proposed a simplified implementation of Heckman's estimator.

method by focusing on the joint distribution of observations after the initial period, conditional on initial observations. As such, Wooldridge (2005) specified the conditional distribution of the unobserved heterogeneity given the initial values and the within-means (over time) of the time-varying covariates (Mundlak, 1978). In our analysis, we use the method of Wooldridge (2005) to address the problem of endogenous initial conditions.

One last issue that remains to be solved is related to the acknowledgement of Wooldridge (2005) that a misspecified latent heterogeneity distribution generally results in inconsistent parameter estimates. Therefore, we let this distribution be unspecified. To this end, we impose a nonparametric structure on it, which is built upon the concept of Dirichlet Process (DP) prior (Ferguson, 1973). This prior has been widely exploited in Bayesian nonparametric modeling and it is a powerful tool for modeling unknown, random distributions. The attractiveness of the DP prior is attributed to its theoretical properties. In this chapter, we offer a brief introduction to this prior. A more detailed description of the Dirichlet process prior is provided, among others, by Navarro, Griffiths, Steyver, and Lee (2006) and Ghosal (2010).

Semiparametric Bayesian Poisson regression models based on DP priors have been considered by Jochmann and Len-Gonzlez (2004) and Zheng (2008). Jochmann and Len-Gonzlez (2004) proposed a Poisson panel data model with multiple semiparametric random effects and parametric stochastic disturbances, whereas Zheng (2008) set up a cross-sectional Poisson model with a semiparametric idiosyncratic error term. However, none of these studies has accounted for the three sources of persistence in panel counts (true state dependence, spurious state dependence, and autocorrelated disturbances) and/or the initial values problem. This is a gap in the Bayesian literature that we attempt to fill.

To estimate our semiparametric Poisson panel models, we develop Markov Chain Monte Carlo (MCMC) algorithms that enable us to sample from the posterior distribution of the parameters of interest. We also show how we can calculate the quantities of average partial effects, because the direct interpretation of the regression coefficient is not possible because of the nonlinear nature of panel count data models. We also display two criteria, the Deviance Information Criterion (DIC) of Spiegelhalter, Best, Carlin, and Van Der Linde (2002) and cross-validation predictive densities that can be used for model comparison. Computer codes for implementing the MCMC methodologies of this chapter also are provided.[2]

The MCMC sampling schemes that we propose rely heavily on two major Bayesian tools, the Gibbs sampling tool and the Metropolis-Hastings tool. Both these MCMC simulation techniques are described briefly in the next section. For a more detailed exposition of the Markov Chain theory behind these tools,

2. These codes can be downloaded from the author's website: https://sites.google.com/site/sdimitrakopoulosweb/publications.

refer to the papers of Chib and Greenberg (1995) and Chib (2001, 2004), as well as to the standard Bayesian textbooks of Robert and Casella (2004) and of Gelman et al. (2013).

The organization of the chapter is as follows. In Section 2 we introduce the reader to the basic tools, while we also describe the main statistical/theoretical properties of the Dirichlet process prior. Sections 3 and 4 present several parametric and semiparametric extensions of the static panel Poisson model, while Section 5 exposes the reader to the MCMC algorithms that were used to estimate the parameters of the proposed model specifications, as well as to the calculation of the average partial effects and the model comparison criteria. Section 6 concludes.

2 Bayesian Preliminaries

2.1 Bayesian Statistics

In order to conduct Bayesian analysis one first has to specify a probability model for the data to be analyzed. Suppose that the observed data ia $\boldsymbol{y} = (y_1, \ldots, y_n)'$ and that $p(\boldsymbol{y}\,|\,\boldsymbol{\theta})$ is the conditional density of $\boldsymbol{y}$ given a k-dimensional vector of unknown parameters $\boldsymbol{\theta} = (\theta_1, \ldots, \theta_k)$. The density $p(\boldsymbol{y}\,|\,\boldsymbol{\theta})$ is known as the likelihood function. After the data model has been selected, we need to define a prior distribution for $\boldsymbol{\theta}$. This distribution, denoted by $p(\boldsymbol{\theta})$, reflects our uncertainty about $\boldsymbol{\theta}$ prior to seeing the data $\boldsymbol{y}$. The goal is to make inference about $\boldsymbol{\theta}$ given the data $\boldsymbol{y}$ (i.e., a posteriori). Therefore, the conditional distribution $p(\boldsymbol{\theta}\,|\,\boldsymbol{y})$, known as the posterior distribution of $\boldsymbol{\theta}$, is of fundamental interest in Bayesian statistics and is obtained by applying the Baye's rule

$$p(\boldsymbol{\theta}|\,\boldsymbol{y}) = \frac{p(\boldsymbol{\theta}) \times p(\boldsymbol{y}|\,\boldsymbol{\theta})}{p(\boldsymbol{y})}, \tag{1}$$

where $p(\boldsymbol{y}) = \int p(\boldsymbol{\theta}) \times p(\boldsymbol{y}\,|\,\boldsymbol{\theta})d\boldsymbol{\theta}$ is the normalizing constant (also known as the marginal likelihood).

Descriptive measures related to the posterior distribution are the posterior mean

$$E(\boldsymbol{\theta}|\,\boldsymbol{y}) = \int_{-\infty}^{+\infty} \boldsymbol{\theta} p(\boldsymbol{\theta}|\,\boldsymbol{y})d\boldsymbol{\theta}, \tag{2}$$

and the posterior variance

$$Var(\boldsymbol{\theta}|\,\boldsymbol{y}) = \int_{-\infty}^{+\infty} (\boldsymbol{\theta} - E(\boldsymbol{\theta}|\,\boldsymbol{y}))^2 p(\boldsymbol{\theta}|\,\boldsymbol{y})d\boldsymbol{\theta}. \tag{3}$$

2.2 Markov Chain Monte Carlo Simulation Methods

Nowadays, Monte Carlo simulation methods based on Markov chains are very popular for sampling from high dimensional nonstandard probability distributions in statistics and econometrics. This algorithm is called Monte Carlo Markov Chain (MCMC). We construct a Markov chain, the limiting distribution of which is the correct posterior distribution from which we want to sample. We start from some arbitrary (but sensible) initial values for the parameters and then the chain proceeds by updating each parameter of the model (or suitably defined groups of parameters) sequentially. After some initial period, which is discarded as burn-in and accounts for the time needed to reach the limit distribution, the samples obtained are taken as samples from the true posterior distribution of the model parameters.

The next two sections describe two particular Markov chains that can be constructed by the Gibbs algorithm and the Metropolis-Hastings algorithm.

2.2.1 The Gibbs Sampler

The Gibbs sampling scheme (see, for example, Chib (2001)) is an MCMC method that allows us to simulate intractable joint posterior distributions by breaking them down to lower dimensional distributions, which are generally easy to sample from.

Suppose that $p(\boldsymbol{\theta}|\mathbf{y})$ has an unknown distribution or one that is extremely difficult to sample from. If we can sample from the conditional distribution of each parameter $\theta_p, p = 1, \ldots, k$, in $\boldsymbol{\theta}$, given $\mathbf{y}$ and all the remaining parameters of $\boldsymbol{\theta}$, denoted by $\boldsymbol{\theta}_{-p} = (\theta_1, \ldots, \theta_{p-1}, \theta_{p+1}, \ldots, \theta_k)$, then we use the Gibbs sampler, In other words, we cannot simulate from the full posterior distribution $p(\boldsymbol{\theta}|\mathbf{y})$, but we can simulate from each of the full conditional distributions $p(\theta_p|\boldsymbol{\theta}_{-p}, \mathbf{y})$. During this procedure, the most updated values for the conditioning parameters are used. The Gibbs sampler works as follows:

1. Define an arbitrary starting value $\boldsymbol{\theta}^{(0)} = (\theta_1^{(0)}, \ldots, \theta_k^{(0)})$ and set $i = 0$.
2. Given $\boldsymbol{\theta}^{(0)} = (\theta_1^{(0)}, \ldots, \theta_k^{(0)})$,
   generate $\theta_1^{(i+1)}$ from $p(\theta_1|\boldsymbol{\theta}_{-1}^{(i)}, \mathbf{y})$.
   generate $\theta_2^{(i+1)}$ from $p(\theta_2|\boldsymbol{\theta}_{-2}^{(i)}, \mathbf{y})$.
   ⋮
   generate $\theta_k^{(i+1)}$ from $p(\theta_k|\boldsymbol{\theta}_{-k}^{(i)}, \mathbf{y})$.
3. Set $i = i + 1$ and go to step 2.

We can save these draws from each iteration of the sampler and use them in order to conduct posterior inference. For example, we might want to calculate posterior means and variances as defined in Eqs. (2)–(3).

2.2.2 The Metropolis-Hastings Algorithm

In many real-life applications the full conditional distributions in the Gibbs sampler are nonstandard. As such, one can instead use the Metropolis-Hastings (M-H) algorithm; see, for example, Chib and Greenberg (1995). It is another MCMC method, which is designed to sample from conditional posterior distributions that do not have closed forms.

The logic behind the M-H method is to generate a proposal (candidate) value from a proposal density (also known as candidate generating density), from which we can easily sample, and then reject or accept this value according to a probability of move.

To be more specific, suppose that the posterior $p(\boldsymbol{\theta}|\boldsymbol{y})$ from which we want to generate a sample, is broken into the Gibbs conditionals $p(\theta_p|\boldsymbol{\theta}_{-p}, \boldsymbol{y})$, $p=1, \ldots, k$, some of which might be unknown distributions. The sampling scheme of the M-H method (to be more specific, a Metropolis-within-Gibbs sampler) is summarized as follows:

1. Initialize $\boldsymbol{\theta}^{(0)}$ and set $i=0$.
2. Given $\boldsymbol{\theta}^{(i)}=(\theta_1^{(i)}, \ldots, \theta_k^{(i)})$ (the current state of the chain), generate a candidate value θ_p^*, based on $\theta_p^{(i)}$, by using the proposal density $q(\theta_p^{(i)}, \theta_p^*)$. The value θ_p^* is accepted as a current value ($\theta_p^{(i+1)}=\theta_p^*$) with probability

$$\alpha\left(\theta_p^{(i)}, \theta_p^*\right)=\min\left(\frac{p\left(\theta_p^*|\boldsymbol{\theta}_{-p}^{(i)}, \boldsymbol{y}\right)\times q\left(\theta_p^*, \theta_p^{(i)}\right)}{p\left(\theta_p^{(i)}|\boldsymbol{\theta}_{-p}^{(i)}, \boldsymbol{y}\right)\times q\left(\theta_p^{(i)}, \theta_p^*\right)}, 1\right).$$

   Otherwise, set $\theta_p^{(i+1)}=\theta_p^{(i)}$. Repeat for $p=1, \ldots, k$.
3. Set $i=i+1$ and go to step 2.

It is not necessary to know the normalizing constant of the target density because this term is canceled from the construction of the acceptance probability. Furthermore, there are many ways to choose the proposal density $q(\theta_p^{(i)}, \theta_p^*)$. Generally, it is a good idea to make this proposal distribution as close to the target distribution (i.e., the full conditional distribution) as possible. For those parameters that have known full conditional distributions, the proposal distribution is taken to be the target distribution and the M-H step is basically a Gibbs step (it is easy to show that the acceptance probability is equal to 1).

In this chapter, we will apply the so-called independence M-H algorithm (Hastings, 1970) according to which the proposed value θ_p^* is independent of the current value $\theta_p^{(i)}$, that is, $q(\theta_p^{(i)}, \theta_p^*)=q_2(\theta_p^*)$.

2.3 Bayesian Nonparametric Models

The term "Bayesian nonparametric models" might seem to be an oxymoron, because in a Bayesian setting, one needs to have some parameters in the model. Perhaps, the most intuitive way to think about these models is as probability models with infinitely many parameters (Bernardo & Smith, 1994), in which case they are directly comparable to the classical (nonBayesian) nonparametric models.

There are a few ways to introduce infinite number of parameters in a model. Some examples of infinite-dimensional models include species sampling models, introduced by Pitman (1996), Pólya trees, introduced by Ferguson (1974) and developed by Lavine (1992, 1994), and Bernstein polynomials. For a more detailed review of Bayesian nonparametric methods, see Müller and Quintana (2004).

The most usual way in the Bayesian semiparametric literature to introduce an infinite number of parameters is to consider some probability measures, which also are considered random quantities. This way, if these measures are defined on an infinite-dimensional probability space (which is the case in most practical applications in econometrics), we end up with an infinite number of parameters. Such probability measures are called Random Probability Measures (RPMs); see, for example, Crauel (2002).

Alternatively, as mentioned by Ferguson (1974), RPMs can be thought of as random variables whose values are probability measures. Being in a Bayesian setting, we need to assign a prior distribution to each of these. The far more widely used prior is the Dirichlet process (DP), introduced by Ferguson (1973) and is described in the next section. Other choices include the normalized inverse-Gaussian process (N-IGP), which was proposed by Lijoi, Mena, and Prünster (2005), and Pólya trees.

2.3.1 The Dirichlet Process and the Dirichlet Process Mixture Model

In this section, we present the Dirichlet Process and its statistical properties. We begin by defining the Dirichlet distribution.

Definition:

Let Z be a n-dimensional continuous random variable $Z = (Z_1, \ldots, Z_n)$ such that $Z_1, Z_2, \ldots, Z_n > 0$ and $\sum_{i=1}^{n} Z_i = 1$. The random variable Z will follow the Dirichlet distribution, denoted by $Dir(\alpha_1, \ldots, \alpha_n)$, with parameters $\alpha_1, \ldots, \alpha_n > 0$, if its density is

$$f_Z(z_1, z_2, \ldots, z_n) = \frac{\Gamma(\alpha_1 + \ldots + \alpha_n)}{\Gamma(\alpha_1)\Gamma(\alpha_2)\ldots\Gamma(\alpha_n)} \prod_{i=1}^{n} z_i^{\alpha_i - 1}, z_1, z_2, \ldots, z_n > 0, \sum_{i=1}^{n} z_i = 1, \tag{4}$$

where Γ is the gamma function.

The Dirichlet distribution is a useful property for random variables defined in the unit simplex. It includes the well-known beta distribution as a special case, for $n = 2$.

Consider, now a probability space $(\Omega, \mathcal{F}, P)$ and a finite measurable partition of Ω, $\{B_1, \ldots, B_l\}$, with each $B_i \in \mathcal{F}$. A random probability distribution G is said to follow a Dirichlet process with parameters a and G_0 if the random vector $(G(B_1), \ldots, (G(B_l))$ is finite-dimensional Dirichlet distributed for all possible partitions; that is, if

$$(G(B_1), \ldots, G(B_l)) \sim Dir(aG_0(B_1), \ldots, aG_0(B_l)), \tag{5}$$

where $G(B_k)$ and $G_0(B_k)$ for $k = 1, \ldots, l$ are the probabilities of the partition B_k under G and G_0, respectively.

The Dirichlet Process prior is denoted as $DP\ (a, G_0)$ and we write $G \sim DP\ (a, G_0)$. The distribution G_0, which is usually a parametric distribution, is called the baseline distribution and it defines the "location" of the DP; it also can be considered our prior best guess about G. The parameter a is called concentration parameter and it is a positive scalar quantity. It determines the strength of our prior belief regarding the stochastic deviation of G from G_0. This interpretation can be seen from the following moment results

$$\forall B \in \mathcal{F}, \mathrm{E}(G(B)) = G_0(B), \mathrm{Var}(G(B)) = \frac{G_0(B)(1 - G_0(B))}{1 + a}. \tag{6}$$

The reason for the success and popularity of the DP as a prior is its nice theoretical and practical properties. The two moments in expression (6) are examples of the former, whereas a few of the latter will be presented later. These practical properties allow for relatively easy simulation of models involving the DP, when combined with MCMC methods.

A property that, in fact, characterizes the DP, is its conjugacy: given a sample $(\theta_1, \theta_2, \ldots, \theta_N)$ from $G \sim \mathrm{DP}(a, G_0)$, the posterior distribution of G is also a DP with parameters $a + N$ and $G_0 + \sum_{i=1}^{n} \delta_{\theta_i}$; namely,

$$G|\theta_1, \theta_2, \ldots, \theta_N \sim \mathrm{DP}\left(a + N, G_0 + \sum_{i=1}^{N} \delta_{\theta_i}\right), \tag{7}$$

where δ_x denotes the Dirac measure giving mass 1 to the value x.

In more practical issues, an important property of the DP is its Pólya-urn representation. Suppose that the sample $(\vartheta_1, \vartheta_2, \ldots, \vartheta_N)$ is simulated from G with $G \sim DP\ (a, G_0)$. Blackwell and MacQueen (1973) showed that, by integrating out G, the joint distribution of these draws can be described by the Pólya-urn process

$$\begin{aligned} p(\vartheta_1, \ldots, \vartheta_N) &= \prod_{i=1}^{N} p(\vartheta_i | \vartheta_1, \ldots, \vartheta_{i-1}) = \int \prod_{i=1}^{N} p(\vartheta_i | \vartheta_1, \ldots, \vartheta_{i-1}, G) p(G | \vartheta_{1:i-1}) dG \\ &= G_0(\vartheta_1) \prod_{i=2}^{N} \left\{ \frac{a}{a + i - 1} G_0(\vartheta_i) + \frac{1}{a + i - 1} \sum_{j=1}^{i-1} \delta_{\vartheta_j}(\vartheta_i) \right\}. \end{aligned} \tag{8}$$

The intuition behind Eq. (8), is rather simple. The first draw ϑ_1 is always sampled from the base measure G_0 (the urn is empty). Each next draw ϑ_i, conditional on the previous values, is either a fresh value from G_0 with probability $a/(a + i - 1)$ or is assigned to an existing value ϑ_j, $j = 1, \ldots, i - 1$ with probability $1/(a + i - 1)$.

According to Eq. (8), the concentration parameter a determines the number of clusters in $(\vartheta_1, \ldots, \vartheta_N)$. For larger values of a, the realizations G are closer to G_0 and the probability that a new ϑ_i is equal to one of the existing values is smaller. For smaller values of a the probability mass of G is concentrated on a few atoms; in this case, we see few unique values in $(\vartheta_1, \ldots, \vartheta_N)$, and realizations of G resemble finite mixture models.

By using the distinct values of ϑ's, denoted by ϑ^*'s, the conditional distribution of ϑ_i given $\vartheta_1, \ldots, \vartheta_{i-1}$ becomes

$$\vartheta_i|\vartheta_1,\ldots,\vartheta_{i-1},G_0 \sim \frac{a}{a+i-1}G_0(\vartheta_i) + \frac{1}{a+i-1}\sum_{m=1}^{M^{(i)}} n_m^{(i)} \delta_{\vartheta_m^{*(i)}}(\vartheta_i), \tag{9}$$

where $(\vartheta_1^{*(i)}, \ldots, \vartheta_{M^{(i)}}^{*(i)})$ are the distinct values in $(\vartheta_1, \vartheta_2, \ldots, \vartheta_{i-1})$. The term $n_m^{(i)}$ represents the number of already drawn values ϑ_l, $l < i$ that are associated with the cluster $\vartheta_m^{*(i)}$, $m = 1, \ldots, M^{(i)}$, where $M^{(i)}$ is the number of clusters in $(\vartheta_1, \vartheta_2, \ldots, \vartheta_{i-1})$ and $\sum_{m=1}^{M^{(i)}} n_m^{(i)} = i - 1$. The probability that ϑ_i is assigned to one of the existing clusters $\vartheta_m^{*(i)}$ is equal to $n_m^{(i)}/(a + i - 1)$.

Furthermore, expressions (8–9) show the exchangeability of the draws, which implies that the conditional distribution of ϑ_i has the same form for any i. To be more specific, because of the exchangeability of the sample $(\vartheta_1, \ldots, \vartheta_N)$, any value ϑ_i, $i = 1, \ldots, N$ can be treated as the last value ϑ_N, so that the prior conditional of ϑ_i given $\boldsymbol{\vartheta}_{-i}$ is given by

$$\vartheta_i|\boldsymbol{\vartheta}_{-i},G_0 \sim \frac{a}{a+N-1}G_0(\vartheta_i) + \frac{1}{a+N-1}\sum_{m=1}^{M^{(i)}} n_m^{(i)} \delta_{\vartheta_m^{*(i)}}(\vartheta_{-i}), \tag{10}$$

where $\boldsymbol{\vartheta}_{-i}$ denotes the vector of the random parameters $\boldsymbol{\vartheta}$ with ϑ_i removed, that is, $\boldsymbol{\vartheta}_{-i} = (\vartheta_1, \ldots, \vartheta_{i-1}, \vartheta_{i+1}, \ldots, \vartheta_N)'$. As a result, one can easily sample from a DP using the Pólya-urn representation in expression (10), which forms the basis for the posterior computation of DP models. This general representation also is used in the posterior analysis of this chapter.

Various techniques have been developed to fit models that include the DP. One such method is the Pólya-urn Gibbs sampling, which is based on the updated version of the Pólya-urn scheme of expression (10); see Escobar and West (1995) and MacEachern and Müller (1998). These methods are called marginal methods, because the DP is integrated out. In this way, we do not need to generate samples directly from the infinite dimensional G.

Another important property of the DP is that it can be represented, using what it is called the stick-breaking representation (Sethuraman, 1994; Sethuraman & Tiwari, 1982): If $G \sim \mathrm{DP}(a, G_0)$, then

$$\begin{aligned} G(\cdot) &= \sum_{h=1}^{\infty} w_h \delta_{\theta_h^{**}}(\cdot), \text{ where } \theta_h^{**} \overset{iid}{\sim} G_0, \ w_h \\ &= V_h \prod_{j<h} (1 - V_j), \text{ where } V_h \overset{iid}{\sim} \mathrm{Be}(1, a) \end{aligned} \tag{11}$$

Expression (11) verifies the infinite dimension of G, because G can be considered to be an infinite weighted average of point masses $\delta_{\theta_h^{**}}$, where the atoms $\{\vartheta_h^{**}\}_{h=1}^{\infty}$ are drawn from the baseline distribution G_0, while the sequence

$\{V_h\}_{h=1}^{\infty}$ forms a collection of independent and identically distributed (*iid*) random variables that follow the Beta distribution.[3]

The term "stick-breaking process" arises because of the way the random weights $\{w_h\}_{h=1}^{\infty}$ are constructed. Imagine that we break a unit length stick infinitely many times. Let the first broken piece have length V_1 and that it is assigned to the atom ϑ_1^{**}. Then, the proportion left to be allocated to the remaining atoms is $1-V_1$. A proportion V_2 of $1-V_1$ is broken off and is hence assigned to ϑ_2^{**}, leaving a remainder $(1-V_1)(1-V_2)$ and so on.

Another implication of expression (11) is that any realization of the DP is, with probability 1, a discrete distribution. This discreteness creates ties in the sample $(\vartheta_1, \ldots, \vartheta_N)$, a result that is verified by expressions (8)–(10), and allows for clustering the values of a random distribution following a DP. Depending on the magnitude of a, the population distribution G can either mimic the baseline distribution or a finite mixture model with few atoms.

It is also important to note that G_0 usually is taken to be a continuous distribution. This is in order to guarantee that all clusters will be different, and therefore all ties in the sample are caused only by the clustering behavior of the DP, and not by having matching draws from G_0, if it were discrete.

In cases of continuous data, and in order to overcome the discreteness of the realizations of the DP, the use of mixtures of DPs has been proposed by Lo (1984). The idea is to assume that some continuous data $y_1, \ldots, y_N$ follow a distribution $f(y_i \mid \theta_i, \lambda)$, where (some of) the parameters (in this case, θ_i) follow a distribution $G \sim DP$. This popular model is called the Dirichlet process mixture (DPM) model and its general form is

$$\begin{aligned} Y_i &\sim f(Y_i; \boldsymbol{\theta}_i, \boldsymbol{\zeta}),\ i=1,2,\ldots,n \\ \theta_i &\overset{iid}{\sim} G \\ G &\sim \mathrm{DP}(M, G_0(\psi)) \\ M \sim h_1(M), &\boldsymbol{\zeta} \sim h_2(\boldsymbol{\zeta}), \psi \sim h_3(\psi) \end{aligned} \tag{12}$$

where $\boldsymbol{\zeta}$ are any other parameters in the likelihood f not modeled using the DP, $\boldsymbol{\psi}$ are any parameters in G_0, and h_1, h_2, h_3 are suitable prior distributions.

Notice that the distribution of each Y_i is given by convolving f with $G \sim$ DP:

$$f(Y_i; \boldsymbol{\zeta}) = \int f(Y_i; \boldsymbol{\theta}, \boldsymbol{\zeta}) dG(\boldsymbol{\theta}_i), \text{ where } G \sim DP(M, G_0(\psi))$$

and this, together with the discrete nature of the realizations of the DP, will lead to an infinite mixture model for Y_i (Antoniak, 1974).

3. Notationally, ϑ_h^{**} represents the h-th of the atoms in the stick-breaking representation and ϑ_m^{**} represents the m-th of the clusters in the sample of N individuals.

3 Parametric Panel Count Data Regression Models

3.1 The Static Poisson Model

We start our analysis with the Poisson model that does not control for dynamics, latent heterogeneity, or autocorrelated errors.

Suppose that y_{it} is a nonnegative integer-valued observed outcome for individual $i = 1, \ldots, N$ at time $t = 1, \ldots, T$, which is Poisson distributed with probability mass function

$$f(y_{it}; \lambda_{it}) = \frac{\lambda_{it}^{y_{it}} \exp(-\lambda_{it})}{y_{it}!}, \tag{13}$$

where λ_{it} is the mean parameter (also known as the intensity or rate parameter). We denote the Poisson model by $Poisson(\lambda_{it})$.

For the Poisson distribution it holds $E(y_{it};\ \lambda_{it}) = V\ (y_{it};\ \lambda_{it}) = \lambda_{it}$. In other words, the conditional mean $E(y_{it};\ \lambda_{it})$ is equal to the conditional variance $E(y_{it};\ \lambda_{it})$, which are both equal to the mean parameter λ_{it}. This property of the Poisson distribution is known as equidispersion and often is violated in real-life applications. Alternative count panel data models can be used to overcome this type of problem (e.g., the negative Binomial model). However, because the scope of this chapter is the Bayesian estimation of count panel data regression models, we focus on the Poisson model, which is the simplest of all.

In regression analysis, y_{it} is allowed to be determined by a set of covariates $\mathbf{x}it = (x1,it, \ldots, xk,it)'$. The Poisson regression model parameterizes the mean parameter as

$$\lambda_{it} = \exp\left(\mathbf{x}'_{it}\boldsymbol{\beta}\right), \tag{14}$$

or

$$\lambda_{it} = \exp\left(\mathbf{x}'_{it}\boldsymbol{\beta} + \epsilon_{it}\right), \quad \epsilon_{it} \overset{iid}{\sim} N\left(0, \sigma_{\epsilon}^2\right), \tag{15}$$

where the idiosyncratic error term ϵ_{it} follows a normal distribution with mean zero and variance σ_{ϵ}^2. Also, ϵ_{it} is assumed to be uncorrelated with the regressors such that $E(\epsilon_{it};\ x_{i1}, \ldots, x_{iT}) = 0,\ \forall t,\ t = 1, \ldots, T$.

Equations (14)–(15), are called exponential mean functions and guarantee that λ_{it} is strictly positive. Throughout the chapter we consider only models with exponential conditional mean.

The Poisson model with exponential mean function also is known as the log-linear model because the logarithm of the conditional mean $E(y_{it}; \mathbf{x}_{it})$ is linear in the parameters. For example, using Eq. (14), we have that log log $E(y_{it}; \mathrm{x}_{it}) = \mathbf{x}'_{it}\boldsymbol{\beta}$.

3.2 Extension I: The Dynamic Poisson Model

A more realistic approach would allow the current value of the observed outcome y_{it} to depend on past realizations $y_{i,t-k}$, $k > 0$. The literature on count panel models has proposed a variety of dynamic specifications (Blundell, Griffith, & Windmeijer, 2002; Crepon & Duguet, 1997; Zeger & Qaqish, 1988). An extensive review of various dynamic models for count panel data is given in Chapters 7 and 9 of the textbook by Cameron and Trivedi (2013).

In this chapter we model dynamics by considering the exponential feedback model (EFM).

For the case of a single one-period lagged dependent variable ($k = 1$), the EFM is defined as

$$\lambda_{it} = \exp\left(\mathbf{x}_{it}'\boldsymbol{\beta} + \gamma y_{it-1}\right), \tag{16}$$

or

$$\lambda_{it} = \exp\left(\mathbf{x}_{it}'\boldsymbol{\beta} + \gamma y_{it-1} + \epsilon_{it}\right), \quad \epsilon_{it} \overset{iid}{\sim} N\left(0, \sigma_\epsilon^2\right). \tag{17}$$

Equations (16)–(17), introduce autoregressive dependence via the exponential mean function, where the current realization of the count y_{it} depends on its previous realization y_{it-1} and the coefficient γ measures the strength of true state dependence.

Furthermore, these equations, as they stand, suffer from a serious problem. It is easy to see that, for example, the conditional mean in Eq. (16) becomes explosive if $\gamma > 0$ because $y_{it-1} \geq 0$. This problem is rectified by replacing y_{it-1} by the logarithm of y_{it-1}, $\ln y_{it-1}$. In this case, Eq. (16) for example, becomes $exp(\mathbf{x}_{it}'\boldsymbol{\beta})y_{it-1}^{\gamma}$, which entails that $\lambda_{it} = 0$ for $y_{it-1} = 0$. As such, we adopt a strictly positive transformation when $y_{it-1} = 0$. In particular, the zero values of y_{it-1} are rescaled to a constant c according to the rule $y_{it-1}^{*} = \max(y_{it-1}, c)$, $c \in (0, 1)$. Often the constant c is set to be equal to 0.5. See, also, Zeger and Qaqish (1988). Similar analysis holds for Eq. (17).

Taking into account these considerations, Eqs. (16)–(17), obtain the following form

$$\lambda_{it} = \exp\left(\mathbf{x}_{it}'\boldsymbol{\beta} + \gamma \ln y_{it-1}^{*}\right), \tag{18}$$

or

$$\lambda_{it} = \exp\left(\mathbf{x}_{it}'\boldsymbol{\beta} + \gamma \ln y_{it-1}^{*} + \epsilon_{it}\right), \quad \epsilon_{it} \overset{iid}{\sim} N\left(0, \sigma_\epsilon^2\right), \tag{19}$$

respectively.

3.3 Extension II: The Dynamic Poisson Model With Latent Heterogeneity

The Poisson models of previous sections partially account for unobserved heterogeneity, because the Poisson mean varies across i (and t). Yet, there might still be latent heterogeneity, which cannot be explained by the previous models. This unexplained heterogeneity can be captured, though, by adding the random effect term φ_i in the conditional mean function as follows

$$\lambda_{it} = \exp\left(\mathbf{x}_{it}'\boldsymbol{\beta} + \gamma \ \ln y_{it-1}^{*} + \varphi_i\right), \tag{20}$$

or

$$\lambda_{it} = \exp\left(\mathbf{x}_{it}'\boldsymbol{\beta} + \gamma \ \ln y_{it-1}^{*} + \varphi_i + \epsilon_{it}\right), \ \ \epsilon_{it} \overset{iid}{\sim} N\left(0, \sigma_\epsilon^2\right), \tag{21}$$

with φ_i being normally distributed, $\varphi_i \overset{iid}{\sim} N\left(\mu_\varphi, \sigma_\varphi^2\right)$. The nonzero mean μ_ϕ excludes the presence of a constant term from the covariate vector $\mathbf{x}_{it}$ for identification reasons. The random effect component φ_i captures spurious state dependence.

The Poisson model with exponential conditional mean given by Eq. (20), but without the lagged component (dynamics), has been considered, in a Bayesian framework, by Chib, Greenberg, and Winkelmann (1998), Jochmann and Len-Gonzlez (2004), Zheng (2008), and Mukherji, Roychoudhury, Ghosh, and Brown (2016).

The Poisson distribution in Eq. (13), and the exponential mean function in Eq. (20), can be regarded as a Poisson-lognormal model as the heterogeneity term $z_i = exp(\varphi_i)$ is lognormal with mean one.

To tackle the initial values problem that we mentioned in the Introduction we need to make some additional assumptions about the relationship between the initial conditions and the random effects. We follow the approach of Wooldridge (2005) and model ϕ_i in Eqs. (20)–(21), as follows:

$$\varphi_i = h_{i1} \ \ln y_{i0}^{*} + \overline{\mathbf{x}}'_i \mathbf{h}_{i2} + u_i, \ \ i = 1, \ldots, N. \tag{22}$$

As before, if the first available count in the sample for individual i, y_{i0}, is zero, it is rescaled to a constant c, that is, $y_{i0}^{*} = \ max\,(y_{i0}, c)$, $c \in (0, 1)$. Also, $\overline{\mathbf{x}}_i$ is the time average of $\mathbf{x}_{it}$ and u_i is a stochastic disturbance, which is assumed to be uncorrelated with y_{i0} and $\overline{\mathbf{x}}_i$. For identification reasons, time-constant regressors that might be included in $\mathbf{x}_{it}$ should be excluded from $\overline{\mathbf{x}}_i$. The slope parameters h_{i1} and $\mathbf{h}_{i2}$ in Eq. (22), are heterogeneous because they are allowed to change across i. This is a better way to capture cross-sectional heterogeneity.

It is usually assumed that the error term u_i of the auxiliary regression is normal, that is,

$$u_i | \mu_u, \sigma_u^2 \overset{iid}{\sim} N\left(\mu_u, \sigma_u^2\right), \tag{23}$$

where μ_u and σ_u^2 are the mean and variance of u_i, respectively.

3.4 Extension III: The Dynamic Poisson Model With Latent Heterogeneity and Serial Error Correlation

So far, the idiosyncratic error terms ϵ_{it} were iid distributed. One can relax this assumption and assume that the error terms are independently distributed over i

but are serially correlated, having a first-order stationary autoregressive structure

$$\epsilon_{it} = \rho\epsilon_{it-1} + v_{it}, \quad -1 < \rho < 1, v_{it} \overset{iid}{\sim} N\left(0, \sigma_v^2\right). \tag{24}$$

The random variables v_{it} are independently and identically normally distributed across all i and t with mean zero and variance σ_v^2. We assume that v_{it} and ϕ_i are mutually independent.

4 Semiparametric Panel Count Data Regression Models

As we mentioned, the error terms u_i usually belongs to some parametric family of distributions; see, for example, expression (23). However, to ensure that our conclusions about persistence are robust to various forms of unobserved heterogeneity, the unconditional distribution of u_i is modeled nonparametrically. In particular, we assume that u_i follows the Dirichlet process mixture (DPM) model, which is defined as

$$\begin{aligned}
&u_i|\mu_i, \sigma_i^2 \overset{iid}{\sim} N\left(\mu_i, \sigma_i^2\right), \\
&\begin{pmatrix}\mu_i \\ \sigma_i^2\end{pmatrix}|G \overset{iid}{\sim} G, \qquad G|a, \\
&G_0 \overset{iid}{\sim} DP(a, G_0), \\
&G_0\left(\mu_i, \sigma_i^2\right) \equiv N\left(\mu_i; \mu_0, \tau_0\sigma_i^2\right)\mathcal{IG}\left(\sigma_i^2; \frac{e_0}{2}, \frac{f0}{2}\right), \\
&a \overset{iid}{\sim} \mathcal{G}\left(\underline{c, d}\right).
\end{aligned} \tag{25}$$

Conditional on the mean μ_i and variance σ_i^2, the u_i are independent and normally distributed. The parameters μ_i and σ_i^2 are generated from an unknown distribution G on which the Dirichlet process (DP) prior is imposed. The DP prior is defined by the prior baseline distribution G_0, which is a conjugate normal-inverse gamma distribution, and a nonnegative concentration parameter a that follows a gamma prior. Using the stick breaking representation of Sethuraman and Tiwari (1982) and Sethuraman (1994)—see also Eq. (11)—it follows that the DPM model is equivalent to an infinite mixture model; namely,

$$u_i|f_N \sim \sum_{h=1}^{\infty} w_h f_N\left(\cdot \mid \mu_h^*, \sigma_h^{2*}\right), \tag{26}$$

where $f_N(\cdot|\mu_h^*, \sigma_h^{2*})$ is the Gaussian density with mean μ_h^* and variance σ_h^{2*}. The mixture parameters (atoms), (μ_h^*, σ_h^{2*}), have the same normal-inverse gamma prior as the parameters (μ_i, σ_i^2). The random weights w_h are constructed by the process $w_h = V_h\prod_{k=1}^{h-1}(1 - V_k)$, where the sequence $\{V_h\}_{h=1}^{\infty}$ is a collection of beta distributed random variables, that is, $V_h \overset{iid}{\sim} Beta(1, a)$, where a is the concentration parameter.

An implication of expression (26) is the discreteness of the realizations from the DP. Therefore, there will be ties in the parameters μ_i and σ_i^2. Because of the discreteness of the DP, the countably infinite mixture of normal densities reduces to a finite mixture distribution with an unknown (random) number of components.

A nonparametric structure in the form of a DPM model can also be assigned to the error term ϵ_{it} in Eq. (21), or to the error term v_{it} in Eq. (24). In addition, the DPM model can be imposed on the composite error term $e_{it} = u_i + \epsilon_{it}$ that follows from Eqs. (21)–(22) or on the composite error term $r_{it} = u_i + v_{it}$ that follows from Eqs. (22) and (24). In any case, these semiparametric versions of the Poisson model are possible as long as there is some reasonable economic justification. In this chapter we consider exclusively the case where the DPM model is used for the construction of the semiparametric structure of the random effect φ_i.

5 Prior-Posterior Analysis

5.1 The Models of Interest

Based on the various extensions of the static Poisson model that were presented in the two previous sections, we estimate the following three specifications.

Model 1

$$\begin{aligned} & y_{it}|\lambda_{it} \sim Poisson(\lambda_{it}), \\ & \lambda_{it} = \exp\left(\mathbf{x}_{it}'\boldsymbol{\beta} + \gamma \ \ln y_{it-1}^* + \varphi_i + \epsilon_{it}\right), \\ & \epsilon_{it} = \rho\epsilon_{it-1} + v_{it}, \ -1 < \rho < 1, \ v_{it} \overset{iid}{\sim} N\left(0, \sigma_v^2\right), \\ & \varphi_i = h_{i1} \ \ln y_{i0}^* + \overline{\mathbf{x}'}_i \mathbf{h}_{i2} + u_i, \end{aligned} \tag{27}$$

where u_i follows the DPM model of expression (25).

Model 2

$$\begin{aligned} & y_{it}|\lambda_{it} \sim Poisson(\lambda_{it}), \\ & \lambda_{it} = \exp\left(\mathbf{x}_{it}'\boldsymbol{\beta} + \gamma \ \ln y_{it-1}^* + \varphi_i + \epsilon_{it}\right), \ \epsilon_{it} \overset{iid}{\sim} N\left(0, \sigma_\epsilon^2\right), \\ & \varphi_i = h_{i1} \ \ln y_{i0}^* + \overline{\mathbf{x}'}_i \mathbf{h}_{i2} + u_i, \end{aligned} \tag{28}$$

where again u_i follows the DPM model of expression (25).

Model 3

$$\begin{aligned} & y_{it}|\lambda_{it} \sim Poisson(\lambda_{it}), \\ & \lambda_{it} = \exp\left(\mathbf{x}_{it}'\boldsymbol{\beta} + \gamma \ \ln y_{it-1}^* + \varphi_i\right), \\ & \varphi_i = h_{i1} \ \ln y_{i0}^* + \overline{\mathbf{x}'}_i \mathbf{h}_{i2} + u_i, \end{aligned} \tag{29}$$

where u_i follows the DPM model of expression (25).

5.2 Prior Specification

The Bayesian analysis of the models in question requires priors over the parameters $(\boldsymbol{\delta}, \mathbf{h}_i, \sigma_v^2, \sigma_\epsilon^2, \rho)$, where $\boldsymbol{\delta} = (\boldsymbol{\beta}', \gamma)'$ and $\mathbf{h}_i = (h_{i1}, \mathbf{h}_{i2})'$. Therefore, we assume the following priors

$$
\begin{gathered}
p(\boldsymbol{\delta}) \propto 1, \mathbf{h}_i \sim \mathbf{N}_{k+1}\left(\tilde{\mathbf{h}}, \tilde{\mathbf{H}}\right), \tilde{\mathbf{h}} \sim \mathbf{N}\left(\tilde{\mathbf{h}}_0, \Sigma\right), \tilde{\mathbf{H}} \sim IW\left(\delta, \Delta^{-1}\right), \\
\sigma_v^{-2} \sim \mathcal{G}\left(\frac{e_1}{2}, \frac{f_1}{2}\right), \sigma_\epsilon^{-2} \sim \mathcal{G}\left(\frac{e_2}{2}, \frac{f_2}{2}\right), \rho \sim N\left(\rho_0, \sigma_\rho^2\right) I_{(-1,\,1)}(\rho).
\end{gathered} \tag{30}
$$

In particular, the prior distribution for $\boldsymbol{\delta}$ is flat, $p(\boldsymbol{\delta}) \propto 1$. A joint normal prior is imposed on the heterogeneous slope parameters, $\mathbf{h}_i \sim \mathbf{N}_{k+1}\left(\tilde{\mathbf{h}}, \tilde{\mathbf{H}}\right)$, where $\tilde{\mathbf{h}}$ follows a multivariate normal $\mathbf{N}\left(\tilde{\mathbf{h}}_0, \Sigma\right)$ and $\tilde{\mathbf{H}}$ follows an Inverse Wishart distribution $IW(\delta, \Delta^{-1})$. Because the autoregressive parameter is restrictive to the stationary region, we propose a truncated normal for ρ, $N(\rho_0, \sigma_\rho^2) I_{(-1,1)}(\rho)$, where $I_{(-1,1)}(\rho)$ is an indicator function that equals one if $\rho \in (-1, 1)$ and zero otherwise. For the inverse error variance σ_v^{-2} a gamma prior is used, $\sigma_v^{-2} \sim \mathcal{G}\left(\frac{e_1}{2}, \frac{f_1}{2}\right)$. A similar prior is used for the error variance σ_ϵ^{-2}, that is, $\mathcal{G}\left(\frac{e_2}{2}, \frac{f_2}{2}\right)$.

5.3 Posterior Sampling

In this section we present the MCMC schemes, which are used to estimate the parameters for each model.

5.3.1 MCMC for Model 1

Following Tanner and Wong (1987), we augment the parameter space to include the latent variables $\{\lambda_{it}^*\}_{i \geq 1, t \geq 1}$, where $\lambda_{it}^* = \mathbf{w}_{it}'\boldsymbol{\delta} + \varphi_i + \epsilon_{it}$ and $\mathbf{w}_{it}' = (\mathbf{x}_{it}', \ln y_{it-1}^*)$. The estimation procedure for model 1 consists of two parts.

In part I, we update at each iteration the parameters $\left(\{\lambda_{it}^*\}_{i \geq 1, t \geq 1}, \boldsymbol{\delta}, \{\varphi_i\}, \{\mathbf{h}_i\}, \tilde{\mathbf{h}}, \tilde{\mathbf{H}}, \sigma_v^2, \rho\right)$ and recover the errors $\{u_i\}$ deterministically, using the auxiliary regression of Wooldridge (2005). In part II, we update the Dirichlet process parameters $\vartheta_i = (\mu_i, \sigma_i^2)$, $i = 1, \ldots, N$, and a.

If we stack the latent equation $\lambda_{it}^* = \mathbf{w}_{it}'\boldsymbol{\delta} + \varphi_i + \epsilon_{it}$ over t we get

$$
\lambda_i^* = \mathbf{W}_i \boldsymbol{\delta} + \mathrm{i}_T \varphi_i + \epsilon_i, \tag{31}
$$

where $\mathbf{W}_i = (\mathbf{w}_{i1}, \ldots, \mathbf{w}_{iT})'$, $\mathbf{i}_T$ is a $T \times 1$ vector of ones and $\boldsymbol{\epsilon}_i = (\epsilon_{i1}, \ldots, \epsilon_{iT})'$ follows a multivariate normal with mean $\mathbf{0}$ and covariance matrix $\sigma_v^2 \Omega_i$, which is symmetric and positive definite with

$$\Omega_i = \frac{1}{1-\rho^2}\begin{pmatrix} 1 & \rho & \rho^2 & \cdots & \rho^{T-1} \\ \rho & 1 & \rho & \cdots & \rho^{T-2} \\ \rho^2 & \rho & 1 & \cdots & \rho^{T-3} \\ \vdots & \vdots & \vdots & \ddots & \vdots \\ \rho^{T-1} & \rho^{T-2} & \rho^{T-3} & \cdots & 1 \end{pmatrix}$$

Part I

- We sample σ_v^{-2}, $\delta \mid \{\lambda_i^*\}$, $\{\Omega_i\}$, $\{\varphi_i\}$, e_1, f_1 in one block by sampling.

(a) $\sigma_v^{-2}|\{\lambda_i^*\},\{\Omega_i\},\{\varphi_i\},e_1,f_1 \sim \mathcal{G}\left(\frac{\overline{e_1}}{2},\frac{\overline{f_1}}{2}\right)$, where $\overline{e_1}=e_1+NT-k-1,\overline{f_1}=f_1+\left(\overline{\lambda}^*-\mathbf{W}\hat{\delta}\right)'\Omega^{-1}\left(\overline{\lambda}^*-\mathbf{W}\hat{\delta}\right)$, $\overline{\lambda}^*$ contains the elements $\tilde{\lambda}_{it}^*=\lambda_{it}^*-\varphi_i$, $i=1,\ldots N,t=1,\ldots,N$ that have been stacked over i and t, $\mathbf{W}=(\mathbf{W}_1',\ \ldots\ ,\ \mathbf{W}_N')'$, $\hat{\delta}$ is the OLS estimator of δ given by $\hat{\delta}=\left(\mathbf{W}'\Omega^{-1}\mathbf{W}\right)^{-1}\mathbf{W}'\Omega^{-1}\tilde{\lambda}^*$ and Ω is a block diagonal matrix

$$\Omega = \begin{pmatrix} \Omega_1 & & & \\ & \Omega_2 & & \\ & & \ddots & \\ & & & \Omega_N \end{pmatrix}.$$

(b) $\delta|\{\lambda_i^*\},\sigma_v^2,\{\Omega_i\},\{\varphi_i\} \sim N\left(\hat{\delta},\left(\frac{1}{\sigma_v^2}\mathbf{W}'\Omega^{-1}\mathbf{W}\right)^{-1}\right)$.

- We sample $\varphi_i \mid \lambda_i^*$, $\mathbf{h}_i$, δ, Ω_i, σ_v^2, $\vartheta_i \sim N(d_0,D_0)$, $i=1,\ldots,N$, where $D_0=\left(\frac{1}{\sigma_i^2}+\sigma_v^{-2}\mathbf{i}_T'\Omega_i^{-1}\mathbf{i}_T\right)^{-1}$ and $d_0=D_0\left(\frac{\mathrm{k}_i'\mathrm{h}_i+\mu_i}{\sigma_i^2}+\sigma_v^{-2}\mathbf{i}_T'\Omega_i^{-1}\left(\lambda_i^*-\mathbf{W}_i\delta\right)\right)$ with $\mathbf{k}_i'=(\ \ln y_{i0}^*,\overline{\mathbf{x}}_i')$.
- We sample $\mathbf{h}_i|\varphi_i,\tilde{\mathbf{h}},\tilde{\mathbf{H}},\vartheta_i \sim \mathrm{N}(d_{\mathrm{h}_i},D_{\mathrm{h}_i}),i=1,\ldots,N$, where $d_{\mathrm{h}_i}=D_{\mathrm{h}_i}\left(\tilde{\mathbf{H}}^{-1}\tilde{\mathbf{h}}+\frac{\mathrm{k}_i(\varphi_i-\mu_i)}{\sigma_i^2}\right)$ and $D_{\mathrm{h}_i}=\left(\tilde{\mathbf{H}}^{-1}+\frac{\mathrm{k}_i\mathrm{k}_i'}{\sigma_i^2}\right)^{-1}$.
- We sample $\tilde{\mathbf{h}}|\{\mathrm{h}_i\},\tilde{\mathbf{H}},\Sigma,\tilde{\mathbf{h}}_0 \sim \mathrm{N}(d_1,D_1)$, where $d_1=D_1\left(\Sigma^{-1}\tilde{\mathbf{h}}_0+\tilde{\mathbf{H}}^{-1}\right.$ $\left.\sum_{i=1}^N\mathrm{h}_i\right)$ and $D_1=\left(\Sigma^{-1}+N\tilde{\mathbf{H}}^{-1}\right)^{-1}$.
- We sample $\tilde{\mathbf{H}}|\{\mathrm{h}_i\},\tilde{\mathbf{h}},\Delta^{-1},\delta \sim IW\left(N+\delta,\sum_{i=1}^N\left(\mathrm{h}_i-\tilde{\mathbf{h}}\right)\left(\mathrm{h}_i-\tilde{\mathbf{h}}\right)'+\Delta^{-1}\right)$.
- We sample $\lambda_i^*, i=1,\ \ldots\ ,N$ from $\lambda_i^* \mid \delta,\sigma_v^2,\Omega_i,\varphi_i,\boldsymbol{y}_i$, which is proportional to $N(\lambda_i^*|\mathbf{W}_i\delta+\mathbf{i}_T\varphi_i,\sigma_v^2\Omega_i)$ *Poisson* $(\boldsymbol{y}_i|exp(\lambda_i^*))$, where $\boldsymbol{y}_i=\{y_{it}\}_{t\geq 1}$. This density

does not have closed form. Therefore, we use an independence Metropolis-Hastings algorithm to update each $\boldsymbol{\lambda}_i^*$. In this chapter, we orthogonalize the correlated errors so that the elements within each $\boldsymbol{\lambda}_i^*$ can be sampled independently of one another (Chib & Greenberg, 1995).

In particular, we decompose the covariance matrix Ω_i as $\Omega_i = \xi \boldsymbol{I}_T + \tilde{R}_i$, where $\boldsymbol{I}_T$ is the $T \times T$ identity matrix, ξ is an arbitrary constant that satisfies the constraint $\overline{\xi} > \xi > 0$, where $\overline{\xi}$ is the minimum eigenvalue of Ω_i and $\tilde{R}_i$ is a symmetric positive definite matrix. The algorithm becomes stable by setting $\xi = \overline{\xi}/2$ (Chib & Greenberg, 1995). $\tilde{R}_i$ can be further decomposed into $\tilde{R}_i = C_i' C_i$ (Cholesky decomposition). Therefore, $\Omega_i = C_i' C_i + \xi \boldsymbol{I}_T$..

Using this decomposition, the latent regression for $\boldsymbol{\lambda}_i^*$, $i = 1, \dots, N$ can be written as

$$\boldsymbol{\lambda}_i^* = \mathbf{W}_i \boldsymbol{\delta} + \mathbf{i}_T \varphi_i + C_i' \eta_i + e_i, \tag{32}$$

where $\boldsymbol{\eta}_i \sim N(0, \sigma_v^2 \boldsymbol{I}_T)$ and $e_i \sim N(0, \xi \sigma_v^2 \boldsymbol{I}_T)$. Using Eq. (32), the (intractable) full conditional distribution of each λ_{it}^*, $i = 1, \dots, N$, $t = 1, \dots, T$ is given by

$$p\left(\lambda_{it}^* | \boldsymbol{\delta}, \sigma_v^2, \rho, \varphi_i, y_{it}\right) \propto \exp\left(-\exp\left(\lambda_{it}^*\right) + \lambda_{it}^* y_{it} - \exp\left(\frac{1}{2\xi\sigma_v^2}\left(\lambda_{it}^* - \mathrm{w}_{it}' \boldsymbol{\delta} - \varphi_i - q_{it}\right)^2\right)\right), \tag{33}$$

where q_{it} is the $t-th$ element of $q_i = C_i' \boldsymbol{\eta}_i$. Let $St\left(\lambda_{it}^* | \hat{\lambda}_{it}^*, c_1 V_{\lambda_{it}^*}, v_1\right)$ denote a Student-t distribution, where $\hat{\lambda}_{it}^*$ denotes the modal value of the $logp$ $(\lambda_{it}^* | \boldsymbol{\delta}, \sigma_v^2, \rho, \varphi_i, y_{it})$ with respect to λ_{it}^*, $V_{\lambda_{it}^*} = (-H_{\lambda_{it}^*})^{-1}$ is defined as the inverse of the negative second-order derivative of the $logp(\lambda_{it}^* | \boldsymbol{\delta}, \sigma_v^2, \rho, \varphi_i, y_{it})$ evaluated at $\hat{\lambda}_{it}^*$, v_1 is the degrees of freedom and c_1 is a positive-valued scale parameter. Both v_1 and c_1 are essentially tuning parameters, which are determined by the user prior to the main MCMC loop.

To obtain the modal value we use a few Newton-Raphson rounds implemented in the first-order derivative

$$\hat{\lambda}_{it}^* = -\exp\left(\lambda_{it}^*\right) + y_{it} - \frac{1}{\xi\sigma_v^2}\left(\lambda_{it}^* - \mathrm{w}_{it}' \boldsymbol{\delta} - \varphi_i - q_{it}\right),$$

and the second-order derivative

$$H_{\lambda_{it}^*} = -\exp\left(\lambda_{it}^*\right) - \frac{1}{\xi\sigma_v^2}.$$

of $logp(\lambda_{it}^* | \boldsymbol{\delta}, \sigma_v^2, \rho, \varphi_i, y_{it})$,

Then, sample a proposal value $\lambda_{it}^{*(p)}$ from the density $St\left(\lambda_{it}^* | \hat{\lambda}_{it}^*, c_1 V_{\lambda_{it}^*}, v_1\right)$ and move to $\lambda_{it}^{*(p)}$ given the current point $\lambda_{it}^{*(c)}$ with probability of move

$$\min\left(\frac{p\left(\lambda_{it}^{*(p)} | \boldsymbol{\delta}, \sigma_v^2, \rho, \varphi_i, y_{it}\right) St\left(\lambda_{it}^* | \hat{\lambda}_{it}^{*(c)}, c_1 V_{\lambda_{it}^*}, v_1\right)}{p\left(\lambda_{it}^{*(c)} | \boldsymbol{\delta}, \sigma_v^2, \rho, \varphi_i, y_{it}\right) St\left(\lambda_{it}^{*(p)} | \hat{\lambda}_{it}^*, c_1 V_{\lambda_{it}^*}, v_1\right)}, 1\right).$$

• To update $q_i = C_i' \boldsymbol{\eta}_i$, $i = 1, \ldots, N$ in each iteration we sample $\boldsymbol{\eta}_i$ from $\boldsymbol{\eta}_i \mid \boldsymbol{\lambda}_i^*, \boldsymbol{\delta}$, φ_i, $\sigma_v^2 \sim N(p_1, P_1)$, where $p_1 = P_1 \left(\frac{c_i \left(y_i^* - \mathbf{W}_i \boldsymbol{\delta} - \mathbf{i}_T \varphi_i \right)}{\xi \sigma_v^2} \right)$ and $P_1 = \left(\frac{I_T}{\sigma_v^2} + \frac{C_i C_i'}{\xi \sigma_v^2} \right)^{-1}$.

• We sample $\rho \mid \boldsymbol{\epsilon}$, σ_v^2, ρ_0, $\sigma_\rho^2 \propto \Psi(\rho) \times N(d_2, D_2) I_{(-1,1)}(\rho)$, where $\boldsymbol{\epsilon} = (\boldsymbol{\epsilon}_1', \ldots, \boldsymbol{\epsilon}_N')'$, $\epsilon_{it} = \lambda_{it}^* - \mathbf{w}_{it}' \boldsymbol{\delta} - \varphi_i$, $\Psi(\rho) = \sqrt{(1-\rho^2)^N} \times \exp\left(-\frac{(1-\rho^2)}{2\sigma_v^2} \sum_{i=1}^N \epsilon_{i1}^2 \right)$,

$$d_2 = D_2 \left(\frac{\rho 0}{\sigma_\rho^2} + \sigma_v^{-2} \sum_{i=1}^N \sum_{t=2}^T \epsilon_{it} \epsilon_{it-1} \right) \text{ and } D_2 = \left(\frac{1}{\sigma_\rho^2} + \sigma_v^{-2} \sum_{i=1}^N \sum_{t=2}^T \epsilon_{it-1}^2 \right)^{-1}.$$

We use an independence Metropolis-Hastings algorithm in order to simulate ρ. A candidate value ρ' is generated from the density $N(d_2, D_2) I_{(-1.1)}(\rho)$ and is accepted as the next value in the chain with probability $\min(\Psi(\rho')/\Psi(\rho), 1)$; otherwise, the current value ρ is taken to be the next value in the sample.

• We obtain deterministically the errors u_i from $u_i = \varphi_i - h_{i1} \ln y_{i0} - \overline{\mathbf{x}}_1' \mathbf{h}_{i2}$, $i = 1, \ldots, N$.

Part II

• To improve efficiency of sampling from $\boldsymbol{\theta} \mid \{u_i\}$, μ_0, τ_0, e_0, f_0, we sample from the equivalent distribution $\boldsymbol{\theta}^*$, $\boldsymbol{\psi} \mid \{u_i\}$, μ_0, τ_0, e_0, f_0, where $\boldsymbol{\theta} = (\vartheta_1, \ldots, \vartheta_N)'$, $\boldsymbol{\theta}^* = (\vartheta_1^*, \ldots, \vartheta_M^*)'$, $M \leq N$ contains the set of unique values from the $\boldsymbol{\theta}$ with ϑ_m^*, $m = 1, \ldots, M$ representing a cluster location and $\boldsymbol{\psi} = (\psi_1, \ldots, \psi_N)'$ is the vector of the latent indicator variables such that $\psi_i = m$ iff $\vartheta_i = \vartheta_m^*$. Together $\boldsymbol{\theta}^*$ and $\boldsymbol{\psi}$ completely define $\boldsymbol{\theta}$ (MacEachern, 1994). Let also $\boldsymbol{\theta}^{*(i)} = (\vartheta_1^{*(i)}, \ldots, \vartheta_{M^{(i)}}^{*(i)})'$ denote the distinct values in $\boldsymbol{\theta}^{(i)}$, which is the $\boldsymbol{\theta}$ with the element ϑ_i deleted. Also, the number of clusters in $\boldsymbol{\theta}^{*(i)}$ is indexed from $m = 1$ to $M^{(i)}$. Furthermore, we define $n_m^{(i)} = \sum_j 1(\psi_j = m, j \neq i)$, $m = 1, \ldots, M^{(i)}$ to be the number of elements in $\boldsymbol{\theta}^{(i)}$ that take the distinct element $\vartheta_m^{*(i)}$.

We follow a two-step process in order to draw from $\boldsymbol{\theta}^*$, $\boldsymbol{\psi} \mid \{u_i\}$, μ_0, τ_0, e_0, f_0. In the first step, we sample $\boldsymbol{\psi}$ and M by drawing ϑ_i, $i = 1, \ldots, N$ from

$$\vartheta_i | \boldsymbol{\theta}^{(i)}, u_i, G_0 \sim c \frac{a}{a+N-1} q_{i0} p(\vartheta_i | u_i, \mu_0, \tau_0, e_0, f_0) + \sum_{m=1}^{M^{(i)}} \frac{c}{a+N-1} n_m^{(i)} q_{im} \delta_{\vartheta_m^{*(i)}}(\vartheta_i),$$

setting $\psi_i = M^{(i)} + 1$ and $\vartheta_i = \vartheta_{M \oplus 1}^*$ when $\vartheta_{M \oplus 1}^*$ is sampled from $p(\vartheta_i | u_i, \mu_0, \tau_0, e_0, f_0)$ or $\psi_i = m$, when $\vartheta_i = \vartheta_m^{*(i)}$, $m = 1, \ldots, M^{(i)}$. c is the normalizing constant and $\delta_{\vartheta_j}(\theta_i)$ represents a unit point mass at $\vartheta_i = \vartheta_j$. The new cluster value $\vartheta_{M \oplus 1}^*$ is sampled from $p(\vartheta_i | u_i, \mu_0, \tau_0, e_0, f_0)$, which is the posterior density of ϑ_i under the prior G_0. By conjugacy we have

$$\vartheta_i = \left(\mu_i, \sigma_i^2 \right) | u_i, \mu_0, \tau_0, e_0, f_0 \sim N\left(\mu_i | \overline{\mu_0}, \overline{\tau_0} \sigma_i^2 \right) \mathcal{IG}\left(\sigma_i^2 | \frac{\overline{e_0}}{2}, \frac{\overline{f_0}}{2} \right),$$

where

$$\overline{\mu_0} = \frac{\mu_0 + \tau_0 u_i}{1+\tau_0}, \quad \overline{\tau_0} = \frac{\tau_0}{1+\tau_0}, \quad \overline{e_0} = e_0 + 1, \quad \overline{f_0} = f_0 + \frac{(u_i - \mu_0)^2}{\tau_0 + 1}.$$

The probability of assigning ψ_i to a new cluster is proportional to the marginal density of u_i, $\tilde{q}_{i0} = \int f(u_i|\vartheta_i)dG_0(\vartheta_i) = q_t(u_i|\mu_0, (1+\tau_0)f_0/e_0, e_0)$, where q_t is the Student-t distribution, μ_0 is the mean, e_0 is the degrees of freedom, and $(1+\tau_0)f_0/e_0$ is the scale factor. The probability of ψ_i equaling an existing cluster $m = 1, \ldots, M^{(i)}$ is proportional to $n_m^{(i)} q_{im}$, where $\tilde{q}_{im}$ is the normal distribution of u_i evaluated at $\vartheta_m^{*(i)}$; hence, $\tilde{q}_{im} = n_m^{(i)} \exp\left(-\frac{1}{2}\left(u_i - \mu_m^{*(i)}\right)^2 / \sigma_m^{*2(i)}\right)$.

In the second step, given M and $\boldsymbol{\psi}$, we draw each ϑ_m^*, $m = 1, \ldots, M$ from

$$\vartheta_m^* = \left(\mu_m^*, \sigma_m^{*2}\right)|\{u_i\}_{i\in F_m}, \mu_0, \tau_0, e_0, f_0 \sim N\left(\mu_m^* | \overline{\mu_m}, \overline{\tau_m}\sigma_m^{*2}\right)\mathcal{IG}\left(\sigma_m^{*2} | \frac{\overline{e_m}}{2}, \frac{\overline{f_m}}{2}\right),$$

where

$$\overline{\mu_m} = \frac{\mu_0 + \tau_0 \sum_{i\in F_m} u_i}{1+\tau_0 n_m}, \quad \overline{\tau_m} = \frac{\tau_0}{1+\tau_0 n_m},$$

$$\overline{e_m} = e_0 + n_m, \quad \overline{f_m} = f_0 + \frac{n_m\left(\frac{1}{n_m}\sum_{i\in F_m} u_i - \mu_0\right)^2}{1+\tau_0 n_m} + \sum_{i\in F_m}\left(u_i - \frac{1}{n_m}\sum_{i\in F_m} u_i\right)^2,$$

and $F_m = \{i : \vartheta_i = \vartheta_m^*\}$ is the set of individuals that share the same parameter ϑ_m^*.

• To sample the precision parameter a, we first sample $\tilde{\eta}$ from $\tilde{\eta}|a, N \sim Beta(a+1, N)$, where $\tilde{\eta}$ is a latent variable and then sample a from a mixture of two gammas, $a|\tilde{\eta}, \underline{c}, \underline{d}, M \sim \pi_{\tilde{\eta}}\mathcal{G}(\underline{c}+M, \underline{d} - \ln(\tilde{\eta})) + (1-\pi_{\tilde{\eta}})\mathcal{G}(\underline{c}+M-1, \underline{d} - \ln(\tilde{\eta}))$ with the mixture weight $\pi_{\tilde{\eta}}$ satisfying $\pi_{\tilde{\eta}}/(1-\pi_{\tilde{\eta}}) = (\underline{c}+M-1)/N(\underline{d} - \ln(\tilde{\eta}))$. For details, see Escobar and West (1995).

Average Marginal Effects for Model 1

Because of the nonlinear nature of the Poisson panel models, the direct interpretation of the coefficients can be misleading. To overcome this problem, we calculate the marginal effects. For model 1, the marginal effect for the *i*th component with respect to the *k*-th continuous regressor is

$$ME_{kit} = \frac{\partial E(y_{it}| \mathbf{w}_{it}, \boldsymbol{\delta}, \varphi_i, q_{it})}{\partial x_{k,it}} = \beta_k \exp\left(\mathbf{w}_{it}'\boldsymbol{\delta} + \varphi_i + q_{it}\right).$$

By integrating out all the unknown parameters (including the random effects), the posterior distribution of $M\,E_{kit}$ is

$$\pi(ME_{kit}|\,data) = \int \pi(ME_{kit}|\,\boldsymbol{\delta}, \varphi_i, q_{it}, data)d\pi(\boldsymbol{\delta}, \varphi_i, q_{it}|\,data).$$

Using the composition method, we can produce a sample of $M\,E_{kit}$ values, using the posterior draws of $\boldsymbol{\delta}$, ϕ_i, q_{it}. Chib and Hamilton (2002) also used this method to calculate average treatment effects. Given a posterior sample of $M\,E_{kit}$ values obtained from $\pi(M\,E_{kit}\,|\,data)$, which we denote by $\{ME_{kit}^{(l)}\}$, the average marginal effect ($AM\,E$) can be defined as

$$AME_k = \frac{\sum_{l=1}^{L}\sum_{i=1}^{N}\sum_{t=1}^{T} ME_{kit}^{(l)}}{L\times N\times T},$$

where $ME_{kit}^{(l)} = \beta_k^{(l)}\ exp\ (\mathbf{w}_{it}'\boldsymbol{\delta}^{(l)} + \varphi_i^{(l)} + q_{it}^{(l)})$ and L is the total number of iterations after the burn-in period.

If $x_{k,it}$ is binary, the partial effect is

$$\begin{aligned}\Delta_j(x_{k,it}) = \exp\left(\left(\mathbf{w}_{it}'\boldsymbol{\delta} - x_{k,it}\beta_k\right) + \beta_k + \varphi_i + q_{it}\right)\\ - \exp\left(\left(\mathbf{w}_{it}'\boldsymbol{\delta} - x_{k,it}\beta_k\right) + \varphi_i + q_{it}\right).\end{aligned}$$

5.3.2 MCMC for Model 2

The updating of $\{\mathbf{h}_i\}$, $\tilde{\mathbf{h}}$, $\tilde{\mathbf{H}}$, $\{u_i\}$, $\{\vartheta_i\}$ and a is the same as in model 1. In addition, one has to update the latent variables $\{\varphi_i\}$ and $\{\lambda_{it}^*\}$ as well as the parameters $\boldsymbol{\delta}$ and σ_ϵ^2. In this case, we use the equation

$$\lambda_{it}^* = \mathbf{w}_{it}'\boldsymbol{\delta} + \varphi_i + \epsilon_{it}, \tag{34}$$

where now ϵ_{it} is iid distributed.

- We sample the random effects, φ_i, $i = 1, \ldots, N$, from $N\ (d_0,\ D_0)$, where $D_0 = \left(\frac{1}{\sigma_i^2} + \frac{T}{\sigma_\epsilon^2}\right)^{-1}$ and $d_0 = \frac{\sum_{t=1}^{T}(\lambda_{it}^* - \mathbf{w}_{it}'\boldsymbol{\delta})}{\sigma_\epsilon^2} + \frac{\mathbf{k}_i'\mathbf{h}_i + \mu_i}{\sigma_i^2}$.
- We sample $\boldsymbol{\delta}$ and σ_ϵ^2 in one block again:

(a) First, sample σ_ϵ^2 marginalized over $\boldsymbol{\delta}$ from

$$\sigma_\epsilon^{-2}|\{\boldsymbol{\lambda}_i^*\}, \{\mathbf{W}_i\}, \{\varphi_i\}, e_2, f_2 \sim \mathcal{G}\left(\frac{\overline{e_2}}{2}, \frac{\overline{f_2}}{2}\right),$$

where $\overline{e_2} = e_2 + NT - k - 1, \overline{f_2} = f_2 + \sum_{i=1}^{N}\sum_{t=1}^{T}\left(\lambda_{it}^* - \mathbf{w}_{it}'\hat{\boldsymbol{\delta}} - \varphi_i\right)^2$, and $\hat{\boldsymbol{\delta}} = \left(\sum_{i=1}^{N}\sum_{t=1}^{T}\mathbf{w}_{it}\mathbf{w}_{it}'\right)^{-1} \times \left[\sum_{i=1}^{N}\sum_{t=1}^{T}\mathbf{w}_{it}\left(\lambda_{it}^* - \varphi_i\right)\right]$.

(b) Second, sample $\boldsymbol{\delta}$ from its full posterior distribution:

$$\boldsymbol{\delta}|\sigma_\epsilon^2, \{\lambda_i^*\}, \{\mathbf{W}_i\}, \{\mathbf{W}_i\}, \{\varphi_i\} \sim N\left(\hat{\boldsymbol{\delta}}, \left(\frac{1}{\sigma_\epsilon^2}\sum_{i=1}^{N}\sum_{t=1}^{T}\mathbf{w}_{it}\mathbf{w}_{it}'\right)^{-1}\right).$$

- As in model 1, the posterior distribution of λ_{it}^* for $i = 1, \ldots, N$ and $t = 1, \ldots, T$ is intractable and is given by

$$p\left(\lambda_{it}^*| \boldsymbol{\delta}, \sigma_\epsilon^2, \varphi_i, y_{it}\right) \propto \exp\left(-\exp\left(\lambda_{it}^*\right) + \lambda_{it}^* y_{it} - \exp\left(\frac{1}{2\sigma_\epsilon^2}\left(\lambda_{it}^* - \mathbf{w}_{it}'\boldsymbol{\delta} - \varphi_i\right)^2\right)\right), \tag{35}$$

which is a modified version of Eq. (33). Again, we use a Metropolis-Hastings step similar to that of model 1.

Average Marginal Effects for Model 2

For model 2, the marginal effect for the *it*-th component with respect to the *k*-th continuous regressor is

$$ME_{kit} = \frac{\partial E(y_{it}|\, \mathbf{w}_{it}, \boldsymbol{\delta}, \varphi_i)}{\partial x_{k,it}} = \beta_k \exp\left(\mathbf{w}_{it}'\boldsymbol{\delta} + \varphi_i + \epsilon_{it}\right),$$

and the calculation of the average partial effects is similar to that of model 1.

5.3.3 MCMC for Model 3

The conditional distributions for $\mathbf{h}_i$, $\tilde{\mathbf{h}}$ and $\tilde{\mathbf{H}}$ are the same as those in model 1. The same holds for the update of the DP parameters and the deterministic update of u_i.

The posterior densities of φ_i and $\boldsymbol{\delta} = (\boldsymbol{\beta}', \gamma)'$ in model 3 are intractable and therefore we use the independence Metropolis-Hastings algorithm to make draws from their posteriors.

In particular, the posterior distribution of φ_i, $i = 1, \ldots, N$ is given by

$$p\left(\varphi_i|\, \{y_{it}\}_{t\geq 1}, \mathbf{h}_i, \boldsymbol{\delta}, \mu_i, \sigma_i^2\right) \propto \exp\left(-\frac{1}{2\sigma_i^2}\left(\varphi_i - \mathbf{k}_i'\mathrm{h}_i - \mu_i\right)^2\right)$$
$$\times \prod_{t=1}^{T} \frac{\exp\left[-\exp\left(\mathbf{w}_{it}'\boldsymbol{\delta} + \varphi_i\right)\right]\left[\exp\left(\mathbf{w}_{it}'\boldsymbol{\delta} + \varphi_i\right)\right]^{y_{it}}}{y_{it}!}.$$

A proposed draw $\varphi_i^{(p)}$ is generated from the Student-*t* distribution $St\left(\varphi_i^{(p)}|\, \hat{\varphi}_i, c_2 V_{\varphi_i}, v_2\right)$, where $\hat{\varphi}_i = a_{\varphi_i} rgmaxlogp\left(\varphi_i|\, \{y_{it}\}_{t\geq 1}, \mathbf{h}_i, \boldsymbol{\delta}, \mu_i, \sigma_i^2\right)$ is the modal value of the logarithm of the posterior distribution of φ_i, $V_\varphi i = (-H_\varphi i)^{-1}$

is the inverse of the negative Hessian of $logp(\varphi_i | \{y_{it}\}_{t\geq 1}, \mathbf{h}_i, \boldsymbol{\delta}, \mu_i, \sigma_i^2)$ evaluated at $\hat{\varphi}_i$, v_2 is the degrees of freedom and $c_2 > 0$ is a constant. To obtain the modal value we use the Newton-Raphson method that requires the calculation of the gradient

$$g_{\varphi_i} = -\left(\varphi_i - \mathbf{k}_i'\mathbf{h}_i - \mu_i\right)/\sigma_i^2 + \sum_{t=1}^{T}\left[y_{it} - \exp\left(\mathbf{w}_{it}'\boldsymbol{\delta} + \varphi_i\right)\right],$$

where $\mathbf{k}_i' = \left(\ln y_{i0}^*, \overline{\mathbf{x}}_i'\right)$ and the Hessian

$$H_{\varphi_i} = -\sigma_i^{-2} - \sum_{t=1}^{T}\exp\left(\mathbf{w}_{it}'\boldsymbol{\delta} + \varphi_i\right)$$

Given the current value $\varphi_i^{(c)}$, we move to the proposed point $\varphi_i^{(p)}$ with probability

$$a_p\left(\varphi_i^{(c)}, \varphi_i^{(p)}\right) = \min\left(\frac{p\left(\varphi_i^{(p)} | \{y_{it}\}_{t\geq 1}, \mathbf{h}_i, \boldsymbol{\delta}, \mu_i, \sigma_i^2\right) St\left(\varphi_i^{(c)} | \hat{\varphi}_i, c_2 V_{\varphi_i}, v_2\right)}{p\left(\varphi_i^{(c)} | \{y_{it}\}_{t\geq 1}, \mathbf{h}_i, \boldsymbol{\delta}, \mu_i, \sigma_i^2\right) St\left(\varphi_i^{(p)} | \hat{\varphi}_i, c_2 V_{\varphi_i}, v_2\right)}, 1\right).$$

The target density of $\boldsymbol{\delta}$ is also intractable,

$$p(\boldsymbol{\delta} | \{y_{it}\}_{i\geq 1, t\geq 1}, \{\varphi_i\}) \propto \sum_{i=1}^{N}\sum_{t=1}^{T}\exp\left[\frac{-\exp\left(\mathbf{w}_{it}'\boldsymbol{\delta} + \varphi_i\right)\left[\exp\left(\mathbf{w}_{it}'\boldsymbol{\delta} + \varphi_i\right)\right]^{y_{it}}}{y_{it}!}\right].$$

To generate $\boldsymbol{\delta}$ from its full conditional we use a multivariate Student-t distribution $MVt\left(\boldsymbol{\delta} | \hat{\boldsymbol{\delta}}, c_3\hat{\Sigma}_{\delta}, v_3\right)$, where $\hat{\boldsymbol{\delta}} = ar_{\delta}gmaxlogp(\boldsymbol{\delta} | \{y_{it}\}_{i\geq 1, t\geq 1}\{\varphi_i\})$ is the mode of the logarithm of the right side of the earlier conditional distribution and $\hat{\Sigma}_{\delta} = [-H_{\delta}]^{-1}$ is the negative inverse of the Hessian matrix of $p(\boldsymbol{\delta} | \{y_{it}\}_{i\geq 1, t\geq 1}, \{\phi_i\})$ at the mode $\hat{\boldsymbol{\delta}}$. The degrees of freedom v_3 and the scaling factor c_3 are, as before, adjustable parameters. The maximizer Newton-Raphson procedure with gradient vector $\hat{\boldsymbol{\delta}}$ is obtained by using the

$$g_{\delta} = \sum_{i=1}^{N}\sum_{t=1}^{T}\left[y_{it} - \exp\left(\mathbf{w}_{it}'\boldsymbol{\delta} + \varphi_i\right)\right]\mathbf{w}_{it},$$

and Hessian matrix

$$H_{\delta} = -\sum_{i=1}^{N}\sum_{t=1}^{T}\left[\exp\left(\mathbf{w}_{it}'\boldsymbol{\delta} + \varphi_i\right)\right]\mathbf{w}_{it}\mathbf{w}_{it}'.$$

The algorithm to generate $\boldsymbol{\delta}$ works as follows:

(1) Let $\boldsymbol{\delta}^{(c)}$ be the current value.

(2) Generate a proposed value $\boldsymbol{\delta}^{(p)}$ from $MVt\left(\boldsymbol{\delta}|\,\hat{\boldsymbol{\delta}}, c_3\hat{\Sigma}_{\delta}, v_3\right)$.

(3) A move from $\boldsymbol{\delta}^{(c)}$ to $\boldsymbol{\delta}^{(p)}$ is made with probability

$$\min\left(\frac{p\left(\boldsymbol{\delta}^{(p)}|\,\{y_{it}\}_{i\geq 1,t\geq 1}, \{\varphi_i\}\right)MVt\left(\boldsymbol{\delta}^{(c)}|\,\hat{\boldsymbol{\delta}}, c_3\hat{\Sigma}_{\delta}, v_3\right)}{p\left(\boldsymbol{\delta}^{(c)}|\,\{y_{it}\}_{i\geq 1,t\geq 1}, \{\varphi_i\}\right)MVt\left(\boldsymbol{\delta}^{(p)}|\,\hat{\boldsymbol{\delta}}, c_3\hat{\Sigma}_{\delta}, v_3\right)}, 1\right).$$

Average Marginal Effects for Model 3

For model 3, the marginal effect for the *it*th component with respect to the *k*-th continuous regressor is

$$ME_{kit} = \frac{\partial E(y_{it}|\,\mathbf{w}_{it}, \boldsymbol{\delta}, \varphi_i)}{\partial x_{k,it}} = \beta_k \exp\left(\mathbf{w}_{it}'\boldsymbol{\delta} + \varphi_i\right),$$

and the calculation of the average partial effects is similar to that of model 1.

5.4 Model Comparison

In this section we explain how we can conduct model comparison, using the Deviance Information Criterion (DIC), proposed by Spiegelhalter et al. (2002) and cross-validation predictive densities.

The Deviance Information Criterion (DIC) can be calculated easily because it uses the conditional likelihood of the model. For model 1, where the idiosyncratic errors are serially correlated, the DIC also can be computed because of the orthogonalization of the error terms.

The DIC is based on the deviance $D(\boldsymbol{\Theta}) = -2\ln f(\mathbf{y}\,|\,\boldsymbol{\Theta})$, where $\mathbf{y}$ is the vector of observations, $\ln f(\mathbf{y}\,|\,\boldsymbol{\Theta})$ is the log-likelihood function and $\boldsymbol{\Theta}$ is the vector of all model parameters. The DIC is defined as $DIC = \overline{D(\Theta)} + p_D$, where $\overline{D(\Theta)} = -2\mathbf{E}_{\Theta}[\log f(\mathrm{y}|\,\Theta)|\,\mathrm{y}]$ is the posterior mean deviance that measures how well the model fits the data. The term p_D measures model complexity and is defined as $p_D = \overline{D(\Theta)} - D\left(\overline{\Theta}\right)$, where $D\left(\overline{\Theta}\right) = -2\log f\left(\mathrm{y}|\,\overline{\Theta}\right)$ and $\log f\left(\mathrm{y}|\,\overline{\Theta}\right)$ is the log-likelihood evaluated at $\overline{\Theta}$, the posterior mean of $\boldsymbol{\Theta}$. The DIC is, therefore, defined as $\mathrm{DIC} = \overline{D(\Theta)} + p_D = 2\overline{D(\Theta)} - D\left(\overline{\Theta}\right)$. The model with the smallest DIC has the best model fit. The DIC can be computed using MCMC samples of the parameters, $\{\boldsymbol{\Theta}^{(l)}\}$, where $\boldsymbol{\Theta}^{(l)}$ is the value of $\boldsymbol{\Theta}$ at iteration $l = 1, \ldots, L$. Lower DIC values indicate better model fit.

An alternative model comparison criterion is based on cross-validation predictive densities. In particular, we apply the leave-one-out cross validation

(CV) method that requires the calculation of the conditional predictive ordinate (CPO),

$$CPO_{it} = f(y_{it}|\, y_{-it}) = \int f(y_{it}|\, \Theta) f(\Theta|\, y_{-it}) = \mathrm{E}_{\Theta|y-it}[f(y_{it}|\, \Theta)], \quad i = 1,\ldots,N, \quad t = 1,\ldots,T,$$

where $y_{-it} = \mathbf{y} \setminus \{y_{it}\}$. Gelfand and Dey (1994) and Gelfand (1996) proposed a Monte Carlo integration of CPO. More specifically,

$$C\hat{P}O_{it} = \hat{f}(y_{it}|\, y_{-it}) = \left(\frac{1}{L}\sum_{l=1}^{L}\left(f\left(y_{it}|\, y_{-it}, \Theta^{(l)}\right)\right)^{-1}\right)^{-1},$$

where L is the number of iterations after the burn-in period. Then, for each model we calculate the average of the estimated CPO values, $\frac{1}{NT}\sum_{i=1}^{N}\sum_{t=1}^{T}\hat{f}(y_{it}|\, y_{-it})$. Higher values of this average imply better "goodness of fit" of a model.

6 Conclusions

In this chapter we presented various Markov Chain Monte Carlo algorithms for estimating various versions of the panel Poisson model. These versions controlled for dynamic, random effects, and serial error correlation. Furthermore, we assigned a nonparametric structure to the distribution of the random effects, using the Dirichlet process prior. We also tackled the initial conditions problem from which models of this type suffer. As a byproduct of the posterior algorithms, we showed how the average partial effects can be calculated, while we used two Bayesian criteria for model comparison, the Deviance Information Criterion (DIC) and cross-validation predictive densities.

References

Antoniak, C.E., 1974. Mixtures of Dirichlet processes with applications to Bayesian nonparametric problems. The Annals of Statistics 2 (6), 1152–1174.

Arulampalam, W., Stewart, M.B., 2009. Simplified implementation of the Heckman estimator of the dynamic probit model and a comparison with alternative estimators. Oxford Bulletin of Economics and Statistics 71 (5), 659–681.

Bernardo, J.M., Smith, A.F.M., 1994. Bayesian theory, 1st ed. Wiley series in probability and mathematical statistics: Probability and mathematical statisticsJohn Wiley & Sons Ltd, Chichester.

Blackwell, D., MacQueen, J.B., 1973. Ferguson distributions via Pólya urn schemes. The Annals of Statistics 1 (2), 353–355.

Blundell, R., Griffith, R., Windmeijer, F., 2002. Individual effects and dynamics in count data models. Journal of Econometrics 108 (1), 113–131.

Cameron, A.C., Trivedi, P.K., 2013. Regression analysis of count data, second ed. Cambridge University Press, Cambridge.

Cameron, A.C., Trivedi, P.K., 2014. Count panel data. In: Baltagi, B. (Ed.), Oxford hand-book of panel data. Oxford University Press, Oxford, pp. 233–256.

Chib, S., 2001. Markov chain Monte carlo methods: computation and inference. In: Heckman, J.J., Leamer, E. (Eds.), Handbook of econometrics. In: Vol. 5. North Holland, Amsterdam, pp. 3569–3649.

Chib, S., 2004. MCMC technology. In: Gentle, J., Hardle, W., Mori, Y. (Eds.), Handbook of computational statistics: Concepts and fundamentals. In: Vol. I. Springer-Verlag, Heidelberg, pp. 71–102.

Chib, S., Greenberg, E., 1995. Understanding the Metropolis-Hastings algorithm. The American Statistician 49 (4), 327–335.

Chib, S., Greenberg, E., Winkelmann, R., 1998. Posterior simulation and Bayes factors in panel count data models. Journal of Econometrics 86 (1), 33–54.

Chib, S., Hamilton, B.H., 2002. Semiparametric Bayes analysis of longitudinal data treatment models. Journal of Econometrics 110 (1), 67–89.

Crauel, H., 2002. Random probability measures on Polish spaces, 1st ed. Stochastics monographs 11Taylor & Francis, London.

Crepon, B., Duguet, E., 1997. Estimating the innovation function from patent numbers: GMM on count data. Journal of Applied Econometrics 12 (3), 243–264.

Escobar, M.D., West, M., 1995. Bayesian density estimation and inference using mixtures. Journal of the American Statistical Association 90 (430), 577–588.

Ferguson, T.S., 1973. A Bayesian analysis of some nonparametric problems. The Annals of Statistics 1 (2), 209–230.

Ferguson, T.S., 1974. Prior distributions on spaces of probability measures. The Annals of Statistics 2 (4), 615–629.

Fotouhi, A.R., 2005. The initial conditions problem in longitudinal binary process: a simulation study. Simulation Modelling Practice and Theory 13 (7), 566–583.

Gelfand, A.E., 1996. Model determination using sampling-based methods. In: Gilks, W.R., Richardson, S., Spiegelhalter, D.J. (Eds.), Markov Chain Monte Carlo in practice. Chapman & Hall, London, pp. 145–161.

Gelfand, A.E., Dey, D.K., 1994. Bayesian model choice: asymptotics and exact calculations. Journal of the Royal Statistical Society, Series B (Statistical Methodology) 56 (3), 501–514.

Gelman, A., Carlin, J.B., Stern, H.S., Dunson, D.B., Vehtari, A., Rubin, D.B., 2013. Bayesian data analysis, 3rd ed. Chapman & Hall/CRC, New York.

Ghosal, S., 2010. The Dirichlet process, related priors and posterior asymptotics. In: Hjort, N., Holmes, C., Müller, P., Walker, S.G. (Eds.), Bayesian nonparametrics: Principles and practice. Cambridge University Press, Cambridge.

Hastings, W.K., 1970. Monte Carlo sampling methods using Markov chains and their applications. Biometrika 57 (1), 97–109.

Heckman, J.J., 1981a. Heterogeneity and state dependence. In: Rosen, S. (Ed.), Studies in labor markets. University of Chicago Press, Chicago, pp. 91–140.

Heckman, J.J., 1981b. The incidental parameters problem and the problem of initial conditions in estimating a discrete time-discrete data stochastic process. In: Manski, C.F., McFadden, D. (Eds.), Structural analysis of discrete data with econometric applications. The MIT Press, Cambridge, p. 179196.

Jochmann, M., Len-Gonzlez, R., 2004. Estimating the demand for health care with panel data: a semiparametric Bayesian approach. Health Economics 13 (10), 1003–1014.

Lavine, M., 1992. Some aspects of Pólya tree distributions for statistical modelling. The Annals of Statistics 20 (3), 1222–1235.

Lavine, M., 1994. More aspects of Pólya tree distributions for statistical modelling. The Annals of Statistics 22 (3), 1161–1176.

Lijoi, A., Mena, R.H., Prünster, I., 2005. Hierarchical mixture modeling with normalized inverse-Gaussian priors. Journal of the American Statistical Association 100 (472), 1278–1291.

Lo, A.Y., 1984. On a class of Bayesian nonparametric estimates. I. Density estimates. The Annals of Statistics 12 (1), 351–357.

MacEachern, S.N., 1994. Estimating normal means with a conjugate style Dirichlet process prior. Communications in Statistics: Simulation and Computation 23 (3), 727–741.

MacEachern, S.N., Müller, P., 1998. Estimating mixture of Dirichlet process models. Journal of Computational and Graphical Statistics 7 (2), 223–238.

Mukherji, A., Roychoudhury, S., Ghosh, P., Brown, S., 2016. Estimating health demand for an aging population: A flexible and robust Bayesian joint model. Journal of Applied Econometrics 31 (6), 1140–1158.

Müller, P., Quintana, F.A., 2004. Nonparametric Bayesian data analysis. Statistical Science 19 (1), 95–110.

Mundlak, Y., 1978. On the pooling of time series and cross-section data. Econometrica 46 (1), 69–85.

Navarro, D.J., Griffiths, T.L., Steyver, M., Lee, M.D., 2006. Modeling individual differences using Dirichlet processes. Journal of Mathematical Psychology 50 (2), 101–122.

Pitman, J., 1996. Some developments of the Blackwell-MacQueen urn scheme. In: Ferguson, T.S., Shapley, L.S., MacQueen, J.B. (Eds.), Statistics, probability and game theory: Papers in honor of David Blackwell, IMS lecture notes-monograph series. Vol. 30. pp. 245–267. Hayward, CA.

Robert, C., Casella, G., 2004. Monte Carlo statistical methods, second ed. Springer-Verlag, New York.

Sethuraman, J., 1994. A constructive definition of Dirichlet priors. Statistica Sinica 4 (2), 639–650.

Sethuraman, J., Tiwari, R.C., 1982. Convergence of Dirichlet measures and the interpre tation of their parameter. Statistical Decision Theory and Related Topics III.2, pp. 305–315.

Spiegelhalter, D., Best, N., Carlin, B., Van Der Linde, A., 2002. Bayesian measures of model complexity and fit. Journal of the Royal Statistical Society, Series B (Statistical Methodology) 64 (4), 583–639.

Tanner, M.A., Wong, W.H., 1987. The calculation of posterior distributions by data augmentation. Journal of the American Statistical Association 82 (398), 528–540.

Winkelmann, R., 2008. Econometric analysis of count data, fifth ed. Springer-Verlag, Berlin.

Wooldridge, J.M., 2005. Simple solutions to the initial conditions problem in dynamic, nonlinear panel data models with unobserved heterogeneity. Journal of Applied Econometrics 20 (1), 39–54.

Zeger, S.L., Qaqish, B., 1988. Markov regression models for time series: a quasi-likelihood approach. Biometrics 44 (4), 1019–1031.

Zheng, X., 2008. Semiparametric Bayesian estimation of mixed count regression models. Economics Letters 100 (3), 435–438.

Further Reading

Chib, S., Jeliazkov, I., 2006. Inference in semiparametric dynamic models for binary longitudinal data. Journal of the American Statistical Association 101 (474), 685–700.

Chapter 7

Fixed Effects Likelihood Approach for Large Panels

Chihwa Kao* and Fa Wang[†]
*Department of Economics, University of Connecticut, Storrs, CT, United States, [†]Faculty of Finance, Cass Business School, London, United Kingdom

Chapter Outline

1 Introduction

Panel data has the advantage of controlling unobserved heterogeneity by including individual effects and time effects. The random effects approach assumes the unobserved effects are random and their distributions conditioning on the regressors satisfy some special conditions. These conditions are crucial for identification but cannot be verified easily. The fixed effects approach treats the unobserved effects as parameters to be estimated, therefore allowing arbitrary correlation between the unobserved effects and the regressors. Estimation of the unobserved effects, however, brings in the incidental parameter problem.

Under the fixed T framework, some smart methods, such as differencing or conditioning on sufficient statistics, are developed to get consistent estimator of the regressor coefficients, e.g., Manski (1987), Honore (1992) and many others. In general, however, the fixed T framework has limitations in dealing with the incidental parameter problem. With the increased availability of large panels, the literature gradually switched to the large T framework. Under this new

Panel Data Econometrics. https://doi.org/10.1016/B978-0-12-814367-4.00007-1

asymptotic scheme, the estimated regression coefficients are shown to be asymptotically normal with biased mean, and various bias correction methods are developed to provide valid confidence intervals. For example, see Hahn and Newey (2004), Fernandez-Val and Weidner (2016), and Dhaene and Jochmans (2015).

In this chapter, we focus only on the techniques used to derive the limit distribution of the estimated regression coefficients. Bias correction methods will not be discussed here, nor panel with interactive effects and other extensions. For a comprehensive survey, see Arellano and Hahn (2007) and Fernandez-Val and Weidner (2017). These surveys mainly focus on the results, and only briefly discuss the intuition for deriving these results. Understanding the joint limits[1] asymptotic theory for the estimated parameters is still difficult and time-consuming. Different papers use different notations and different techniques, some are similar in nature, while others are totally different. This chapter seeks to provide a unified framework to introduce and explain the main techniques used in the literature.

When the number of parameters is fixed, consistency and limit distribution of maximum likelihood estimator are well-established (see Newey & McFadden, 1994). These classical results are not directly applicable for fixed effects panel data models, because the number of parameters $K+N+T$ goes to infinity jointly with the sample size. The fixed effects panel models, however, have certain sparsity structure, i.e.,

$$\begin{aligned}
\partial_{\lambda_i} l_{jt}(\cdot) &= 0 \text{ if } i \neq j, \\
\partial_{f_t} l_{is}(\cdot) &= 0 \text{ if } s \neq t, \\
\partial_{\lambda_i \lambda_j} l_{it}(\cdot) &= 0 \text{ if } i \neq j, \\
\partial_{f_t f_s} l_{it}(\cdot) &= 0 \text{ if } s \neq t, \\
\partial_{\lambda_i f_t} l_{js}(\cdot) &= 0 \text{ if } i \neq j \text{ or } s \neq t, \\
\partial_{\beta \lambda_j} l_{it}(\cdot) &= 0 \text{ if } i \neq j, \\
\partial_{\beta f_s} l_{it}(\cdot) &= 0 \text{ if } s \neq t, \\
\partial_{\beta \lambda_i \lambda_j} l_{it}(\cdot) &= 0 \text{ if } i \neq j, \\
&\cdots\cdots
\end{aligned}$$

where $l_{it}(\cdot)$ is the likelihood function of the ith individual at time t. The fixed effects panel literature uses this structure in extending the classical theory of MLE to reestablish the consistency and limit distribution of $\hat{\beta}$. For linear dynamic panel with individual effects, see Hahn and Kuersteiner (2002). For linear dynamic panel with individual effects and time effects, see Hahn and Moon (2006). For nonlinear static panel with individual effects, see Hahn and Newey (2004). For nonlinear dynamic panel with individual effects, see

1. N and T tend to infinity jointly.

Hahn and Kuersteiner (2011). For nonlinear dynamic panel with individual effects and time effects, see Fernandez-Val and Weidner (2016). Among these papers, Hahn and Newey (2004) and Fernandez-Val and Weidner (2016) are most representative for the techniques used to handle the incidental parameters problem. Understanding these two papers is almost halfway to understanding all of the bias correction literature. We provide detailed discussion about their working mechanism.

Throughout the paper, $(N, T) \to \infty$ denotes N and T going to infinity jointly. $\xrightarrow{d}$ denotes convergence in distribution. For matrix A, let $\rho_{\min}(A)$ denote its smallest eigenvalue, $\|A\|$ and $\|A\|_{\max}$ denote its spectral norm and max norm respectively. For vector a, let $\|a\|$ and $\|a\|_4$ denote its Euclidean norm and 4-norm. Note that when a is high dimensional, different norms are not equivalent. The rest of the chapter is organized as follows: Section 2 introduces notations and preliminaries. Section 3, Section 4, and Section 5 provide asymptotic theory for the fixed dimensional case, for panel with only individual effects and for panel with both individual and time effects, respectively. Section 6 offers conclusions.

2 Notations and Preliminaries

For panel models with both individual effects and time effects, the log-likelihood function is

$$L(\beta, \lambda, f) = \sum_{i=1}^{N} \sum_{t=1}^{R} l_{it}\left(x_{it}'\beta + \lambda_i + f_t\right), \tag{1}$$

where $l_{it}(\pi_{it}) = \log\ g_{it}(y_{it} | \pi_{it})$ and $\pi_{it} = x_{it}'\beta + f_t + \lambda_i$. y_{it} is the dependent variable. x_{it} is a K dimensional vector of regressors. Lagged dependent variables are allowed for. The functional form of $g_{it}(\cdot|\cdot)$ is allowed to vary across i and t. Let $\lambda = (\lambda_1, \ldots, \lambda_N)'$, $f = (f_1, \ldots, f_T)'$, $\phi = (\lambda', f')'$ and $\theta = (\beta', \lambda', f')'$. When letters have superscript 0, they denote the true parameters. For example, $\pi_{it}^0 = x_{it}'\beta^0 + f_t^0 + \lambda_i^0$, $\lambda^0 = (\lambda_1^0, \ldots, \lambda_N^0)'$ and $f^0 = (f_1^0, \ldots, f_T^0)'$. Also, let $\partial_\pi l_{it}(\pi_{it})$, $\partial_{\pi^2} l_{it}(\pi_{it})$, $\partial_{\pi^3} l_{it}(\pi_{it})$ and $\partial_{\pi^4} l_{it}(\pi_{it})$ denote the first, second, third and fourth order derivatives of $l_{it}(\cdot)$ evaluated at π_{it}, respectively.

Both individual effects and time effects are treated as parameters to be estimated through maximum likelihood. For any λ_i, f_t and constant b, $\lambda_i + b$ and f_t - b has the same likelihood as λ_i and f_t. Thus $\sum_{i=1}^{N} \lambda_i^0$ and $\sum_{t=1}^{T} f_t^0$ are not identified. We simply assume $\sum_{i=1}^{N} \lambda_i^0 = \sum_{t=1}^{T} f_t^0$, and add the penalty

$$P(\lambda, f) = -\frac{b}{2}\left(\sum_{i=1}^{N} \lambda_i - \sum_{t=1}^{T} f_t\right)^2 \tag{2}$$

to the log-likelihood to get unique solution, where b is an arbitrary positive constant.

Therefore, the criterion function is

$$Q(\beta, \lambda, f) = L(\beta, \lambda, f) + P(\lambda, f), \tag{3}$$

and the fixed effects estimator is

$$\hat{\theta} = \left(\hat{\beta}', \hat{\lambda}', \hat{f}'\right)' = \arg\max Q(\beta, \lambda, f). \tag{4}$$

Also, let $\hat{\phi} = \left(\hat{\lambda}', \hat{f}'\right)'$ and $\hat{\pi}_{it} = x_{it}'\hat{\beta} + \hat{\lambda}_i + \hat{f}_t$. For the first-order derivatives, let

$$\begin{aligned}
S_\beta(\theta) &= \partial_\beta Q(\theta),\\
S_\lambda(\theta) &= \partial_\lambda Q(\theta),\\
S_f(\theta) &= \partial_f Q(\theta),\\
S_\phi(\theta) &= \partial_\phi Q(\theta),\\
S(\theta) &= \partial_\theta Q(\theta).
\end{aligned}$$

It follows that $S_\phi(\theta) = (S'_\lambda(\theta), S_f'(\theta))'$ and $S(\theta) = (S_\beta'(\theta), S_\phi'(\theta))'$. For the second-order derivatives, let

$$H(\theta) = \partial_{\theta\theta'} Q(\theta)$$

be the Hessian matrix. When the argument of a function is suppressed, the true values of the parameters are plugged in. For example, $S = S(\theta^0)$ and $H = H(\theta^0)$. Because $\sum_{i=1}^N \lambda_i^0 = \sum_{t=1}^T f_t^0$, we have $\partial_\lambda P = \partial_f P = 0$. Therefore,

$$S_\beta(\theta) = \sum_{i=1}^N \sum_{t=1}^T \partial_\pi l_{it} x_{it}, \tag{5}$$

$$S_\lambda(\theta) = \sum_{t=1}^T \partial_\pi l_{1t}, \ldots, \sum_{t=1}^T \partial_\pi l_{Nt}, \tag{6}$$

$$S_f(\theta) = \sum_{i=1}^N \partial_\pi l_{i1}, \ldots, \sum_{i=1}^N \partial_\pi l_{iT}. \tag{7}$$

The Hessian matrix can be written as:

$$H(\theta) = \begin{bmatrix} H_{\beta\beta'}(\theta) & H_{\beta\phi'}(\theta) \\ H_{\phi\beta'}(\theta) & H_{\phi\phi'}(\theta) \end{bmatrix}.$$

Let $H_{L\phi\phi'}(\phi) = \partial_{\phi\phi'} L(\phi)$ and $H_{P\ \phi\phi'}(\phi) = \partial_{\phi\phi'} P(\phi)$. We have

$$H_{\beta\beta'}(\theta) = \sum_{i=1}^N \sum_{t=1}^T \partial_{\pi^2} l_{it}(\pi_{it}) x_{it} x_{it}', \tag{8}$$

$$\begin{aligned}
H_{\beta\phi'}(\theta) = (&\sum_{t=1}^T \partial_{\pi^2} l_{1t}(\pi_{1t}) x_{1t}, \ldots, \sum_{t=1}^T \partial_{\pi^2} l_{Nt}(\pi_{Nt}) x_{Nt},\\
&\sum_{i=1}^N \partial_{\pi^2} l_{i1}(\pi_{i1}) x_{i1}, \ldots, \sum_{i=1}^N \partial_{\pi^2} l_{iT}(\pi_{iT}) x_{iT}),
\end{aligned} \tag{9}$$

$$H_{\phi\phi'}(\theta) = H_{L\phi\phi'}(\theta) + H_{P\phi\phi'}(\phi). \tag{10}$$

$H_{L\phi\phi'}(\theta)$ can be further decomposed as

$$H_{L\phi\phi'}(\theta) = \begin{bmatrix} H_{L\lambda\lambda'}(\theta) & H_{L\lambda f'}(\theta) \\ H_{Lf\lambda'}(\theta) & H_{Lff'}(\theta) \end{bmatrix}. \tag{11}$$

$H_{L\lambda\lambda'}(\theta)$ is an $N \times N$ diagonal matrix and the ith diagonal element is $\sum_{t=1}^{T}\partial_{\pi^2}l_{it}(\pi_{it})$. $H_{Lff'}(\theta)$ is a $T \times T$ diagonal matrix and the tth diagonal element is $\sum_{t=1}^{T}\partial_{\pi^2}l_{it}(\pi_{it})$. $H_{L\lambda f'}(\theta)$ is an $N \times T$ matrix and the (i, t)th element is $\partial_{\pi^2}l_{it}(\pi_{it})$. $H_{Lf\lambda'}(\theta)$ is the transpose of $H_{L\lambda f'}(\theta)$. Let 1_N and 1_T be vectors of ones with dimension N and T, respectively, and let $v = (1_N', -1_T')'$. We have

$$H_{P\phi\phi'}(\phi) = -bvv'. \tag{12}$$

Finally, let $\partial_{\theta\theta'\theta}Q(\theta)$ be the tensor cube of third-order partial derivatives evaluated at θ. Each cross section of $\partial_{\theta\theta'\theta}Q(\theta)$ is a matrix of dimension $\dim(\theta) \times \dim(\theta)$, and the ith cross section is $\partial_{\theta\theta'\theta_i}Q(\theta)$. Thus $\partial_{\theta\theta'\theta}Q(\theta)$ contains $\partial_{\beta\beta'\beta}Q(\theta)$, $\partial_{\phi\phi'\beta}Q(\theta)$, etc. as subcubes. Also, let $\partial_{\theta\theta'\theta}Q(s) = \partial_{\theta\theta'\theta}Q\left(\theta^0 + s\left(\hat{\theta} - \theta^0\right)\right)$ and define $\partial_{\beta\beta'\beta}Q(s)$, $\partial_{\phi\phi'\beta}Q(s)$, etc. similarly.

The procedure for deriving the limit distribution of $\hat{\beta}$ has three steps: consistency, asymptotic expansion, and bias calculation. We start from the classical fixed dimension case discussed in Newey and McFadden (1994).

3 Fixed Dimensional Case

Following the notation of Section 2, let θ, $\hat{\theta}$, $l_t(\theta)$, $Q(\theta)$, $S(\theta)$, $H(\theta)$, and T denote the parameter, the estimator, the likelihood function, the criterion function, the score, the Hessian, and the sample size, respectively. Also, let d denote the dimension of the parameter space.

3.1 Consistency

Let Θ denote the parameter space of θ and $\bar{Q}(\theta) = \mathbb{E}Q(\theta)$. Consistency follows from the following conditions:

1. $\hat{\theta} = \arg\max_{\theta\in\Theta} Q(\theta)$ and is unique.
2. $\theta^0 = \arg\max_{\theta\in\Theta} \bar{Q}(\theta)$ and is unique.
3. $Q(\theta)$ converges uniformly in probability to $\bar{Q}(\theta)$, i.e., $\sup_{\theta\in\Theta}\left|Q(\theta) - \bar{Q}(\theta)\right| = o_p(1)$.
4. $\bar{Q}(\theta)$ is continuous.
5. Θ is compact.

Conditions (1), (2), (4), and (5) can be considered as regularity conditions. Condition (3) is crucial. Details about how to establish condition (3) for econometric models can be found in Newey and McFadden (1994).

Conditions (1)–(3) together implies that, for any $\epsilon > 0$,

$$\bar{Q}(\theta^0) > \bar{Q}(\hat{\theta}) > Q(\hat{\theta}) - \varepsilon > Q(\theta^0) - \varepsilon > \bar{Q}(\theta^0) - 2\varepsilon, \tag{13}$$

with probability approaching 1 (w.p.a.1). The four inequalities follow from conditions (2), (3), (1), and (3) respectively. For any small $c > 0$, $\Theta \cap \|\theta - \theta^0\| \geq c$ is a closed subset of a compact set, and therefore is also compact. This together with condition (4) implies that $\theta^* = \arg \max_{\theta\in\Theta. \|\theta-\theta^0\|\geq c} \bar{Q}(\theta)$ exists. Condition (2) implies $\bar{Q}(\theta^0) > \bar{Q}(\theta^*)$. Now choose ϵ such that $2\varepsilon < \bar{Q}(\theta^0) - \bar{Q}(\theta^*)$, then we have $\bar{Q}(\hat{\theta}) > \bar{Q}(\theta^*)$ w.p.a.1, which implies $\|\hat{\theta} - \theta^0\| < c$ w.p.a.1.

3.2 Asymptotic Expansion

The first-order conditions are $\partial_\theta Q(\hat{\theta}) = 0$. Expand these conditions to the third order,[2] we have

$$0 = \partial_\theta Q(\hat{\theta}) = S + H \times (\hat{\theta} - \theta^0) + R, \tag{14}$$

where $R = (R_1, \ldots, R_d)'$, $R_i = (\hat{\theta} - \theta^0)' \left[\int_0^1 \int_0^{s_1} \partial_{\theta\theta'\theta_i} Q(s_2) ds_2 ds_1\right] (\hat{\theta} - \theta^0)$ and $Q(s) = Q(\theta^0 + s(\hat{\theta} - \theta^0))$. It follows that

$$\hat{\theta} - \theta^0 = -H^{-1}S - H^{-1}R. \tag{15}$$

Because the dimension d is fixed, it is not difficult to show that

$$\|H^{-1}\| = O_p(T^{-1}), \tag{16}$$

$$\|R\| = O_p(1). \tag{17}$$

Let $\overline{H}(\theta) = \mathbb{E}H(\theta)$ denote the expected Hessian. $\lim_{T\to\infty} T^{-1}\overline{H}$ is assumed to be positive definite. First, after weak dependence conditions are imposed, each element of $T^{-1}H$ converges in probability to its corresponding element of $T^{-1}\overline{H}$. Because the dimension is fixed, this implies $\|T^{-1}H - T^{-1}\overline{H}\|$ is $o_p(1)$. This implies that $\rho_{\min}(T^{-1}H)$ converges in probability to $\rho_{\min}(T^{-1}\overline{H})$ since $|\rho_{\min}(T^{-1}H) - \rho_{\min}(T^{-1}\overline{H})| \leq \|T^{-1}H - T^{-1}\overline{H}\|$. $\rho_{\min}(T^{-1}\overline{H})$ is bounded away from zero, thus $\|(T^{-1}H)^{-1}\|$ is $O_p(1)$. This proves equation Eq. (16).

Now consider R. Given consistency of $\hat{\theta}$, it can be easily shown that for each i, each element of the $K \times K$ matrix $\int_0^1 \int_0^{s_1} \partial_{\theta\theta'\theta_i} Q(s_2) ds_2 ds_1$ is $O_p(T)$. Because the dimension d is fixed, this implies that $\|\int_0^1 \int_0^{s_1} \partial_{\theta\theta'\theta_i} Q(s_2) ds_2 ds_1\|$ is also $O_p(T)$, and thus $|R_i| = O_p\left(T\|\hat{\theta} - \theta^0\|^2\right)$. Again, because the dimension is fixed, we have $\|R\| = O_p\left(T\|\hat{\theta} - \theta^0\|^2\right)$. This, together with Eqs. (15) and (16), shows that

$$\hat{\theta} - \theta^0 = -H^{-1}S + O_p\left(\|\hat{\theta} - \theta^0\|^2\right) = -H^{-1}S + o_p(\|\hat{\theta} - \theta^0\|). \tag{18}$$

It is easy to see that $\|S\|$ is $O_p\left(T^{\frac{1}{2}}\right)$ after weak dependence condition is imposed. Therefore, $\|\hat{\theta} - \theta^0\|$ is $O_p\left(T^{-\frac{1}{2}}\right)$, which further implies that

2. Note that mean value theorem for vector-valued functions does not exist. We use the integral form of the mean value theorem for vector-valued functions.

$$\hat{\theta}-\theta^0=-H^{-1}S+O_p\left(T^{-1}\right). \tag{19}$$

3.3 Bias Calculation

When dimension is fixed, we have $T^{-\frac{1}{2}}S \xrightarrow{d} N\left(0,\overline{H}\right)$. We have shown that $\left\|T^{-1}H-T^{-1}\overline{H}\right\|$ is $o_p(1)$. Therefore, we have $T^{\frac{1}{2}}\left(\hat{\theta}-\theta^0\right) \xrightarrow{d} N\left(0,\overline{H}^{-1}\right)$, that is, the asymptotic bias is zero.

4 Panel With Individual Effects

In extending the fixed dimensional MLE previously discussed to panel models with individual effects, we face two difficulties: consistency and asymptotic expansion. For consistency, the main difficulty is that we need to show uniform convergence in probability of $Q(\theta)$ to $\bar{Q}(\theta)$ when the dimension of the parameter space tends to infinity jointly with the sample size. For asymptotic expansion, the difficulty is that the dimensions of H, $\int_0^1\int_0^{s_1}\partial_{\theta\theta'\theta_i}Q(s_2)ds_2ds_1$, and R all tend to infinity jointly with the sample size. The key step of asymptotic expansion is to evaluate the magnitude of $\|H^{-1}\|$ and $\|R\|$. The increasing dimension makes this step much harder, if not impossible. Now we introduce how Hahn and Newey (2004) overcome these two difficulties.

Following the notation of Section 2, for panel models with only individual effects, the log-likelihood function is $L(\beta,\lambda)=\sum_{i=1}^N\sum_{t=1}^T l_{it}(x_{it}'\beta+\lambda_i)$, where $l_{it}(\pi_{it})=\log g_{it}(y_{it}\mid\pi_{it})$ and $\pi_{it}=x_{it}'\beta+\lambda_i$ is the dependent variable. x_{it} is a K dimensional vector of regressors. Lagged dependent variables are allowed for. The functional form of $g_{it}(\cdot|\cdot)$ is allowed to vary across i and t. Since λ_i^0 is uniquely identified when there are no time effects, we have $Q(\beta,\lambda)=L(\beta,\lambda)$. Let $\lambda=(\lambda_1,\ldots,\lambda_N)'$ and $\theta=(\beta',\lambda')'$. Let λ^0 and θ^0 denote the true parameters and $\hat{\theta}=\left(\hat{\beta}',\hat{\lambda}'\right)'$ $=$ arg max $Q(\beta,\lambda)$ denote the estimator. Also, $\hat{\theta}-\theta^0=\left(\left(\hat{\beta}-\beta^0\right)',\left(\hat{\lambda}-\lambda^0\right)'\right)'$, $R=(R_\beta',R_\lambda')'$ and the Hessian matrix is

$$H=\begin{bmatrix} H_{\beta\beta'} & H_{\beta\lambda'} \\ H_{\lambda\beta'} & H_{\lambda\lambda'} \end{bmatrix}.$$

$H_{\lambda\lambda'}$ is diagonal and the ith diagonal element is $\sum_{t=1}^T\partial_{\pi^2}l_{it}$.

4.1 Consistency

In general, we do not have uniform convergence in probability of $Q(\theta)$ to $\bar{Q}(\theta)$ when the dimension of θ tends to infinity. Hahn and Newey (2004) and Hahn and Kuersteiner (2011) overcome this issue by using the individual effects model specification. More specifically, given the model setup, we have $Q(\theta)=\sum_{i=1}^N Q_i(\beta,\lambda_i)$ and $Q_i(\beta,\lambda_i)=\sum_{t=1}^T l_{it}(x_{it}'\beta+\lambda_i)$. Therefore, $N^{-1}T^{-1}Q(\theta)$

is the average of $T^{-1}Q_i(\beta,\ \lambda_i)$. Similarly, $N^{-1}T^{-1}\bar{Q}(\theta)$ is the average of $T^{-1}\bar{Q}_i(\beta,\lambda_i)$, where $\bar{Q}_i(\beta,\lambda_i)=\mathbb{E}Q_i(\beta,\lambda_i)$. For each i, it would not be difficult to show uniform convergence in probability of $T^{-1}Q_i(\beta,\ \lambda_i)$ to $T^{-1}\bar{Q}_i(\beta,\lambda_i)$ because $(\beta,\ \lambda_i)$ is fixed dimensional. After we have uniform convergence for each i, it suffices to show this uniform convergence is uniform over i, i.e.,

$$\max_{1\leq i\leq N}\sup_{\beta,\lambda_i}\left|T^{-1}\left(Q_i(\beta,\lambda_i)-\bar{Q}_i(\beta,\lambda_i)\right)\right|=o_p(1), \tag{20}$$

because $\sup_\theta\left|N^{-1}T^{-1}\left(Q(\theta)-\bar{Q}(\theta)\right)\right|\leq\max_{1\leq i\leq N}\sup_{\beta,\lambda_i}\left|T^{-1}\left(Q_i(\beta,\lambda_i)-\bar{Q}_i\ (\beta,\lambda_i)\right)\right|$.

To show Eq. (20), Hahn and Newey (2004) and Hahn and Kuersteiner (2011) show that

$$P\left(\sup_{\beta,\lambda_i}\left|\ T^{-1}\left(Q_i(\beta,\lambda_i)-\bar{Q}_i(\beta,\lambda_i)\right)\right|\ \geq\eta\right)=o\left(T^{-2}\right). \tag{21}$$

This is because $N=O(T)$ and $P\left(\max_{1\leq i\leq N}\sup_{\beta,\lambda_i}\left|T^{-1}\left(Q_i(\beta,\lambda_i)-\bar{Q}_i\ (\beta,\lambda_i)\right)\right|\geq\eta\right)$ is not larger than $\sum_{i=1}^N P\left(\sup_{\beta,\lambda_i}T^{-1}\left(Q_i(\beta,\lambda_i)-\bar{Q}_i(\beta,\lambda_i)\right)\geq\eta\right)$.

4.2 Asymptotic Expansion

The first-order conditions (14) is still valid and can be written as

$$0=S_\beta+H_{\beta\beta'}\left(\hat{\beta}-\beta^0\right)+H_{\beta\lambda'}\left(\hat{\lambda}-\lambda^0\right)+R_\beta, \tag{22}$$

$$0=S_\lambda+H_{\lambda\beta'}\left(\hat{\beta}-\beta^0\right)+H_{\lambda\lambda'}\left(\hat{\lambda}-\lambda^0\right)+R_\lambda, \tag{23}$$

and R_β and R_λ have the following expression:

$$\begin{aligned}
R_\beta&=R_{\beta\beta\beta}+R_{\beta\lambda\beta}+R_{\lambda\lambda\beta},\\
R_{\beta\beta\beta}&=\left(\hat{\beta}-\beta^0\right)'\left(\int_0^1\int_0^{s_1}\partial_{\beta\beta'\beta}Q(s_2)ds_2ds_1\right)\left(\hat{\beta}-\beta^0\right),\\
R_{\beta\lambda\beta}&=2\left(\hat{\beta}-\beta^0\right)'\left(\int_0^1\int_0^{s_1}\partial_{\beta\lambda'\beta}Q(s_2)ds_2ds_1\right)\left(\hat{\lambda}-\lambda^0\right),\\
R_{\lambda\lambda\beta}&=\left(\hat{\lambda}-\lambda^0\right)'\left(\int_0^1\int_0^{s_1}\partial_{\lambda\lambda'\beta}Q(s_2)ds_2ds_1\right)\left(\hat{\lambda}-\lambda^0\right),\\
R_\lambda&=R_{\beta\beta\lambda}+R_{\beta\lambda\lambda}+R_{\lambda\lambda\lambda},\\
R_{\beta\beta\lambda}&=\left(\hat{\beta}-\beta^0\right)'\left(\int_0^1\int_0^{s_1}\partial_{\beta\beta'\lambda}Q(s_2)ds_2ds_1\right)\left(\hat{\beta}-\beta^0\right),\\
R_{\beta\lambda\lambda}&=2\left(\hat{\beta}-\beta^0\right)'\left(\int_0^1\int_0^{s_1}\partial_{\beta\lambda'\lambda}Q(s_2)ds_2ds_1\right)\left(\hat{\lambda}-\lambda^0\right),\\
R_{\lambda\lambda\lambda}&=\left(\hat{\lambda}-\lambda^0\right)'\left(\int_0^1\int_0^{s_1}\partial_{\lambda\lambda'\lambda}Q(s_2)ds_2ds_1\right)\left(\hat{\lambda}-\lambda^0\right).
\end{aligned} \tag{24}$$

Eq. (22) subtracts Eq. (23) left multiplied by $H_{\beta\lambda'}H_{\lambda\lambda'}^{-1}$, we have

$$\hat{\beta}-\beta^0 = -\left(H_{\beta\beta'}-H_{\beta\lambda'}H_{\lambda\lambda'}^{-1}H_{\lambda\beta'}\right)^{-1}\left(S_\beta-H_{\beta\lambda'}H_{\lambda\lambda'}^{-1}S_\lambda\right) \\ -\left(H_{\beta\beta'}-H_{\beta\lambda'}H_{\lambda\lambda'}^{-1}H_{\lambda\beta'}\right)^{-1}\left(R_\beta-H_{\beta\lambda'}H_{\lambda\lambda'}^{-1}R_\lambda\right). \tag{25}$$

First, consider the matrix $H_{\beta\beta\prime} - H_{\beta\lambda\prime}H_{\lambda\lambda\prime}^{-1}H_{\lambda\beta\prime}$. This expression does not rely on any econometric model structure, because expression Eq. (25) is always true. What's special is that $H_{\beta\beta\prime}$ is sum of NT terms, while $H_{\beta\lambda\prime}$ is a vector of dimension N and each element is sum of T terms, and $H_{\lambda\lambda\prime}$ is a diagonal matrix of dimension N and each diagonal element is sum of T terms. This specialty comes from the individual effects model specification. Because of this specialty, we are able to show

$$\|\left(H_{\beta\beta'}-H_{\beta\lambda'}H_{\lambda\lambda}^{-1},H_{\lambda\beta'}\right)^{-1}\| = O_p\left(N^{-1}T^{-1}\right), \tag{26}$$

which is not true in general. To show Eq. (25), let $\overline{H}_{\beta\beta'} = \mathbb{E}H_{\beta\beta'}$, $\overline{H}_{\beta\lambda'} = \mathbb{E}H_{\beta\lambda'}$ and $\overline{H}_{\lambda\lambda'} = \mathbb{E}H_{\lambda\lambda'}$. After relevant regularity conditions are imposed, it's easy to show that $\|H_{\beta\beta'}-\overline{H}_{\beta\beta'}\|$ is o_p (NT) $\|H_{\beta\lambda'}-\overline{H}_{\beta\lambda'}\|$ is $o_p\left(N^{\frac{1}{2}}T\right)$ and $\left\|H_{\lambda\lambda'}^{-1}-\overline{H}_{\lambda\lambda'}^{-1}\right\|$ is $o_p(T^{-1})$. These together imply that $\|\left(H_{\beta\beta'}-H_{\beta\lambda'}H_{\lambda\lambda'}^{-1}H_{\lambda\beta'}\right) -\left(\overline{H}_{\beta\beta'}-\overline{H}_{\beta\lambda'}\overline{H}_{\lambda\lambda'}^{-1}\overline{H}_{\lambda\beta'}\right)\|$ is $o_p(NT)$. Because $\lim_{(N,T)\to\infty} N^{-1}T^{-1}\left(\overline{H}_{\beta\beta'}-\overline{H}_{\beta\lambda'}\overline{H}_{\lambda\lambda'}^{-1}\overline{H}_{\lambda\beta'}\right)$ is assumed to be positive definite,[3] this proves Eq. (25).

Next consider $S_\beta - H_{\beta\lambda\prime}H_{\lambda\lambda\prime}^{-1}S_\lambda$. This term can be written as

$$S_\beta-H_{\beta\lambda'}H_{\lambda\lambda'}^{-1}S_\lambda = S_\beta-\overline{H}_{\beta\lambda'}H_{\lambda\lambda}^{-1},S_\lambda-\left(H_{\beta\lambda'}-\overline{H}_{\beta\lambda'}\right)H_{\lambda\lambda'}^{-1}S_\lambda- \\ \overline{H}_{\beta\lambda'}\left(H_{\lambda\lambda'}^{-1}-\overline{H}_{\lambda\lambda'}^{-1}\right)S_\lambda-\left(H_{\beta\lambda'}-\overline{H}_{\beta\lambda'}\right)\left(H_{\lambda\lambda'}^{-1}-\overline{H}_{\lambda\lambda'}^{-1}\right)S_\lambda. \tag{27}$$

Given relevant regularity conditions and noting that both $H_{\lambda\lambda\prime}$ and $\overline{H}_{\lambda\lambda'}$ are diagonal, it would not be difficult to show that

$$\begin{aligned}
\|S_\beta-\overline{H}_{\beta\lambda'}H_{\lambda\lambda}^{-1},S_\lambda\| &= O_p\left(N^{\frac{1}{2}}T^{\frac{1}{2}}\right),\\
\|H_{\beta\lambda'}-\overline{H}_{\beta\lambda'}\| &= O_p\left(N^{\frac{1}{2}}T^{\frac{1}{2}}\right),\\
\|\overline{H}_{\beta\lambda'}\| &= O_p\left(N^{\frac{1}{2}}T\right),\\
\|S_\lambda\| &= O_p\left(N^{\frac{1}{2}}T^{\frac{1}{2}}\right),\\
\left\|\overline{H}_{\lambda\lambda'}^{-1}\right\| &= O_p\left(T^{-1}\right),\\
\|H_{\lambda\lambda'}-\overline{H}_{\lambda\lambda'}\| &= O_p\left(T^{\frac{1}{2}}\right)\\
\|H_{\lambda\lambda'}^{-1}\| &= O_p\left(T^{-1}\right),\\
\left\|H_{\lambda\lambda'}^{-1}-\overline{H}_{\lambda\lambda'}^{-1}\right\| &= O_p\left(T^{-\frac{3}{2}}\right).
\end{aligned} \tag{28}$$

3. This is the standard identification condition that appears in almost all nonlinear panel literature.

Therefore, the four terms on the right side of Eq. (27) are $O_p\left(N^{\frac{1}{2}}T^{\frac{1}{2}}\right)$, $O_p(N)$, $O_p(N)$, and $O_p\left(NT^{-\frac{1}{2}}\right)$, respectively. Thus

$$\left\|\left(H_{\beta\lambda'} - \overline{H}_{\beta\lambda'}\right)\left(H_{\lambda\lambda'}^{-1} - \overline{H}_{\lambda\lambda'}^{-1}\right)S_\lambda\right\| = O_p\left(NT^{-\frac{1}{2}}\right), \tag{29}$$

$$\left\|S_\beta - H_{\beta\lambda'}H_{\lambda\lambda'}^{-1}S_\lambda\right\| = O_p\left(N^{\frac{1}{2}}T^{\frac{1}{2}}\right) + O_p(N). \tag{30}$$

Now consider $R_\beta - H_{\beta\lambda'}H_{\lambda\lambda'}^{-1}R_\lambda$. Assume[4] that there exists $c > 0$ such that third-order derivatives of $l_{it}(\beta, \lambda_i)$ with respect to β and λ_i are[5] uniformly bounded in absolute value by $M(x_{it}, y_{it})$ within the neighborhood $\|\beta - \beta^0\| \le c$ and $\|\lambda_i - \lambda_i^0\| \le c$, and $\mathbb{E}(M(x_{it}, y_{it}))^4$ is uniformly bounded over i and t. Based on this assumption, using consistency of $\hat{\beta}$ and $\hat{\lambda}_i$, and using Eq. (24), direct calculation shows that[6]

$$\begin{aligned}
\|R_{\beta\beta\beta}\| &= O_p\left(NT\|\hat{\beta} - \beta^0\|^2\right),\\
\|R_{\beta\lambda\beta}\| &= O_p\left(N^{\frac{1}{2}}T\|\hat{\beta} - \beta^0\|\|\hat{\lambda} - \lambda^0\|\right),\\
\|R_{\lambda\lambda\beta}\| &= O_p\left(T\|\hat{\lambda} - \lambda^0\|^2\right),\\
\|R_{\beta\beta\lambda}\| &= O_p\left(N^{\frac{1}{2}}T\|\hat{\beta} - \beta^0\|^2\right),\\
\|R_{\beta\lambda\lambda}\| &= O_p(T\|\hat{\beta} - \beta^0\|\|\hat{\lambda} - \lambda^0\|),\\
\|R_{\lambda\lambda\lambda}\| &= O_p\left(T\|\hat{\lambda} - \lambda^0\|_4^2\right).
\end{aligned} \tag{31}$$

To evaluate the six expressions in Eq. (31), consistency of $\hat{\beta} - \beta^0$ and $\hat{\lambda}_i - \lambda_i^0$ alone is not enough; we need their convergence rates. An important intuition shared by the nonlinear panel literature is that $\hat{\lambda} - \lambda^0 \approx H_{\lambda\lambda'}^{-1}S_\lambda$. For the moment, let's just suppose $\hat{\lambda} - \lambda^0 = H_{\lambda\lambda'}^{-1}S_\lambda$ and $\|\hat{\beta} - \beta^0\| = O_p\left(N^{-\frac{1}{2}}T^{-\frac{1}{2}}\right)$ to evaluate Eq. (31) first. The third and fifth equations of Eq. (28) imply $\|\hat{\lambda} - \lambda^0\|$

---

4. This assumption is quite common for nonlinear panel models.
5. For example, $\partial_{\beta_k\beta_k\beta_k} l_{it}(\beta, \lambda_i)$, $\partial_{\beta_k\beta_k\lambda_i} l_{it}(\beta, \lambda_i)$, … , $\partial_{\lambda_i\lambda_i\lambda_i} l_{it}(\beta, \lambda_i)$.
6. For example, consider $R_{\beta\beta\lambda}$. It is easy to see that $\left\|\int_0^1\int_0^{s_1}\partial_{\beta\beta'\lambda_i}Q(s_2)ds_2ds_1\right\| \le \frac{1}{2}\sup_{0\le s\le 1}\|\partial_{\beta\beta'\lambda_i}Q(s)\|$ and $\sup_{0\le s\le 1}\|\partial_{\beta\beta'\lambda_i}Q(s)\| \le K\sum_{t=1}^T M(x_{it}, y_{it})$ w.p.a.1. Thus $\|R_{\beta\beta\lambda}\|$ is bounded by $\frac{1}{2}K\|\hat{\beta} - \beta^0\|^2\left[T\sum_{i=1}^N\sum_{t=1}^T(M(x_{it}, y_{it}))^2\right]^{\frac{1}{2}}$, which is $O_p\left(N^{\frac{1}{2}}T\|\hat{\beta} - \beta^0\|^2\right)$.

$=O_p\left(N^{\frac{1}{2}}T^{-\frac{1}{2}}\right)$. It is not difficult to show that $\|\hat{\lambda}-\lambda^0\|_4=O_p\left(N^{\frac{1}{2}}T^{-\frac{1}{2}}\right)$, because $(\sum_{t=1}^{T}\partial_{\pi^2}l_{it})^{-1}(\sum_{t=1}^{T}\partial_{\pi}l_{it})$ is $O_p\left(T^{-\frac{1}{2}}\right)$. It follows that

$$\begin{aligned}
\|R_{\beta\beta\beta}\| &= O_p(1),\\
\|R_{\beta\lambda\beta}\| &= O_p\left(N^{\frac{1}{2}}\right),\\
\|R_{\lambda\lambda\beta}\| &= O_p(N),\\
\|H_{\beta\lambda'}H_{\lambda\lambda'}^{-1}R_{\beta\beta\lambda}\| &= O_p(1),\\
\|H_{\beta\lambda'}H_{\lambda\lambda'}^{-1}R_{\beta\lambda\lambda}\| &= O_p\left(N^{\frac{1}{2}}\right),\\
\|H_{\beta\lambda'}H_{\lambda\lambda'}^{-1}R_{\lambda\lambda\lambda}\| &= O_p(N).
\end{aligned} \tag{32}$$

Therefore, given $N/T\to\kappa$, $R_{\beta\beta\beta}$, $R_{\beta\lambda\beta}$, $H_{\beta\lambda'}H_{\lambda\lambda'}^{-1}R_{\beta\beta\lambda}$, and $H_{\beta\lambda'}H_{\lambda\lambda'}^{-1}R_{\beta\lambda\lambda}$ are asymptotically negligible compared to $S_\beta - H_{\beta\lambda'}H_{\lambda\lambda'}^{-1}S_\lambda$. $R_{\lambda\lambda\beta}$ and $H_{\beta\lambda'}H_{\lambda\lambda'}^{-1}R_{\lambda\lambda\lambda}$ are not negligible and will contribute to asymptotic bias. First, given consistency of $\hat{\beta}-\beta^0$ and $\hat{\lambda}_i-\lambda_i^0$, we have

$$\begin{aligned}
\int_0^1\int_0^{s_1}\partial_{\lambda\lambda'\beta}Q(s_2)ds_2ds_1 &\approx \frac{1}{2}\mathbb{E}\partial_{\lambda\lambda'\beta}Q,\\
H_{\beta\lambda'}H_{\lambda\lambda'}^{-1}\left(\int_0^1\int_0^{s_1}\partial_{\lambda\lambda'\lambda}Q(s_2)ds_2ds_1\right) &\approx \frac{1}{2}\overline{H}_{\beta\lambda'}\overline{H}_{\lambda\lambda'}^{-1}\mathbb{E}\partial_{\lambda\lambda'\lambda}Q.
\end{aligned}$$

This together with $\hat{\lambda}-\lambda^0\approx\overline{H}_{\lambda\lambda'}^{-1}S_\lambda$ and the fourth and eighth equations of Eq. (24) implies that

$$\begin{aligned}
R_{\lambda\lambda\beta} &\approx \frac{1}{2}S_\lambda'\overline{H}_{\lambda\lambda'}^{-1}\left(\mathbb{E}\partial_{\lambda\lambda'\beta}Q\right)\overline{H}_{\lambda\lambda'}^{-1}S_\lambda,\\
R_{\lambda\lambda\lambda} &\approx \frac{1}{2}S_\lambda'\overline{H}_{\lambda\lambda'}^{-1}\left(\overline{H}_{\beta\lambda'}\overline{H}_{\lambda\lambda'}^{-1}\mathbb{E}\partial_{\lambda\lambda'\lambda}Q\right)\overline{H}_{\lambda\lambda'}^{-1}S_\lambda.
\end{aligned} \tag{33}$$

Taking the previous analyses together, we have

$$\begin{aligned}
\hat{\beta}-\beta^0 =& -\left(\overline{H}_{\beta\beta'}-\overline{H}_{\beta\lambda'}\overline{H}_{\lambda\lambda'}^{-1}\overline{H}_{\lambda\beta'}\right)^{-1}\left(S_\beta-\overline{H}_{\beta\lambda'}\overline{H}_{\lambda\lambda'}^{-1}S_\lambda\right)\\
&+\left(\overline{H}_{\beta\beta'}-\overline{H}_{\beta\lambda'}\overline{H}_{\lambda\lambda'}^{-1}\overline{H}_{\lambda\beta'}\right)^{-1}\\
&[(H_{\beta\lambda'}-\overline{H}_{\beta\lambda'})\overline{H}_{\lambda\lambda'}^{-1}S_\lambda+\overline{H}_{\beta\lambda'}\left(H_{\lambda\lambda'}^{-1}-\overline{H}_{\lambda\lambda'}^{-1}\right)S_\lambda-\\
&\frac{1}{2}S_\lambda'\overline{H}_{\lambda\lambda'}^{-1}\left(\mathbb{E}\partial_{\lambda\lambda'\beta}Q-\overline{H}_{\beta\lambda'}\overline{H}_{\lambda\lambda'}^{-1}\mathbb{E}\partial_{\lambda\lambda'\lambda}Q\right)\overline{H}_{\lambda\lambda'}^{-1}S_\lambda]\\
&+O_p\left(T^{-\frac{3}{2}}\right)+o_p\left(N^{-\frac{1}{2}}T^{-\frac{1}{2}}\right).
\end{aligned} \tag{34}$$

Eq. (34) can be used to calculate the asymptotic variance and bias, which will be shown later. The first term on the right side will have normal distribution with zero mean in the limit. The second term will contribute to the asymptotic bias. The third and fourth terms are asymptotically negligible if $N/T \to \kappa$. Therefore, the equation clearly shows the relationship between the asymptotic variance and bias of $\hat{\beta}-\beta^0$ and the score, the Hessian, and third-order derivatives.

In deriving Eq. (34), we already have used $\hat{\lambda}-\lambda^0 \approx H_{\lambda\lambda'}^{-1}S_\lambda$ and $\|\hat{\beta}-\beta^0\| = O_p\left(N^{-\frac{1}{2}}T^{-\frac{1}{2}}\right)$, which has not been proved yet. So far, we have only consistency for each i, which is not enough to derive Eq. (34). Therefore, the remaining issue is how to prove $\hat{\lambda}-\lambda^0 \approx H_{\lambda\lambda'}^{-1}S_\lambda$ and $\|\hat{\beta}-\beta^0\| = O_p\left(N^{-\frac{1}{2}}T^{-\frac{1}{2}}\right)$ based on consistency of $\hat{\beta}-\beta^0$ and $\|\hat{\lambda}_i-\lambda_i^0\|$. This is exactly where the difficulty occurs when using first-order conditions Eqs. (22) and (23) to derive the limit distribution. So far, it is unknown how to tackle this difficulty directly.[7]

Now we introduce how Hahn and Newey (2004) and Hahn and Kuersteiner (2011) solve this difficulty. First, β, λ, and (x_{it}, y_{it}) correspond to θ, γ and x_{it}, respectively in these two papers. These two papers use empirical likelihood method to transform the first-order derivatives from function of β and λ to function of β and ϵ, where ϵ is defined as: $F(\epsilon)=\epsilon T^{\frac{1}{2}}\left(\hat{F}-F\right)$ for $\epsilon \in \left[0, T^{-\frac{1}{2}}\right]$, $F = (F_1, \ldots, F_N)$ and F_i is the (marginal) distribution function of (x_{it}, y_{it}), $\hat{F}=\left(\hat{F}_1, \ldots, \hat{F}_N\right)$ and $\hat{F}_i$ is the empirical distribution function of subject i. By Eqs. (22) and (23), $\hat{\beta}-\beta^0$ is an implicit function of $\hat{\lambda}-\lambda^0$. After the transformation, $\hat{\beta}-\beta^0$ becomes a function of ϵ, so that we do not need to deal with $\hat{\lambda}-\lambda^0$ directly. This is crucial for asymptotic expansion because ϵ is a number and we know its magnitude $\left(|\epsilon| \le T^{-\frac{1}{2}}\right)$, while $\hat{\lambda}-\lambda^0$ is a high dimensional vector and we do not know how to prove its magnitude.

More details about the transformation follows. Let $\hat{\lambda}_i(\beta) = \arg\max_{\lambda_i} \sum_{t=1}^T l_{it}(\beta, \lambda_i)$ and $\hat{\beta} = \arg\max_{\beta} \sum_{i=1}^N l_{it}\left(\beta, \hat{\lambda}_i(\beta)\right)$. The first-order conditions are

$$\sum_{t=1}^T \partial_{\lambda_i} l_{it}\left(\beta, \hat{\lambda}_i(\beta)\right) = 0, \tag{35}$$

$$\sum_{i=1}^N \sum_{t=1}^T \partial_\beta l_{it}\left(\hat{\beta}, \hat{\lambda}_i\left(\hat{\beta}\right)\right) = 0. \tag{36}$$

7. Because the dimension of $\hat{\lambda}-\lambda^0$ tends to infinity jointly as sample size, $\|\hat{\lambda}_i-\lambda_i^0\| = o_p(1)$ for each i even does not necessarily imply $\|\hat{\lambda}_i-\lambda_i^0\| = o_p\left(N^{\frac{1}{2}}\right)$.

Let $\rho_{i0} = \frac{\mathbb{E}\left(\partial_{\beta\lambda_i} l_{it}\right)}{\mathbb{E}\left(\partial_{\lambda_i\lambda_i} l_{it}\right)}$ and $U_i(x_{it}, y_{it}; \beta, \lambda_i) = \partial_\beta\, l_{it}(\beta, \lambda_i) - \rho_{i0}\partial_{\lambda_i}\, l_{it}(\beta, \lambda_i)$. Then Eqs. (35) and (36) imply that

$$\sum\nolimits_{i=1}^{N}\sum\nolimits_{t=1}^{T} U_i\left(x_{it}, y_{it}; \hat{\beta}, \hat{\lambda}_i\left(\hat{\beta}\right)\right) = 0. \tag{37}$$

Now for each given ϵ, let $\lambda_i(\beta, \epsilon)$ be the solution of

$$\int \partial_{\lambda_i} l_{it}(x_{it}, y_{it}; \beta, \lambda_i(\beta, \epsilon))dF_i(\epsilon) = 0, \tag{38}$$

and let $\hat{\beta}(\varepsilon)$ be the solution of

$$\sum\nolimits_{i=1}^{N}\int U_i\left(x_{it}, y_{it}; \hat{\beta}(\epsilon), \lambda_i\left(\hat{\beta}(\epsilon), \epsilon\right)\right)dF_i(\epsilon) = 0. \tag{39}$$

By Eqs. (38) and (39), $\hat{\beta}(\epsilon)$ is an implicit function of ϵ, and it's not difficult to see that $\hat{\beta} = \hat{\beta}\left(T^{-\frac{1}{2}}\right)$ and $\beta^0 = \hat{\beta}(0)$. Apply Taylor expansion to $\hat{\beta}(\epsilon)$, we have

$$\hat{\beta} - \beta^0 = T^{-\frac{1}{2}}\beta^\epsilon(0) + \frac{1}{2}T^{-1}\beta^{\epsilon\epsilon}(0) + \frac{1}{6}T^{-\frac{3}{2}}\beta^{\epsilon\epsilon\epsilon}(\widetilde{\epsilon}), \tag{40}$$

where $\beta^\epsilon(\epsilon) = d\hat{\beta}(\epsilon)/d\epsilon$, $\beta^{\epsilon\epsilon}(\epsilon) = \mathrm{d}^2\hat{\beta}(\epsilon)/d\epsilon^2$, $\beta^{\epsilon\epsilon\epsilon}(\epsilon) = d^3\hat{\beta}(\epsilon)/d\epsilon^3$, and $\widetilde{\epsilon} \in \left[0, T^{-\frac{1}{2}}\right]$.

Eqs. (38) and (39) can be used to calculate $\beta^\epsilon(\epsilon)$, $\beta^{\epsilon\epsilon}(\epsilon)$ and $\beta^{\epsilon\epsilon\epsilon}(\epsilon)$. Let $h_i(x_{it}, y_{it}; \epsilon) = U_i\left(x_{it}, y_{it}; \hat{\beta}(\epsilon), \lambda_i\left(\hat{\beta}(\epsilon), \epsilon\right)\right)$. Eq. (39) can be written as

$$N^{-1}\sum\nolimits_{i=1}^{N}\int h_i(x_{it}, y_{it}; \epsilon)dF_i(\epsilon) = 0. \tag{41}$$

Differentiating repeatedly with respect to ϵ, we have

$$N^{-1}\sum\nolimits_{i=1}^{N}\int\frac{dh_i(x_{it}, y_{it}; \epsilon)}{d\epsilon}dF_i(\epsilon) + N^{-1}\sum\nolimits_{i=1}^{N}\int h_i(x_{it}, y_{it}; \epsilon)d\Delta_{iT} = 0, \tag{42}$$

$$N^{-1}\sum\nolimits_{i=1}^{N}\int\frac{d^2h_i(x_{it}, y_{it}; \epsilon)}{d\epsilon^2}dF_i(\epsilon) + 2N^{-1}\sum\nolimits_{i=1}^{N}\int\frac{dh_i(x_{it}, y_{it}; \epsilon)}{d\epsilon}d\Delta_{iT} = 0, \tag{43}$$

$$N^{-1}\sum\nolimits_{i=1}^{N}\int\frac{d^3h_i(x_{it}, y_{it}; \epsilon)}{d\epsilon^3}dF_i(\epsilon) + 3N^{-1}\sum\nolimits_{i=1}^{N}\int\frac{d^2h_i(x_{it}, y_{it}; \epsilon)}{d\epsilon^2}d\Delta_{iT} = 0, \tag{44}$$

where $\Delta_{iT} = T^{\frac{1}{2}}\left(\hat{F}_i - F_i\right)$. Using these three equations together and Eq. (38), we can get expressions of $\beta^\epsilon(0)$ and $\beta^{\epsilon\epsilon}(0)$, and show that $T^{-\frac{3}{2}}\beta^{\epsilon\epsilon\epsilon}(\widetilde{\epsilon})$ is $o_p\left(N^{-\frac{1}{2}}T^{-\frac{1}{2}}\right)$. This step is tedious but not difficult. For detailed calculation procedure, see the Appendices of Hahn and Newey (2004) and Hahn and Kuersteiner (2011). It can be verified that $\beta^\epsilon(0)$ and $\beta^{\epsilon\epsilon}(0)$ corresponds to the first and the second term on the right side of Eq. (34), respectively.

4.3 Bias Calculation

Now we use Eq. (34) to calculate the limit distribution. Assume $W = -\lim_{(N,T)\to\infty} N^{-1}T^{-1}\left(\overline{H}_{\beta\beta'} - \overline{H}_{\beta\lambda'}\overline{H}_{\lambda\lambda'}^{-1}\overline{H}_{\lambda\beta'}\right)$ exists. W also is assumed to be positive definite. It can be verified that W corresponds to $\mathcal{I}$ in Hahn and Newey (2004) and Hahn and Kuersteiner (2011). The calculation contains the following four steps.

(1) $N^{-\frac{1}{2}}T^{-\frac{1}{2}}\left(S_\beta - \overline{H}_{\beta\lambda'}\overline{H}_{\lambda\lambda'}^{-1}S_\lambda\right) \xrightarrow{d} \mathcal{N}(0, W)$.

In the literature, the DGP of (x_{it}, y_{it}) is assumed such that $\partial_\pi l_{it}$ and $\partial_\pi l_{it}x_{it}$ are independent across i and $\mathbb{E}(\partial_\pi l_{it}\partial_\pi l_{is}) = 0$ and $E(\partial_\pi l_{it}\partial_\pi l_{is}x_{it}x_{is}') = 0$ for $s \neq t$.

Then it is easy to see that $N^{-\frac{1}{2}}T^{-\frac{1}{2}}S_\beta \xrightarrow{\text{d}} \mathcal{N}\left(0, -\overline{H}_{\beta\beta'}\right), N^{-\frac{1}{2}}T^{-\frac{1}{2}}\overline{H}_{\beta\lambda'}\overline{H}_{\lambda\lambda'}^{-1}S_\lambda \xrightarrow{\text{d}} \mathcal{N}\left(0, -\overline{H}_{\beta\lambda'}\overline{H}_{\lambda\lambda'}^{-1}\overline{H}_{\lambda\beta'}\right)$ and $\mathbb{E}\left(S_\beta'\overline{H}_{\beta\lambda'}\overline{H}_{\lambda\lambda'}^{-1}S_\lambda\right) = -\overline{H}_{\beta\lambda'}\overline{H}_{\lambda\lambda'}^{-1}\overline{H}_{\lambda\beta'}$.

(2) $N^{-\frac{1}{2}}T^{-\frac{1}{2}}\left(H_{\beta\lambda'} - \overline{H}_{\beta\lambda'}\right)\overline{H}_{\lambda\lambda'}^{-1}S_\lambda = \sqrt{\kappa}N^{-1}\sum_{i=1}^{N}\frac{\sum_{t=1}^{T}\sum_{s=1}^{t}\mathbb{E}\left(\partial_\pi l_{is}\partial_{\pi^2}l_{it}x_{it}\right)}{\sum_{t=1}^{T}\mathbb{E}\left(\partial_{\pi^2}l_{it}\right)} + o_p(1)$.

This is straightforward.

(3) $N^{-\frac{1}{2}}T^{-\frac{1}{2}}\overline{H}_{\beta\lambda'}\left(H_{\lambda\lambda'}^{-1} - \overline{H}_{\lambda\lambda'}^{-1}\right)S_\lambda$

$$= -\sqrt{\kappa}N^{-1}\sum_{i=1}^{N}\frac{\sum_{t=1}^{T}\sum_{s=1}^{t}\mathbb{E}(\partial_\pi l_{is}\partial_{\pi^2}l_{it})\sum_{t=1}^{T}\mathbb{E}(\partial_{\pi^2}l_{it}x_{it})}{\sum_{t=1}^{T}\mathbb{E}(\partial_{\pi^2}l_{it})\quad\sum_{t=1}^{T}\mathbb{E}(\partial_{\pi^2}l_{it})} + o_p(1).$$

This is because $H_{\lambda\lambda'}^{-1} - \overline{H}_{\lambda\lambda'}^{-1} = -\overline{H}_{\lambda\lambda'}^{-1}\left(H_{\lambda\lambda'} - \overline{H}_{\lambda\lambda'}\right)H_{\lambda\lambda'}^{-1}$ and $\left(H_{\lambda\lambda'}^{-1} - \overline{H}_{\lambda\lambda'}^{-1}\right)S_\lambda = o_p\left(N^{\frac{1}{2}}T^{-1}\right)$.

(4) $-\frac{1}{2}N^{-\frac{1}{2}}T^{-\frac{1}{2}}S_\lambda'\overline{H}_{\lambda\lambda'}^{-1}\left(\mathbb{E}\partial_{\lambda\lambda'\beta}Q - \overline{H}_{\beta\lambda'}\overline{H}_{\lambda\lambda'}^{-1}\mathbb{E}\partial_{\lambda\lambda'\lambda}Q\right)\overline{H}_{\lambda\lambda'}^{-1}S_\lambda$

$$= \frac{1}{2}\sqrt{\kappa}N^{-1}\sum_{i=1}^{N}\left(\frac{\sum_{t=1}^{T}\mathbb{E}(\partial_{\pi^3}l_{it}x_{it})}{\sum_{t=1}^{T}\mathbb{E}(\partial_{\pi^2}l_{it})} - \frac{\sum_{t=1}^{T}\mathbb{E}(\partial_{\pi^3}l_{it})\sum_{t=1}^{T}\mathbb{E}(\partial_{\pi^2}l_{it}x_{it})}{\sum_{t=1}^{T}\mathbb{E}(\partial_{\pi^2}l_{it})\sum_{t=1}^{T}\mathbb{E}(\partial_{\pi^2}l_{it})}\right) + o_p(1).$$

This is because $\mathbb{E}\partial_{\lambda\lambda'\beta}Q$ is diagonal and the ith diagonal element is $\sum_{t=1}^{T}\mathbb{E}(\partial_{\pi^3}l_{it}x_{it})$, $\mathbb{E}\left(S_\lambda S_\lambda'\right) = -\overline{H}_{\lambda\lambda'}$, and $\overline{H}_{\beta\lambda'}\overline{H}_{\lambda\lambda'}^{-1}\mathbb{E}\partial_{\lambda\lambda'\lambda}Q$ is also diagonal and the ith diagonal element is $\frac{\sum_{t=1}^{T}\mathbb{E}\left(\partial_{\pi^2}l_{it}x_{it}\right)\sum_{t=1}^{T}\mathbb{E}\left(\partial_{\pi^3}l_{it}\right)}{\sum_{t=1}^{T}\mathbb{E}\left(\partial_{\pi^2}l_{it}\right)}$.

5 Panel With Individual Effects and Time Effects

There are some difficulties in extending Hahn and Newey (2004) and Hahn and Kuersteiner (2011) to panels with both individual and time effects. First, the proof of consistency cannot be extended to allow both individual and time effects because, when time effects are present, the criterion function cannot be written as the average of a sequence of functions, with each function depending on only a finite number of parameters. Second, it would be very tedious, if not infeasible, to extend Hahn and Newey (2004)'s empirical likelihood method for asymptotic expansion to allow both individual and time effects. Now, we introduce Fernandez-Val and Weidner (2016)'s method.

5.1 Consistency

Let $\mathcal{B}(r_\beta,\beta^0)$ be a shrinking neighborhood of β^0 and $r_\beta = o\left((NT)^{-\frac{1}{2q}-\varepsilon}\right)$ for $0<\epsilon<\frac{1}{8}-\frac{1}{2q}$ and $q>4$. Fernandez-Val and Weidner (2016)'s argument of consistency can be summarized as follows. First, $\partial_\beta Q(\beta,\hat{\phi}(\beta))$ has a zero point within $\mathcal{B}(r_\beta,\beta^0)$. Second, $\partial_\beta Q(\beta,\hat{\phi}(\beta))$ has unique zero point because $Q(\beta,\hat{\phi}(\beta))$ is globally concave. These two together implies that the zero point of $\partial_\beta Q(\beta,\hat{\phi}(\beta))$ must lie in $\mathcal{B}(r_\beta,\beta^0)$. More specifically, from Eqs. (55) and (58)–(62), we have

$$\partial_\beta Q(\beta,\hat{\phi}(\beta)) = \left(H_{\beta\beta'} - H_{\beta\phi'}H_{\phi\phi'}^{-1}H_{\phi\beta'}\right)(\beta-\beta^0) + U + o_p\left(N^{\frac{1}{2}}T^{\frac{1}{2}}\right) + o_p\left(NT\|\beta-\beta^0\|\right), \tag{45}$$

uniformly within $\mathcal{B}(r_\beta,\beta^0)$, where

$$U = \left(S_\beta - H_{\beta\phi'}H_{\phi\phi'}^{-1}S_\phi\right) + \frac{1}{2}S_\phi' H_{\phi\phi'}^{-1}\left(\partial_{\phi\phi'\beta}Q - H_{\beta\phi'}H_{\phi\phi'}^{-1}\partial_{\phi\phi'\phi}Q\right)H_{\phi\phi'}^{-1}S_\phi.$$

It is not difficult to show that $H_{\beta\beta'} - H_{\beta\phi'}H_{\phi\phi'}^{-1}H_{\phi\beta'}$ is $O_p(NT)$ and U is $O_p\left(N^{\frac{1}{2}}T^{\frac{1}{2}}\right)$. Let $\eta = -2(H_{\beta\beta'} - H_{\beta\phi'}H_{\phi\phi'}^{-1}H_{\phi\beta'})^{-1}\ |U|$, then η is $O_p\left(N^{-\frac{1}{2}}T^{-\frac{1}{2}}\right)$. Thus $\beta^0+\eta$ and $\beta^0-\eta$ are both in $\mathcal{B}(r_\beta,\beta^0)$ w.p.a.1. From Eq. (45), it is not difficult to see that

$$\partial_\beta Q(\beta^0+\eta,\hat{\phi}(\beta^0+\eta)) \le 0 \le \partial_\beta Q(\beta^0-\eta,\hat{\phi}(\beta^0-\eta)).$$

Because $\partial_\beta Q(\hat{\beta},\hat{\phi}(\hat{\beta}))=0$ and $\partial_\beta Q(\beta,\hat{\phi}(\beta))$ is strictly decreasing in β (because $Q(\beta,\hat{\phi}(\beta))$ is strictly concave in β), we have $\beta^0-\eta\le\hat{\beta}\le\beta^0+\eta$. Therefore, $|\hat{\beta}-\beta^0|\le\eta=O_p\left(N^{-\frac{1}{2}}T^{-\frac{1}{2}}\right)$. This proves for the case $\dim(\beta)=1$. The previous argument can be generalized to case with $\dim(\beta)>1$, see Fernandez-Val and Weidner (2016) for details.

5.2 Asymptotic Expansion

With λ replaced by ϕ, Eqs. (22)–(25) and Eq. (27) still hold. Therefore, we have the following equations:

$$0 = S_\beta + H_{\beta\beta'}(\hat{\beta}-\beta^0) + H_{\beta\phi'}(\hat{\phi}-\phi^0) + R_\beta, \tag{46}$$

$$0 = S_\phi + H_{\phi\beta'}(\hat{\beta} - \beta^0) + H_{\phi\phi'}(\hat{\phi} - \phi^0) + R_\phi, \tag{47}$$

$$\begin{aligned} \hat{\beta} - \beta^0 = & -\left(H_{\beta\beta'} - H_{\beta\phi'}H_{\phi\phi'}^{-1}H_{\phi\beta'}\right)^{-1}\left(S_\beta - H_{\beta\phi'}H_{\phi\phi'}^{-1}S_\phi\right) \\ & -\left(H_{\beta\beta'} - H_{\beta\phi'}H_{\phi\phi'}^{-1}H_{\phi\beta'}\right)^{-1}\left(R_\beta - H_{\beta\phi'}H_{\phi\phi'}^{-1}R_\phi\right), \end{aligned} \tag{48}$$

$$\begin{aligned} S_\beta - H_{\beta\phi'}H_{\phi\phi'}^{-1}S_\phi = & S_\beta - \overline{H}_{\beta\phi'}\overline{H}_{\phi\phi'}^{-1}S_\phi - (H_{\beta\phi'} - \overline{H}_{\beta\phi'})\overline{H}_{\phi\phi'}^{-1}S_\phi - \\ & \overline{H}_{\beta\phi'}\left(H_{\phi\phi'}^{-1} - \overline{H}_{\phi\phi'}^{-1}\right)S_\phi - (H_{\beta\phi'} - \overline{H}_{\beta\phi'})\left(H_{\phi\phi'}^{-1} - \overline{H}_{\phi\phi'}^{-1}\right)S_\phi, \end{aligned} \tag{49}$$

$$\begin{aligned} R_\beta &= R_{\beta\beta\beta} + R_{\beta\phi\beta} + R_{\phi\phi\beta}, \\ R_{\beta\beta\beta} &= (\hat{\beta} - \beta^0)'\left(\int_0^1\int_0^{s_1} \partial_{\beta\beta'\beta}Q(s_2)ds_2ds_1\right)(\hat{\beta} - \beta^0), \\ R_{\beta\phi\beta} &= 2(\hat{\beta} - \beta^0)'\left(\int_0^1\int_0^{s_1} \partial_{\beta\phi'\beta}Q(s_2)ds_2ds_1\right)(\hat{\phi} - \phi^0), \\ R_{\phi\phi\beta} &= (\hat{\phi} - \phi^0)'\left(\int_0^1\int_0^{s_1} \partial_{\phi\phi'\beta}Q(s_2)ds_2ds_1\right)(\hat{\phi} - \phi^0), \\ R_\phi &= R_{\beta\beta\phi} + R_{\beta\phi\phi} + R_{\phi\phi\phi}, \\ R_{\beta\beta\phi} &= (\hat{\beta} - \beta^0)'\left(\int_0^1\int_0^{s_1} \partial_{\beta\beta'\phi}Q(s_2)ds_2ds_1\right)(\hat{\beta} - \beta^0), \\ R_{\beta\phi\phi} &= 2(\hat{\beta} - \beta^0)'\left(\int_0^1\int_0^{s_1} \partial_{\beta\phi'\phi}Q(s_2)ds_2ds_1\right)(\hat{\phi} - \phi^0), \\ R_{\phi\phi\phi} &= (\hat{\phi} - \phi^0)'\left(\int_0^1\int_0^{s_1} \partial_{\phi\phi'\phi}Q(s_2)ds_2ds_1\right)(\hat{\phi} - \phi^0). \end{aligned} \tag{50}$$

We want to show that with λ replaced by ϕ, Eq. (34) still holds, i.e.,

$$\begin{aligned} \hat{\beta} - \beta^0 = & -\left(\overline{H}_{\beta\beta'} - \overline{H}_{\beta\phi'}\overline{H}_{\phi\phi'}^{-1}\overline{H}_{\phi\beta'}\right)^{-1}\left(S_\beta - \overline{H}_{\beta\phi'}\overline{H}_{\phi\phi'}^{-1}S_\phi\right) \\ & + \left(\overline{H}_{\beta\beta'} - \overline{H}_{\beta\phi'}\overline{H}_{\phi\phi'}^{-1}\overline{H}_{\phi\beta'}\right)^{-1}[\\ & (H_{\beta\phi'} - \overline{H}_{\beta\phi'})\overline{H}_{\phi\phi'}^{-1}S_\phi + \overline{H}_{\beta\phi'}\left(H_{\phi\phi'}^{-1} - \overline{H}_{\phi\phi'}^{-1}\right)S_\phi - \\ & \frac{1}{2}S_\phi'\overline{H}_{\phi\phi'}^{-1}\left(\mathbb{E}\partial_{\phi\phi'\beta}Q - \overline{H}_{\beta\phi'}\overline{H}_{\phi\phi'}^{-1}\mathbb{E}\partial_{\phi\phi'\phi}Q\right)\overline{H}_{\phi\phi'}^{-1}S_\phi] \\ & + o_p\left(N^{-\frac{1}{2}}T^{-\frac{1}{2}}\right). \end{aligned} \tag{51}$$

In last section, when we show Eq. (34), we first show Eqs. (26), (29), (30), (32), and (33). Given relevant regularity conditions, Eq. (26) relies on the last equation of Eq. (28), Eqs. (29) and (30) rely on Eq. (28), and Eqs. (32) and (33) rely on Eq. (31), $\|\hat{\beta} - \beta^0\| = O_p\left(N^{-\frac{1}{2}}T^{-\frac{1}{2}}\right)$, $\|\hat{\lambda} - \lambda^0\| = O_p\left(N^{\frac{1}{2}}T^{-\frac{1}{2}}\right)$,

$\|\hat{\lambda}-\lambda^0\|_4 = O_p\left(N^{\frac{1}{4}}T^{-\frac{1}{2}}\right)$ and $\hat{\lambda}-\lambda^0 \approx H_{\lambda\lambda'}^{-1}S_\lambda$. Therefore, to show equation (51), with $N/T \to \kappa$, it suffices to show

1. $\|\hat{\beta}-\beta^0\| = O_p\left(N^{-\frac{1}{2}}T^{-\frac{1}{2}}\right), \|\hat{\phi}-\phi^0\| = O_p(1), \|\hat{\phi}-\phi^0\|_4 = O_p\left(T^{-\frac{1}{4}}\right)$ and $\hat{\phi}-\phi^0 \approx H_{\phi\phi'}^{-1}S_\phi$.
2. Eqs. (28) and (31), with λ replaced by ϕ.

These two are the difficulties using first-order conditions (46) and (47) to derive the limit distribution. We have encountered the first in panels with only individual effects. For the second, the difficulty is that the proof of Eq. (28) needs to use diagonality of $H_{\lambda\lambda'}$, but $H_{\phi\phi'}$ is not diagonal.[8] For example, the seventh equation of Eq. (28) is $\|H_{\lambda\lambda'}^{-1}\| = O_p(T^{-1})$. Although $H_{\lambda\lambda'}$ is high dimensional, this is not difficult to show since $H_{\lambda\lambda'}$ is diagonal and each diagonal element is sum of T terms. Since $H_{\phi\phi'}$ is nondiagonal, to show $\|H_{\phi\phi'}^{-1}\| = O_p(T^{-1})$ is much more difficult. The second is the extra difficulty of models with both individual and time effects, compared to models with only individual effects. In the following, we introduce how Fernandez-Val and Weidner (2016)'s method solves these difficulties.

Note that $\lambda, f, Q(\beta,\phi), H_{\phi\phi'}$ and S_ϕ here corresponds to α, γ, $N^{\frac{1}{2}}T^{\frac{1}{2}}\mathcal{L}(\beta,\phi)$, $-N^{\frac{1}{2}}T^{\frac{1}{2}}\mathcal{H}$ and $N^{\frac{1}{2}}T^{\frac{1}{2}}\mathcal{S}$ of Fernandez-Val and Weidner (2016), respectively.

For the second difficulty, Fernandez-Val and Weidner (2016)'s idea is to show that $H_{\phi\phi'}$ can be approximated by a diagonal matrix. Lemma D.1 of Fernandez-Val and Weidner (2016) shows that[9]

$$\left\|\overline{H}_{\phi\phi'}^{-1} - \operatorname{diag}\left(\overline{H}_{L\lambda\lambda'}^{-1}, \overline{H}_{Lff'}^{-1}\right)\right\|_{\max} = O_p(N^{-1}T^{-1}), \tag{52}$$

where $diag\left(\overline{H}_{L\lambda\lambda'}^{-1}, \overline{H}_{Lff'}^{-1}\right)$ is a diagonal matrix with left-upper block $\overline{H}_{L\lambda\lambda'}^{-1}$ and lower-right block $\overline{H}_{Lff'}^{-1}$. Lemma S.1(ii) in the supplementary appendix of Fernandez-Val and Weidner (2016) shows that

$$\left\|H_{\phi\phi'}^{-1} - \overline{H}_{\phi\phi'}^{-1}\right\| = o_p\left(T^{-\frac{5}{4}}\right). \tag{53}$$

These two solve the main difficulty in proving Eqs. (31) (with λ replaced by ϕ).

Now consider the first difficulty. By Eqs. (22) and (23), $\hat{\beta}-\beta^0$ is an implicit function of $\hat{\lambda}-\lambda^0$. Hahn and Newey (2004) and Hahn and Kuersteiner (2011) use empirical likelihood method to transform the first-order derivatives so that

---

8. Eq. (31) (with λ replaced by ϕ) can be proved by direct calculation.
9. Note that the likelihood function in Fernandez-Val and Weidner (2016) equals the likelihood function here divided by $N^{\frac{1}{2}}T^{\frac{1}{2}}$.

$\hat{\beta}-\beta^0$ becomes a function of ϵ. Fernandez-Val and Weidner (2016) use Legendre transformation to transform the criterion function $Q(\beta, \phi)$ from function of β and ϕ to function of β and s, $Q^*(\beta, s)$. Here, s denotes score and its true value is S_ϕ. They correspond to S and $\mathbf{S}$ in Fernandez-Val and Weidner (2016) respectively. This transformation is crucial for asymptotic expansion because (1) after the transformation, the third-order terms in the asymptotic expansion would be functions of S_ϕ, (2) S_ϕ has explicit analytical expression so that we can calculate the magnitude of $\|S_\phi\|_q$ for $q = 1, 2, \ldots$, which can be used to truncate the remainder terms in the Taylor expansion. More details about the Legendre transformation method follows.

Consider the shrinking neighborhood $\mathcal{B}(r_\beta,\beta^0) \times \mathcal{B}_q(r_\phi,\phi^0)$ of the true parameters (β^0, ϕ^0). Within this neighborhood, define

$$Q^*(\beta, s) = \max_{\phi \in \mathcal{B}_q(r_\phi, \phi^0)} [Q(\beta, \phi) - \phi' s],$$
$$\Phi(\beta, s) = \arg \max_{\phi \in \mathcal{B}_q(r_\phi, \phi^0)} [Q(\beta, \phi) - \phi' s].$$

Given β, $Q^*(\beta, s)$ as function of s is called Legendre transformation of $Q(\beta, \phi)$ as function of ϕ. Since $Q(\beta, \phi)$ is strictly concave w.p.a.1 within $\mathcal{B}(r_\beta,\beta^0) \times \mathcal{B}_q(r_\phi,\phi^0)$, $Q^*(\beta, s)$ is well-defined w.p.a.1. Define the corresponding shrinking neighborhood of (β^0, S_ϕ),

$$\mathcal{SB}_r(\beta^0, \phi^0) = \{(\beta, s) \in R^{\dim\beta + \dim\phi} : (\beta, \Phi(\beta, s)) \in \mathcal{B}(r_\beta, \beta^0) \times \mathcal{B}_q(r_\phi, \phi^0)\}.$$

Fernandez-Val and Weidner (2016) prove within $\mathcal{SB}_r(\beta^0, \phi^0)$, $Q^*(\beta, s)$ is four times continuously differentiable. Thus $Q^*(\beta, s)$ is well-behaved and Taylor expansion can be used. In the following, for $Q^*(\beta, s)$, we also suppress the argument when its true value (β^0, S_ϕ) is plugged in.

It is not difficult to see that $\Phi(\beta, 0) = \hat{\phi}(\beta)$ and $Q^*(\beta, 0) = Q(\beta, \hat{\phi}(\beta))$. Therefore, we have $\partial_\beta Q^*(\beta, 0) = \partial_\beta Q(\beta, \hat{\phi}(\beta))$. It follows that the first-order conditions for $\hat{\beta}$ is.

$$\partial_\beta Q^*(\hat{\beta}, 0) = \partial_\beta Q(\hat{\beta}, \hat{\phi}(\hat{\beta})) = 0. \tag{54}$$

Using the integral form of mean value theorem to expand $\partial_\beta Q^*(\beta, 0)$ at (β^0, S_ϕ),

$$\partial_\beta Q^*(\beta, 0) = \partial_\beta Q^* + (\partial_{\beta\beta'} Q^*)(\beta - \beta^0) - (\partial_{\beta s'} Q^*) S_\phi + R^*(\beta), \tag{55}$$

$$\begin{aligned} R^*(\beta) =& \frac{1}{2}(\beta - \beta^0)' \left(\int_0^1 \int_0^{a_1} \partial_{\beta\beta'\beta} Q^*(a_2) da_2 da_1 \right) (\beta - \beta^0) \\ &+ \frac{1}{2}(\beta - \beta^0)' \left(\int_0^1 \int_0^{a_1} \partial_{\beta s'\beta} Q^*(a_2) da_2 da_1 \right) S_\phi \\ &+ \frac{1}{2} S_\phi' \left(\int_0^1 \int_0^{a_1} \partial_{ss'\beta} Q^*(a_2) da_2 da_1 \right) S_\phi, \end{aligned} \tag{56}$$

where $Q^*(a) = Q(\beta^0 + a(\beta - \beta^0), S_\phi + a(-S_\phi))$. It follows that

$$\hat{\beta} - \beta^0 = -\left(\partial_{\beta\beta'}Q^*\right)^{-1}\left(\partial_\beta Q^* - \left(\partial_{\beta s'}Q^*\right)S_\phi\right) - \left(\partial_{\beta\beta'}Q^*\right)^{-1}R^*\left(\hat{\beta}\right). \tag{57}$$

By definition of Legendre transformation, the derivatives of $Q^*(\beta, s)$ have a special relationship with derivatives of $Q(\beta, \phi)$. For example, $S_\phi(\beta, \Phi(\beta, s)) = s$, and after taking derivative with respect to s, we have

$$\partial_{\phi'}S_\phi(\beta, \Phi(\beta, s))\partial_{s'}\Phi(\beta, s) = I_{N+T}.$$

By definition, we have $\Phi(\beta, s) = -\partial_s Q^*(\beta, s)$. Thus $-\partial_{ss'}Q^*(\beta, s) = [\partial_{\phi'} S_\phi(\beta, \Phi(\beta, s))]^{-1} = [H(\beta, \Phi(\beta, s))]^{-1}$. Using this kind of special relationship, part (ii) of Lemma S.2 proves that

$$\partial_{\beta\beta'}Q^* = H_{\beta\beta'} - H_{\beta\phi'}H_{\phi\phi}^{-1}H_{\phi\beta'}, \tag{58}$$

$$\partial_\beta Q^* = S_\beta, \tag{59}$$

$$\partial_{\beta s'}Q^* = H_{\beta\phi'}H_{\phi\phi}^{-1}, \tag{60}$$

$$\partial_{ss'\beta}Q^* = H_{\phi\phi'}^{-1}\partial_{\phi\phi'\beta}QH_{\phi\phi'}^{-1} - H_{\phi\phi'}^{-1}\left(H_{\beta\phi'}H_{\phi\phi'}^{-1}\partial_{\phi\phi'\phi}Q\right)H_{\phi\phi}^{-1}. \tag{61}$$

Because $R^*(\beta)$ is function of S_ϕ, Fernandez-Val and Weidner (2016) are able to show that

$$R_1(\beta) = R^*(\beta) - \frac{1}{2}S_\phi'\left(\partial_{ss'\beta}Q^*\right)S_\phi = o_p\left(N^{\frac{1}{2}}T^{\frac{1}{2}}\right) + o_p\left(NT\|\beta - \beta^0\|\right), \tag{62}$$

uniformly over $\beta \in \mathcal{B}(r_\beta, \beta^0)$. See part (2) of Fernandez-Val and Weidner (2016)'s Theorem B.1 for detailed proof. This is why the Legendre transformation works. Eqs. (57)–(62) together show that

$$\begin{aligned}\hat{\beta} - \beta^0 = &-\left(H_{\beta\beta'} - H_{\beta\phi'}H_{\phi\phi'}^{-1}H_{\phi\beta'}\right)^{-1}\left(S_\beta - H_{\beta\phi'}H_{\phi\phi'}^{-1}S_\phi\right)\\ &-\left(H_{\beta\beta'} - H_{\beta\phi'}H_{\phi\phi'}^{-1}H_{\phi\beta'}\right)^{-1}[\frac{1}{2}S_\phi'H_{\phi\phi'}^{-1}\left(\partial_{\phi\phi'\beta}Q - H_{\beta\phi'}H_{\phi\phi'}^{-1}\partial_{\phi\phi'\phi}Q\right)H_{\phi\phi'}^{-1}S_\phi\\ &+o_p\left(N^{\frac{1}{2}}T^{\frac{1}{2}}\right) + o_p\left(NT\|\hat{\beta} - \beta^0\|\right)].\end{aligned} \tag{63}$$

After we have Eq. (63), proof of Eq. (51) is straightforward.

5.3 Bias Calculation

Now we use Eq. (51) to calculate the asymptotic variance and bias. The procedure is similar to the case with only individual effects.

(1) $N^{-\frac{1}{2}}T^{-\frac{1}{2}}\left(S_\beta - \overline{H}_{\beta\phi'}\overline{H}_{\phi\phi'}^{-1}S_\phi\right) \xrightarrow{d} \mathcal{N}(0, W)$,
where $W = -\lim_{(N,T)\to\infty} N^{-1}T^{-1}\left(\overline{H}_{\beta\beta'} - \overline{H}_{\beta\phi'}\overline{H}_{\phi\phi'}^{-1}\overline{H}_{\phi\beta'}\right)$ is assumed to be positive definite.[10] W also has the following interpretation:

$$W = \lim_{(N,T)\to\infty} \sum_{i=1}^{N}\sum_{t=1}^{T}\mathbb{E}\left(-\partial_{\pi^2}l_{it}z_{it}z_{it}'\right), \tag{64}$$

where $z_{it} = x_{it} - \eta_i - h_t$ and η_i and h_t are solutions of the following weighted least squares problem:

$$\min \sum_{i=1}^{N}\sum_{t=1}^{T}\mathbb{E}(-\partial_{\pi^2}l_{it})\left\|\frac{\mathbb{E}(\partial_{\pi^2}l_{it}x_{it})}{\mathbb{E}(\partial_{\pi^2}l_{it})} - \eta_i - h_t\right\|^2. \tag{65}$$

To see this, write out the first-order conditions of (65),

$$\sum_{t=1}^{T}\mathbb{E}(\partial_{\pi^2}l_{it})\left(\frac{\mathbb{E}(\partial_{\pi^2}l_{it}x_{it})}{\mathbb{E}(\partial_{\pi^2}l_{it})} - \eta_i - h_t\right) = 0 \quad \text{for } i = 1, \ldots, N, \tag{66}$$

$$\sum_{i=1}^{N}\mathbb{E}(\partial_{\pi^2}l_{it})\left(\frac{\mathbb{E}(\partial_{\pi^2}l_{it}x_{it})}{\mathbb{E}(\partial_{\pi^2}l_{it})} - \eta_i - h_t\right) = 0 \quad \text{for } t = 1, \ldots, T. \tag{67}$$

Let $\eta = (\eta_1, \ldots, \eta_N)'$ and $h = (h_1, \ldots, h_T)'$, then Eqs. (66) and (67) imply that $(\eta', h') = \overline{H}_{\beta\phi'}\overline{H}_{L\phi\phi'}^{-1}$ and $\sum_{i=1}^{N}\sum_{t=1}^{T}\mathbb{E}(\partial_{\pi^2}l_{it})\left(\frac{\mathbb{E}(\partial_{\pi^2}l_{it}x_{it})}{\mathbb{E}(\partial_{\pi^2}l_{it})} - \eta_i - h_t\right)(\eta_i + h_t)' = 0$. It follows that

$$\begin{aligned}
&\sum_{i=1}^{N}\sum_{t=1}^{T}\mathbb{E}(\partial_{\pi^2}l_{it})(\eta_i + h_t)(\eta_i + h_t)' \\
&= \sum_{i=1}^{N}\sum_{t=1}^{T}\mathbb{E}(\partial_{\pi^2}l_{it}x_{it})(\eta_i + h_t)' = \overline{H}_{\beta\phi'}\overline{H}_{L\phi\phi'}^{-1}\overline{H}_{\phi\beta'} = \overline{H}_{\beta\phi'}\overline{H}_{\phi\phi'}^{-1}\overline{H}_{\phi\beta'}.
\end{aligned}$$

This proves Eq. (64).

$$\begin{aligned}
&(2)\, N^{-\frac{1}{2}}T^{-\frac{1}{2}}\left(H_{\beta\phi'} - \overline{H}_{\beta\phi'}\right)\overline{H}_{\phi\phi'}^{-1}S_\phi \\
&= N^{-\frac{1}{2}}T^{-\frac{1}{2}}\left(H_{\beta\phi'} - \overline{H}_{\beta\phi'}\right)\left(\left(\overline{H}_{L\lambda\lambda'}^{-1}S_\lambda\right)', \left(\overline{H}_{Lff'}^{-1}S_f\right)'\right)' + o_p(1) \\
&= \sqrt{\kappa}N^{-1}\sum_{i=1}^{N}\frac{\sum_{t=1}^{T}\sum_{s=1}^{t}\mathbb{E}(\partial_\pi l_{is}\partial_{\pi^2}l_{it}x_{it})}{\sum_{t=1}^{T}\mathbb{E}(\partial_{\pi^2}l_{it})} \\
&+ \frac{1}{\sqrt{\kappa}}T^{-1}\sum_{t=1}^{T}\frac{\sum_{i=1}^{N}\mathbb{E}(\partial_\pi l_{it}\partial_{\pi^2}l_{it}x_{it})}{\sum_{i=1}^{N}\mathbb{E}(\partial_{\pi^2}l_{it})} + o_p(1).
\end{aligned}$$

The first equality uses Eq. (52).

10. Note that $\mathbb{E}\left(S_\beta'\overline{H}_{\beta\phi'}\overline{H}_{\phi\phi'}^{-1}S_\phi\right) = -\overline{H}_{\beta\phi'}\overline{H}_{\phi\phi'}^{-1}\overline{H}_{\phi\beta'}$ and $\mathbb{E}\left(S_\phi S_\phi'\right) = \overline{H}_{L\phi\phi'} \neq \overline{H}_{\phi\phi'}$, but $\overline{H}_{\beta\phi'}\overline{H}_{\phi\phi'}^{-1}\overline{H}_{L\phi\phi'}\overline{H}_{\phi\phi'}^{-1}\overline{H}_{\phi\beta'} = \overline{H}_{\beta\phi'}\overline{H}_{\phi\phi'}^{-1}\overline{H}_{\phi\beta'}$. This is because $\overline{H}_{\phi\phi'} = \overline{H}_{L\phi\phi'} - bvv'$, $\overline{H}_{L\phi\phi'}v = 0$ and $\overline{H}_{\beta\phi'}v = 0$.

$$(3)\, N^{-\frac{1}{2}}T^{-\frac{1}{2}}\overline{H}_{\beta\phi'}\left(H_{\phi\phi'}^{-1}-\overline{H}_{\phi\phi'}^{-1}\right)S_{\phi}$$

$$=-N^{-\frac{1}{2}}T^{-\frac{1}{2}}\overline{H}_{\beta\phi'}\overline{H}_{\phi\phi'}^{-1}\left(H_{\phi\phi'}-\overline{H}_{\phi\phi'}\right)\left(\left(\overline{H}_{L\lambda\lambda'}^{-1}S_{\lambda}\right)',\left(\overline{H}_{Lff'}^{-1}S_{f}\right)'\right)'+o_p(1).$$

$$=-\sqrt{\kappa}N^{-1}\sum\nolimits_{i=1}^{N}\frac{\sum\nolimits_{t=1}^{T}\sum\nolimits_{s=1}^{t}\mathbb{E}((\eta_i+h_t)\partial_{\pi}l_{is}\partial_{\pi^2}l_{it})}{\sum\nolimits_{t=1}^{T}\mathbb{E}(\partial_{\pi^2}l_{it})}$$

$$=-\frac{1}{\sqrt{\kappa}}T^{-1}\sum\nolimits_{t=1}^{T}\frac{\sum\nolimits_{i=1}^{N}\mathbb{E}((\eta_i+h_t)\partial_{\pi}l_{it}\partial_{\pi^2}l_{it})}{\sum\nolimits_{i=1}^{N}\mathbb{E}(\partial_{\pi^2}l_{it})}+o_p(1).$$

$$(4)\, -\frac{1}{2}N^{-\frac{1}{2}}T^{-\frac{1}{2}}S_{\phi}'\overline{H}_{\phi\phi'}^{-1}\left(\mathbb{E}\partial_{\phi\phi'\beta}Q-\overline{H}_{\beta\phi'}\overline{H}_{\phi\phi'}^{-1}\mathbb{E}\partial_{\phi\phi'\phi}Q\right)\overline{H}_{\phi\phi'}^{-1}S_{\phi}$$

$$=\frac{1}{2}\sqrt{\kappa}N^{-1}\sum\nolimits_{i=1}^{N}\frac{\sum\nolimits_{t=1}^{T}\mathbb{E}(\partial_{\pi^3}l_{it}z_{it})}{\sum\nolimits_{t=1}^{T}\mathbb{E}(\partial_{\pi^2}l_{it})}+\frac{1}{2}\frac{1}{\sqrt{\kappa}}T^{-1}\sum\nolimits_{t=1}^{T}\frac{\sum\nolimits_{i=1}^{N}\mathbb{E}(\partial_{\pi^3}l_{it}z_{it})}{\sum\nolimits_{i=1}^{N}\mathbb{E}(\partial_{\pi^2}l_{it})}+o_p(1).$$

Take (2)–(4) together, the asymptotic bias is $W^{-1}b$, and

$$b=-\sqrt{\kappa}N^{-1}\sum\nolimits_{i=1}^{N}\frac{\sum\nolimits_{t=1}^{T}\sum\nolimits_{s=1}^{t}\mathbb{E}(\partial_{\pi}l_{is}\partial_{\pi^2}l_{it}z_{it})+\sum\nolimits_{t=1}^{T}\mathbb{E}\left(\frac{1}{2}\partial_{\pi^3}l_{it}z_{it}\right)}{\sum\nolimits_{t=1}^{T}\mathbb{E}(\partial_{\pi^2}l_{it})}$$

$$-\frac{1}{\sqrt{\kappa}}T^{-1}\sum\nolimits_{i=1}^{N}\frac{\sum\nolimits_{i=1}^{N}\mathbb{E}(\partial_{\pi}l_{it}\partial_{\pi^2}l_{it}z_{it})+\sum\nolimits_{i=1}^{N}\mathbb{E}\left(\frac{1}{2}\partial_{\pi^3}l_{it}z_{it}\right)}{\sum\nolimits_{i=1}^{N}\mathbb{E}(\partial_{\pi^2}l_{it})}.$$

6 Conclusions

This chapter provides detailed discussion for the working mechanism of the techniques used in Hahn and Newey (2004) and Fernandez-Val and Weidner (2016) to deal with high dimensional MLE, and their relationship with the classical fixed dimensional MLE. It can be considered as a translation and reorganization of the main techniques of fixed effects panel models. Therefore, it could be a starting point for researchers who have interests in the theoretical derivation. This chapter also provides a map for asymptotic analysis of more general models. For example, the discussion in Section 5 clearly shows where the difficulty is in extending to panels with interactive effects. Knowing where the difficulty is also could help us understand how general the specification of the unobserved effects could be.

Acknowledgment

We would like to thank Martin Weidner for very helpful discussion.

References

Arellano, M., Hahn, J., 2007. Understanding bias in nonlinear panel models: Some recent developments. Vol. 43. Econometric Society Monographs, p. 381.

Dhaene, G., Jochmans, K., 2015. Split-panel jackknife estimation of fixed-effect models. Review of Economic Studies 82, 991–1030.

Fernandez-Val, I., Weidner, M., 2016. Individual and time effects in nonlinear panel models with large N, T. Journal of Econometrics 192, 291–312.

Fernandez-Val, I., Weidner, M., 2017. Fixed effect estimation of large t panel data models. (arXiv preprint arXiv:1709.08980).

Hahn, J., Kuersteiner, G., 2002. Asymptotically unbiased inference for a dynamic panel model with fixed effects when both N and T are large. Econometrica 70, 1639–1657.

Hahn, J., Kuersteiner, G., 2011. Bias reduction for dynamic nonlinear panel models with fixed effects. Econometric Theory 27, 1152–1191.

Hahn, J., Moon, H.R., 2006. Reducing bias of mle in a dynamic panel model. Econometric Theory 22, 499–512.

Hahn, J., Newey, W., 2004. Jackknife and analytical bias reduction for nonlinear panel models. Econometrica 72, 1295–1319.

Honore, B., 1992. Trimmed LAD and least squares estimation of truncated and censored regression models with fixed effects. Econometrica 60, 533–565.

Manski, C., 1987. Semiparametric analysis of random effects linear models from binary panel data. Econometrica 55, 357–362.

Newey, W.K., McFadden, D., 1994. Large sample estimation and hypothesis testing. Handbook of Econometrics 4, 2111–2245.

Chapter 8

Panel Vector Autoregressions With Binary Data

Bo E. Honoré* **and Ekaterini Kyriazidou**†
*Department of Economics, Princeton University, Princeton, NJ, United States, †Department of Economics, Athens University of Economics and Business, Athens, Greece

Chapter Outline

1 Introduction

Discrete choice models play an important role in theoretical and applied econometric research. Static and dynamic models have been used to explain decisions such as labor force participation, brand choice, whether to invest, go to college, and predict a recession. Inference methods have been developed for cross-section data in univariate parametric (Berkson, 1944; Bliss, 1934), semiparametric (Cosslett, 1983; Ichimura, 1993; Klein & Spady, 1993; Manski, 1975, 1985), and nonparametric settings (Matzkin, 1992), among others.

Multivariate parametric discrete choice models for cross-sectional data have been considered in the literature for the logistic case in Theil (1969) and Nerlove and Press (1973a, 1973b). Schmidt and Strauss (1975) considered a simultaneous logit model. Substantive literature also is found in statistics, such as Carey, Zeger, and Diggle (1993) and Glonek and McCullagh (1995), who proposed generalizations of the binary logistic model. Ashford and Sowden (1970) and Amemiya (1974) focused on generalizing the binary probit model

Panel Data Econometrics. https://doi.org/10.1016/B978-0-12-814367-4.00008-3

to a multivariate setting in a static framework. The main difficulty in probit models lies in evaluating the likelihood function. Chib and Greenberg (1998) developed a simulation-based Bayesian and non-Bayesian approach; Song and Lee (2005) relied on the expectation maximization algorithm to evaluate the likelihood function for a multivariate probit model. Huguenin, Pelgrin, and Holly (2009) have shown that a multivariate probit model cannot be estimated accurately using simulation methods, as generally is done in the literature. Its estimation instead requires the derivation of the exact maximum-likelihood function. All these papers are in a static framework with strictly exogenous explanatory variables and assume a large n.

Dynamic discrete choice models for univariate time series data case have been considered among others by Eichengreen, Watson, and Grossman (1985), Dueker (1997, 2005), Chauvet and Potter (2005), and Kauppi and Saikkonen (2008).[1] The last develop a unified model framework that accommodates most previously analyzed dynamic binary time series models as special cases. Chauvet and Potter (2005) apply a Bayesian approach to a dynamic probit model. Candelon, Dumitrescu, Hurlin, and Palm (2013) generalize Kauppi and Saikkonen (2008) to a multivariate setting. Multivariate dynamic discrete choice models also are considered by Eichler, Manner, and Türk (2015), Nyberg (2014), and Winkelmann (2012). All these papers take a fully parametric approach, and they require a large T.

The literature about univariate and multivariate discrete choice models for panel data is much more limited, because these models are difficult to estimate, especially in short panels with individual specific heterogeneity if one is unwilling to make assumptions about how the latter is related to the observable exogenous covariates and initial conditions. See Chamberlain (1985) for static as well as pure (i.e., without exogenous covariates) dynamic fixed effects logit models and Magnac (2000) for multinomial dynamic panel logit models; Manski (1987) for the semiparametric static case; and Honoré and Kyriazidou (2000) for dynamic logit and semiparametric models with exogenous covariates. Most of the research, however has focused on univariate models. Static bivariate panel logit models with random effects (i.e., with parameterized heterogeneity) have been considered by Ten Have and Morabia (1999) and dynamic random effects models by Bartolucci and Farcomeni (2009). Narendranathan, Nickell, and Metcalf (1985) consider a simple case of the type of models analyzed in this chapter.

We consider inference in dynamic multivariate discrete choice panel data models with fixed effects, in the sense that we avoid making assumptions about the nature of the individual effects and their relationship with the initial conditions and/or the exogenous covariates. We show that in the logit pure VAR(1) case (i.e., without exogenous covariates), the parameters are identified with four

1. Validity of dynamic probit ML estimation has been proven by DeJong and Woutersen (2011).

waves of observations and therefore can be estimated consistently at rate $\sqrt{n}$ with an asymptotic normal distribution.[2] We show that the identification strategy of Honoré and Kyriazidou (2000) carries over in the multivariate case when strictly exogenous covariates are included in the model. We also present an extension of the bivariate simultaneous logit model of Schmidt and Strauss (1975) to the panel case, allowing for contemporaneous cross-equation dependence both in a static framework and a dynamic framework. The results of this chapter are of particular interest for short panels, that is, for small T.

The chapter is organized as follows: Section 2 discusses univariate static and dynamic panel logit models. Section 3 introduces the bivariate pure VAR(1) logit model and discusses identification with four periods of data. Section 4 introduces strictly exogenous covariates in the bivariate logit model of Section 3. Section 5 provides the identification condition for the general M-variate general T case. Section 6 presents extensions of the simultaneous logit model of Schmidt and Strauss (1975) to the panel case. Finally, Section 7 contains some simple Monte Carlo simulations for the model of Section 3 for different sample sizes ($n=100$, 400, 1600) and different panel lengths ($T=4, 6, 8$). Section 8 offers conclusions and discusses directions of future research.

2 The Univariate Logit Model

2.1 Static Case

We first review the static panel data logit model with strictly exogenous explanatory variables. Recall the cross-sectional logit model:

$$y_i = 1\{x_i'\beta + \varepsilon_i \geq 0\}.$$

If we assume that ε_i is logistically distributed conditional on the explanatory variable, x_i, that is,

$$\Pr(\varepsilon_i \leq z | x_i) = \frac{\exp(z)}{1+\exp(z)} = \Lambda(z)$$

then

$$\Pr(y_i = 1 | x_i) = \frac{\exp(x_i\beta)}{1+\exp(x_i\beta)} = \Lambda(x_i'\beta).$$

Estimation of β can be done by maximizing the log-likelihood function

$$\mathcal{L}(b) = \sum_{i=1}^{n} y_i \log \Lambda(x_i'b) + (1-y_i)\log(1-\Lambda(x_i'b)) = \sum_{i=1}^{n} \log\left(\frac{\exp(x_i'b)y_i}{1+\exp(x_i'b)}\right).$$

2. Fernández-Val and Weidner (2016) show how to estimate parameters and obtain partial effects in a variety of nonlinear panel models with fixed effects, including the ones we consider here, assuming, however, large T.

We now turn to the panel data version of the simple logit model. The setup considered throughout this chapter is one in which the econometrician has access to a data set on a large number of observations, n, each observed across a relatively small number of time periods. The static panel data binary choice model with individual effects is

$$y_{it} = 1\{x_{it}'\beta + \alpha_i + \varepsilon_{it} \geq 0\} \quad t = 1, \ldots, T$$

where we assume that ε_{it} is distributed logistically conditional on $x_i = (x_{i1}, x_{i2}, \ldots, x_{iT})'$ and α_i and independent over time. The assumption that ε_{it} is independent over time assumption implies that the y_{it}'s are independent over time conditional on x_i and α_i. As above, we have that

$$\begin{aligned}
\Pr(y_{it} = 1 | x_i, \alpha_i) &= \Pr(\varepsilon_{it} \geq -x_{it}'\beta - \alpha_i | x_i, \alpha_i) \\
&= \Pr(\varepsilon_{it} \leq x_{it}'\beta + \alpha_i | x_i, \alpha_i) \\
&= \frac{\exp(x_{it}'\beta + \alpha_i)}{1 + \exp(x_{it}'\beta + \alpha_i)} \\
&= \Lambda(x_{it}'\beta + \alpha_i).
\end{aligned}$$

In this model, α_i plays the same role as a so-called fixed effect in a linear panel data model, and the challenge is to estimate β without making assumptions about the relationship between $x_i = (x_{i1}, x_{i2}, \ldots, x_{iT})$ and α_i. In a linear model, this can be accomplished by differencing. Such differencing does not work in nonlinear models.

One generic approach that sometimes can be used to estimate β is to condition on a sufficient statistic for α_i. Specifically, assume that for each i we can find a function of the data, S_i, such that the distribution of $y_i = (y_{i1}, y_{i2}, \ldots, y_{iT})$ conditional on (S_i, x_i, α_i) does not depend on α_i, and that the distribution of y_i conditional on (S_i, x_i, α_i) depends on the parameter of interest (here, β). Then we can estimate the parameter of interest by maximum likelihood using the conditional distribution of the data given (S_i, x_i). This is referred to as the conditional maximum likelihood estimator. See Andersen (1970). The main limitation of this approach is that it often is impossible to find such a sufficient statistic S_i.

In the logit model, it turns out that $\Sigma_t y_{it}$ is a sufficient statistic for α_i. See Rasch (1960). To see why, consider, for example, the case where $T = 2$. In this case

$$\Pr(y_{it} = 1 | y_{i1} + y_{i2} = 0, x_i, \alpha_i) = 0$$

$$\Pr(y_{it} = 1 | y_{i1} + y_{i2} = 2, x_i, \alpha_i) = 1$$

i.e., individuals who do not switch states (i.e., who are 0 or 1 in both periods) do not offer any information about β. Consider the events in which the individual switches states, $\mathcal{A}_{01} = \{y_{i1} = 0,\ y_{i2} = 1\}$ and $\mathcal{A}_{10} = \{y_{i1} = 1,\ y_{i2} = 0\}$.

Here $\mathcal{A}_{01} \cup \mathcal{A}_{10}$ is the event $y_{i1} + y_{i2} = 1$. It then is easy to see that because of independence over time

$$\begin{aligned}\Pr(\mathcal{A}_{01}|\, x_i, \alpha_i) &= \Pr(y_{i1} = 0, y_{i2} = 1|\, x_i, \alpha_i)\\ &= \Pr(y_{i1} = 0|\, x_i, \alpha_i) \cdot \Pr(y_{i2} = 1|\, x_i, \alpha_i)\\ &= \frac{1}{1 + \exp\left(x'_{i1}\beta + \alpha_i\right)} \cdot \frac{\exp\left(x'_{i2}\beta + \alpha_i\right)}{1 + \exp\left(x'_{i2}\beta + \alpha_i\right)}\end{aligned}$$

and

$$\Pr(\mathcal{A}_{10}|\, x_i, \alpha_i) = \frac{\exp\left(x'_{i1}\beta + \alpha_i\right)}{1 + \exp\left(x'_{i1}\beta + \alpha_i\right)} \frac{1}{1 + \exp\left(x'_{i2}\beta + \alpha_i\right)}.$$

Therefore,

$$\begin{aligned}\Pr(\mathcal{A}_{01}|\, \mathcal{A}_{01} \cup \mathcal{A}_{10}, x_i, \alpha_i) &= \frac{\Pr(\mathcal{A}_{01} \cap (\mathcal{A}_{01} \cup \mathcal{A}_{10})|\, x_i, \alpha_i)}{\Pr(\mathcal{A}_{01} \cup \mathcal{A}_{10}|\, x_i, \alpha_i)}\\ &= \frac{\Pr(\mathcal{A}_{01}|\, x_i, \alpha_i)}{\Pr(\mathcal{A}_{01}|\, x_i, \alpha_i) + \Pr(\mathcal{A}_{10}|\, x_i, \alpha_i)}\\ &= \frac{1}{1 + \dfrac{\Pr(\mathcal{A}_{10}|\, x_i, \alpha_i)}{\Pr(\mathcal{A}_{01}|\, x_i, \alpha_i)}}\\ &= \frac{1}{1 + \exp\left((x_{i1} - x_{i2})'\beta\right)}\\ &= 1 - \Lambda\left((x_{i1} - x_{i2})'\beta\right)\end{aligned}$$

and

$$\Pr(\mathcal{A}_{10}|\, \mathcal{A}_{01} \cup \mathcal{A}_{10}, x_i, \alpha_i) = 1 - \Pr(\mathcal{A}_{01}|\, \mathcal{A}_{01} \cup \mathcal{A}_{10}, x_i, \alpha_i) = \Lambda\left((x_{i1} - x_{i2})'\beta\right).$$

In other words, conditional on the individual switching states (from 0 to 1 or from 1 to 0) so that $y_{i1} + y_{i2} = 1$, the probability of observing $\{0, 1\}$ or $\{1, 0\}$ depends on β (i.e., contains information about β) but is independent of α_i. For $T = 2$, estimation of β can be based on maximizing the conditional log-likelihood

$$\begin{aligned}\mathcal{L}_C(b) &= \sum_{i=1}^{N} 1\{y_{i1} + y_{i2} = 1\} \left[y_{i1} \log\left(\Lambda\left((x_{i1} - x_{i2})'b\right)\right)\right.\\ &\quad \left. + (1 - y_{i1}) \log\left(1 - \Lambda\left((x_{i1} - x_{i2})'b\right)\right)\right]\\ &= \sum_{i=1}^{N} 1\{y_{i1} + y_{i2} = 1\} \log\left(\frac{\exp\left((x_{i1} - x_{i2})'b\right) y_{i1}}{1 + \exp\left((x_{i1} - x_{i2})'b\right)}\right) \qquad (1)\end{aligned}$$

which is nothing but logit estimation with first-differenced regressors performed on the individuals who switch states in the two periods.

For general T, the conditional log-likelihood can be shown to be

$$\mathcal{L}_C(b) = \sum_{i=1}^{N} \log\left(\frac{\exp\left(\sum_t y_{it}x_{it}'b\right)}{\sum_{(d_1, \ldots, d_T)\in B} \exp\left(\sum_t d_t x_{it}'b\right)}\right)$$

where

$$B = \left\{(d_1, \ldots, d_T) \text{ such that } d_t = 0 \text{ or } 1 \text{ and} \sum_t d_t = \sum_t y_{it}\right\}.$$

For $T = 2$, this gives

$$\begin{aligned}\mathcal{L}_C(b) = &\sum_{i=1}^{N} 1\{y_{i1}+y_{i2}=0\}\log\left(\frac{\exp(0)}{\exp(0)}\right)\\ &+\sum_{i=1}^{N} 1\{y_{i1}+y_{i2}=2\}\log\left(\frac{\exp\left(x_{i1}'\beta+x_{i2}'\beta\right)}{\exp\left(x_{i1}'\beta+x_{i2}'\beta\right)}\right)\\ &+\sum_{i=1}^{N} 1\{y_{i1}+y_{i2}=1\}\log\left(\frac{\exp\left(y_{i1}x_{i1}'b+y_{i2}x_{i2}'b\right)}{\exp\left(1\cdot x_{i1}'b+0\cdot x_{i2}'b\right)+\exp\left(0\cdot x_{i1}'b+1\cdot x_{i2}b'\right)}\right).\end{aligned}$$

Obviously, those i that have $y_{i1} = y_{i2} = 1$ have no contribution to the log-likelihood (we obtain $\log\left(\frac{\exp\left(x_{i1}'\beta+x_{i2}'\beta\right)}{\exp\left(x_{i1}'\beta+x_{i2}'\beta\right)}\right) = \log(1) = 0$, and similarly for those with $y_{i1} = y_{i2} = 0$ since $\log\left(\frac{\exp(0)}{\exp(0)}\right) = \log(1) = 0$. Therefore, we can write

$$\begin{aligned}\mathcal{L}_C(b) &= \sum_{i=1}^{N} 1\{y_{i1}+y_{i2}=1\}\log\left(\frac{\exp\left(y_{i1}x_{i1}'b+y_{i2}x_{i2}b'\right)}{\exp\left(x_{i1}'b\right)+\exp\left(x_{i2}'b\right)}\right)\\ &= \sum_{i=1}^{N} 1\{y_{i1}+y_{i2}=1\}\log\left(\frac{\exp\left(y_{i1}x_{i1}'b+(1-y_{i1})x_{i2}'b\right)}{\exp\left(x_{i1}'b\right)+\exp\left(x_{i2}'b\right)}\right)\\ &= \sum_{i=1}^{N} 1\{y_{i1}+y_{i2}=1\}\log\left(\frac{\exp\left(y_{i1}(x_{i1}-x_{i2})'b\right)}{1+\exp(x_{i1}-x_{i2})'b}\right)\end{aligned}$$

which agrees with the expression we obtained previously.

2.2 Dynamic Case (Pure AR(1))

The conditional maximum likelihood approach also can be used to estimate panel data logit models with individual effects and lags of the dependent variable, provided that there are no other explanatory variables and that there are at least four observations per individual (see Cox (1958), Chamberlain (1985), and Magnac (2000)). The panel AR (1) logit model is

$$\Pr(y_{i1}=1|\,\alpha_i)=p_1(\alpha_i) \tag{2}$$

$$\Pr(y_{it}=1|\,\alpha_i,y_{i1},\ldots,y_{it-1})=\Pr(y_{it}=1|\,\alpha_i,y_{it-1})=\frac{\exp(\gamma y_{it-1}+\alpha_i)}{1+\exp(\gamma y_{it-1}+\alpha_i)}$$

$$t=2,\ldots,T;T\geq 4$$

where y_{i1} is observed, although the model need not be specified in the initial period. The underlying errors are assumed here independent of initial conditions and identically distributed with logistic distribution. Eq. (2) does not make any assumptions about the distribution of the initial y and how it depends on α_i.

To gain intuition, consider the case with four observations per individual ($T=4$). Inference on γ then is based on individuals switching states in the two middle periods, 2 and 3. Consider the events:

$$\mathcal{A}_{01}=\{y_{i1},y_{i2}=0,y_{i3}=1,y_{i4}\}$$
$$\mathcal{A}_{10}=\{y_{i1},y_{i2}=1,y_{i3}=0,y_{i4}\}.$$

By sequential decomposition of the joint probability and by the first-order Markovian property of y, the probabilities of events $\mathcal{A}_{01}$ and $\mathcal{A}_{10}$ can be written as follows

$$\begin{aligned}\Pr(\mathcal{A}_{01}|\,\alpha_i)=&\Pr(y_{i1}|\,\alpha_i)\cdot\Pr(y_{i2}=0|\,\alpha_i,y_{i1})\cdot\\&\Pr(y_{i3}=1|\,\alpha_i,y_{i2}=0)\cdot\Pr(y_{i4}|\,\alpha_i,y_{i3}=1)\\&=p_1(\alpha_i)^{y_{i1}}(1-p_1(\alpha_i))^{1-y_{i1}}\frac{1}{1+\exp(\gamma y_{i1}+\alpha_i)}\cdot\\&\frac{\exp(\alpha_i)}{1+\exp(\alpha_i)}\cdot\frac{\exp(y_{i4}\gamma+y_{i4}\alpha_i)}{1+\exp(\gamma+\alpha_i)}\end{aligned}$$

and

$$\begin{aligned}\Pr(\mathcal{A}_{10}|\,\alpha_i)=&\Pr(y_{i1}|\,\alpha_i)\cdot\Pr(y_{i2}=1|\,\alpha_i,y_{i1})\cdot\\&\Pr(y_{i3}=0|\,\alpha_i,y_{i2}=1)\cdot\Pr(y_{i4}|\,\alpha_i,y_{i3}=0)\\&=p_1(\alpha_i)^{y_{i1}}(1-p_1(\alpha_i))^{1-y_{i1}}\cdot\frac{\exp(\gamma y_{i1}+\alpha_i)}{1+\exp(\gamma y_{i1}+\alpha_i)}\cdot\\&\frac{1}{1+\exp(\gamma+\alpha_i)}\cdot\frac{\exp(y_{i4}\alpha_i)}{1+\exp(\alpha_i)}.\end{aligned}$$

Therefore,

$$\Pr(\mathcal{A}_{01}|\,\mathcal{A}_{01}\cup\mathcal{A}_{10},\alpha_i)=\frac{1}{1+\dfrac{\Pr(\mathcal{A}_{10}|\,\alpha_i)}{\Pr(\mathcal{A}_{01}|\,\alpha_i)}}=\frac{1}{1+\exp(\gamma(y_{i1}-y_{i4}))}$$

$$\Pr(\mathcal{A}_{10}|\,\mathcal{A}_{01}\cup\mathcal{A}_{10},\alpha_i)=1-\Pr(\mathcal{A}_{01}|\,\mathcal{A}_{01}\cup\mathcal{A}_{10},\alpha_i)=\frac{\exp(\gamma(y_{i1}-y_{i4}))}{1+\exp(\gamma(y_{i1}-y_{i4}))}$$

which do not depend on the individual effects. The conditional log-likelihood of the model for $T=4$ periods is:

$$\mathcal{L}_C(g)=\sum_{i=1}^{n}1\{y_{i2}+y_{i3}=1\}\log\left(\frac{\exp(g(y_{i1}-y_{i4}))^{y_{i2}}}{1+\exp(g(y_{i1}-y_{i4}))}\right). \tag{3}$$

The conditional log-likelihood is similar in the static Eq. (1) and dynamic case Eq. (3). For general T, the conditional log-likelihood is based on the fact that

$$\Pr\left(y_{i1},y_{i1},\ldots,y_{iT}\,|\,y_{i1},y_{iT},\sum_{t=2}^{T}y_{it},\alpha_i\right)=\frac{\exp\left(\gamma\sum_{t=2}^{T}y_{it}y_{it-1}\right)}{\sum_{(d_0,\ldots,d_T)\in B}\exp\left(\gamma\sum_{t=2}^{T}d_t d_{t-1}\right)}$$

where

$$\mathcal{B}=\left\{(d_0,\ldots,d_T)\text{ such that }d_t\in\{0,1\}\text{ and}\sum_{t=1}^{T}d_t=\sum_{t=1}^{T}y_{it}\right\}.$$

See Cox (1958) and Magnac (2000) for higher order AR models.

2.3 Dynamic Case With Exogenous Covariates

Honoré and Kyriazidou (2000) propose conditional maximum likelihood type estimators for an extension of the AR(1) panel data logit model that also allows for strictly exogenous regressors.[3] They consider models of the form

$$\Pr(y_{i1}=1\,|\,x_i,\alpha_i)=p_1(x_i,\alpha_i)$$
$$\Pr(y_{it}=1\,|\,x_i,\alpha_i,y_{i1},y_{it-1})=\Pr(y_{it}=1\,|\,x_i,\alpha_i,y_{it-1})=\frac{\exp\left(x_{it}'\beta+\gamma y_{it-1}+\alpha_i\right)}{1+\exp\left(x_{it}'\beta+\gamma y_{it-1}+\alpha_i\right)}$$

where $x_i=(x_{i1},x_{i2},x_3,x_{i4})$. The model is unspecified for the initial period. The x's need not be observed in that period though, that is, x_{i1} need not be observed. Similar to the previous AR(1) logit, Honoré and Kyriazidou consider the events:

$$\mathcal{A}_{01}=\{y_{i1},y_{i2}=0,y_{i3}=1,y_{i4}\}$$
$$\mathcal{A}_{10}=\{y_{i1},y_{i2}=1,y_{i3}=0,y_{i4}\}.$$

By sequential decomposition of the joint probability, the probabilities of events $\mathcal{A}_{01}$ and $\mathcal{A}_{10}$ can be written as follows

3. D'Addio and Honoré (2010) generalized the approach in Honoré and Kyriazidou (2000) to a model with two lags.

$$\Pr(\mathcal{A}_{01}|\,\alpha_i, x_i) = \Pr(y_{i1}|\,\alpha_i, x_i)\cdot \Pr(y_{i2}=0|\,\alpha_i, y_{i1}, x_i)\cdot$$
$$\Pr(y_{i3}=1|\,\alpha_i, y_{i2}=0, x_i)\cdot \Pr(y_{i4}|\,\alpha_i, y_{i3}=1, x_i)$$
$$= p_1(\alpha_i, x_i)^{y_{i1}}(1-p_1(\alpha_i, x_i))^{1-y_{i1}}\cdot \frac{1}{1+\exp\left(x_{i2}'\beta+\gamma y_{i1}+\alpha_i\right)}\cdot$$
$$\frac{\exp\left(x_{i3}'\beta+\alpha_i\right)}{1+\exp\left(x_{i3}'\beta+\alpha_i\right)}\cdot\frac{\exp\left(y_{i4}x_{i4}'\beta+y_{i4}\gamma+y_{i4}\alpha_i\right)}{1+\exp\left(x_{i4}'\beta+\gamma+\alpha_i\right)}$$

and

$$\Pr(\mathcal{A}_{10}|\,\alpha_i, x_i) = \Pr(y_{i1}|\,\alpha_i, x_i)\cdot \Pr(y_{i2}=1|\,\alpha_i, y_{i1}, x_i)\cdot$$
$$\Pr(y_{i3}=0|\,\alpha_i, y_{i2}=1, x_i)\cdot \Pr(y_{i4}|\,\alpha_i, y_{i3}=0, x_i)$$
$$= p_1(\alpha_i, x_i)^{y_{i1}}(1-p_1(\alpha_i, x_i))^{1-y_{i1}}\cdot \frac{\exp\left(x_{i2}'\beta+\gamma y_{i1}+\alpha_i\right)}{1+\exp\left(x_{i2}'\beta+\gamma y_{i1}+\alpha_i\right)}\cdot$$
$$\frac{1}{1+\exp\left(x_{i3}'\beta+\gamma+\alpha_i\right)}\cdot\frac{\exp\left(y_{i4}x_{i4}'\beta+y_{i4}\alpha_i\right)}{1+\exp\left(x_{i4}'\beta+\alpha_i\right)}.$$

Identification of β and γ in this model is based on the fact that if $x_{i2}=x_{i3}$, then

$$\Pr(\mathcal{A}_{01}|\,\mathcal{A}_{01}\cup\mathcal{A}_{10}, \alpha_i, x_i, x_{i3}=x_{i4}) = \frac{1}{1+\exp\left((x_{i2}-x_{i3})'\beta+\gamma(y_{i1}-y_{i4})\right)}$$

$$\Pr(\mathcal{A}_{10}|\,\mathcal{A}_{01}\cup\mathcal{A}_{10}, \alpha_i, x_i, x_{i3}=x_{i4}) = \frac{\exp\left((x_{i2}-x_{i3})'\beta+\gamma(y_{i1}-y_{i4})\right)}{1+\exp\left((x_{i2}-x_{i3})'\beta+\gamma(y_{i1}-y_{i4})\right)}$$

that is, they are independent of α_i. We can estimate β and γ by maximizing the weighted log-likelihood function where (discrete) explanatory variables, x_{it}, satisfy the condition $\Pr(x_{i2}=x_{i3})>0$:

$$\sum_{i=1}^{n} 1\{y_{i2}+y_{i3}=1\}1\{x_{i3}-x_{i4}=0\}\log\left(\frac{\exp\left((x_{i2}-x_{i3})'b+g(y_{i1}-y_{i4})\right)^{y_{i2}}}{1+\exp\left((x_{i2}-x_{i3})'b+g(y_{i1}-y_{i4})\right)}\right), \tag{4}$$

leading to root-n asymptotically normal and consistent estimators of β and γ. The objective function Eq. (4) is similar to the log-likelihood in the static Eq. (1) and pure AR(1) dynamic case Eq. (3).

Although inference based only on observations for which $x_{i3}=x_{i4}$ might be reasonable in some cases (in particular, experimental cases where the distribution of x_i is in the control of the researcher), it is not useful in many economic applications. The idea then is to replace the indicator functions $1\,\{x_{i3}-x_{i4}=0\}$ in the previous objective function with weights that depend inversely on the magnitude of the difference $x_{i3}-x_{i4}$, giving more weight to observations for which x_{i3} is close to x_{i4}. Specifically, they propose estimating β_0 and γ_0 by maximizing

$$\sum_{i=1}^{n} 1\{y_{i2}+y_{i3}=1\} K\left(\frac{x_{i3}-x_{i4}}{h_n}\right) \log\left(\frac{\exp\left((x_{i2}-x_{i3})'b+g(y_{i1}-y_{i4})\right)^{y_{i2}}}{1+\exp\left((x_{i2}-x_{i3})'b+g(y_{i1}-y_{i4})\right)}\right) \tag{5}$$

with respect to b and g over some compact set. Here $K(\cdot)$ is a kernel density function that gives appropriate weight to observation i, and h_n is a bandwidth that shrinks to 0 as n increases. The asymptotic theory will require that $K(\cdot)$ be chosen so that a number of regularity conditions, such as $K(\nu) \to 0$ as $|\nu| \to \infty$, are satisfied. The estimators are shown to be consistent and asymptotically normal although the rate of convergence in distribution is slower than the usual $\sqrt{n}$. The proposed estimators are extremum or M-estimators. The key idea behind the estimation is that the limit of the previous objective function, is uniquely maximized at the true parameter values, under appropriate assumptions. It is clear that identification of the model will require that $x_{i3} - x_{i4}$ be continuously distributed with support in a neighborhood of 0, and that $x_{i2} - x_{i3}$ have sufficient variation conditional on the event that $x_{i3} - x_{i4} = 0$.

3 The Bivariate Pure VAR(1) Logit Case

Narendranthan et al. (1985) considered a bivariate extension of the univariate dynamic logit model:

$$y_{1,it} = 1\{y_{1,it-1}\gamma_{11} + y_{2,it-1}\gamma_{12} + \alpha_{1,i} + \varepsilon_{1,it} \geq 0\}$$
$$y_{2,it} = 1\{y_{1,it-1}\gamma_{21} + y_{2,it-1}\gamma_{22} + \alpha_{2,i} + \varepsilon_{2,it} \geq 0\}$$

where $\{\varepsilon_{1,it}\}_{t=1}^{T}$ and $\{\varepsilon_{2,it}\}_{t=1}^{T}$ are independent i.i.d. sequences of logistic errors, independent of the individual effects $\alpha_{1,i}$ and $\alpha_{2,i}$. The model holds (at least) for periods $t = 2, \ldots, T$ while it is not parametrically specified for the first (initial) period, that is, $P\left(\begin{pmatrix} y_{1,i1} \\ y_{2,i1} \end{pmatrix} \middle| \alpha_{1,i}, \alpha_{2,i}\right)$ is not parameterized. $\alpha_{1,i}$ and $\alpha_{2,i}$ are fixed effects in the sense that they can be correlated arbitrarily while their relationship with the initial conditions is not specified. In the sequel, we suppress the i subscript for notational simplicity. Under these assumptions

$$\begin{aligned}
& P\left(\begin{pmatrix} y_{1t} \\ y_{2t} \end{pmatrix} \middle| \left\{\begin{pmatrix} y_{1s} \\ y_{2s} \end{pmatrix}\right\}_{s<t}, \begin{pmatrix} \alpha_1 \\ \alpha_2 \end{pmatrix}\right) \\
&= P\left(\begin{pmatrix} y_{1t} \\ y_{2t} \end{pmatrix} \middle| \begin{pmatrix} y_{1t-1} \\ y_{2t-1} \end{pmatrix}, \begin{pmatrix} \alpha_1 \\ \alpha_2 \end{pmatrix}\right) \\
&= P\left(y_{1t} \middle| \begin{pmatrix} y_{1t-1} \\ y_{2t-1} \end{pmatrix}, \alpha_1\right) \cdot P\left(y_{2t} \middle| \begin{pmatrix} y_{1t-1} \\ y_{2t-1} \end{pmatrix}, \alpha_2\right) \\
&= \frac{\exp\left((\alpha_1 + y_{1t-1}\gamma_{11} + y_{2t-1}\gamma_{12})y_{1t}\right)}{1+\exp\left((\alpha_1 + y_{1t-1}\gamma_{11} + y_{2t-1}\gamma_{12})\right)} \cdot \frac{\exp\left((\alpha_2 + y_{2,t-1}\gamma_{21} + y_{t-1}\gamma_{22})y_{2t}\right)}{1+\exp\left((\alpha_2 + y_{1t-1}\gamma_{21} + y_{2t-1}\gamma_{22})\right)}.
\end{aligned}$$

We will first discuss identification in the $T = 4$ case. Using the same key insight as in the univariate 4-period case, namely that conditioning on the individual switching states in the middle two periods, that is, for $t = 2, 3$, eliminates the individual effect, we consider first the case that both y's switch states from 0 to 1. We have that

$$P\left(\begin{pmatrix} y_{11} \\ y_{21} \end{pmatrix}, \begin{pmatrix} y_{12} \\ y_{22} \end{pmatrix} = \begin{pmatrix} 0 \\ 0 \end{pmatrix}, \begin{pmatrix} y_{13} \\ y_{23} \end{pmatrix} = \begin{pmatrix} 1 \\ 1 \end{pmatrix}, \begin{pmatrix} y_{14} \\ y_{24} \end{pmatrix} \middle| \alpha_1, \alpha_2\right)$$
$$= P\left(\begin{pmatrix} y_{11} \\ y_{21} \end{pmatrix} \middle| \alpha_1, \alpha_2\right) \cdot \frac{1}{1 + \exp(\alpha_1 + y_{11}\gamma_{11} + y_{21}\gamma_{12})} \frac{1}{1 + \exp(\alpha_2 + y_{11}\gamma_{21} + y_{21}\gamma_{22})}$$
$$\cdot \frac{\exp(\alpha_1)}{1 + \exp(\alpha_1)} \frac{\exp(\alpha_2)}{1 + \exp(\alpha_2)} \cdot \frac{\exp((\alpha_1 + \gamma_{11} + \gamma_{12})y_{14})}{1 + \exp(\alpha_1 + \gamma_{11} + \gamma_{12})} \frac{\exp((\alpha_2 + \gamma_{21} + \gamma_{22})y_{24})}{1 + \exp(\alpha_2 + \gamma_{21} + \gamma_{22})}$$

and

$$P\left(\begin{pmatrix} y_{11} \\ y_{21} \end{pmatrix}, \begin{pmatrix} y_{12} \\ y_{22} \end{pmatrix} = \begin{pmatrix} 1 \\ 1 \end{pmatrix}, \begin{pmatrix} y_{13} \\ y_{23} \end{pmatrix} = \begin{pmatrix} 0 \\ 0 \end{pmatrix}, \begin{pmatrix} y_{14} \\ y_{24} \end{pmatrix} \middle| \alpha_1, \alpha_2\right)$$
$$= P\left(\begin{pmatrix} y_{11} \\ y_{21} \end{pmatrix} \middle| \alpha_1, \alpha_2\right) \cdot \frac{\exp(\alpha_1 + y_{11}\gamma_{11} + y_{21}\gamma_{12})}{1 + \exp(\alpha_1 + y_{11}\gamma_{11} + y_{21}\gamma_{12})} \frac{\exp(\alpha_2 + y_{11}\gamma_{21} + y_{21}\gamma_{22})}{1 + \exp(\alpha_2 + y_{11}\gamma_{21} + y_{21}\gamma_{22})}$$
$$\cdot \frac{1}{1 + \exp(\alpha_1 + \gamma_{11} + \gamma_{12})} \frac{1}{1 + \exp(\alpha_2 + \gamma_{21} + \gamma_{22})} \cdot \frac{\exp(\alpha_1 y_{14})}{1 + \exp(\alpha_1)} \frac{\exp(\alpha_2 y_{24})}{1 + \exp(\alpha_2)}.$$

Define

$$\mathcal{A}_{jk,lm} = \left\{\begin{pmatrix} y_{11} \\ y_{21} \end{pmatrix}, \begin{pmatrix} y_{12} \\ y_{22} \end{pmatrix} = \begin{pmatrix} j \\ k \end{pmatrix}, \begin{pmatrix} y_{13} \\ y_{23} \end{pmatrix} = \begin{pmatrix} l \\ m \end{pmatrix}, \begin{pmatrix} y_{14} \\ y_{24} \end{pmatrix}\right\}$$

for $j, k, l, m \in \{0, 1\}$.

It is not difficult to see that

$$\frac{P(\mathcal{A}_{11,00} | y_{11}, y_{21}, y_{14}, y_{24}, \alpha_1, \alpha_2)}{P(\mathcal{A}_{00,11} | y_{11}, y_{21}, y_{14}, y_{24}, \alpha_1, \alpha_2)}$$
$$= \exp(\gamma_{11}(y_{11} - y_{14}) + \gamma_{12}(y_{21} - y_{14}) + \gamma_{21}(y_{11} - y_{24}) + \gamma_{22}(y_{21} - y_{24}))$$

and therefore

$$P(\mathcal{A}_{00,11} | y_{11}, y_{21}, y_{14}, y_{24}, \alpha_1, \alpha_2, \mathcal{A}_{00,11} \cup \mathcal{A}_{11,00})$$
$$= \frac{P(\mathcal{A}_{00,11} | y_{11}, y_{21}, y_{14}, y_{24}, \alpha_1, \alpha_2)}{P(\mathcal{A}_{00,11} | y_{11}, y_{21}, y_{14}, y_{24}, \alpha_1, \alpha_2) + P(\mathcal{A}_{11,00} | y_{11}, y_{21}, y_{14}, y_{24}, \alpha_1, \alpha_2)}$$
$$= \frac{1}{1 + \dfrac{P(\mathcal{A}_{11,00} | y_{11}, y_{21}, y_{14}, y_{24}, \alpha_1, \alpha_2)}{P(\mathcal{A}_{00,11} | y_{11}, y_{21}, y_{14}, y_{24}, \alpha_1, \alpha_2)}}$$
$$\frac{1}{1 + \exp(\gamma_{11}(y_{11} - y_{14}) + \gamma_{12}(y_{21} - y_{14}) + \gamma_{21}(y_{11} - y_{24}) + \gamma_{22}(y_{21} - y_{24}))}. \tag{6}$$

We observe that Eq. (6) does not depend on the fixed effects, while it identifies the dependence parameters, the γ's, from the variation of responses between the first and the fourth periods.

Similarly, for individuals whose y_1 switches from 0 to 1 and y_2 switches from 1 to 0 in the middle two periods ($t = 2, 3$) we have that

$$P\left(\begin{pmatrix} y_{11} \\ y_{21} \end{pmatrix}, \begin{pmatrix} y_{12} \\ y_{2} \end{pmatrix} = \begin{pmatrix} 0 \\ 1 \end{pmatrix}, \begin{pmatrix} y_{13} \\ y_{3} \end{pmatrix} = \begin{pmatrix} 1 \\ 0 \end{pmatrix}, \begin{pmatrix} y_{14} \\ y_{24} \end{pmatrix} = \begin{pmatrix} y_{14} \\ y_{24} \end{pmatrix} \middle| \alpha_1, \alpha_2 \right)$$
$$= P\left(\begin{pmatrix} y_{11} \\ y_{21} \end{pmatrix} \middle| \alpha_1, \alpha_2 \right) \cdot \frac{1}{1+\exp(\alpha_1 + y_{11}\gamma_{11} + y_{21}\gamma_{12})} \frac{\exp(\alpha_2 + y_{11}\gamma_{21} + y_{21}\gamma_{22})}{1+\exp(\alpha_2 + y_{11}\gamma_{21} + y_{21}\gamma_{22})}$$
$$\cdot \frac{\exp(\alpha_1 + \gamma_{12})}{1+\exp(\alpha_1 + \gamma_{12})} \frac{1}{1+\exp(\alpha_2 + \gamma_{22})} \cdot \frac{\exp((\alpha_1 + \gamma_{11})y_{14})}{1+\exp(\alpha_1 + \gamma_{11})} \frac{\exp((\alpha_2 + \gamma_{21})y_{24})}{1+\exp(\alpha_2 + \gamma_{21})}$$

and

$$P\left(\begin{pmatrix} y_{11} \\ y_{21} \end{pmatrix}, \begin{pmatrix} y_{12} \\ y_{22} \end{pmatrix} = \begin{pmatrix} 1 \\ 0 \end{pmatrix}, \begin{pmatrix} y_{13} \\ y_{23} \end{pmatrix} = \begin{pmatrix} 0 \\ 1 \end{pmatrix}, \begin{pmatrix} y_{14} \\ y_{24} \end{pmatrix} \middle| \alpha_1, \alpha_2 \right)$$
$$= P\left(\begin{pmatrix} y_{11} \\ y_{21} \end{pmatrix} \middle| \alpha_1, \alpha_2 \right) \cdot \frac{\exp(\alpha_1 + y_{11}\gamma_{11} + y_{21}\gamma_{12})}{1+\exp(\alpha_1 + y_{11}\gamma_{11} + y_{21}\gamma_{12})} \frac{1}{1+\exp(\alpha_2 + y_{11}\gamma_{21} + y_{21}\gamma_{22})}$$
$$\cdot \frac{1}{1+\exp(\alpha_1 + \gamma_{11})} \frac{\exp(\alpha_2 + \gamma_{21})}{1+\exp(\alpha_2 + \gamma_{21})} \cdot \frac{\exp((\alpha_1 + \gamma_{12})y_{14})}{1+\exp(\alpha_1 + \gamma_{12})} \frac{\exp((\alpha_2 + \gamma_{22})y_{24})}{1+\exp(\alpha_2 + \gamma_{22})}$$

and therefore

$$P(\mathcal{A}_{01,10} | \, y_{11}, y_{21}, y_{14}, y_{24}, \alpha_1, \alpha_2, \mathcal{A}_{10,01} \cup \mathcal{A}_{01,10})$$
$$= \frac{1}{1+\exp(\gamma_{11}(y_{11} - y_{14}) + \gamma_{12}(y_{14} + y_{21} - 1) + \gamma_{21}(1 - y_{11} - y_{24}) + \gamma_{22}(y_{24} - y_{21}))}.$$

All sequences where at least one switch occurs contain information about at least some of the unknown parameters. For example, consider the case where y_1 changes from 0 to 1 between periods 2 and 3, while y_2 is 0 in both periods:

$$P\left(\begin{pmatrix} y_{11} \\ y_{21} \end{pmatrix}, \begin{pmatrix} y_{12} \\ y_{22} \end{pmatrix} = \begin{pmatrix} 0 \\ 0 \end{pmatrix}, \begin{pmatrix} y_{13} \\ y_{23} \end{pmatrix} = \begin{pmatrix} 1 \\ 0 \end{pmatrix}, \begin{pmatrix} y_{14} \\ y_{24} \end{pmatrix} \middle| \alpha_1, \alpha_2 \right)$$
$$= P\left(\begin{pmatrix} y_{11} \\ y_{21} \end{pmatrix} \middle| \alpha_1, \alpha_2 \right) \cdot \frac{1}{1+\exp(\alpha_1 + y_{11}\gamma_{11} + y_{21}\gamma_{12})} \frac{1}{1+\exp(\alpha_2 + y_{11}\gamma_{21} + y_{21}\gamma_{22})}$$
$$\cdot \frac{\exp(\alpha_1)}{1+\exp(\alpha_1)} \frac{1}{1+\exp(\alpha_2)} \cdot \frac{\exp((\alpha_1 + \gamma_{11})y_{14})}{1+\exp(\alpha_1 + \gamma_{11})} \frac{\exp((\alpha_2 + \gamma_{21})y_{24})}{1+\exp(\alpha_2 + \gamma_{21})}$$

and

$$P\left(\begin{pmatrix} y_{11} \\ y_{21} \end{pmatrix}, \begin{pmatrix} y_{12} \\ y_{22} \end{pmatrix} = \begin{pmatrix} 1 \\ 0 \end{pmatrix}, \begin{pmatrix} y_{13} \\ y_{23} \end{pmatrix} = \begin{pmatrix} 0 \\ 0 \end{pmatrix}, \begin{pmatrix} y_{14} \\ y_{24} \end{pmatrix} \middle| \alpha_1, \alpha_2 \right)$$
$$= P\left(\begin{pmatrix} y_{11} \\ y_{21} \end{pmatrix} \middle| \alpha_1, \alpha_2 \right) \cdot \frac{\exp(\alpha_1 + y_{11}\gamma_{11} + y_{21}\gamma_{12})}{1+\exp(\alpha_1 + y_{11}\gamma_{11} + y_{21}\gamma_{12})} \frac{1}{1+\exp(\alpha_2 + y_{11}\gamma_{21} + y_{21}\gamma_{22})}$$
$$\cdot \frac{1}{1+\exp(\alpha_1 + \gamma_{11})} \frac{1}{1+\exp(\alpha_2 + \gamma_{21})} \cdot \frac{\exp(\alpha_1 y_{14})}{1+\exp(\alpha_1)} \frac{\exp(\alpha_2 y_{24})}{1+\exp(\alpha_2)}.$$

Therefore

$$\frac{P(\mathcal{A}_{10,00} | y_{11}, y_{21}, y_{14}, y_{24}, \alpha_1, \alpha_2)}{P(\mathcal{A}_{00,10} | y_{11}, y_{21}, y_{14}, y_{24}, \alpha_2, \alpha_2)} = \exp(\gamma_{11}(y_{11} - y_{14}) + \gamma_{12} y_{21} - \gamma_{21} y_{24})$$

and

$$P(\mathcal{A}_{00,10} | y_{11}, y_{21}, y_{14}, y_{24}, \alpha_1, \alpha_2, \mathcal{A}_{10,00} \cup \mathcal{A}_{00,10})$$
$$= \frac{1}{1+\exp(\gamma_{11}(y_{11} - y_{14}) + \gamma_{12} y_{21} - \gamma_{21} y_{24})}.$$

In this case, the parameter of the own lag (γ_{22}) of the process with no switches in the two middle periods (y_2) is not identified.

4 The Bivariate Logit Model With Exogenous Covariates

We now add exogenous variables to the model and demonstrate how the ideas of Honoré and Kyriazidou (2000) can be applied to obtain identification and construct estimators. The model takes the form

$$y_{1,it} = 1\{y_{1,it-1}\gamma_{11} + y_{2,it-1}\gamma_{12} + x'_{1,it}\beta_1 + \alpha_{1,i} + \varepsilon_{1,it} \geq 0\}$$
$$y_{2,it} = 1\{y_{1,it-1}\gamma_{21} + y_{2,it-1}\gamma_{22} + x'_{2,it}\beta_2 + \alpha_{2,i} + \varepsilon_{2,it} \geq 0\}$$

where $\{\varepsilon_{1,it}\}_{t=1}^{T}$ and $\{\varepsilon_{2,it}\}_{t=1}^{T}$ are independent i.i.d. sequences of logistic errors. $\alpha_{1,i}$ and $\alpha_{2,I}$ are fixed effects, and $x_{it} = (x_{1,it} \cup x_{2,it})$ is a set of strictly exogenous variables. Again, the initial conditions $P\left(\begin{pmatrix} y_{1,i1} \\ y_{2,i1} \end{pmatrix} \middle| \alpha_{1,i}, \alpha_{2,i}, x_{i1}, x_{i2}, x_{i3}, x_{i4} \right)$ are left unspecified. The model for periods $t = 2, \ldots, T$ is (dropping the i subscripts)

$$P\left(\begin{pmatrix} y_{1t} \\ y_{2t} \end{pmatrix} \middle| \left\{\begin{pmatrix} y_{1s} \\ y_{2s} \end{pmatrix}\right\}_{s<t}, \begin{pmatrix} \alpha_1 \\ \alpha_2 \end{pmatrix}, x \right)$$
$$= \frac{\exp\left(\left(\alpha_1 + y_{1t-1}\gamma_{11} + y_{2t-1}\gamma_{12} + x'_{1t}\beta_1\right) y_{1t}\right)}{1+\exp\left(\left(\alpha_1 + y_{1t-1}\gamma_{11} + y_{2t-1}\gamma_{12} + x'_{1t}\beta_1\right)\right)} \frac{\exp\left(\left(\alpha_2 + y_{2,t-1}\gamma_{21} + y_{t-1}\gamma_{22} + x'_{2t}\beta_2\right) y_{2t}\right)}{1+\exp\left(\left(\alpha_2 + y_{1t-1}\gamma_{21} + y_{2t-1}\gamma_{22} + x'_{2t}\beta_2\right)\right)}$$

where $x = (x_1, x_2, x_3, x_4)$. As in the univariate case, we need not observe x_1.

Concentrating again on sequences where there is at least one switch of state in the middle two periods in a 4-period panel, we have that

$$P\left(\begin{pmatrix} y_{11} \\ y_{21} \end{pmatrix}, \begin{pmatrix} y_{12} \\ y_{22} \end{pmatrix} = \begin{pmatrix} 0 \\ 0 \end{pmatrix}, \begin{pmatrix} y_{13} \\ y_{23} \end{pmatrix} = \begin{pmatrix} 1 \\ 1 \end{pmatrix}, \begin{pmatrix} y_{14} \\ y_{24} \end{pmatrix} \middle| \alpha_1, \alpha_2, x\right)$$
$$= P\left(\begin{pmatrix} y_{11} \\ y_{21} \end{pmatrix} \middle| \alpha_1, \alpha_2, x\right) \cdot$$
$$\frac{1}{1+\exp\left(\alpha_1+y_{11}\gamma_{11}+y_{21}\gamma_{12}+x_{12}'\beta_1\right)} \frac{1}{1+\exp\left(\alpha_2+y_{11}\gamma_{21}+y_{21}\gamma_{22}+x_{22}'\beta_2\right)} \cdot$$
$$\frac{\exp\left(\alpha_1+x_{13}'\beta_1\right)}{1+\exp\left(\alpha_1+x_{13}'\beta_1\right)} \frac{\exp\left(\alpha_2+x_{23}'\beta_2\right)}{1+\exp\left(\alpha_2+x_{23}'\beta_2\right)}$$
$$\frac{\exp\left(\left(\alpha_1+\gamma_{11}+\gamma_{12}+x_{14}'\beta_1\right)y_{14}\right)}{1+\exp\left(\alpha_1+\gamma_{11}+\gamma_{12}+x_{14}'\beta_1\right)} \frac{\exp\left(\left(\alpha_2+\gamma_{21}+\gamma_{22}+x_{24}'\beta_2\right)y_{24}\right)}{1+\exp\left(\alpha_2+\gamma_{21}+\gamma_{22}+x_{24}'\beta_2\right)}$$

and

$$P\left(\begin{pmatrix} y_{11} \\ y_{21} \end{pmatrix}, \begin{pmatrix} y_{12} \\ y_{22} \end{pmatrix} = \begin{pmatrix} 1 \\ 1 \end{pmatrix}, \begin{pmatrix} y_{13} \\ y_{23} \end{pmatrix} = \begin{pmatrix} 0 \\ 0 \end{pmatrix}, \begin{pmatrix} y_{14} \\ y_{24} \end{pmatrix} \middle| \alpha_1, \alpha_2, x\right)$$
$$= P\left(\begin{pmatrix} y_{11} \\ y_{21} \end{pmatrix} \middle| \alpha_1, \alpha_2, x\right) \cdot$$
$$\frac{\exp\left(\alpha_1+y_{11}\gamma_{11}+y_{21}\gamma_{12}+x_{12}'\beta_1\right)}{1+\exp\left(\alpha_1+y_{11}\gamma_{11}+y_{21}\gamma_{12}+x_{12}'\beta_1\right)} \frac{\exp\left(\alpha_2+y_{11}\gamma_{21}+y_{21}\gamma_{22}+x_{22}'\beta_2\right)}{1+\exp\left(\alpha_2+y_{11}\gamma_{21}+y_{21}\gamma_{22}+x_{22}'\beta_2\right)} \cdot$$
$$\frac{1}{1+\exp\left(\alpha_1+\gamma_{11}+\gamma_{12}+x_{13}'\beta_1\right)} \frac{1}{1+\exp\left(\alpha_2+\gamma_{21}+\gamma_{22}+x_{23}'\beta_2\right)} \cdot$$
$$\frac{\exp\left(\left(\alpha_1+x_{14}'\beta_1\right)y_{14}\right)}{1+\exp\left(\alpha_1+x_{14}'\beta_1\right)} \frac{\exp\left(\left(\alpha_2+x_{24}'\beta_2\right)y_{24}\right)}{1+\exp\left(\alpha_2+x_{24}'\beta_2\right)}.$$

Therefore, similarly to Honoré and Kyriazidou (2000), if the exogenous variables do not change in the last two periods that is, if $x_3 = x_4$ then

$$\begin{aligned} P(&\mathcal{A}_{00,11} | y_{11}, y_{21}, y_{14}, y_{24}, \alpha_1, \alpha_2, \mathcal{A}_{00,11} \cup \mathcal{A}_{11,00}, x_3 = x_4) \\ &= 1/(1+\exp(\gamma_{11}(y_{11}-y_{14}) + \gamma_{12}(y_{21}-y_{14}) + (x_{13}-x_{12})'\beta_1 \\ &\quad + \gamma_{21}(y_{11}-y_{24}) + \gamma_{22}(y_{21}-y_{24}) + (x_{22}-x_{23})'\beta_2)) \end{aligned}$$

does not depend on the fixed effects.

Similarly, we can show that

$$\begin{aligned} P(&\mathcal{A}_{01,10} | y_{11}, y_{21}, y_{14}, y_{24}, \alpha_1, \alpha_2, \mathcal{A}_{01,10}, x_3 = x_4) \\ &= 1/(1+\exp(\gamma_{11}(y_{11}-y_{14}) + \gamma_{12}(y_{14}+y_{21}-1) + (x_{12}-x_{13})'\beta_1 \\ &\quad + \gamma_{21}(1-y_{11}-y_{24}) + \gamma_{22}(y_{24}-y_{21}) + (x_{23}-x_{22})'\beta_2)). \end{aligned}$$

Because the right side does not depend on α_1 or α_2, the same result holds without conditioning on those,

$$P(\mathcal{A}_{01,10}|\, y_{11}, y_{21}, y_{14}, y_{24}, \mathcal{A}_{01,10} \cup \mathcal{A}_{10,01}, x_3 = x_4)$$
$$= 1/(1+\exp(\gamma_{11}(y_{11}-y_{14})+\gamma_{12}(y_{14}+y_{21}-1)+(x_{12}-x_{13})'\beta_1+\gamma_{21}(1-y_{11}-y_{24})$$
$$+\gamma_{22}(y_{24}-y_{21})+(x_{23}-x_{22})'\beta_2)).$$

This expression can be used to construct a conditional "likelihood" function that can be used to estimate γ_{11}, γ_{12}, γ_{21}, γ_{22}, β_1 and β_2 without making any assumptions about α_1 or α_2 or about the distribution of the initial y's.

The coefficients on the exogenous variables, the β's, are identified from the variation of the x's between periods 2 and 3. Furthermore, both of the β's are identified under the same conditioning event, namely $x_3 = x_4$, even if only one of the y's switches states in the middle two periods while the other remains constant in both periods (a case in which, as we saw in the previous section, only the parameters of the switching process are identified when there are no exogenous variables). Indeed, consider the case in which y_1 changes from 0 to 1 between periods 2 and 3, while y_2 is 0 on both periods:

$$P\left(\begin{pmatrix} y_{11} \\ y_{21} \end{pmatrix}, \begin{pmatrix} y_{12} \\ y_{22} \end{pmatrix} = \begin{pmatrix} 0 \\ 0 \end{pmatrix}, \begin{pmatrix} y_{13} \\ y_{23} \end{pmatrix} = \begin{pmatrix} 1 \\ 0 \end{pmatrix}, \begin{pmatrix} y_{14} \\ y_{24} \end{pmatrix} \middle| \alpha_1, \alpha_2, x\right)$$
$$= P\left(\begin{pmatrix} y_{11} \\ y_{21} \end{pmatrix} \middle| \alpha_1, \alpha_2, x\right) \cdot \frac{1}{1+\exp\left(\alpha_1 + y_{11}\gamma_{11} + y_{21}\gamma_{12} + x_{12}'\beta_1\right)}$$
$$\frac{1}{1+\exp\left(\alpha_2 + y_{11}\gamma_{21} + y_{21}\gamma_{22} + x_{22}'\beta_2\right)} \cdot \frac{\exp\left(\alpha_1 + x_{13}'\beta_1\right).}{1+\exp\left(\alpha_1 + x_{13}'\beta_1\right)} \cdot \frac{1}{1+\exp\left(\alpha_2 + x_{23}'\beta_2\right)}$$
$$\cdot \frac{\exp\left((\alpha_1+\gamma_{11}+x_{14}'\beta_1)y_{14}\right)}{1+\exp\left(\alpha_1+\gamma_{11}+x_{14}'\beta_1\right)} \cdot \frac{\exp\left((\alpha_2+\gamma_{21}+x_{24}'\beta_2)y_{24}\right)}{1+\exp\left(\alpha_2+\gamma_{21}+x_{24}'\beta_2\right)}$$

and

$$P\left(\begin{pmatrix} y_{11} \\ y_{21} \end{pmatrix}, \begin{pmatrix} y_{12} \\ y_{22} \end{pmatrix} = \begin{pmatrix} 1 \\ 0 \end{pmatrix}, \begin{pmatrix} y_{13} \\ y_{23} \end{pmatrix} = \begin{pmatrix} 0 \\ 0 \end{pmatrix}, \begin{pmatrix} y_{14} \\ y_{24} \end{pmatrix}\right)$$
$$= P\left(\begin{pmatrix} y_{11} \\ y_{21} \end{pmatrix} \middle| \alpha_1, \alpha_2, x\right) \cdot \frac{\exp\left(\alpha_1 + y_{11}\gamma_{11} + y_{21}\gamma_{12} + x_{12}'\beta_1\right)}{1+\exp\left(\alpha_1 + y_{11}\gamma_{11} + y_{21}\gamma_{12} + x_{12}'\beta_1\right)}$$
$$\cdot \frac{1}{1+\exp\left(\alpha_2 + y_{11}\gamma_{21} + y_{21}\gamma_{22} + x_{22}'\beta_2\right)} \cdot \frac{1}{1+\exp\left(\alpha_1 + \gamma_{11} + x_{13}'\beta_1\right)} \cdot \frac{1}{1+\exp\left(\alpha_2 + \gamma_{21} + x_{23}'\beta_2\right)}$$
$$\cdot \frac{\exp\left(\left(\alpha_1 + x_{14}'\beta_1\right)y_{14}\right)}{1+\exp\left(\alpha_1 + x_{14}'\beta_1\right)} \cdot \frac{\exp\left(\left(\alpha + x_{24}'\beta_2\right)y_{24}\right)}{1+\exp\left(\alpha_2 + x_{24}'\beta_2\right)}.$$

Conditioning in $x_3 = x_4$ we obtain

$$\frac{P(\mathcal{A}_{10,00}|\, y_{11}, y_{21}, y_{14}, y_{24}, \alpha_1, \alpha_2, x_3 = x_4)}{P(\mathcal{A}_{00,10}|\, y_{11}, y_{21}, y_{14}, y_{24}, \alpha_2, \alpha_2, x_3 = x_4)}$$
$$= \exp\left(\gamma_{11}(y_{11}-y_{14}) + \gamma_{12}y_{21} + (x_{12}' - x_{13}' - x_{14}'y_{14})\beta_1 - \gamma_{21}y_{24} - x_{24}'y_{24}\beta_2\right)$$

Therefore

$$P(A_{00,10}|\, y_{11}, y_{21}, y_{14}, y_{24}, \alpha_1, \alpha_2, x_3 = x_4, A_{00,10} \cup A_{00,10}) = \frac{1}{1 + \exp\left(\gamma_{11}(y_{11} - y_{14}) + \gamma_{12}y_{21} - \gamma_{21}y_{24} + (x_{12} - x_{13})'\beta_1 - x'_{14}y_{14}\beta_1 - x'_{24}y_{24}\beta_2\right)}.$$

5 The General *M*-Variate, General *T* VAR(1) Case

Let $\mathbf{y}_{it}$ denote the vector of M choices of individual i at time t, $(y_{1,it}, y_{2,it}, \ldots, y_{M,it})$. Also let $\gamma_m = (\gamma_{m1}, \gamma_{m2}, \ldots, \gamma_{mM})'$ be the dependence parameters of the m'th choice. The multivariate VAR(1) logit model with fixed effects is

$$P(\mathbf{y}_{it} = \mathbf{y}_t, |\, \mathbf{y}_{i1} = \mathbf{y}_1, \ldots, \mathbf{y}_{it-1} = \mathbf{y}_{t-1}, \alpha_{1,i}, \ldots, \alpha_{M,i}) = \prod_{m=1}^{M} \frac{\exp\left(y_{m,it}\mathbf{y}'_{it-1}\gamma_m + y_{m,it}\alpha_{m,i}\right)}{1 + \exp\left(\mathbf{y}'_{it-1}\gamma_m + \alpha_{m,i}\right)}.$$

Note that $\mathbf{y}_t$ can take 2^M distinct values. Denote each one by B_ℓ for $\ell = 1, \ldots, 2^M$. For $\ell = 1, \ldots, 2^M$, let $N_y(\ell) = \sum_{t=1}^{T-1} 1\{\mathbf{y}_t = B_\ell\}$ be the total number of incidences of the particular set of choices B_ℓ between periods 1 and $T-1$. Let $S_y(m) = \sum_{t=2}^{T} y_{m,t}$ be the total number that the mth choice was made between periods 2 and T. Note that $S_{\mathbf{y}}(m)$ is known if $N_{\mathbf{y}}(\ell)$ and $\mathbf{y}_T$ is given. Then

$$\begin{aligned} P(\mathbf{y}_{i2} = \mathbf{y}_2, \ldots, \mathbf{y}_{iT} = \mathbf{y}_T|\, \mathbf{y}_{i1} = \mathbf{y}_1, \alpha_{1,i}, \ldots, \alpha_{M,i}) &= \prod_{m=1}^{M}\prod_{t=2}^{T} \frac{\exp\left(y_{m,it}\mathbf{y}'_{it-1}\gamma_m + y_{m,it}\alpha_{m,i}\right)}{1 + \exp\left(\mathbf{y}'_{it-1}\gamma_m + \alpha_{m,i}\right)} \\ &= \frac{\exp\left(\sum_{m=1}^{M}\sum_{t=2}^{T} y_{m,it}\mathbf{y}'_{it-1}\gamma_m + S_y(m)\alpha_{m,i}\right)}{\prod_{m=1}^{M}\prod_{\ell=1}^{2^M}\left(1 + \exp\left((B'_\ell\gamma_m + \alpha_{m,i})\right)\right)^{N_y(\ell)}}. \end{aligned}$$

Now consider the ratio of the probabilities for two sequences $(\mathbf{y}_1, \mathbf{y}_2, \ldots, \mathbf{y}_T)$ and $(\mathbf{z}_1, \mathbf{z}_2, \ldots, \mathbf{z}_T)$ with $\mathbf{y}_1 = \mathbf{z}_1$, $\mathbf{y}_T = \mathbf{z}_T$ and $N_{\mathbf{y}}(\ell) = N_{\mathbf{z}}(\ell)$, $\ell = 1, \ldots, 2^M$. This last condition implies that $S_{\mathbf{y}}(m) = S_{\mathbf{z}}(m)$ for $m = 1, \ldots, M$. We then have

$$\frac{P(\mathbf{y}_{i2} = \mathbf{y}_2, \cdots, \mathbf{y}_{iT} = \mathbf{y}_T|\, \mathbf{y}_{i1} = \mathbf{y}_1, \alpha_{i1}, \cdots, \alpha_{iM})}{P(\mathbf{y}_{i2} = \mathbf{z}_2, \ldots, \mathbf{y}_{iT} = \mathbf{z}_T|\, \mathbf{y}_{i1} = \mathbf{y}_1, \alpha_{i1}, \ldots, \alpha_{iM})} = \frac{\exp\left(\sum_{m=1}^{M}\sum_{t=2}^{T} y_{m,it}\mathbf{y}'_{it-1}\gamma_m\right)}{\exp\left(\sum_{m=1}^{M}\sum_{t=2}^{T} z_{m,it}\mathbf{z}'_{it-1}\gamma_m\right)}$$

and therefore

$$P\left(\mathbf{y}_{i2}=\mathbf{y}_2,\ldots,\mathbf{y}_{iT}=\mathbf{y}_T\,|\,\mathbf{y}_{i1}=\mathbf{y}_1,\mathbf{y}_{iT}=\mathbf{y}_T,N_{\mathbf{y}}(\cdot),\alpha_{1,i},\ldots,\alpha_{M,i}\right)$$
$$=\frac{\exp\left(\sum_{m=1}^{M}\sum_{t=2}^{T}y_{m,it}\mathbf{y}'_{it-1}\gamma_m\right)}{\sum_{\mathcal{B}}\exp\left(\sum_{m=1}^{M}\sum_{t=2}^{T}z_{m,it}\mathbf{z}'_{it-1}\gamma_m\right)} \tag{7}$$

where

$$\mathcal{B}=\left\{\mathbf{z}:\mathbf{y}_1=\mathbf{z}_1,\mathbf{y}_T=\mathbf{z}_T\text{ and }N_{\mathbf{y}}(\ell)=N_{\mathbf{z}}(\ell)\text{ for }\ell=1,2^M\right\}.$$

In other words, $\mathbf{y}_1$, $\mathbf{y}_T=\mathbf{z}_T$ and $N_{\mathbf{y}}$ (R) for $R=1,\ldots,2^M$ are sufficient statistics for $\{\alpha_{1,i},\ldots,\alpha_{M,i}\}$. It is clear that the ML estimator of γ based on Eq. (7) will be consistent and $\sqrt{n}$ asymptotically normal.

6 Contemporaneous Cross-Equation Dependence

The setup considered so far assumes that the errors are independent across equations in a given time period. At some level, this is not a strong assumption because the individual-specific fixed effects can be correlated arbitrarily across equations. The individual-specific fixed effects, however, also help govern the dependence in the observed data over time, so the setup implicitly links the dependence over time and the dependence across equations. It is of interest, therefore, to also study a generalization of the model in which the cross-equation dependence is driven by a separate parameter. To do this, we adapt the simultaneous logit model considered by Schmidt and Strauss (1975) to our panel data setting, both in a static and a dynamic context, allowing for cross-equation dependence. To simplify the exposition, we will restrict attention to the case in which there are two outcomes.

6.1 Static Case

Schmidt and Strauss (1975) proposed a cross-section simultaneous equations logit model in which two binary variables are each distributed according to a logit model conditional on the other and on a set of explanatory variables

$$P(y_{1,i}=1|\,y_{2,i},x_{1,i},x_{2,i})=\Lambda\left(x'_{1,i}\beta_1+\rho y_{2,i}\right)$$

and

$$P(y_{2,i}=1|\,y_{1,i},x_{1,i},x_{2,i})=\Lambda\left(x'_{2,i}\beta_1+\rho y_{1,i}\right),$$

where Λ $(\cdot)$ is the logistic cumulative distribution function.

In this section, we adapt this model to a static panel data setting in which each outcome can also depend on an individual-specific fixed effect. Specifically, assume that

$$P\left(y_{1,it}=1|\, y2, it, \{y_{1,is}, y_{2,is}\}_{s<t}, \{x_{1,it}\}_{t=1}^{T}, \{x_{2,it}\}_{t=1}^{T}, \alpha_{1,i}, \alpha_{2,i}\right) \\ =\Lambda\left(\alpha_{1,i}+x_{1,it}'\beta_1+\rho y_{2,it}\right) \tag{8}$$

and

$$P\left(y_{2,it}=1|\, y_{1,it}, \{y_{1,is}, y_{2,is}\}_{s<t}, \{x_{1,it}\}_{t=1}^{T}, \{x_{2,it}\}_{t=1}^{T}, \alpha_{1,i}, \alpha_{2,i}\right) \\ =\Lambda\left(\alpha_{2,i}+x_{2,it}'\beta_2+\rho y_{1,it}\right), \tag{9}$$

In this model, $\alpha_{1,i}$ and $\alpha_{2,i}$ are the fixed effects, $x_{1,it}$ and $x_{2,it}$ are strictly exogenous explanatory variables, and ρ is the cross-equation dependence parameter, which, as Schmidt and Strauss (1975) show, needs to be the same in the two equations given the structure in Eqs. (8) and (9).

Following Schmidt and Strauss (1975), it can be shown that

$$P\left(y_{1,it}=c_1, y_{2,it}=c_2|\, \{y_{1,is}, y_{2,is}\}_{s<t}, \{x_{1,it}\}_{t=1}^{T}, \{x_{2,it}\}_{t=1}^{T}, \alpha_{1,i}, \alpha_{2,i}\right) \\ =\frac{\exp\left(c_1\left(\alpha_{1,i}+x_{1,it}'\beta_1\right)+c_2\left(\alpha_{2,i}+x_{2,it}'\beta_2\right)+c_1c_2\rho\right)}{1+\exp\left(\alpha_{1,i}+x_{1,it}'\beta_1\right)+\exp\left(\alpha_{2,i}+x_{2,it}'\beta_2\right)+\exp\left(\alpha_{1,i}+x_{1,it}'\beta_1+\alpha_{2,i}+x_{2,it}'\beta_2+\rho\right)}$$

for c_1, $c_2 \in \{0, 1\}$.

We now show that all parameters of the model are identified with two time periods ($T=2$). Using the notation adopted in the rest of the chapter, and dropping the i subscripts for simplicity, define the event

$$\mathcal{A}_{jk,lm}-\left\{\begin{pmatrix} y_{11} \\ y_{21}\end{pmatrix}=\begin{pmatrix} j \\ k\end{pmatrix}\begin{pmatrix} y_{12} \\ y_{22}\end{pmatrix}=\begin{pmatrix} l \\ m\end{pmatrix}\right\}$$

for j, k, l, $m \in \{0, 1\}$.

Observe that

$$P\left(\mathcal{A}_{10,00}|\, x, \alpha_1, \alpha_2\right)=\frac{\exp\left(\alpha_1+x_{11}'\beta_1\right)}{1+\exp\left(\alpha_1+x_{11}'\beta_1\right)+\exp\left(\alpha_2+x_{21}'\beta_2\right)+\exp\left(\alpha_1+x_{11}'\beta_1+\alpha_2+x_{21}'\beta_2+\rho\right)} \cdot \\ \frac{1}{1+\exp\left(\alpha_1+x_{12}'\beta_1\right)+\exp\left(\alpha_2+x_{22}'\beta_2\right)+\exp\left(\alpha_1+x_{12}'\beta_1+\alpha_2+x_{22}'\beta_2+\rho\right)}$$

and

$$P\left(\mathcal{A}_{00,10}|\, \alpha_1, \alpha_2\right)=\frac{1}{1+\exp\left(\alpha_1+x_{11}'\beta_1\right)+\exp\left(\alpha_2+x_{21}'\beta_2\right)+\exp\left(\alpha_1+x_{11}'\beta_1+\alpha_2+x_{21}'\beta_2+\rho\right)} \cdot \\ \frac{\exp\left(\alpha_1+x_{12}'\beta_1\right)}{1+\exp\left(\alpha_1+x_{12}'\beta_1\right)+\exp\left(\alpha_2+x_{22}'\beta_2\right)+\exp\left(\alpha_1+x_{12}'\beta_1+\alpha_2+x_{22}'\beta_2+\rho\right)},$$

which implies that

$$\frac{P(\mathcal{A}_{10,00}|\, x, \alpha_1, \alpha_2)}{P(\mathcal{A}_{00,10}|\, x, \alpha_1, \alpha_2)}=\frac{\exp\left(\alpha_1+x_{11}'\beta_1\right)}{\exp\left(\alpha_1+x_{12}'\beta_1\right)}=\exp\left((x_{11}-x_{12})'\beta_1\right).$$

Therefore, β_1 is identified from

$$P(\mathcal{A}_{00,10}|\,\mathcal{A}_{00,10}\cup\mathcal{A}_{10,00},x,\alpha_1,\alpha_2)=\frac{1}{1+P(\mathcal{A}_{10,00}|\,x,\alpha_1,\alpha_2)/P(\mathcal{A}_{00,10}|\,x,\alpha_1,\alpha_2)}$$
$$=\frac{1}{1+\exp\left((x_{11}-x_{12})'\beta_1\right)}.$$

This line of argument uses that fact that conditional on $(y_{2,i1}, y_{2,i2}) = (0, 0)$, $y_{1,it}$ follows the simple static logit panel data model discussed in Section 2.1. We present the explicit derivation to set the stage for the dynamic version of the model in the next section.

The parameter β_2 is identified by the same reasoning.

It is clear from the previous calculations that the cross-equation parameter, ρ, can be made time-specific. We next show explicitly how ρ_t can be identified. Consider

$$P\left(\mathcal{A}_{11,00}|x,\alpha_1,\alpha_2\right)=\frac{\exp\left(\alpha_1+x_{11}'\beta_1+\alpha_2+x_{21}'\beta_2+\rho_1\right)}{1+\exp\left(\alpha_1+x_{11}'\beta_1\right)+\exp\left(\alpha_2+x_{21}'\beta_2\right)+\exp\left(\alpha_1+x_{11}'\beta_1+\alpha_2+x_{21}'\beta_2+\rho_1\right)}\cdot$$
$$\frac{1}{1+\exp\left(\alpha_1+x_{12}'\beta_1\right)+\exp\left(\alpha_2+x_{22}'\beta_2\right)+\exp\left(\alpha_1+x_{12}'\beta_1+\alpha_2+x_{22}'\beta_2+\rho_2\right)}$$

$$P\left(\mathcal{A}_{00,11}|x,\alpha_1,\alpha_2\right)=\frac{1}{1+\exp\left(\alpha_1+x_{11}'\beta_1\right)+\exp\left(\alpha_2+x_{21}'\beta_2\right)+\exp\left(\alpha_1+x_{11}'\beta_1+\alpha_2+x_{21}'\beta_2+\rho_1\right)}\cdot$$
$$\frac{\exp\left(\alpha_1+x_{12}'\beta_1+\alpha_2+x_{22}'\beta_2+\rho_2\right)}{1+\exp\left(\alpha_1+x_{12}'\beta_1\right)+\exp\left(\alpha_2+x_{22}'\beta_2\right)+\exp\left(\alpha_1+x_{12}'\beta_1+\alpha_2+x_{22}'\beta_2+\rho_2\right)}$$

and

$$P\left(\mathcal{A}_{01,10}|x,\alpha_1,\alpha_2\right)=\frac{\exp\left(\alpha_2+x_{21}'\beta_2\right)}{1+\exp\left(\alpha_1+x_{11}'\beta_1\right)+\exp\left(\alpha_2+x_{21}'\beta_2\right)+\exp\left(\alpha_1+x_{11}'\beta_1+\alpha_2+x_{21}'\beta_2+\rho_1\right)}\cdot$$
$$\frac{\exp\left(\alpha_1+x_{12}'\beta_1\right)}{1+\exp\left(\alpha_1+x_{12}'\beta_1\right)+\exp\left(\alpha_2+x_{22}'\beta_2\right)+\exp\left(\alpha_1+x_{12}'\beta_1+\alpha_2+x_{22}'\beta_2+\rho_2\right)}.$$

Because the denominators are the same,

$$\frac{P(\mathcal{A}_{11,00}|\,x,\alpha_1,\alpha_2)}{P(\mathcal{A}_{01,10}|\,x,\alpha_1,\alpha_2)}=\frac{\exp\left(\alpha_1+x_{11}'\beta_1+\rho_1\right)}{\exp\left(\alpha_1+x_{12}'\beta_1\right)}=\exp\left((x_{11}-x_{12})'\beta_1+\rho_1\right)$$

and

$$\frac{P(\mathcal{A}_{00,11}|\,x,\alpha_1,\alpha_2)}{P(\mathcal{A}_{01,10}|\,x,\alpha_1,\alpha_2)}=\frac{\exp\left(\alpha_2+x_{21}'\beta_2+\rho_2\right)}{\exp\left(\alpha_2+x_{22}'\beta_2\right)}=\exp\left((x_{22}-x_{21})'\beta_2+\rho_2\right).$$

Therefore (ρ_1, ρ_2) are identified from

$$P(\mathcal{A}_{01,10}|\,\mathcal{A}_{01,10}\cup\mathcal{A}_{11,00},x,\alpha_1,\alpha_2)=\frac{1}{1+P(\mathcal{A}_{11,00}|\,x,\alpha_1,\alpha_2)/P(\mathcal{A}_{01,10}|\,x,\alpha_1,\alpha_2)}$$
$$=\frac{1}{1+\exp\left((x_{11}-x_{12})'\beta_1+\rho_1\right)}$$

and

$$P(\mathcal{A}_{01,10}|\,\mathcal{A}_{01,10}\cup\mathcal{A}_{00,11},x,\alpha_1,\alpha_2)=\frac{1}{1+P(\mathcal{A}_{00,11}|\,x,\alpha_1,\alpha_2)/P(\mathcal{A}_{01,10}|\,x,\alpha_1,\alpha_2)}$$
$$=\frac{1}{1+\exp\left((x_{22}-x_{21})'\beta_2+\rho_2\right)}.$$

Again, this is not surprising, because $y_{1,it}$ follows the simple static logit panel data model discussed in Section 2.1 conditional on $(y_{2,i1}, y_{2,i2})$ and on the explanatory variables. We present the previous explicit derivation to set the stage for the dynamic version of the following model.

6.2 Dynamic Case

We next consider a dynamic version of the previous model that combines the insights from Schmidt and Strauss (1975) with those in Narendranthan et al. (1985). Assume that

$$\begin{aligned}&P\left(y_{1,it}=1|\,y_{2,it},\{y_{1,is},y_{2,is}\}_{s<t},\alpha_{1,i},\alpha_{2,i}\right)\\&=\Lambda(\alpha_{1,i}+y_{1,it-1}\gamma_{11}+y_{2,it-1}\gamma_{12}+\rho y_{2,it})\end{aligned}\tag{10}$$

and

$$\begin{aligned}&P\left(y_{2,it}=1|\,y_{1,it},\{y_{1,is},y_{2,is}\}_{s<t},\alpha_{1,i},\alpha_{2,i}\right)\\&=\Lambda(\alpha_{2,i}+y_{1,it-1}\gamma_{21}+y_{2,it-1}\gamma_{22}+\rho y_{1,it}).\end{aligned}\tag{11}$$

Similarly to the static case, ρ is the same in the two equations. For our following calculations, however, we need ρ to be constant over time. When $\rho=0$, Eqs. (10) and (11) are the same as the model considered in Section 3.

Similarly to Schmidt and Strauss (1975), it can be shown that

$$P\left(y_{1,it}=c_1,y_{2,it}=c_2|\,\{y_{1,is},y_{2,is}\}_{s<t},\alpha_{1,i},\alpha_{2,i}\right)$$
$$=\frac{\exp\left(c_1(\alpha_{1,i}+y_{1,it-1}\gamma_{11}+y_{2,it-1}\gamma_{12})+c_2(\alpha_{2,i}+y_{1,it-1}\gamma_{21}+y_{2,it-1}\gamma_{22})+c_1c_2\rho\right)}{\Delta_{it}}.$$

where

$$\begin{aligned}\Delta_{it}=1&+\exp\left(\alpha_{1,i}+y_{1,it-1}\gamma_{11}+y_{2,it-1}\gamma_{12}\right)+\exp\left(\alpha_{2,i}+y_{1,it-1}\gamma_{21}+y_{2,it-1}\gamma_{22}\right)\\&+\exp\left(\alpha_{1,i}+y_{1,it-1}\gamma_{11}+y_{2,it-1}\gamma_{12}+\alpha_{2,i}+y_{1,it-1}\gamma_{21}+y_{2,it-1}\gamma_{22}+\rho\right).\end{aligned}$$

We now will study identification in this model. As discussed in the previous section, we can think of the identification result for the static version of the model as an application of the results in Section 2.1. This is not the case there. Conditional on $(y_{2,i1}, y_{2,i2}) = (0, 0)$, $y_{1,it}$ does follow the simple AR(1) logit panel data model discussed in Section 2.2. This implies that γ_{11} is identified. The parameter, γ_{22}, is identified for the same reason. It does not seem that we can recover the remaining parameters, γ_{12}, γ_{21} and ρ, by a similar argument, and we therefore mimic the calculations in Section 3. The outcomes of these calculations will cast light on the identification in this model. Define

$$\mathcal{A}_{00,11} = \left\{ \begin{pmatrix} y_{11} \\ y_{21} \end{pmatrix} = \begin{pmatrix} d_1 \\ d_2 \end{pmatrix}, \begin{pmatrix} y_{12} \\ y_{22} \end{pmatrix} = \begin{pmatrix} 0 \\ 0 \end{pmatrix}, \begin{pmatrix} y_{13} \\ y_{23} \end{pmatrix} = \begin{pmatrix} 1 \\ 1 \end{pmatrix}, \begin{pmatrix} y_{14} \\ y_{24} \end{pmatrix} = \begin{pmatrix} f_1 \\ f_2 \end{pmatrix} \right\}$$

and

$$\mathcal{A}_{11,00} = \left\{ \begin{pmatrix} y_{11} \\ y_{21} \end{pmatrix} = \begin{pmatrix} d_1 \\ d_2 \end{pmatrix}, \begin{pmatrix} y_{12} \\ y_{22} \end{pmatrix} = \begin{pmatrix} 1 \\ 1 \end{pmatrix}, \begin{pmatrix} y_{13} \\ y_{23} \end{pmatrix} = \begin{pmatrix} 0 \\ 0 \end{pmatrix}, \begin{pmatrix} y_{14} \\ y_{24} \end{pmatrix} = \begin{pmatrix} f_1 \\ f_2 \end{pmatrix} \right\}$$

Then

$$\begin{aligned} P\left(\mathcal{A}_{00,11}\alpha_1\alpha_2\right) = P\left(\left(\begin{pmatrix} y_{11} \\ y_{21} \end{pmatrix} = \begin{pmatrix} d_1 \\ d_2 \end{pmatrix}\right) \middle| \alpha_1, \alpha_2\right) \cdot \\ \frac{1}{1+\exp\left(\alpha_1+\gamma_{11}d_1+\gamma_{12}d_2\right)+\exp\left(\alpha_2+\gamma_{21}d_1+\gamma_{22}d_2\right)+\exp\left(\alpha_1+\gamma_{11}d_1+\gamma_{12}d_2+\alpha_2+\gamma_{21}d_1+\gamma_{22}d_2+\rho\right)} \cdot \\ \frac{\exp\left(\alpha_1+\alpha_2+\rho\right)}{1+\exp\left(\alpha_1\right)+\exp\left(\alpha_2\right)+\exp\left(\alpha_1+\alpha_2+\rho\right)} \cdot \\ \frac{\exp\left(f_1\left(\alpha_1+\gamma_{11}+\gamma_{12}\right)+f_2\left(\alpha_2+\gamma_{21}+\gamma_{22}\right)+f_1f_2\rho\right)}{1+\exp\left(\alpha_1+\gamma_{11}+\gamma_{12}\right)+\exp\left(\alpha_2+\gamma_{21}+\gamma_{22}\right)+\exp\left(\alpha_1+\gamma_{11}+\gamma_{12}+\alpha_2+\gamma_{21}+\gamma_{22}+\rho\right)} \end{aligned} \tag{12}$$

and

$$\begin{aligned} P\left(\mathcal{A}_{11,00}|\alpha_1, \alpha_2\right) = P\left(\left(\begin{pmatrix} y_{11} \\ y_{21} \end{pmatrix} = \begin{pmatrix} d_1 \\ d_2 \end{pmatrix}\right) \middle| \alpha_1, \alpha_2\right) \cdot \\ \frac{\exp\left(\alpha_1+\gamma_{11}d_1+\gamma_{12}d_2+\alpha_2+\gamma_{21}d_1+\gamma_{22}d_2+\rho\right)}{1+\exp\left(\alpha_1+\gamma_{11}d_1+\gamma_{12}d_2\right)+\exp\left(\alpha_2+\gamma_{21}d_1+\gamma_{22}d_2\right)+\exp\left(\alpha_1+\gamma_{11}d_1+\gamma_{12}d_2+\alpha_2+\gamma_{21}d_1+\gamma_{22}d_2+\rho\right)} \cdot \\ \frac{1}{1+\exp\left(\alpha_1+\gamma_{11}+\gamma_{12}\right)+\exp\left(\alpha_2+\gamma_{21}+\gamma_{22}\right)+\exp\left(\alpha_1+\gamma_{11}+\gamma_{12}+\alpha_2+\gamma_{21}+\gamma_{22}+\rho\right)} \cdot \\ \frac{\exp\left(f_1\alpha_1+f_2\alpha_2+f_1f_2\rho\right)}{1+\exp\left(\alpha_1\right)+\exp\left(\alpha_2\right)+\exp\left(\alpha_1+\alpha_2+\rho\right)} \end{aligned} \tag{13}$$

The denominators in Eqs. (12) and (13) are the same (note that it is crucial here that ρ be time-invariant), so the ratio of the two is

$$\frac{P(\mathcal{A}_{00,11}|\alpha_1,\alpha_2)}{P(\mathcal{A}_{11,00}|\alpha_1,\alpha_2)}=\frac{\exp(f_1(\gamma_{11}+\gamma_{12})+f_2(\gamma_{21}+\gamma_{22}))}{\exp(\gamma_{11}d_1+\gamma_{12}d_2+\gamma_{21}d_1+\gamma_{22}d_2)}$$

and therefore

$$\begin{aligned}
&P(\mathcal{A}_{11,00}|\mathcal{A}_{00,11}\cup\mathcal{A}_{11,00},\alpha_1,\alpha_2)\\
&=\frac{P(\mathcal{A}_{11,00}|\alpha_1,\alpha_2)}{P(\mathcal{A}_{00,11}|\alpha_1,\alpha_2)+P(\mathcal{A}_{11,00}|\alpha_1,\alpha_2)}\\
&=\frac{1}{1+P(\mathcal{A}_{00,11}|\alpha_1,\alpha_2)/P(\mathcal{A}_{11,00}|\alpha_1,\alpha_2)}\\
&=\frac{\exp(d_1(\gamma_{11}+\gamma_{21})+d_2(\gamma_{12}+\gamma_{22}))}{\exp(f_1(\gamma_{11}+\gamma_{12})+f_2(\gamma_{21}+\gamma_{22}))+\exp(d_1(\gamma_{11}+\gamma_{21})+d_2(\gamma_{12}+\gamma_{22}))}
\end{aligned}$$

does not depend on (α_1, α_2). Setting (d_1, d_2, f_1, f_2) to (0, 0, 1, 0), (0, 0, 0, 1), (0, 1, 1, 1) and (1, 0, 1, 1) identifies $\gamma_{11}+\gamma_{12}$, $\gamma_{21}+\gamma_{22}$, $\gamma_{11}+\gamma_{21}$, and $\gamma_{12}+\gamma_{22}$, respectively. Unfortunately, these alone are not sufficient to identify $(\gamma_{11}, \gamma_{12}, \gamma_{21}, \gamma_{22})$.

Next define

$$\mathcal{A}_{10,01}=\left\{\begin{pmatrix}y_{11}\\y_{21}\end{pmatrix}=\begin{pmatrix}d_1\\d_2\end{pmatrix},\begin{pmatrix}y_{12}\\y_{22}\end{pmatrix}=\begin{pmatrix}1\\0\end{pmatrix},\begin{pmatrix}y_{13}\\y_{23}\end{pmatrix}=\begin{pmatrix}0\\1\end{pmatrix},\begin{pmatrix}y_{14}\\y_{24}\end{pmatrix}=\begin{pmatrix}f_1\\f_2\end{pmatrix}\right\}.$$

and

$$\mathcal{A}_{01,10}=\left\{\begin{pmatrix}y_{11}\\y_{21}\end{pmatrix}=\begin{pmatrix}d_1\\d_2\end{pmatrix},\begin{pmatrix}y_{12}\\y_{22}\end{pmatrix}=\begin{pmatrix}0\\1\end{pmatrix},\begin{pmatrix}y_{13}\\y_{23}\end{pmatrix}=\begin{pmatrix}1\\0\end{pmatrix},\begin{pmatrix}y_{14}\\y_{24}\end{pmatrix}=\begin{pmatrix}f_1\\f_2\end{pmatrix}\right\}.$$

We have that

$$P(\mathcal{A}_{10,01}|\alpha_1,\alpha_2)=P\left(\begin{pmatrix}y_{11}\\y_{21}\end{pmatrix}=\begin{pmatrix}d_1\\d_2\end{pmatrix}\middle|\alpha_1,\alpha_2\right)\cdot$$

$$\frac{\exp(\alpha_1+\gamma_{11}d_1+\gamma_{12}d_2)}{1+\exp(\alpha_1+\gamma_{11}d_1+\gamma_{12}d_2)+\exp(\alpha_2+\gamma_{21}d_1+\gamma_{22}d_2)+\exp(\alpha_1+\gamma_{11}d_1+\gamma_{12}d_2+\alpha_2+\gamma_{21}d_1+\gamma_{22}d_2+\rho)}\cdot$$

$$\frac{\exp(\alpha_2+\gamma_{21})}{1+\exp(\alpha_1+\gamma_{11})+\exp(\alpha_2+\gamma_{21})+\exp(\alpha_1+\gamma_{11}+\alpha_2+\gamma_{21}+\rho)}\cdot$$

$$\frac{\exp(f_1(\alpha_1+\gamma_{12})+f_2(\alpha_2+\gamma_{22})+f_1f_2\rho)}{1+\exp(\alpha_1+\gamma_{12})+\exp(\alpha_2+\gamma_{22})+\exp(\alpha_1+\gamma_{12}+\alpha_2+\gamma_{22}+\rho)}$$

and

$$P\left(\mathcal{A}_{01,10}\alpha_1\alpha_2\right)=P\left(\begin{pmatrix} y_{11} \\ y_{21} \end{pmatrix}=\begin{pmatrix} d_1 \\ d_2 \end{pmatrix}\middle| \alpha_1,\alpha_2\right)\cdot$$

$$\frac{\exp\left(\alpha_2+\gamma_{21}d_1+\gamma_{22}d_2\right)}{1+\exp\left(\alpha_1+\gamma_{11}d_1+\gamma_{12}d_2\right)+\exp\left(\alpha_2+\gamma_{21}d_1+\gamma_{22}d_2\right)+\exp\left(\alpha_1+\gamma_{11}d_1+\gamma_{12}d_2+\alpha_2+\gamma_{21}d_1+\gamma_{22}d_2+\rho\right)}\cdot$$

$$\frac{\exp\left(\alpha_1+\gamma_{12}\right)}{1+\exp\left(\alpha_1+\gamma_{12}\right)+\exp\left(\alpha_2+\gamma_{22}\right)+\exp\left(\alpha_1+\gamma_{12}+\alpha_2+\gamma_{22}+\rho\right)}\cdot$$

$$\frac{\exp\left(f_1\left(\alpha_1+\gamma_{11}\right)+f_2\left(\alpha_2+\gamma_{21}\right)+f_1f_2\rho\right)}{1+\exp\left(\alpha_1+\gamma_{11}\right)+\exp\left(\alpha_2+\gamma_{21}\right)+\exp\left(\alpha_1+\gamma_{11}+\alpha_2+\gamma_{21}+\rho\right)}$$

which implies that

$$\frac{P(\mathcal{A}_{10,01}|\,\alpha_1,\alpha_2)}{P(\mathcal{A}_{01,10}|\,\alpha_1,\alpha_2)}=\frac{\exp(\gamma_{11}d_1+\gamma_{12}d_2)\exp(\gamma_{21})\exp(f_1\gamma_{12}+f_2\gamma_{22})}{\exp(\gamma_{21}d_1+\gamma_{22}d_2)\exp(\gamma_{12})\exp(f_1\gamma_{11}+f_2\gamma_{21})}$$

and therefore

$$\begin{aligned}
&P\left(\mathcal{A}_{01,10}|\,\mathcal{A}_{10,01}\cup\mathcal{A}_{01,10},\alpha_1,\alpha_2\right)\\
&=\frac{P\left(\mathcal{A}_{01,10}|\,\alpha_1,\alpha_2\right)}{P\left(\mathcal{A}_{10,01}|\,\alpha_1,\alpha_2\right)+P\left(\mathcal{A}_{01,10}|\,\alpha_1,\alpha_2\right)}\\
&=\frac{1}{1+P\left(\mathcal{A}_{10,01}|\,\alpha_1,\alpha_2\right)/P\left(\mathcal{A}_{01,10}|\,\alpha_1,\alpha_2\right)}\\
&=\frac{\exp\left(\gamma_{21}d_1+\gamma_{22}d_2\right)\exp\left(\gamma_{12}\right)\exp\left(f_1\gamma_{11}+f_2\gamma_{21}\right)}{\exp\left(\gamma_{21}d_1+\gamma_{22}d_2\right)\exp\left(\gamma_{12}\right)\exp\left(f_1\gamma_{11}+f_2\gamma_{21}\right)+\exp\left(\gamma_{11}d_1+\gamma_{12}d_2\right)\exp\left(\gamma_{21}\right)\exp\left(f_1\gamma_{12}+f_2\gamma_{22}\right)}.
\end{aligned}$$

Setting (d_1, d_2, f_1, f_2) to (1, 0, 0, 0) and (0, 1, 0, 0) identifies $\gamma_{11}-\gamma_{12}$ and $\gamma_{21}-\gamma_{22}$. Because $\gamma_{11}+\gamma_{12}$ and $\gamma_{21}+\gamma_{22}$ already were identified from $P(\mathcal{A}_{00,11}|\mathcal{A}_{00,11}\cup\mathcal{A}_{11,00})$, this identifies $(\gamma_{11}, \gamma_{12}, \gamma_{21}, \gamma_{22})$. Note that ρ is not identified by this argument.

It is not difficult to show that strictly exogenous covariates can be incorporated in the model similar to Section 4.

7 Monte Carlo Experiments

In this section, we report results from a small Monte Carlo experiment. We generate data according to the bivariate pure panel VAR(1) logit model of Section 3 with $\gamma_{11}=0.1$, $\gamma_{12}=0.2$, $\gamma_{21}=0.3$, $\gamma_{22}=0.4$. Mean bias and root mean squared error (RMSE) across 1000 replications are reported for $N=100$, 400, 1600 in Tables 1–3 for $T=4$, 6, 8, respectively. Biases in this correctly specified model are small, not larger than approximately 20%, even with the smallest samples ($N=100$, $T=4$). As expected, RMSE is approximately halved as sample size (N) quadruples and is smaller for bigger T.

TABLE 1 $T = 4$

	$N = 100$		$N = 400$		$N = 1600$	
	Bias	*RMSE*	*Bias*	*RMSE*	*Bias*	*RMSE*
γ_{11}	0.01727	0.58733	0.00595	0.24058	0.00031	0.12155
γ_{12}	−0.00592	0.53998	−0.0002	0.24146	0.00546	0.11358
γ_{21}	0.03683	0.53702	0.01512	0.23583	−0.00032	0.11447
γ_{22}	0.06807	0.62488	0.00975	0.26795	−0.00047	0.13008

TABLE 2 $T = 6$

	$N = 100$		$N = 400$		$N = 1600$	
	Bias	*RMSE*	*Bias*	*RMSE*	*Bias*	*RMSE*
γ_{11}	−0.00151	0.27358	0.00562	0.1326	−0.00116	0.07211
γ_{12}	0.00174	0.26474	0.00604	0.13038	0.00446	0.06732
γ_{21}	0.00004	0.28008	0.00478	0.13485	0.00129	0.06806
γ_{22}	−0.00141	0.29543	−0.00973	0.1451	−0.00224	0.07129

TABLE 3 $T = 8$

	$N = 100$		$N = 400$		$N = 1600$	
	Bias	*RMSE*	*Bias*	*RMSE*	*Bias*	*RMSE*
γ_{11}	0.00269	0.20842	0.00164	0.11059	−0.00414	0.05461
γ_{12}	−0.00924	0.20885	−0.00045	0.10485	−0.00028	0.05342
γ_{21}	0.00054	0.21731	0.00049	0.10801	−0.00076	0.05397
γ_{22}	0.00889	0.21606	−0.00080	0.10674	0.00333	0.05337

8 Conclusions

The chapter discusses an identification strategy for multivariate dynamic logit models in short panels and how it relates to the conditional maximum likelihood approach for univariate panel data logit models. Furthermore, it provides an extension of the simultaneous logit model of Schmidt and Strauss (1975) to a panel context. Although the fixed effects approach adopted is robust to the presence of unobserved individual heterogeneity of the usual (additive) form that can be correlated arbitrarily with initial conditions, it suffers from the usual critique, namely, it cannot identify coefficients of time-invariant variables, nor can it provide predictions. Furthermore, the estimators in certain dynamic models with exogenous covariates typically will not have the parametric $\sqrt{n}$ rate of convergence. Although the logistic assumption adopted throughout this chapter can be restrictive, we conjecture that this assumption can be relaxed similarly to Honoré and Kyriazidou (2000). It might also be of interest to consider identification in models with more than one lag.

Acknowledgments

An earlier version of this paper was presented at Conference on Research in Economic Theory and Econometrics (CRETE) 2016, at the 2016 European Meetings of the Econometric Society and at the University of Warwick. We thank Wiji Arulampalam for useful comments. This research was supported by the Gregory C. Chow Econometric Research Program at Princeton University and by the National Science Foundation (Grant Number SES-1530741). Evangelos Paravalos and Rachel S. Anderson provided invaluable research assistance.

References

Amemiya, T., 1974. Bivariate Probit analysis: minimum chi-square methods. Journal of the American Statistical Association 69 (348), 940–944.

Andersen, E., 1970. Asymptotic properties of conditional maximum likelihood estimators. Journal of the Royal Statistical Society, Series B 32, 283–301.

Ashford, J.R., Sowden, R.R., 1970. Multi-variate Probit analysis. Biometrics 26 (3), 535–546.

Bartolucci, F., Farcomeni, A., 2009. A multivariate extension of the dynamic logit model for longitudinal data based on a latent Markov heterogeneity structure. Journal of the American Statistical Association 104 (486), 816–831.

Berkson, J., 1944. Application of the logistic function to bio-assay. Journal of the American Statistical Association 39, 357–365.

Bliss, C.I., 1934. The method of Probits. Science 79 (2037), 38–39.

Candelon, B., Dumitrescu, E.-I., Hurlin, C., Palm, F.C., 2013. Multivariate dynamic probit models: an application to financial crises mutation. Advances in Econometrics 32, 395–427.

Carey, V., Zeger, S.L., Diggle, P., 1993. Modelling multivariate binary data with alternating logistic regressions. Biometrika 80 (3), 517–526.

Chamberlain, G., 1985. Heterogeneity, omitted variable bias, and duration dependence. In: Heckman, J.J., Singer, B. (Eds.), Longitudinal analysis of labor market data. Cambridge University Press, Cambridge.

Chauvet, M., Potter, S., 2005. Forecasting recessions using the yield curve. Journal of Forecasting 24, 77–103.

Chib, S., Greenberg, E., 1998. Analysis of multivariate probit models. Biometrika 85, 347–361.

Cosslett, S.R., 1983. Distribution-free maximum likelihood estimator of the binary choice model. Econometrica 51, 765–782.

Cox, D.R., 1958. The regression analysis of binary sequences. Journal of the Royal Statistical Society, Series B 20 (2), 215–242.

D'Addio, A., Honoré, B., 2010. Duration dependence and timevarying variables in discrete time duration models. Brazilian Review of Econometrics. 30 (2)(Special Volume in Honor of Ricardo Paes de Barros).

DeJong, R.M., Wouteresen, T., 2011. Dynamic time series binary choice. Econometric Theory 27 (2011), 673–702.

Dueker, M.J., 1997. Strengthening the case for the yield curve as a predictor of U.S. recessions. Federal Reserve Bank of St. Louis Review in Business & Finance 2, 41–51.

Dueker, M.J., 2005. Dynamic forecasts of qualitative variables: a qual VAR model of U.S. recessions. Journal of Business & Economic Statistics 23 (1), 96–104.

Eichengreen, B., Watson, M., Grossman, R., 1985. Bank rate policy under the interwar gold standard: a dynamic probit model. Economic Journal 95, 725–745.

Eichler, M., Manner, H., Türk, D., 2015. Dynamic copula based multivariate discrete choice models with applications. unpublished manuscript.

Fernández-Val, I., Weidner, M., 2016. Individual and time effects in nonlinear panel models with large N, T. Journal of Econometrics 192 (1), 291–312.

Glonek, G.F., McCullagh, P., 1995. Multivariate logistic models. Journal of the Royal Statistical Society Series B: Methodological 57, 533–546.

Honoré, B., Kyriazidou, E., 2000. Panel data discrete choice models with lagged dependent variables. Econometrica 68, 839–874.

Huguenin, J., Pelgrin, F., Holly, A., 2009. Estimation of multivariate Probit models by exact maximum likelihood, working paper no 09-02. Univ. of Lausanne.

Ichimura, H., 1993. Semiparametric least squares (SLS) and weighted SLS estimation of single-index models. Journal of Econometrics 58, 71–120.

Kauppi, H., Saikkonen, P., 2008. Predicting US recessions with dynamic binary response. The Review of Economics and Statistics 90 (4), 777–791.

Klein, R., Spady, R.H., 1993. An efficient semiparametric estimator for binary response models. Econometrica 61 (2), 387–421.

Magnac, T., 2000. Subsidised training and youth employment: distinguishing unobserved heterogeneity from state dependence in labour market histories. The Econometrics Journal 110, 805–837.

Manski, C.F., 1975. Maximum score estimation of the stochastic utility model of choice. Journal of Econometrics 3, 205–228.

Manski, C.F., 1985. Semiparametric analysis of discrete response: asymptotic properties of the maximum score estimator. Journal of Econometrics 27, 313–333.

Manski, C.F., 1987. Semiparametric analysis of random effects linear models from binary panel data. Econometrica 55, 357–362.

Matzkin, R.L., 1992. Nonparametric and distribution-free estimation of the binary threshold crossing and the binary choice models. Econometrica 60, 239–270.

Narendranthan, W., Nickell, S., Metcalf, D., 1985. An investigation into the incidence and dynamic structure of sickness and unemploymentin Britain. Journal of the Royal Statistical Society, Series A (General) 148, 254–267.

Nerlove, M., Press, S.J., 1973a. Mutlivariate log linear models for the analysis of qualitative data, Discussion Paper #1. Center for Statistics and Probability.

Nerlove, M., Press, S.J., 1973b. Univariate and mutlivariate log linear and logistic models. Rand Co. Discussion Paper #R-1306.

Nyberg, H., 2014. A bivariate autoregressive Probit model: Business cycle linkages and transmission of recession probabilities. Macroeconomic Dynamics 18 (4), 838–862.

Rasch, G., 1960. Probabilistic models for some intelligence and attainmenzt tests. Denmark Pædagogiske Institut, Copenhagen.

Schmidt, P., Strauss, R.P., 1975. Estimation of models with jointly dependent qualitative variables: a simultaneous logit approach. Econometrica 43 (4), 745–755.

Song, X., Lee, S., 2005. A multivariate probit latent variable model for analyzing dichotomous responses. Statistica Sinica 15 (3), 645–664.

Ten Have, T.R., Morabia, A., 1999. Mixed effects models with bivariate and univariate association parameters for longitudinal bivariate binary response data. Biometrics 55 (1), 85–93.

Theil, H., 1969. A multivariate extension of the logit model. International Economic Review 10, 251–259.

Winkelmann, R., 2012. Copula bivariate Probit models with an application medical expenditures. Health Economics 21, 1444–1455.

Chapter 9

Implementing Generalized Panel Data Stochastic Frontier Estimators

Subal C. Kumbhakar* and Christopher F. Parmeter†
*Department of Economics, State University of New York at Binghamton, Binghamton, NY, United States, †Department of Economics, University of Miami, Miami, FL, United States

Chapter Outline

1 Introduction

The use of panel data in models examining efficiency and productivity are ubiquitous. The prevalence of panel data appears at the academic level and by regulators and policymakers. This is no coincidence. The academic interest in stochastic frontier analysis with panel data stems from the ability to decompose various forms of heterogeneity into noise and inefficiency and to examine the behavior of technology over time. For policymakers and regulators, how firms respond to regulation and benchmarks warrants use of panel data almost by definition, and the increase in observations has the potential to improve estimation efficiency and add power to any inference that is conducted. Thus, panel data stochastic frontier models are legion and of broad appeal.

More recently, a sea change has arisen in how one views panel data stochastic frontier models. As the literature has evolved, so too have the views of these models and what they are capable of explaining. For example, until recently it

Panel Data Econometrics. https://doi.org/10.1016/B978-0-12-814367-4.00009-5

was a commonly held belief that firm heterogeneity, firm-specific inefficiency, and time-varying inefficiency could not all be modeled. This turned out to be false and what has arisen is the four-component stochastic frontier model, or the generalized panel data stochastic frontier model. Given the nascency of these models, coupled with the lack of in-depth treatment of these models (though there is some coverage in the recent reviews of Kumbhakar, Parmeter, & Zelenyuk, 2018; Parmeter & Kumbhakar, 2014), this chapter seeks to provide a rigorous overview of the various approaches to estimation and inference specific for the four-component stochastic frontier model.

The discussion is important beyond academic interest. As noted by Kumbhakar and Lien (2018, pg. 35), "Given that the efficiency estimates vary widely depending on whether one models transient inefficiency, persistent inefficiency, or both, the regulator ought to take extra care in using the appropriate model and the correct efficiency measures in practice, especially when the efficiency measures are used to reward/punish companies as an incentive for better performance." Proper understanding of the most recent panel data stochastic frontier models is important for practitioners so that they have the best information to put forth when constructing benchmarks and recommending policy.

2 Earlier Models and Shortcomings

A wide variety of panel data stochastic frontier models have been proposed, dating to the earliest work of Pitt and Lee (1981). A variety of texts have discussed these models (Greene, 2008; Kumbhakar & Lovell, 2000; Parmeter & Kumbhakar, 2014). We will highlight several of the more recently developed models and discuss why they are still insufficient with respect to the generalized panel data stochastic frontier model.

The time-invariant stochastic frontier model of Pitt and Lee (1981) can be viewed as a standard panel data model in which α_i is the unobservable individual effect and standard panel data fixed- and random-effects (REs) estimators are applied to estimate the model parameters including α_i. The estimated value of α_i then is transformed to obtain estimates of u_i.

A notable drawback of this approach is that individual heterogeneity cannot be distinguished from inefficiency: All time-invariant heterogeneity is confounded with inefficiency, and therefore $\hat{u}_i$ will capture heterogeneity in addition to, or even instead of, inefficiency. Another potential issue of the model is the time-invariant assumption of inefficiency. If T is large, it seems implausible that the level of inefficiency of a firm will stay constant for an extended period of time or that a firm that was persistently inefficient would survive in a competitive market.

The question is: Should one view the time-invariant component as persistent inefficiency or as individual heterogeneity that captures the effects of (unobserved) time-invariant covariates and has nothing to do with inefficiency?

If the latter setting holds, then the results from the time-invariant inefficiency models are incorrect. A less rigid perspective is that the truth lies somewhere in the middle; inefficiency might be decomposed into a component that is persistent over time and a component that varies over time. Unless persistent inefficiency is separated from the time-invariant individual effects, one has to choose either the model in which α_i represents persistent inefficiency or the model in which α_i represents an individual-specific effect (heterogeneity).

First, we consider models in which inefficiency is time-varying, and the time-invariant component is firm heterogeneity. Therefore, the models we focus on is

$$y_{it} = \alpha_i + \boldsymbol{x}_{it}'\boldsymbol{\beta} + v_{it} - u_{it}, \tag{1}$$

where y_{it} is the (natural) logarithm of output for firm i in period t, $\boldsymbol{x}_{it}$ is a vector of the logarithm of inputs, v_{it} is stochastic noise, and u_{it} is time-varying inefficiency. Compared to a standard panel data model, we have the additional time-varying inefficiency term, u_{it}, in Eq. (1).

If one treats α_i, $i = 1, \cdots, N$ as a random variable that is correlated with $\boldsymbol{x}_{it}$ but does not capture inefficiency, then the model presented earlier becomes what has been termed the true fixed-effects (TFE) panel stochastic frontier model (Greene, 2005b). The model is labeled as the true random-effects (TRE) stochastic frontier model when α_i is treated as uncorrelated with $\boldsymbol{x}_{it}$.

Estimation of the model in Eq. (1) is not straightforward. When α_i, $i = 1, \cdots, N$, are embedded in the fixed-effects (FE) framework, the model encounters the incidental parameters problem. The incidental parameters problem arises when the number of parameters to be estimated increases with the number of cross-sectional units in the data, which is the case with the α_i in Eq. (1). In this situation, consistency of the parameter estimates is not guaranteed even if $N \to \infty$ because the number of α_i increases with N.

For a standard linear panel data model, one that does not have $-u_{it}$, the literature has developed estimation methods to deal with this problem. The methods involve transforming the model so that α_i is removed before estimation. One can use the within-transformation or the first-difference transformation model to remove α_i. Without α_i in the transformed model, the incidental parameters problem no longer exists and the number of parameters to be estimated is not large. Greene (2005b) ignored the incidental parameter problem and proposed estimating all the β and α_i parameters using the ML method. More specifically, he assumes u_{it} follows a simple i.i.d. half-normal distribution and includes N dummy variables directly into the model for α_i, $i = 1, \cdots, N$ and then estimates the model by MLE without any transformation. Greene's (2005b) results show that the incidental parameters problem does not cause significant bias to the model parameters ($\boldsymbol{\beta}$) when T is large.

The problem using the transformed model was the derivation of the likelihood function based on the within (or first-difference) transformation. Chen, Schmidt, and Wang (2014) solved the problem by using the result that the error term in the transformed model has a closed skew normal (CSN) distribution. Thus the log-likelihood function has a closed form expression and ML estimation of the parameter is possible. One also can use the approach of Jondrow, Lovell, Materov, and Schmidt (1982) to estimate u_{it}.

Wang and Ho (2010) solve the TFE problem in Greene (2005b) by proposing a class of stochastic frontier models in which either the within or first-difference transformation on the model can be carried out while also providing a closed form likelihood function. The main advantage of such a model is that because the α_is are removed from the model, the incidental parameters problem is avoided entirely. As such, consistency of the estimates is obtained for either $N \to \infty$ or $T \to \infty$, which is invaluable for applied settings. A further computational benefit is that the elimination of α_is reduces the number of parameters to be estimated by N. The model, however, is quite complicated to estimate, commonly encountering convergence issues, using the ML method.

Formally, the Wang and Ho (2010) model is:

$$y_{it} = \alpha_i + \boldsymbol{x}_{it}'\boldsymbol{\beta} + \varepsilon_{it}, \tag{2}$$

with $v_{it} \sim N(0, \sigma_v^2)$, $u_{it} = g_{it}u_i^*$ and $u_i^* \sim N^+(\mu, \sigma_u^2)$, the now-familiar scaling property model with a truncated normal distribution for the basic distribution of inefficiency. For the scaling function, Wang and Ho (2010) set $g_{it} = \exp(z_{u,\,it}{}'\delta^u)$. The key feature that allows the model transformation to be applied is the scaling property. Because u_i^* does not change with time, the within and the first-difference transformations remove α_i leaving the stochastic u_i^* intact, which helps in the derivation of the likelihood function. The transformed model becomes

$$\Delta y_{it} = \Delta \boldsymbol{x}_{it}'\boldsymbol{\beta} + \Delta \varepsilon_{it}, \tag{3}$$

using the notation $\Delta w_{it} = w_{it} - w_{it-1}$ for variable w_{it}. The error terms $\Delta \varepsilon_{it} = \Delta v_{it} - [g_{it}(.) - g_{it-1}(.)]u_i^*$, the pdf of which can be easily derived following the distributional assumptions on v_{it} and u_i^*.

Let the stacked vector of Δw_{it}, for a given i and $t = 2, \ldots, T$, be defined as $\Delta \widetilde{w}_i = (\Delta w_{i2}, \Delta w_{i3}, \ldots, \Delta w_{iT})'$ the log-likelihood function for the ith cross-sectional unit is (Wang & Ho, 2010, p. 288)

$$\begin{aligned} \ln \mathcal{L}_i^D = & -\frac{1}{2}(T-1)\ln(2\pi) - \frac{1}{2}\ln(T) - \frac{1}{2}(T-1)\ln\left(\sigma_v^2\right) \\ & -\frac{1}{2}\Delta\widetilde{\varepsilon}_i'\Sigma^{-1}\Delta\widetilde{\varepsilon}_i + \frac{1}{2}\left(\frac{\mu_*^2}{\sigma_*^2} - \frac{\mu^2}{\sigma_u^2}\right) \\ & + \ln\left(\sigma_*\Phi\left(\frac{\mu_*}{\sigma_*}\right)\right) - \ln\left(\sigma_u\Phi\left(\frac{\mu}{\sigma_u}\right)\right), \end{aligned} \tag{4}$$

where

$$\mu_{*i} = \frac{\mu/\sigma_u^2 - \Delta\widetilde{\varepsilon}_i'\Sigma^{-1}\Delta\widetilde{h}_i}{\Delta\widetilde{h}_i'\Sigma^{-1}\Delta\widetilde{h}_i + 1/\sigma_u^2}; \quad \sigma_{*i}^2 = \frac{1}{\Delta\widetilde{h}'_i\Sigma^{-1}\Delta\widetilde{h}_i + 1/\sigma_u^2},$$

and $\Delta\widetilde{\varepsilon}_i = \Delta\widetilde{y}_i - \Delta\widetilde{x}_i\boldsymbol{\beta}$.

The $(T-1)\times(T-1)$ variance-covariance matrix Σ of $\Delta\widetilde{v}_i$ is

$$\Sigma=\begin{bmatrix} 2\sigma_v^2 & -\sigma_v^2 & 0 & \cdots & 0 \\ -\sigma_v^2 & 2\sigma_v^2 & -\sigma_v^2 & \cdots & 0 \\ 0 & \ddots & \ddots & \ddots & \vdots \\ \vdots & \ddots & \ddots & \ddots & -\sigma_v^2 \\ 0 & 0 & \cdots & -\sigma_v^2 & 2\sigma_v^2 \end{bmatrix} \tag{5}$$

The matrix has $2\sigma_v^2$ on the diagonal and $-\sigma_v^2$ on the off-diagonals. The final log-likelihood function is

$$\ln\mathcal{L}=\sum_{i=1}^{N}\ln\mathcal{L}_i^D.$$

After the model parameters have been estimated, the observation-specific inefficiency index is computed from

$$E(u_{it}|\,\Delta\widetilde{\varepsilon}_i)=h_{it}\left[\mu_{*i}+\sigma_{*i}\left\{\frac{\phi\left(\mu_{*i}/\sigma_{*i}\right)}{\Phi\left(\mu_{*i}/\sigma_{*i}\right)}\right\}\right], \tag{6}$$

evaluated at $\Delta\widetilde{\varepsilon}_i=\Delta\hat{\widetilde{\varepsilon}}_i$. The model of Wang and Ho (2010) represents another demonstration of the usefulness of the scaling property in applied settings. A limitation of their model is that it does not completely separate persistent and time-varying inefficiency. Moreover, both the mean and the variance of u_{it} are functions of the scaling function that can complicate interpretation.

Although several models that can separate firm-heterogeneity from time-varying inefficiency exist, none of these models considers persistent technical inefficiency. Identifying the magnitude of persistent inefficiency is important, especially in short panels, because it reflects the effects of inputs such as management and unobserved inputs that vary across firms but not over time. Unless there is a change in something that affects the management practices at the firm level (such as changes in ownership or new government regulations), it is unlikely that persistent inefficiency will change. Alternatively, time-varying efficiency can change over time without operational changes in the firm. This distinction between the time-varying and persistent components is important from a policy perspective because each yields different implications.

To help formalize this issue more clearly consider the model

$$y_{it}=\beta_0+\boldsymbol{x}_{it}'\boldsymbol{\beta}+\varepsilon_{it}=\beta_0+\boldsymbol{x}_{it}'\boldsymbol{\beta}+v_{it}-(\eta_i+\tau_{it}). \tag{7}$$

The error term, ε_{it}, is decomposed as $\varepsilon_{it}=v_{it}-u_{it}$ where u_{it} is technical inefficiency and v_{it} is statistical noise. The technical inefficiency part is further decomposed as $u_{it}=\eta_i+\tau_{it}$ where η_i is the persistent component (for example, time-invariant ownership) and τ_{it} is the residual (time-varying) component of technical inefficiency, both of which are nonnegative. The former is only firm-specific, while the latter is both firm- and time-specific. These models were introduced by Kumbhakar (1991), Kumbhakar and Heshmati (1995), Kumbhakar and Hjalmarsson (1993), and Kumbhakar and Hjalmarsson (1998).

In this model, the size of overall inefficiency, as well as the components, are important to know because they convey different types of information. For example, if the residual inefficiency component for a firm is relatively large in a particular year, then it might be argued that inefficiency is caused by something that is unlikely to be repeated in the next year. If the persistent inefficiency component is large for a firm, however, then it is expected to operate with a relatively high level of inefficiency over time, unless some changes in policy and/or management take place. Thus, a high value of η_i is of more concern from a long-term point of view because of its persistent nature than a high value of τ_{it}.

The advantage of the current specification is that one can test the presence of the persistent nature of technical inefficiency without imposing any parametric form of time-dependence. Further, by including time in the $\boldsymbol{x}_{it}$ vector, we separate exogenous technical change from technical inefficiency.

The model can be estimated using a single-step ML method (as a special case of the four-component model to be discussed later) using say half-normal distributions on η_i and τ_{it} along with the normality assumption on v_{it}. It also can be estimated using a multistep procedure. Again, see the work of Kumbhakar (1991), Kumbhakar and Heshmati (1995), and Kumbhakar and Hjalmarsson (1993), and Kumbhakar and Hjalmarsson (1998).

3 The Generalized Panel Data Stochastic Frontier Model

To begin, consider the benchmark parametric panel data regression model:

$$y_{it} = m(\boldsymbol{x}_{it}; \boldsymbol{\beta}) + c_i + v_{it}. \tag{8}$$

Until assumptions are made regarding the structure of c_i and v_{it}, this model is nothing more than the classical panel data model that is common across applied econometrics when $m(\boldsymbol{x}_{it}; \boldsymbol{\beta})$ is linear in $\boldsymbol{\beta}$. This model is adapted to the stochastic frontier setting by including inefficiency. Two specific forms of inefficiency are included. First, there is persistent inefficiency, which varies across firms, but not time. Second, there is transient inefficiency, which varies across both firms and time. When both of these terms are included, it is the generalized panel data stochastic frontier model (GPDSFM) or more colloquially as the four-component stochastic frontier model.

The linear GPDSFM is

$$y_{it} = m(\boldsymbol{x}_{it}; \boldsymbol{\beta}) + c_i - \eta_i + v_{it} - u_{it} = \boldsymbol{x}'_{it}\boldsymbol{\beta} + \alpha_i + \varepsilon_{it}, \tag{9}$$

where $\alpha_i = c_i - \eta_i$ with c_i capturing time-invariant heterogeneity and η_i encapsulating time-invariant (persistent) inefficiency, while $\varepsilon_{it} = v_{it} - u_{it}$ with u_{it} representing time-varying (transient) inefficiency. The panel data SFM is identical to the panel data regression model in Eq. (8), except that, because pf

$u_{it} > 0$, ε_{it} no longer has mean zero, and α_i no longer solely captures individual specific heterogeneity.

Rote application of the linear panel data regression model faces a common dilemma regarding the relationship between c_i and $\boldsymbol{x}_{it}$. The most common assumptions for modeling this relationship are the fixed-effects framework and the random-effects (RE) framework. The benefit of the FE framework is that no specific relationship need be specified between $\boldsymbol{x}_{it}$ and c_i; the parameters of the frontier, $\boldsymbol{\beta}$, can be estimated consistently using the within or first-difference transformation (Baltagi, 2013). Operating in the RE framework, $\boldsymbol{x}_{it}$ and c_i are required to be uncorrelated, leading to OLS being a consistent, but ultimately inefficient, estimator. A feasible generalized least squares approach is available to obtain asymptotically efficient estimators of the parameters of the regression model in this case. Alternative approaches, such as a Hausman and Taylor (1981) or correlated random-effects (CRE) approach also could be deployed. We do not cover those cases because, to our knowledge, they have not been applied to estimate a stochastic frontier model. An approach akin to the work of Mundlak (1978) does exist; and we will have some brief remarks about this later.

Until recently, econometricians and applied researchers estimated variants of the four-component model in (2) because it was unclear how specifically to estimate all of the parameters of the model in a consistent fashion. This changed with the proposals of Colombi, Kumbhakar, Martini, and Vittadini (2014), Kumbhakar, Lien, and Hardaker (2014), and Tsionas and Kumbhakar (2014), all of which use the one-sided structure of the two inefficiency terms to develop estimators for the model.

In the GPDSFM, each of the four components takes into account different factors affecting output, given inputs. As in Greene (2005b, 2005a), c_i captures heterogeneity that varies across firms but is time constant. Because this is not inefficiency, it needs to be accounted for separately beyond persistent inefficiency. Failure to do so will result in an overstatement of time-constant inefficiency. Persistent inefficiency, η_i, collects features that serve to lower firm output but do not change over time. This component first was included in panel data stochastic frontier models by Kumbhakar and Hjalmarsson (1993), Kumbhakar and Heshmati (1995), and Kumbhakar and Hjalmarsson (1998). The noise component, v_{it} captures stochastic shocks beyond control of the firm (which has always appeared in any panel data stochastic frontier model). Lastly, transient or time-varying inefficiency, u_{it}, represents inefficiency levels that, in some sense, can be corrected by the firm. This component is similar to many of the earliest panel data stochastic frontier models, including Kumbhakar (1990) and Battese and Coelli (1992).

There are many reasons why practitioners should embrace estimation of the GPDSFM. First, while earlier models that include time-varying inefficiency can accommodate firm heterogeneity, these models fail to acknowledge the presence of persistent inefficiency. Next, those panel data stochastic frontier models that allow time-varying inefficiency commonly assume that the inefficiency level of the firm at time t is independent of its previous level of inefficiency; it is more reasonable to assume that a firm can eliminate some of its inefficiency by mitigating short-run rigidities, yet other sources of inefficiency might remain over time. It is these rigidities that are captured by the time-varying component, but the sources that remain are more aptly characterized through η_i. Lastly, although several earlier panel data stochastic frontier models have considered time-invariant inefficiency, they have not simultaneously accounted for the presence of unobserved firm heterogeneity. In doing so, these models confound time-invariant inefficiency with firm effects (heterogeneity). Regulators and policymakers should jump at the opportunity to separately capture firm specific heterogeneity, persistent, and transient inefficiency. The ability to characterize each of these aspects of variation in firm output should aid in benchmarking, yardstick competition, carrot-and-stick policies, and more.

Given what we hope is an earnest motivation of the GPDSFM, we now turn to estimation. A variety of proposals have been made recently, and, given the nascency of this model in applied milieus, we believe it prudent to detail each of these strategies. All of the approaches we will discuss center on maximum likelihood estimation based on assumptions of half-normality imposed on each of the inefficiency components and normality imposed on firm-specific heterogeneity and idiosyncratic noise.

3.1 Plug-in Estimation

We begin discussion of estimation of the GPDSFM in Eq. (9) through a simple, multistep procedure originally proposed in (Kumbhakar et al., 2014). This approach is what is known as pseudo- or plug-in likelihood estimation (see Andor & Parmeter, 2017).

First, rewrite the model in Eq. (9) as

$$y_{it} = \beta_0^* + \boldsymbol{x}_{it}'\boldsymbol{\beta} + \alpha_i^* + \varepsilon_{it}^*, \tag{10}$$

where $\beta_0^* = \beta_0 - E[\eta_i] - E[u_{it}]$; $\alpha_i^* = c_i - \eta_i + E[\eta_i]$; and $\varepsilon_{it}^* = v_{it} - u_{it} + E[u_{it}]$. With this specification, both α_i^* and ε_{it}^* are zero mean and constant variance random variables. Additionally, we will assume that v_{it} is i.i.d. $N(0, \sigma_u^2)$ and u_{it} is i.i.d. $N_+(0, \sigma_\eta^2)$ while c_i is i.i.d. $N(0, \sigma_u^2)$, η_i is i.i.d. $N_+(0, \sigma_\eta^2)$. The parameters of the model are estimated in three steps. We discuss estimation of this model under the RE framework.

Step 1: Use any of the standard random effect panel data estimators (Amemiya, 1971; Nerlove, 1971; Swamy & Arora, 1972) to estimate $\boldsymbol{\beta}$. Use $\hat{\boldsymbol{\beta}}$ to generate predicted values of α_i^* and ε_{it}^*, denoted by $\hat{\alpha}_i^*$ and $\hat{\varepsilon}_{it}^*$. This step does not require any distributional assumptions.

Step 2: Time-varying technical inefficiency, u_{it}, is estimated using the information contained in $\hat{\varepsilon}_{it}^*$ from Step 3.1. We have $\varepsilon_{it}^* = v_{it} - u_{it} + \sqrt{2/\pi}\sigma_u$ under the assumption of half-normality. The parameters for the distributions of v and u can be estimated using maximum likelihood. Doing so produces predictions of the time-varying technical inefficiency component u_{it}, $E[e^{-u_{it}}][\varepsilon_{it}^*]$, which Kumbhakar et al. (2018) term relenting technical efficiency (RTE).

Step 3: Estimate η_i following a similar strategy as in Step 3.1. For this, we use $\hat{\alpha}_i^*$ from Step 3.1. Again, based on the common distributional assumptions, $\alpha_i^* = c_i - \eta_i + \sqrt{2/\pi}\sigma_\eta$ can be estimated using maximum likelihood. Estimates of the persistent technical inefficiency (PTE) component, can be obtained from $E\,[e^{-\eta i}|\alpha_i^*]$. Overall technical efficiency (OTE) is constructed as the product of PTE and RTE, OTE = PTE × RTE.

One must be careful in the implementation of maximum likelihood to recognize that the likelihood functions for ε_{it} (α_i) differ from that of $\varepsilon_{it}^*(\alpha_i^*)$. This stems from the fact that $\varepsilon_{it}^*(\alpha_i^*)$ is centered at zero, which requires subtraction of $E[u_{it}]$ ($E[\eta_i]$), which in turn depends on σ_u (σ_η). If one were to erroneously pass the time-varying (time-constant) residuals from a panel data routine calculated in the first stage to a standard stochastic frontier estimation algorithm, it will produce biased estimates of all the parameters in Step 2 or 3. The reason is the failure to recognize the centering. This requires a slight modification of the likelihood function (see Andor & Parmeter, 2017; Fan, Li, & Weersink, 1996). It is possible to extend the model just described (in Steps 3.1 and 3.1) to include PTE and RTE that is distributed as truncated-normal or exponential as opposed to half-normal.

The three-step approach of Kumbhakar et al. (2014) inefficiency to full maximum likelihood, yet is straightforward to implement. Previous work has shown that various stepwise approaches tend to perform nearly equally as well as maximum likelihood in small sample settings. Olson, Schmidt, and Waldman (1980) and Coelli (1995) both find that the corrected ordinary least squares estimator (COLS) has similar performance to application of the normal-half normal stochastic frontier model. Andor and Parmeter (2017) document that pseudo likelihood has nearly identical performance to maximum likelihood as well. These results suggest that concerns about loss of efficiency in applying stepwise or corrected procedures might be overstated. No comparative study, however, has been undertaken to determine if migrating from the cross-sectional setting to the panel affects these conclusions in any way. This is an interesting investigation for future study.

An alternative multistep approach based on COLS follows from Kumbhakar and Lien (2018). Rather than performing maximum likelihood estimation in steps 2 and 3, method of moments are deployed to recover estimates of the unknown distributional parameters. A benefit of this approach is that a modified likelihood function is not needed, and these estimators can be constructed with a few lines of code in any matrix-oriented statistical software. To see this, under the assumption of normal-half normal for either α_i or ε_{it}, the variance parameters can be constructed using the second and third moments of these terms. That is, for the second and third moments of, say, $\hat{\zeta}_{it}$:

$$\hat{m}_2(\hat{\zeta}) = (nT)^{-1}\sum_{i=1}^{n}\sum_{t=1}^{T}\hat{\zeta}_{it}^2 \tag{11}$$

and

$$\hat{m}_3(\hat{\zeta}) = (nT)^{-1}\sum_{i=1}^{n}\sum_{t=1}^{T}\hat{\zeta}_{it}^3, \tag{12}$$

the variance components can be estimated via:

$$\hat{\sigma}_u^2 = \max\left\{0, \left[\sqrt{\frac{\pi}{2}}\left(\frac{\pi}{\pi-4}\right)\hat{m}_3(\hat{\varepsilon}^*)\right]^{2/3}\right\} \tag{13}$$

$$\hat{\sigma}_v^2 = \hat{m}_2(\hat{\varepsilon}^*) - \left(\frac{\pi-2}{\pi}\right)\hat{\sigma}_u^2. \tag{14}$$

For the estimation of the variance components of the time-constant components, we have.

$$\hat{\sigma}_\eta^2 = \max\left\{0, \left[\sqrt{\frac{\pi}{2}}\left(\frac{\pi}{\pi-4}\right)\hat{m}_3(\hat{\alpha}^*)\right]^{2/3}\right\} \tag{15}$$

$$\hat{\sigma}_\mu^2 = \hat{m}_2(\hat{\alpha}^*) - \left(\frac{\pi-2}{\pi}\right)\hat{\sigma}_\eta^2. \tag{16}$$

As in standard cross-sectional settings, if either $\hat{\alpha}_i^*$ or $\hat{\varepsilon}_{it}^*$ have the wrong skew, then the variance estimate of the corresponding inefficiency term will be zero (Olson, Schmidt, & Waldman, 1980). It is also possible to obtain negative variance estimates (what Olson et al. (1980) term a type 2 error) for the normally distributed components, c_i and v_{it}, but this is rare empirically.

In either of these stepwise procedures, if inference is to be done on the distributional parameters, then specific variance estimates are needed. The first stage standard errors for the estimates of $\boldsymbol{\beta}$ can be used directly, but the approach detailed in Olson et al. (1980) is necessary for standard errors for the parameters of the one-sided distributions. As pointed out by Olson et al. (1980), the first six moments of the composed error term are needed to correctly calculate standard errors (see also Coelli, 1995). In Olson et al. (1980), the cross-sectional case is dealt with, but their application can be extended easily to the GPDSFM just described. One application of this method would apply to the random effects, and another application of this method to the time-varying model errors. The variance of the intercept would change because it is now dependent upon both the mean of time-varying and persistent inefficiency, whereas in Olson et al. (1980) the intercept depends only on the mean of the cross-sectional inefficiency. Alternatively, a bootstrap approach could be deployed, though we have not seen this issue discussed in the literature deploying COLS.

3.1.1 Estimation in the Fixed-Effects Framework

So far, the discussion has centered on estimation in the RE framework, but one can just as easily operate in the FE framework. In step 1 of Section 3.1, rather than estimate $\boldsymbol{\beta}$ using GLS, either first differencing or the within transformation could be deployed. Here the first-differencing approach introduced by Chen et al. (2014) delivers.

$$\Delta y_{it} = \Delta \boldsymbol{x}'_{it}\boldsymbol{\beta} + \Delta \varepsilon_{it}. \tag{17}$$

The intercept and firm-specific heterogeneity terms are removed with the differencing, and the first differenced residual does not contain the mean shift because the differencing makes this obsolete. All of the pertinent information can be derived from Eq. (31). A two-step procedure is detailed:

Step 1: Estimate (31) using OLS to obtain consistent estimates of $\boldsymbol{\beta}$. Use these estimates to construct $\widehat{\Delta \varepsilon_{it}} = \Delta y_{it} - \Delta \boldsymbol{x}'_{it}\hat{\boldsymbol{\beta}}$. No distributional assumptions are made here.

Step 2: Time-varying technical inefficiency, u_{it}, is estimated using the information contained in $\widehat{\Delta \varepsilon_{it}}$ from Step 3.1. The parameters for the distributions of v and u can be estimated using maximum likelihood. Doing so produces predictions of the time-varying technical inefficiency component u_{it}, $E[e^{-u_{it}}|\varepsilon^*_{it}]$, termed relenting technical efficiency (RTE), as in the RE setting.

A COLS procedure could be used alternatively if maximum likelihood is not invoked. The caveats we detailed earlier hold here in the FE framework as well. What is interesting about the FE framework is that PTE can be present, and is allowed to be correlated with the covariates, but we cannot separately identify it from individual heterogeneity. The reason is that it is no longer clear how η_i is distributed if it is allowed to be correlated with $\boldsymbol{x}$. This approach is simpler to implement than the one found in Chen et al. (2014) because they also invoke distributional assumptions on v_{it} and u_{it} but propose estimation of the full likelihood function. Moreover, they treat all time-constant variation as unobserved heterogeneity, but this is not required for the implementation we describe.

3.1.2 The FE Versus the RE Framework

In the FE framework, we have just outlined why it is not possible to identify both persistent inefficiency and individual heterogeneity. Unfortunately, under the RE framework, there is always the concern that omitted variable bias might lead to inconsistent parameter estimates (therefore, the appeal of operating in the FE framework). An alternative approach follows from the seminal work of Mundlak (1978). In this case, unobserved heterogeneity is modeled as.

$$c_i = \overline{\boldsymbol{x}}'_{i\cdot}\phi + \omega_i, \tag{18}$$

where the jth element of $\overline{\boldsymbol{x}}_i$ is equal to $\overline{x}_{ji\cdot} = T^{-1}\sum_{t=1}^{T} x_{jit}$ and ω_i is assumed to be uncorrelated with $\boldsymbol{x}$. In this case, after $\overline{\boldsymbol{x}}_i$ has been controlled, there no longer exists correlation between the covariates and the unobserved heterogeneity, so we migrate from the FE framework to the RE framework.

If this approach is followed, the GPDSFM takes the form.

$$y_{it} = \beta_0^* + \mathbf{x}_{it}'\boldsymbol{\beta} + \overline{\mathbf{x}}_{i.}'\boldsymbol{\phi} + \alpha_i^* + \varepsilon_{it}^*, \tag{19}$$

where $\alpha_i^* = \omega_i - \eta_i E[\eta_i]$ and ε_{it}^* and β_0^* are as before. This model can be estimated following the three-step approach listed for the RE framework. Both Filippini and Greene (2016) and Filippini and Zhang (2016) use this approach in their applications.

We note that the modeling of unobserved heterogeneity in this framework ignores any dependence on time-persistent inefficiency. This is intended. If η_i depends in a meaningful way on some set of time-constant covariates, then this should be modeled through the distributional assumptions, a point we will return later when we discuss the approach of Badunenko and Kumbhakar (2017).

3.2 Full Maximum Likelihood

Although the approaches we have just detailed are insightful and shed light onto practical approaches to estimate the GPDSFM, there is always the desire to implement a full-fledged maximum likelihood analysis that, under correct distributional assumptions, will produce estimates that are, theoretically, superior to the stepwise approaches. To obtain a tractable likelihood function, Colombi et al. (2014) invoked normal-half-normal assumptions about each distributional pair of errors, noting that adding a normal random variable and a half-normal random variable produces a random variable that has a skew normal distribution. The elegance of this is that the skew normal distribution is a more general distribution than the normal distribution, allowing for asymmetry (Azzalini, 1985) and is closed under various operations (such as subtraction), making attainment of the likelihood function a less treacherous undertaking.

Colombi et al. (2014) provide the likelihood function using the following matrix representation of model (8). Let $\mathbf{1}_T$ be a vector of ones, $\mathbf{0}_T$ a vector of zeros; and $\boldsymbol{I}_T$ the identity matrix of dimension T. Moreover, $\boldsymbol{y}_i$ is a vector of the T observations on the ith unit; $\boldsymbol{X}_i$ is the $T \times p$ matrix with rows $\boldsymbol{x}_{it}'$, $\boldsymbol{u}_i$ is the $(T+1)$ vector with components $\eta_i, u_{i1}, u_{i2}, \ldots, u_{iT}$; and $\boldsymbol{v}_i$ is the vector of the idiosyncratic random components of the ith unit. From Eq. (8), it follows that:

$$\boldsymbol{y}_i = \mathbf{1}_T(\beta_0 + c_i) + \boldsymbol{X}_i\boldsymbol{\beta} + \boldsymbol{A}\boldsymbol{u}_i + \boldsymbol{v}_i, \tag{20}$$

where $\boldsymbol{A} = -[\mathbf{1}_T \boldsymbol{I}_T]$. $\boldsymbol{A}$ assigns the inefficiency terms, both persistent and time-varying, to output. This setup also can be modified easily to handle unbalanced panel data.

Let $\varphi_q(\boldsymbol{x}, \boldsymbol{\mu}, \boldsymbol{\Omega})$ be the density function of a q-dimensional normal random variable with expected value $\boldsymbol{\mu}$ and variance $\boldsymbol{\Omega}$, while $\overline{\Phi}_q(\boldsymbol{\mu}, \boldsymbol{\Omega})$ is the probability that a q-variate normal random variable of expected value $\boldsymbol{\mu}$ and variance matrix $\boldsymbol{\Omega}$ belongs to the positive orthant.[1]

A random vector z, $-\infty < z < \infty$, has an (o, q) closed-skew normal distribution with parameters $\boldsymbol{\mu}$, $\boldsymbol{\Gamma}$, $\boldsymbol{D}$, $\boldsymbol{\nu}$, $\boldsymbol{\Delta}$ if its probability density function is (Arellano-Valle & Azzalini, 2006; González-Farías et al., 2004):

$$f(z,\boldsymbol{\mu},\boldsymbol{\Gamma},\boldsymbol{D},\boldsymbol{\nu},\boldsymbol{\Delta},o,q)=\frac{\phi_o(z,\boldsymbol{\mu},\boldsymbol{\Gamma})\overline{\Phi}_q(\boldsymbol{D}(z-\boldsymbol{\mu})-\boldsymbol{\nu},\boldsymbol{\Delta})}{\overline{\Phi}_q(-\boldsymbol{\nu},\boldsymbol{\Delta}+\boldsymbol{D}\boldsymbol{\Gamma}\boldsymbol{D}')}. \tag{21}$$

The dimensions of the matrices $\boldsymbol{\Gamma}$, $\boldsymbol{D}$, $\boldsymbol{\Delta}$ and of the vectors $\boldsymbol{\mu}$, $\boldsymbol{\nu}$ are determined by the dimensionality o of the o-dimensional normal probability density function and by the dimensionality q of the q-dimensional normal distribution function. Aside from the boldface and matrix notation, this is nothing more than the multivariate generalization of the univariate skew normal distribution that arises from the baseline cross-sectional stochastic frontier model. The $\overline{\Phi}_q(-\boldsymbol{\nu},\boldsymbol{\Delta}+\boldsymbol{D}\boldsymbol{\Gamma}\boldsymbol{D}')$ term appearing in the denominator of Eq. (21) is to ensure integration to 1 so that a theoretically consistent probability density function arises. For clarity, consider the cross-sectional setup in which we would have a $(1, 1)$ probability density. Letting $\boldsymbol{\mu}=0$, $\boldsymbol{\Gamma}=\sigma^2=\sigma_u^2+\sigma_v^2$, $\boldsymbol{\nu}=0$, $\boldsymbol{D}=-\lambda=\sigma_u/\sigma_v$ and $\boldsymbol{\Delta}=\sigma^2$ would produce $f(\varepsilon)=\frac{2}{\sigma}\phi(\varepsilon/\sigma)\Phi(-\lambda\varepsilon/\sigma)$. When $\boldsymbol{D}=0$ the o-dimensional normal results. Thus, $\boldsymbol{D}$ controls the skewness, which is akin to how we view λ in the stochastic frontier setting. When $\boldsymbol{\Delta}+\boldsymbol{D}\boldsymbol{\Gamma}\boldsymbol{D}'$ is a diagonal matrix, then $\overline{\Phi}_q(\boldsymbol{0},\boldsymbol{\Delta}+\boldsymbol{D}\boldsymbol{\Gamma}\boldsymbol{D}')=2^q$.

To minimize the notational burden introduce the following matrices:

$$\boldsymbol{V}=\begin{bmatrix}\sigma_\eta^2 & 0_T' \\ 0_T & \sigma_u^2\boldsymbol{I}_T\end{bmatrix}, \Sigma=\sigma_v^2\boldsymbol{I}_T+\sigma_c^2\boldsymbol{1}_T\boldsymbol{1}_T'$$

$$\boldsymbol{\Lambda}=\boldsymbol{V}-\boldsymbol{V}\boldsymbol{A}'(\Sigma+\boldsymbol{A}\boldsymbol{V}\boldsymbol{A}')^{-1}\boldsymbol{A}\boldsymbol{V}=\left(\boldsymbol{V}^{-1}+\boldsymbol{A}'\Sigma^{-1}\boldsymbol{A}\right)^{-1},$$

$$\boldsymbol{R}=\boldsymbol{V}\boldsymbol{A}'(\Sigma+\boldsymbol{A}\boldsymbol{V}\boldsymbol{A}')^{-1}=\boldsymbol{\Lambda}\boldsymbol{A}'\Sigma^{-1}.$$

Colombi et al. (2014) show, conditional on $\boldsymbol{X}_i$, that the random vector $\boldsymbol{y}_i$ has a $(T, T+1)$ closed-skew normal distribution with the parameters: $\boldsymbol{\nu}=\boldsymbol{0}$, $\boldsymbol{\mu}=\boldsymbol{1}_T\beta_0+\boldsymbol{X}_i\boldsymbol{\beta}$, $\boldsymbol{\Gamma}=\boldsymbol{\Sigma}+\boldsymbol{A}\boldsymbol{V}\boldsymbol{A}'$, $\boldsymbol{D}=\boldsymbol{R}$; and $\boldsymbol{\Delta}=\boldsymbol{\Lambda}$. From this, conditional on $\boldsymbol{X}_i$, the density of $\boldsymbol{y}_i$ is.

$$f(\boldsymbol{y}_i)=\phi_T(\boldsymbol{y}_i,\boldsymbol{1}_T\beta_0+\boldsymbol{X}_i\boldsymbol{\beta},\Sigma+\boldsymbol{A}\boldsymbol{V}\boldsymbol{A}')\frac{\overline{\Phi}_{T+1}(\boldsymbol{R}(\boldsymbol{y}_i-\boldsymbol{X}_i\boldsymbol{\beta}-\boldsymbol{1}_T\beta_0),\boldsymbol{\Lambda})}{2^{-(T+1)}} \tag{22}$$

1. The multiple random-component SF model is related to the SF model introduced by Domínguez-Molina, González-Farías, and Ramos-Quiroga (2003) and to the linear mixed models proposed by Lin and Lee (2008) and Arellano-Valle, Bolfarine, and Lachos (2005). Domínguez-Molina et al. (2003) were the first to recognize the relevance of the closed-skew normal distribution in SF analysis, but they did not examine multiple-random-component SF models. Lin and Lee (2008) and Arellano-Valle et al. (2005) used the closed-skew normal distribution to relax the normality assumption in the mixed-regression models.

It can be checked easily that it is not necessary to include both time invariant and time-varying inefficiency to obtain a closed-skew normal distribution of the error components. For example, a (*T*, *T*) closed-skew normal results in the Kumbhakar (1987), Battese and Coelli (1988), and Greene (2005a, 2005b) models. When time-varying inefficiency is omitted, a (*T*, 1) closed-skew normal density arises, and, when the random firm-effects are omitted, the joint distribution is given by the previous results with $\sigma_c^2 = 0$.

The log-likelihood for the *nT* observations from Eq. (22) is:

$$\ln \mathcal{L} = \sum_{i=1}^{n} \left[\ln \phi_T(\boldsymbol{y}_i - \boldsymbol{X}_i\boldsymbol{\beta}, \mathbf{1}_T\beta_0, \Sigma + \boldsymbol{A}\boldsymbol{V}\boldsymbol{A}') + \ln \overline{\Phi}_{T+1}(\boldsymbol{R}(\boldsymbol{y}_i - \boldsymbol{X}_i\boldsymbol{\beta} - 1_T\beta_0), \boldsymbol{\Lambda}) \right] \tag{23}$$

the sum of the log-likelihood for each of the *n* independent closed-skew normal random variables $\boldsymbol{y}_i - \boldsymbol{X}_i\boldsymbol{\beta}$. For $T > 2$ the computational complexity involved to maximize the log-likelihood function is high. This stems from the *T* integrals in $\overline{\Phi}_{T+1}(\boldsymbol{R}(\boldsymbol{y}_i - \boldsymbol{X}_i\boldsymbol{\beta} - 1_T\beta_0), \boldsymbol{\Lambda})$. Adroit users can avail themselves of the R packages csn (Pavlyuk & Girtcius, 2015) and sn (Azzalini, 2018) to access a range of commands that allow for command line calculation of closed-skew normal densities, distribution, and random number generation. This allows greater ease of implementation rather than hard coding everything by oneself.

3.2.1 Prediction of the Random Components

Aside from estimating $\boldsymbol{\beta}$ and the parameters of the distributions of the random components, predictors of both technical inefficiency and firm effects still are needed. To do this, some additional notation is useful:

$$\widetilde{\sigma}_\mu^2 = \sigma_\mu^2 - \sigma_\mu^4 \mathbf{1}_T' \Delta \mathbf{1}_T, \quad \Omega = (\Sigma + \boldsymbol{A}\boldsymbol{V}\boldsymbol{A}')^{-1}, \quad \widetilde{\boldsymbol{\Lambda}} = \boldsymbol{\Lambda} - \boldsymbol{R}\mathbf{1}_T\mathbf{1}_{T'}\boldsymbol{R}'\frac{\sigma_\mu^4}{\widetilde{\sigma}_\mu^2}.$$

Denote the errors as $\boldsymbol{r}_i = \boldsymbol{y}_i - \boldsymbol{X}_i\boldsymbol{\beta} - \mathbf{1}_T\beta_0$. With this, Colombi et al. (2014) list the distributions of μ_i and $\boldsymbol{u}_i$ conditional on $\boldsymbol{y}_i$ as.

$$f(\mu_i | \boldsymbol{y}_i) = \phi\left(\mu_i, \sigma_\mu^2 \mathbf{1}'\Omega r_i, \widetilde{\sigma}_\mu^2\right) \frac{\overline{\Phi}_{T+1}\left(\boldsymbol{R}\boldsymbol{r}_i - \boldsymbol{R}\mathbf{1}_T\sigma_\mu^2\widetilde{\sigma}_\mu^{-2}\left(\mu_i - \sigma_\mu^2\mathbf{1}_{T'}\Omega\boldsymbol{r}_i\right), \widetilde{\boldsymbol{\Lambda}}\right)}{\overline{\Phi}_{T+1}(\boldsymbol{R}\boldsymbol{r}_i, \boldsymbol{\Lambda})}; \tag{24}$$

$$f(\boldsymbol{u}_i | \boldsymbol{y}_i) = \frac{\phi_{T+1}(\boldsymbol{u}_i, \boldsymbol{R}\boldsymbol{r}_i, \boldsymbol{\Lambda})}{\overline{\Phi}_{T+1}(\boldsymbol{R}\boldsymbol{r}_i, \boldsymbol{\Lambda})}, \boldsymbol{u}_i \geq 0. \tag{25}$$

These distributions can be used to derive the conditional moments of both the unobserved firm effects and time-varying and time invariant technical inefficiency. This is done using the moment generating function of the (o, q) closed-skew normal distribution:

$$E(\exp\{t'z\}) = \frac{\overline{\Phi}_q(\boldsymbol{D}\boldsymbol{\Gamma}\boldsymbol{t} - \boldsymbol{\nu}, \boldsymbol{\Delta} + \boldsymbol{D}\boldsymbol{\Gamma}\boldsymbol{D}')}{\overline{\Phi}_q(-\boldsymbol{\nu}, \boldsymbol{\Delta} + \boldsymbol{D}\boldsymbol{\Gamma}\boldsymbol{D}')} \exp\left\{\boldsymbol{t}'\boldsymbol{\mu} + \frac{1}{2}\boldsymbol{t}'\boldsymbol{\Gamma}\boldsymbol{t}\right\}. \tag{26}$$

Using the moment generating function, Colombi et al. (2014) provide the conditional means of the random effects as (in their model $\boldsymbol{y}$ is in logarithmic form):

$$E(e^{\mu_i} \mid \boldsymbol{y}_i) = \frac{\overline{\Phi}_{T+1}\left(\boldsymbol{R}\boldsymbol{r}_i - \boldsymbol{R}\mathbf{1}_T\sigma_\mu^2, \boldsymbol{\Lambda}\right)}{\overline{\Phi}_{T+1}(\boldsymbol{R}\boldsymbol{r}_i, \boldsymbol{\Lambda})} e^{\sigma_\mu^2 1_T' \boldsymbol{\Delta} r_i + \frac{1}{2}\tilde{\sigma}_\mu^2}; \tag{27}$$

$$E\left(e^{t' u_i} \mid \boldsymbol{y}_i\right) = \frac{\overline{\Phi}_{T+1}(\boldsymbol{R}\boldsymbol{r}_i + \boldsymbol{\Lambda}\boldsymbol{t}, \boldsymbol{\Lambda})}{\overline{\Phi}_{T+1}(\boldsymbol{R}\boldsymbol{r}_i, \boldsymbol{\Lambda})} e^{t'\boldsymbol{R}\boldsymbol{r}_i + \frac{1}{2}t'\boldsymbol{\Lambda}\boldsymbol{t}}. \tag{28}$$

The first element of Eq. (28) is the conditional expected value of time-invariant inefficiency for firm i. Conditional on $\boldsymbol{r}_i$, the firm effect μ_i, does not have a normal distribution as is the case in the standard random effects panel model (Baltagi, 2013).

3.3 Maximum Simulated Likelihood

Although the log-likelihood of the generalized panel data stochastic frontier model appears daunting to implement, Filippini and Greene (2016) recently proposed a simulation-based optimization routine that circumvents many of the challenges that can arise from brute force optimization in this setting. Using the insights of Butler and Moffitt (1982), Filippini and Greene (2016) note that the density in Eq. (22) can be simplified greatly by conditioning on μ_i and η_i. In this case, the conditional density is the product over time of T univariate closed-skew normal densities. Thus, only a single integral, as opposed to $T+1$ integrals needs to be calculated.

The conditional density, following Butler and Moffitt (1982), is.

$$f(y_i) = \int_{-\infty}^{\infty} \prod_{t=1}^{T} \left[\frac{2}{\sigma}\phi(\varepsilon_{it}/\theta)\Phi(-\lambda\varepsilon_{it}/\sigma)\right] \frac{2}{\theta}\phi(\delta_i/\theta)\Phi(-\gamma\delta_i/\theta)d\delta_i, \tag{29}$$

where $\epsilon_{it} = y_{it} - \alpha - \boldsymbol{x}_{it}'\boldsymbol{\beta} - \delta_i$ and $\delta_i = \mu_i - \eta_i$. We use the common $\lambda = \sigma_u/\sigma_v$ and $\sigma = \sqrt{\sigma_v^2 + \sigma_u^2}$ notation for the time-varying skew normal density and $\theta = \sqrt{\sigma_\mu^2 + \sigma_\eta^2}$ and $\gamma = \sigma_\eta/\sigma_\mu$ for the time constant skew normal density. Provided we can generate random draws for δ_i, we can replace the one dimension integral in Eq. (29) with a simple average.

Our simulated log-likelihood function is.

$$\ln \mathcal{L}_s = \sum_{i=1}^{N} \ln\left(R^{-1}\sum_{r=1}^{R}\prod_{t=1}^{T}\left[\frac{2}{\sigma}\phi(\widetilde{\varepsilon}_{it}/\theta)\Phi(-\lambda\widetilde{\varepsilon}_{it}/\sigma)\right]\right), \tag{30}$$

where $\widetilde{\varepsilon}_{it} = y_{it} - \beta_0 - \boldsymbol{x}_{it}'\boldsymbol{\beta} - \widetilde{\delta}_{ir}$ and $\widetilde{\delta}_{ir} = \sigma_\tau W_{ir} - \sigma_\eta |H_{ir}|$ and W_{ir} and H_{ir} are independent draws from a standard normal distribution. Maximization of this simulated log-likelihood is not more complicated from the cross-sectional case, aside from the additional parameters. With the milestone work of Colombi et al. (2014) and Filippini and Greene (2016), estimation of the generalized panel data stochastic frontier model is accessible to applied researchers.

3.3.1 Rudiments of Maximum Simulated Likelihood Implementation

Simulated maximum likelihood has a rich history in applied econometrics (Train, 2009). Two key implementation issues that the practitioner faces are the generation of the draws to build the simulated maximum likelihood function and the production of the primitive draws across the simulation. For most statistical software, it is quite easy to generate random draws from a standard normal distribution for W_{ir} and H_{ir}. It is imperative, however, for the user to ensure that the same draws of W_{ir} and H_{ir} are used at each iteration of the optimization routine. Failure to fix the draws across iterations will produce discontinuities in the function being optimized.

Although the cost of generating random standard normal variates is inexpensive, it is well known (Bhat, 2001; Train, 2009) that the use of nonrandom sequences can produce sharply improved results over quasi-random generation. This stems from the fact that nonrandom sequences can better cover the area over which the draws are to be produced, say from [0, 1]. This will lead to better approximation of the integral, which is what is desired. A popular, and common, nonrandom technique to take draws is through a Halton sequence. In the case of generating normal draws, the researcher could first construct a Halton sequence, which lies between 0 and 1, and then use the quantile function of the standard normal to produce the random draws from the normal distribution.

What is left to determine is the number of draws to take. Although there is no optimal selection, Greene (2003, pg. 186) mentions that use of Halton draws can cut down the required number of draws by a factor of 10.

4 Including Determinants of Inefficiency

Perhaps one of the most popular implementations undertaken by applied efficiency and productivity researchers has been to model the parameters of the inefficiency distributions with a set of covariates, the determinants of inefficiency (Parmeter & Kumbhakar, 2014). It is standard to model the variance parameters, in this case σ_η^2 and σ_u^2, as exponential functions. Because u_{it} and η_i vary across different aspects of the model, they naturally would be modeled with different sets of variables. The most common approach is to use exponential functions to ensure positivity.

More specifically, for the distributional assumptions, $\eta_i \sim N+(0, \sigma_{\eta,\ i}^2)$, $u_{it} \sim N_+(0, \sigma_{u,\ it}^2)$, $c_i \sim N(0, \sigma_{c,\ i}^2)$, and $v_{it} \sim N(0, \sigma_{v,\ it}^2)$. These distributional assumptions are imposed so that the sum of the time invariant composed errors

$(c_i - \eta_i)$ and the sum of the time-varying composed errors $(v_{it} - u_{it})$ each follow the skew normal distribution. Each of the variance parameters of the four components is dependent upon a set of covariates and specified as an exponential function: $\sigma^2_{\eta,\,i} = \sigma^2_\eta e^{z_{\eta,\,i}\boldsymbol{\delta}^\eta}$, $\sigma^2_{c,\,i} = \sigma^2_c e^{z_{c,\,i}\boldsymbol{\delta}^c}$, $\sigma^2_{u,\,it} = \sigma^2_u e^{z_{u,\,it}\boldsymbol{\delta}^u}$, and $\sigma^2_{v,\,it} = \sigma^2_v e^{z_{v,\,it}\boldsymbol{\delta}^v}$. The time-constant and time-varying z vectors can overlap because the assumed distributional assumptions, that is, zc,i can share elements with $z_{\eta,i}$ and $z_{u,it}$ can share elements with $z_{v,it}$. Therefore, we could have $\sigma_\eta = c_\eta e^{\delta_\eta z}{}_i$ and $\sigma_u = c_u e^{\delta_u z}{}_{it}$ where c_η and c_u are scaling constants on the exponential functions and z_i and z_{it} are the vectors of determinants to model the persistent and time-varying inefficiency components, respectively.

Including any of $z_{\eta,i}$, $z_{c,i}$, $z_{u,it}$, and $z_{v,it}$ is straightforward. The researcher can simply replace σ_η, σ_c, σ_u and/or σ_v in Eq. (23) directly and optimize over the relevant parameter space. Alternatively, this approach also can be undertaken in the maximum simulated likelihood context, which was proposed by Badunenko and Kumbhakar (2017) following the logic of Filippini and Greene (2016).[2]

As before, the benefit of this approach is that, rather than having T integrals to evaluate, by conditioning on $c_i - \eta_i$, the likelihood function can be written as the product of T univariate integrals. Simulation methods are required to construct draws of $c_i - \eta_i$ inside the convolution density. The final log-likelihood function is.

$$\mathcal{L} = \sum_{i=1}^{n} \log\left(R^{-1} \sum_{r=1}^{R} \left[\prod_{t=1}^{T} \frac{2}{\sigma_{it}} \phi\left(\frac{\varepsilon_{itr}}{\sigma_{it}}\right) \Phi\left(\frac{\varepsilon_{itr}\lambda_{it}}{\sigma_{it}}\right) \right] \right), \tag{31}$$

where $\sigma_{it} = \sqrt{e^{z'_{u,it}\delta_u} + e^{z'_{v,it}\delta_v}}$, $\lambda_{it} = \sqrt{e^{z'_{u,it}\delta_u - z'_{v,it}\delta_v}}$, $\varepsilon_{itr} = \varepsilon_{it} - \left(\sqrt{e^{z'_{c,i}\delta_c}} V_{ir} - \sqrt{e^{z'_\eta \delta_\eta}} |U_{ir}|\right)$ and $\epsilon_{it} = y_{it} - m(\boldsymbol{x}_{it}; \boldsymbol{\beta})$. R is the number of draws over which to numerically evaluate the integral. Lastly, both V_{ir} and U_{ir} are random draws from a standard normal distribution. Implementation of this routine is straightforward if one has access to a standard normal random number generator (typically available in any general statistical software). After draws for V_{ir} and U_{ir} have been constructed, the likelihood is evaluated for the current set of parameters $(\boldsymbol{\beta}, \boldsymbol{\delta}_u, \boldsymbol{\delta}_v, \boldsymbol{\delta}_\eta, \boldsymbol{\delta}_C)$. This process then is iterated over different sets of parameter values. Naturally, one can impose constancy at various parts of the error components by restricting $\boldsymbol{\delta}_\ell = 0$ for $\ell \in \{u, v, c, \eta\}$.

An even simpler approach is available to the researcher without requiring maximum likelihood methods (simulated or direct). Assume for simplicity that $\sigma^2_{c,i} = \sigma^2_i$ and $\sigma^2_{v,it} = \sigma^2_v$. In this setup, we have that $E[\eta_i] = \sqrt{\frac{2}{\pi}}\sigma_{\eta,i} = \sqrt{\frac{2}{\pi}}\sigma_\eta e^{z'_{\eta,i}\delta_\eta/2}$ and $E[u_{it}] = \sqrt{\frac{2}{\pi}}\sigma_{u,it} = \sigma_u e^{z'_{u,it}\delta_u/2}$. If we first difference the model in Eq. (10), we have.

2. See also Lai and Kumbhakar (2018).

$$\Delta y_{it} = \Delta \boldsymbol{x}'_{it}\boldsymbol{\beta} - \sqrt{\frac{2}{\pi}}\left(e^{z'_{u,it}\delta_u/2} - e^{z'_{u,it-1}\delta_u/2}\right) + \Delta\varepsilon_{it}, \tag{31}$$

where $\Delta\varepsilon_{it} = \Delta v_{it} - (\Delta u_{it} - E[\Delta u_{it}])$. Thus, $E[\Delta\varepsilon_{it}] = 0$.

Estimation of this model using nonlinear least squares will provide $\hat{\boldsymbol{\beta}}$ and $\hat{\boldsymbol{\delta}}_u$. $\hat{\boldsymbol{\delta}}_u$ then can be used to estimate $E[u_{it}]$. $\boldsymbol{\delta}_\eta$ can be estimated by noting that

$$y_{it} - \boldsymbol{x}'_{it}\boldsymbol{\beta} + u_{it} = \beta_0 + c_i - \eta_i + v_{it} \equiv \gamma_{it},$$

which can be rewritten as

$$\begin{aligned}\gamma_{it} &= \beta_0 - \sqrt{\frac{2}{\pi}}\sigma_\eta e^{z'_{\eta,i}\delta_\eta/2} + c_i - (\eta_i - E[\eta_i]) + v_{it} \\ &\equiv \beta_0 - \sqrt{\frac{2}{\pi}}\sigma_\eta e^{z'_{\eta,i}\delta_\eta/2} + \xi_{it},\end{aligned}$$

where $E[\xi_{it}] = 0$ (though it does not have constant variance). We can replace γ_{it} with $y_{it} - \boldsymbol{x}'_{it}\hat{\boldsymbol{\beta}} + E\widehat{[u_{it}]}$ and then use nonlinear least squares a second time to recover $\boldsymbol{\delta}_\eta$. $E[\eta_i]$ then can be estimated using $\hat{\boldsymbol{\delta}}_\eta$.

This simple approach offers two advantages to the researcher. First, c_i and v_{it} are not required to follow normal distributions, only that their means are zero. Second, we do not need η_i or u_{it} to have a particular distribution. Although we have written the previous text in the context of both terms having distinct half-normal distributions, one can simply assume the scaling property (Alvarez, Amsler, Orea, & Schmidt, 2006) and follow the same logic. A potential third benefit is that this approach lets the researcher estimate $E[u_{it}]$ and $E[\eta_i]$ without resorting to the conditional mean approach of Jondrow et al. (1982), which would require distributional assumptions on both c_i and v_{it}, as well as η_i and u_{it}.

4.1 Semiparametric Approaches

An even more recent approach to estimating the GPDSFM in the presence of determinants of inefficiency stems from the work of Lien, Kumbhakar, and Alem (2018). This paper uses the insights of Tran and Tsionas (2009) and Parmeter, Wang, and Kumbhakar (2017) to model the production frontier in a parametric fashion, and the conditional mean of inefficiency in a fully non-parametric fashion, what is known as a semiparametric model. The approach taken by Lien et al. (2018) is to assume that firm heterogeneity falls under the random effects framework and that only time-varying inefficiency depends on determinants. In this setup, the model of interest is.

$$y_{it} = \boldsymbol{x}'_{it}\boldsymbol{\beta} + c_i - \eta_i + v_{it} - u(z_{it}). \tag{32}$$

This model is identical to the standard model discussed in Eq. (9) except that time-varying inefficiency now depends on z_{it}. To minimize reliance on parametric assumptions the distribution of u is left unspecified. Recentering the model so that the error terms have zero mean, and letting $g(z_{it}) = E[u(z_{it})]$, we have.

$$y_{it} = g^*(z_{it}) + \boldsymbol{x}_{it}'\boldsymbol{\beta} + \alpha_i^* + \varepsilon_{it}^*, \tag{33}$$

where $g^*(z_{it}) = -(E[\eta_i] + g(z_{it}))$. As before, both α_i^* and ε_{it}^* are mean zero. The frontier and the conditional mean of time-varying inefficiency can be estimated following Tran and Tsionas (2009) and Parmeter, Wang, and Kumbhakar (2017), who in turn use the partly linear estimator proposed by Robinson (1988). This estimator works in three steps.

To begin, take the conditional on z_{it} expectation of both sides of Eq. (33). This produces.

$$E[y_{it}|\, z_{it}] = g^*(z_{it}) + E[\boldsymbol{x}_{it}|\, z_{it}]'\boldsymbol{\beta}, \tag{34}$$

where $E[\alpha_i^*|\, z_{it}] = 0$ and $E[\varepsilon_{it}^*|\, z_{it}] = 0$ by assumption. This is then subtracted from Eq. (35), producing.

$y_{it} - E[yit|\, z_{it}] = (\boldsymbol{x}_{it} - E[\boldsymbol{x}_{it}|\, z_{it}])'\boldsymbol{\beta} + \alpha_i^* + \varepsilon_{it}^*$, (35) which, upon estimation of $E[y_{it}|\, z_{it}]$ and $E[\boldsymbol{x}_{it}|\, z_{it}]$, is nothing more than traditional random effects estimation and does not require distributional assumptions about the error components. What complicates this approach is that the conditional means of y_{it} and $\boldsymbol{x}_{it}$ are unknown. Robinson's (1988) insight was to estimate these conditional means nonparametrically.

After $\hat{\boldsymbol{\beta}}$ has been recovered, the random effects, α_i^* can be predicted and the variance components, σ_η and σ_c can be recovered using either method of moments or maximum likelihood as detailed earlier. Lastly, the unknown, shifted, conditional mean of u_{it} is estimated by using the shifted residuals.

$$\widetilde{\varepsilon}_{it}^* = y_{it} - \boldsymbol{x}_{it}'\hat{\boldsymbol{\beta}} - \hat{\alpha}_i^* \tag{36}$$

and running a nonparametric regression of $\widetilde{\varepsilon}_{it}^*$ on z_{it}. Lien et al. (2018) proposed a parametric structure for $g(z_{it})$ in their three-step procedure, which limits some of the appeal of the modeling aspect for practical purposes. This parametric structure, which also requires distributional assumptions, is really necessary only if one wishes to correct the shift in the inefficiency function for the unknown mean of the persistent inefficiency component. Additionally, for identification purposes, the production frontier itself cannot have an intercept because it is not identified. Therefore, without further assumptions, only $g^*(z_{it})$ can be identified. This is not viewed as a real problem for empirical researchers because one still can rank firms by looking at differences across the various estimates, and the impact of z_{it} on inefficiency can be determined directly by looking at the derivatives of the estimated function (Parmeter et al., 2017). For more details relating to the estimation of the partly linear model, we refer to Li and Racine (2007) and Henderson and Parmeter (2015).

This model also could be estimated under the fixed-effects framework. In this case, a slightly different estimation approach, known as profile least squares, is required (Su & Ullah, 2006). We refer to the reader to Chapter 4 of Parmeter and Racine (2019) in this volume for a robust discussion about profile least squares estimation and the work of Zhou, Parmeter, and Kumbhakar (2018) for more details about implementation of the GPDSFM under the FE framework. As we mentioned above, under the FE framework, we cannot separate persistent inefficiency from time heterogeneity in this approach.

5 Recent Applications of the Generalized Panel Data Stochastic Frontier Model

In applications, the ability to parse persistent from time-varying inefficiency is important for practitioners. Moreover, also being able to control for unobserved heterogeneity lends considerable insight into any policy recommendations that might stem from such an analysis. As Filippini and Zhang (2016, pg. 1319) note "… [the practitioner needs to] use an econometric specification that takes into account of the presence of time-invariant unobserved heterogeneity variables, time-invariant or persistent inefficiency, and transient inefficiency." With advances in the estimation of the generalized panel data stochastic frontier model, it is no wonder that a range of applications have appeared that have deployed this model to determine the structure of inefficiency and the presence (or lack thereof) of inefficiency.

Filippini and Zhang (2016) study energy demand, which they use to assess energy efficiency across 29 Chinese provinces in the early 2000s.[3] They estimate four different variants of panel data stochastic frontier models, but none is the generalized panel data stochastic frontier model. Although they note the complexity in estimating this model, this offers little comfort with respect to their findings. The models that include only persistent inefficiency suggest strong levels of persistent inefficiency, and the models that allow only time-varying inefficiency find strong levels of inefficiency (albeit with much less variation). In this case, one might expect that a model that allows both (the GPDSFM) to outperform any of these models, and yet the authors passed on using such a model. The different models also suggest that the estimates of persistent and transient energy efficiency are not highly correlated. Interestingly, Beijing is classified as inefficient with regards to time-varying energy inefficiency and efficient with regards to persistent energy inefficiency. Although this might make sense if these two terms were included together, the fact that they stem from different, nonnested models makes direct interpretation difficult. The rank correlations between the panel data stochastic frontier models, which include either persistent or time-varying inefficiency, is also quite low. This is indicative that using the GPDSFM is apt to provide insights in practice that one would miss when using a more restrictive/limited model.

Ajayi, Weyman-Jones, and Glass (2017) study cost efficiency of the power generation sector between OECD nations across 30 years. They consider models that allow for only time-invariant inefficiency or only time-varying inefficiency, as well as implementing the four-component model in the manner suggested by

3. See Marin and Palma (2017) for a similar study, with similar methods, for energy demand in the United States.

Kumbhakar et al. (2014). In their application, it is determined that little persistent inefficiency exists, and only time-varying inefficiency is indicative of the power generation sector. What is most interesting from this perspective is that a model that includes only persistent inefficiency finds high levels of it. It appears in this instance that what is being picked up is not really persistent inefficiency, but time-varying inefficiency that is masquerading as persistent inefficiency. Their preferred model is the true fixed-effects model of Greene (2005b).

Blasch, Boogen, Filippini, and Kumar (2017) use the GPDSFM to estimate efficiency of electricity use in Swiss households following the maximum simulated likelihood approach of Filippini and Greene (2016). The GPDSFM is well suited to their setup, as they note that "... residential consumers are typically very heterogeneous." They find high levels of both persistent and transient inefficiency with an unbalanced sample across 1994 households. Further, the level of persistent efficiency is much higher when the energy demand function does not account for energy services provided. Transient scores are lower without accounting for energy services. Lastly, Blasch et al. (2017) note that investment literacy plays an important role in the overall level of both persistent and transient inefficiency. The difference between households deemed literate can be >10 percentage points on the efficiency scores, which has important implications for policy analysis.

Kumbhakar and Lien (2018) deploy the GPDSFM, estimated using the COLS approach described earlier, to study efficiency of Norwegian electricity distribution from 2000 to 2013. Their approach is based on a translog input distance function for total expenditures. Kumbhakar and Lien (2018) estimate models that consider only both persistent and time-varying inefficiency (but no unobserved heterogeneity) along with a panel data stochastic frontier model that accounts only for time-varying inefficiency as well to provide a base for comparison with the GPDSFM estimates. The model that omits unobserved heterogeneity finds low levels of persistent efficiency and high levels of time-varying efficiency (0.532 and 0.962, respectively, on average).[4] These contrast with the estimates from the GPDSFM, which also allows for unobserved heterogeneity, where much higher levels of persistent efficiency are found (0.935 on average) and the degree of time-varying efficiency is still high, although lower than the more restrictive model (0.885 on average).[5]

The key from Kumbhakar and Lien's (2018) work is that overall technical efficiency is substantially different (both on average and in distribution) between these two models. The fact that unobserved heterogeneity is ignored

---

4. Here and in the remainder of the paragraph, we are reporting Kumbhakar and Lien's (2018) estimates of efficiency, so inefficiency would be 1 minus the level of reported efficiency.

5. Not only does the average level change, but the variance also is greatly affected. Kumbhakar and Lien (2018) surmise that this is because the firm effects can be positive for some electric generation plants and negative for others. Therefore, it is likely see a larger dispersion of the persistent efficiency estimates.

implies that persistent inefficiency is, in this setting, higher than when this heterogeneity is acknowledged and properly modeled. Moreover, the large differences in these efficiency estimates are important to acknowledge because they are used by the Norwegian regulator to construct the revenue-cap allocation for firms, and allocations based on incorrect/inaccurate estimates of inefficiency likely would send poor signals to the firms. Interestingly, all three models have similar average estimates of returns to scale and technical change, which is suggestive that the first-stage estimation of $\boldsymbol{\beta}$ is consistent regardless of how the time constant term is treated.

6 Conclusion

This chapter has detailed the workings and intuition of the generalized panel data stochastic frontier model. This model marks the culmination of >30 years of research in properly modeling both heterogeneity and inefficiency in a panel data framework. This model is flexible and fully identified, making it an exemplar for the foreseeable future. Various alternative modeling and estimation strategies still exist, but the basic structure and intuition of the model have been refined and applied in just the past several years. We also mention that, although users might find these new methods daunting to apply, the COLS methods described in Section 3.1 are quite easy to implement in any matrix-oriented programming language while NLOGIT/LIMDEP offers maximum simulated likelihood estimation. Recently, R code, also offering maximum simulated likelihood, has appeared in the psfm call (see www.davidharrybernstein.com/software).

Overall, the GPDSFM is an excellent addition to the armamentarium of the applied researcher and offers many areas for continued expansion. An interesting investigation would be a comparison of the various estimation methods for the GPDSFM. Currently, no such study exists, and we have no indication which of these approaches is likely to dominate. For an unlimited sample size, full maximum likelihood is theoretically optimal, but the work of both Olson et al. (1980) and Andor and Parmeter (2017) have revealed that COLS and pseudo-likelihood methods perform nearly as well as maximum likelihood in the cross-sectional setting. The transferrence of these insights to the panel setting would be well worth the effort.

Acknowledgment

The authors thank David Bernstein for reviewing this paper and providing detailed comments. All errors are ours alone.

References

Ajayi, V., Weyman-Jones, T., Glass, A., 2017. Cost efficiency and electricity market structure: a case study of OECD countries. Energy Economics 65, 283–291.

Alvarez, A., Amsler, C., Orea, L., Schmidt, P., 2006. Interpreting and testing the scaling property in models where inefficiency depends on firm characteristics. Journal of Productivity Analysis 25 (2), 201–212.

Amemiya, T., 1971. The estimation of variances in a variance components model. International Economic Review 12 (1), 13.

Andor, M., Parmeter, C.F., 2017. Pseudolikelihood estimation of the stochastic frontier model. Applied Economics 49, 5651–5661.

Arellano-Valle, R.B., Azzalini, A., 2006. On the unification of families of skew-normal distributions. Scandinavian Journal of Statistics 33 (3), 561–574.

Arellano-Valle, R.B., Bolfarine, H., Lachos, H., 2005. Skew-normal linear mixed models. Journal of Data Science 3 (4), 415–438.

Azzalini, A., 1985. A class of distributions which includes the normal ones. Scandinavian Journal of Statistics 12 (2), 171–178.

Azzalini, A., 2018. The R package **sn**: The Skew-Normal and Related Distributions such as the Skew-t (version 1.5-2). Universit'a di Padova, Italia. http://azzalini.stat.unipd.it/SN.

Badunenko, O., Kumbhakar, S.C., 2017. Economies of scale, technical change and persistent and time-varying cost efficiency in Indian banking: Do ownership, regulation and heterogeneity matter? European Journal of Operational Research 260, 789–803.

Baltagi, B.H., 2013. Econometric analysis of panel data, 5th ed John Wiley and Sons, Great Britain.

Battese, G.E., Coelli, T.J., 1988. Prediction of firm-level technical efficiencies with a generalized frontier production function and panel data. Journal of Econometrics 38, 387–399.

Battese, G.E., Coelli, T.J., 1992. Frontier production functions, technical efficiency and panel data: With application to paddy farmers in India. Journal of Productivity Analysis 3, 153–169.

Bhat, C.R., 2001. Quasi-random maximum simulated likelihood estimation of the mixed multinomial logit model. Transportation Research Part B: Methodological 35 (7), 677–693.

Blasch, J., Boogen, N., Filippini, M., Kumar, N., 2017. Explaining electricity demand and the role of energy and investment literacy on end-use efficiency of Swiss households. Energy Economics 68, 89–102.

Butler, J., Moffitt, R., 1982. A computationally efficient quadrature procedure for the one factor multinomial probit model. Econometrica 50, 761–764.

Chen, Y.-Y., Schmidt, P., Wang, H.-J., 2014. Consistent estimation of the fixed effects stochastic frontier model. Journal of Econometrics 181 (1), 65–76.

Coelli, T.J., 1995. Estimators and hypothesis tests for a stochastic frontier function: a Monte Carlo analysis. Journal of Productivity Analysis 6 (4), 247–268.

Colombi, R., Kumbhakar, S., Martini, G., Vittadini, G., 2014. Closed-skew normality in stochastic frontiers with individual effects and long/short-run efficiency. Journal of Productivity Analysis 42 (2), 123–136.

Domínguez-Molina, J.A., González-Farías, G., Ramos-Quiroga, R., 2003. Skew normality in stochastic frontier analysis. (Comunicaci'on T'ecnica No I-03-18/06-10-2003 (PE/CIMAT).

Fan, Y., Li, Q., Weersink, A., 1996. Semiparametric estimation of stochastic production frontier models. Journal of Business & Economic Statistics 14 (4), 460–468.

Filippini, M., Greene, W., 2016. Persistent and transient productive inefficiency: a maximum simulated likelihood approach. Journal of Productivity Analysis 45, 187–196.

Filippini, M., Zhang, L., 2016. Estimation of the energy efficiency in Chinese provinces. Energy Efficiency 9, 1315–1328.

González-Farías, G., Domínguez-Molina, J.A., Gupta, A.K., 2004. The closed skew normal distribution. In: Genton, M. (Ed.), Skew elliptical distributions and their applications: A journal beyond normality. Chapman and Hall/CRC, Boca Raton, Florida. Chapter 2.

Greene, W.H., 2003. Simulated likelihood estimation of the normal-gamma stochastic frontier function. Journal of Productivity Analysis 19 (2), 179–190.

Greene, W.H., 2005a. Fixed and random effects in stochastic frontier models. Journal of Productivity Analysis 23 (1), 7–32.

Greene, W.H., 2005b. Reconsidering heterogeneity in panel data estimators of the stochastic frontier model. Journal of Econometrics 126 (2), 269–303.

Greene, W.H., 2008. The econometric approach to efficiency analysis. In: Fried, C.A.K.L.H.O., Schmidt, S.S. (Eds.), The measurement of productive efficiency and productivity change. Oxford University Press, Oxford, United Kingdom (Chapter 2).

Hausman, J.A., Taylor, W.E., 1981. Panel data and unobservable individual effects. Econometrica 49, 1377–1398.

Henderson, D.J., Parmeter, C.F., 2015. Applied Nonparametric Econometrics. Cambridge University Press, Cambridge, Great Britain.

Jondrow, J., Lovell, C.A.K., Materov, I.S., Schmidt, P., 1982. On the estimation of technical efficiency in the stochastic frontier production function model. Journal of Econometrics 19 (2/3), 233–238.

Kumbhakar, S.C., 1987. The specification of technical and allocative inefficiency in stochastic production and profit frontiers. Journal of Econometrics 34 (1), 335–348.

Kumbhakar, S.C., 1990. Production frontiers, panel data, and time-varying technical inefficiency. Journal of Econometrics 46 (1), 201–211.

Kumbhakar, S.C., 1991. The measurement and decomposition of cost-inefficiency: The translog cost system. Oxford Economic Papers 43 (6), 667–683.

Kumbhakar, S.C., Heshmati, A., 1995. Efficiency measurement in Swedish dairy farms: An application of rotating panel data, 1976-88. American Journal of Agricultural Economics 77 (3), 660–674.

Kumbhakar, S.C., Hjalmarsson, L., 1993. Technical efficiency and technical progress in Swedish dairy farms. In: Fried, K.L.H., Schmidt, S. (Eds.), The measurement of productive efficiency. Oxford University Press, Oxford, United Kingdom.

Kumbhakar, S.C., Hjalmarsson, L., 1998. Relative performance of public and private ownership under yardstick competition: electricity retail distribution. European Economic Review 42 (1), 97–122.

Kumbhakar, S.C., Lien, G., 2018. Yardstick regulation of electricity distribution—disentangling short-run and long-run inefficiencies. The Energy Journal 38, 17–37.

Kumbhakar, S.C., Lien, G., Hardaker, J.B., 2014. Technical efficiency in competing panel data models: a study of Norwegian grain farming. Journal of Productivity Analysis 41 (2), 321–337.

Kumbhakar, S.C., Lovell, C.A.K., 2000. Stochastic frontier analysis. Cambridge University Press.

Kumbhakar, S.C., Parmeter, C.F., Zelenyuk, V., 2018. Stochastic frontier analysis: foundations and advances II. In: Ray, S., Chambers, R., Kumbhakar, S.C. (Eds.), Handbook of production economics. Springer. Forthcoming.

Lai, H.-P., Kumbhakar, S.C., 2018. Panel data stochastic frontier model with determinants of persistent and transient inefficiency. European Journal of Operational Research 271, 746–755.

Li, Q., Racine, J., 2007. Nonparametric econometrics: Theory and practice. Princeton University Press.

Lien, G., Kumbhakar, S.C., Alem, H., 2018. Endogeneity, heterogeneity, and determinants of inefficiency in Norwegian crop-producing farms. International Journal of Production Economics 201, 53–61.

Lin, T., Lee, C., 2008. Estimation and prediction in linear mixed models with skew-normal random effects for longitudinal data. Statistics in Medicine 27 (9), 1490–1507.

Marin, G., Palma, A., 2017. Technology invention and adoption in residential energy consumption a stochastic frontier approach. Energy Economics 66, 85–98.

Mundlak, Y., 1978. On the pooling of time series and cross section data. Econometrica 64 (1), 69–85.

Nerlove, M., 1971. Further evidence on the estimation of dynamic economic relations from a time-series of cross-sections. Econometrica 39, 359–382.

Olson, J.A., Schmidt, P., Waldman, D.A., 1980. A Monte Carlo study of estimators of stochastic frontier production functions. Journal of Econometrics 13, 67–82.

Parmeter, C.F., Kumbhakar, S.C., 2014. Efficiency analysis: A primer on recent advances. Foundations and Trends in Econometrics 7 (3–4), 191–385.

Parmeter, C.F., Racine, J.S., 2019. Nonparametric estimation and inference for panel data models. In: Tsionas, M. (Ed.), Panel data econometrics. Academic Press, Elsevier, pp. 97–129

Parmeter, C.F., Wang, H.-J., Kumbhakar, S.C., 2017. Nonparametric estimation of the determinants of inefficiency. Journal of Productivity Analysis 47 (3), 205–221.

Pavlyuk, D., Girtcius, E., 2015. csn: Closed Skew-Normal Distribution. R Package Version 1.1.3. https://CRAN.R-project.org/package=csn.

Pitt, M.M., Lee, L.-F., 1981. The measurement and sources of technical inefficiency in the Indonesian weaving industry. Journal of Development Economics 9 (1), 43–64.

Robinson, P.M., 1988. Root-n consistent semiparametric regression. Econometrica 56, 931–954.

Su, L., Ullah, A., 2006. Profile likelihood estimation of partially linear panel data models with fixed effects. Economics Letters 92 (1), 75–81.

Swamy, P.A.V.B., Arora, S.S., 1972. The exact finite sample properties of the estimators of coefficients in the error components regression models. Econometrica 40, 261–275.

Train, K., 2009. Discrete choice methods with simulation, 2nd ed. Cambridge University Press.

Tran, K.C., Tsionas, E.G., 2009. Estimation of nonparametric inefficiency effects stochastic frontier models with an application to British manufacturing. Economic Modelling 26, 904–909.

Tsionas, E.G., Kumbhakar, S.C., 2014. Firm heterogeneity, persistent and transient technical inefficiency: a generalized true random-effects model. Journal of Applied Econometrics 29 (1), 110–132.

Wang, H.-J., Ho, C.-W., 2010. Estimating fixed-effect panel stochastic frontier models by model transformation. Journal of Econometrics 157 (2), 286–296.

Zhou, J., Parmeter, C.F., Kumbhakar, S.C., 2018. Nonparametric estimation of the determinants of inefficiency in the presence of firm heterogeneity. University of Miami Working Paper.

Chapter 10

Panel Cointegration Techniques and Open Challenges

Peter Pedroni
Williams College, Williamstown, MA, United States

Chapter Outline

1 Introduction

In this chapter, I discuss the development and status of panel cointegration techniques and some of the open challenges that remain. During the past quarter-century, the investigation of panel cointegration methods has involved many dozens of econometric papers that have studied and developed methodology and many hundreds of economic papers that have employed the techniques. This chapter is not intended to be a survey of the vast literature about the topic. Rather, it is written as a guide to some of the key aspects of the concepts and implementation of panel cointegration analysis in a manner that is intended to be intuitive and accessible to applied researchers. It also is written from the perspective of a personal assessment of the status of panel cointegration techniques and the open challenges that remain.

Panel Data Econometrics. https://doi.org/10.1016/B978-0-12-814367-4.00010-1

Notwithstanding the overall approach of the chapter, some occasional overview is instructive to understanding some of the key motivations that have helped to shape the literature and the associated challenges. One of the earliest motivations for panel cointegration methods in my Ph.D. dissertation, Pedroni (1993), was the desire to import some of the remarkable features of the time series properties of cointegration into a panel data framework where they could be exploited in the context of data series that often are far too short for reliable cointegration analysis in a conventional time series context. In particular, what was at the time a relatively young field of cointegration analysis for pure time series provided considerable promise in its potential to circumvent traditional concerns regarding endogeneity of regressors because of certain forms of reverse causality, simultaneity, omitted variables, measurement errors, and so forth. The potential robustness with respect to these features stems fundamentally from the superconsistency properties under cointegration, which are described in the next section.

Bringing superconsistency associated with cointegration to panel analysis, however, naturally brought to the front numerous challenges for panel data analysis that became more apparent in the treatment of the type of aggregate level data that is typically used in cointegration analysis. In particular, although cointegration analysis in panels reduces the need for series to be as long as one would require for cointegration analysis in a pure time series context, it does require the panels to have moderately long length, longer than we typically would require for more conventional panel data techniques that are oriented toward microeconomic data analysis. This leads many of the panels that are used for cointegration analysis to be composed of aggregate level data, which are more often observed over longer periods of time and therein fall into the realm of what has come to be known as time series panels.

Typical data include formats such as multicountry panels of national level data, multiregional panels, or panels composed of relatively aggregated industry level data. With these data formats, the need to address cross-sectional heterogeneity becomes apparent, not just in the form of fixed effects, as was typical in earlier panel data methods that were oriented toward microeconomic data, but more importantly heterogeneity in both short-run and long-run dynamics. Another challenge that becomes more readily apparent from these types of data structures is that the nature of cross-sectional dependency is likely to be more complex than was typical in the treatment of earlier micro-oriented panel methods, particularly in the sense that the cross-sectional dependency is likely to be intertwined with temporal dependencies. In short, both the cross-sectional heterogeneity and the cross-sectional dependency interact with an essential feature of time series panels, namely temporal dependence.

The panel cointegration techniques discussed in this chapter can be applied equally well to microeconomic data panels given sufficient length of the panels. But by addressing the challenges that arise from the typical applications to aggregate-level macro panels, they have helped to highlight some of the attractive features of panel time series techniques in general, which has helped to fuel the growth of the literature. One way to better appreciate this is to compare these methods in broad terms to alternative strategies for empirical analysis of aggregate-level data. For example, at one end of the spectrum, we can consider simply using cross-sectional methods to study aggregate country level data. Although this has the attraction of providing ample variation in macroeconomic conditions along the cross-sectional dimension, it runs into the usual challenges in treating endogeneity and searching for underlying structural causation. Furthermore, when the cross sections represent point in time observations, the estimation can reflect the arbitrariness of the time period, and similarly, when the cross sections represent averages over time, the estimation can reflect a relationship that exists among the unconditional time averages rather than for a well-defined sense of a long-run steady state relationship.

Another strategy might be to use more conventional static micro panel methods for aggregate data. In fact, static micro panel methods can be viewed as essentially repeated cross sections, observed in multiple time periods. But aside from offering controls for unobserved fixed effects or random effects, in the absence of cointegration, the challenges in treating endogeneity and the issues associated with the temporal interpretation still pertain for these methods. Although dynamic panel methods such as those of Holz-Eakin, Newey, and Rosen (1988), and Arellano and Bond (1991), among others, exist for micro data that can help give more precise meaning to temporal interpretations, the difficulty with these approaches is that they require the dynamics to be strictly homogeneous among the individual members of the panel. When this assumption is violated, as would be typical for most aggregate data, then, as noted in Pesaran and Smith (1995) and discussed in detail in Section 3 of this chapter, it leads to inconsistent estimation, even for the average dynamic relationships, which makes these dynamic panel methods unattractive for the analysis of dynamics in aggregate level macro type data.

At the other end of the spectrum of alternatives, it is worth considering what we learn from time series estimation applied to the series of an individual country. In this context, plenty of methods exist for treating endogeneity without the need for external instruments, and providing specific temporal interpretations often is central to these methods. By using the data from an individual country, however, the sample variation that pertains to a particular question of interest can be limited. For example, learning about the economic consequences of changing from one type of monetary policy regime to another type is difficult when the time series data from a country spans only one regime. For this, cross-sectional variation that spans both regimes in the form of multicountry time series data becomes important and useful.

Viewed from this perspective, panel time series methods, which includes panel cointegration techniques, provide an opportunity to blend the attractive features of time series with potential aggregate level cross-sectional variation in data settings where the time series length are moderate. Furthermore, as we will see, when the challenges posed by the interaction of temporal dependencies with cross-sectional heterogeneity and cross-sectional dependence are addressed properly, the techniques offer a further opportunity to study the underlying determinants of the cross-sectional variation.

The remainder of this chapter is structured as follows. In the next section, I use a simple bivariate example to review the concepts behind the superconsistency result that is key to understanding the robustness properties that cointegration brings to panel data analysis. In Sections 3–7, I describe how the challenge of addressing cross-sectional heterogeneity in the dynamics has shaped testing, estimation, and inference in cointegrated panels, including testing for directions of long-run causality in panels. In Sections 8 and 9, I discuss how addressing the interaction of both cross-sectional heterogeneity and cross-sectional dependencies continue to drive some of the open challenges in panel cointegration analysis, and in Section 10, I conclude with a discussion about some open challenges being explored currently that are associated with generalizing panel cointegration analysis to allow for time varying heterogeneity and nonlinearities in the long-run relationships. Again, this chapter is not intended as a comprehensive or even partial survey, because the panel cointegration literature on the whole is vast, and there are by necessity topics that are not touched upon in detail here, including, for example, nonclassical, Bayesian approaches, because they are reserved for another chapter.

2 Cointegration and the Motivation for Panels

In this section, I discuss the property of superconsistency and the motivation that this gives to bringing cointegration to a panel setting in order to allow for estimation that is robust to myriad issues typically associated with endogenous regressors. In particular, to gain some intuition, I illustrate these concepts using a simple bivariate OLS regression framework.

Consider the following simple and standard example taken from a classical time series perspective. Let

$$y_t = \alpha + \beta x_t + \mu_t \tag{1}$$

for $t = 1, \ldots, T$ be the data generating process that describes the true unknown relationship between y_t and x_t for some unknown error process μ_t. For simplicity of notation, we will work with the time demeaned versions of the variables, so that $y_t^* = y_t - T^{-1}\sum_{t=1}^{T} y_t$ and similarly $x_t^* = x_t - T^{-1}\sum_{t=1}^{T} x_t$. Then we know that the OLS estimator for β can be written as

$$\hat{\beta}_{OLS} = \frac{\frac{1}{T}\sum_{t=1}^{T} x_i^* \left(\beta x_i^* + \mu_t\right)}{\frac{1}{T}\sum_{i=1}^{T} x_t^{*2}} = \beta + R_T \tag{2}$$

$$\text{where } R_T = \frac{R_{1T}}{R_{2T}}, \quad R_{1T} = \frac{1}{T}\sum_{t=1}^{T} x_i^* \mu_t, \quad R_{2T} = \frac{1}{T}\sum_{t=1}^{T} x_i^{*2} \tag{3}$$

Thus, OLS is a consistent estimator of the true value β only when the remainder term, R_T, is eliminated, and much of the use and adaptation of OLS for empirical work revolves around the conditions under which this occurs.

When x_t and μ_t are both covariance stationary, and in the simplest special case are i.i.d. serially uncorrelated over time, then as we envision the sample growing large and consider $T \to \infty$, the probability limit of both the numerator and denominator go to constants, such that $R_{1,T} \to E_T[x_t^* \mu_t] = \sigma_{x,\mu}$ and $R_{2,T} \to E_T[x_t^{*2}] = \sigma_x^2$. Thus, OLS becomes consistent such that $\hat{\beta}_{OLS} \to \beta$ only when x_t and μ_t are orthogonal, such that $E_T[x_t^* \mu_t] = \sigma_{x,\mu} = 0$. When the condition is violated, one classic solution is to look for an external instrumental variable, z_t, such that $E_T[z_t^* \mu_t] = 0$ and $E_T[z_t^* x_t^*] \neq 0$, which often can be difficult to justify in practice, particularly for aggregate time series data.

In a different scenario, however, wherein x_t and μ_t are not both covariance stationary, but rather x_t is unit root nonstationary, denoted $x_t \sim I(1)$, while μ_t is covariance stationary, denoted $\mu_t \sim I(0)$, then y_t and x_t are said to be cointegrated, in which case the large sample OLS properties become very different. Specifically, in this case, OLS becomes consistent in the sense that $\hat{\beta}_{OLS} \to \beta$ regardless of whether the regressor is orthogonal to the residual μ_t, and regardless of any serial correlation dynamics that endogenously relate the changes in x_t to μ_t. In a nutshell, this occurs because when x_t is nonstationary, its variance is no longer finite but rather grows indefinitely with respect to the sample size, while by contrast, under cointegration, because of the stationarity of μ_t, the covariance between x_t and μ_t does not similarly diverge.

To see this more precisely, it is worth introducing a few concepts that typically are used in the analysis of nonstationary time series, which also will be useful in other sections of this chapter. For example, to allow for fairly general vector stationary processes with jointly determined serial correlation dynamics, we typically assume that the conditions are present for a multivariate functional central limit theorem, which essentially generalizes more standard central limit theorems to allow for time-dependent processes. Specifically, if we let $\xi_t = (\mu_t, \eta_t)'$ where $\Delta x = \eta_t$ is the stochastic process that describes how x_t changes, then we can replace the standard central limit theorem for i.i.d. processes with one that allows for endogenous, jointly determined dependent process by writing

$$\frac{1}{\sqrt{T}}\sum_{t=1}^{[Tr]} \xi_t \Rightarrow B_r(\Omega) \text{ as } T \to \infty \text{ for } r \in [0, 1], \tag{4}$$

where $B_r(\Omega)$ is a vector of demeaned Brownian motion with long-run covariance Ω. This functional central limit theorem applies for a broad class of processes for ξ_t, including for example linear time series representations such as VARs.

If we define the vector $Z_t = Z_{t-1} + \xi_t$, it is fairly straightforward to show based on Eq. (4) and what is known as the continuous mapping theorem, that

$$\frac{1}{T}\sum_{t=1}^{T} Z_t\xi_t' \Rightarrow \int_{r=0}^{1} B_r(\Omega)dB_r(\Omega) + \Lambda + \Omega_0 \text{ as } T \to \infty \tag{5}$$

$$\frac{1}{T^2}\sum_{t=1}^{T} Z_t Z_t' \Rightarrow \int_{r=0}^{1} B_r(\Omega)B_r(\Omega)'dr \text{ as } T \to \infty. \tag{6}$$

These expressions simply indicate that the sample statistics on the left of the thick arrows converge in distribution to the expressions on the right of the thick arrow, which are multivariate stable distributions expressed in terms of Brownian motion, known as Brownian motion functionals. In the case of Eq. (5), the distribution is further uncentered by constants, which come from the decomposition of the long-run covariance matrix into its forward spectrum, Λ, and standard covariance, Ω_0, components such that $\Omega = \Lambda + \Lambda' + \Omega_0$. But for our current purposes, the more important detail to notice is that the OLS remainder terms from Eq. (3) are closely related to the sample statistics on the left sides of Eqs. (5) and (6), such that the numerator and denominator terms correspond to off-diagonal and lower diagonal elements of these matrix expressions, so that $R_{1T} = \left(\frac{1}{T}\sum_{t=1}^{T} Z_t\xi_t'\right)_{21}$ and $R_{2T} = \left(\frac{1}{T}\sum_{t=1}^{T} Z_t Z_t'\right)_{22}$. Therefore, according to Eq. (5), R_{1T} converges to a stable distribution as the sample grows large. By contrast, according to Eq. (6), R_{2T} is off by a factor of T. In order to converge to a stable distribution, one would need to divide R_{2T} by an additional factor of T. By not doing so in the construction of the OLS estimator, the implication is that R_{2T} diverges to infinity at rate T so that the remainder term $R_T = R_{2T}^{-1} R_{1T}$ collapses to zero as the sample size grows large. Therefore, under cointegration we have

$$R_{1T} \Rightarrow \left(\int_{r=0}^{1} B_r(\Omega)dB_r(\Omega)\right)_{21} + \Lambda_{21} + \Omega_{0,21} \text{ as } T \to \infty \tag{7}$$

$$R_{2T} \to \infty,\ R_T \to 0,\ \hat{\beta}_{OLS} \to \beta, \text{ as } T \to \infty. \tag{8}$$

Notice that under cointegration, this occurs regardless of the covariance structure between x_t and μ_t in the DGP. Furthermore, because under Eq. (4) the vector process for μ_t and $\Delta x_t = \eta_t$ is permitted to have very general forms of dynamic dependence, the parameter β can be interpreted as the relationship between x_t and y_t that is invariant to any stationary and therefore transitional dynamics associated with either changes in x_t or changes in y_t conditional on x_t. In this way, the parameter β also can be interpreted as reflecting the stable steady state relationship that exists between x_t^* and y_t^*, which under cointegration can be estimated consistently even when the transition dynamics are unknown and omitted from the estimation.

For these reasons, the presence of cointegration brings with it a form of robustness to many of the classic empirical problems that lead to the so-called violation of exogeneity condition for the regressors. Obvious examples include omitted variables, measurement error, simultaneity, reverse causality, or anything that leads the data generating process, for $\Delta x_t = \eta_t$ to be jointly determined with the data generating process, hereafter referred to as the DGP, for μ_t. To be clear, one must make sure that the reasons for the violation are not so extreme as to essentially break the cointegration and thereby induce μ_t to become unit root nonstationary. For example, measurement error that is stationary but unknown will not affect consistency of the OLS estimator, nor will omission of a stationary variable, nor will omission of stationary transition dynamics, and so forth. But if the measurement error is itself unit root nonstationary, or the omitted variable is unit root nonstationary and belongs in the cointegrating relationship such that without it μ_t is nonstationary, then robustness is lost. This is just another way to state the fact that y_t and x_t are not cointegrated, in which case there is no claim to the robustness. In practice, one can either assert on an a priori basis that the cointegration is likely to hold based on economic reasoning, or more commonly, one can test whether the cointegrating relationship appears to hold empirically, as I discuss in the next section.

Of course, these arguments are based on asymptotics, and the practical question is how closely these properties hold as approximations in small samples. If the empirical interest were limited only to the actual estimation of the steady state relationship by OLS under cointegration, then one could say that estimation performs reasonably well in small samples, though precisely how well it performs depends on amyriad of details about what the regression omits relative to the DGP.

The bigger practical issue, however, pertains to the performance of the various tests typically associated with cointegration analysis. For example, one often is interested in confirming by empirical test whether a relationship is cointegrated, so that one has greater confidence that the robustness properties associated with cointegration are in play. Similarly, beyond robustly estimating the coefficients associated with the long-run steady-state relationship, we are interested in conducting inferential tests regarding the estimated coefficients or simply reporting standard errors or confidence bands. In contrast to what is required in order to consistently and robustly estimate the steady-state relationship, each of these inferential aspects of cointegration analysis require us to account for the stationary transitional dynamics, most commonly through estimation either parametrically or nonparametrically. The classic methods for these also are based on asymptotic arguments, and it is these methods for treating the dynamics that often require distressingly long time series in order to perform well. It is in this context that panels can help to substantially reduce the length of the series required in order for the tests to perform well and for the inference to be reliable.

By using cross-sectional variation to substitute for temporal variation in the estimation of the transitional dynamics, however, this is the context in which the challenges posed by the interaction of temporal dependencies with cross-sectional heterogeneity and cross-sectional dependence arise. This is an important theme for the next section, in which I discuss how these challenges help to shape the strategies for testing cointegration in time series panels and constructing consistent and robust methods of inference in cointegrated panels.

3 Strategies for Treating Cross-Sectional Heterogeneity in Cointegration Testing and Inference

In the next several sections, I discuss some the key aspects of using panels to test for the presence of cointegration and to test hypotheses about cointegrating relationships in panels. As discussed in the previous section, classic approaches to this in time series contexts invariably require the estimation of dynamics. An important challenge for panels occurs when these dynamics are cross-sectionally heterogeneous, as one would expect for virtually all aggregate level data, and I detail the challenge that this creates. Specifically, cross-sectional heterogeneity in the dynamics rules out standard approaches to pooling data cross sectionally as is done in tradition micro panel methods. This is because if one pools the data when the true dynamics are heterogeneous, it leads to inconsistent estimation of all coefficients of the regression. More precisely, as pointed out in Pesaran and Smith (1995), in the presence of heterogeneity, the pooled coefficients on lagged dependent variables do not converge to he average of the underlying heterogeneous parameters.

To see this point more clearly, consider a simple illustration for a dynamic process characterized by a first-order autoregressive process. For example, imagine that for a panel y_{it} with $i = 1, \ldots, N$ cross-sectional units, which I call members of the panel, and $t = 1, \ldots, T$ time periods, the data generating process for the dynamics in stationary form can be represented as

$$\Delta y_{it} = \alpha_i + \phi_i \Delta y_{it-1} + \mu_{it}, \tag{9}$$

$$\phi_i = \phi + \eta_i, \quad \eta_i \sim iid\left(0, \sigma_\eta^2\right), \quad \sigma_\eta^2 < \infty, |\phi_j| < 1 \forall i, \tag{10}$$

so that the coefficient reflecting the stationary transition dynamics, ϕ_i, is heterogeneous among the members of the panel, i. But imagine that, in the process of estimation, the dynamic coefficient is pooled across i, so that estimation takes the form

$$\Delta y_{it} = \alpha_i + \phi \Delta y_{it-1} + v_{it}, \tag{11}$$

so that we have imposed the homogeneity restriction $\phi_i = \phi \ \forall i$, when in truth $\phi_i = \phi + \eta_i$. This would not be a problem if the pooled estimation for $\hat{\phi}$ consistently estimated the average or some other notion of the typical value of ϕ_i among the members of the panel. But as noted by Pesaran and Smith (1995), this is not what happens. To see this, notice that for the estimated residuals in Eq. (11) we have

$$v_{it} = \mu_{it} + \eta_i \Delta y_{it-1}, \tag{12}$$

which now consists of both the original stochastic term μ_{it} from the DGP plus a contamination term $\eta_i \Delta y_{it-1}$. Consequently, $E[(\Delta y_{it-1} - \Delta \overline{y}_{it-1}) v_{it}] \neq 0$ and the usual condition for consistency is violated so that the pooled OLS estimator no longer estimates the average value for ϕ_i in the sense that $\hat{\phi}_{POLS} \nrightarrow \phi$. Most importantly, there is no easy solution to this problem when the heterogeneous coefficients are pooled, because the same value Δy_{it-1} appears in both the regressor and the residuals, so that instrumentation is not possible. This is a simple illustrative example, but the principle generalizes to higher order dynamics and multivariate dynamics. Indeed, this issue is pervasive in any panel time series methods that estimate dynamics, and because both testing for the presence of cointegration and constructing consistent tests for hypotheses about cointegrating relationships typically require estimation of dynamics, this issue must be addressed in most panel cointegration techniques.

4 Treating Heterogeneity in Residual Based Tests for Cointegration

In this section, I focus on the challenges that cross-sectional heterogeneity in the dynamics creates for testing for the presence of cointegration in panels, with an initial focus on residual based tests. Furthermore, it is important to understand that in addition to the issue of heterogeneity in the stationary transition dynamics as discussed in the previous section, the specifics of testing for the presence of cointegration introduces another important heterogeneity issue, which is possible heterogeneity of long-run steady-state dynamics. This was an important theme regarding cointegration testing in Pedroni (1993), as presented at the 1994 Econometric Society meetings, then circulated as Pedroni (1995), and then published as part of Pedroni (1999, 2004). To understand this issue, which is fairly unique specifically to testing for the presence of cointegration, consider a panel version of the DGP described in Eq. (1) so that we have

$$y_{it} = \alpha_i + \beta_i x_{it} + e_{it}. \tag{13}$$

Imagine, analogous to the discussion surrounding heterogeneity of stationary transition dynamics, that the cointegration slope of steady-state dynamics also are heterogeneous, so that by analogy

$$\beta_i = \beta + \eta_i, \quad \eta_i \sim iid\left(0, \sigma_\eta^2\right), \quad \sigma_\eta^2 < \infty. \tag{14}$$

Again, imagine that in the process of estimation, the cointegration slope coefficient is pooled across i, so that estimation takes the form

$$y_{it} = \alpha_i + \beta x_{it} + v_{it}. \tag{15}$$

so that the homogeneity restriction $\beta_i = \beta \ \forall i$ has been imposed when in truth $\beta_i = \beta + \eta_i$. Now, similar to when we were studying the consequences of ignoring heterogeneity in stationary dynamics, the regression error term in Eq. (15) becomes

$$v_{it} = e_{it} + \eta_i x_{it}, \tag{16}$$

which consists of both the original stochastic term e_{it} from the DGP plus a contamination term $\eta_i x_{it}$.

In this case, the consequences we wish to consider are specifically for testing whether y_{it} and x_{it} are cointegrated. If the linear combination is stationary, so that e_{it} is stationary, denoted $e_{it} \sim I(0)$, then y_{it} and x_{it} are cointegrated, whereas if the linear combination is unit root nonstationary, so that e_{it} follows a nonstationary unit root process, denoted $e_{it} \sim I(1)$, then y_{it} and x_{it} are not cointegrated. Based on Eq. (16), $v_{it} \sim I(1)$ follows a unit root process because the contamination term $\eta_i x_{it}$ inherits a unit root from $x_{it} \sim I(1)$. This implies that $v_{it} \sim I(1)$ regardless of whether y_{it} and x_{it} are cointegrated. Consequently, if the true cointegrating relationships are heterogeneous across i in the sense that $\beta_i \neq \beta \ \forall i$, then tests constructed from pooled regressions that treat $\beta_i = \beta \ \forall i$ will produce inconsistent tests, in that they cannot distinguish between the presence or absence of cointegration regardless of the sample size. Even when the degree of heterogeneity is small in the sense that η_i is small, because it multiplies a unit root variable x_{it}, substantial contamination of the stationary component of v_{it} occurs even for very small deviations from a false homogeneity assumption. Therefore, the relatively small possible gain in the degrees of freedom obtained from pooling is rarely worth the risk of misspecification, particularly because panel cointegration methods typically already have very high power under standard conditions. For these reasons, although there are later exceptions such as Kao (1999) that pools both the long-run steady-state dynamics and the stationary transition dynamics, most other methods for testing for the presence of cointegration allow for heterogeneity of both the short-run transition dynamics and the long-run steady state dynamics, as reflected in the heterogeneity of the cointegration slope.

By now, many different approaches proposed for constructing tests for the presence of cointegration take into account heterogeneity in both the transition dynamics and the steady-state cointegrating relationship. Rather than surveying all of the various approaches, I will focus on conveying the central idea of treating the cross-sectional heterogeneity in both the short-run and long-run dynamics. I will use examples based on residual-based tests in this section, as well as ECM-based tests in the next section. The first two examples are taken from Pedroni (1999, 2004). Somewhat ironically, because of the lengthy and uneven publication process, the 2004 paper is actually the original paper, with the 1999 one being the follow-up paper, which reported numerical adjustment values that applied to the case in which larger numbers of variables were used in the cointegrating regressions. Both papers studied seven different statistics spanning various parametric and semiparametric approaches, but I will focus on only the parametric ADF-based test statistics to illustrate two different general methods for treating heterogeneous stationary transition dynamics.

The first method uses a technique that conditions out the heterogeneity in the pooled dynamics; the second uses a simple group mean technique for accommodating heterogeneous dynamics. I will use a bivariate regression example, although all of the techniques generalize to multivariate regressions.

Because all of these methods account for potential heterogeneity, in long-run steady-state dynamics, the first-stage regression of the residual-based methods always takes the form

$$y_{it} = \alpha_i + \beta_i x_{it} + e_{it}. \tag{17}$$

for the bivariate case. The only difference in the various methods of testing lies in how the estimated residuals $\hat{e}_{it}$ from this regression are treated, either semi-parametrically using long-run variance estimators or parameterically using ADF principles, as I discuss here.

The first, taken from Pedroni (1999, 2004), is based on constructing a pooled ADF regression on the estimated residuals $\hat{e}_{it}$ by conditioning out the heterogenous dynamics. Toward that end, rather than estimating the full ADF regression with lagged differences, we estimate a simple DF type of regression, but with the dynamics conditioned out individually for each member of the panel, for both the regressor and regressand. Specifically, the regression takes the form

$$\hat{v}_{it} = \rho \hat{\eta}_{i,t-1} + u_{it} \tag{18}$$

where $\hat{v}_{it}$ and $\hat{\eta}_{i,t-1}$ are obtained as the estimated residuals from the regressions

$$\Delta \hat{e}_{i,t} = \sum_{k=1}^{K_{1i}} \hat{\gamma}_{1i,k} \Delta \hat{e}_{i,t-k} + v_{it} \tag{19}$$

$$\hat{e}_{i,t-1} = \sum_{k=1}^{K_{2i}} \hat{\gamma}_{2i,k} \Delta \hat{e}_{i,t-k} + \eta_{i,t-1} \tag{20}$$

applied to each of the members of the panel individually. Notice that Eqs. (19) and (20) condition out the member-specific dynamics for the significance of ρ in the pooled DF style regression Eq. (18).

This method for conditioning out the heterogeneous dynamics is analogous to the approach taken in Levin, Lin, and Chu's (2002) panel unit root test. A further refinement, consistent with LLC's approach, can be made for the cross-sectional heteroscedasticity of the long-run variances, in which case it is known as the weighted pooled ADF-based test. As shown in Pedroni (2004), however, this refinement is not necessary for the consistency of the test, even when the dynamics and, therefore, the long-run variances are heterogeneous across i, provided that the dynamics are conditioned out via regressions Eqs. (19) and (20). The unweighted pooled version computes the t-statistic associated with the pooled estimator for ρ in Eq. (18), which we will denote here as t_{POLS}.

The final step is to adjust the statistic in a manner that will allow it to converge in distribution as the sample size grows large. The adjustment takes the form

$$Z_{PADF} = \frac{t_{POLS,\rho} - \mu_{PADF,\rho}\sqrt{N}}{\sqrt{v_{PADF,\rho}}}. \tag{21}$$

The adjustment terms $\mu_{PADF,\rho}$ and $\nu_{PADF,\rho}$ are numerical values that are either computed analytically or simulated based on the properties of the distribution of $t_{POLS,\rho}$, and depend on the moments of the underlying Wiener functionals that describe the distributions. The numerical values that result from these computations or simulations differ depending on details of the hypothesized cointegrating relationship Eq. (17), such as whether intercepts or trends are included, and on the number of regressors that are included, and are reported accordingly in Pedroni (2004) for the case of a single regressor, and in Pedroni (1999) for the case of multiple regressors. The adjusted statistic is distributed as standard normal under the null hypothesis of no cointegration and diverges to the left under the alternative of cointegration, so that for example -1.28 and -1.64 are the 10% and 5% critical values required to reject the null in favor of cointegration.

As noted previously, conditioning out the member specific dynamics prior to pooling is just one strategy for dealing with heterogeneous transition dynamics. Another, more common technique is to use group mean methods rather than the combination of pooling with heterogenous dynamic conditioned out of the regression. Group mean methods have become more popular in large part because they are relatively easier to implement and interpret. To illustrate this, I use a second example taken from Pedroni (1999, 2004), namely the group mean ADF residual-based test. To implement this test, we begin by estimating the individual ADF regressions using the estimated residuals from the hypothesized cointegrating regression Eq. (17), so that we estimate

$$\Delta\hat{e}_{i,t} = \rho_j\hat{e}_{i,t-1} + \sum_{k=1}^{K_i}\gamma_{i,k}\Delta\hat{e}_{i,t-k} + u_{i,t} \tag{22}$$

by OLS individually for each member i of the panel. The group mean ADF t-statistic for the null of cointegration then is computed as $t_{GOLS,\rho} = N^{-1}\sum_{i=1}^{N} t_{i,ADF}$, where $t_{i,ADF}$ is the standard ADF t-statistic for significance of ρ_i for member i. The statistic is adjusted to ensure it converges in distribution as the sample grows large, so that

$$Z_{GADF} = \frac{t_{GOLS,\rho}\sqrt{N} - \mu_{GADF,\rho}\sqrt{N}}{\sqrt{v_{GADF,\rho}}}. \tag{23}$$

where $\mu_{GADF,\rho}$ and $\nu_{GADF,\rho}$ are numerical values that are either computed analytically or simulated based on the properties of the distribution of $t_{GOLS,\rho}$, and depend on the moments of the underlying Wiener functionals that describe the distributions. Although these values differ from those of $\mu_{PADF\rho}$ and $\nu_{PADF\rho}$, they also depend on the details of the hypothesized cointegrating relationship Eq. (17), such as whether intercepts or trends are included, and also on the number of regressors that are included and are reported accordingly in Pedroni (2004) for the case of a single regressor, and in Pedroni (1999) for the case of multiple regressors. The statistic is distributed as standard normal under the null hypothesis of no cointegration and diverges to the left under the alternative of cointegration, so that for example -1.28 and -1.64 are the 10% and 5% critical values required to reject the null in favor of cointegration.

Monte Carlo simulation studies reported in Pedroni (2004) show that for all of the residual-based test statistics studied in the paper, including the two ADF-based tests described previously, size distortions are low and power is extremely high even in modestly dimensioned panels. For example, even when the time series length, T, is too short for reliable inferences in a conventional time series context, in the panel framework, panels with similarly short lengths for T and modest N dimensions can in many cases deliver close to 100% power with relatively small degrees of size distortion.

5 Comparison of Residual Based and Error Correction Based Testing

Although residual-based methods are the most common approach, there are also other methods for testing for cointegration in time series, which have been extended to heterogeneous panel frameworks. One such example involves error correction methods, and it is worth comparing these to residual methods in order to understand the trade-offs. For example, Westerlund (2007) studied the use of single-equation ECMs in panels with heterogeneous dynamics, including a group mean version. In contrast to residual-based methods, single-equation ECM approaches require the assumption of weak exogeneity. The basic idea is to exploit this assumption in order to estimate the error correction loading parameter from a single equation and use it to test for the null of no cointegration.

The first step is to estimate by OLS what is known as an augmented form of the ECM equation as

$$\Delta y_{it} = c_i + \lambda_{1,i}\ y_{i,t-1} + \gamma_i x_{i,t-1} + \sum_{j=1}^{K_i} R_{i,j,11} \Delta y_{i,t-j} + \sum_{j=-K_i}^{K_i} R_{i,j,12} \Delta x_{i,t-j} + \varepsilon_{1,it}, \tag{24}$$

where $\gamma_i = -\lambda_{1,i}\ \beta_i$. The equation has been augmented relative to the standard ECM equation by the inclusion of lead terms of the differences in Δx_{it}, rather than just the usual lagged terms of Δx_{it}. This allows us to loosen the exogeneity requirements on x_{it} to one of weak exogeneity, rather than stronger forms of exogeneity. As discussed later, imposing weak exogeneity in this context can be interpreted as imposing the a priori restriction that causality runs in only one direction in the long-run cointegrating relationship, from innovations in x_{it} to y_{it}. Imposing such an exogeneity restriction is contrary to the full endogeneity that typically is permitted for most panel cointegration methods, and the implications are discussed in the following.

Under the maintained assumption of weak exogeneity in the relationship between y_{it} and x_{it}, the null of no cointegration between y_{it} and x_{it} can be determined by testing whether $t_{i,\lambda} = 0$, and the group mean test is constructed by computing the average value of the t-statistics associated with these such that $t_{GOLS,\lambda} = N^{-1}\sum_{i=1}^{N} t_{i,\lambda}$, where $t_{i,\lambda}$ are the individual t-statistics for significance of λ_{1i} for each member i. Analogous to the other tests, this statistic can be standardized as

$$Z_{G\lambda} = \frac{t_{GOLS,\lambda}\sqrt{N} - \mu_{GOLS,\lambda}\sqrt{N}}{\sqrt{\nu_{GOLS,\lambda}}}. \tag{25}$$

where $\mu_{GOLS,\lambda}$ and $\nu_{GOLS,\lambda}$ are the numerical adjustment values based on the properties of the distribution of $t_{GOLS,\lambda}$, so that $Z_{G\lambda}$ is similarly distributed as standard normal under the null hypothesis of no cointegration and diverges to the left under the alternative of cointegration.

To better understand the motivation for the ECM-based approach in relation to residual based approaches and to see the consequences of violating the specialized weak exogeneity condition, it is worth comparing the details of the ECM estimation equation to the residual-based estimation equation. In particular, consider rearranging the various terms in Eq. (24) as

$$\begin{aligned} \Delta y_{it} - \beta_i \Delta x_{it} = \lambda_{1,i}(y_{it-1} - \beta_i x_{it-1}) + \sum_{j=1}^{K_i} R_{ij,11}\Delta y_{it-j} + \sum_{j=1}^{K_i} R_{ij,11}\beta_i \Delta x_{it-j} \\ + \sum_{j=0}^{K_i} R_{ij,12}\Delta x_{it-j} - \sum_{j=0}^{K_i} R_{ij,11}\beta_i \Delta x_{it-j} + \varepsilon_{1,it} \end{aligned} \tag{26}$$

where, for ease of notation, I have dropped the deterministics, c_i, and the leads of Δx_{it} from the equation because they are not central to the issues I discuss next. Specifically, the previous form is convenient because it allows us to substitute e_{it} for $y_{it} - \beta_i x_{it}$ and similarly for $\Delta e_{it} = \Delta y_{it} - \beta_i \Delta x_{it}$ where they appear in the first line of Eq. (26). This gives us the form

$$\Delta e_{it} = \lambda_{1,i} e_{it-1} + \sum_{j=1}^{K_i} R_{ij,11}\Delta e_{it-j} + \sum_{j=0}^{K_i} R_{ij,12}\Delta x_{it-j} - \sum_{j=0}^{K_i} R_{ij,11}\beta_i \Delta x_{it-j} + \varepsilon_{1,it}, \tag{27}$$

which allows us to easily compare what the ECM equation is estimating relative to what the residual-based methods are estimating. In particular, for a given finite lag truncation K_i, we can see from Eq. (27) that estimating the ADF regression for the residuals e_{it} is equivalent to setting $\sum_{j=0}^{K_i} R_{ij,12}\Delta x_{it-j} = \sum_{j=0}^{K_i} R_{ij,11}\beta_i \Delta x_{it-j}$. This is the so-called common factor restriction. One of the motivations for ECM-based approaches is that residual-based tests ignore that these two factors need not be the same, and ignoring this can add variance to the small sample distribution of the $\lambda_{1,i}$ estimator. This, however, is not a form of misspecification that leads to inconsistency. The key is that the lag truncation is not treated as given in residual-based methods and can increase to absorb any additional serial correlation because of these terms. Therefore, the gain from using the ECM form for the estimation is a potential increase in small sample power, although it is not guaranteed to increase power, because this depends on the tradeoff between the number of lag coefficients estimated by the ADF regression versus the number of coefficients estimated by the ECM.

The tradeoff for this potential increase in small sample power, however, is the specialized assumption of weak exogeneity. In light of this, it is worth considering what the consequences can be when this assumption does not hold, yet the single-equation ECM test is used. In general, for the case in which y_{it} and x_{it} are cointegrated, the VECM representation provides for a two-equation system with the error correction coefficient taking the form $\lambda_i \beta_i'$ where λ_i is a loading vector with two elements such that $\lambda_i = (\lambda_{1i}, \lambda_{2i})'$. Cointegration between y_{it} and x_{it} requires that at least one of the values for λ_i is nonzero. In this context, the weak exogeneity assumption can be interpreted as an a priori assumption that $\lambda_{2i} = 0$. Therefore, because λ_{2i} is zero by assumption, then in order for y_{it} and x_{it} to be cointegrated, λ_{1i} must be nonzero, and therefore the test for the null of no cointegration proceeds by testing whether $\lambda_{1i} = 0$ via Eq. (24). The risk with this strategy, however, is that if the a priori maintained assumption that $\lambda_{2i} = 0$ corresponding to weak exogeneity turns out not to be true, then the test risks becoming inconsistent because it cannot distinguish the null of no cointegration from the alternative of cointegration no matter how large the sample size.

To see this, consider what the first equation of the VECM form looks like when the weak exogeneity assumption is not true, so that potentially both elements of λ_i appear in front of the error correction term, which can be written as

$$\Delta y_{it} = (\lambda_{1,i} - R_{i0,12}\lambda_{2,i})(y_{it-1} - \beta_i x_{it-1}) + \sum_{j=1}^{K_i} R_{ij,11}\Delta y_{i,t-j} + \sum_{j=1}^{K_i} R_{ij,12}\Delta x_{i,t-j} + \varepsilon_{1,it}. \tag{28}$$

In this context, the single-equation ECM-based approach can be interpreted as testing whether $\lambda_{1,i} - R_{i0,12}\lambda_{2,i} = 0$ under the null of no cointegration. In general, however, the value for $R_{i0,12}\lambda_{2,i}$ is unrestricted under cointegration. Therefore, if we consider the scenarios in which $R_{i0,12}\lambda_{2,i} < 0$ and $\lambda_{1,i} < 0$, but $|R_{i0,12}\lambda_{2,i}| > |\lambda_{1,i}|$, then $(\lambda_{1,i} - R_{i0,12}\lambda_{2,i}) > 0$, and the test will fail to reject the null of cointegration with certainty as the sample size grows, despite the fact that the null is false. In contrast to residual-based tests, the test becomes inconsistent because it will be unable to reject a false null even for large samples if the maintained assumption of weak exogeneity is not true. The tradeoff between residual-based tests, therefore, amounts to a tradeoff between a potential gain in small sample power at the expense of robustness in the sense that the test risks become meaningless if the weak exogeneity condition is violated. Because small sample power already is fairly large in almost all tests for the null of no cointegration in panels, in most applications the potential gain is unlikely to be worth the risk if one is not absolutely a priori certain of the weak exogeneity assumption.

So far, I have discussed panel cointegration tests that are designed to test the classic null of no cointegration against the alternative of cointegration. For some applications, we might be interested in reversing the null hypothesis, however, so that the null becomes cointegration against the alternative of no cointegration. It can be useful to consider both types of tests, in particular when the empirical application is likely to be such that results might be mixed—some members of the panel are best described as cointegrated but others might not be cointegrated. Although a test for the null of cointegration does not resolve the issue of mixed panel applications, which we will discuss later, the combination of both types of tests sometimes can narrow the fraction of individual members that are consistent with either alternative as discussed and illustrated in Pedroni (2007). There are many proposed tests in the literature for the null of cointegration in panels, starting with McCoskey and Kao (1998), which develop a pooled panel version of the Shin (1994) time series test for the null of cointegration. The difficulty with virtually all of the tests that have been proposed in the literature, however, is that, similar to the corresponding time series based tests, they inherit the property of high size distortion and low power in finite samples, and they are unable to mitigate this problem even for fairly large panels. Hlouskova and Wagner (2006) document these difficulties through a series of large-scale Monte Carlo simulations for tests for the null of stationarity that also apply to tests for the null of cointegration. A generalized solution to this problem and the related problem associated with inference for mixed panel applications remains an open challenge, which I will discuss later.

6 Estimation and Testing of Cointegrating Relationships in Heterogeneous Panels

For panels in which cointegration has been established or is expected to hold, the typical next step is to estimate the cointegrating relationships and construct consistent tests of hypotheses pertaining to the cointegrating relationships. Discussion follows about some simple methods that account for heterogeneous dynamics. As discussed previously, static OLS provides an immediate solution for obtaining superconsistent estimates because it is robust to any features that lead to endogeneity of the regressors, including the omitted dynamics. The problem that presents itself with OLS, however, is that the associated standard errors are not consistently estimated when the regressors are endogenous, even when cointegration is present. The methods discussed here are designed to correct for this, such that both the estimates of the cointegrating relationship and the associated standard errors are consistently estimated so that standard test statistics that rely on standard error estimates, such as t-statistics or F-statistics, can be used.

Many ways of constructing cointegration estimators also produce consistent standard error estimates for the purposes of testing hypotheses about cointegrating relationships. Two relatively easy-to-understand approaches are based on the time series principles of fully modified OLS estimation and dynamic OLS estimation. In both cases, the primary strategy is to adjust for a second-order bias that arises from the dynamic feedback because of the endogeneity of the regressors by using dynamics of the regressors as an internal instrument. Fully modified OLS makes these adjustments via nonparametric estimates of the autocovariances, while dynamic OLS makes these adjustments by parametric estimates using the leads and lags of the differenced regressors. Because dynamics are estimated in both of these cases, an important issue for panels is to accommodate any heterogeneity in the dynamics that is likely to be present among the members of the panel. Analogous to previous discussions, we can use either a pooled approach that conditions out the member-specific heterogeneous dynamics or a group mean approach.

Group mean approaches are popular in that they are easy to implement, and the group mean estimates can be interpreted as the average cointegrating relationship among the members of the panel. Another attractive advantage for group mean approaches is that they produce a sample distribution of estimated cointegration relationships for the individual members of the panel, which can be further exploited in order to study what characteristics of the members are associated with different values for the cointegrating relationships as illustrated in Pedroni (2007). Following are the details of the group mean fully modified OLS (FMOLS) approach developed in Pedroni (2000, 2001) and the group mean dynamic OLS (DOLS) approach introduced in Pedroni (2001).

The group mean FMOLS approach simply makes the FMOLS adjustments to each member of the panel individually, and then computes the average of the corresponding cointegration estimators. For example, continuing with the bivariate example of this chapter, the first step is to obtain the estimated residuals $\hat{e}_{it}$ from the OLS regression for the cointegrating relationship, as described in Eq. (17). These residuals are paired with the differences in the regressors to create the panel vector series $\hat{\xi}_{it} = (\hat{e}_{it}, \Delta x_{it})'$. From this, the vector of autocovariances $\hat{\Psi}_{ij} = T^{-1}\sum_{t=j+1}^{T} \hat{\xi}_{it}\hat{\xi}'_{it-j}$ are estimated and then weighted using the Bartlett kernel as per the Newey-West estimator to estimate the various elements of the long-run covariance matrix

$$\hat{\Omega}_i = \hat{\Sigma}_i + \hat{\Gamma}_i + \hat{\Gamma}'_i, \quad where \quad \hat{\Gamma}_i = \sum_{j=1}^{K_i}\left(1 - \frac{j}{K_i + 1}\right)\hat{\Psi}_{ij}, \; \hat{\Sigma}_i = \hat{\Psi}_{i0} \tag{29}$$

for each member i for some bandwidth K_i, typically set according to the sample length as $K_i = 4\left(\frac{T_i}{100}\right)^{\frac{2}{9}}$, rounded down to nearest integer. These are used to create the modification to the usual OLS estimator such that the FMOLS estimator for each member i becomes

$$\hat{\beta}_{FMOLS,i} = \frac{\sum_{t=1}^{T} x_{it}^{*}\widetilde{y}_{it}^{*} - T\hat{\gamma}_i}{\sum_{t=1}^{T} x_{it}^{*2}}, \tag{30}$$

where analogous to earlier in the chapter, $y_{it}^{*} = y_{it} - T^{-1}\sum_{t=1}^{T} y_{it}$ and $x_{it}^{*} = x_{it} - T^{-1}\sum_{t=1}^{T} x_{it}$ are the time demeaned versions of the variables, and the FMOLS corrections are now such that

$$\widetilde{y}_{it}^{*} = y_{it}^{*} - \frac{\hat{\Omega}_{21,i}}{\hat{\Omega}_{22,i}}\Delta x_{it}, \quad \hat{\gamma}_i = \hat{\Gamma}_{21,i} + \hat{\Sigma}_{21,i} - \frac{\hat{\Omega}_{21,i}}{\hat{\Omega}_{22,i}}\left(\hat{\Gamma}_{22,i} + \hat{\Sigma}_{22,i}\right) \tag{31}$$

To understand the role of these adjustment terms, it is worth pointing out that, according to Eq. (7), the numerator of the OLS estimator converges to a distribution with a stochastic nonzero mean because of the feedback effect that arises from the endogeneity of the regressors. After the adjustment terms Eq. (31) are made, the distribution for the FMOLS estimator becomes centered around zero, so that when the FMOLS t-statistic is computed based on the variance of the distribution, the t-statistic becomes asymptotically standard normal. In the special case in which the regressors are exogenous, the off-diagonal elements of the autocovariances between Δx_{it} and e_{it} go to zero, so that $\widetilde{y}_{it}^{*} \to y_{it}^{*}$ and $\hat{\gamma}_i \to 0$, and therefore the $\hat{\beta}_{FMOLS,i}$ estimator becomes identical to the $\hat{\beta}_{OLS,i}$ estimator.

After the $\beta_{FMOLS,i}$ estimator is computed, the associated FMOLS t-statistic is constructed on the basis of Eq. (30) in a manner analogous to conventional t-statistics, except that in place of the usual standard deviation the standard deviation of the long-run variance $\hat{\Omega}_{11,i}$ is used as estimated by Eq. (29), so that the FMOLS t-statistic becomes

$$t_{FMOLS,i} = \frac{\hat{\beta}_{FMOLS,i}^{*} - \beta_{o,i}}{\sqrt{\hat{\Omega}_{11,i}^{-1}\sum_{t=1}^{T} x_{it}^{*2}}}. \tag{32}$$

The group mean FMOLS estimator and group mean t-statistic are computed as

$$\hat{\beta}_{GFMOLS} = N^{-1}\sum_{i=1}^{N}\hat{\beta}_{FMOLS,i}, \quad t_{GFMOLS} = N^{-1/2}\sum_{i=1}^{N} t_{FMOLS,i} \tag{33}$$

where $\hat{\beta}_{FMOLS,i}$ and $t_{FMOLS,i}$ are the individual member FMOLS estimator and t-statistic from Eq. (30) and Eq. (32), respectively. Because the individual t-statistics have an asymptotic distribution that is standard normal, there is no need to use the usual μ, v adjustment terms to render the group mean asymptotically normal, and under the null $t_{GFMOLS} \Rightarrow N(0, 1)$ and under the alternative $t_{GFMOLS} \rightarrow \pm\infty$ as a two-tailed test, the critical values are the familiar ± 1.96 for the 5% p-value, and so forth.

In pure time series applications, FMOLS is suffers from small sample size distortion, which is inherited to some degree by pooled FMOLS as documented in Pedroni (1996). As documented in Pedroni (2000), however, group mean FMOLS has remarkably high power and very little size distortion in small samples. Intuitively, this appears to be because although the individual FMOLS t-statistic distributions have fairly fat tails that lead to size distortion in short samples, they are nevertheless fairly symmetric so that, as the cross sectional dimension N increases, the group mean t-statistic converges quickly and is well approximated by a standard normal even in short panels.

DOLS also appears to behave similarly, with the pooled version inheriting the poor small sample properties, while the grouped version appears to do well. As noted previously, DOLS also makes the adjustments to OLS that are necessary in order to obtain consistent standard errors and thus produce standard tests such as t-statistics that are consistent and nuisance parameter free under the null. In contrast to FMOLS that uses estimated autocovariances to make the adjustments, however, DOLS accomplished the adjustments via a parametric strategy that uses leads and lags of Δx_{it} directly in the regression. In order to construct the group mean DOLS estimator as described in Pedroni (2001), we first estimate the individual DOLS regression for each member of the panel as

$$y_{it} = \alpha_i + \beta_i x_{it} + \sum_{j=-K_i}^{K_i} \phi_{i,j} \Delta x_{it-j} + e_{it}. \tag{34}$$

The inclusion of the leads and lags of Δx_{it} serve to center the distribution of the numerator of the estimator for β_i here, which we refer to as $\hat{\beta}_{DOLS,i}$, much in the same way that the adjustment with the autocovariances in FMOLS served to center the distribution. Again, analogous to the t-statistic for FMOLS, the DOLS t-statistic then is constructed on the basis of Eq. (34) in a manner analogous to conventional t-statistics, except that in place of the usual standard deviation, the standard deviation of the long-run variance $\hat{\Omega}_{11,i}$ is used, which can be estimated by Eq. (29). The corresponding group mean DOLS estimators and t-statistics then become

$$\hat{\beta}_{DOLS} = N^{-1} \sum_{i=1}^{N} \hat{\beta}_{DOLS,i}, \quad t_{DOLS} = N^{-1/2} \sum_{i=1}^{N} t_{DOLS,i} \tag{35}$$

and again there is no need to use μ, v adjustment terms to render the group mean asymptotically normal, and under the null $t_{DOLS} \Rightarrow N(0, 1)$ and under the alternative $t_{DOLS} \rightarrow \pm\infty$ as a two-tailed test, so that the critical values here are also the familiar ± 1.96 for the 5% p-value, and so forth.

Pooled approaches are also possible, as for example, the pooled FMOLS approaches studied in Pedroni (1996) and Phillips and Moon (1999) and the pooled DOLS studied in Kao and Chiang (2000). In the DOLS approach the dynamics are pooled, which can be problematic for reasons discussed previously, but one can easily imagine conditioning out the heterogeneous dynamics in a pooled DOLS approach. Another approach that is used sometimes is the panel autoregressive distributed lag approach of Pesaran, Shin, and Smith (1999). Although autoregressive distributed lag approaches are, in general, built around the assumption that the regressors are fully exogenous, the approach in Pesaran et al. (1999) is able to relax the restriction to one of weak exogeneity, analogous to the assumption discussed previously for the Westerlund (2007) ECM-based approach. By contrast, FMOLS and DOLS approaches allow for full endogeneity of the regressors as is typical in the panel cointegration literature. Finally, rank-based tests using VECM approaches also are possible, but we defer this to a more general discussion of rank-based tests later in this chapter, and instead turn to the use of the panel VECM framework for the purposes of causality testing in cointegrated panels.

7 Testing Directions of Long-Run Causality in Heterogeneous Cointegrated Panels

Although cointegration analysis in panels is in general robust to the presence of full endogeneity of the regressors, as with any econometric method, consistent estimation in the presence of endogeneity is not synonymous with establishing a direction of causality. In order to establish causality, we need to impose further restrictions that relate the structure of the estimated relationship to exogenous processes, which, in general, requires additional a priori assumptions when the observed processes are endogenous, and, therefore, is not synonymous with consistency of estimation under endogeneity. In this regard, cointegration analysis is on par with any other econometric method that treats endogeneity to establish consistency of estimation. Additional structure is needed to establish the nature of the causal relationships.

In this context, cointegration can be interpreted as a type of identification that already implicitly imposes some structure on dynamic systems, so that the additional a priori structure that is needed to establish causal relationships can be relatively easy to come by. As discussed previously, the presence of cointegration in dynamic systems can be interpreted to imply the existence of a long-run steady-state relationship among the variables. Continuing with the bivariate example of this chapter, the implication is that if y_{it} and x_{it} are cointegrated, then a long-run causal effect must exist that links the two variables in their steady state. The long run causal effect, however, can run in either direction. It can originate in something that induces an innovation in x that causes y to move in the long run, or it can originate in something that induces an innovation in y that causes x to move in the long run, or it can be both. In the following,

I describe the panel VECM long-run causality tests introduced in Canning and Pedroni (1997) and published in Canning and Pedroni (2008).

The technique relies on the panel VECM form to estimate the vector loadings, which provide the basis to construct panel tests. Both the direction of causality and the sign of the causal effect can be tested in this way. It is worth considering how some of the implications of cointegration lead to a natural test for these. I will use a simple bivariate example to illustrate, but to economize on notation, I will use polynomial operator notation. Cointegration has three important implications that can be used to understand the nature of the tests. First, cointegration between y_{it} and x_{it} implies that their relationship can be represented in VECM form as

$$R_i(L)\Delta Z_{it} = c_i + \lambda_i \beta_i' Z_{it-1} + \mu_{it},\ \ R_i(L) = I - \sum_{j=1}^{P_i} R_{i,j} L^j \tag{36}$$

where $Z_{it} = (y_{it}, x_{it})'$ is the vector of variables, $R_i(L)$ contains the coefficients for the lagged differences that reflect the heterogenous dynamics specific to member i, μ_{it} are the i.i.d. white noise innovations, and $\beta_i' Z_{it-1}$ is the error correction term. Because β_i typically is unknown, when Eq. (36) is estimated for the purposes of constructing long-run causality tests, this error correction term must be estimated individually for each member, and it is important that it be estimated in a manner that has no asymptotic second-order bias, such that the associated standard errors are estimated consistently. Therefore, the Johansen procedure can be used to estimate the VECM, or alternatively we can use estimated residuals, computed on the basis of the FMOLS or DOLS estimator, so that for example

$$\hat{e}_{FMOLS,it} = y_{it}^* - \hat{\beta}_{i,FMOLS} x_{it}^* \tag{37}$$

is used in place of $\beta_i' Z_{it-1}$ in (36). When $\hat{e}_{FMOLS,it}$ is used in place of $\beta_i' Z_{it-1}$, then each of the equations of Eq. (36) can be estimated individually by OLS for each member i to obtain consistent estimates of the loadings λ_i, and the associated t-statistics will be asymptotically standard normal.

The second, fairly trivial implication is that a stationary vector moving average representation exists for the differenced data, ΔZ_{it}, which we write as

$$\Delta Z_{it} = c_i + F_i(L)\mu_{it}, \quad F_i(L) = \sum_{j=0}^{Q_i} F_{i,j} L^j, \quad F_{i,0} = I. \tag{38}$$

When we evaluate the polynomial $F_i(L)$ at $L = 1$, it gives us the total sum $F(1) = \sum_{j=0}^{Q_i} F_{i,j}$, which can be interpreted as the total accumulated response of ΔZ_{it} to the innovations μ_{it}, which is equivalent to the long run steady state response of the levels Z_{it} to the innovations. Therefore, the off-diagonal elements of $F_i(1)$ can be interpreted as the long-run responses of the variables to each other's innovations, so that, for example, $F_i(1)_{21}$ represents the long-run response of x_{it} to a $\mu_{it,1}$ unanticipated innovation in y_{it} and therefore can be interpreted as a measure of the causal effect from y to x.

The third and, in this context, most substantial implication of cointegration, is known as the Granger representation theorem, which ties together the first two implications. It tells us that the relationship between the loadings on the error correction terms and the long-run steady-state responses of the levels is restricted via a singularity such that

$$F_i(1)\lambda_i = 0. \tag{39}$$

If, for example, we are interested to test hypotheses regarding the long-run causal effect represented by $F_i(1)_{21}$, then we can use one of the characteristic equations of Eq. (39) to see the implications in terms of the loadings, λ_i. Specifically, Eq. (39) implies that

$$F_i(1)_{21}\lambda_{i,1} + F_i(1)_{22}\lambda_{i,2} = 0. \tag{40}$$

Under cointegration, both elements of λ_i cannot be zero, because in this case the error correction term would drop out of Eq. (36). If we make the fairly innocuous assumption that x causes itself to move in the long run, so that $F(1)_{i,22} \neq 0$, then Eq. (40) implies that $F_i(1)_{21} = 0$ if and only if $\lambda_{i,2} = 0$. This implies that the construction of a test for the null hypothesis that $\lambda_{i,2} = 0$ becomes a test for the null of no long-run causality running from y to x. A grouped panel version of the t-statistic for this test can be constructed as

$$Z_{GLRC} = N^{-1/2}\sum_{i=1}^{N} t_{i,\lambda_2} \tag{41}$$

where $t_{i,\lambda 2}$ is the individual t-statistic for the significance of $\lambda_{i,2}$ for unit i. Under the null hypothesis of no long-run causality running from y to x, the grouped test is asymptotically standard normal, while, under the alternative, the test diverges to positive or negative infinity. By substituting t_{i,λ_1} in place of t_{i,λ_2} in Eq. (41) we can test for the null hypothesis of no long-run causality running from x to y.

Because these are two-tailed tests, it is possible that positive and negative values for the loadings average out over the i dimension, so that the test effectively asks whether there is no long-run causality on average. To address the extent to which this might occur, we can use the same individual $t_{i,\lambda 2}$ values to compute the corresponding Fischer style statistic, which is constructed as

$$P_\lambda = -2\sum_{i=1}^{N} \ln p_i, \tag{42}$$

where $\ln p_i$ is the natural log of the p-value associated with either t_{i,λ_1} or t_{i,λ_2} depending on which causal direction one wishes to test. Under the null hypothesis of no causality, the P_λ statistic is distributed as χ^2_{2N}, that is, a chi-square with $2N$ degrees of freedom. Because this is a one-tailed test with only positive values, there is no canceling out of positive and negative values, and the test can be interpreted as a test of how pervasive noncausality is in the long run from y to x or x to y, depending on which element of λ_i is used.

Another advantage of this general framework is that we can use the implications of Eq. (40) to test the sign of the long-run causal effect. For example, imagine we have rejected the null of no long-run causality running from y to x so that $\lambda_{i,2} \neq 0$ and therefore $F_i(1)_{21} \neq 0$. If we are willing to make a sign normalization such that we call an innovation to x positive if it increases x in the long run and negative if it decreases x in the long run, so that $F_i(1)_{22} > 0$, then Eq. (40) implies that the sign of $F_i(1)_{21}$ is the opposite of the sign of the ratio of the two elements of the loading vector. If causality runs both directions in the long run, so that neither $\lambda_{i,2}$ nor $\lambda_{i,1}$ are zero, then

$$\text{sign}\left[F_i(1)_{21}\right] = \text{sign}\left[-\frac{\lambda_{i,2}}{\lambda_{i,1}}\right]. \tag{43}$$

so that this ratio can be used to test the sign of the long-run causal effect. If $\lambda_{i,1} = 0$, there is no need to compute such a ratio, because in that case causality runs in only one direction and the sign of the OLS or FMOLS estimator reflects the sign of the remaining long-run causal effect. Constructing the panel version of a test based on the ratio is not as straightforward as some of the other tests discussed in this chapter. This is because the ratio in Eq. (43) is distributed as a Cauchy, which does not have a defined mean and variance. Instead the median, which is defined for the Cauchy, is used to recenter the distribution, and the panel distribution then is simulated by bootstrap from the estimated version of Eq. (36).

In contrast to the other techniques discussed in this chapter, for which the bivariate examples were illustrations of techniques that work for any number of variables, the panel long-run causality tests are best suited for simple bivariate investigations. In this regard, they can be interpreted easily as total derivative causal effects rather than partial derivative causal effects. If we are interested in investigating multivariate channels, it is possible to generalize to larger systems of variables. The generalizations are not trivial, however, because they require additional restrictions beyond the normalization assumptions made for the bivariate case. If they are to be justified on the basis of economic restrictions, then the approach begins to look like the heterogeneous panel SVAR approach developed in Pedroni (2013), which also can be used to test for long-run directions of causality whether or not cointegration is present. Embedding an error correction term in the panel structural VAR approach of Pedroni (2013) is conceptually straightforward, although the properties of the approach specifically when the ECM term is embedded is a topic that will benefit from further study.

8 Strategies for Treating Cross-Sectional Dependence in Heterogeneous Panels

The emphasis so far in this chapter has been on the treatment of heterogeneity in the dynamics. As discussed in Section 1, however, it is also imperative to consider how the heterogeneity of the temporal dependencies interacts with the cross-sectional, or spatial, dependencies in such panels. In this section, I discuss a number of approaches, each of which can be applied to the techniques discussed so far in this chapter.

One the earliest and simplest ways that was used to treat cross-sectional dependencies was to use time effects, much in the way fixed effects were used regularly. For this, we simply compute the time effects as $\overline{y}_t = N^{-1}\Sigma_{i=1}^{N} y_{it}$, $\overline{x}_t = N^{-1}\Sigma_{i=1}^{N} x_{it}$, which can be used to purge the raw data so that $\widetilde{y}_{it} = y_{it} - \overline{y}_t$, $\widetilde{x}_{it} = x_{it} - \overline{x}_t$. Keeping with our bivariate example, we can proceed to use the purged data in place of the raw data for any of the techniques discussed in this chapter. Mechanically, this treatment is symmetric with the treatment of fixed effects discussed earlier, such that they were computed as the means over time for each member and subtracted from the raw data. Keeping with our bivariate example, if we account for both time effects and fixed effects, then we can represent the prototypical cointegrating regression as

$$\widetilde{y}_{it}^{*} = \beta_i \widetilde{x}_{it}^{*} + e_{it} \tag{44}$$

where the * denotes that fixed effects also have been extracted, so that for example $\widetilde{y}_{it}^{*} = \widetilde{y}_{it} - T^{-1}\sum_{t=1}^{T} \widetilde{y}_{it}$ where $\widetilde{y}_{it}$ is as defined, and similarly for $\widetilde{x}_{it}^{*}$. The advantage of this approach is that it is easy to implement, and it can be applied to the raw data as a standalone solution, which then can be fed into any one of the techniques discussed in this chapter, as was typically done in empirical applications. Furthermore, the asymptotic properties of estimators and tests are unaffected.

Economically, the solution can be justified when most of the cross-sectional dependency in the data derives from sources that commonly affect all members of the panel. This is a typical assumption in microeconomic applications where the members of the panel are small, and it can be a reasonable first approximation in macroeconomic applications when, for example, the panel consists of a large number of small open economies that are responding to the global economy, but do not have much effect individually on the global economy. Similar justifications can be used for regions of a large country or disaggregated industries of a large economy.

In many applications, however, time effects might not be sufficient to accommodate all of the cross-sectional dependency. This can occur most obviously when the individuals that constitute the members of the panel are large enough to affect one another rather than merely being affected by a commonality. More importantly, the cross-sectional dependencies can be intertwined with the temporal dependencies so that one member affects another member over time. In other words, conceptually, one can think of autocovariances that run across both time and space for the cross-sectional dimension, so that there is an $N \times N$ long-run covariance matrix. A GLS approach for cointegration and unit root testing in panels based on such a long-run covariance matrix estimation was explored in a conference paper by Pedroni (1997).

Although the approach studied in Pedroni (1997) allows for a generalization of the dependency structure relative to time effects, it suffers from two important shortcomings. The first is that it requires the time series dimension to be substantially longer than what one requires for time effects. The second is that it falls apart when the cross-sectional dependencies that run across the members of the panel are not temporally transitory, but are permanent. In other words, it is possible that series are cointegrated not simply across variables for a given member of the panel, but also for variables from different members of the panel, sometime referred to as cross-member or cross-unit cointegration, so that for example y_{it} might be cointegrated with y_{jt} for $i \neq j$ regardless of whether y_{it} is cointegrated with x_{it}. In this case, the long-run covariance becomes singular, and the estimators used for GLS might not be good approximations of the true dependency.

A more elegant solution is a generalization that is more closely related to the time effects solution, which is to model the commonalities in terms of a dynamic factor model. One can think of time effects as a special case in which a single common factor drives the dependency structure in the panel. The factor model approach generalizes this in two regards. First, it allows for multiple factors and allows the individual members of the panel to respond in a heterogeneous manner by allowing member-specific loadings for the common factors. Secondly, the factors themselves can be thought of as dynamic so that there is temporal dependence in the evolution of the vector of common factors. This is the approach taken for example in Bai and Ng (2004), among others.

Bai and Ng (2004) suggest estimating the common factors by principle components and conducting the subsequent analysis on the defactored data. Bai and Ng originally proposed the approach in the context of panel unit root testing and showed that treating the cross-sectional dependency in this manner did not affect the asymptotic properties of the subsequent panel unit root tests. Similar to time effects, we can think of this as a standalone treatment that can be performed prior to using the data for any of the techniques discussed in this chapter. The technique works well for a small known number of factors. When the number of factors is unknown and must itself be estimated, the technique can be sensitive to misspecification of the number of factors. The practical consequence is that, when the number of factors is unknown, inference regarding unit roots and cointegration can be sensitive to the number of chosen factors.

Another related approach advocated by Pesaran in numerous papers, including Pesaran (2007), is to use the cross-sectional averages directly in the panel regressions, in what is known as cross-sectional augmentation. This is equivalent to estimating the time effects from the data as previously described, but rather than extracting them, we include them in the regressions. This has the consequence of allowing the individual members of the panel to respond in a heterogeneous manner to the time effects similar to the common factor approach but without the need to estimate principle components. Pesaran (2007) also proposed the method in the context of panel unit root testing, but the approach also can be used in the context of any type of panel cointegration technique. One important implication, in contrast to other approaches, however, is that using the time effects in this way does affect the asymptotic distributions of subsequent tests. This stems from the fact that member-specific coefficients on the cross-sectional averages must be estimated jointly within the same equation as we estimate for the panel analysis. In contrast to the principle components based factor model approach, the cross-sectional augmentation technique should not be thought of as a standalone treatment for the data prior to analysis, but rather as a method for adapting existing techniques. Westerlund and Urbain (2015) compare the cross-sectional based approach versus the principle-component based approach analytically and in Monte Carlo simulations to draw out comparisons of the relative merits of the two approaches.

Although simple time effects extraction, common factor extraction, and conditioning regressions on cross-sectional averages have econometric appeal, an important practical concern stems from the idea that their implementation has the potential to alter the economic interpretation of the results, depending on what has been extracted. For cointegration analysis, this is particularly relevant when the commonality that has been extracted or conditioned out potentially follows a unit root process. To give a simple empirical example, imagine that we are testing whether long-run purchasing power parity holds for a panel of real exchange rates. Imagine, furthermore, that the truth is that the parity condition fails because of a unit root process in the common total factor productivity frontier shared by countries, which causes differential terms of trade effects in different economies in the spirit of the Balassa-Samuelson hypothesis. The researcher, however, is unaware of this truth and simply wants to control for possible cross-sectional dependency by extracting a common factor by principle components or conditioning out the effect of the common factor by means of a cross-sectional average. In this case, we expect the raw data to reject PPP as the individual real exchange rates will follow a unit root process because of the common TFP unit root, while the data that has been treated for cross-sectional dependency in either of these ways will fail to reject PPP. It would be a mistake, however, to conclude that PPP holds in the data. In the name of controlling for cross-sectional dependency, we would have unwittingly eliminated the very factor that is responsible for failure of PPP. This manner of controlling for cross-sectional dependency is not innocuous, in that it has the potential to have a substantial impact on the economic interpretation of the results in unknown ways if we do not know what the commonality is that has been eliminated. Rather than working with defactored data, it would be preferable to work with the raw data in a way that accounted for the dependency without potentially changing the interpretation of the results.

There are several avenues for alternative approaches to controlling for cross-sectional dependency that can work in modestly dimensioned panels without the need to eliminate the source that creates the dependency. One such approach is to account for the dependencies via bootstrap methods. Estimating and replicating by bootstrap general forms of dynamic cross-sectional dependency parametrically is not feasible in moderately dimensioned panels, so that sieve bootstrap methods are likely to be a nonstarter if the hope is generality in the dependence structure. By contrast, block bootstrap methods have the potential to accommodate fairly general processes, as for example the approach developed in Palm, Smeekes, and Urbain (2011). The basic idea is to sample blocks of random temporal length, $T_n < T$ for each draw n that span the entire cross-sectional dimension with width N for each draw. In this way, whatever form of cross-sectional dependency is present in the data will be captured and replicated within the block with each draw. Performance of the bootstrap is sensitive to some of the details, such as choices by which randomization of the block length occurs, and at this point the Palm, Urbain, and Smeekes approach is designed specifically for panel unit root testing rather than for cointegration applications. This remains a promising area of current and future research.

In the next two sections, I discuss some other lines of research, which, although not exclusively focused on the treatment of cross-sectional dependency, nevertheless offer broad alternative solutions to accounting for general unknown forms of cross-sectional and temporal dependencies in a manner that does not alter the economic interpretation of the results, as potentially occurs when commonalities are extracted.

9 A Nonparametric Rank Based Approach to Some Open Challenges

In this section, I discuss a method for testing cointegration rank in panels using robust methods and its relationship to some of the challenges in the literature. In particular, the approach addresses four important challenges, some of which have been touched upon in earlier sections of this chapter. One key challenge is the ability to address the interaction of temporal dependencies with both cross-sectional heterogeneities and dependencies in a general manner that does not require the extraction of commonalities, as discussed in the previous section. A second, related challenge is to do so in a way that creates sensitivity to ad hoc choices. Examples of potentially ad hoc choices include not only choices related to numbers of common factors when treating the cross-sectional dependence, but also choices with respect to choosing lag length or the number of autocovariances for the bandwidth when treating the cross-sectionally heterogeneous temporal dependence. A third challenge discussed previously in this chapter is the problem of mixed panels, whereby different members of the panel can exhibit different properties with regard to cointegration and unit roots. Finally, a challenge for many of the techniques is that they tend not to perform well when incidental member-specific deterministic trends are present and estimated in the regressions. For all of these challenges, it would be good to have techniques that perform well without the need for exceedingly large panels.

As it turns out, these challenges are interrelated and can be viewed as stemming fundamentally from the overriding challenge presented by the classic curse of dimensionality problem. To see the connection, imagine treating a panel of time series as if it were a large vector of time series to be investigated, a large dimensional unrestricted VECM, with each member of the panel contributing variables and equations to the VECM. For example, imagine a panel with N members, each one of which includes $M = 2$ variables, y_{it}, x_{it}. This could be loaded into an $MN \times 1$ dimensional vector to produce a VECM of dimension $MN \times MN$. This is appropriate conceptually, because without restrictions, the VECM would allow for both full heterogeneity of the dynamics among the members as well as full unrestricted dynamic cross-sectional dependencies among the members. The dependencies could include nontransitory, permanent dependencies across the variables analogous to cross-member cointegration, which would be reflected in a reduction in the rank of the VECM.

The question of rank is also of interest here because it relates to the issue of mixed panels discussed earlier in this chapter. It is common to think of the problem of mixed panels in terms of questions about how many members of the panel are consistent with the alternative when we reject the null. For example, if we reject the null of a unit root or the null of no cointegration, if the empirical application allows for the possibility that the answer differs across members of the panel, then how many of the members are consistent with the alternative? There is a conceptual problem in thinking about the question in this way, however, when one recognizes that the members of the panel might be linked through cross-member cointegration. For example, imagine a panel consisting of a hypothetical state GDP price deflator series for the 50 states of the United States. Imagine that each of the series follows a unit root process, but that the unit root in each of these series is because of their common link to the US dollar, which creates a unit root for the US national GDP deflator. In other words, the panel has a cointegration rank of 1 rather than 50. In this case, depending on our perspective, we could argue either that 50 of the state deflators have unit roots, or, after accounting for the cross-sectional dependence structure, we could argue that, in effect, there is really only one unit root shared among all 50. More generally, in applications with unknown forms of cross-sectional dependency and unknown degrees of cross-member cointegration dependencies, the answer can lie anywhere in between. I believe that in this case, conceptually the more salient question is not how many members have unit roots but rather what is the rank of the panel. In effect, we would like to know how many unit roots are responsible for determining the properties of the panel and whether the rank is large and close to full rank, or whether the rank is low and close to zero. The same applies if we are asking about the number of members for which two variables within the same member appear to cointegrate.

Although the VECM approach helps us to sort through these various issues conceptually, it is not feasible to apply the VECM form directly because the number of parameters that would need to be estimated is far too large. Consider the example described previously, where we have $N = 30$ members with $M = 2$ variables, and, say, $K = 8$ lags. Estimating the VECM would require the estimation of $N^2M^2(K + 1) + NM$ parameters, which comes to 32,460 parameters. If we require at least 10 data points per parameter in order to allow enough degrees of freedom, which is likely an understatement, then we should look for panels of length $T = 10x(32{,}460/30)$, hence panels of length $T = 10{,}820$. This makes the approach infeasible and contrary to the spirit of the panel cointegration literature, which attempts to find techniques that work well in panels of moderate length.

One way to think about this is that the vast majority of the parameters that would need to be estimated for such a VECM approach are parameters that are associated with nuisance features of the data, which are not necessarily central to the questions of interest. A different strategy is to look for approaches that do not require that the nuisance features be controlled for by estimation of the associated parameters. This is central to the approach discussed in this section, as well the very different approach discussed in the next section. In this section, I discuss the approach taken in Pedroni, Vogelsang, Wagner, and Westerlund (2015) to test for the cointegration rank in panels in a way that is robust to the interaction of cross-sectional dynamic heterogeneity and cross-sectional dynamic dependence of unknown form. The approach is based on using untruncated kernel estimation. An added advantage to the untruncated kernel estimation is that it does not require the choice of any tuning parameters, such as numbers of lags or autocovariances or common factors to be estimated, and, therefore, eliminates the sensitivity to them. Because the dependence structure is not explicitly modeled or estimated, the method can be implemented with much shorter panels, provided that the time series dimension, T, is greater than the cross-sectional dimension, N. Finally, freeing up degrees of freedom in this way leaves enough room for the tests to perform almost as well with the inclusion of member-specific deterministic trends as without.

To gain some understanding about the technique, imagine that we are interested whether a single series or potentially cointegrated linear combination of series follows a unit root or is stationary. We will take the series to be μ_t to denote the idea that any deterministics, such as intercepts or trends, are accounted for by regressing the individual member series against an intercept and possibly also a trend. Then consider estimating the untruncated kernel for μ_t. This is equivalent to estimating Eq. (29) for a single series for a single member, but with the bandwidth K_i set to the maximum possible for the sample, so that $K_i = T$. Ordinarily, this would not be done if we are interested in estimating the long-run covariance, because it will lead to an inconsistent estimation of the long-run variance. In this context, however, the nature of the inconsistent estimation turns out to be useful. Specifically, Kiefer and Vogelsang (2002) show that when μ_t follows a unit root process

$$T^{-2}\hat{\omega}^2 \Rightarrow 2\sigma^2 D_1 \quad \text{as} \quad T \rightarrow \infty, \tag{45}$$

where $\hat{\omega}^2$ is the untruncated Bartlett kernel estimate of μ_t, σ^2 is the true long-run variance, and D_1 is a known nuisance parameter-free distribution based on a Brownian bridge. If one computes the standard variance for a process that follows a unit root, then

$$T^{-1}\hat{s}^2 \Rightarrow 2\sigma^2 D_2 \quad \text{as} \quad T \rightarrow \infty, \tag{46}$$

where $\hat{s}^2$ is the standard variance estimate of μ_t, σ^2 is the true long-run variance, and D_2 is a different but known nuisance parameter-free distribution based on a Wiener functional. The implication of Eqs. (45) and (46) is that for their ratio we have

$$T^{-1}\frac{\hat{\omega}^2}{\hat{s}^2} \Rightarrow 2\frac{D_1}{D_2} \quad \text{as} \quad T \rightarrow \infty, \tag{47}$$

so that the ratio converges to a known nuisance parameter-free distribution when μ_t follows a unit root. By contrast, if μ_t is stationary, then $\hat{s}^2 \rightarrow s^2$ converges to a constant given by the true standard variance, while $T^{-1}\hat{\omega}^2 \rightarrow 0$, so that the ratio in Eq. (47) collapses to zero as $T \rightarrow \infty$. In this way, the ratio in Eq. (47) can be used to test consistently whether μ_t follows a unit root process against the alternative that it is stationary without the need to consistently estimate and control for the unknown dynamics associated with σ^2.

Consider now the case of a panel imagined as a large vector of variables. This can be for a univariate case, or for the case in which the variable represents a linear combination of unit root variables that are hypothesized to be cointegrated for each member i of the panel. In this case, μ_t becomes an $N \times 1$ vector of variables. If we use these to compute the untruncated Bartlett kernel, we obtain the analogous symmetric matrix estimate such that

$$T^{-2}\hat{\Omega} \Rightarrow 2\Omega^{1/2} D_{1,R} \Omega'^{1/2} \quad \text{as} \quad T \rightarrow \infty, \tag{48}$$

where $\hat{\Omega}$ is the untruncated kernel estimate, Ω is the true unknown long-run covariance structure, and $D_{1,R}$ is a known nuisance parameter-free vector Brownian bridge of dimension R, which will be explained shortly. For the standard covariance matrix estimator, we obtain

$$T^{-1}\hat{\Sigma} \Rightarrow \Omega^{1/2} D_{2,R} \Omega'^{1/2} \quad \text{as} \quad T \rightarrow \infty, \tag{49}$$

where $\hat{\Sigma}$ is the standard covariance estimate, Ω is the same true unknown long-run covariance structure, and $D_{2,R}$ is a different but known nuisance parameter-free vector Wiener functional, also of dimension R. The long-run covariance matrix Ω summarizes all possible heterogeneous temporal and cross-sectional dependencies and is unknown. Unfortunately, it is no longer the case that these simply cancel out if we form the ratio $\hat{\Omega}\hat{\Sigma}^{-1}$. Fortunately, however, if we perform the trace operation over the ratio, then the Ω terms do cancel out, so that

$$T^{-1}\hat{\Omega}\hat{\Sigma}^{-1} \Rightarrow D_{1,R}D_{2,R}^{-1} \text{ as } T \to \infty. \tag{50}$$

Notice what this has accomplished. Because the Ω terms that contain all the information about the heterogeneous temporal and cross-sectional dynamic dependencies has dropped out, there is no need to estimate any of them, and we are left with a pure nuisance parameter-free known distribution, which can be used for testing in a manner that is robust to the temporal and cross-sectional dependencies. The dimensionality R of the vector distributions and, therefore, the tail values of the distributions, depend on the rank of the vector μ_t, so that we can use them to test the rank of the panel. In this light, conventional panel unit root tests can be viewed as testing hypotheses that are special cases. In the simplest interpretation of conventional panel unit root tests such that they are used in applications in which the individual members either all follow a unit root or are all stationary, conventional panel unit root tests can be interpreted as special cases of the rank test of this section whereby the null of full rank $R = N$ is tested against the alternative of zero rank $R = 0$. In more nuanced mixed panel applications of conventional panel unit root tests, in which individual members are free to follow either a unit root process or a stationary process, a conventional test can be interpreted as a special case of the rank test whereby we test the null of full rank $R = N$ against the alternative of any reduced rank $R < N$. By contrast, here we have a continuum of possibilities to test for the null as well as the alternative, ranging anywhere between full rank to zero rank. Pedroni et al. (2015) describe a sequential step-down procedure to determine the rank.

Although the test has high power even in the presence of deterministic trends to distinguish full rank from zero rank, or in general high rank from low rank, the test does not have sufficient power to reliably distinguish the exact numerical ranks in moderately dimensioned panels. The precise numerical rank, however, is not likely to be of interest in most economic applications. For example, it is hard to foresee many economic hypotheses that revolve around whether a panel of dimension $N = 30$ has a rank of say 17 or 18. Instead, I believe that what is typically of interest is whether the rank of the panel is relatively high or relatively low so that we know whether there are many or only a few unit roots that drive the properties of the panel. This also can be useful as a type of empirical cross-check for more conventional panel unit root and panel cointegration tests. Imagine, for example, that we have confirmed through panel cointegration testing that the null of no cointegration has been rejected. In mixed applications, if we would like confirmation that the fraction of members consistent with this rejection is high, then we can use this type of rank test to check the rank of the residuals. If the rank is low, then the fraction of the members consistent with the rejection is high. Because we estimate $N \times N$ untruncated kernels, we require $T > N$ to implement the rank test. In cases where $T < N$, however, it is always possible to break the panel into smaller subsets of members for the purposes of rank testing.

In unpublished versions of the study, tests for the null of stationarity also were explored initially, but were dropped in order to focus on the pure rank tests, and that the general approach of using untruncated kernels also holds promise for constructing tests for the null of stationarity or the null of cointegration that have good small sample properties. In general, the testing framework of this section is one in which we obtain robustness to unknown forms of temporal and cross-sectional dependencies in panels of moderate sample length because we do not need to estimate the associated parameters. In the next section, I continue this discussion with some more recent techniques that do so in a completely different manner while attempting to address further open challenges.

10 New Directions and Challenges for Nonlinear and Time Varying Long-Run Relationships

In this section, I discuss some new directions and their relationships to the open challenges of treating nonlinearities and time varying relationships in heterogeneous cross-sectionally dependent panels. In particular, I discuss some of the details of an approach introduced by application in Al Masri and Pedroni (2016) and studied econometrically in terms of its asymptotic and small sample properties in Pedroni and Smeekes (2018).

The basic idea is to exploit some the desired robustness properties discussed in this chapter and to estimate long-run nonlinear relationships and, potentially, time varying long-run relationships by using the form

$$y_{it} = f(X_{it'}, Z_i) \tag{51}$$

for some vector of unit root variables X_{it}, possibly conditional on the value of some vector of cross-sectional observations Z_i. This is a challenging goal because cointegration was developed in the time series literature as a fundamentally linear concept, and, although nonlinearities have been explored in the recent time series literature, it often is hard to retain the superconsistency robustness properties that come from cointegration after nonlinearities are introduced. To gain some understanding for this, imagine a nonlinear relationship among unit root variables naively estimated by grouped OLS in the following form

$$y_{it} = \gamma_0 + \gamma_1 x_{it} + \gamma_2 x_{it}^2 + e_{it}. \tag{52}$$

The problem with this format relates to the way in which unit root variables contribute to the regression properties when they appear in nonlinear form. For example, imagine that y_{it} and x_{it} follow unit roots and are cointegrated. If we then square the x_{it} variable, the stochastic properties are altered and it becomes difficult to think about y_{it} being cointegrated with both x_{it} and x_{it}^2 in a way that preserves the conventional superconsistency. Conversely, if we start by thinking about y_{it} being cointegrated with x_{it}^2, it is difficult to imagine that it also is cointegrated with the square root of this variable in a way that preserves the superconsistency associated with cointegration in a conventional sense.

Therefore, the approach we take is not to estimate anything like the format in Eq. (52), but is entirely unrelated to existing approaches to treating nonlinearities in nonstationary time series. Rather, we take an approach that is uniquely possible only in a heterogeneous panel context. The result allows us to estimate a general class of functions of unknown form in a way that is robust to any of the forms of temporal and cross-sectional dependency discussed in this chapter, including dependencies in the form of cross-member cointegration, which we will not need to extract or identify in order to estimate the function. The approach works by estimating what can be interpreted as the Taylor polynomial approximation to Eq. (51) in a way that envisions different members i of the panel as being realizations along different portions of the domain of the function Eq. (51). A cross-sectional sampling of a linear approximation of the polynomial is taken across these different portions of the domain that correspond to the different units of the panel. This is then interacted with fixed point in time observations, s, of the regressors X_i (s) via a second-stage regression in order to approximate the Taylor polynomial.

If we continue with the bivariate example used throughout this chapter, we can describe the technique as composed of two key steps. The first step is to estimate a static time series regression for each unit of the panel in the form

$$y_{it} = \alpha_i + \beta_i x_{it} + \mu_{it}. \tag{53}$$

The second stage is to take the heterogeneous estimated slope values, $\hat{\beta}_i$ from Eq. (53), and use them in a second-stage cross-sectional regression as

$$\hat{\beta}_i = \sum_{j=0}^{P} c_{j,s} x_i^j(s) + v_i \tag{54}$$

where the order of the polynomial P in Eq. (54) is chosen by data dependent methods, and x_i (s) is a point in time observation of x_{it} at any fixed point in time s from the observed sample. In practice, Eq. (54) can repeated for any and all available values of s. Furthermore, if the data generating process is understood to be time invariant, then the group mean values can be used to obtain the time invariant estimates $\hat{c}_j = S^{-1}\Sigma_{s=1}^{S}\hat{c}_{j,s}$ for any value j. If instead the data generating process is understood to be time varying, subject to smoothness constraints, then one can use individual or rolling window averages of the $\hat{c}_{j,s}$ to trace their evolution over time.

To gain some further understanding about the technique, consider a simple case in which the polynomial being estimated is relatively low order. For example, imagine that the chosen value for P in Eq. (54) is $P = 1$. If we take the fitted values from Eq. (54) and imagine plugging them into the fitted values of Eq. (53), for the case of $P = 1$, we obtain

$$y_{it} = \alpha_i + c_0 x_{it} + c_1 x_i(s) x_{it}, \tag{55}$$

so that by setting $P = 1$ in Eq. (54) we obtain a quadratic relationship in x for Eq. (55). The quadratic term in Eq. (55), however, is specialized in that it is not x_{it}^2, but rather $x_i(s)x_{it}$. It is this detail that allows us to use variation in the domain realizations of $x_i(s)$ over the cross-sectional dimension i to trace out the polynomial. Specifically, if we picture the polynomial as having the curvature of a quadratic, take a fixed point $x_i(s)$, and then vary x_{it} over t around this point, we obtain a line representing the tangency of the curve at that location. If we do this at various points along the x axis corresponding to the different i realizations for $x_i(s)$, with enough variation over i, we begin to trace out the entire polynomial. In this way, we exploit the heterogeneity among the i realizations to map out the details of the polynomial. The same principle applies when we take higher order values for P, so that we are, in effect, taking a higher order expansion around the linear relationship between y_{it} and x_{it} corresponding to unit i.

Although the regressions Eq. (53) and Eq. (54) are both static and linearly additive, the data generating process y_{it} and x_{it} is permitted to be dynamic, cross-sectionally dependent and potentially nonlinear, with the idea being that these regressions are able to consistently estimate the underlying nonlinear long-run relationship between y and x in a way that is robust to these features, without the need to specify and estimate the dynamics and cross-sectional dependencies. The robustness properties owe much to the fact that the nonlinear panel form has been decomposed into two simple sets of regressions, the first a static time series regression for each member i and the second an additively linear cross-sectional regression for each fixed time point s. In particular, the first-stage regressions Eq. (53) needs to estimate a linear approximation that is appropriate for the range over which the data is realized for each member i. Because these are unit-root variable, stationary transition dynamics play only a second-order role in this estimation and vanishes asymptotically as the number of observations for the range associated with a given i increases.

In the second-stage regressions Eq. (54), the cross-sectional distribution of these estimates is related to the corresponding cross-sectional distributions of observations taken at a given point in time s. Because this step is done as a cross-sectional regression for a given period s, dynamic cross-sectional dependencies do not play a role in the consistency of the estimation viewed from the perspective of the cross-sectional estimation as the number of members grows large. More broadly, the fact that the interaction of the linear approximation based on the relationship between y_{it} and x_{it} and the cross-sectional point in time observations on $x_i(s)$ are used to obtain the robustness properties can be interpreted as exploiting the fact that the specific historical realizations $x_i(s)$ matter in the way they interact in the incremental relationship between x_{it} and y_{it} to create the nonlinearities that we observe.

Another interesting aspect of the approach is that, because for the first-stage regressions Eq. (53) we do not require the variables to be cointegrated in the conventional sense of a linear combination of variables that are stationary, the technique also is robust to the omission of unit-root common factors that would, in a more conventional setting, break the cointegrating relationship between y_{it} and x_{it}. In this regard, the technique also offers the possibility of a type of robustness for mixed panel applications, because we do not require each member to be individually cointegrated in the conventional sense. Monte Carlo simulations for both the Al Masri and Pedroni (2016) and Pedroni and Smeekes (2018) studies show that the technique works well even when the length of the panel is relatively short, even in the presence of omitted dynamics and common factors. Pedroni and Smeekes (2018) study the conditions under which the distributions are asymptotically normal, and under which standard t-statistics have good size and strong power even in relatively short samples.

I have described a simple bivariate example, but as shown in both studies, and as applied in Al Masri and Pedroni (2016), the technique also can be used in the general case when X_{it} is an $M \times 1$ vector, and the corresponding multivariate polynomials also can be conditioned on cross-sectional variables. Because the generalization is less obvious than for some of the other techniques discussed in this chapter, it is worth elaborating briefly on how this is done. When Eq. (53) is replaced with a multivariate regression of the form

$$y_{it} = \alpha_i + \beta_i' X_{it} + \mu_{it} \tag{56}$$

where X_{it} is an $M \times 1$ vector, the second-stage regressions now take the form

$$\hat{\beta}_i = \sum_{j=0}^{P} C_{j,s} X_i^j(\mathrm{s}) + v_i, \tag{57}$$

which represents a system of equations, one for each estimate of the $M \times 1$ vector $\hat{\beta}_i$ from Eq. (56), where $X_i(s)$ is an $M \times 1$ vector realization of X_{it} for some fixed time period s and the C_j are the $M \times M$ estimated matrices, which is diagonal for $j = 0$, symmetric for $j = 1$ and unrestricted for $j > 1$. In this way, the form of the approximating polynomial is interacted among the various elements of the vector version of Eq. (51). For example, in Al Masri and Pedroni (2016) arguments, $X_{1,it}$ and $X_{2,it}$ reflecting measures of development of financial institutions and measures of development of financial markets, respectively, are allowed to interact with one another in their relationship to per capita income. By taking time derivatives of the estimated relationships, we can infer the implications of different relative rates of development in financial institutions versus financial markets for various types of countries.

Furthermore, it is also possible to condition these polynomial relationships on any vector of cross-sectional observables, Z_i. In such cases, Eq. (58) can be extended to take the form

$$\hat{\beta}_i = \sum_{j=0}^{P} C_{j,s} X_i^j(s) + \sum_{k=1}^{K} \sum_{j=0}^{P} D_{k,j} X_i^j(s) Z_{k,i} + v_i \tag{58}$$

Z_i is $K \times 1$ vector of unit specific variables and $D_{k,j}$ are conformably dimensioned $M \times M$ matrices. In practice, Z_i can take the form of static cross-sectional variables, or either point in time realizations or time averaged realizations of stationary time series variables. In this way, cross-sectional and stationary variables also can have a role in shaping the form of the polynomials. For example, Al Masri and Pedroni (2016) show how the relationships between the different types of financial development and long-run economic growth depend in part on the degree of financial openness, which is incorporated as a static conditioning variable, Z_i, that reflects the financial openness of the member. Furthermore, by estimating the relationship over a rolling window for s, we can see the evolution of the polynomials over time.

Although this general line of research about nonlinear and time varying long-run relationships is in its early stages, it should be clear that the promise is fairly high for addressing some of the open challenges about panel cointegration that remain and for having broad empirical applicability. In that spirit, far from being an exhaustive survey of the literature on panel cointegration methods, this chapter has instead selectively touched on a simple manner about what I believe to be some of the key challenges that have helped to shape the literature, as well as some the key challenges that I expect are likely to be a part of what continues to motivate the literature, both in its theoretical development and its broad empirical applicability.

References

Al Masri, D., Pedroni, P., 2016. Nonlinearities in financial development; The good, the bad and the beautiful, working paper. Williams College.

Arellano, M., Bond, S., 1991. Some tests of specification for panel data: Monte Carlo evidence and an application to employment equations. Review of Economic Studies 58, 277–297.

Bai, J., Ng, S., 2004. A PANIC attack on unit roots and cointegration. Econometrica 72, 1127–1177.

Canning, D., Pedroni, P., 1997. Does infrastructure cause economic growth, working paper. Queen's University of Belfast.

Canning, D., Pedroni, P., 2008. Infrastructure, long run economic growth and causality test for cointegrated panels. The Manchester School 76, 504–527.

Hlouskova, J., Wagner, M., 2006. The performance of panel unit root and stationarity tests: results from a large scale simulation study. Econometric Reviews 25, 85–116.

Holz-Eakin, D., Newey, W., Rosen, H., 1988. Estimating vector autoregressions with panel data. Econometrica 56, 1371–1395.

Kao, C., 1999. Spurious regression and residual-based tests for cointegration in panel data. Journal of Econometrics 90, 1–44.

Kao, C., Chiang, M.H., 2000. On the estimation and inference of a cointegrated regression in panel data. In: Baltagi, B (Ed.), Nonstationary panels, panel cointegration, and dynamic panels (advances in econometrics). JAI Press, Amsterdam, pp. 161–178.

Kiefer, N., Vogelsang, T., 2002. Heteroskedasticity-autocorrelation robust standard errors using the Bartlett kernel without truncation. Econometrica 70, 2093–2095.

Levin, A., Lin, C., Chu, C., 2002. Unit root tests in panel data: asymptotic and finite-sample properties. Journal of Econometrics 108, 1–22.

McCoskey, S., Kao, C., 1998. A residual-based test of the null of cointegration in panel data. Econometric Reviews 17, 57–84.

Palm, F., Smeekes, S., Urbain, J., 2011. Cross-sectional dependence robust block bootstrap panel unit root tests. Journal of Econometrics 163, 85–104.

Pedroni, P., 1993. Panel cointegration, endogenous growth and business cycles in open economies, Ph.D. Thesis. Columbia University, University Microfilms International.

Pedroni, P., 1995. Panel cointegration: Asymptotic and finite sample properties of pooled time series tests with an application to the PPP hypothesis, Indiana University working paper, No. 95-013. .

Pedroni, P., 1996. Fully modified OLS for heterogeneous cointegrated panels and the case of purchasing power parity, Indiana University working paper, No. 96-020.

Pedroni, P., 1997. Cross sectional dependence in cointegration tests of purchasing power parity in panels, Indiana University working paper.

Pedroni, P., 1999. Critical values for cointegration tests in heterogeneous panels with multiple regressors. Oxford Bulletin of Economics and Statistics 61, 653–670.

Pedroni, P., 2000. Fully modified OLS for heterogeneous cointegrated panels. In: Advances in econometrics: Nonstationary panels, panel cointegration and dynamic panels.Vol. 15, pp. 93–130.

Pedroni, P., 2001. Purchasing power parity tests in cointegrated panels. The Review of Economics and Statistics 83, 727–731.

Pedroni, P., 2004. Panel cointegration: asymptotic and finite sample properties of pooled time series tests with an application to the PPP hypothesis. Econometric Theory 20, 597–625.

Pedroni, P., 2007. Social capital, barriers to production and capital shares: implications for the importance of parameter heterogeneity from a nonstationary panel approach. Journal of Applied Econometrics 22, 429–451.

Pedroni, P., 2013. Structural panel VARs. Econometrics 1, 180–206.

Pedroni, P., Smeekes, S., 2018. A new approach to estimating nonlinearities in nonstationary panels, working paper. Williams College.

Pedroni, P., Vogelsang, T., Wagner, M., Westerlund, J., 2015. Nonparametric rank tests for non-stationary panels. Journal of Econometrics 185 (2), 378–391.

Pesaran, M.H., 2007. A simple panel unit root test in the presence of cross section dependence. Journal of Applied Econometrics 22, 265–312.

Pesaran, M.H., Shin, Y., Smith, R., 1999. Pooled mean group estimation of dynamic heterogeneous panels. Journal of the American Statistical Association 94, 621–634.

Pesaran, M.H., Smith, R., 1995. Estimating long-run relationships from dynamic heterogeneous panels. Journal of Econometrics 68, 79–113.

Phillips, P., Moon, H., 1999. Linear regression limit theory for nonstationary panel data. Econometrica 67, 1057–1111.

Shin, Y., 1994. A residual-based test of the null of cointegration against the alternative of no cointegration. Econometric Theory 10, 91–115.

Westerlund, J., 2007. Testing for error correction in panel data. Oxford Bulletin of Economics and Statistics 69, 709–748.

Westerlund, J., Urbain, J., 2015. Cross-sectional averages versus principal components. Journal of Econometrics 185, 372–377.

Chapter 11

Alternative Approaches to the Econometrics of Panel Data

P.A.V.B. Swamy*, Peter von zur Muehlen*, Jatinder S. Mehta† and I-Lok Chang‡

*Federal Reserve Board (Retired), Washington, DC, United States, †Department of Mathematics (Retired), Temple University, Philadelphia, PA, United States, ‡Department of Mathematics (Retired), American University, Washington, DC, United States

Chapter Outline

Panel Data Econometrics. https://doi.org/10.1016/B978-0-12-814367-4.00011-3

1 Introduction

Econometricians have traditionally used one of three types of data sets for estimation: single cross-section, single time series, and panel data. Data on a number of units for a single time period with one observation per unit constitute a single cross-section. A time series is a realization of a stochastic process, being a sequence of observations on a single unit, usually ordered in time. Panel data refer to time-series of cross-sectional data obtained by assembling cross-sections over several periods, with the same cross-section units appearing in all periods. Cross-section units can be households, firms, or any microeconomic unit. Sometimes countries, states, or regions are used as cross-section units. The periods for which time-series data are available can be years, quarters, months, hours, or intervals shorter than an hour, such as observations received from satellites. Market interest rates, such as the federal funds rate, change every minute. In this chapter, we are concerned exclusively with panel data. We do not consider data with missing values and combined single time series and single cross-section data.

Depending on the type of data, various complications in estimation can occur. In cross-sectional data, we might need to account for interindividual heterogeneity. This heterogeneity varies depending on whether cross-section units are micro units or aggregates. For example, if the cross-section units are countries rather than firms, then economy-wide production functions do not exist even though firm-level production functions exist, as aggregation theories show (see Felipe & Fisher, 2003). Thus, in the study of any economic relationship, one must consider issues of existence first. Another complication, arising in capital theory and first identified by Sraffa (1960) and Robinson (1953–54), concerns the phenomenon of re-switching, which denies any unique relationship between capital intensity and the rate of profits. To analyze yet another complication, consider Shephard's duality theorem which, as restated by Diewert (1971, p. 482), asserts that "technology may be equivalently represented by a production function, satisfying certain regularity conditions, or a cost function, satisfying certain regularity conditions," which he enumerated. Later, Swamy, Tavlas, and Hall (2015) defined uniqueness of the coefficients and error term of any model and proved that production and cost functions having unique coefficients and error terms and satisfying Diewert's regularity conditions are difficult to find. For example, to handle the typically unknown correct functional form of a production or cost function, Swamy, Tavlas, and Hall (2015) employed a rich class of functional forms that can cover the unknown correct functional form as a special case. With this approach, however, there remains an issue of deciding whether the correct but unknown functional form, covered as a special case of a class of functional forms, satisfies the regularity conditions because it is difficult to apply Shephard's duality theorem under these circumstances. If we relinquish uniqueness, however, the results will be incorrect, as we will show. For this reason, we study cost and production functions with unique coefficients and error terms, without applying Shephard's duality theorem. Keeping this in mind, we assert that intercountry heterogeneity in the case of economywide production functions is a nonexistent problem, because such functions do not exist, whereas interfirm heterogeneity in the case of firm-level production functions with unique coefficients and error terms and intercountry heterogeneity in the case of aggregate consumption functions and other functions with unique coefficients and error terms do constitute real and solvable problems.

In time series, successive observations might be dependent, and such dependence, if present, should be taken into account. In the time-series literature, a distinction is made between stationary and nonstationary processes.[1] Time-varying coefficients models define nonstationary processes for their dependent variables.[2] In panel-data analyses, both interindividual heterogeneity and temporal dependence of observations, and nonstationary processes generating observations on dependent variables should be analyzed carefully. This chapter shows how this could be done. Another point to note is that researchers have been able to use panel data to examine issues that could not be studied in either cross-sectional or time-series data alone, such as the separate estimation of economies of scale and technological change, as exemplified by Greene (2012, p. 345), who believed that data about output and factors of production for a number of firms, each observed over several years, can provide estimates of both the rate of technological change over time and economies of scale for different firms at each point in time. We will point out several difficulties raised by this procedure.

Swamy, Mehta, and Chang (2017) (hereafter SMC) showed that when the error term of an econometric model is made up of omitted relevant regressors, its coefficients and error term are nonunique. Such nonuniqueness is far more prevalent in econometric practice than nonuniqueness of the relationship between capital intensity and the rate of profits noted by Sraffa and Robinson. Again, when the error term of a model is made up of omitted relevant regressors, the assumption that the included regressors are independent of the error term is the same as the assumption that the included regressors are independent of the omitted regressors. Pratt and Schlaifer (1988) (hereafter PS) pointed out that

1. The statistical properties of stationary processes do not change over time. All processes that do not possess this property are called nonstationary (see Priestley, 1981, p. 14).

2. In the time domain, a model with time-varying coefficients is used to define a class of functional forms to cover the unknown true functional form of the model as a special case, as will be made clear later. By contrast, in the case of general types of nonstationary processes, it is not possible to estimate the spectrum at a particular instant of time, but if the spectrum changes only smoothly over time, then using estimates that involve only local functions of the data, an attempt can be made to estimate some form of average spectrum of the process in the neighborhood of any particular time instant (see Priestley, 1981, p. 818).

this is a meaningless assumption. SMC (2017) further showed that nonuniqueness of the coefficients and error term of a model implies that none of the included regressors can be exogenous, and therefore nonunique coefficients are not identifiable. Unfortunately, unidentifiable coefficients are not consistently estimable. Therefore, there is a problem, one that we intend to solve in this chapter by extending techniques applied to our previous models having unique coefficients and error terms to a case involving panel data. The essence of the problem to be solved is to find a way to estimate separately an omitted-regressor bias component and a bias-free component that are inherent in the unique coefficients of the proposed model. As we will show, using appropriate coefficient drivers, to be defined later, we can solve this problem.

The remainder of this chapter is divided into five sections. Section 2 gives the reasons why models with nonunique coefficients and error terms produce incorrect inferences. To do away with these models, Section 3 develops models with unique coefficients and error terms for panel data. The section shows how such a model, in conjunction with time-series data on each individual in a panel data set, can be used to estimate the causal effects of the included nonconstant regressors on the dependent variable. The difficult part of this estimation is separating the estimates of causal effects from those of omitted-regressor and measurement-error biases. For this separation, certain coefficient drivers are needed. The section shows the impediments to estimating the causal effects using the entire panel data. Under a reasonable assumption about interindividual heterogeneity, only mean effects can be estimated using non-Bayesian methods and the entire available panel data set. We provide two examples to highlight a number of problems with existing methods of handling spatial autocorrelation and cross-section dependence in the econometrics literature. Section 4 discusses the difficulties in using Bayesian methods to estimate mean effects and proposes a method for improving the precision of the estimators of causal effects based on time series data for each individual. This section also proposes a correction to the existing method of simulation-based estimation and inference. Section 5 presents empirical estimates of the causal effects of wives' education on their earnings. Section 6 provides our conclusions.

2 Models With Nonunique Coefficients and Error Terms for Panel Data

In this section, we provide a definition of uniqueness of the coefficients and error term of any model for panel data and discuss problems that arise when this uniqueness condition is not satisfied. Typically, panel data contain a large number of cross-section units and only a few periods. For such data, time-series methods requiring long time series can be problematic, but useful techniques can be focused on cross-sectional variation, or, equivalently, on interindividual heterogeneity.

To achieve greater flexibility in modeling differences in behavior across individuals than a cross-section allows, econometricians have been studying panel data sets. A model setup considered in the econometric literature for the analysis of such a data set is

$$y_{it} = x_{it}'\beta + \varsigma_i'\alpha + \tau_t'\xi + \varepsilon_{it}. \tag{1}$$

where i (= 1, ..., n) indexes individuals, t (= 1, ..., T) in Eq. (1) indexes time, and y is a dependent variable. There are K regressors in x_{it} (including a constant term), called the included regressors. The scalars $\varsigma_i'\alpha$ and $\tau_t'\xi$ can be represented by μ_i and φ_t, respectively. The term $\varsigma_i'\alpha$ represents interindividual heterogeneity, with ς_i being a vector of time-invariant and individual-specific variables, such as race, sex, location, individual skill, ability, and preferences, some of which can be observed. Note that ς_i does not contain a constant term.[3] The term $\tau_t'\xi$ is the time effect, with τ_t being a vector of individual-invariant and time-varying variables, not all of which may be unobserved. The vector τ_t also does not contain a constant term. Model (1), which Swamy (1971) and Swamy and Arora (1972) estimated under certain assumptions, and Mehta, Narasimham, and Swamy (1978) used to estimate a dynamic demand function for gasoline, is called the random effects model if $\varsigma_i'\alpha$ and $\tau_t'\xi$ are treated as random variables. One of these assumptions is that every element of β has the interpretation of a partial derivative.

Assumption A1:

$$\beta = \partial E(y_{it} | x_{it}) / \partial x_{it}. \tag{2}$$

When x_{it} is random, the conditional expectation, $E(y_{it} | x_{it})$, exists if the conditions of Lemma 1 stated next are satisfied.

Lemma 1 If, for all i and t, $\varsigma_i'\alpha$ and $\tau_t'\xi$ are such that $g(x_{it})$ is a Borel function of x_{it}, and $E|y_{it}| < \infty$, $E|y_{it}g(x_{it})| < \infty$, then $E(y_{it}|x_{it})$ in $E[g(x_{it})(y_{it}|x_{it})] = g(x_{it})$ $E(y_{it}|x_{it})$ exists such that $E\{g(x_{it})[y_{it} - E(y_{it}|x_{it})]\} = 0$.

Proof

See Rao (1973, p. 97).

Under the conditions of Lemma 1, Assumption A1 follows from Eq. (1), provided $E(y_{it}|x_{it})$ is a continuous function of x_{it}. We will describe some situations in which the conditions of Lemma 1 are not satisfied. In these situations, the interpretation that ε_{it} containing μ_i and φ_t is the deviation of y_{it} from the conditional mean, $E(y_{it}|x_{it})$, might not hold.

The main objective of the analysis is to obtain a consistent and efficient estimator of β. The question of whether this objective can be achieved cannot be answered without first providing a real-world interpretation of ε_{it}, as Pratt and Schlaifer (1984, p. 11) pointed out.

$$\textit{Interpretation I} \text{ of } \varepsilon_{it}: \ \varepsilon_{it} = \mathbf{w}_{it}'\boldsymbol{\omega} \tag{3}$$

where $w_{it} = (w_{1it}, \ldots, w_{Lit})'$ is a vector of omitted relevant regressors other than ς_i and τ_t, L is the unknown number of such regressors, and $\omega = (\omega_1, \ldots, \omega_L)'$ is the vector of the coefficients of omitted relevant regressors. In words, the error term ε_{it} of Eq. (1) is made up of all relevant regressors w_{it} omitted from Eq. (1).

3. A better method of modeling interindividual heterogeneity is presented in Section 3 below.

These are called omitted regressors. None of these regressors is time-invariant or individual-invariant because such variables are already removed from w_{it} and are put in either ς_i or τ_t in Eq. (1).

Substituting $w_{it}'\omega$ for ε_{it} in Eq. (1) gives

$$y_{it} = x_{it}'\beta + \varsigma_i'\alpha + \tau_t'\xi + w_{it}'\omega \tag{4}$$

Treating this as a linear deterministic equation, Pratt and Schlaifer (1988, p. 13) showed that the omitted regressors w_{it}, and the coefficients β and ω are not unique. By the same logic, the vectors ς_i, τ_t and the coefficient vectors α and ξ also are not unique if ς_i and τ_t are not observed. We adopt the following definition of uniqueness:

Definition (Uniqueness): The coefficients and the error term of any econometric equation are unique if they are invariant under the addition and subtraction of the product of the coefficient of any omitted relevant regressor and any included regressor on the right-hand side of the equation.

Axiom by Pratt and Schlaifer (1988, *p. 34*)*:* The condition that the included regressors be independent of "the" omitted regressors themselves is meaningless unless the definite article is deleted and then can be satisfied only for certain sufficient sets of omitted regressors, some if not all of which must be defined in a way that makes them unobservable as well as unobserved.

These considerations, which will become clear as we proceed further in this chapter, have been useful in our earlier research.

Theorem 1 Under interpretation I of ε_{it} in Eq. (3), the coefficient vectors, β and ω, and omitted regressors (w_{it}) in Eq. (4) are not unique; the included regressors x_{it} cannot be uncorrelated with every omitted regressor in w_{it}; and the econometrician's reduced-form equations and instrumental variables do not exist.

Proof

Using interpretation I of ε_{it} in Eq. (3), rewrite Eq. (4) as

$$y_{it} = \beta_0 + \sum_{j=1}^{K-1} x_{jit}\beta_j + \varsigma_i'\alpha + \tau_t'\xi + \sum_{\ell=1}^{L} w_{\ell it}\omega_\ell \tag{5}$$

where this equation is the same as Eq. (4). Let j' be one of the values the subscript j takes and ℓ' be one of the values the subscript ℓ takes. Following the definition of uniqueness, add and subtract the product $x_{j'it}\omega_{\ell'}$ on the right-hand side of Eq. (5). Doing so gives

$$y_{it} = \beta_0 + \sum_{\substack{j=1\\ j\neq j'}}^{K-1} x_{jit}\beta_j + x_{j'it}\left(\beta_{j'} + \omega_{\ell'}\right) + \varsigma_i'\alpha + \tau_t'\xi + \sum_{\substack{\ell=1\\ \ell\neq \ell'}}^{L} w_{\ell it}\omega_\ell + \left(w_{\ell' it} - x_{j'it}\right)\omega_{\ell'} \tag{6}$$

Eq. (6) is the same as (5), but going from Eq. (5) to Eq. (6) changes the coefficient of $x_{j'it}$ from $\beta_{j'}$ to ($\beta_{j'}$ + $\omega_{\ell'}$) and further changes an omitted regressor from $w_{\ell' it}$ to ($w_{\ell' it}$ − $x_{j'it}$). These changes would be inadmissible if the coefficients and the error term of Eq. (5) were known, but they are not. Because the subscripts j' and ℓ' are arbitrary, we conclude from Eqs. (5), (6) that the coefficients and the error term of Eq. (5) are nonunique for all i and t, thus confirming the Pratt and Schlaifer (1984, p. 13) result.

Not knowing anything about the omitted regressor $w_{\ell' it}$ in Eq. (5), we cannot say whether it is uncorrelated with the included regressor $x_{j' it}$. But in Eq. (6), the included regressor $x_{j' it}$ is definitely correlated with the omitted regressor $(w_{\ell' it} - x_{j' it})$ because $x_{j' it}$ is common to both $x_{j' it}(\beta_{j'} + \omega_{\ell'})$ and $(w_{\ell' it} - x_{j' it})\omega_{\ell'}$. Therefore, an assertion that $x_{j' it}$ and $w_{\ell' it}$ are correlated can be made to be uncertain and certain at the whim of an arbitrary choice between the two equivalent Eqs. (5) and (6). This proves that the lack of correlation between $x_{j' it}$ and $w_{\ell' it}$ is not based on reality. Here we should take guidance from Pratt and Schlaifer (1984, p. 14), who proved that x_{it} in Eq. (4) cannot be uncorrelated with every omitted relevant regressor in Eq. (5). Given that the subscripts j' and ℓ' are arbitrary, we conclude from Eq. (5) and Eq. (6) that under interpretation I of ε_{it} in Eq. (3), x_{it} cannot be uncorrelated with every element of the vector w_{it} and therefore cannot be exogenous. Pratt and Schlaifer (1988, p. 34) even proved the stronger result that the condition that the included regressor $x_{j' it}$ be independent of "the" omitted regressor $w_{\ell' it}$ itself is meaningless. In this case, it is usual to assume that there exists a set of m (m $\geq$ K) instrumental variables, denoted by z_{it}^*, such that z_{it}^* is correlated with x_{it}, but not with ε_{it}. The method of instrumental variables uses such a vector z_{it}^* to construct an estimator of β. However, the proof of the consistency of this estimator given in the econometric literature is unsatisfactory because it does not take into account the nonuniqueness of β and w_{it} in the case where interpretation I of ε_{it} in Eq. (3) holds. In the presence of this nonuniqueness, any method of finding instrumental variables should take both $w_{\ell' it}$ and $(w_{\ell' it} - x_{j' it})$ as the plausible values of the ℓ'th omitted regressor. Therefore, we see that any attempt to find an instrumental variable that is correlated with $x_{j' it}$ and uncorrelated with both $w_{\ell' it}$ and $(w_{\ell' it} - x_{j' it})$ will fail. This argument shows that we should accept the conclusion that instrumental variables do not exist when interpretation I of ε_{it} in Eq. (3) holds.

If the included regressors in Eq. (5) cannot be uncorrelated with the error term $\sum_{\ell=1}^{L} w_{\ell it}\omega_{\ell}$, then Eq. (5) cannot be a reduced-form equation. Because Eq. (5) is an arbitrary equation, we can conclude from the previous argument that any equation with nonunique coefficients and error term cannot be a reduced-form equation.

Lemma 2 If, for all i and t, $f(x_{it}, t = 1, \ldots)$ is a Borel function of the vectors x_{it}, $t = 1, \ldots$, $E|\mu_i| < \infty$, $E|\mu_i f(x_{it}, t = 1, \ldots)| < \infty$, then $E(\mu_i | x_{it}, t = 1, \ldots)$ in $E[f(x_{it}, t = 1, \ldots)(\mu_i | x_{it})] = f(x_{it}, t = 1, \ldots)E(\mu_i | x_{it})$ exists.

Proof

See Rao (1973, p. 97).

In the econometric literature, Eq. (1) is estimated under different assumptions about $E(\mu_i | x_{it}, t = 1, \ldots)$. When $x_{it}, t = 1, \ldots$ are all endogenous, the conditions of Lemma 2 are not satisfied, and these estimations lead to inconsistent estimators.

To show some problems that Theorem 1 leads to, we consider the following assumption:

Assumption A2: For all i and t, $E(\varepsilon_{it}|x_{t1}, x_{t2}, \ldots) = E(\varepsilon_{it}) = 0$.

Assumption A2 is stronger than the assumption that the x_{it}, $t = 1, 2, \ldots$, are uncorrelated with ε_{it} for all i and t.[4] Some econometricians take this stronger assumption to mean that the x_{it}, $t = 1, 2, \ldots$, are exogenous for all i and t (see Greene, 2012, p. 52). Under interpretation I of ε_{it} in (3), Assumption A2 is false, as Theorem 1 shows. In the context of endogenous regressors, it is useful to recall Greene's (2012, p. 320) demonstration that the ratio of the first differences in two endogenous variables is meaningless without first determining what caused the change in the denominator variable. But nowhere in the econometric literature do we find the partial derivative of an endogenous variable with respect to another endogenous variable. Therefore, the partial derivatives in Assumption A1 should be questioned, because x_{it} is endogenous under interpretation I of ε_{it} in Eq. (3).

The econometric literature features four tests: the tests of hypotheses on β in Eq. (1); the Lagrange multiplier test of the null hypothesis that the variance of the random effects $\varsigma_i'\alpha$ is zero; the specification test for a random effects model; and the test for fixed versus random effects. All these tests are based on Assumption A2. It follows from Theorem 1 that under interpretation I of ε_{it} in Eq. (3), Assumption A2 is false, the conditions of Lemma 1 are not satisfied, and all these tests are invalid.

3 Models With Unique Coefficients and Error Terms for Panel Data

Section 2 teaches us that when omitted regressors constitute the error term ε_{it} of Eq. (1), its coefficient vector β and its error term $w_{it}'\omega$ are not unique. The section also shows us the undesirable consequences of this nonuniqueness. To develop a model with unique coefficients and error term, we proceed as follows:

3.1 Linear-in-Variables and Nonlinear-in-Coefficients Functional Form for Economic Relationships

$$y_{it}^* = \alpha_{0it}^* + \sum_{j=1}^{K-1} x_{jit}^* \alpha_{jit}^* + \sum_{\ell=1}^{L_{it}} w_{\ell it}^* \omega_{\ell it}^* \tag{7}$$

where y_{it}^* is the dependent variable, the x_{jit}^*'s are K – 1 determinants of y_{it}^*, the $w_{\ell it}^*$'s are the remaining determinants of y_{it}^*, and the values with asterisks are the unobserved true values. The $w_{\ell it}^*$'s include time-invariant, individual-specific

4. For a proof of this statement, see Swamy and von zur Muehlen (1988, p. 110).

(ς_i) and individual-invariant, period-specific (τ_t) determinants of y_{it}^*, and all relevant pre-existing conditions. In Eq. (4), we provide a reason why the coefficients on nonconstant regressors cannot be treated as partial derivatives. For the same reason, in Eq. (7) for $j > 0$ and $\ell > 0$, we do not treat α_{jit}^* as the partial derivative of y_{it}^* with respect to x_{jit}^* and $\omega_{\ell it}^*$ as the partial derivative of y_{it}^* with respect to $w_{\ell it}^*$. The total number of $w_{\ell it}^*$ may depend on both i and t and is denoted by L_{it}. By assuming that L_{it} is unknown, we avoid missing any relevant $w_{\ell it}^*$.

3.2 A Deterministic Law

Eq. (7) contains the full set of the determinants of its dependent variable. We will show that the functional form of the unknown true (or real-world) relationship between y_{it}^* and its determinants is not misspecified in Eq. (7). Therefore, it satisfies Pratt and Schlaifer's (1984) definition of a deterministic law. It is the first deterministic law for panel data, in the sense that it is proposed here for the first time for such data.

Definitions of measurement errors: Let $y_{it} = y_{it}^* + \nu_{0it}^*$ and let $x_{jit} = x_{jit}^* + \nu_{jit}^*$, $j = 1, \ldots, K-1$ where ν_{0it}^* is the measurement error in y_{it} and for $j = 1, \ldots, K-1$, ν_{jit}^* is the measurement error in x_{jit}.

The asterisks mean that the indicated variables are not observed. The variables without asterisks are observed. We do not assume that measurement errors are random variables. This assumption is weaker than the assumption that they are distributed with mean zero. In what follows, we call the x_{jit} "the included regressors" and the $w_{\ell it}^*$ "omitted regressors."

Spurious and True Correlations: We define the $w_{\ell it}^*$'s as including all relevant pre-existing conditions. If Eq. (7) involves some spurious correlations, then they disappear when we control for all relevant pre-existing conditions, as Skyrms (1988, p. 59) pointed out. He further observed that "statistical causation is positive statistical relevance which does not disappear when we control for all relevant pre-existing conditions." We will show how we control for all such conditions.

Interindividual Heterogeneity: Allowing all the coefficients of Eq. (7) to differ among individuals both at a point in time and through time is a sure way of capturing interindividual heterogeneity. This much generality in the type of variation in the coefficients of Eq. (7) is convenient in the absence of knowledge about the type of variation needed to capture interindividual heterogeneity in our cross-sectional data. The constant coefficient vector β in Eq. (1), even with the inclusion of terms $\varsigma_i'\alpha$ and $\tau_t'\xi$, cannot represent interindividual heterogeneity. Another justification for the specification in Eq. (7) is given in the next paragraph.

A rich class of functional forms: We assume that the functional form of the true (real-world) relationship between y_{it}^* and its determinants is not known. In this case, any particular functional form we specify may actually be incorrect.

Choosing a sufficiently rich class of functional forms, however, allows us to cover the true functional form as a special case. We believe that the functional form of Eq. (7) represents such a class in that variations in its coefficients generate a rich class of nonlinear functional forms that can cover the true functional form as a special case and, as a bonus, turns out to be one that is easy to work with. We refer to the functional form of Eq. (7) as "linear in variables and nonlinear in coefficients."

Real-world relations: We say that any mis-specifications-free equation is a real-world relationship. Accordingly, Eq. (7) with the correct functional form, being free of misspecifications, represents a real-world relationship. This claim would have been false had we used a stationarity inducing transformation of observable y_{it} or $\log y_{it}$ as the dependent variable of Eq. (7) (see Basmann, 1988, p. 98). In that event, Eq. (7) would not have been free of the most serious objection, that is, nonuniqueness. According to Basmann (1988), there is nothing wrong with using the word "causality" to designate a property of the real world.[5]

True functional forms: Intrinsic functional forms of real-world relationships are, by definition, true. Conversely, any relationship expressed with an incorrect functional form cannot be a mis-specifications-free relationship.

Potential-outcome notation: Rubin (1978) showed that Eq. (7) cannot be a causal law unless it is stated in terms of Neyman's potential-outcome notation. Such outcomes are denoted by Y^*_{xit}, which is the value that outcome Y^* would take for individual i at time t, had the value of the regressor vector x^*_{it} been at level x (see PS 1988). This is how we interpret the outcome variable y^*_{it} in Eq. (7), although, for notational simplicity, we suppress the subscript x.

Sufficient sets of omitted regressors: If we treat the last term $\sum_{\ell=1}^{L_{it}} w^*_{\ell it}\omega^*_{\ell it}$ on the right-hand side of Eq. (7) as its error term, then it must be considered as being made up of omitted regressors. But then we are back to the case of a model with nonunique coefficients and nonunique error term. To avoid this situation, we adopt the previously stated axiom by PS (1988, p. 34) introducing sufficient sets. The question then arises: How do we find these sufficient sets? We will answer this question presently.

3.3 Derivation of the Unique Error Term From the Deterministic Law

Stochastic law: For $\ell = 1, \ldots, L_{it}$, let

$$w^*_{\ell it} = \lambda^*_{\ell 0it} + \sum_{j=1}^{K-1} x^*_{jit}\lambda^*_{\ell jit} \; (\ell = 1, \ldots, L_{it}) \tag{8}$$

5. Basmann (1988) used the term "real-world relations." We also use it after giving it a definition of our own choice. Some econometricians prefer the term "data-generating process" to the term "real-world relation." We do not believe that the former term is appropriate to our model containing omitted regressors because any notion of data generating process says nothing about omitted regressors.

where each omitted regressor of Eq. (7) is related to the included regressors. Not all of these L_{it} relationships can be absent because Pratt and Schlaifer (1984, p. 14) proved that the included regressors on the right-hand side of Eq. (8) cannot be uncorrelated with every omitted regressor on its left-hand side. As in Eq. (7), the functional form of Eq. (8) is linear in variables and nonlinear in coefficients. For this functional form, the equality sign in Eq. (8) is easily satisfied because the λ's are allowed to vary freely. The intercept $\lambda^*_{\ell 0it}$ of Eq. (8) is the remainder of the omitted regressor $w^*_{\ell it}$ after the effect $\sum_{j=1}^{K-1} x^*_{jit}\lambda^*_{\ell jit}$ of the x^*_{jit}'s on $w^*_{\ell it}$ has been removed from it. Pratt and Schlaifer (1984, p. 14) proved the important result that although the x^*_{jit}'s cannot be independent of every omitted regressor $w^*_{\ell it}$ that affects y^*_{it}, they can be independent of the remainder of every such regressor. While Pratt and Schlaifer (1984, p. 13) treated the $\lambda^*_{\ell 0it}$, $\ell = 1, \ldots, L$, as L-dimensional, independently and identically distributed (i.i.d.) random vectors with mean vector zero, we treat $\lambda^*_{\ell 0it}$ as a random variable. Eq. (8) satisfies Pratt and Schlaifer's (1984, p. 13) definition of a stochastic law and therefore constitutes the first set of stochastic laws for panel data.

Because some of the $w^*_{\ell it}$'s are relevant pre-existing conditions, Eq. (8) permits us to control for these conditions by controlling the included regressors. These controls serve the important purpose of removing any spurious correlations implied by Eq. (7) (see Skyrms, 1988, p. 59). The point of Eq. (8) is that it takes into account Theorem 1, which invalidates a condition of exogeneity on any of the included regressors in Eq. (7), a condition, moreover, that has been widely, albeit erroneously, used in studies about small and large-sample properties of the estimators of the coefficients of econometric models.

3.4 Stochastic Law With Unique Coefficients and Error Term

Substituting the right-hand side of Eq. (8) for $w^*_{\ell it}$ in Eq. (7) gives

$$y^*_{it} = \alpha^*_{0it} + \sum_{\ell=1}^{L_{it}} \lambda^*_{\ell 0it}\omega^*_{\ell it} + \sum_{j=1}^{K-1} x^*_{jit}\left(\alpha^*_{jit} + \sum_{\ell=1}^{L_{it}} \lambda^*_{\ell jit}\omega^*_{\ell it}\right) \quad (9)$$

where the remainders $\lambda^*_{\ell 0it}$, $\ell = 1, \ldots, L_{it}$, of omitted regressors in conjunction with the included regressors x^*_{jit}, $j = 0, 1, \ldots, K-1$, are at least sufficient to determine the value of y^*_{it} exactly. This is the reason why PS (1988, p. 50) called the $\lambda^*_{\ell 0it}$, $\ell = 1, \ldots, L_{it}$, "sufficient sets of omitted regressors, $w^*_{\ell it}$, $\ell = 1, \ldots, L_{it}$, respectively." Following Pratt and Schlaifer (1984, p. 13), we treat Eq. (9) as a stochastic law, which is derived from the deterministic and stochastic laws in Eq. (7) and Eq. (8), respectively.[6] Eq. (9) is the first stochastic law for panel data.[7]

---

6. Many economists believe that there are no well-established laws in economics and Zellner (1988, p. 12) was one of them. Eq. (9) will enable us to establish economic laws.
7. Model (9) was extended to autoregressive models in Swamy, Chang, Mehta, and Tavlas (2003).

Interpretation II of the Error Term $\sum_{\ell=1}^{L_{it}} \lambda_{\ell 0it}^* \omega_{\ell it}^*$ *of Eq. (9):* This error term is made up of certain sufficient sets of all omitted relevant regressors contained in the vector, w_{it}.

Eq. (9) has the following properties:

1. The second term $\sum_{\ell=1}^{L_{it}} \lambda_{\ell 0it}^* \omega_{\ell it}^*$ on the right-hand side of Eq. (9) is its error term (see Pratt & Schlaifer, 1984, p. 12). This error term is not the same as the deviation of y_{it}^* from its conditional expectation $E(y_{it}^* | x_{jit}^*, j = 1, \ldots, K - 1)$, even when it exists. We will clarify that we do not assign a mean zero to the error term $\sum_{\ell=1}^{L_{it}} \lambda_{\ell 0it}^* \omega_{\ell it}^*$.
2. This error term enters additively into Eq. (9).
3. The included regressors (x_{jit}^*, $j = 1, \ldots, K - 1$) can be independent of the sufficient sets ($\lambda_{\ell 0it}^*$, $\ell = 1, \ldots, L_{it}$) of omitted regressors ($w_{\ell it}^*$, $\ell = 1, \ldots, L_{it}$). This statement is based on PS' (Pratt & Schlaifer, 1984, p. 14; Pratt & Schlaifer, 1988, p. 34) assertion that, although the included regressors (x_{jit}^*, $j = 1, \ldots, K - 1$) cannot be uncorrelated with every omitted regressor (i.e., with every $w_{\ell it}^*$, $\ell = 1, \ldots, L_{it}$) that affects y_{it}^*, they can be independent of the remainder ($\lambda_{\ell 0it}^*$) of every such variable. For this reason, the included regressors (x_{jit}^*, $j = 1, \ldots, K - 1$) can be considered as exogenous without the need to find instrumental variables that are highly correlated with the included regressors and uncorrelated with the sufficient sets of omitted regressors. The included regressors (x_{jit}^*, $j = 1, \ldots, K - 1$) are endogenous under interpretation I in Eq. (3) of the error term of Eq. (4), as shown by Theorem 1, and are exogenous under Interpretation II of the error term of (9), as shown by PS (Pratt & Schlaifer, 1984; Pratt & Schlaifer, 1988).
4. The coefficients and the error term of Eq. (9) are unique—a consequence of Eq. (8). This uniqueness supports our treatment of Eq. (9) as a causal relationship because causal relations are unique in the real world, as Basmann (1988, p. 73) pointed out. For the convenience of the reader, we reproduce Swamy, Mehta, Tavlas, and Hall's (2014) proof of this uniqueness in Appendix A.
5. The *bias-free component* of the coefficient on x_{jit}^* is α_{jit}^*. Another name for this component is the direct effect of x_{jit}^* on y_{it}^*. In another article dealing with empirical measurement of treatment effects, Swamy, Hall, Tavlas, Chang, Gibson, Greene, Mehta (2016, p. 8) expressed the effect of the treatment x_{jit}^* on the ith treated individual by $x_{jit}^* \alpha_{jit}^*$. The direct effect is not unique because the coefficients of Eq. (7) are not unique.
6. The *omitted-regressor bias* of the coefficient on x_{jit}^* in Eq. (9) is $\sum_{\ell=1}^{L_{it}} \lambda_{\ell jit}^* \omega_{\ell it}^*$, which can also be called an indirect effect of x_{jit}^* on y_{it}^*. The sum of products, $\lambda_{\ell jit}^* \omega_{\ell it}^*$, is the indirect effect because of the effect of x_{jit}^* on each omitted relevant regressor, which appears in Eq. (8), and the effects of omitted relevant regressors on y_{it}^* that appear in Eq. (7). The indirect effect of each x_{jit}^* is nonunique because the coefficients of Eq. (7) and Eq. (8) are nonunique. The sum of direct and indirect effects

of x_{jit}^* is its total effect, which appears in Eq. (9). Importantly, the total effects of included regressors are unique because the coefficients of Eq. (9) are unique. Another property of the total effect of each x_{jit}^* is that although its components, that is, its separate direct and indirect effects depend on the omitted relevant regressors chosen to define them, the total effect does not. As a consequence, when omitted relevant regressors are not identified, total effects can be estimated meaningfully, even though no meaningful distinction exists between direct and indirect effects. We note that PS (Pratt & Schlaifer, 1984, 1988) proved all the results stated in this paragraph.

7. *Simpson's paradox:* This paradox refers to a phenomenon whereby the association between a pair of variables X and Y reverses sign upon conditioning of a third variable Z, regardless of the value taken by Z. *Resolution:* Eq. (9) has $K - 1$ nonconstant regressors. In this equation, either the conversion of any one of its omitted relevant regressors into an included regressor or the deletion of any one of its included regressors changes only the omitted-regressor bias components but not the bias-free components of the coefficients on its included regressors. It is only the bias-free component of the coefficient on an included regressor that measures the causal relationship between the regressor and the dependent variable. This proves that Simpson's paradox cannot arise if the coefficients and error term of a relationship are unique, as in Eq. (9) (see Swamy, Mehta, Tavlas, & Hall, 2015).
8. For all j, the bias-free and omitted-regressor-bias components of the coefficient on x_{jit}^* appear additively in Eq. (9).
9. Manifestations of defects such as the wrong sign or a wrong magnitude of an estimate of a coefficient in a fixed-coefficient econometric model of a conventional type can be explained as arising from: (a) nonuniqueness of the coefficient lacking a distinction between its bias-free and omitted-regressor bias components, (b) nonuniqueness of the model's error term, (c) the incorrect restriction of exogeneity on some or all of the model's regressors, (d) the use of an incorrect functional form, and (e) measurement errors that have been ignored. Given this list, chances are high that any model with nonunique coefficients and error term leads to incorrect inferences.
10. The advantage of the linear-in-variables and nonlinear-in-coefficients functional-form of Eq. (7) is that it has all the good properties of PS' (Pratt & Schlaifer, 1984, p. 13) linear stochastic law, without its limitations.

Production functions and Diewert's (1971) *regularity conditions:* Suppose that Eq. (9) is a microproduction function with y_{it}^* denoting the output produced by the ith firm at time t, and the x_{jit}^* denoting a set of inputs used in the production of y_{it}^*. The functional form of Eq. (9) is not misspecified because it is derived from the class of functional forms in Eqs. (7), (8) that covers the unknown true functional form of the production function as a special case. Therefore, the production function in Eq. (9) is mis-specifications free and therefore can be treated as a real-world relationship. According to Basmann (1988), causality designates a property of the real world. It cannot be shown, however, that the true functional form of Eqs. (9) covered as a special case of the class of the functional forms in Eqs. (7), (8) satisfies the regularity conditions of Diewert (1971, pp. 484–485). Therefore, Shephard's duality theorem may not apply to Eq. (9). This is the consequence of working with a class of functional forms. If we do not work with a class of functional forms, however, then any specific functional form that satisfies the regularity conditions can be misspecified. But causal effects can be measured only using appropriate real-world relationships; and unfortunately, production functions with misspecified functional forms are not real-world relationships. Let us compare Eq. (9) with the following Diewert production function satisfying regularity conditions: $y = h\left(\sum_{j=1}^{K}\sum_{\ell=1}^{K} a_{j\ell} x_j^{1/2} x_\ell^{1/2}\right)$ where $a_{j\ell} = a_{\ell j} \geq 0$, and h is a continuous, monotonically increasing function that tends to plus infinity and has $h(0) = 0$. This specification has three problems: its functional form may be misspecified, its coefficients are not unique, and it has no error term. Note that merely adding a nonunique error term to $y = h\left(\sum_{j=1}^{K}\sum_{\ell=1}^{K} a_{j\ell} x_j^{1/2} x_\ell^{1/2}\right)$ before estimation leads to inconsistent estimators of the $a_{j\ell}$'s because (i) the included x_j's cannot be independent of every omitted relevant regressor constituting the added nonunique error term, (ii) omitted-regressor biases are completely ignored, and (iii) a possibly wrong functional form is applied to data.[8] In this chapter, the framework encompassing the class of functional forms giving rise to models with unique coefficients and error terms would be more attractive if, within it, Diewert's regularity conditions were to be satisfied. Unfortunately, the dual goal of achieving uniqueness and meeting the regularity conditions is not attainable in the current context.

3.5 Stochastic Law in Terms of Observable Variables

Using previously given symbols for measurement errors, Eq. (9) can be written as

$$y_{it} = \gamma_{0it} + \sum_{j=1}^{K-1} x_{jit}\gamma_{jit} \tag{10}$$

where

8. Here we hasten to point out that we are only expressing our difficulties without criticizing Diewert, who is doubtless a brilliant mathematical economist and whose work we admire. Had we not understood his work, we would have misapplied Shephard's duality theorem to our production or cost function with unique coefficients and error term. We are grateful for his role in our avoiding this mistake.

$$\gamma_{0it} = \nu^*_{0it} + \alpha^*_{0it} + \sum_{\ell=1}^{L_{it}} \lambda^*_{\ell 0it} \omega^*_{\ell it} \tag{11}$$

and

$$\gamma_{jit} = \left(1 - \frac{\nu^*_{jit}}{x_{jit}}\right)\left(\alpha^*_{jit} + \sum_{\ell=1}^{L_{it}} \lambda^*_{\ell jit} \omega^*_{\ell it}\right) \tag{12}$$

Note that the choice of x_{jit}'s to be included in Eq. (10) is entirely dictated by the causal effects one wants to learn.

Measurement-Error Bias Components of the Coefficients of the Stochastic Law in (10): For $j = 1, \ldots, K - 1$, they are

$$\left(-\frac{\nu^*_{jit}}{x_{jit}}\right)\left(\alpha^*_{jit} + \sum_{\ell=1}^{L_{it}} \lambda^*_{\ell jit} \omega^*_{\ell it}\right) \tag{13}$$

For all $j = 1, \ldots, K - 1$, measurement-error bias of the coefficient of x_{jit} enters multiplicatively into Eq. (10).

Latent stochastic law: Suppose that the dependent variable in Eq. (10) is not observable and that only the outcome of a binary choice depending on the sign of the regression on the right-hand side of (10) is observable. Then model (10) can be called "a latent regression model" that algebraically resembles Greene's (2012, p. 686) latent regression model. This resemblance suggests that the coefficients and the error term of the latter latent regression model can be made unique by deriving it from Eq. (9). The maximum likelihood method of estimating such a model is considered in Swamy et al. (2016).

Special features of the stochastic law in (9) and (10): (i) The coefficients and error term of (9) are unique, (ii) the observable dependent variable (y_{it}) and regressors (x_{jit}'s) satisfy a general equation in (10), with coefficients that differ among individuals both at a point in time and through time. Each of these coefficients contains three components, and (iii) given that (9) is a real-world relationship with unique coefficients and error term, the bias-free component of the coefficient on each of its nonconstant regressor is used to measure the (direct) causal effect of the regressor on the dependent variable, as shown by property (5) of (9).

Main objective of the analysis and nature of the approach to be followed: The objective is to accurately estimate causal effects, with accuracy referring to the size of deviations from the true causal effects. The suggested approach contrasts with past econometric practice in studies of small and large sample properties of econometric estimators of what turn out to be nonunique coefficients in econometric models containing some exogenous regressors and nonunique error terms without an understanding that the regressors considered as exogenous are not really exogenous, as shown by Theorem 1. Moreover, because such nonunique coefficients do not implicitly contain omitted-regressor and measurement-error biases, there has been no perceived need to deal with the problem of separating the estimators of bias-free components from those of omitted-regressor and measurement-error bias components of hopefully unique model coefficients. The purpose of this chapter, then, is to confront this problem head-on by answering the question: How does one formulate unbiased or consistent estimators of the bias-free components of the coefficients of (10)?

3.6 Simultaneous Estimation of the Bias-Free and Omitted-Regressor Bias Components of the Coefficient on Each Nonconstant Regressor of a Stochastic Law

An inherent message in Eq. (10) is that the estimates of its coefficients cannot be obtained sensibly by a mere regression of panel data y_{it} on panel data x_{it} but that, instead, we need to estimate this equation subject to the restriction that its coefficients satisfy Eqs. (11) and (12). For this purpose, we parameterize (10) using the following coefficient equations: for $j = 0, 1 \ldots, K-1$, define

$$\gamma_{jit} = \pi_{j0i} + \sum_{h=1}^{p-1} \pi_{jhi} z_{hit} + u_{jit} \tag{14}$$

where the z_{hit}'s are observed and are called "the coefficient drivers" with the restriction that they have the same range as γ_{jit}, the π's do not depend on t, and the u's are random error terms.[9] The restrictions that the π's do not vary over time are needed to estimate them using the time-series data set of every individual in the given panel data set. Because the π's in Eq. (14) cannot be shown to be unique, we make sure that they have strong connections with the unique coefficients of (9).

We have designed the K equations in (14) so that not all coefficient drivers in (14) appear in all those equations. Therefore, some of the π's in each equation in (14) will be zero. An example of such exclusion restrictions is given in Swamy, Mehta, Tavlas, and Hall (2014, p. 213).

It is important to note that Eqs. (7)–(10) and (14) provide a method of eliminating models with nonunique coefficients and error terms from the econometric literature because such models are shown to be misspecified in Section 2. Inserting the right-hand side of Eq. (14) for γ_{jit} in (10) gives

$$y_{it} = \pi_{00i} + \sum_{h=1}^{p-1} \pi_{0hi} z_{hit} + u_{0it} + \sum_{j=1}^{K-1} x_{jit} \left(\pi_{j0i} + \sum_{h=1}^{p-1} \pi_{jhi} z_{hit} + u_{jit} \right) \tag{15}$$

which is a fixed-coefficient model for a given i. In this model, the coefficient drivers, the x_{jit}, and the interactions of each x_{jit} with the coefficient drivers

9. Models appear with different labels, such as "hierarchical models," "mixed models," "random parameters models," or "random effects models," in different fields (see Greene, 2012, pp. 639–641). These models, which algebraically resemble the model in (10) and (14), have nonunique coefficients and error terms and therefore have all the problems the models in Section 2 have.

appear as regressors, and the error term $u_{0it} + \sum_{j=1}^{K-1} x_{jit} u_{jit}$ is heteroscedastic. We call the π's of Eq. (15) "time invariant and individual-specific coefficients of the stochastic law." Another way of looking at the dependent variable of (15) is that for each i, $\{y_{it}\}$ is a nonstationary process.

Sources of the error terms of Eq. (15): These are the sufficient sets of omitted regressors in (9) and the coefficients of (10). These two sources of the error terms justify our treatment of the coefficients of (10) as stochastic. Our assumptions about the u's in (14) follow. Complete explanations of the components of the dependent variable of (14) might require some additional coefficient drivers to those included in (14). These omitted drivers justify our inclusion of the error terms in (14), which, in turn, justify our treatment of the coefficients of (10) as stochastic.[10] It follows from Eq. (14) that the error term of (9) has a nonzero mean if some of the π_{0hi}'s in (14) are nonzero.

Conditions for the appropriateness and adequacy of coefficient drivers: We assert that the coefficient drivers included in (14) are appropriate and adequate, and our guesses about $\nu_{jit}^*, j = 1, \ldots, K-1$, are appropriate if, for $j = 1, \ldots, K-1$, $\left(1 - \frac{\nu_{jit}^*}{x_{jit}}\right)\left(\alpha_{jit}^* + \sum_{\ell=1}^{L_{it}} \lambda_{\ell jit}^* \omega_{\ell it}^*\right) = \pi_{j0i} + \sum_{h=1}^{p-1} \pi_{jhi} z_{hit} + u_{jit}$ such that the following decomposition of γ_{jit} holds:

$$\text{(i) } \alpha_{jit}^* = \left(1 - \frac{\nu_{jit}^*}{x_{jit}}\right)^{-1} \pi_{j0i} \text{ and (ii) } \sum_{\ell=1}^{L_{it}} \lambda_{\ell jit}^* \omega_{\ell it}^* = \left(1 - \frac{\nu_{jit}^*}{x_{jit}}\right)^{-1} \left(\sum_{h=1}^{p-1} \pi_{jhi} z_{hit} + u_{jit}\right) \quad (16)$$

for all i and t. It is this mapping of the terms on the right-hand side of (14) on to the terms on the right-hand side of (12) that determines the decomposition of γ_{jit} into its components. The equations in (16) establish strong connections between the π's and the unique coefficients of (9). All variables except π_{j0i} in Eqs. (16)(i) and all variables except the π_{jhi}'s in Eqs. (16)(ii) are allowed to vary over time. Given that we cannot allow the π's to vary over time to help estimation of (15) by using the time-series data on each individual of the given panel data set, it is desirable to allow the other variables in (16)(i) and (16)(ii) to vary over time. This requirement motivates the conditions that in (16)(i), time variation in α_{jit}^* should match that in $\left(1 - \frac{\nu_{jit}^*}{x_{jit}}\right)^{-1}$, and in (16)(ii), time variation in $\sum_{\ell=1}^{L_{it}} \lambda_{\ell jit}^* \omega_{\ell it}^*$ should match that in $\left(1 - \frac{\nu_{jit}^*}{x_{jit}}\right)^{-1}$ $\left(\sum_{h=1}^{p-1} \pi_{jhi} z_{hit} + u_{jit}\right)$. If these conditions hold, then we can say that the coefficient drivers included in (14) are appropriate and adequate. The time-invariance restrictions on π's in (16)(i) are the restrictions

10. Not all econometricians accept the notion that coefficients of econometric models can be random.

on the estimators of the bias-free components of the coefficients of (9), and the time-invariance restrictions on the π's in (16)(ii) are the restrictions on the estimators of the omitted-regressor biases of the coefficients of (9).

Conditions (i) and (ii) in (16) mean that for $j = 1, \ldots, K - 1$, the bias-free component α^*_{jit} of the coefficient γ_{jit} on x_{jit} in (10) should be made to depend on the coefficient π_{j0i} on x_{jit} in (15) but not on the coefficients on the interactions of x_{jit} with the coefficient drivers in (15), and the omitted-regressor bias component of the coefficient γ_{jit} on x_{jit} in (10) should be made to depend on the coefficients on the interactions of x_{jit} with the coefficient drivers in (15) but not on the coefficient on x_{jit} in (15).

Later, we develop the estimator of π_{j0i} in $\left[\left(1-\frac{\nu^*_{jit}}{x_{jit}}\right)^{-1}\pi_{j0i}\right]$, the estimators of π_{jhi}'s, and the predictor of u_{jit} in $\left(1-\frac{\nu^*_{jit}}{x_{jit}}\right)^{-1}\left(\sum_{h=1}^{p-1}\pi_{jhi}z_{hit} + u_{jit}\right)$, $j = 1 \ldots K - 1$.

Properties of estimators (16)(i) and (16)(ii): The coefficient drivers in (14) are chosen to achieve the following results: (i) The smaller the magnitude of u_{jit}, the closer the sum $\pi_{j0i} + \sum_{h=1}^{p-1}\pi_{jhi}z_{hit}$ to the sum $\left(1-\frac{\nu^*_{jit}}{x_{jit}}\right)\left(\alpha^*_{jit} + \sum_{\ell=1}^{L_{it}}\lambda^*_{\ell jit}\omega^*_{\ell it}\right)$. (ii) The sign of α^*_{jit} is the correct sign of $\left(1-\frac{\nu^*_{jit}}{x_{jit}}\right)^{-1}\pi_{j0i}$ in (16)(i), which can be known a priori from economic theory. (iii) The magnitude of α^*_{jit} is the correct magnitude of $\left(1-\frac{\nu^*_{jit}}{x_{jit}}\right)^{-1}\pi_{j0i}$, which is not usually known a priori. (iv) Data about $\left(1-\frac{\nu^*_{jit}}{x_{jit}}\right)^{-1}$, $j = 1, \ldots, K - 1$, are rarely, if ever, available, so we need to make some plausible assumptions about them. (v) For $j = 1, \ldots, K - 1$, the z-variables that rightly belong in the omitted-regressor bias component (16)(ii) of the jth coefficient of (10) should be included as the coefficient drivers on the right-hand side of (14). Such coefficient drivers are related to the omitted-regressor bias component of the jth coefficient of (10). How one deals with issues (i)-(v) in estimating the causal effects of wives' education on their earnings is discussed in Section 5. To the extent the available data permit, it is always a good practice to experiment with different sets of relevant coefficient drivers and different plausible assumptions about the factors $\left(1-\frac{\nu^*_{jit}}{x_{jit}}\right)^{-1}$ and compare the results.

Given that all models with nonunique coefficients and error terms should be rejected in favor of models of the type (9), the question that naturally arises is: Where and how do we find valid coefficient drivers? The choice of regressors to be included in (10) is dictated entirely by the causal effects one wants to learn.

A good estimate of the bias-free component of the coefficient on an included regressor, such as x_{jit}, is needed to estimate the causal effect of x_{jit} on the dependent variable y_{it}. Eq. (16)(i) is formed to obtain the estimate of this bias-free component. This estimate will be accurate if the coefficient drivers included on the right-hand side of (14) satisfy the equality sign in (16)(ii).[11] It is easy to see from (16)(ii) that such coefficient drivers are those variables that completely absorb the omitted-regressor bias component of the coefficient γ_{jit} on x_{jit}. The omitted-regressor bias component of γ_{jit} is given by $\sum_{\ell=1}^{L_{it}} \lambda_{\ell jit}^{*} \omega_{\ell it}^{*}$ in (16)(ii). The $\omega_{\ell it}^{*}$'s are the coefficients on omitted regressors in (7), and the $\lambda_{\ell jit}^{*}$'s are the coefficients on the included regressors in (8). Obviously, variables that perform well in explaining most of the variation in $\sum_{\ell=1}^{L_{it}} \lambda_{\ell jit}^{*} \omega_{\ell it}^{*}$ are valid coefficient drivers. The metric for judging performance is: When the coefficient γ_{jit} is equated to a function of these coefficient drivers with nonzero intercept plus an error, as in (14), the coefficient drivers should have the same range as the coefficient, γ_{jit}. We follow this same procedure to find the coefficient drivers that absorb the omitted-regressor bias components in the other coefficients of (10).

Desirable Properties of the Model in (10) and (14) not shared by Model (4): (i) Model (10) is not based on the assumption that the included regressors are independent of the relevant omitted regressors. That such an assumption would be meaningless was first pointed out by PS (1988, p. 34). (ii) The coefficients of (10) are derived from the unique coefficients of (9) with unique error term without ignoring omitted-regressor biases. (iii) The coefficients of (10) account for any measurement errors present in the available data on the dependent variable and on the included regressors of (10) for $i = 1, \ldots, n$ and $t = 1, \ldots, T$. (iv) Spurious correlations are made to disappear from (10) by controlling for all relevant pre-existing conditions via (8). (v) No incorrect exogeneity restrictions are imposed on the regressors of (10).

Difficulties in Separating Economies of Scale and Technological Change: Suppose that (15) is a production function, with y_{it} representing output, x_{it}, and the $w_{\ell it}^{*}$'s, not including all relevant pre-existing conditions, representing the vector of inputs used in the production of y_{it}, i indexing firms, and t indexing time. As we pointed out earlier, the production function in (15) is not without virtues. Those who have followed the Cambridge-Cambridge capital controversy are aware of the problems of measuring capital services used in the production of y_{it}, but there are other problems. "Returns to scale" describes the output response to a proportionate increase of all inputs. To determine that response, we should introduce a proportionate increase of all inputs in (7) and then work out its effect on the dependent variable of (10). After doing so, we should search for coefficient drivers that should be included in (14) and (16)(ii). After these coefficient drivers are found, the formulas to measure the bias-free and omitted-regressor bias components of the coefficients on inputs are given in (16). The next step is to use Chang, Hallahan, and

11. Accuracy refers to the size of deviations from the true bias-free component.

Swamy's (1992) and Chang, Swamy, Hallahan, and Tavlas' (2000) method of iteratively rescaled generalized least squares (IRSGLS) to estimate the coefficients π_{j0i} on x_{jit}, $j = 1, \ldots, K - 1$, in (15). From these estimates, it may not be easy to obtain estimates of bias-free economies of scale and bias-free technological change for the ith firm as time progresses.

Matrix Formulations of (10), (14), and (15): Let $i = 1, \ldots, n$ and let $t = 1, \ldots, T$ where T is large.[12] Then (10) in vector form is

$$y_{it} = (1\, x_{1it}, \ldots, x_{K-1,it}) \begin{pmatrix} \gamma_{0it} \\ \gamma_{1it} \\ \vdots \\ \gamma_{K-1,it} \end{pmatrix}$$

$$y_{it} = x'_{it}\gamma_{it} \tag{17}$$

In matrix form model (14) is

$$\gamma_{it} = \Pi_i z_{it} + u_{it} \tag{18}$$

where Π_i is a $K \times p$ matrix having $(\pi_{j0i}, \pi_{j1i}, \ldots, \pi_{j,\, p-1,\, i})$ as its jth row, $z_{it} = (1, z_{1it}, \ldots, z_{p-1,\, it})'$ is p-vector of coefficient drivers, and $u_{it} = (u_{0it}, u_{1it}, \ldots, u_{K-1,\, it})'$ is a K-vector of random variables. The following condition should be imposed on x_{it} for our method of estimating the equations in (17) and (18) to be valid.

Admissibility condition: The vector $Z_{it} = (1, Z_{1it}, \ldots, Z_{p-1,\, it})'$ in Eq. (18) is an admissible vector of coefficient drivers if, given Z_{it}, the value that the coefficient vector (γ_{it}) of Eq. (17) takes for individual i at time t is independent of $X_{it} = (1, X_{1it}, \ldots, X_{K-1,\, it})'$ for all i and t whenever $X_{it} = (1, X_{1it}, \ldots, X_{K-1,\, it})'$ takes the value $x_{it} = (1, x_{1it}, \ldots, x_{K-1,\, it})'$.

By definition, in any panel data set, one time-series data set is associated with each individual $i = 1, \ldots, n$. The next section turns to the assumptions that one needs to make about time series properties for each individual. Following a note about prediction in Section 3.7.1, Section 3.8 discusses parallel assumptions about cross-section properties at each period of time.

3.7 Assumptions Appropriate to Time-Series Data Sets Within a Given Panel Data Set

Assumption A3: For each $i = 1, \ldots, n$, the errors u_{it} ($t = 1, \ldots, T$) are the realizations of a stationary stochastic process following the first-order vector autoregressive equation.

12. Greene (2012, p. 378) pointed out that for the typical panel data set "it does not make sense to assume that T increases without bound or, in some cases, at all." In these cases, we have to be careful not to let T increase without bound.

$$u_{it} = \Phi_i u_{i,t-1} + a_{it} \tag{19}$$

where Φ_i is a $K \times K$ matrix and $\{a_{it}\}$, (t = 1, …, T), is a sequence of uncorrelated K-vector variables with

$$E(a_{it} | z_{it}, x_{it}) = 0, E(a_{it} a'_{i't'} | z_{it}, x_{it}) = \begin{cases} \sigma_{ai}^2 \Delta_{ai} & \text{if } i=i' \text{ and } t=t' \\ 0 & \text{if } i \neq i' \text{ and } t \neq t' \end{cases} \tag{20}$$

where Δ_{ai} is a $K \times K$ nonnegative definite matrix.

We set $\Phi_i = 0$ if T is small and set $\Phi_i \neq 0$ and do the following otherwise. Swamy and Tinsley (1980) assumed that $\{u_{it}\}$ can be represented by a vector autoregressive and moving average processes of finite orders, for which Chang et al. (1992), and Chang et al. (2000) developed IRSGLS. The latter two studies together answer our question: How general can the process $\{u_{it}\}$ become before an IRSGLS method of estimating the Swamy and Tinsley model stops stabilizing? The answer is that the process $\{u_{it}\}$ cannot be more general than (19), where Φ_i is diagonal, its diagonal elements lie between -1 and 1, and Δ_{ai} is nondiagonal.

The issue of parsimony: Parsimony, a relative and possibly subjective term, is highly prized in econometrics, so the seemingly complex causal model in Eqs. (17)–(20) might strike some readers as unparsimonious. This impression, however, would rely on what we believe to be a superficial interpretation of parsimony. Our preferred definition is: of two models, both of which perform equally well in prediction and explanation, the one with fewer unknown parameters is more parsimonious.

Thus, parsimony is a relative term. Without the qualification, "perform equally well in prediction and explanation," the above definition of parsimony is meaningless.

Inserting Eq. (18) into Eq. (17) gives, for the ith individual,

$$y_{it} = (z'_{it} \otimes x'_{it}) vec(\Pi_i) + x'_{it} u_{it} \ (t = 1, \ldots, T) \tag{21}$$

where $\otimes$ denotes the Kronecker product, and where the $Kp \times 1$ vector $vec(\Pi_i)$ is a column stack of the $K \times p$ matrix Π_i.

Non-existence of instrumental variables: From Eq. (21) we see that instrumental variables that are highly correlated with x_{it} but not with $x_{it}{}' u_{it}$ do not exist.

This conclusion follows directly, because all the coefficients, that is, the elements of the vector γ_{it} on x_{it}, including the intercept in (17), are equal to $\Pi_i z_{it} + u_{it}$ on the right-hand side of (18). The forms of Eqs. (17) and (18) are the weakest of all possible forms, and therefore specification errors can arise if they are written in any other form.

From Eqs. (19) and (20) it follows that for $t = 1, \ldots, T$, $E(u_{it} | z_{it}, x_{it}) = 0$, and the $TK \times TK$ conditional covariance matrix of the $TK \times 1$ vector $u_i = (u_{i1}', \ldots, u_{iT}')'$ given z_{it} and x_{it}, is

$$E\left(u_i u_i' | z_{it}, x_{it}\right) = \sigma_{ai}^2 \Omega_{ui} = \sigma_{ai}^2 \begin{bmatrix} \Gamma_{0i} & \Gamma_{0i}\Phi_i' & \Gamma_{0i}\Phi_i'^2 & \cdots & \Gamma_{0i}\Phi_i'^{T-1} \\ \Phi_i\Gamma_{0i} & \Gamma_{0i} & \Gamma_{0i}\Phi_i' & \cdots & \Gamma_{0i}\Phi_i'^{T-2} \\ \vdots & \vdots & \vdots & & \vdots \\ \Phi_i^{T-1}\Gamma_{0i} & \Phi_i^{T-2}\Gamma_{0i} & \Phi_i^{T-3}\Gamma_{0i} & \cdots & \Gamma_{0i} \end{bmatrix} \tag{22}$$

where $E(u_{it}u_{it}' \mid z_{it}, x_{it}) = \sigma_{ai}^2\Gamma_{0i} = \Phi_i\sigma_{ai}^2\Gamma_{0i}\Phi_i' + \sigma_{ai}^2\Delta_{ai}$ is a $K \times K$ matrix (see Chang et al., 1992, p. 45).

Let $y_i = (y_{i1} \ldots y_{iT})'$ be the $T \times 1$ vector. Then the conditional covariance matrix of y_i, given z_{it} and x_{it}, is

$$\sigma_{ai}^2 \Sigma_{yi} = D_{xi}\sigma_{ai}^2 \Omega_{ui} D_{xi}' \tag{23}$$

where $D_{xi} = \text{diag}[x_{i1}' \ldots x_{iT}']$ is a $T \times TK$ block diagonal matrix, and where the covariance matrices Ω_{ui}, Γ_{0i}, and Σ_{yi} are nonnegative definite.

Because the covariance matrices, Δ_{ai}, Γ_{0i}, Ω_{ui}, and Σ_{yi} are symmetric nonnegative definite matrices, they have the factorizations

$$\Delta_{ai} = W_{ai}W_{ai}', \Gamma_{0i} = W_{0i}W_{0i}', \Omega_{ui} = W_{ui}W_{ui}' \text{ and } \Sigma_{yi} = D_{xi}W_{ui}W_{ui}'D_{xi}' \tag{24}$$

such that W_{ai}, W_{0i}, and W_{ui} are lower triangular matrices, where W_{ui} can be explicitly written in terms of Φ_i, W_{ai}, and W_{0i}, as Chang, Hallahan, and Swamy (1992, p. 45) have done.

The unknown parameters of model (21) consist of the unknown elements of Π_i, the diagonal elements of Φ_i, σ_{ai}^2, and the diagonal and above-diagonal elements of Δ_{ai}. If the ratio of T to the number of these unknown parameters is not large, then it may not be possible to obtain precise and unique estimates of all the unknown parameters. The T equations of model (21) can be written compactly as

$$y_i = X_{zi}\pi_i + D_{xi}u_i \; (i = 1, \ldots, n) \tag{25}$$

where X_{zi} is $T \times Kp$ having $(z_{it}' \otimes x_{it}')$ as its tth row, $\pi_i = vec(\Pi_i)$ is $Kp \times 1$, and u_i is $TK \times 1$.

Generalized least squares estimation of π_i and u_i: The generalized least squares (GLS) estimator of π_i is

$$\hat{\pi}_i = \left(X_{zi}'\Sigma_{yi}^{-1}X_{zi}\right)^{-1} X_{zi}'\Sigma_{yi}^{-1}y_i \tag{26}$$

where the regular inverses of Σ_{yi} and $X_{zi}'\Sigma_{yi}^{-1}X_{zi}$ can be changed to the appropriate generalized inverses whenever the former inverses do not exist (see Chang et al., 1992).

Under the assumption that $E(D_{xi}u_i | x_i, z_i) = 0$, $\hat{\pi}_i$ is the minimum variance linear unbiased estimator of π_i. The covariance matrix of $\hat{\pi}_i$ is

$$\sigma_{ai}^2 \left(X_{zi}'\Sigma_{yi}^{-1}X_{zi}\right)^{-1} \tag{27}$$

Swamy and Mehta (1975b, p. 595) showed that the minimum variance linear unbiased predictor of u_i is

$$\hat{u}_i = \Omega_{ui} D'_{xi} \Sigma_{yi}^{-1} (y_i - X_{zi} \hat{\pi}_i) \tag{28}$$

where the regular inverse of Σ_{yi} can be changed to an appropriate generalized inverse whenever the former inverse does not exist.[13]

Feasible generalized least squares estimation of π_i and u_i: The IRSGLS method of estimating π_i, based on the residual-based estimates of Φ_i, σ_{ai}^2, and Δ_{ai}, $i = 1, \ldots, n$, proceeds as follows: for each i, starting with the initial values $\Phi_i = 0$ and $\Delta_{ai} = \text{I}$, iteratively solve Eqs. (26) and (28) to find the estimates, $\hat{\pi}_i$ and $(\hat{\Phi}_i, \hat{\Delta}_{ai}, \hat{\sigma}_{ai}^2)$, until they are stabilized. In their studies, Chang et al. (1992), and Chang et al. (2000) accepted estimates of π_i, Φ_i, σ_{ai}^2, and Δ_{ai} obtained in the last iteration of this method, and so named it "an iteratively rescaled generalized least squares (IRSGLS) method." The purpose of iterating is to (i) eliminate the effects of the arbitrary initial values on the estimates of the unknown parameters, Π_i, Φ_i, σ_{ai}^2, and Δ_{ai}, obtained in the last iteration, and (ii) make consistent the estimators of all these parameters used in the last iteration. After estimating all these unknown parameters, the degrees of freedom that remain unused are positive if $T > Kp + K + 1 + K(K + 1)/2$.

Let the IRSGLS estimator of π_i be denoted as

$$\hat{\hat{\pi}}_i = \left(X'_{zi} \hat{\Sigma}_{yi}^{-1} X_{zi} \right)^{-1} X'_{zi} \hat{\Sigma}_{yi}^{-1} y_i \; (i = 1, \ldots, n) \tag{29}$$

where $\hat{\Sigma}_{yi}$ is obtained by using the IRSGLS estimates of Φ_i, σ_{ai}^2, and Δ_{ai} in place of their true values used in Σ_{yi}.

The approximate covariance matrix of $\hat{\hat{\pi}}_i$ is

$$\hat{\sigma}_{ai}^2 \left(X'_{zi} \hat{\Sigma}_{yi}^{-1} X_{zi} \right)^{-1} \tag{30}$$

Sampling properties of estimator (29): Under our admissibility condition for the coefficient drivers shown previously, x_{it} and u_{it} are conditionally independent, given z_{it} for all i and t. Independence permits us to make use of Cavanagh and Rothenberg's (1995) derivation with some modifications. These authors considered a linear regression model with nonunique coefficients and error term not dependent on D_{xi} in Eq. (25) and constructed for its coefficient vector the standardized arbitrary linear combinations of the elements of the vector of generalized and feasible generalized least squares estimators. To avoid all the problems that arise with nonuniqueness of the coefficients and error term in Cavanagh and Rothenberg's (1995) model, we replace their model by (25) and their standardized arbitrary linear combinations of the elements of vector generalized and feasible generalized least squares estimators

13. Rao (2003, p. 96) attributed predictor (28) to Henderson (1950).

with $A = c'(\hat{\pi}_i - \pi_i)/\left[c'\sigma_{ai}^2\left(X_{zi}'\Sigma_{yi}^{-1}X_{zi}\right)^{-1}c\right]^{1/2}$ and $\hat{A} = c'\left(\hat{\hat{\pi}}_i - \pi_i\right)/\left[c'\sigma_{ai}^2\left(X_{zi}'\Sigma_{yi}^{-1}X_{zi}\right)^{-1}c\right]^{1/2}$, where $\boldsymbol{c}$ is a $Kp \times 1$ vector of arbitrary constants, respectively. Their method gives us the $o(T^{-1})$ approximation to the difference between the distributions of $\hat{A}$ and A. Earlier, Swamy, Tavlas, Hall, and Hondroyiannis (2010, pp. 18–20) extended Cavanagh and Rothenberg's method to model (25) for a single individual i by setting the υ_{jit}^*, $j = 1, \ldots, K - 1$, equal to zero and examining the $o(T^{-1})$ approximation to the difference between the distributions of $\hat{A}$ and A. This study gives conditions under which $\hat{A}$ and A have the same mean, skewness, and kurtosis. To present these conditions, we introduce the following notation.

Let θ_i be a vector containing the unknown distinct elements of $(\Phi_i, \Delta_{ai}, \sigma_{ai}^2)$ (for the ith individual), and let $\hat{\theta}_i$ be a vector containing the distinct, nonzero elements of $(\hat{\Phi}_i, \hat{\Delta}_{ai}, \hat{\sigma}_{ai}^2)$. The elements of $\hat{\theta}_i$ are written in the same order as those of θ_i. Because these elements are obtained from the residuals $D_{xi}\hat{u}_i = y_i - X_{zi}\hat{\hat{\pi}}_i$, following Cavanagh and Rothenberg (1995), we call $\hat{\theta}_i$ "the residual-based estimator" of θ_i. Suppose that $\hat{\theta}_i$ is a consistent estimator of θ_i satisfying the conditions under which $d = \sqrt{T}\left(\hat{\theta}_i - \theta_i\right)$ converges in law to a normal distribution uniformly on compact intervals of θ_i.[14] We assume that the vector $\boldsymbol{b} = \partial\hat{A}/\partial\hat{\theta}_i\big|_{\hat{\theta}_i=\theta_i}$ and the matrix $C = \frac{1}{2}\partial^2\hat{A}/\partial\hat{\theta}_i\partial\hat{\theta}_i'\Big|_{\hat{\theta}_i=\theta_i}$ are stochastically bounded as $T \to \infty$. Cavanagh and Rothenberg (1995, p. 279) use the matrix symbol Σ_{bd} and the vector symbol σ_{Ad} to denote the asymptotic covariance matrix for the vectors $\boldsymbol{b}$ and d and the asymptotic covariance between A and d, respectively.

Our conjecture is that the following propositions follow from Cavanagh and Rothenberg's (1995) results:

(i) The variable A is asymptotically independent of $\boldsymbol{b}$ and C.

(ii) Based on moments of the $o(T^{-1})$ Edgeworth approximation to the distributions, (a) the skewness of $\hat{A}$ is always the same as that of A; (b) if $\Sigma_{bd} = 0$, then the mean of $\hat{A}$ is the same as that of A; (c) if $\sigma_{Ad} = 0$, then the kurtosis of $\hat{A}$ is the same as that of A.

(iii) To a second order of approximation, the difference in location and shape between the $\hat{\pi}_i$ and $\hat{\hat{\pi}}_i$ distributions depends only on the asymptotic covariances σ_{Ad} and Σ_{bd}.

(iv) If d is asymptotically independent of A and $\boldsymbol{b}$, then $\hat{\pi}_i$ and $\hat{\hat{\pi}}_i$ have approximate distributions differing only in covariance matrix.

---

14. The definition of uniform convergence is given in Lehmann (1999, pp. 93-97).

For $j = 1, \ldots, K-1$, an estimate of the intercept (π_{j0i}) of (14) is needed to estimate the bias-free component of the coefficient on the jth nonconstant regressor of (10) which, in turn, is needed to measure the causal effect of the regressor on y_{it}. Therefore, the sampling properties of the estimators in (29) of these intercepts are of interest. However, the sampling properties of the estimators in (29) of the coefficients $\pi_{jhi}, j = 1, \ldots, K-1$ and $h = 1, \ldots, p-1$ of (14) may not be of interest, since these coefficients appear in the estimators of omitted-regressor bias components ((16)(ii)) of the coefficients of (10). For $j = 1, \ldots, K-1$, when the regular inverses in (29) exist, the estimators in (29) of the intercepts of (14) are unbiased if $E(u_i|X_{zi}, z_{it}) = 0$, and the u_i's are normally distributed (see Swamy et al., 2014, pp. 219–223).

An estimator of $E\{(\hat{\hat{\pi}}_i - \pi_i)(\hat{\hat{\pi}}_i - \pi_i)'|x_{it}, z_{it}\}$ to the desired order of approximation when u_i is normal and $\Phi_i = 0$, is given in Swamy et al. (2014, pp. 223–225). In Appendix B, we provide the conditions under which estimator (29) is consistent.

The estimators of the components of the coefficients of (10) for the ith individual provided by estimator (29) are:

Estimator of the bias-free component of the coefficient γ_{jit} of (10):

$$\left(1 - \frac{\hat{\nu}^*_{jit}}{x_{jit}}\right)^{-1} \hat{\hat{\pi}}_{j0i}\ (j = 1, \ldots, K-1) \tag{31}$$

Estimator of the omitted-regressor bias component of the coefficient γ_{jit} of (10):

$$\left(1 - \frac{\hat{\nu}^*_{jit}}{x_{jit}}\right)^{-1} \left(\sum_{h=1}^{p-1} \hat{\hat{\pi}}_{jhi} z_{hit} + \hat{\hat{u}}_{jit}\right) (j = 1, \ldots, K-1) \tag{32}$$

In formulas (31) and (32), the $\hat{\hat{\pi}}$'s are the IRSGLS estimates given by (29), $\hat{\hat{u}}_{jit}$ is the feasible best linear unbiased predictor of u_{jit} involving the IRSGLS estimates of Φ_i, σ^2_{ai}, and Δ_{ai}, and $\hat{\nu}^*_{jit}$, which is our guess about ν^*_{jit}. The IRSGLS estimators are consistent under general conditions. The accuracy of the estimates given by (31) depends on the appropriateness and adequacy of the coefficient drivers included in (14) and on the accuracy of our guesses $\hat{\nu}^*_{jit}$ of the ν^*_{jit}.[15] We can establish the relevance of the coefficient drivers in (14) using economic theories. Thus, selected coefficient drivers and guessed $\hat{\nu}^*_{jit}$ used to obtain the estimates in (31) of bias-free components are inappropriate and ill-chosen if the signs and magnitudes of the estimates are implausible. A further guide is the prior based on theory. Another is comparison of the estimates in (31) with the estimates of these bias-free components obtained in other studies.

The vector $\hat{\hat{\pi}}_{0i} = \left(\hat{\hat{\pi}}_{10i}, \ldots, \hat{\hat{\pi}}_{K-1,0i}\right)$ is a subvector of the vector $\hat{\hat{\pi}}_i$ in (29). The $o(T^{-1})$ approximate distribution of $\hat{\hat{\pi}}_{0i}$, its approximate covariance matrix,

15. Accuracy refers to the size of deviations from the true value, ν^*_{jit}.

and the approximate distribution of the ratio of an element of $\hat{\hat{\pi}}_{0i}$ to its standard error can be found following the method of Cavanagh and Rothenberg (1995) in work that needs yet to be done. The matrix $\hat{\sigma}_{ai}^2\left(X_{zi}'\hat{\Sigma}_{yi}^{-1}X_{zi}\right)^{-1}$ can give a very crude approximation to the $o(T^{-1})$ approximation to the exact covariance matrix of $\hat{\hat{\pi}}_i$. According to Cavanagh and Rothenberg (1995), the distribution of $\hat{\hat{\pi}}_{0i}$ is not normal unless the distribution of u_i is normal.

t-Ratios: A rule followed by econometricians is to accept (or reject) the null hypothesis that a single slope coefficient in a regression model is equal to zero, if the *t*-ratio, defined as the ratio of the least squares estimate of the coefficient to its standard error, is less (or greater) than 2 in absolute value.[16] Theorem 1 proves that under Interpretation I of the error term in (3), this rule is incorrect. To remedy this situation, we use the model in (10) and (14), where extra information in the form of coefficient drivers is used and $(K-1)(p-1)$ degrees of freedom are spent in estimating omitted-regressor biases (see (32)). The ratio of the IRSGLS estimator of π_{j0i}, with $0 < j < K$, to its standard error given by the square root of the corresponding diagonal element of the matrix in (30) can be called a *t*-ratio.[17] To distinguish this *t* from its conventional counterpart, let our *t*-ratios be denoted by $Newt_j$, $j = 1, \ldots, K-1$. Under certain conditions, Cavanagh and Rothenberg's (1995, p. 287) method can be used to derive the $o(T^{-1})$ approximate distribution of $(Newt_j)$. They also provided the conditions under which $Newt_j$ is approximately distributed as Student's *t* with $T-Kp$ degrees of freedom. Under these conditions, if $|(Newt_j)| > t_{(1\text{-}\alpha/2),\ [T\text{-}Kp]}$, where $t_{(1\text{-}\alpha/2),\ [T\text{-}Kp]}$ is the $100(1-\alpha/2)$ percent critical value from the *t* distribution with $(T-Kp)$ degrees of freedom, then the null hypothesis that π_{j0i} is zero is rejected and the estimated π_{j0i} is said to be statistically significant (see Greene, 2012, p. 116).

If all the $(p-1)$ coefficient drivers are dropped from (21), then the estimate of the bias-free component of the coefficient on any included nonconstant regressor of (10) cannot be separated from that of the omitted-regressor bias component of the coefficient. Certain sentences in PS (Pratt & Schlaifer, 1984, p. 14) can be interpreted as implying that exclusion of a coefficient driver because its estimated coefficient is not statistically significant can make sense when one wants to predict y_{it}, given a naturally occurring x_{it}, but not when one wants to know how x_{it} affects y_{it}.

We say that model (15) performs well in explanation if, for $j = 1, \ldots, K-1$, (31) is an accurate estimate of the bias-free component of the coefficient on each of the included nonconstant regressors.

16. The definition of "*t*-ratio" is given in Greene (2012, p. 116).
17. We like to replace this definition with Cavanagh and Rothenberg (1995) definition of the *t*-ratio.

3.7.1 Prediction

Suppose that all the distinct nonzero elements of π_i, Φ_i, σ_{ai}^2, and Δ_{ai} are known. Then the problem of predicting a single drawing of the dependent variable y_{it}, given the vectors x_{it} and z_{it} for the prediction period, can be solved. The actual drawing for each $i = 1, \ldots, n$ and for the post-sample period $T + s$ will be

$$y_{i,T+s} = \left(z'_{i,T+s} \otimes x'_{i,T+s}\right)\pi_i + x'_{i,T+s}u_{i,T+s} \tag{33}$$

The criterion of minimum mean square error linear predictor is explained in Swamy and Tinsley (1980, p. 111). Using their derivation, we have

$$\hat{u}_{i,T+s} = \Phi_i^s \Omega'_{Tui} D'_{xi} \Sigma_{yi}^{-1}(y_i - X_{zi}\pi_i) \tag{34}$$

where $\hat{u}_{i,T+s}$ is the $K \times 1$ vector of the predictions of the errors in the coefficients of (17), Φ_i is the $K \times K$ diagonal matrix appearing in the autoregressive process of order 1 in (19), Ω_{Tui} is the $TK \times K$ matrix formed by the last K columns of Ω_{ui} in Eq. (22), Σ_{yi} is defined in Eq. (23), and y_i, X_{zi} and π_i are defined in Eq. (25).

The feasible error vector, denoted by $\hat{\hat{u}}_{i,T+s}$, is obtained by using the sample estimates of π_i, Φ_i, σ_{ai}^2, and Δ_{ai} in place of their true values used in $\hat{u}_{i,T+s}$. Similarly, the feasible minimum mean square error linear predictor, denoted by $\hat{\hat{y}}_{i,T+s}$, also is obtained by using $\hat{\hat{\pi}}_i$ and $\hat{\hat{u}}_{i,T+s}$ in place of π_i and $u_{i,T+s}$ used in Eq. (33), respectively. An estimator of $E\,[(\hat{\hat{y}}_{i,T+s} - y_{i,T+s})^2 | x_{it}, z_{it}]$ to the desired degree of approximation when u_i is normal is given in Swamy, Yaghi, Mehta, and Chang (2007, pp. 3388 and 3389).

Our practical experience with $\hat{\hat{y}}_{i,T+s}$ has taught us that the magnitude of the absolute relative forecast error $|(\hat{\hat{y}}_{i,T+s} - y_{i,T+s})/y_{i,T+s}|$ will be smaller if $\Phi_i \neq 0$ than if $\Phi_i = 0$. In some models, removing the coefficient drivers can decrease the absolute relative forecast error. This can happen if the chosen coefficient drivers are inappropriate, thus providing a further clue to the validity of their selection.

Omitted-regressor biases are rarely, if ever, constant. For this reason, constant coefficient models without coefficient drivers cannot perform as well in prediction as model (21) with appropriate coefficient drivers. Working with real data, Swamy et al. (2007) observed this result. The time-varying coefficient model in (10) without the equations in (14) for its coefficients can predict the out-of-sample values of its dependent variable better than model (21) in those cases where appropriate coefficient drivers are difficult to find. Making the coefficients of Eq. (14) also time-varying Yokum, Wildt, and Swamy (1998) conducted very informative simulation experiments and noted the following:

This paper addresses the problem of forecasting economic data generated by causal models exhibiting structural change. The structural change is represented by unexpected systematic coefficient shifts superimposed on random variation and is denoted as disjoint data structures. An extensive simulation compares four

> *app-roximate coefficient structures, including constant and stochastic, on their ability to discount six different structural shocks to the true coefficients and still maintain adequate forecast accuracy over multiple forecast horizons. The results indicate that stochastic first-order autoregressive coefficient structures, especially those represented by the Swamy-Tinsley estimation procedure, yield more accurate forecasts.*
>
> Yokum, Wildt, and Swamy (1998, p. 1)

The preceding conclusions extend to full panel data, because in any given panel data, one cross-sectional data set will be in each time period $t = 1, \ldots, T$.

3.8 Assumptions Appropriate to Cross-Sectional Data Sets Within a Given Panel Data Set

Reconsider (25): $y_i = X_{zi}\pi_i + D_{xi}u_i$ for individual i. Recall Assumption A3 about u_i. In Section 3.7, each individual is considered separately. We will change this treatment in this section. Suppose that i indexes micro units. Then the following assumption may be appropriate.

Assumption A4: For $i - 1, \ldots, n$, $\pi_i = \bar{\pi} + \eta_i$, where the vectors η_i for different i are independently distributed with mean vector 0 and covariance matrix Δ.

This assumption, first proposed by Zellner (1969) and later adopted by Swamy (1970, 1971, 1974), Feige and Swamy (1974), Swamy and Mehta (1975b), and Swamy et al. (2007), states that the coefficient vectors π_i, $i = 1, \ldots, n$, for different individuals are independent drawings from the same multivariate distribution.[18] As Zellner (see Swamy, 1971, p. 18) pointed out, Assumption A4 stands between the limiting assumptions that the π_i's are fixed and the same, and that the π_i's are fixed and different. Given that micro units are possibly different in their behavior, the former assumption is often found to be restrictive, although the latter assumption requires the use of many parameters and therefore is not always satisfactory or even feasible in the analysis of panel data pertaining to many individuals.

Assumption A4 permits us to write Eq. (25) as

$$y_i = X_{zi}\bar{\pi} + X_{zi}\eta_i + D_{xi}u_i \; (i = 1, \ldots, n) \tag{35}$$

Stacking these equations gives

$$y = X_z\bar{\pi} + D_{Xz}\eta + D_{Dx}u \tag{36}$$

where $y = (y_1', \ldots, y_n')'$ is $nT \times 1$, y_i, $i = 1, \ldots, n$, are as defined in Eq. (25), $X_z = (X_{z1}', \ldots, X_{zn}')'$ is $nT \times Kp$, X_{zi}, $i = 1, \ldots, n$, are as defined in Eq. (25), $\bar{\pi}$ is $Kp \times 1$, $D_{Xz} = \text{diag}(X_{z1}, \ldots, X_{zn})$ is $nT \times nKp$, X_{zi}, $i = 1, \ldots, n$, are as defined in Eq. (25), $\eta = (\eta_1', \ldots, \eta_n')'$ is $nKp \times 1$, η_i is $Kp \times 1$, it is as defined in Eq. (35), $D_{Dx} = \text{diag}(D_{x1}, \ldots, D_{xn})'$ is $nT \times nTK$, D_{xi}, $i = 1, \ldots, n$, are as defined in (25), $u = (u_1{}', \ldots, u_n{}')'$ is $nTK \times 1$, and u_i, $i = 1, \ldots, n$ are as defined in Eq. (25).[19]

---

18. Hildreth and Houck (1968) did not consider panel data (see Swamy, 1971, pp. 10–11).

19. Model (36) removes all the defects of Swamy's (1970, 1971, 1974) model for panel data. The defects of this model arise as a direct consequence of the nonuniqueness of its coefficients and error term.

Assumption A5: (i) The vector η_i is independent of u_i for all i. (ii) The u_i, $i = 1$, ..., n, are independently distributed with the same mean vector 0, and the covariance matrix of u_i is given in Eq. (22).

Comparison of Model (35) with Lehmann and Casella's (1998, p. 253) *Hierarchical Bayes model:* In specifying the hierarchical Bayes model, Lehmann and Casella (1998, p. 253) (LC hereafter) were not at all concerned with omitted-regressor and measurement-error biases. Model (35), involving such biases, is derived from Eqs. (7)–(16). Of these, Eq. (9), derived from Eqs. (7) and (8), has unique coefficients and error term, so LC (1998, p. 176) are not able to achieve uniqueness of coefficients and the error term in their normal linear model. Eq. (10) expresses Eq. (9) in terms of observed variables. The equations in (14) decompose the coefficients on the nonconstant regressors of (10) into their respective components, as in (16). Although (16) distinguishes between the bias-free component and the omitted-regressor and measurement-error bias components of the coefficient on each non-constant regressor of (10), LC's normal linear model does not. To make the mean of the error term of (9) nonzero, this error term is made to be related to the coefficient drivers in (14). LC's normal linear model has an error term with mean zero, but like all models with nonunique coefficients and error terms described in Section 2, LC's hierarchical Bayes model is bound to provide incorrect inferences.

Under Assumptions A3–A5, $E[(D_{Xz}\eta + D_{Dx}u)|X_z] = 0$ and the covariance matrix of the error term of Eq. (36) is

$$\begin{aligned}\Sigma_y &= E\left[(D_{Xz}\eta + D_{Dx}u)(D_{Xz}\eta + D_{Dx}u)' | X_z\right] \\ &= D_{Xz}(\mathrm{I}_n \otimes \Delta)D'_{Xz} + D_{Dx}\Omega D'_{Dx}\end{aligned} \tag{37}$$

where $\Omega = \mathrm{diag}[\sigma_{a1}^2\Omega_{u1}, \ldots, \sigma_{an}^2\Omega_{un}]$ and $\sigma_{ai}^2\Omega_{ui}$ is as shown in Eq. (22).

Generalized least squares estimation of $\bar{\pi}$, η, and u: The generalized least squares estimator of $\bar{\pi}$ is

$$\hat{\bar{\pi}} = \left(X_z'\Sigma_y^{-1}X_z\right)^{-1}X_z'\Sigma_y^{-1}y \tag{38}$$

and its covariance matrix is

$$\left(X_z'\Sigma_y^{-1}X_z\right)^{-1} \tag{39}$$

Following derivations in Swamy (1974, pp. 163) and Swamy and Tinsley (1980), the minimum variance linear unbiased predictors of η and u are[20]

$$\begin{pmatrix}\hat{\eta}\\ \hat{u}\end{pmatrix} = \begin{bmatrix}(\mathrm{I}_n \otimes \Delta) & 0\\ 0 & \Omega\end{bmatrix}\begin{pmatrix}D'_{Xz}\\ D'_{Dx}\end{pmatrix}\Sigma_y^{-1}\left(y - X_z\hat{\bar{\pi}}\right) \tag{40}$$

20. The formula in (40) corrects an error in a formula given in Swamy & Mehta (1975b, p. 600, (3.7)).

Estimation of Δ*:* In Section 3.7, we discussed estimation of all the unknown parameters involved in Ω. The only matrix that remains is Δ, the estimator of which we now present. That estimator (38) can be written as

$$\hat{\bar{\pi}} = \left[\sum_{i=1}^{n} X'_{zi}\left(X_{zi}\Delta X'_{zi} + D_{xi}\sigma_{ai}^2\Omega_{ui}D'_{xi}\right)^{-1}X_{zi}\right]^{-1} \times \left[\sum_{i=1}^{n} X'_{zi}\left(X_{zi}\Delta X'_{zi} + D_{xi}\sigma_{ai}^2\Omega_{ui}D'_{xi}\right)^{-1}y_i\right] \quad (41)$$

which can be given another more convenient form via a matrix identity in Rao (1973, p. 33, Problem 29). Application of this identity to $(X_{zi}\Delta X_{zi}{}' + D_{xi}\sigma_{ai}^2\Omega_{ui}D_{xi}{}')^{-1}$ gives

$$\begin{aligned}
&\left(\sigma_{ai}^2 D_{xi}\Omega_{ui}D'_{xi} + X_{zi}\Delta X'_{zi}\right)^{-1} = \left(\sigma_{ai}^2 D_{xi}\Omega_{ui}D'_{xi}\right)^{-1} - \\
&\left(\sigma_{ai}^2 D_{xi}\Omega_{ui}D'_{xi}\right)^{-1}X_{zi}\left[X'_{zi}\left(\sigma_{ai}^2 D_{xi}\Omega_{ui}D'_{xi}\right)^{-1}X_{zi}\right]^{-1}X'_{zi}\left(\sigma_{ai}^2 D_{xi}\Omega_{ui}D'_{xi}\right)^{-1} + \\
&\left(\sigma_{ai}^2 D_{xi}\Omega_{ui}D'_{xi}\right)^{-1}X_{zi}\left[X'_{zi}\left(\sigma_{ai}^2 D_{xi}\Omega_{ui}D'_{xi}\right)^{-1}X_{zi}\right]^{-1}\left\{\left[X'_{zi}\left(\sigma_{ai}^2 D_{xi}\Omega_{ui}D'_{xi}\right)^{-1}X_{zi}\right]^{-1} + \Delta\right\}^{-1} \times \\
&\qquad\left[X'_{zi}\left(\sigma_{ai}^2 D_{xi}\Omega_{ui}D'_{xi}\right)^{-1}X_{zi}\right]^{-1}X'_{zi}\left(\sigma_{ai}^2 D_{xi}\Omega_{ui}D'_{xi}\right)^{-1}
\end{aligned} \quad (42)$$

Inserting the right-hand side of Eq. (42) for its left-hand side in Eq. (41) gives

$$\begin{aligned}
\hat{\bar{\pi}} = &\left(\sum_{i=1}^{n}\left\{\left[X'_{zi}\left(\sigma_{ai}^2 D_{xi}\Omega_{ui}D'_{xi}\right)^{-1}X_{zi}\right]^{-1} + \Delta\right\}^{-1}\right)^{-1}\sum_{i=1}^{n}\left\{\left[X'_{zi}\left(\sigma_{ai}^2 D_{xi}\Omega_{ui}D'_{xi}\right)^{-1}X_{zi}\right]^{-1} + \Delta\right\}^{-1} \\
&\times\left[X'_{zi}\left(D_{xi}\Omega_{ui}D'_{xi}\right)^{-1}X_{zi}\right]^{-1}X'_{zi}\left(D_{xi}\Omega_{ui}D'_{xi}\right)^{-1}y_i
\end{aligned} \quad (43)$$

This estimator $\hat{\bar{\pi}}$ is a matrix-weighted average of the estimators, $\hat{\pi}_i = [X'_{zi}(D_{xi}\Omega_{ui}D'_{xi})^{-1}X_{zi}]^{-1}X'_{zi}(D_{xi}\Omega_{ui}D'_{xi})^{-1}y_i$, $i = 1, \ldots, n$, the weight of $\hat{\pi}_i$ being equal to

$$\left(\sum_{i=1}^{n}\left\{\left[X'_{zi}(\sigma_{ai}^2 D_{xi}\Omega_{ui}D'_{xi})^{-1}X_{zi}\right]^{-1} + \Delta\right\}^{-1}\right)^{-1}\left\{\left[X'_{zi}(\sigma_{ai}^2 D_{xi}\Omega_{ui}D'_{xi})^{-1}X_{zi}\right]^{-1} + \Delta\right\}^{-1} \quad (44)$$

The estimator $\hat{\pi}_i$ here is the same as (26), with prediction error

$$\hat{\pi}_i - \pi_i = \left(X'_{zi}\Sigma_{yi}^{-1}X_{zi}\right)^{-1}X'_{zi}\Sigma_{yi}^{-1}D_{xi}u_i \quad (45)$$

This error is a linear function of u_i involving the unknown covariance matrix, $\sigma_{ai}^2\Omega_{ui}$. Now define

$$S_{\hat{\pi}} = \sum_{i=1}^{n} \hat{\pi}_i \hat{\pi}_i' - \frac{1}{n} \sum_{i=1}^{n} \hat{\pi}_i \sum_{i=1}^{n} \hat{\pi}_i' \tag{46}$$

where $\frac{S_{\hat{\pi}}}{n-1}$ is the sample covariance matrix of the $\hat{\pi}_i$. We justify this label by treating, $\hat{\pi}_i$, $i = 1 \ldots n$, as a random sample of size n, $\hat{\pi}_i$ being the ith draw. The matrix $S_{\hat{\pi}}$ is nonsingular if $n > Kp$.

Taking expectations on both sides of Eq. (46) gives

$$\begin{aligned} ES_{\hat{\pi}} &= n(\Delta + \bar{\pi}\bar{\pi}') + \sum_{i=1}^{n} \sigma_{ai}^2 \left(X_{zi}' \Sigma_{yi}^{-1} X_{zi}\right)^{-1} - (\Delta + \bar{\pi}\bar{\pi}') - (n-1)\bar{\pi}\bar{\pi}' \\ &\quad - \frac{1}{n} \sum_{i=1}^{n} \sigma_{ai}^2 \left(X_{zi}' \Sigma_{yi}^{-1} X_{zi}\right)^{-1} \\ &= (n-1)\Delta + \frac{(n-1)}{n} \sum_{i=1}^{n} \sigma_{ai}^2 \left(X_{zi}' \Sigma_{yi}^{-1} X_{zi}\right)^{-1} \end{aligned}$$

$$\hat{\Delta} = \frac{S_{\hat{\pi}}}{n-1} - \frac{1}{n} \sum_{i=1}^{n} \sigma_{ai}^2 \left(X_{zi}' \Sigma_{yi}^{-1} X_{zi}\right)^{-1} \tag{47}$$

An operational version of this estimator is

$$\hat{\hat{\Delta}} = \frac{\hat{S}_{\hat{\pi}}}{n-1} - \frac{1}{n} \sum_{i=1}^{n} \hat{\sigma}_{ai}^2 \left(X_{zi}' \hat{\Sigma}_{yi}^{-1} X_{zi}\right)^{-1} \tag{48}$$

where $\hat{S}_{\hat{\pi}} = \sum_{i=1}^{n} \hat{\hat{\pi}}_i \hat{\hat{\pi}}'_i - \frac{1}{n} \sum_{i=1}^{n} \hat{\hat{\pi}}_i \sum_{i=1}^{n} \hat{\hat{\pi}}'_i$.

Here $\hat{\hat{\pi}}_i$ is defined in Eq. (29), and the estimators $\hat{\Sigma}_{yi}$ and $\hat{\sigma}_{ai}^2$ are defined using the methods of Chang et al. (1992).

The estimator (48), however, can create a problem in that, in small samples, some or all of the diagonal elements of $\hat{\hat{\Delta}}$ can turn out to be negative, even though $n > Kp$ and the estimand Δ is known to be nonnegative definite. Therefore, $\hat{\hat{\Delta}}$ is an inadmissible estimator of Δ against any loss function for which the risk function exists (see Lehmann & Casella, 1998, p. 323). The difficulty can be avoided by replacing $\hat{\hat{\Delta}}$ by a nonnegative definite matrix, denoted by B, that is closest to $\hat{\hat{\Delta}}$ in the sense that the Euclidean norm of $\hat{\hat{\Delta}} - B$ is smallest, i.e., $\inf_B \|\hat{\hat{\Delta}} - B\|$ (see Rao, 1973, p. 63, 1f.2 (v)). Let $\lambda_1 \geq \cdots \geq \lambda_{Kp}$ be the eigenvalues of $\hat{\hat{\Delta}}$, and let P_1, … , P_{Kp} be the corresponding eigenvectors. Suppose that $m\,(<Kp)$ eigenvalues of $\hat{\hat{\Delta}}$ are nonnegative and the remaining are negative. Then the nonnegative definite matrix $B = \lambda_1 P_1 P_1{}' + \cdots + \lambda_m P_m P'_m$ provides the closest fit to $\hat{\hat{\Delta}}$.

$$\textit{IRSGLS nonnegative definite estimator of } \Delta : B \tag{49}$$

The efficiency of B exceeds that of $\hat{\hat{\Delta}}$ because the former estimator is obtained by putting the correct constraint of nonnegative definiteness on the latter estimator. A proof of the consistency of $\hat{\hat{\Delta}}$ can be constructed, as in Swamy (1971, p. 117).

Under conditions set out by Swamy (1971, p. 117), the problem of negative diagonal elements of $\hat{\hat{\Delta}}$ disappears for large T because the second term on the right-hand side of Eq. (48) converges in probability to the null matrix as $T \to \infty$. If for a small T, all the diagonal elements of $\hat{\Delta}$ are negative, then $\hat{\Delta}$ without its second term on the right-hand side of Eq. (48) can be used. Under this modification, $\hat{\hat{\Delta}}$ is still consistent.

Feasible Generalized Least Squares Estimation of $\bar{\pi}$*:* Turning to $\bar{\pi}$, its IRSGLS estimator is

$$\hat{\hat{\bar{\pi}}} = \left(X_z'\hat{\Sigma}_y^{-1}X_z\right)^{-1}X_z'\hat{\Sigma}_y^{-1}y \tag{50}$$

where the IRSGLS estimates of Δ, Φ_i, and $\sigma_{ai}^2\Delta_{ai}$, $i = 1, \ldots, n$, replace their respective true values used in $\Sigma_y = D_{Xz}(\mathrm{I}_n \otimes \Delta)D_{Xz}' + D_{Dx}\Omega D_{Dx}'$ (see Eq. (37)).[21]

We note the following properties of the estimator $\hat{\hat{\bar{\pi}}}$: (1) It gives the estimates of the means of the coefficients of all equations in (14). (2) A subvector of $\hat{\hat{\bar{\pi}}}$ that is of interest is $\hat{\hat{\bar{\pi}}}_0 = \left(\hat{\hat{\bar{\pi}}}_{10}, \cdots, \hat{\hat{\bar{\pi}}}_{K-1,0}\right)'$. This subvector gives the estimates of the means of the intercepts of all equations in (14). (3) The distribution of $\hat{\hat{\bar{\pi}}}$ to order $o((\mathrm{nT})^{-1})$ and its approximate covariance matrix can be found by extending the method of Cavanagh and Rothenberg (1995, p. 279). (4) The matrix $(X_z'\Sigma_y^{-1}X_z)^{-1}$ with Σ_y replaced by its sample estimate $\hat{\Sigma}_y^{-1}$, developed earlier, can give a crude approximation to the $o((nT)^{-1})$ approximation to the exact covariance matrix of $\hat{\hat{\bar{\pi}}}$. (5) Based on results in Cavanagh and Rothenberg (1995), one may guess that the distribution of $\hat{\hat{\bar{\pi}}}$ is not normal, unless the distributions of η and u are normal. Their derivation can be extended to find all the properties of $\hat{\hat{\bar{\pi}}}$ implied by its first four moments.

From the estimator $\hat{\hat{\bar{\pi}}}$ we obtain the following estimators:

Average value of the bias-free component of the coefficient γ_{jit} *with* $j > 0$ *of model (10):*

$$\frac{1}{nT}\sum_{i=1}^{n}\sum_{t=1}^{T}\left[1 - \frac{\hat{\nu}_{jit}^*}{x_{jit}}\right]^{-1}\hat{\hat{\bar{\pi}}}_{j0}\ (j = 1, \ldots, K-1) \tag{51}$$

where $\hat{\hat{\bar{\pi}}}_{j0}$ is the $(j, 0)$ element of (50).

Average value of the omitted-regressor bias component of γ_{jit} *with* $j > 0$ *in model (10):*

21. Conditions for the consistency of $\hat{\hat{\bar{\pi}}}$ are given in Appendix B.

$$\frac{1}{nT}\sum_{i=1}^{n}\sum_{t=1}^{T}\left[1-\frac{\hat{\nu}_{jit}^{*}}{x_{jit}}\right]^{-1}\left(\sum_{h=1}^{p-1}\hat{\hat{\pi}}_{jh}z_{hit}+\hat{\hat{u}}_{jit}\right)(j=1,\ldots,K-1) \quad (52)$$

where $\hat{\hat{\pi}}_{jh}$ is the (j,h) element of (50), and $\hat{\hat{u}}_{jit}$ is the jth element of $\hat{\hat{u}}_{it}$ which is a subvector of the feasible version of $\hat{u}$ in Eq. (40).

We assert that model (10) performs well in explanation if, for $j = 1, \ldots, K-1$, (51) is an accurate estimate of the average bias-free component of model (10)'s jth coefficient.[22]

Two examples of cases when Assumptions A4 and A5(ii) are not satisfied: If i indexes countries, states, or regions, then Assumptions A4 and A5(ii) are not satisfied in the presence of spatial or cross-section dependence. To explore this contingency, we analyze model (25) under either kind of dependence using two models for panel data, where either spatial autocorrelation or a kind of cross-section dependence is present.

Example 1 *(Model of Spatial Autocorrelation):* Let i index regions or countries. Then effects of neighboring locations could spill over into each other resulting in clustering effects, as described in Greene (2012, pp. 352–354 and 390–391). To capture such effects, Greene worked with the following model:

$$y_{it} = x_{it}'\beta + \varepsilon_{it} + \mu_i \quad (53)$$

where the common μ_i is the unit (e.g., country) effect. The correlation across space is implied by the spatial autocorrelation model

$$\varepsilon_{it} = \varphi\sum_{j=1}^{n}W_{ij}\varepsilon_{jt} + \tau_t \quad (54)$$

where the scalar φ is the spatial autoregressive coefficient, the W_{ij}'s are contiguity weights that are assumed known, and τ_t is random time effect. It is further assumed that μ_i and τ_t have zero means, variances σ_μ^2 and σ_τ^2, and are independent across countries and of each other.

Greene (2012, p. 391) pointed out that φ has no natural residual-based estimator. Rao (2003, p. 86) pointed out that if i indexes neighborhoods, then a drawback of the model in (53) and (54) is that it depends on how neighborhoods are defined. Upon addition of a normality assumption, the unknown parameters of Eqs. (53) and (54) are estimated using the method of maximum likelihood. Because of its heavy computational burden for large n, a generalized method of moments estimation was developed for the model in (53) and (54).

However, there remains a basic nonuniqueness of the coefficient vector β and the error components ε_{it} and μ_i resulting from the discrepancies $x_{it}'\beta \neq (\alpha_{0it}^{*} + \sum_{j=1}^{K-1}x_{jit}\gamma_{jit})$ and $(\varepsilon_{it} + \mu_i) \neq (\nu_{0it}^{*} + \sum_{\ell=1}^{L_{it}}\lambda_{\ell 0it}^{*}\omega_{\ell it}^{*})$, between model (10) and the model in (53) with all the undesirable implications discussed in

22. Accuracy refers to the size of deviations from the true average bias-free component.

Section 2. The complexity of model in (53) and (54) becomes unmanageable if μ_i is dropped, and the restrictive assumption that β is fixed and does not vary across individuals is changed to the assumption that β_i varies randomly across individuals. Thus, the interindividual heterogeneity reflected in random β_i's and spatial autocorrelation in (54) cannot be handled simultaneously. Further, the functional form of (53) may also be incorrect.

To remove nonuniqueness of the coefficients and error components of (53), we resort to the methodology advanced in this chapter by introducing cross-section dependence into model (21): $y_{it} = (z_{it}' \otimes x_{it}')vec(\Pi_i) + x_{it}' u_{it}$ because of its superior properties. This model has K error terms, whereas (53) has only one nonunique error term and one nonunique common unit effect, μ_i. We next use u_{it} to develop a vector spatial autocorrelation structure. Let (21) be written as

$$y_t = X_{zt}\pi + D_{xt}u_t \tag{55}$$

where $y_t = (y_{1t}, \ldots, y_{nt})'$ is $n \times 1$, X_{zt} is an $n \times Kp$ matrix having $(z_{it}' \otimes x_{it}')$ as its ith row, π is $vec(\Pi_i)$ which is restricted not to vary across individuals and is $Kp \times 1$, $D_{xt} = \text{diag}(x_{1t}', \ldots, x_{nt}')$ is $n \times nK$, $u_t = (u_{1t}', \ldots, u_{nt}')'$ is $nK \times 1$, and $u_{it} = (u_{0it}, \mathrm{u}_{1it}, \ldots, \mathrm{u}_{K-1,\,it})'$ is $K \times 1$.

For $j = 0, 1, \ldots, K-1$, let the jth element of u_{it}, denoted by u_{jit}, be equal to

$$u_{jit} = \rho_j \sum_{i'-1}^{n} W_{ii'} u_{ji't} + \mathrm{v}_{jt} \tag{56}$$

where ρ_j is the spatial autoregression coefficient and the elements $W_{ii'}$ are spatial (or contiguity) weights that are assumed known. Eq. (56) can be written as

$$u_{jt} = \rho_j W u_{jt} + \mathrm{v}_{jt}\iota \tag{57}$$

where $u_{jt} = (u_{j1t}, \ldots, u_{jnt})'$ is $n \times 1$, W is an $n \times n$ known spatial weight matrix that is symmetric, has zero diagonal elements, and is usually row-normalized, v_{jt} is a remainder effect that is assumed to be i.i.d. $(0, \sigma_{jj})$, and ι is an $n \times 1$ vector of 1's.

There are two methods of assigning values to the elements of W. In one method, the element $W_{ii'}$ will equal one for (i, i') pairs that are neighbors, and zero otherwise. In another method, $W_{ii'}$ can reflect distances across space, so that $W_{ii'}$ decreases with increases in $|i - i'|$. When $|\rho_j| < 1$ and the elements of W are such that $(\mathrm{I} - \rho_j W)$ is nonsingular, we can write $u_{jt} = (\mathrm{I} - \rho_j W)^{-1}\mathrm{v}_{jt}\iota$. For $i = 1, \ldots, n$ and $t = 1, \ldots, T$, the conditional covariance matrix of u_{jt} given z_{it} and x_{it}, is

$$(\mathrm{I} - \rho_j W)^{-1} [\sigma_{jj}\iota\iota'] (\mathrm{I} - \rho_j W)^{-1} \tag{58}$$

The conditional covariance matrix between u_{jt} and $u_{j't}$, given z_{it} and x_{it}, is

$$(\mathrm{I} - \rho_j W)^{-1} [\sigma_{jj'}\iota\iota'] (\mathrm{I} - \rho_{j'} W)^{-1} \tag{59}$$

Let $u_t = (u'_{0t}, u'_{1t}, \ldots, u'_{K-1,t})'$ where $u_{jt}, j = 0, 1, \ldots, K-1$, are given in (57). Let Ω_{ut} denote the covariance matrix of u_t. The jth diagonal block of Ω_{ut} is given in (58) and (j, j') above the diagonal block of Ω_{ut} is given in (59). The dimension of Ω_{ut} is $nK \times nK$.

In (55) and (56), we have a model with spatially correlated disturbances, derived from model (9), which has unique coefficients and error term. The task before us is to determine the best feasible method of estimating the parameters of the model in (55), (58), and (59). A disconcerting result is that when Assumption A5(ii) is not satisfied, model (56) cannot be estimated without restricting the coefficient vector π of model (55) to be individual-invariant, a restriction not imposed on the coefficient vectors of models (25) and (36). In the model in (55) and (56), interindividual heterogeneity is assumed away.

Example 2 (Pesaran's (2007) *Simple dynamic panel with cross-section dependence*)*:* Let

$$y_{it} = (1 - \phi_i)\mu_i + \phi_i y_{i,t-1} + u_{it} \tag{60}$$

where Pesaran assumed that the initial value y_{i0} has a given density function with a finite mean and variance, and the error term u_{it} has the single-factor structure

$$u_{it} = \gamma_i f_t + \varepsilon_{it} \tag{61}$$

where the symbol f_t is the unobserved common effect, and ε_{it} is the individual-specific (idiosyncratic) error. It is the common factor f_t that produces cross-section dependence. Using the model in (60) and (61), Pesaran (2007) conducted the unit-root test of the hypothesis $\phi_i = 1$. Again, the differences $(1 - \phi_i)\mu_i + \phi_i y_{i,\, t-1} \neq (\alpha^*_{0it} + \sum_{j=1}^{K-1} x_{jit}\gamma_{jit})$ and $u_{it} \neq (\nu^*_{0it} + \sum_{\ell=1}^{L_{it}} \lambda^*_{\ell 0it}\omega^*_{\ell it})$ between the model in (60) and (61) and model (10) imply nonuniqueness of the coefficients and error term of the former model. As in the preceding example, we conjecture that this nonuniqueness can seriously affect the consistency properties of Pesaran's unit-root test.

4 Bayesian Analysis of Panel Data

Recall that the covariance matrix Σ_y in (37) depends on (i) the unknown elements of the $K \times K$ diagonal matrices Φ_i, $i = 1, \ldots, n$, (ii) the unknown scalar variances σ^2_{ai}, $i = 1, \ldots, n$, (iii) the unknown distinct elements of the $K \times K$ nonnegative definite matrices Δ_{ai}, $i = 1, \ldots, n$, and (iv) the unknown distinct elements of the $Kp \times Kp$ nonnegative definite matrix Δ. Thus, the number of unknown parameters on which Σ_y depends is $n[K + 1 + K(K + 1)/2] + Kp(Kp + 1)/2$. Even though this number depends on n, no incidental parameter problem arises if Assumptions A4 and A5 hold, as shown by Swamy (1971). To ease the computational burden, we can set $K = 2$, that is, model Eq. (10) as containing one intercept and a single included regressor. To begin, write all the unknown parameters on which Σ_y depends in the form of a vector, θ. Let the means of the intercepts of (14) needed to measure the causal effects of the non-constant regressors of (10) on its dependent variable be included in the vector $\bar{\pi}_0 = (\bar{\pi}_{10} \cdots \bar{\pi}_{K-1,0})'$ and the remaining elements of $\bar{\pi}$ be included in the vector, $\bar{\pi}_1$, so that $\bar{\pi} = (\bar{\pi}_0', \bar{\pi}_1')'$.

The elements of the vector $(\bar{\pi}_0', \bar{\pi}_1', \theta')'$ are fixed but unknown. It is knowledge about these unknowns that Bayesians model as random, using a method that, after careful reflection, considers all the possible alternatives in order to distribute among them in a way that will appear most appropriate, one's own expectations and perceptions of probability (see Swamy & Mehta, 1983). Such a method provides the prior probability density function (pdf) for $(\bar{\pi}_0', \bar{\pi}_1', \theta')'$. The prior distribution is improper if it has infinite mass. Use of Bayes' theorem shows that the posterior pdf for $(\bar{\pi}_0', \bar{\pi}_1', \theta')'$ is proportional to the product of the likelihood function of $(\bar{\pi}_0', \bar{\pi}_1', \theta')'$ and the prior pdf for $(\bar{\pi}_0', \bar{\pi}_1', \theta')'$. Therefore, we can write

$$p\left(\left(\bar{\pi}_0', \bar{\pi}_1', \theta'\right)' | y, X_z\right) \propto p\left(\left(\bar{\pi}_0', \bar{\pi}_1', \theta'\right)'\right) L\left(\left(\bar{\pi}_0', \bar{\pi}_1', \theta'\right)' | y, X_z\right) \quad (62)$$

where $p((\bar{\pi}_0', \bar{\pi}_1', \theta')'|y,X_z)$ is the posterior pdf for $(\bar{\pi}_0', \bar{\pi}_1', \theta')'$, $p((\bar{\pi}_0', \bar{\pi}_1', \theta')')$ is the prior pdf for $(\bar{\pi}_0', \bar{\pi}_1', \theta')'$, and $L((\bar{\pi}_0', \bar{\pi}_1', \theta')'|y,X_z)$ is the likelihood function, which is defined as the sample density $p(y|X_z, (\bar{\pi}_0', \bar{\pi}_1', \theta')')$ considered as a function of $(\bar{\pi}_0', \bar{\pi}_1', \theta')'$for fixed y and X_z.

The elements of the vector $\bar{\pi}_0$ are the parameters of interest. If the joint posterior density for $(\bar{\pi}_0', \bar{\pi}_1', \theta')'$ in (62) is proper, then the marginal posterior density for $\bar{\pi}_0$ can be obtained by integrating out $(\bar{\pi}_1', \theta')'$. In (62), the posterior density is proper if the prior density is proper. In some cases, the posterior density for an improper prior density is proper, but improper posterior densities are meaningless. A word of caution: In applying Bayesian analysis to (36), a case of misapplication of Bayes' theorem occurs when the likelihood function of a parameter vector, such as β, is multiplied by the unmatched prior pdf for $R\beta$, where $R \neq I$. This insight comes from Kashyap, Swamy, Mehta, and Porter (1988), who studied a case in which attempts to avoid this misapplication resulted in prior and posterior distributions of β that do not possess density functions.

Bayesians emphasize the importance of carefully assessing both the likelihood function and the prior pdf before inserting them into Bayes' formula (62). As statisticians are aware, however, likelihood functions adopted for such purposes are typically model based, which raises a concern because, generally, models cannot be completely trusted, especially if, as we proved, their coefficients and error terms are not unique. This would certainly be true if $L((\bar{\pi}_0', \bar{\pi}_1', \theta')'|y,X_z)$ were based on a model with nonunique coefficients and error term.[23] However, as we have indicated, $L((\bar{\pi}_0', \bar{\pi}_1', \theta')'|y,X_z)$ is based on models

23. Such a model can be written as $y_{it} = x_{it}'\beta_i + \varepsilon_{it}$ where $\beta_i = \beta + \Pi z_i + u_i$ and $\varepsilon_{it} = w_{it}'\omega_{it}$ and is called "a hierarchical linear model" in the econometrics literature (see Greene, 2012, p. 639). In Section 2, we showed that this model has nonunique coefficients and error term. Nevertheless, it is used in some estimation methods, including simulation-based estimation and inference (see Greene, 2012, p. 639–641).

(25) and (36), which are constructed carefully to be unique and therefore trustworthy. We note further that the function $L((\bar{\pi}_0', \bar{\pi}_1', \theta')'|y,X_z)$ is the result of simultaneous rather than two-step estimation in (16), (51), and (52), a choice made necessary because the coefficients on the nonconstant regressors of (10) contain more than one component. This choice is fortuitous because simultaneous estimation is, in principle, superior to two-step estimation.

Statisticians also like to assert that likelihood functions become less satisfactory as the number of parameters involved is raised and apply this criticism to the model in Eqs. (10) and (14). This would be mistaken, however, because after following all the steps in Eqs. (7)–(10), (14), (19), and (20), and applying Assumptions A4 and A5, it becomes evident that reducing the $n[K+1 + K(K+1)/2] + Kp + Kp(Kp+1)/2$ unknown parameters of the model in (36) to a smaller number would lead to serious specification errors and otherwise gain nothing.

If a proper prior pdf for $(\bar{\pi}_0', \bar{\pi}_1', \theta')'$ is available, then it should be used in place of $p((\bar{\pi}_0', \bar{\pi}_1', \theta')')$ in Eq. (62). If such a prior pdf is not available, then we should use only those improper prior pdf's for $(\bar{\pi}_0', \bar{\pi}_1', \theta')'$ that, when used in place of $p((\bar{\pi}_0', \bar{\pi}_1', \theta')')$ in Eq. (62), give the proper joint posterior distributions and consistent generalized Bayes estimators of $(\bar{\pi}_0', \bar{\pi}_1', \theta')'$.[24] Any generalized Bayes estimator is not a proper Bayes estimator, because it is obtained by using an improper prior distribution. It can be conditionally admissible, even though its average risk (Bayes risk) is infinite.[25] In general, the Bayes estimator of $\bar{\pi}_0$ under squared error loss is given by the mean of the marginal posterior distribution of $\bar{\pi}_0$. To avoid unacceptable posterior distributions, Swamy and Mehta (1973) used improper prior pdf's recommended by Stone and Springer (1965) in a Bayesian analysis of the random effects model in (1). In a pair of other studies in models with missing observations, Mehta and Swamy (1973) and Swamy and Mehta (1975a) used certain improper priors to get proper posterior pdf's.

Lindley (1971, p. 8) pointed out that within the framework of coherence, statements, such as "a prior distribution does not exist in this problem," is "demonstrably" not true. DeGroot (1970) pursued this framework and presented an axiomatic system for subjective probabilities originally due to Savage, including a proposal for a method of specifying a unique prior pdf using a uniform distribution. The importance of uniqueness was emphasized by Lehmann and Casella (1998. p. 323), who gave a proof of the admissibility of any unique Bayes estimator. Brown (1990) showed earlier that conditionally admissible estimators might be unconditionally inadmissible, meaning that they must be rejected in favor of estimators that are admissible both conditionally and unconditionally, provided the latter estimators are available. Finally, we stress PS' (Pratt & Schlaifer, 1988, p. 49) admonition regarding Bayesian analysis of a

24. The definitions of Bayes and generalized Bayes estimators are given in Lehmann and Casella (1998, pp. 228 and 239). The latter Bayes estimator is based on an improper prior pdf.
25. The definition of admissible estimators is given in Lehmann and Casella (1998, p. 48).

stochastic law: "... a Bayesian will do much better to search like a non-Bayesian for concomitants that absorb ... ['proxy effects' for excluded variables]." This is the intent behind Eq. (16)(ii), where the coefficient drivers included in (14) estimate omitted-regressor bias components of the coefficients of (10). With the exception of Pratt and Schlaifer (1984, 1988), statisticians have so far not managed to develop models with unique coefficients and error terms.

Lehmann and Casella (1998) pointed out that "it is not the case that all generalized Bayes estimators are admissible." (p. 383), so we should not use an improper prior pdf if it leads to an inadmissible generalized Bayes estimator of $(\bar{\pi}_0', \bar{\pi}_1', \theta')'$.[26] Consistency being a desirable property of estimators, Brown (1990) pointed out that "Ordinary notions of consistency demand use of procedures ... [that] are valid and admissible both conditionally and unconditionally" (p. 491).[27] He further pointed out that "estimators which are formally Bayes with respect to prior measures having infinite mass [otherwise known as improper prior distributions] may easily be conditionally admissible and yet unconditionally inadmissible" (p. 491). Lehmann and Casella (1998, p. 239) note that

> *From a Bayesian view, estimators that are limits of Bayes estimators are somewhat more desirable than generalized Bayes estimators. This is because, by construction, a limit of Bayes estimators must be close to a proper Bayes estimator. In contrast, a generalized Bayes estimator may not be close to any proper Bayes estimator.*[28]

Assumption A6: The conditional distribution of the dependent variable y in Eq. (36) is multivariate normal, given X_z, with mean $X_z\bar{\pi}$ and covariance matrix Σ_y defined in Eq. (37).

Under this assumption, the noninformative prior postulates are that $\bar{\pi}$, Δ, and Ω are independent with improper densities, $p(\bar{\pi}) \propto$ const, $p(\Delta) \propto |\Delta|^{-1/2}$ and the MDIP pdf for Ω, respectively. In this case, the posterior distribution of $(\bar{\pi}_0', \bar{\pi}_1', \theta')'$ in Eq. (62) is improper, so that the calculation of a posterior expectation is meaningless. Instead, let us consider the noninformative prior postulates that $\bar{\pi}$ and Σ_y are independent with improper densities $p(\bar{\pi}) \propto$ const and $p(\Sigma_y) \propto |\Sigma_y|^{-1/2}$, respectively. The posterior distribution of $(\bar{\pi}, \Sigma_y)$ is then proper. This posterior, however, is also not acceptable because the noninformative prior $p(\Sigma_y) \propto |\Sigma_y|^{-1/2}$ depends on the likelihood function, an outcome not generally acceptable to Bayesians.

---

26. Arnold Zellner, whose work included specifying carefully and appropriately selected improper prior distributions, is widely acknowledged as the father of Bayesian econometrics. In his early work, Zellner used Jeffreys' ideas to select improper prior pdf's, and in his later work, he created what are known as maximal data information prior (MDIP) pdf's (see Zellner, 1971, 1977), which, we emphasize, are also improper prior pdf's.

27. Note that this shows the connection between consistency and admissibility.

28. The definition of a limit of Bayes estimators is given in Lehmann and Casella (1998, p. 239).

4.1 Improvements in the Precisions of the Estimators of Time-Invariant and Individual-Specific Coefficients of the Stochastic Law

Our interest centers on the estimators in Eq. (31) because they are needed to estimate the causal effects of the nonconstant regressors of Eq. (10) on this equation's dependent variable. Since we assume that these effects are different for different individuals because of interindividual heterogeneity, the estimators in Eq. (51) provide only average causal effects for all n individuals. But there may not be much interest in these average effects. Therefore, we investigate whether there is any way the mean-square errors of the estimators in Eq. (29) can be reduced.

For $i = 1, \ldots, n$, an estimator of π_i is

$$\hat{\pi}_{i\mu} = \left(\frac{X_{zi}'\Sigma_{yi}^{-1}X_{zi}}{\sigma_{ai}^2} + \mu\Delta^{-1}\right)^{-1}\left(\frac{X_{zi}'\Sigma_{yi}^{-1}y_i}{\sigma_{ai}^2} + \mu\Delta^{-1}\bar{\pi}\right) \tag{63}$$

This estimator is obtained by minimizing the Lagrangean $(y_i - X_{zi}\pi_i)'\frac{\Sigma_{yi}^{-1}}{\sigma_{ai}^2}(y_i - X_{zi}\pi_i) + \mu\left[(\pi_i - \bar{\pi})'\Delta^{-1}(\pi_i - \bar{\pi}) - r^2\right]$ (see Swamy & Mehta, 1976) and Chang, Swamy, Hallahan, and Tavlas (2000, pp. 125 and 126)). Chang et al. (2000, p. 125) pointed out that estimator (63) can be used to estimate π_i, subject to certain equality and inequality restrictions. Estimator (63) is a biased estimator of π_i, and when $\mu = 1$, it is the minimum mean square error linear estimator of π_i, as shown by Chipman (1964, pp. 1104-1107), who attributed the estimator with $\mu = 1$ to Foster (1961).

Lehmann and Casella (1998) proved the admissibility of several estimators under a sum-of-squared-errors loss. This loss function is inappropriate for our purposes because an error of fixed size is much more serious for values of the sub-vector $\bar{\pi}_0$ of $\bar{\pi}$ than for values of its other sub-vector $\bar{\pi}_1$. Therefore, we proceed as follows: Swamy and Mehta (1977) proved that a necessary and sufficient condition for the second-order moment matrix $E(\hat{\pi}_i - \pi_i)(\hat{\pi}_i - \pi_i)'$ of estimator (26) around the true value of π_i to exceed the second-order moment matrix $E\left(\hat{\pi}_{i\mu} - \pi_i\right)\left(\hat{\pi}_{i\mu} - \pi_i\right)'$ of estimator (63) around the same true value by a positive semidefinite matrix is

$$(\pi_i - \bar{\pi})'\left\{\left(\frac{2}{\mu}\right)\Delta + \sigma_{ai}^2\left(X_{zi}'\Sigma_{yi}^{-1}X_{zi}\right)^{-1}\right\}^{-1}(\pi_i - \bar{\pi}) \le 1 \tag{64}$$

The importance of this result is that it gives a necessary and sufficient condition under which the superiority of the biased linear estimator in (63) over the minimum variance linear unbiased estimator in (26) will be reflected in any positive semidefinite weighted sum of mean square and mean product errors and also in the generalized mean square error, i.e.,

$$E\left(\hat{\pi}_{i\mu} - \pi_i\right)'\Psi\left(\hat{\pi}_{i\mu} - \pi_i\right) \le E(\hat{\pi}_i - \pi_i)'\Psi(\hat{\pi}_i - \pi_i) \text{ for all positive semidefinite } \Psi \tag{65}$$

and

$$|E(\hat{\pi}_{i\mu} - \pi_i)(\hat{\pi}_{i\mu} - \pi_i)'| \leq |E(\hat{\pi}_i - \pi_i)(\hat{\pi}_i - \pi_i)'| \quad (66)$$

where $\hat{\pi}_i$ is defined in (26).

If Δ is singular, then condition (64) can be satisfied, but (63) does not exist. In this case, using a formula in Swamy and Mehta (1976, p. 811), estimator (63) can be rewritten as

$$\hat{\pi}_{i\mu} = \Delta X'_{zi}(X_{zi}\Delta X'_{zi} + \sigma^2_{ai}\Sigma_{yi})^{-1} y_i + \left[I - \Delta X'_{zi}(X_{zi}\Delta X'_{zi} + \sigma^2_{ai}\Sigma_{yi})^{-1} X_{zi}\right]\bar{\pi} \quad (67)$$

which exists when Δ is singular.

The availability of the minimum mean square error estimator of π_i in (67) is important because its feasible form can provide more efficient estimators of the causal effects of the nonconstant regressors of (10) on its dependent variable than (31).

Computation of estimator (63) merely requires a priori values of ($\bar{\pi}$, Δ). In terms of prior information, estimator (63) is less demanding than Bayes' formula in (62) because, by examining the sample estimates given by (49) and (50) based on a previous sample, we can more easily formulate our prior beliefs about ($\bar{\pi}$, Δ) than about the prior pdf $p((\bar{\pi}'_0, \bar{\pi}'_1, \theta')')$. Swamy and Mehta (1979) considered the case where σ^2_{ai} and μ are sample estimates. For this case, they proposed a new estimator by introducing suitable constants at the appropriate places in estimator (63) and derived a necessary and sufficient condition for $E(\hat{\pi}_i - \pi_i)(\hat{\pi}_i - \pi_i)'$ of a much simpler version of (26) to exceed the second-order moment matrix about π_i of the new estimator by a positive semidefinite matrix. Swamy, Mehta, and Rappoport's (1978) methods of evaluating a ridge regression estimator can be extended to find methods of evaluating (63) using the available data.

4.1.1 A Complete Inference System

The preceding establishes that a complete system of inferences is composed of the following elements:

I. A model: Eqs. (10), (14).

IIA. Estimators of the bias-free components of the coefficients of the model: Eq. (31).

IIB. Improved estimators of the bias-free components of the coefficients of the model based on the estimators in (63).

IIC. Kernel density estimates using the point estimates and the improved point estimates of the bias-free components of the coefficients of the model.

III. Predictions of the out-of-sample values of the dependent variable of the model: Eqs. (33), (34).

4.2 Simulation-Based Estimation and Inference

In Section 2, we have demonstrated that models with nonunique coefficients and error terms, in other words, models that have typically been employed in the past for simulation-based estimation and inference, yield incorrect inferences. For his simulation-based estimation and inference, Greene (2012, p. 643) considered a sampling density based on a hierarchical model with nonunique coefficients and error term.[29] We modify this model to make its coefficients and error term unique, because models with nonunique coefficients and error terms yield incorrect results, as we have already shown.

From (21) and Assumption A3, it follows that conditional on (x_{it}, z_{it}, π_i), y_{it} has sampling density.

$$p\left(y_{it}\middle|\, x_{it}, z_{it}, \pi_i, \Phi_i, \sigma_{ai}^2 \Delta_{ai}\right) \tag{68}$$

and conditional on $\bar{\pi}$ and Δ, π_i has prior density $p(\pi_i|\bar{\pi},\Delta)$ for all i. This is a single prior Bayes model for each i. From this model, we calculate the posterior distribution, $p(\pi_i|y_i,X_{zi},\Phi_i,\sigma_{ai}^2\Delta_{ai},\bar{\pi},\Delta)$ for individual i. The virtue of the pdf in (68) comes from model (21) because the latter is derived from model (9) having unique coefficients and error term.

The joint pdf of y_i and π_i is

$$p\left(y_i, \pi_i\middle|\, X_{zi}, \Phi_i, \Delta_{ai}, \sigma_{ai}^2, \bar{\pi}, \Delta\right) = p\left(y_i\middle|\, X_{zi}, \pi_i, \Phi_i, \Delta_{ai}, \sigma_{ai}^2\right) p(\pi_i|\, \bar{\pi}, \Delta) \tag{69}$$

Suppose that Φ_i, Δ_{ai}, σ_{ai}^2, $\bar{\pi}$, and Δ are known. Then using Bayes' theorem gives

$$\begin{aligned} p\left(\pi_i\middle|\, y_i, X_{zi}, \Phi_i, \sigma_{ai}^2\Delta_{ai}, \bar{\pi}, \Delta\right) &= \frac{p\left(y_i\middle|\, X_{zi}, \pi_i, \Phi_i, \sigma_{ai}^2\Delta_{ai}\right) p(\pi_i|\, \bar{\pi}, \Delta)}{p\left(y_i\middle|\, X_{zi}, \Phi_i, \sigma_{ai}^2\Delta_{ai}, \bar{\pi}, \Delta\right)} \\ &= \frac{p\left(y_i\middle|\, X_{zi}, \pi_i, \Phi_i, \sigma_{ai}^2\Delta_{ai}\right) p(\pi_i|\, \bar{\pi}, \Delta)}{\int_{\pi_i} p\left(y_i, \pi_i\middle|\, X_{zi}, \Phi_i, \sigma_{ai}^2\Delta_{ai}, \bar{\pi}, \Delta\right) d\pi_i} \\ &= \frac{p\left(y_i\middle|\, X_{zi}, \pi_i, \Phi_i, \sigma_{ai}^2\Delta_{ai}\right) p(\pi_i|\, \bar{\pi}, \Delta)}{\int_{\pi_i} p\left(y_i\middle|\, X_{zi}, \pi_i, \Phi_i, \sigma_{ai}^2\Delta_{ai}\right) p(\pi_i|\, \bar{\pi}, \Delta) d\pi_i} \end{aligned} \tag{70}$$

where the pdf for π_i is used as the prior density. This is in contrast to (62), in which the distribution of π_i is used as part of the likelihood function. The advantage of Bayes' formula in (62) is that the sample data in (25) can be used to estimate $\bar{\pi}$ and Δ, as in (49) and (50).

29. See also Train (2003).

The Bayes estimator under squared error loss is given by

$$E\left(\pi_i \mid y_i, X_{zi}, \Phi_i, \sigma_{ai}^2\Delta_{ai}, \bar{\pi}, \Delta\right) = \frac{\int\limits_{\pi_i} \pi_i p\left(y_i \mid X_{zi}, \pi_i, \Phi_i, \sigma_{ai}^2\Delta_{ai}\right) p(\pi_i \mid \bar{\pi}, \Delta) d\pi_i}{\int\limits_{\pi_i} p\left(y_i \mid X_{zi}, \pi_i, \Phi_i, \sigma_{ai}^2\Delta_{ai}\right) p(\pi_i \mid \bar{\pi}, \Delta) d\pi_i} \tag{71}$$

Unfortunately, Greene's (2012, p. 644, (15–39)) equation cannot be used to compute the integral in Eq. (71), because the error term of Eq. (21) is both heteroscedastic and serially correlated. We need reasonably straightforward and general methods of evaluating the integral in Eq. (71) and, to this end, we consider using a theory based on Markov chain limiting behavior defined in Lehmann and Casella (1998, pp. 306–307). If this theory can be extended to make it applicable to the model with heteroscedastic serially correlated disturbances in Eq. (21), then we may use the extended theory to evaluate the integral in Eq. (71). If it cannot be extended, then we can use only the non-Bayesian estimators in Eqs. (29) and (31).

The estimators (29) and (71) are of the same π_i but are obtained using two different methods. The question then becomes: Which of the two do we choose? To decide this, consider the following: An inference based on Eq. (29) proceeds conditionally on X_{zi}, where potential difficulties in choosing a prior density in Eq. (69) are no serious impediment. By contrast, an inference based on the posterior pdf in Eq. (70) is more complex in that (i) it is appropriate only if the distribution of π_i is used as the prior, and proceeds conditionally (ii) on the T observations in (y_i and X_{zi}) available for the ith individual and (iii) on the values of the parameters $(\Phi_i, \sigma_{ai}^2\Delta_{ai}, \bar{\pi}, \Delta)$ which are assumed to be known. Because the parameters $(\Phi_i, \sigma_{ai}^2\Delta_{ai}, \bar{\pi}, \Delta)$ are not known, any inference based on Eq. (70) is heavily dependent on the accuracy of their non-Bayesian estimates. For estimator (29), the ease or difficulty of managing the unknown parameters $(\Phi_i, \sigma_{ai}^2\Delta_{ai})$ is intrinsic to the probabilistic structure of the particular problem with which we are dealing. Thus, although estimator (71) appears to cope easily with the unknown parameters that estimator (29) finds difficult, this benefit is earned at the expense of assuming away this obstacle in the form of a convenient integral in Eq. (71). Therefore, there is really not much advantage of Eq. (71) over Eq. (29). We now turn to an example.

5 Empirical Evidence of the Causal Effects of Wives' Education on Their Earnings

To illustrate the methods discussed in Sections 2 and 3, we use the following example of Eq. (10):

$$\text{earnings}_i = \gamma_{0i} + \gamma_{1i}\text{education}_i \tag{72}$$

where i indexes individuals, earnings$_i$ = the ith wife's earnings measured as hourly wage times hours worked, and education$_i$ = the ith wife's education measured in years of schooling. Because time-series data about these variables are not available for any i, Eq. (72) can be considered a special case of (10), where subscript t is suppressed, the dependent variable is replaced by the variable "earnings," K is set equal to 2, x_{1i} is replaced by the variable "education," and corresponding changes are made in (7)–(9) above. It then follows from (11) that γ_{0i} = [(measurement error in earnings$_i$) + (the intercept of (7)) +(the error term of (9))]. It further follows from (12) that γ_{1i} = [(Bias-Free Component (BFC) + omitted-regressor bias component)(1 – the proportion of measurement error in education$_i$)]. The BFC of γ_{1i} is needed to measure the causal effect of the ith wife's education on her earnings, as shown in (9) (see Property (5) of (9)). We assume that both earnings$_i$ and education$_i$ in (72) are measured with error. The variable education$_i$ is the sole regressor in (72) because we are interested in learning only the causal effect of education$_i$ on earnings$_i$. In the following, we provide an example of (14) to complete the specification of (72).

To estimate the BF and omitted-regressor bias components of γ_{1i} separately, we need to make γ_{0i} and γ_{1i} functions of appropriate coefficient drivers, as in (14). Before we do so, we examine three previous studies on the earnings-education relationship to determine if they contain any useful ideas about the coefficient drivers that we will need for our estimation. Also, we will attempt to find out to what extent the specification of model (72) can remedy apparent defects in extant models for earnings attainment and elite college attendance. Model (72) is most conveniently described in the context of earlier work, of which we give three examples.

Krueger and Dale's model:

$$\log(\text{earnings}) = x'\beta + \delta T + \varepsilon \tag{73}$$

where individual earnings are for a given time period, x is education in number of years, and T equals 1 for those who attended an elite college and is zero otherwise.

Mincer's Model:

$$\log(\text{earnings}) = a + bS + cx + dx^2 + \varepsilon \tag{74}$$

where S denotes years of completed education, and x denotes the number of years an individual of age A could have worked, assuming he or she started school at age 6, finished schooling in exactly S years and began working immediately thereafter: $x = A - S - 6$, and ε is an added random error term.

The sources of models (73) and (74) are Greene (2012, p. 251) and Card (1999), respectively. Card's paper surveyed a number of studies about the earnings and education relationship done before 1999. Finally, Greene offers three approaches of his own to modeling the effects of education on earnings:

Greene's Models:

(i) *Semi-log equation.*

$$\log(\text{earnings}) = \beta_1 + \beta_2\text{age} + \beta_3\text{age}^2 + \beta_4\text{education} + \beta_5\text{kids} + \varepsilon \tag{75}$$

where hourly wage times hours worked are used to measure "earnings," "education" is measured in years of schooling, and "kids" is a binary variable that equals one if there are children under 18 in the household.

(ii) *Exponential equation.*

$$\begin{aligned}\text{Income} = \exp(&\beta_1 + \beta_2\text{Age} + \beta_3\text{Age}^2 + \beta_4\text{Education} + \beta_5\text{Female} + \beta_6\text{Female} \times \text{Education} + \\ &\beta_7\text{Age} \times \text{Education}) + \varepsilon\end{aligned} \tag{76}$$

where two interaction terms are included as regressors.

(iii) *Discrete choice.*

$$\text{Prob}(LFP_i = 1) = \Phi(\beta_1 + \beta_2\text{Age}_i + \beta_3\text{Age}_i^2 + \beta_4\text{Education}_i + \beta_5\text{Kids}_i + \gamma\text{HHrs}_i) \tag{77}$$

where LFP_i denotes the ith wife's labor force participation, and $HHrs_i$ denotes the husband's hours defined as

$$\text{HHrs}_i = \alpha_1 + \alpha_2\text{HAge}_i + \alpha_3\text{HEducation}_i + \alpha_4\text{Family Income}_i + u_i \tag{78}$$

Greene (2012, pp. 14–15, 195 and 708) explains the selection of regressors in models (75)–(77) as follows: (i) Most people have higher incomes when they are older than when they are young, regardless of their education. This justifies the inclusion of age as a regressor in models (75)–(77). (ii) Income tends to rise less rapidly in the later earning years than in the early ones. This justifies the inclusion of age^2 as a regressor in (75)–(77). (iii) Labor force participation is the outcome of a market process whereby the demanders of labor services are willing to offer a wage based on expected marginal product, and individuals themselves make a decision whether to accept the offer, depending on whether it exceeded their own reservation wage. Employers' expected marginal product depends on education, among other things, and female employees' reservation wage depends on such variables as age, the presence of children in the household, other sources of income (husband's), and marginal tax rates on labor income. These arguments justify the inclusion of some or all of the variables (kids, family income, and HHrs) as regressors in (75)–(77).

To study models (72)–(77), consider first their functional forms. In light of this chapter's main theme, estimation of the causal effects of education on earnings requires an underlying real-world relationship between earnings and education (EE). When the true functional form of such a relationship is unknown, as it usually is, the specific semi-log form of (73)–(77) can be false. A commitment to such a specific form then might yield incorrect inferences. For this reason, we posit the far more general alternative equation in (72), which is derived from a model that is linear in all relevant observed and unobserved regressors but nonlinear in all coefficients that are cross-sectionally varying. Because of its generality, this functional form can cover the true (but unknown) functional form of the real-world relationship between EE as a special case. Applying Basmann's (1988, p. 98) argument to (73)–(77) means that these equations are not free of the most serious of defects: non-uniqueness. Lack of uniqueness arises from two sources: functional form, because the log of earnings instead of earnings themselves is used as the dependent variable, and nonuniqueness of the coefficients and error terms. Such models cannot represent a real-world relationship and therefore cannot be causal. It follows that the coefficient of T in Eq. (73), the coefficient of S in Eq. (74), and the coefficients of education in Eqs. (75)–(77) cannot describe causal effects. Needless to say, these comments also apply to other models covered by Card (1999).

As specified, the error terms in Eqs. (73)–(78), as well as those in the models examined by Card (1999), comprise omitted relevant regressors, as in Eq. (4) of Section 2. Consequently, the assumption that the regressors included in these models are independent of the error term consisting of "the" omitted regressors is meaningless for all the reasons outlined earlier. Therefore, the least square estimators of the coefficients of Eqs. (73)–(76) and the maximum likelihood estimators of the coefficients of Eqs. (77) and (78) are inconsistent, as are the instrumental variable estimators of the coefficients of models tabulated by Card (1999), as Theorem 1 proves.

Another problem with Eq. (73), pointed out by Greene (2012, p. 220), is that some unobserved determinants of lifetime earnings, such as ambition, inherent abilities, and persistence, can also determine whether the individual had an opportunity to attend an elite college in the first place. The least squares estimator of δ then will inappropriately attribute the effect to the treatment rather than to these underlying factors. This incorrect attribution produces correlation between T and ε, which results in inconsistency of the least squares estimator of δ.

In Eq. (72), a correlation between education and the component of γ_{0i}, called "the error term of (9)", cannot arise because, in the formulation of Eq. (72), every omitted regressor is first split into two pieces: a "sufficient" piece, and a piece consisting of the effect of the included regressor, education, on each omitted regressor, using a functional form that is linear in the included regressor and nonlinear in its coefficients (see Eq. 8). The proposed protocol is then (i) to define sufficient pieces—certain "sufficient" sets of omitted regressors—as the arguments of a function called the unique error term, and (ii) to use the effect of the included regressor on each omitted regressor piece as an argument of the function called omitted-regressor biases of the coefficient on the included regressor (education). It can be shown that this regressor is uncorrelated with the unique error term, which is a function of sufficient sets of omitted regressors. Omitted-regressor bias components, which in our proposed model (72) constitute a formal accounting of such biases, are missing from the coefficients of Eqs. (73)–(78). Their absence renders all coefficients and error terms in these models nonunique, so that they cannot be estimated consistently.

By construction, Eq. (72) is without specification errors, meaning that it can be a real-world relationship. The explanation that follows Eq. (72) clarifies that the components of its coefficients are exactly of the type that the coefficients of an equation must have if it is derived from a real-world relationship, with algebraic expressions for their components being given in (10)–(12). Property (5) of (9) further implies that the causal effect of the *i*th wife's education on her earnings is exactly the bias-free component of γ_{1i} × the true value of education$_i$.

To estimate this causal effect, we need to estimate the components of γ_{1i} separately. For this purpose, we seek coefficient drivers strongly related to the omitted-regressor bias component of γ_{1i} and select them accordingly on the basis of arguments that follow Eq. (78) and originally provided by Greene (2012, pp. 14 and 15, 683 and 684, 699–701, 708–711, 888). The selected coefficient drivers are: z_{1i} = Wife's Age$_i$, z_{2i} = Wife's Age$_i^2$, z_{3i} = Kids$_i$, z_{4i} = Husband's Age$_i$, z_{5i} = Husband's education$_i$, z_{6i} = Family income$_i$. The difference between Greene's approach (2012, pp. 116 and 117) and ours is that we employ as coefficient drivers of (72) the same variables he used directly as regressors in a fixed-coefficient latent regression of earnings in (77). Accordingly, for $j = 0, 1$, the *j*th coefficient in (72) becomes an equation like (14).

$$\gamma_{ji} = \pi_{j0} + \pi_{j1} z_{1i} + \ldots + \pi_{j6} z_{6i} + u_{ji} \tag{79}$$

Substituting (79) for both $j = 0$ and $j = 1$ in (72) gives a fixed-coefficients model where not only education and the coefficient drivers but also the interactions of education with each of the coefficient drivers appear as regressors. Indeed, one of these interaction terms also appeared in Greene's (2012, pp. 699–701) model not shown here. Of course, we can put different exclusion restrictions on the coefficients of γ_{0i} and γ_{1i}. Eq. (79) is an example of (14).[30]

Greene's (2012, p. 116) Appendix Table F5.1 contains 753 observations used in Mroz's study of the labor supply behavior of married women. Of the 753 individuals in the sample, 428 were participants in the formal labor market. For these 428 individuals, we fit the fixed coefficients model implied by (72) and (79) under the assumptions that for $i, i' = 1, \ldots, 428$: $u_i = (u_{0i}, u_{1i})'$,

30. We note as an aside that the present discussion is related to the debate about discrimination in the work place, which prominently relied on a so-called reverse linear regression, reproduced in Greene (2012, pp. 176–178). But here, as proved in Theorem 1, we emphasize that least squares estimators of the coefficients from such a regression are inconsistent if the error term is made up of relevant regressors omitted from the regression, so that the conclusion regarding the presence or absence of work place discrimination based on that work needs to be viewed with skepticism.

$$E(u_i|\, z_{1i},\, \dots,\, z_{6i},\, \text{education}_i) = 0, E\left(u_i u_i'|\, z_{1i},\, \dots,\, z_{6i},\, \text{education}_i\right) = \sigma_u{}^2 \Delta_u, \text{and}\, E\left(u_i u_{i'}'|\, z_{1i},\, \dots,\, z_{6i},\, \text{education}_i\right) = 0\, \text{if}\, i \neq i' \tag{80}$$

Because Mroz's data provide a single crosss-section data set only, we must assume that the coefficients of (79) do not vary across individuals. Still, this assumption is not as strong as the assumption that γ_{0i} and γ_{1i} are constant. This is because under our assumption that, although the coefficients of (79) do not vary across i, γ_{0i} and γ_{1i} still vary with the z's. For estimation, we choose IRSGLS to fit the data. We also will seek empirical best linear unbiased predictors of u_{0i} and u_{1i}, denoted by $\hat{u}_{0i}$ and $\hat{u}_{1i}$. Using the IRSGLS estimates of π's in (79) we get

$$\begin{array}{ll} \hat{\gamma}_{0i} = & \underset{(-0.051158)}{-1573.3} + \underset{(0.2262)}{351.72} z_{1i} - \underset{(-0.07653)}{1.3316} z_{2i} + \underset{(1.3315)}{3304.6}\, z_{3i} \\ (t-\text{ratio}) & - \underset{(-1.0455)}{298.11}\, z_{4i} - \underset{(-0.070343)}{21.843} z_{5i} + \underset{(0.78745)}{0.063717}\, z_{6i} \end{array} \tag{81}$$

$$\begin{array}{ll} \hat{\gamma}_{1i} = & \underset{(0.1964)}{505.17} \underset{(-0.14541)}{-18.922}\, z_{1i} + \underset{(0.0028917)}{0.0042111}\, z_{2i} \\ (t\text{–ratio}) & - \underset{(-1.9074)}{390.58}\, z_{3i} + \underset{(0.88043)}{20.847}\, z_{4i} - \underset{(-0.67717)}{17.520}\, z_{5i} + \underset{(1.0908)}{0.0070177} z_{6i} \end{array} \tag{82}$$

where the errors in (79) are set at their zero-mean values and the figures in parentheses below the estimates of π's are the t-ratios.

The estimate of the BFC of γ_{1i} in Eq. (72) given by Eq. (82) is:

$$\underset{(0.1964)}{505.17} \tag{83}$$

This is the first estimate on the right-hand side of Eq. (82) and is the same as one we would have obtained had we used the formula in (31) after equating $\hat{\hat{\pi}}_{j0i}$ with the IRSGLS estimate of π_{j0} with $j = 1$ in (79), setting $\hat{\nu}^*_{jit}$ equal to zero, because no data about measurement errors are available, and setting K to 2.

Suppose that the correct functional form of the BFC of the coefficient, γ_{1i}, on education$_i$ in (72) is a constant and does not vary across individuals. In this case, the estimate of BFC is the same as that of the intercept of Eq. (79), which is $505.17_{(0.1964)}$. Because it has the correct positive sign for all i, the causal effect of the ith married woman's education on her earnings is unambiguously $505.17_{(0.1964)}$ $\times$education$_i$). Constancy of the BFC of γ_{1i} does not mean that γ_{1i} is a constant because its omitted-regressor bias component varies as a function of the coefficient drivers, as in (32).

Because the estimates of individual causal effects are too numerous to display in tabular form, we show them in Fig. 1 as a histogram and its implied kernel density of the causal effect ($505.17_{(0.1964)}$ $\times$ education$_i$) of the ith wife's education on her earnings, the total number of married women being 428.

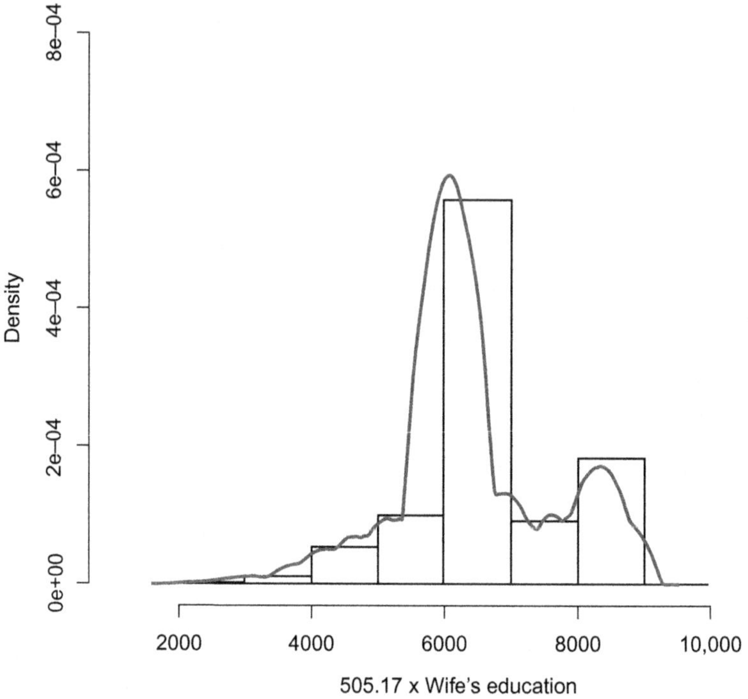

FIG. 1 Histogram and kernel density estimate for the causal effects of different married woman's education on their earnings when the BFC of γ_{1i} is a constant.

The formula $\left(\hat{\hat{\pi}}_{10} \times \text{education}_i\right)$ is the estimate of the causal effect of the ith married woman's education on her earnings, shown in dollars on the horizontal axis in Fig. 1, with frequencies indicated on the vertical axis. Note the bimodal nature of the implied distribution.

Calculations (not reported here) show that if the causal effect of a married woman's education on her earnings is her actual earnings, given by the dependent variable of (72), then the estimate $0.0070177_{(1.0908)} \times \text{Family income}_i \times \text{education}_i$ generally is closer to the actual earnings$_i$ than the estimate $505.17_{(0.1964)} \times \text{education}_i$, meaning that it is more *accurate*.[31] The intercept (π_{10}) of γ_{1i} in (79), however, is actually the coefficient on education$_i$ in the fixed coefficient model implied by Eqs. (72) and (79). So it is proper to interpret an estimate of the coefficient (π_{10}) times education$_i$ as an estimate of the causal effect of

31. Here, *accuracy* refers to the size of deviations from the true causal effect, whereas *precision*, widely used in statistical work, refers to the size of deviations from the expectation of an estimator of a causal effect.

education$_i$ on the dependent variable of Eq. (72). A great advantage of this approach is that this fixed coefficient model eliminates all specification errors in Eqs. (73)–(77).[32]

One can object that our estimates of causal effects in (79), displayed in Fig. 1, are obtained with a statistically insignificant estimated intercept of (79) for $j = 1$. What these estimates then tell us is that we may have used too many coefficient drivers in (79) with $j = 0$ and 1, or perhaps not even a relevant set thereof. If by including any combination of six coefficient drivers in Eq. (79) for γ_{0i} and γ_{1i}, we cannot increase the t-ratio of the estimated intercept with $j = 1$ to above 2 in absolute value, then we must conclude that none of the coefficient drivers in (79) having ranges different from that of γ_{0i} (or γ_{1i}) is appropriate for γ_{0i} (or γ_{1i}), requiring a renewed search for a new set. This eventuality, however, is not grounds for rejecting the methodology that led to estimator (31), for which we have given principled reasons based on uniqueness and consistency. We emphasize that the method proposed here may not guarantee the discovery of truth for a single set of coefficient drivers; it merely prevents our committing to a path that prevents discovery for sure. It is to clarify our position that a failure to find "statistically significant" estimate for the intercept of Eq. (79) with $j = 1$ is not grounds for reverting to conventional models with nonunique coefficients and error terms that we provide a numerical example, based on the same data.

Before we do, it is important to emphasize that, when testing between the hypotheses, H_0: $\pi_{10} = 0$ and H_1: $\pi_{10} \neq 0$, the mere specification of a 5% type I probability of error for the t-test used, and of the decision, accept H_0, reached, often is viewed as an unsatisfactory form of the conclusion to our problem. This uneasiness was well articulated by Kiefer (1977) and was shared by all the discussants of his paper. The example given in Kiefer (1977) might clarify this apprehension further.

Example 3 Suppose we observe a normally distributed random variable X with mean θ and unit variance, and must decide between the two simple hypotheses, H_0: $\theta = -1$ and H_1: $\theta = 1$. The symmetric Neyman-Pearson test rejects H_0 if $X \geq 0$ and has (type I and II probabilities of errors) = (0.16, 0.16). Thus we make the same decision d_1 in favor of H_1 whether $X = 0.5$ or $X = 5$, but the statement of error probabilities and decision reached, "(the type I and II probabilities of errors, decision) = (0.16, 0.16, d_1)" that we make for either of these sample

32. In practical terms, this chapter is able to determine how much, say, $1000 spent on education will increase a woman's earnings. Suppose that in Eq. (7) of Section 3.1, y_{it}^* represents earnings, x^*_{1it} represents education, and all other relevant regressors are omitted regressors. Then $\alpha_{1it}^*(x_{1it}'' - x_{1it}')$ is the amount by which y_{it}^* will necessarily be greater if on any one observation x_{1it}^* is deliberately set equal to x_{1it}'' rather than x_{1it}' where α_{1it}^* is the bias-free component of the coefficient on education in (72) and $(x_{1it}'' - x_{1it}')$ is the difference between two different values of x_{1it}^*. It also should be noted that $(x_{1it}'' - x_{1it}')$ is measured in years and y_{it}^* is measured in dollars.

values does not exhibit any detailed data-dependent measure of conclusiveness that conveys our stronger feeling in favor of H_1 when $X = 5$, than when $X = 0.5$.

From this Kiefer's (1977, p. 789) example, it follows that in (82), our specification of 0.05 type I probability of error, our lack of knowledge of the corresponding type II probability of error for a t-test of the null hypothesis, H_0: $\pi_{10} = 0$ against the alternative hypothesis H_1: $\pi_{10} \neq 0$, and our decision to accept H_0: $\pi_{10} = 0$, do not exhibit any detailed data-dependent measure of conclusiveness that conveys our stronger feeling in favor of H_1 when the estimate of π_{10} is 505.17. In his article, Kiefer (1977) gave an exposition and discussion of a systematic approach to stating statistical conclusions with the suggestion that incorporating a measure of conclusiveness that depends on the sample may assuage the uneasiness he and the discussants of his paper expressed. It is difficult, however, to apply Kiefer's procedures to the model in Eqs. (7)–(20).

5.1 Illuminating the Contrast Between (72) and (79) and an Estimated Earnings and Education Relationship Based on an Incorrectly Specified Error Term in (4)

A direct comparison between our estimate $505.17_{(0.1964)}$ for the intercept of (79) with $j = 1$ and any of the estimates of the coefficient on education in Greene (2012) and Card (1999) is not strictly possible, because, although our model is in level form, their models use the logarithm of earnings as the dependent variable. To allow comparison, however, consider

$$\text{earnings}_i = \beta_0 + \beta_1 z_{1i} + \beta_2 z_{2i} + \beta_3 z_{3i} + \beta_4 \text{education}_i + u_i \tag{84}$$

where all the coefficients are unknown but misspecified to be constants. Unlike the error term of (72), the error term u_i of (84) is equal to the sum of the products, $\omega_\ell w_{i\ell}$, $\ell = 1, \ldots, L$, where the $w_{i\ell}$'s are relevant regressors omitted from Eq. (84), ω_ℓ is the unknown constant coefficient of $w_{i\ell}$, and L is the unknown number of relevant regressors omitted from (84).

Because the error term of (84) is composed of omitted relevant regressors, the following propositions, echoing earlier assertions in this chapter, must hold: (i) The condition that the regressors included in (84) be independent of "the" regressors omitted from (84) is meaningless, and (ii) the error term and the coefficients of (84) are not unique. (iii) From statement (i) it follows that $E(u_i | z_{1i}, z_{2i}, z_{3i}, \text{education}_i) \neq 0$ or, equivalently, all the included regressors in (84) are endogenous. As noted at the beginning, a proof of statement (i) is given in PS (1988, p. 34), and the proofs of propositions (ii) and (iii) appear in Section 2. These observations apply this chapter's central theme to arrive at the conclusion that least squares estimators of the coefficients of (84) are inconsistent whenever its error term is made up of omitted relevant regressors.

Least squares applied to (84) leads to

$$\begin{aligned}\text{earnings}_i = & -\underset{(-1.595)}{9656.827} + \underset{(1.520)}{436.735}\, z_{1i} - \underset{(-1.509)}{5.103}\; z_{2i} \\ & - \underset{(-3.184)}{1609.335}\, z_{3i} + \underset{(6.311)}{545.890}\,\text{education}_i + \hat{u}_i \end{aligned} \tag{85}$$

where the figures in parentheses beneath the coefficient estimates are the t-ratios. Because these estimates are based on inconsistent least squares estimators, all the given "t-ratios" in parentheses are invalid, and therefore uninterpretable. It is clear then that a mere failure to obtain a statistically significant intercept for (79) with $j=1$ does not justify resorting to models with nonunique coefficients and error terms, even though the estimated coefficient on education in Eq. (85) is numerically not too far from the estimate of the intercept in (79) with $j=1$ in (83).

Therefore, we return to our model in (72) and (79). Suppose that with extensive experimentation, we could find the appropriate and adequate number of coefficient drivers and included them in (79) with $j=0, 1$. Now assume the model in (72) and (79) is true. From this, we can generate the misspecified model in (84) by setting $\pi_{04}=\pi_{05}=\pi_{06}=\pi_{11}=\pi_{12}=\pi_{13}=\pi_{14}=\pi_{15}=\pi_{16}=0$ in (79) and assuming that the distribution of u_{1i} in (79) with $j=1$ is degenerate at zero. This being the case, the estimates in (85) are then, from everything that has been said so far, subject to omitted-regressor biases as well as biases because of the misspecification of the distribution of u_{1i}. The two conditions that (i) "causality" is a property of the real world and (ii) a real-world relationship must be mis-specifications-free imply that the BFC of the coefficient on education in the mis-specifications-free model in (72) is needed to estimate the causal effect of education on earnings. In light of this demonstration, it is now obvious that the coefficient on education in the misspecified model in (85) cannot be the causal effect of education on earnings.

6 Conclusions

This chapter has sought to bring together strands from time-series modeling and cross-section analysis by proposing a coherent approach to modeling panel data combining features from both disciplines, based on concepts developed in previous work about time series and cross sections. We take seriously admonitions by PS (1984, 1988) and Basmann (1988) that models purporting to represent causal relationships must be unique in the sense that their error terms and coefficients be unique. Our proof that nonunique models yield inconsistent estimators and inferences—that is, statistically uninterpretable results—leads us directly to the approach advocated in Section 3 of this chapter, which we then apply in Section 5. Having developed a methodology that unambiguously produces models for panel data with unique coefficients and error terms, we are confronted with the task of estimating simultaneously a "bias-free component," an "omitted-regressor bias component," and a "measurement-error bias component." We estimate these components simultaneously, because, in principle, simultaneous estimation is superior to any two-step estimation. Accordingly, the coefficient on each included regressor of a model is regressed on a set of coefficient drivers with nonzero intercept and nonzero error term, and this intercept times a factor is then identified as the bias-free component of that coefficient. The sum of the products of coefficient drivers and their respective coefficients plus the error term, after this whole quantity is multiplied by a factor, becomes the omitted-regressor bias component of the coefficient in question. Estimates of these separate elements are necessary because it is the bias-free component of the coefficient on a nonconstant regressor that is needed to measure the causal effect of the regressor on the model's dependent variable. As we indicate, the most challenging aspect of the theory and the proposed technique outlined here is the search for necessary coefficient drivers able to provide both an accurate estimate of the omitted-regressor bias component and a statistically significant estimate of the bias-free component of the coefficient on each nonconstant regressor in a model. It is here where intuition, theory, and prior experience play important roles.

Appendix A Proof of the Uniqueness of the Coefficients and Error term of a Stochastic Law

Without loss of generality, we present this proof for the simple case of one included regressor and one omitted regressor. For such a case, Eq. (7) becomes

$$y_{it}^* = \alpha_{0it}^* + x_{1it}^*\alpha_{1it}^* + w_{1it}^*\omega_{1it}^* \tag{A.1}$$

where x_{1it}^* is the included regressor, w_{1it}^* is an omitted regressor, and $w_{1it}^*\omega_{1it}^*$ is the error term made up of this omitted regressor. Eq. (A.1) is treated as deterministic.

We add and subtract the product $\omega_{1it}^* x_{1it}^*$ on the right-hand side of Eq. (A.1) without changing it. Doing so gives

$$y_{it}^* = \alpha_{0it}^* + x_{1it}^*\left(\alpha_{1it}^* + \omega_{1it}^*\right) + \left(w_{1it}^* - x_{1it}^*\right)\omega_{1it}^* \tag{A.2}$$

This equation shows that the coefficients and error term of (A.1) are not unique. To make them unique, we introduce the version of Eq. (8) that is appropriate to Eq. (A.1):

$$w_{1it}^* = \lambda_{10it}^* + x_{1it}^*\lambda_{11it}^* \tag{A.3}$$

where λ_{10it}^* is the random error term.

Substituting the right-hand side of Eq. (A.3) for w_{1it}^* in (A.1) gives

$$y_{it}^* = \alpha_{0it}^* + \lambda_{10it}^*\omega_{1it}^* + x_{1it}^*\left(\alpha_{1it}^* + \lambda_{11it}^*\omega_{1it}^*\right) \tag{A.4}$$

In (A.2), $(w_{1it}^* - x_{1it}^*)$ is the omitted regressor. For this omitted regressor (A.3) becomes

$$w_{1it}^* - x_{1it}^* = \lambda_{10it}^* + x_{1it}^*\left(\lambda_{11it}^* - 1\right) \tag{A.5}$$

Substituting the right-hand side of this equation for $(w_{1it}^* - x_{1it}^*)$ in (A.2) gives

$$y_{it}^* = \alpha_{0it}^* + x_{1it}^*\left(\alpha_{1it}^* + \omega_{1it}^*\right) + \left[\lambda_{10it}^* + x_{1it}^*\left(\lambda_{11it}^* - 1\right)\right]\omega_{1it}^* \tag{A.6}$$

This equation is the same as Eq. (A.4). The equality between Eqs. (A.4) and (A.6) proves that in the presence of (A.3), the coefficients and error term of (A.4) are unique. This proof can be generalized easily to prove that the coefficients and the error term of (9) are unique in the presence of (8). The above proof is from Swamy et al. (2014).

Appendix B Conditions for the Consistency of Certain Estimators of the Coefficients of a Stochastic Law

Conditions under which $\hat{\hat{\pi}}_i$ in Eq. (29) is asymptotically equivalent to $\hat{\pi}_i$ in Eq. (26) are

$$\text{plim}\left[\left(\frac{1}{T}X_{zi}'\hat{\Sigma}_{yi}^{-1}X_{zi}\right) - \left(\frac{1}{T}X_{zi}'\Sigma_{yi}^{-1}X_{zi}\right)\right] = 0 \tag{B.1}$$

and

$$\text{plim}\left[\left(\frac{1}{\sqrt{T}}X_{zi}'\hat{\Sigma}_{yi}^{-1}D_{xi}u_i\right) - \left(\frac{1}{\sqrt{T}}X_{zi}'\Sigma_{yi}^{-1}D_{xi}u_i\right)\right] = 0 \tag{B.2}$$

Conditions for $\hat{\hat{\pi}}$ in Eq. (50) to be asymptotically equivalent to $\hat{\pi}$ in Eq. (38) are

$$\text{plim}\left[\left(\frac{1}{nT}X_z'\hat{\Sigma}_y^{-1}X_z\right) - \left(\frac{1}{nT}X_z'\Sigma_y^{-1}X_z\right)\right] = 0 \tag{B.3}$$

and

$$\text{plim}\left[\left(\frac{1}{\sqrt{nT}}X_z'\hat{\Sigma}_y^{-1}(D_{Xz}\eta + D_{Dx}u)\right) - \left(\frac{1}{\sqrt{nT}}X_z'\Sigma_y^{-1}(D_{Xz}\eta + D_{Dx}u)\right)\right] = 0 \tag{B.4}$$

All four conditions in (B.1)–(B.4) can be verified using the methods of Cavanagh and Rothenberg (1995).

References

Basmann, R.L., 1988. Causality tests and observationally equivalent representations of econometric models. Journal of Econometrics 39 (1/2), 69–104 (special issue).

Brown, L.D., 1990. The 1985 Wald memorial lecture: an ancillarity paradox which appears in multiple linear regression (with discussion). The Annals of Statistics 18 (2), 471–538.

Card, D., 1999. The causal effect of education on earnings. In: Ashenfelter, O., Card, D. (Eds.), Handbook of Labor Economics. In: Vol. 3. Elsevier Science B.V.

Cavanagh, C.L., Rothenberg, T.J., 1995. Generalized least squares with nonnormal errors. In: Maddala, G.S., Phillips, P.C.B., Srinivasan, T.N. (Eds.), Advances in econometrics and quantitative economics. Basil Blackwell Ltd, Cambridge, pp. 276–290.

Chang, I., Hallahan, C., Swamy, P.A.V.B., 1992. Efficient computation of stochastic coefficients models. In: Amman, H.M., Belsley, D.A., Pau, L.F. (Eds.), Computational economics and econometrics. Kluwer Academic Publishers, Boston, pp. 43–52.

Chang, I., Swamy, P.A.V.B., Hallahan, C., Tavlas, G.S., 2000. A computational approach to finding causal economic laws. Computational Economics 16 (1–2), 105–136.

Chipman, J.S., 1964. On least squares with insufficient observations. Journal of the American Statistical Association 59, 1078–1111.

DeGroot, M.H., 1970. Optimal Statistical Decisions. McGraw-Hill, New York (Chapter 11).

Diewert, W.E., 1971. An application of the Shephard duality theorem: a generalized Leontief production function. Journal of Political Economy 79, 481–507.

Feige, E.L., Swamy, P.A.V.B., 1974. A random coefficient model of the demand for liquid assets. Journal of Money, Credit and Banking 6, 241–252.

Felipe, J., Fisher, F.M., 2003. Aggregation in production functions: what applied economists should know. Metroeconomica 54, 208–262.

Foster, M., 1961. An application of the Wiener-Kolmogorov smoothing theory to matrix inversion. Journal of the Society for Industrial and Applied Mathematics 9, 387–392.

Greene, W.H., 2012. Econometric Analysis, Seventh ed. Prentice Hall/Pearson, Upper Saddle River, NJ.

Henderson, C.R., 1950. Estimation of genetic parameters (abstract). Annals of Mathematical Statistics 21, 309–310.

Hildreth, C., Houck, J.P., 1968. Some estimators for a model with random coefficients. Journal of the American Statistical Association 63, 584–595.

Kashyap, A.K., Swamy, P.A.V.B., Mehta, J.S., Porter, R.D., 1988. Further results on estimating linear regression models with partial prior information. Economic Modelling 5, 49–57.

Kiefer, J., 1977. Conditional confidence statements and confidence estimators (with discussion). Journal of the American Statistical Association 72, 789–827.

Lehmann, E.L., 1999. Elements of Large-Sample Theory. Springer, New York.

Lehmann, E.L., Casella, G., 1998. Theory of Point Estimation, Second ed. Springer, New York.

Lindley, D.V., 1971. Bayesian Statistics—A review, regional conference series in applied mathematics. Society for Industrial and Applied Mathematics, Philadelphia.

Mehta, J.S., Narasimham, G.V.L., Swamy, P.A.V.B., 1978. Estimation of a dynamic demand function for gasoline with different schemes of parameter variation. Journal of Econometrics 7, 263–279.

Mehta, J.S., Swamy, P.A.V.B., 1973. Bayesian analysis of a bivariate normal distribution with incomplete observations. Journal of the American Statistical Association 68, 922–927.

Pesaran, M.H., 2007. A simple panel unit root test in the presence of cross-section dependence. Journal of Applied Econometrics 22, 265–312.

Pratt, J.W., Schlaifer, R., 1984. On the nature and discovery of structure. Journal of the American Statistical Association 79, 9–21.

Pratt, J.W., Schlaifer, R., 1988. On the interpretation and observation of laws. Journal of Econometrics 39, 23–52.

Priestley, M.B., 1981. Spectral Analysis and Time Series. Academic Press, New York.

Rao, C.R., 1973. Linear Statistical Inference and Its Applications, second ed. John Wiley & Sons, New York.

Rao, J.N.K., 2003. Small Area Estimation. John Wiley & Sons, New Jersey.

Robinson, J., 1953–54. The production function and the theory of capital. Review of Economic Studies 21, 81–106.

Rubin, D.B., 1978. Bayesian inference for causal effects. Annals of Statistics 6, 34–58.

Skyrms, B., 1988. Probability and causation. Journal of Econometrics 39, 53–68.

Sraffa, P., 1960. Production of Commodities by Means of Commodities. Cambridge University Press, Cambridge.

Stone, M., Springer, B.G.F., 1965. A paradox involving quasi prior distributions. Biometrika 52, 623–627.

Swamy, P.A.V.B., 1970. Efficient inference in a random coefficient regression model. Econometrica 38, 311–323.

Swamy, P.A.V.B., 1971. Statistical Inference in Random Coefficient Regression Models. Springer-Verlag, New York.

Swamy, P.A.V.B., 1974. Linear models with random coefficients. In: Zarembka, P. (Ed.), Frontiers in Econometrics. Academic Press, New York.

Swamy, P.A.V.B., Arora, S.S., 1972. The exact finite sample properties of the estimators of coefficients in the error components regression models. Econometrica 40, 261–275.

Swamy, P.A.V.B., Chang, I., Mehta, J.S., Greene, W.H., Hall, S.G.F., Tavlas, G.S., 2016. Removing specification errors from the usual formulation of the binary choice models. Econometrics 4, 26. https://doi.org/10.3390/econometrics4020026.

Swamy, P.A.V.B., Chang, I., Mehta, J.S., Tavlas, G.S., 2003. Correcting for omitted-variables and measurement-error bias in autoregressive model estimation with panel data. Computational Economics 22, 225–253.

Swamy, P.A.V.B., Hall, S.G.F., Tavlas, G.S., Chang, I., Gibson, H.D., Greene, W.H., et al., 2016. A method of measuring treatment effects on the treated without randomization. Econometrics 4, 19. https://doi.org/10.3390/econometrics4020019.

Swamy, P.A.V.B., Mehta, J.S., 1973. Bayesian analysis of error components regression models. Journal of the American Statistical Association 68, 648–658.

Swamy, P.A.V.B., Mehta, J.S., 1975a. Bayesian estimation of seemingly unrelated regressions when some observations are missing. Journal of Econometrics 3, 157–170.

Swamy, P.A.V.B., Mehta, J.S., 1975b. Bayesian and non-Bayesian analysis of switching regressions and of random coefficient regression models. Journal of the American Statistical Association 70, 593–602.

Swamy, P.A.V.B., Mehta, J.S., 1976. Minimum average risk estimators for coefficients in linear models. Communications in Statistics: Theory and Methods A5, 803–818.

Swamy, P.A.V.B., Mehta, J.S., 1977. A note on minimum average risk estimators for coefficients in linear models. Communications in Statistics-Theory and Methods A6, 1181–1186.

Swamy, P.A.V.B., Mehta, J.S., 1979. Estimation of common coefficients in two regression equations. Journal of Econometrics 10, 1–14.

Swamy, P.A.V.B., Mehta, J.S., 1983. Ridge regression estimation of the Rotterdam model. Journal of Econometrics 22, 365–390.

Swamy, P.A.V.B., Mehta, J.S., Chang, I., 2017. Endogeneity, time-varying coefficients, and incorrect vs. correct ways of specifying the error terms of econometric models. Econometrics 5, 8. https://doi.org/10.3390/econometrics/5010008.

Swamy, P.A.V.B., Mehta, J.S., Rappoport, P.N., 1978. Two methods of evaluating Hoerl and Kennard's ridge regression. Communications in Statistics, Part A – Theory and Methods A7, 1133–1155.

Swamy, P.A.V.B., Mehta, J.S., Tavlas, G.S., Hall, S.G.F., 2014. Small area estimation with correctly specified linking models. In: Ma, J., Wohar, M. (Eds.), Recent Advances in Estimating Nonlinear Models. Springer, New York (Chapter 10).

Swamy, P.A.V.B., Mehta, J.S., Tavlas, G.S., Hall, S.G.F., 2015. Two applications of the random coefficient procedure: Correcting for misspecifications in a small area level model and resolving Simpson's paradox. Economic Modelling 45, 93–98.

Swamy, P.A.V.B., Tavlas, G.S., Hall, S.G.F., 2015. Microproduction functions with unique coefficients and errors: A reconsideration and respecification. Macroeconomic Dynamics 19, 311–333.

Swamy, P.A.V.B., Tavlas, G.S., Hall, S.G.F., Hondroyiannis, G., 2010. Estimation of parameters in the presence of model misspecification and measurement error. Studies in Nonlinear Dynamics & Econometrics 14, 1–33.

Swamy, P.A.V.B., Tinsley, P.A., 1980. Linear prediction and estimation methods for regression models with stationary stochastic coefficients. Journal of Econometrics 12, 103–142.

Swamy, P.A.V.B., von zur Muehlen, P., 1988. Further thoughts on testing for causality with econometric models. Journal of Econoetrics 39, 105–147.

Swamy, P.A.V.B., Yaghi, W., Mehta, J.S., Chang, I., 2007. Empirical best linear unbiased prediction in misspecified and improved panel data models with an application to gasoline demand. Computational Statistics & Data Analysis 51, 3381–3392.

Train, K., 2003. Discrete Choice Models with Simulation. Cambridge University Press, Cambridge.

Yokum, J.T., Wildt, A.R., Swamy, P.A.V.B., 1998. Forecasting disjoint data structures using approximate constant and stochastic coefficient models. Journal of Applied Statistical Science 8, 29–49.

Zellner, A., 1969. On the aggregation problem: a new approach to a troublesome problem. In: Fox, K.A., Sengupta, J.K., Narasimham, G.V.L. (Eds.), Economic Models, Estimation and Risk Programming: Essays in Honor of Gerhard Tintner. Springer-Verlag, New York.

Zellner, A., 1971. Introduction to Bayesian Inference in Econometrics. John Wiley and Sons, New York.

Zellner, A., 1977. Aykac, A., Brumat, C. (Eds.), Maximal data information prior distribution. North-Holland Publishing Co., Amsterdam, pp. 201–215

Zellner, A., 1988. Causality and causal laws in economics. Journal of Econometrics 39, 7–21.

Further Reading

Baltagi, B.H., Pirotte, A., 2010. Panel data inference under spatial dependence. Economic Modelling 27 (6), 1368–1381.

Chapter 12

Analysis of Panel Data Using R

Arne Henningsen* and Géraldine Henningsen†
*Department of Food and Resource Economics, University of Copenhagen, Frederiksberg C, Denmark, †Department of Management Engineering, Technical University of Denmark, Kgs. Lyngby, Denmark

Chapter Outline

Panel Data Econometrics. https://doi.org/10.1016/B978-0-12-814367-4.00012-5

1 Introduction

Imagine we want to estimate a model for the demand for natural gas in both residential and industrial buildings. We have aggregated data for only 36 states of the United States, however, so that a cross-sectional analysis with several explanatory variables and only 36 observations might suffer from a small number of degrees of freedom. We are lucky, however, that our data set contains the state-level aggregated demand for 13 years (1950–1962). This is the setting that Balestra and Nerlove (1966) faced when they kick-started the application of panel data models in economics with their study. Balestra and Nerlove (1966) first used ordinary least-squares (OLS) to estimate a dynamic demand model based on the pooled data set. This estimation returned implausible results, e.g., for the depreciation rate of gas-related appliances. These results put them on track: Could it be that unobserved state effects messed up their results? After they started to control for these effects, their results started to make sense. Balestra and Nerlove (1966) did not develop any of the modern panel data estimators that we use today, but they made the scientific community aware of problems when applying pooled OLS to panel data.

Initially, the uptake of panel data analysis was slow, with only sporadic publications in the 1960s and 1970s. During the 1990s, however, panel data econometrics experienced a quantum leap, and today, it has become standard material in econometrics textbooks.

At the same time, panel data sets have become increasingly available for researchers and analysts. In fact, we are in the middle of a new development in panel data econometrics, as the number of panel data sets that include both a large number of individuals (n) and a large number of time periods (T) is increasing rapidly. Panel data sets that include a large number of time periods (T) create new challenges because the statistical inference of commonly used panel data estimators is based on the assumption that the data sets have a large n and a small T, which used to be the case for most panel data sets. Later in this chapter, we will discuss how a large T dimension affects the suitability of dynamic panel data models.

According to Hsiao (2007), the usage of panel data has the following advantages compared to cross-sectional data ($T = 1$) or time series data ($n = 1$):

- more accurate inference of model parameters because of more degrees of freedom,
- greater capacity to capture complicated behavioral processes because of:
  - greater capacity to construct and test complex behavioral assumptions (e.g., when testing effects of policies),
  - the possibility to control for the impact of omitted variables,
  - greater capacity to uncover dynamic relationships,
  - more accurate predictions for individual outcomes than predictions based on a time series for a single individual, and
  - the ability to provide a micro-foundation for aggregate data analysis, and
- surprisingly, often simpler computation and statistical inference.[1]

In short, in comparison to cross-sectional or time series data, panel data contain more information, and therefore, allow for more elaborate analyses.

In this chapter, we demonstrate how the statistical software R (R Core Team, 2018) can be used to analyze panel data.

2 Loading Data

R can import data sets in many different formats. Several different procedures to import (and export) data in different formats are described in the (official) R manual "R Data Import/Export" (`https://cran.r-project.org/doc/manuals/r-release/R-data.html`). For example, the add-on package *foreign* can be used to import data files in formats used by other (statistical) software packages such as SPSS, STATA, or SAS. The add-on package *readstata13* can be used to read data files from all STATA versions (including versions 13 and 14), while the "standard" function for reading STATA data files (`read.dta()` in package *foreign*) can read data files only for STATA versions 5–12.

The R software and many add-on packages include data sets that can be loaded with the `data()` command. In this chapter, we will use two data sets that are included in the *plm* package:

- The data set `EmplUK` was used by Arellano and Bond (1991) and is an unbalanced firm-level panel data set that focuses on employment. It contains observations of 140 firms from 1976 to 1984 with 1031 observations in total.
- The data set `Grunfeld` was used initially by Grunfeld (1958) and was used later in many other publications and textbooks (see, e.g., Kleiber & Zeileis,

1. See Hsiao (2007) for more details on theses points.

2010). This is a balanced firm-level panel data set that focuses on investments and contains observations of 10 firms from 1935 to 1954, i.e., it has $10 \times 20 = 200$ observations in total.

The following commands load these two data sets:

```
data( "EmplUK", package="plm" )
data( "Grunfeld", package="plm" )
```

More detailed information about these data sets, e.g., a description of the variables that are included in these data sets, can be obtained from their help pages:

```
help( "EmplUK", package="plm" )
help( "Grunfeld", package="plm" )
```

3 Exploring the Data Sets

Panel data sets by definition contain a cross-sectional dimension ($i = 1, \ldots, n$) and a time dimension ($t - 1, \ldots, T$). Panel data sets, however, can have more complicated structures and hierarchies, e.g., observations from firm i in city j in country k at time t. Furthermore, panel data sets can be balanced or unbalanced. A balanced panel data set includes observations from all possible combinations of the cross-sectional dimension ($i = 1, \ldots, n$) and the time dimension ($t = 1, \ldots, T$) so that its total number of observations is $N = n \times T$. In contrast, in an unbalanced panel data set, observations are missing for some combinations of the cross-sectional dimension ($i = 1, \ldots, n$) and the time dimension ($t = 1, \ldots, T$) so that its total number of observations is $N < n \times T$ and individual time series can differ in length. Unbalanced panel data sets can sometimes cause problems with certain tests, and not all estimators in the *plm* package can handle these panel data sets. Therefore, in order to know what we are dealing with, it is wise to first explore the data set at hand.

In this section, we explore the employment data set (`EmplUK`). The investment data set (`Grunfeld`) can be explored in the same way. Exploring the investment data set is even simpler than exploring the employment data set because the investment data set is a balanced panel data set, while the employment data set is an unbalanced panel data set.

What are the names of the variables in the data set?

```
names( EmplUK )
```

Display the first six observations:

```
head( EmplUK )
```

What is the number of observations?

```
nrow( EmplUK )
```

What are the identifiers of the firms in the data set?

```
unique( EmplUK$firm )
```

What is the number of firms in the data set?

```
length( unique( EmplUK$firm ) )
```

Which years are included in the data set?

```
unique( EmplUK$year )
```

What is the number of years that are included in the data set?

```
length( unique( EmplUK$year ) )
```

How many duplicate firm-year combinations are in the data set?

```
sum( duplicated( EmplUK[, c("firm", "year")]))
```

There are no duplicate firm-year combinations. Therefore, the number of unique firm-year combinations is equal to the number of observations (1031):

```
nrow( unique( EmplUK[ , c( "firm", "year" ) ] ) )
```

How many observations are included in each of the 9 years?

```
table( EmplUK$year )
```

Illustrate this graphically:

```
barplot( table( EmplUK$year ) )
```

How many firms are how many times (years) included in the data set?

```
table( table( EmplUK$firm ) )
```

Only 14 out of the 140 firms are in the data set for all 9 years, while most of the firms (103) are in the data set for 7 years.

How did the wage rate (unweighted average wage rate of the firms included in the data set) change over time?

```
aggregate( wage ~ year, EmplUK, mean )
```

How did the distribution of the wage rates change over time?

```
boxplot( wage ~ year, data = EmplUK )
lines( aggregate( wage ~ year, EmplUK, mean )$wage,
  col="blue", lwd=2 )
```

How did the distribution of employment change over time? As the distribution of the employment is highly right-skewed (i.e., many firms have a relatively small number of employees and a few firms have a large number of employees), we display the employment in log-scale:

```
boxplot( log( emp ) ~ year, data=EmplUK )
```

4 OLS Regression

4.1 Pooled OLS Regression

We use the investment data set (`Grunfeld`) to estimate a (static) investment equation:

$$inv_{it} = \beta_0 + \beta_1 value_{it} + \beta_2 capital_{it} + u_{it}, \tag{1}$$

where inv_{it} indicates the firm's gross investment, $value_{it}$ indicates the firm's value, $capital_{it}$ indicates the firm's capital stock, u_{it} is an unobserved error term, subscript $i = 1, \ldots, n$ indicates the firm, subscript $t = 1, \ldots, T$ indicates the year, and β_0, β_1, and β_2 are coefficients to be estimated. In case of the investment data set (`Grunfeld`), the number of firms is $n = 10$ and the number of time periods is $T = 20$. The following command estimates this model by OLS and, thus, ignores the panel structure of the data set, any dynamic (nonstatic) processes, and any potential endogeneities of the explanatory variables:

```
invOLS <- lm( inv ~ value + capital, data=Grunfeld )
```

The problem with this approach—as demonstrated in Balestra and Nerlove (1966)—is that a panel data set usually does not fulfill the assumptions of a simple linear regression model such as OLS. A standard linear regression model assumes that the observations $(y_{it}, \mathbf{x}_{it})$ are i.i.d. random draws from a target population with fixed distributional parameters. The model further assumes that the outcome of the dependent variable y_{it} is conditioned on a (column) vector of covariates $\mathbf{x}_{it}$ (potentially including a constant):

$$E(y_{it}|\, \mathbf{x}_{it}) = \mathbf{x}_{it}'\beta \ \forall i,t \tag{2}$$

$$Var(y_{it}|\, \mathbf{x}_{it}) = \sigma^2 \ \forall i,t, \tag{3}$$

where β is a (column) vector of unknown coefficients with the same length as $\mathbf{x}_{it}$ and σ^2 indicates the variance of the conditional distribution of y_{it}. In case of panel data, we often do not have a common conditional probability density function of y_{it} conditional on $\mathbf{x}_{it}$ for all cross-sectional units i at all times t, i.e., the conditional probability density function of y_{it} conditional on $\mathbf{x}_{it}$ differs between cross-sectional units i and/or between time periods t. Often there are time-invariant individual effects and/or individual-invariant time effects (observed or unobserved) that affect individual outcomes. The OLS estimator usually will produce smaller standard errors and, therefore, have higher significance levels than estimates of panel data estimators, such as the fixed- or random-effects estimators, that properly take said effects into account. Ignoring invariant effects, however, leads to inefficient estimators (in every case) and biased ones if the individual effects are correlated with some covariates. Therefore, OLS in a panel data context is likely to produce biased and, thus, potentially misleading estimates.

4.2 Least-Squares Dummy Variables Estimation

If the conditional density of y given $\mathbf{x}$ varies between individuals (i) or between time periods (t), fundamental theorems for statistical inference, such as the law of large numbers and the central limit theorem, are difficult to implement. One way to restore homogeneity across individuals (i) and/or over time periods (t) is to add further explanatory variables, say z_{it}, so that the conditional expectation becomes:

$$E(y_{it}|\,\mathbf{x}_{it}, z_{it}). \tag{4}$$

In order to take into account (at least to some extent) the panel structure of the data set in our example of the investment model, we can add firm-specific (α_j) and/or time-specific (γ_j) effects:

$$inv_{it} = \beta_0 + \beta_1 value_{it} + \beta_2 capital_{it} + \sum_{j=2}^{n} \alpha_j I(i=j) + \sum_{j=2}^{T} \gamma_j I(t=j) + u_{it}, \tag{5}$$

where $I(.)$ is an indicator function that is one if the condition is fulfilled and zero otherwise, α_j ; $j = 2, \ldots, n$ and γ_j; $j = 2, \ldots, T$ are additional coefficients to be estimated, and all other symbols are defined as before.

This model still can be estimated by OLS. If one specifies categorical variables (called `factor` variables in R) as explanatory variables, R automatically generates dummy variables for all but the first levels of these categorical variables. The following commands estimate model (5) with: firm-specific effects only, time-specific effects only, and both firm-specific and time-specific effects:

```
invLSDVi <- lm( inv ~ value + capital + factor( firm ),
  data=Grunfeld )

invLSDVt <- lm( inv ~ value + capital + factor( year ),
  data=Grunfeld )

invLSDV2<- lm( inv ~ value + capital + factor( firm ) +
  factor( year ), data=Grunfeld )
```

Using the investment equation with only one explanatory variable (`capital`) as (simplified) example, the following code creates a figure that demonstrates the effect of taking into account individual time-invariant effects in comparison to a simple pooled OLS regression (thick black line):

```
invLSDVi1<- lm( inv ~ capital + factor( firm ),
  data=Grunfeld )
```

```
invHat <- fitted( invLSDVi1 )
library( "car" )
scatterplot( invHat ~ capital | firm, data=Grunfeld,
  legend=list( coords="bottomright" ) )
abline( lm( inv ~ capital, data=Grunfeld ), lwd=3,
  col="black" )
legend( "topleft", "Pooled OLS regression line",
  col="black", lwd=3 )
```

The resulting Fig. 1 indicates that the intercepts (and, but to a lesser extent, also the slope parameter) notably differ between the 10 firms and the pooled OLS estimates, which demonstrates the bias that results from the pooled estimation. The reasoning is as follows (Balestra & Nerlove, 1966): Let's assume a panel data set with time-invariant individual effects. We then can write the error term as:

$$u_{it} = \alpha_i + \epsilon_{it}. \tag{6}$$

We assume that $E(\alpha_i \epsilon_{it}) = 0$ and that $E(\alpha_i) = E(\epsilon_{it}) = 0$. Furthermore, we assume that:

$$E(\alpha_i \alpha_j) = \begin{cases} \sigma_\alpha^2 & \text{if } i = j \\ 0 & \text{if } i \neq j \end{cases} \tag{7}$$

and that:

$$E(\epsilon_{it} \epsilon_{js}) = \begin{cases} \sigma_\epsilon^2 & \text{if } i = j,\ t = s \\ 0 & \text{otherwise} \end{cases} \tag{8}$$

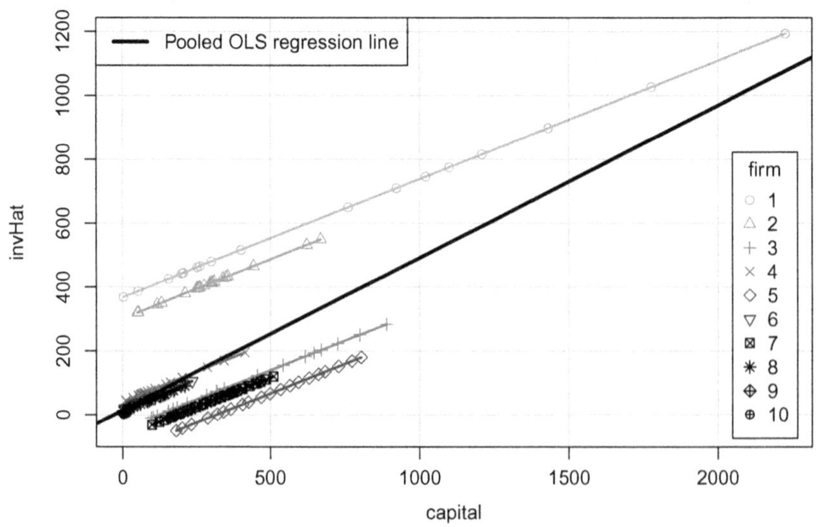

FIG. 1 Pooled regression vs. regression with firm-fixed effects.

For one individual in the panel data set, the covariance matrix of the error term $u_i = (u_{i1}, \ldots, u_{iT})'$ is:

$$E\left(u_i u_i'\right) = \begin{pmatrix} \sigma_\epsilon^2 + \sigma_\alpha^2 & \sigma_\alpha^2 & \cdots & \sigma_\alpha^2 \\ \sigma_\alpha^2 & \sigma_\epsilon^2 + \sigma_\alpha^2 & \cdots & \sigma_\alpha^2 \\ \vdots & \vdots & \ddots & \vdots \\ \sigma_\alpha^2 & \sigma_\alpha^2 & \cdots & \sigma_\epsilon^2 + \sigma_\alpha^2 \end{pmatrix} \forall i. \tag{9}$$

Please note that—by assumption—$E(u_1u_1') = E(u_2u_2') = \ldots = E(u_nu_n')$.

If we assume no cross-sectional dependence or any other disturbances, the covariance matrix of the entire error term $u = (u_1', u_2', \ldots, u_n')'$ is:

$$E(uu') = \begin{pmatrix} E\left(u_1u_1'\right) & 0 & \cdots & 0 \\ 0 & E\left(u_2u_2'\right) & \cdots & 0 \\ \vdots & \vdots & \ddots & \vdots \\ 0 & 0 & \cdots & E\left(u_nu_n'\right) \end{pmatrix}. \tag{10}$$

We can clearly see that the off-diagonal elements of the individual blocks, $E(u_iu_i')$, are nonzero unless the variance of the time-invariant individual effects also is zero, which would remove all individual effects (i.e., $\alpha_i = 0 \ \forall \ i = 1, \ldots, n$) and, therefore, result in the pooled model. If there are individual effects and we conduct a pooled OLS estimation without taking into account the previously discussed error structure, the OLS estimator still will be consistent as long as the composite error u_{it} and, in particular, its component α_i, is independent from the regressors. The OLS estimator, however, will be inefficient, and the OLS estimate of the parameters' covariance matrix and, therefore, the standard errors, will be biased. If, on the contrary, any part of the composite error, and in particular the individual effect, is correlated with the regressors then the OLS estimates for the parameters will be biased and inconsistent as well.

Model specifications as in Eq. (5) that take into account individual or time effects by including dummy variables as additional explanatory variables are safe in this respect, their consistency relying only on the usual exogeneity condition ($E(\epsilon | X) = E(\epsilon)$). They are called "least-squares dummy variables" (LSDV) estimators. However, if a panel data set contains observations from many different individuals or many different time periods, the estimation includes a large number of coefficients of the individual and/or time dummy variables ($n + T - 2$ in case of both individual-specific and time-specific effects), which could result in numerical problems and/or could require computers with large amounts of memory (RAM). A further problem is that the inclusion of such dummy variables can confuse the relationship between y_{it} and $\mathbf{x}_{it}$, which is often the researcher's main interest, because of a considerable loss in degrees of freedom and/or multicollinearity. These are some of the reasons for using specific panel-data specifications for econometric estimations with panel data, for example, those that we will later discuss in this chapter.

5 Organization, Management, and Preparation of Panel Data

5.1 Re-Ordering of Observations

In the investment data set (`Grunfeld`), the observations are ordered primarily according to the firm and secondarily according to the year:

```
Grunfeld[ c( 1:3, 198:200 ), 1:2 ]
##     firm year
## 1      1 1935
## 2      1 1936
## 3      1 1937
## 198   10 1952
## 199   10 1953
## 200   10 1954
```

The following command reorders the observations so that they are ordered primarily according to the year and secondarily according to the firm:

```
GrunfeldSortYear <- Grunfeld[
  order( Grunfeld$year, Grunfeld$firm ), ]
GrunfeldSortYear[ c( 1:3, 198:200 ), 1:2 ]
##     firm year
## 1      1 1935
## 21     2 1935
## 41     3 1935
## 160    8 1954
## 180    9 1954
## 200   10 1954
```

5.2 Conversion between "Long Format" and "Wide Format"

Both the employment data set (`EmplUK`) and the investment data set (`Grunfeld`) are in "long format," that is, each row of the data set corresponds to a specific individual-time (in our examples: firm-year) combination. In this section, we use the investment data set (`Grunfeld`) as an example. The following command converts this data set to "wide format" so that each row of the data set corresponds to one specific firm[2]:

```
GrunfeldFirms <- reshape( Grunfeld, idvar="firm",
  timevar="year", direction="wide" )
dim( GrunfeldFirms )
## [1] 10 61
```

2. Package *tidyr* provides the functions `gather()` and `spread()` that can be used instead of `reshape()` to convert data sets between "long format" and "wide format."

When `reshape()` converts a data set from "long format" to "wide format", it adds an attribute `"reshapeWide"` that provides information about the data structure. When converting a data set that has an attribute `"reshapeWide"` from "wide format" back to "long format," the user does not need to provide additional information on the data structure because this information is available in the attribute `"reshapeWide"`:

```
Grunfeld2 <- reshape(GrunfeldFirms, direction="long")
```

The following command confirms that the resulting data set is identical to the original data set (except for some of the variable names and the ordering of the observations):

```
all.equal(Grunfeld2, GrunfeldSortYear,
  check.attributes = FALSE)
## [1] TRUE
```

The following code removes the attribute `"reshapeWide"` so that we can demonstrate how one can convert a data set from "wide format" to "long format" that has not been converted from a data set in "long format" by using `reshape()` and, thus, does not have an attribute `"reshapeWide"`:

```
attr(GrunfeldFirms, "reshapeWide") <- NULL
Grunfeld2b <- reshape( GrunfeldFirms, idvar="firm",
  timevar="year",
  varying=lapply( c( "inv.", "value.", "capital." ),
    function(x) paste0( x, 1935:1954 ) ),
  times=1935:1954, direction="long" )
all.equal( Grunfeld2, Grunfeld2b, check.attributes = FALSE )
## [1] TRUE
```

Sometimes, we want to obtain a data set in "wide format," where each row of the data set corresponds to one specific time period (e.g., year) rather than to one specific individual (e.g., firm). The following command converts the investment data set (`Grunfeld`) to "wide format" so that each row corresponds to one specific year:

```
GrunfeldYears <- reshape( Grunfeld, idvar="year",
  timevar="firm", direction="wide" )
dim( GrunfeldYears )
## [1] 20 31
```

As before, `reshape()` added an attribute `"reshapeWide"` that provides information about the data structure.

Because the data set `GrunfeldYears` has an attribute `"reshapeWide"`, `reshape()` does not require additional information about the data structure for converting the data set from "wide format" back to "long format":

```
Grunfeld3 <- reshape( GrunfeldYears, direction="long" )
```

The following command confirms that the resulting data set is identical to the original data set (except for some of the variable names and the ordering of the variables):

```
all.equal( Grunfeld3[ , c( 2, 1, 3:5 ) ], Grunfeld,
  check.attributes=FALSE )
## [1] TRUE
```

As before, we remove the attribute "reshapeWide" so that we can demonstrate how one can convert a data set from "wide format" to "long format" that has not been converted from "long format" by using reshape() and, thus, does not have an attribute "reshapeWide":

```
attr( GrunfeldYears, "reshapeWide" ) <- NULL
Grunfeld3b <- reshape( GrunfeldYears, idvar=year,
  timevar="firm",
  varying=lapply( c( "inv.", "value.", "capital." ),
    function(x) paste0( x, 1:10 ) ), direction="long" )
all.equal( Grunfeld3, Grunfeld3b, check.attributes = FALSE )
## [1] TRUE
```

5.3 Creating a Balanced Panel Data Set from an Unbalanced Panel Data Set

Because the investment data set (Grunfeld) already is balanced, we use the employment data set (EmplUK) in this section as an example.

The following command identifies the firms that are in the data set in all of the 9 years that are covered in this data set:

```
firmsAllYears <- names( table(EmplUK$firm) ) [
  table(EmplUK$firm) == 9 ]
```

Now, we can extract the observations of the firms that are in all 9 years of the data set:

```
EmplUKBal <- subset( EmplUK, firm %in% firmsAllYears )
dim( EmplUKBal )
## [1] 126 7
length( unique( EmplUKBal$firm ) )
## [1] 14
length( unique( EmplUKBal$year ) )
## [1] 9
```

The balanced data set has observations from 14 firms and 9 years and, thus, in total $14 \times 9 = 126$ observations.

Alternatively, we can create a balanced panel data set that includes all time periods, for which observations from all individuals are available. The following command identifies the years for which data from all 140 firms are available:

```
yearsAllFirms <- names( table(EmplUK$year) ) [
  table(EmplUK$year) == 140 ]
```

Now, we can extract the observations of the years for which data from all 140 firms are available:

```
EmplUKBalYears <- subset( EmplUK, year %in% yearsAllFirms )
dim( EmplUKBalYears )
## [1] 700 7
length( unique( EmplUKBalYears$year ) )
## [1] 5
length( unique( EmplUKBalYears$firm ) )
## [1] 140
```

This balanced data set has observations from 140 firms and 5 years and, thus, in total $140 \times 5 = 700$ observations.

5.4 Aggregating Panel Data Sets

The following command creates a data set, in which each observation corresponds to one firm and the values of the variables indicate the sums over all of the firm's observations in all available time periods:

```
GrunfeldFirmSum <- aggregate( Grunfeld,
  by=list( Grunfeld$firm ), FUN=sum )
```

The following command creates a data set, where each observation corresponds to one firm and the values of the variables indicate the mean values over all of the firm's observations in all available time periods:

```
GrunfeldFirmMean <- aggregate( Grunfeld,
  by=list( Grunfeld$firm ), FUN=mean )
```

5.5 Preparing the Data Set for Estimations with the *plm* Package

In this chapter, we will use the *plm* package (Croissant & Millo, 2008) to estimate various specifications and to conduct various specification tests of panel data models. The following command loads the *plm* package:

```
library( "plm" )
```

The estimation of panel data models with the *plm* package requires that the data sets are in "long format." If a data set is in "wide format," it can be converted to "long format" using the `reshape()` command as briefly illustrated in Section 5.2. Because the two data sets that we use in our analysis, i.e., the investment data set (`Grunfeld`) and the employment data set (`EmplUK`), are already in "long format," we do not need to convert them.

The `pdata.frame()` function is used in the *plm* package to add information about the panel data structure to the data set, implicitly or explicitly. The following command explicitly adds this information to the investment data set (`Grunfeld`):

```
GrunfeldPdata <- pdata.frame( Grunfeld,
  index=c( "firm", "year" ) )
```

The function `pdata.frame()` modifies the data set in the following ways:

- It sets the class to `"pdata.frame"` (inheriting from class `"data.frame"`):

```
class( GrunfeldPdata )
## [1] "pdata.frame" "data.frame"
```

- It adds an attribute `"index"` to the data set and to each variable in the data set, which is a `data.frame` with two variables, namely the individual identifier and the time identifier:

```
attr(GrunfeldPdata, "index")[c(1:3, 198:200),]
##     firm year
## 1      1 1935
## 2      1 1936
## 3      1 1937
## 198   10 1952
## 199   10 1953
## 200   10 1954
all.equal( attr( GrunfeldPdata, "index" ),
  attr( GrunfeldPdata$inv, "index" ) )
## [1] TRUE
```

- It sets the class of each individual variable to `"pseries"`, inheriting from the original class of the variable, e.g.:

```
class( GrunfeldPdata$inv )
## [1] "pseries" "numeric"
```

- It modifies the row names of the data set so that they indicate the individual identifier and the time identifier:

```
rownames( GrunfeldPdata ) [ c( 1:3, 198:200 ) ]
## [1] "1-1935" "1-1936" "1-1937" "10-1952" "10-1953" "10-1954"
```

- It converts the variables that identify the individuals and the time periods to categorical (`factor`) variables:

```
class( GrunfeldPdata$firm )
## [1] "pseries" "factor"
class( GrunfeldPdata$year )
## [1] "pseries" "factor"
```

The explicit conversion of the data set with pdata.frame() is not necessary if the first variable of the data set is the individual identifier and the second variable is the time identifier. In this case, the data set can be used as is; the conversion will be done internally by the software, transparently to the user.

Because in both of the data sets that we use in our chapter, i.e., the investment data set (Grunfeld) and the employment data set (EmplUK), the first variable is the individual identifier and the second variable is the time identifier, we do not need to use pdata.frame() to prepare our data sets. For example, the function pdim() can identify the panel structure of these two data sets even without having applied pdata.frame() to these data sets:

```
pdim( Grunfeld )
## Balanced Panel: n = 10, T = 20, N = 200
pdim( EmplUK )
## Unbalanced Panel: n=140, T=7-9, N=1031
```

5.6 Lagged Variables and First Differences

If functions lag() and diff() that create lagged variables and first differences of variables, respectively, are applied to variables inside regular data.frames, they do not take into account the panel structure and assume that the values from the previous rows are the values from the previous time periods. If the data set has been transformed into a pdata.frame, then the variables inside will be of class pseries; therefore, the functions lag() and diff() will correctly take into account the panel data structure:

```
cbind(
  firm = Grunfeld$firm,
  year = Grunfeld$year,
  inv = Grunfeld$inv,
  invLag = c( NA, lag( Grunfeld$inv )[ -200 ] ),
  invDiff = c( NA, diff( Grunfeld$inv )[ -200 ] ),
  invLagPanel = lag( GrunfeldPdata$inv ),
  invDiffPanel = diff( GrunfeldPdata$inv ) )[
    c( 1:3, 19:23 ), ]
##         firm year    inv invLag invDiff invLagPanel
## 1-1935    1 1935  317.6     NA      NA          NA
## 1-1936    1 1936  391.8  317.6    74.2       317.6
## 1-1937    1 1937  410.6  391.8    18.8       391.8
## 1-1953    1 1953 1304.4  891.2   413.2       891.2
## 1-1954    1 1954 1486.7 1304.4   182.3      1304.4
## 2-1935    2 1935  209.9 1486.7 -1276.8          NA
## 2-1936    2 1936  355.3  209.9   145.4       209.9
## 2-1937    2 1937  469.9  355.3   114.6       355.3
```

```
##          invDiffPanel
## 1-1935            NA
## 1-1936          74.2
## 1-1937          18.8
## 1-1953         413.2
## 1-1954         182.3
## 2-1935            NA
## 2-1936         145.4
## 2-1937         114.6
```

If functions `lag()` and `diff()` are used directly to specify the model for panel data estimations (in argument `formula`), these functions take into account the panel data structure even if one has not applied `pdata.frame()` to the data set.

6 Estimation of OLS-Based Linear Panel Data Models

To capture the heterogeneity in the data that is not captured by $\mathbf{x}_{it}$, we could assume that the parameter vector $\theta_{it} = (\beta_{it}, \sigma_{it}^2)$ varies with time and over all individuals:

$$E(y_{it} | \mathbf{x}_{it}) = \mathbf{x}_{it}\beta_{it} \tag{11}$$

Such a model is not estimable. Therefore, the idea of panel data estimators is to impose a structure on θ_{it} that levels a compromise between estimability and heterogeneity. This is mainly done by decomposing θ_{it} into $\theta_{it} = (\beta, \lambda_{it}, \sigma^2)$ where β and σ^2 are fixed structural parameters, which are the same over all i and all t, and λ_{it} are incidental parameters, which vary across i and/or t, and, thus, can capture time-invariant individual effects (α_i), individual-invariant time effects (γ_t), or both.

The assumption that all slope parameters β are structural parameters, however, should not be taken lightly. Especially for panel data sets with large T, there is clearly a trade-off between the advantages of a panel data model, as discussed in the introduction, and loss of fit by assuming fixed slope parameters across the individuals. In any case, the poolability of the individual models should be tested.

In this section, we use the investment data set (`Grunfeld`) and various OLS-based panel data specifications to estimate the (static) investment equation (Eq. 1).

6.1 Variable Coefficients Model

The variable coefficients model for panel data allows the coefficients to vary either between individuals or between time periods. Therefore, the (static) investment equation (Eq. 1) would become either:

$$inv_{it} = \beta_{0i} + \beta_{1i} value_{it} + \beta_{2i} capital_{it} + \epsilon_{it} \tag{12}$$

or:

$$inv_{it} = \beta_{0t} + \beta_{1t} value_{it} + \beta_{2t} capital_{it} + \epsilon_{it}, \tag{13}$$

respectively, where $\beta_{ji}; j=0, \ldots, 2; i=1, \ldots, n$ and $\beta_{jt}; j=0, \ldots, 2; t=1, \ldots, T$ are the coefficients to be estimated and all other symbols are defined as before. These two models can be estimated by the following commands:

```
invVCMi <- pvcm( inv ~ value + capital, data = Grunfeld )

invVCMt <- pvcm( inv ~ value + capital, effect = "time",
  data = Grunfeld )
```

The variable coefficients model with individual-specific coefficients (Eq. 12) might be inefficient or even infeasible if the number of time periods (T) is small compared to the number of explanatory variables (k, including a constant) because it requires the estimation of $n \times k$ coefficients with $n \times T$ observations in balanced panel data sets and fewer observations in unbalanced panel data sets. Likewise, the variable coefficients model with time-specific coefficients (Eq. 13) might be inefficient or even infeasible if the number of individuals (n) is small compared to the number of explanatory variables (k, including a constant) because it requires the estimation of $T \times k$ coefficients with $T \times n$ observations in balanced panel data sets and fewer observations in unbalanced panel data sets.

6.2 Fixed-Effects Estimator Based on "Within" Transformation

The most commonly used estimators for linear panel data models are fixed-effects estimators based on the "within" transformation. We demonstrate the "within" transformation with a model that includes individual effects (α_i) but—for simplicity—no time effects (γ_t):

$$y_{it} = \mathbf{x}_{it}'\beta + \alpha_i + \epsilon_{it} \tag{14}$$

We define the following variables:

$$\overline{y}_i \equiv T^{-1} \sum_{t=1}^{T} y_{it} \tag{15}$$

$$\overline{\mathbf{x}}_i \equiv T^{-1} \sum_{t=1}^{T} \mathbf{x}_{it} \tag{16}$$

$$\overline{\epsilon}_i \equiv T^{-1} \sum_{t=1}^{T} \epsilon_{it} \tag{17}$$

$$\widetilde{y}_{it} \equiv y_{it} - \overline{y}_i \tag{18}$$

$$\widetilde{\mathbf{x}}_{it} \equiv \mathbf{x}_{it} - \overline{\mathbf{x}}_i \tag{19}$$

$$\widetilde{\epsilon}_{it} \equiv \epsilon_{it} - \overline{\epsilon}_i \tag{20}$$

Now we can conduct the "within" transformation:

$$\widetilde{y}_i = y_{it} - \overline{y}_i \tag{21}$$

$$\widetilde{y}_i = \mathbf{x}'_{it}\beta + \alpha_i + \epsilon_{it} - T^{-1}\sum_{t=1}^{T} y_{it} \tag{22}$$

$$\widetilde{y}_i = \mathbf{x}'_{it}\beta + \alpha_i + \epsilon_{it} - T^{-1}\sum_{t=1}^{T} \left(\mathrm{x}'_{it}\beta + \alpha_i + \epsilon_{it}\right) \tag{23}$$

$$\widetilde{y}_i = \mathbf{x}'_{it}\beta + \alpha_i + \epsilon_{it} - T^{-1}\sum_{t=1}^{T} \mathbf{x}'_{it}\beta - T^{-1}\sum_{t=1}^{T} \alpha_i - T^{-1}\sum_{t=1}^{T} \epsilon_{it} \tag{24}$$

$$\widetilde{y}_i = \mathbf{x}'_{it}\beta + \alpha_i + \epsilon_{it} - \left(T^{-1}\sum_{t=1}^{T} \mathbf{x}_{it}\right)'\beta - \alpha_i T^{-1}\sum_{t=1}^{T} 1 - \overline{\epsilon}_i \tag{25}$$

$$\widetilde{y}_i = \mathbf{x}_{it}\beta + \alpha_i + \epsilon_{it} - \overline{\mathbf{x}}'_i\beta - \alpha_i - \overline{\epsilon}_i \tag{26}$$

$$\widetilde{y}_i = (\mathbf{x}_{it} - \overline{\mathbf{x}}_i)'\beta + \epsilon_{it} - \overline{\epsilon}_i \tag{27}$$

$$\widetilde{y}_i = \widetilde{\mathbf{x}}'_{it}\beta + \widetilde{\epsilon}_{it} \tag{28}$$

The fixed-effects "within" estimator can be obtained by applying the OLS method to the model with "within" transformed variables (Eq. 28). If the model contains time effects (instead of or in addition to individual effects), the time effects can be removed in a similar way as the individual effects were removed earlier.

In case of the investment equation (Eq. 1), the fixed-effects model is specified as:

$$inv_{it} = \beta_0 + \beta_1 value_{it} + \beta_2 capital_{it} + u_{it} \tag{29}$$

$$u_{it} = \alpha_i + \gamma_t + \epsilon_{it}, \tag{30}$$

where the overall error term u_{it} can be divided into three components, of which α_i; $i = 1, \ldots, n$ picks up firm-specific effects, γ_t; $t = 1, \ldots, T$ picks up time-specific effects, and ϵ_{it} picks up the remaining (idiosyncratic) component of the overall error term u_{it}. The model specified in Eqs. (29) and (30) is the so-called two-ways fixed-effects model because it takes into account both firm-specific effects and time-specific effects. When setting all time-specific effects to zero ($\gamma_t = 0 \; \forall \; t = 1, \ldots, T$), the model specified in Eqs. (29) and (30) becomes a one-way individual-fixed-effects model. Similarly, when setting all individual-specific effects to zero ($\alpha_i = 0 \; \forall \; i = 1, \ldots, n$), the model specified in Eqs. (29) and (30) becomes a one-way time fixed-effects model.

The fixed-effects model allows individual- and/or time-specific effects to be correlated with the covariates $\mathbf{x}_{it}$, which is an advantage over the random-effects estimator, as such correlations are more the rule than the exception. The fixed-effects estimator, however, loses degrees of freedom as n or T increase and the fixed-effects estimator rules out the inclusion of time invariant variables, because their effects are absorbed by the fixed-effects coefficient.

The "within" transformation subtracts the group-specific mean values from the dependent variable and the explanatory variables, which removes the firm-specific effects ($\alpha_i = 0 \ \forall \ i = 1, \ldots, n$) or the time-specific effects ($\gamma_t = 0 \ \forall \ t = 1, \ldots, T$) so that the model can be estimated by applying the OLS method on the "within"-transformed variables.

The following commands use the "within" estimator to estimate the fixed-effects model specified in Eqs. (29) and (30) with: firm-specific effects only, time-specific effects only, and both firm-specific and time-specific effects:

```
invFEi <- plm( inv ~ value + capital, data=Grunfeld )

invFEt <- plm( inv ~ value + capital, effect = "time",
  data = Grunfeld )

invFE2 <- plm( inv ~ value + capital, effect="twoways",
  data = Grunfeld )
```

The slope coefficients estimated by the "within" estimators are equal to the slope coefficients estimated by the corresponding LSDV estimators[3]:

```
all.equal( coef( invFEi ), coef( invLSDVi ) [
  c( "value", "capital" ) ] )
## [1] TRUE
all.equal( coef( invFEt ), coef( invLSDVt ) [
  c( "value", "capital" ) ] )
## [1] TRUE
all.equal( coef( invFE2 ), coef( invLSDV2 ) [
  c( "value", "capital" ) ] )
## [1] TRUE
```

As briefly discussed in Section 4.2, the LSDV has several disadvantages compared to the fixed-effects estimator based on the "within" transformation, e.g., larger memory requirements of the computer and lower numerical accuracy. Therefore, we recommend applying "within" estimators instead of LSDV estimators.

6.3 Pooled Estimation

The pooled model (Eq. 1) that ignores the panel data structure not only can be estimated by the `lm()` function but also by the `plm()` function with argument `model` set to `"pooling"`:

```
invPool <- plm( inv ~ value + capital, model = "pooling",
  data = Grunfeld )
```

---

3. It can be proven mathematically that the least-squares dummy variables (LSDV) estimator and the fixed-effects "within" estimator are identical. Because this proof is lengthy and not essential for understanding panel data econometrics, we do not show it here.

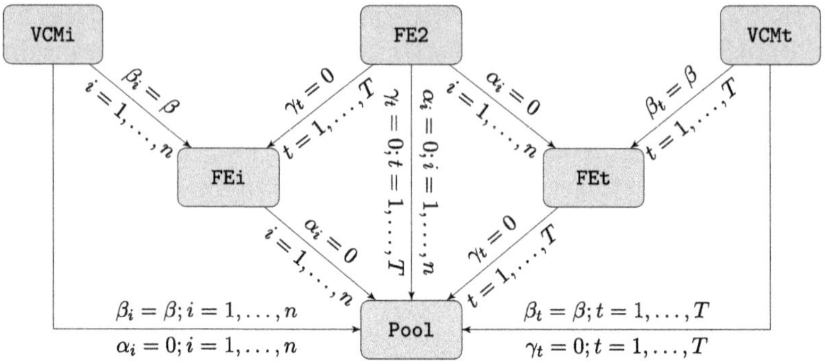

FIG. 2 Relationships between the previously estimated panel data models.

The estimated coefficients and standard errors are identical to those obtained in Section 4.1.

```
all.equal( coef( summary( invPool ) ),
  coef( summary( invOLS ) ), check.attributes = FALSE )
## [1] TRUE
```

6.4 Testing Poolability

The relationships between the previously estimated panel data models are illustrated in Fig. 2. If two models are connected by an arrow, the lower model is nested in the upper model, whereas the implied parameter restrictions are indicated beside the arrow. In the following, the parameter restrictions of all nested relationships between the previously estimated models are tested.

The following two commands conduct the same Wald test (F-test) for testing the null hypothesis that the slope coefficients are equal across all individuals (H_0: $\beta_i = \beta$; $i = 1, \ldots, n$):

```
pooltest( invFEi, invVCMi )
##
##  F statistic
##
## data: inv ~ value + capital
## F = 5.7805, df1 = 18, df2 = 170, p-value = 1.219e-10
## alternative hypothesis: unstability
pooltest( inv ~ value + capital, data = Grunfeld )
##
##  F statistic
##
## data: inv ~ value + capital
## F = 5.7805, df1 = 18, df2 = 170, p-value = 1.219e-10
## alternative hypothesis: unstability
```

The test results indicate that the slope coefficients differ significantly between individuals.

The following two commands conduct the same Wald test (F-test) for testing the null hypothesis that all coefficients (slope coefficients and intercepts/individual effects) are equal across all individuals (H_0: $\beta_i = \beta$; $i = 1, \ldots, n$ and $\alpha_i = 0$; $i = 1, \ldots, n$):

```
pooltest( invPool, invVCMi )
##
##  F statistic
##
## data: inv ~ value + capital
## F = 27.749, df1 = 27, df2 = 170, p-value < 2.2e-16
## alternative hypothesis: unstability
pooltest( inv ~ value + capital, data=Grunfeld,
  model="pooling" )
##
##  F statistic
##
## data: inv ~ value + capital
## F = 27.749, df1 = 27, df2 = 170, p-value < 2.2e-16
## alternative hypothesis: unstability
```

The test results indicate that the slope coefficients and/or the intercepts differ significantly between individuals.

The following two commands conduct the same Wald test (F-test) for testing the null hypothesis that the slope coefficients are equal across all time periods (H_0: $\beta_t = \beta$; $t = 1, \ldots, T$):

```
pooltest( invFEt, invVCMt )
##
##  F statistic
##
## data: inv ~ value + capital
## F = 1.5495, df1 = 38, df2 = 140, p-value = 0.03553
## alternative hypothesis: unstability
pooltest( inv ~ value + capital, data=Grunfeld,
  effect="time" )
##
##  F statistic
##
## data: inv ~ value + capital
## F = 1.5495, df1 = 38, df2 = 140, p-value = 0.03553
## alternative hypothesis: unstability
```

The test results indicate that the slope coefficients differ significantly between time periods at 5% significance level.

The following two commands conduct the same Wald test (F-test) for testing the null hypothesis that all coefficients (slope coefficients and intercepts/time effects) are equal across all time periods (H_0: $\beta_t = \beta$; $t = 1, \ldots, T$ and $\gamma_t = 0$; $t = 1, \ldots, T$):

```
pooltest( invPool, invVCMt )
##
##  F statistic
##
## data: inv ~ value + capital
## F = 1.1204, df1 = 57, df2 = 140, p-value = 0.2928
## alternative hypothesis: unstability
pooltest( inv ~ value + capital, data=Grunfeld,
  effect = "time", model = "pooling" )
##
## F statistic
##
## data: inv ~ value + capital
## F = 1.1204, df1 = 57, df2 = 140, p-value = 0.2928
## alternative hypothesis: unstability
```

The test results do not reject the null hypothesis that all coefficients (slope coefficients and intercepts/time effects) are equal across all time periods.

The following commands test the (joint) null hypothesis that there are no individual effects and no time effects (H_0: $\alpha_i = 0$; $i = 1, \ldots, n$ and $\gamma_t = 0$; $t = 1, \ldots, T$):

```
pooltest( invPool, invFE2 )
##
##  F statistic
##
## data: inv ~ value + capital
## F = 17.403, df1 = 28, df2 = 169, p-value < 2.2e-16
## alternative hypothesis: unstability
pFtest( invFE2, invPool )
##
##  F test for twoways effects
##
## data: inv ~ value + capital
## F = 17.403, df1 = 28, df2 = 169, p-value < 2.2e-16
## alternative hypothesis: significant effects
pFtest( inv ~ value + capital, effect="twoways",
  data=Grunfeld )
##
##  F test for twoways effects
##
## data: inv ~ value + capital
## F = 17.403, df1 = 28, df2 = 169, p-value < 2.2e-16
## alternative hypothesis: significant effects
```

These three commands conduct the same F-test that tests the pooled model against the two-ways fixed-effects model. Therefore, these three commands return exactly the same results.

If the random-effects hypothesis holds, i.e., if correlation between the individual effects (if any) and the regressors is excluded, but one still wants to test whether individual effects are present at all (typically, for deciding whether to use OLS or a random-effects estimator), one can use a Lagrange Multiplier test:

```
plmtest( invPool, effect = "twoways" )
##
##  Lagrange Multiplier Test - two-ways effects (Honda) for
##  balanced panels
##
## data: inv ~ value + capital
## normal = 18.181, p-value < 2.2e-16
## alternative hypothesis: significant effects
```

This command tests the same null hypothesis as the previous three commands, but it conducts the Lagrange multiplier test instead of the F-test. The LM test is appropriate only under the random-effects hypothesis and will be inconsistent if the individual effects are of the correlated (fixed) type. All test results indicate that there are significant individual effects and/or time effects.

The following commands test the null hypothesis that there are no individual effects (H_0: $\alpha_i = 0$; $i = 1, \ldots, n$):

```
library( "lmtest" )
pooltest( invFEt, invFE2 )

##
##  F statistic
##
## data: inv ~ value + capital
## F = 52.362, df1 = 9, df2 = 169, p-value < 2.2e-16
## alternative hypothesis: unstability

waldtest( plm( inv ~ value + capital + factor(firm),
  effect = "time", data = Grunfeld ), 3, test = "F" )

## Wald test
##
## Model 1: inv ~ value + capital + factor(firm)
## Model 2: inv ~ value + capital
##   Res.Df Df      F    Pr(>F)
## 1    169
## 2    178 -9 52.362 <2.2e-16 ***
## ---
## Signif. codes:
   0 '***'0.001 '**'0.01 '*'0.05 '.'0.1 ' ' 1
```

```
pFtest( invFEi, invPool )

##
##  F test for individual effects
##
## data: inv ~ value + capital
## F = 49.177, df1 = 9, df2 = 188, p-value < 2.2e-16
## alternative hypothesis: significant effects

pFtest( inv ~ value + capital, effect="individual",
  data=Grunfeld )

##
##  F test for individual effects
##
## data: inv ~ value + capital
## F = 49.177, df1 = 9, df2 = 188, p-value < 2.2e-16
## alternative hypothesis: significant effects
```

The first command loads package *lmtest* that provides the function `waldtest()`. The following two commands conduct two identical F-tests for individual effects by testing the time-fixed-effects model against the two-ways fixed-effects model (i.e., in the presence of time-fixed effects). The fourth and fifths commands also conduct identical F-tests for individual effects, but these commands test the pooled model against the individual-fixed-effects model (i.e., in the absence of time-fixed effects). All test results indicate that there are significant individual effects.

The following commands test the null hypothesis that there are no time effects (H_0: $\gamma_t = 0$; $t = 1, \ldots, T$):

```
pooltest( invFEi, invFE2 )

##
##  F statistic
##
## data: inv ~ value + capital
## F = 1.4032, df1 = 19, df2 = 169, p-value = 0.1309
## alternative hypothesis: unstability

waldtest( plm( inv ~ value + capital + factor(year),
  data=Grunfeld ), 3, test="F" )

## Wald test
##
## Model 1: inv ~ value + capital + factor(year)
## Model 2: inv ~ value + capital
##    Res.Df  Df       F    Pr(>F)
## 1     169
## 2     188 -19 1.4032    0.1309
```

```
pFtest( invFEt, invPool )

##
##  F test for time effects
##
## data: inv ~ value + capital
## F = 0.23451, df1 = 19, df2 = 178, p-value = 0.9997
## alternative hypothesis: significant effects

pFtest( inv ~ value + capital, effect="time",
  data=Grunfeld )

##
##  F test for time effects
##
## data: inv ~ value + capital
## F = 0.23451, df1 = 19, df2 = 178, p-value = 0.9997
## alternative hypothesis: significant effects

plmtest( invPool, effect="time" )

##
## Lagrange Multiplier Test - time effects (Honda) for
  balanced panels
##
## data: inv ~ value + capital
## normal=-2.5404, p-value=0.9945
## alternative hypothesis: significant effects
```

The first two commands conduct identical F-tests for time effects by testing the individual-fixed-effects model against the two-ways fixed-effects model (i.e., in the presence of individual-fixed effects). The third and fourth commands also conduct identical F-tests for time effects, but these commands test the pooled model against the time-fixed-effects model (i.e., in the absence of individual-fixed effects). The fifth command tests the same null hypothesis as the third and fourth commands, but it conducts the Lagrange multiplier test instead of the F-test, testing the absence of individual effects against the alternative of individual effects of the random type. Neither the F-tests tests nor the Lagrange multiplier test rejects the null hypothesis that there are no time effects. Therefore, we can conclude that the time effects are statistically insignificant.

6.5 Obtaining Estimates of the Fixed Effects

In a "within" model with individual fixed effects (α_i), the estimates of the fixed effects can be obtained by taking the average values of both sides of Eq. (14) over all time periods t for each individual i:

$$T^{-1}\sum_{i=1}^{T} y_{it} = T^{-1}\sum_{i=1}^{T}\left(\mathbf{x}_{it}'\beta + \alpha_i + \epsilon_{it}\right)\forall i \tag{31}$$

$$\bar{y}_i = T^{-1}\sum_{i=1}^{T}\mathbf{x}_{it}\beta + T^{-1}\sum_{i=1}^{T}\alpha_i + T^{-1}\sum_{i=1}^{T}\epsilon_{it}\forall i \tag{32}$$

$$\bar{y}_i = \bar{\mathbf{x}}_i\beta + \alpha_i + \bar{\epsilon}_i\forall i \tag{33}$$

$$\alpha_i = \bar{y}_i - \bar{\mathbf{x}}_i'\beta - \bar{\epsilon}_i\forall i \tag{34}$$

Replacing β by its estimator $\hat{\beta}$ and replacing $\bar{\epsilon}i$ by its expectation (0), we can obtain estimates of the individual effects:

$$\hat{\alpha}_i = \bar{y}_i - \bar{\mathbf{x}}_i'\hat{\beta} \tag{35}$$

These estimates of the fixed effects can be obtained by function `fixef()`[4]:

```
fixef( invFEi )
```

These estimates are individual-specific intercepts that are identical to the intercept of the corresponding least-squares dummy variables (LSDV) model plus the coefficients of the firm-level dummy variables:

```
all.equal( c( fixef( invFEi ) ),
  coef( invLSDVi )[ "(Intercept)" ]+
  c(0, coef( invLSDVi )[
    grep( "firm", names( coef( invLSDVi ) ) ) ] ),
  check.attributes=FALSE )
## [1] TRUE
```

Argument `type` of `fixef()` can be used to specify a different normalization of the estimates of the fixed effects. If this argument is set to `"dfirst"`, differences to the fixed effect of the first individual are returned, which are identical to the coefficients of the firm-level dummy variables in the corresponding least-squares dummy variables (LSDV) model:

```
fixef( invFEi, type="dfirst" )
```

```
all.equal( c( fixef( invFEi, type="dfirst" ) ),
  coef( invLSDVi )[
    grep( "firm", names( coef( invLSDVi ) ) ) ],
  check.attributes = FALSE )
## [1] TRUE
```

If argument `type` is set to `"dmean"`, `fixef()` normalizes the fixed effects so that their mean value is zero:

```
fixef( invFEi, type="dmean" )
```

4. Fixed effects have been used frequently in Fixed Effects Vector Decomposition (FEVD) estimations, i.e., in two-stage analyses, where time-invariant explanatory variables are regressed on the fixed effects in a second stage (Plümper & Troeger, 2011). However, Breusch, Ward, Nguyen, and Kompas (2011a, 2011b) and Greene (2011) have shown that the FEVD is an instrumental variable (IV) estimator that has several problematic properties.

```
all.equal( mean( fixef( invFEi, type="dmean" ) ), 0 )
## [1] TRUE
```

One can test whether the fixed effects differ from zero, from the first fixed effect, or from their mean (depending on argument `type`) by applying the `summary()` method to fixed effects obtained by `fixef()`:

```
summary(fixef(invFEi, type = "dmean"))
##     Estimate    Std. Error      t-value     Pr(>|t|)
## 1   -11.5528      49.7080      -0.2324   0.8164700
## 2   160.6498      24.9383       6.4419   9.627e-10***
## 3 -176.8279      24.4316      -7.2377   1.130e-11***
## 4    30.9346      14.0778       2.1974   0.0292129*
## 5   -55.8729      14.1654      -3.9443   0.0001129***
## 6    35.5826      12.6687       2.8087   0.0054998**
## 7    -7.8095      12.8430      -0.6081   0.5438694
## 8     1.1983      13.9931       0.0856   0.9318489
## 9   -28.4783      12.8919      -2.2090   0.0283821*
## 10  52.1761       11.8269       4.4116   1.725e-05***
## ---
## Signif. codes: 0 '***' 0.001 '**' 0.01 '*' 0.05 '.' 0.1 ' ' 1
```

If `fixef()` is applied to a time fixed-effects model, it returns time effects that can be obtained in a similar way as the individual effects:

```
fixef( invFEt )
```

In the case of a two-ways fixed-effects model, we can set argument `effect` to either `"individual"` or `"time"` in order to obtain either individual effects or time effects:

```
fixef( invFE2, effect="individual" )
fixef( invFE2, effect="time" )
```

6.6 First-Difference Estimator

The first-difference estimator takes the first differences of both the dependent variable and the explanatory variables in order to remove individual effects in panel data models:

$$y_{it} - y_{it-1} = \mathbf{x}'_{it}\beta + \alpha_i + \epsilon_{it} - \mathbf{x}'_{it-1}\beta - \alpha_i - \epsilon_{it-1} \tag{36}$$

$$y_{it} - y_{it-1} = (\mathbf{x}_{it} - \mathbf{x}_{it-1})'\beta + \epsilon_{it} - \epsilon_{it-1} \tag{37}$$

$$\Delta y_{it} = \Delta \mathrm{x}_{it}\beta + \Delta\epsilon_{it} \tag{38}$$

The first-difference estimator is more appealing than the "within" estimator if the errors of the original model are assumed to be nonstationary, as in this case, taking first differences is likely to reduce them to stationarity. If the untransformed model errors are stationary to begin with, however, first-differencing will introduce error correlation and, therefore, make the estimator inefficient.

The first-difference estimator also could be used to remove time effects, but this is generally not done in practice, because there is no natural ordering of the individuals (e.g., firms) so that the first-differencing would depend on the arbitrarily chosen order of the firms in the data set.

Lastly, one should be aware of that using a first-difference model reduces the time dimension by one time period.

Function `plm()` estimates a first-difference model if its argument `model` is set to "fd":

```
invFDi <- plm( inv ~ value + capital, model="fd",
  data=Grunfeld )
```

The same estimates can be obtained manually by:

```
invFDim <- lm( diff( GrunfeldPdata$inv ) ~
  diff( GrunfeldPdata$value ) +
  diff( GrunfeldPdata$capital ) )
all.equal( coef( invFDi ), coef( invFDim ),
  check.attributes=FALSE )
## [1] TRUE
```

According to our derivation in Eq. (38), the first-difference model should not have an intercept. However, `plm( ..., model="fd" )` estimates the first-difference model with an intercept, because this can improve the statistical properties of the estimation (e.g., this guarantees that the residuals sum to zero). The estimated intercept in the first-difference model corresponds to the coefficient of a linear time trend in the original model because a linear time trend as explanatory variable in the original model ($x_{kit} = t$) corresponds to a constant explanatory variable in the first-difference model ($\Delta x_{kit} = x_{kit} - x_{kit-1} = t - (t-1) = 1$). The intercept in the first-difference model can be suppressed by adding "–1" to the model formula:

```
invFDii <- plm( inv ~ value + capital - 1, model="fd",
  data=Grunfeld )

invFDiim <- lm( diff( GrunfeldPdata$inv ) ~
  diff( GrunfeldPdata$value ) +
  diff( GrunfeldPdata$capital ) - 1 )

all.equal( coef( invFDii ), coef( invFDiim ),
  check.attributes=FALSE )
## [1] TRUE
```

In panel data sets with only two time periods, the first-difference estimator gives exactly the same estimates as the corresponding "within" estimator:

```
invFD2y<- plm( inv ~ value + capital - 1, model="fd",
  data=Grunfeld[ Grunfeld$year <= 1936, ] )
```

```
invFE2y<- plm( inv ~ value + capital - 1,
  data=Grunfeld[ Grunfeld$year <= 1936, ] )
all.equal( coef( invFD2y ), coef( invFE2y ) )
## [1] TRUE
```

In panel data sets with more than two time periods, the FD estimator is prone to (negative) serial correlation, because $E[\Delta\epsilon_{it}\,\Delta\epsilon_{i,t-1}] = E[(\epsilon_{it} - \epsilon_{i,t-1})(\epsilon_{i,t-1} - \epsilon_{i,t-2})] = E[\epsilon_{it}\epsilon_{i,t-1} - \epsilon_{it}\epsilon_{i,t-2} - \epsilon^2_{i,t-1} + \epsilon_{i,t-1}\,\epsilon_{i,t-2}]$ is likely negative unless there is strong positive serial correlation in the original disturbance terms, i.e., $E[\epsilon_{it}\epsilon_{i,t-1}] = E[\epsilon_{i,t-1}\,\epsilon_{i,t-2}] \gg 0$. Therefore, one should test for serial correlation. If the errors of a FD model are significantly serially correlated, it is advisable to estimate the model by the "within" estimator or, alternatively, to calculate robust standard errors.

7 "Between" Estimator for Panel Data

7.1 Specification of the "Between" Estimator

The "between" estimator takes only the variance in the cross-sectional dimension into account, averaging over the time dimension. As such, it ignores the information contained in the time dimension. The "between" estimator is basically an OLS estimator applied to a time-averaged equation:

$$\overline{y}_i = \overline{\mathbf{x}}_i\beta + \alpha_i + \overline{u}_i \tag{39}$$

where $\overline{y}_i = T^{-1}\sum_{t=1}^{T} y_{it}$ and $\overline{\mathbf{x}}_{ii} = T^{-1}\sum_{t=1}^{T}\overline{\mathbf{x}}_{it}$. This estimator is not much used in practice, because it is consistent only if the (unobserved) individual effects (α_i) are uncorrelated with the explanatory variables and in this case, the individual random-effects estimator is more efficient than the "between" estimator (Wooldridge, 2010).

7.2 Estimation of the "Between" Estimator

The "between" estimator can be estimated by using `plm()` with argument `model` set to `"between"`:

```
invB <- plm( inv ~ value + capital, data=Grunfeld,
  effect="individual", model="between" )
```

The "between" estimator also can be obtained manually by applying the OLS method to the data set in which each observation corresponds to one firm and the values of the variables indicate the mean values over all of the firm's observations in all available time periods (as created in Section 5.4):

```
invB2<- lm( inv ~ value + capital, data=GrunfeldFirmMean )
all.equal( coef( invB ), coef( invB2 ) )
## [1] TRUE
```

8 Linear Random-Effects Panel Data Models

The random-effects estimator belongs to the group of feasible generalized least-squares (FGLS) estimators. This estimator requires that the individual and/or time effects are uncorrelated with the covariates, while the fixed-effects estimator does not require this assumption. If this assumption is fulfilled, the random-effects estimator is more efficient than the fixed-effects estimator and, therefore, is the preferred estimator. Importantly, however, the random-effects estimator will be inconsistent if it is not.

8.1 Specification of the Random-Effects Model

We can avoid the loss of degrees of freedom resulting from the model specification of the "within" estimator if we assume that the invariant effects λ_{it} are random. In the following discussion, we focus on time-invariant individual effects, α_i, but the discussion also applies for individual-invariant time effects, γ_t. Two-ways effects are more complicated and are therefore omitted.

In this case $\alpha_i \sim IID(0, \sigma_\alpha^2)$ and $\epsilon_{it} \sim IID(0, \sigma_\epsilon^2)$. Also, $E(\alpha_i \epsilon_{it}) = 0$ and—most important—$E(\alpha_i \mathbf{x}_{it}) = 0$ and $E(\epsilon_{it} \mathbf{x}_{it}) = 0$ for all i and t, which means that we assume strict exogeneity between the covariates and the error terms. The random-effects estimator is an appropriate specification if we draw a random sample of N observations from a large population, e.g., a household panel (Baltagi, 2008).

Random-effects models are estimated by means of Feasible GLS estimators, which means that one somehow needs to identify the variance-covariance matrix of the combined error terms $\Omega = E(uu')$. This block-diagonal covariance matrix displays serial correlation over time only between the observations of the same individual or cross-sectional correlation over individuals only between the observations of the same time period. In the case of two-ways effects, however, the covariance matrix becomes more complicated.

Different methods have been proposed to obtain Ω, they can be accessed through option `random.method` in the `plm()` function:

- `"walhus"`: Wallace and Hussain (1969) propose to substitute u by the OLS estimates $\hat{u}_{OLS}$, as under the random-effects model assumptions OLS estimates are inefficient but still unbiased and consistent.
- `"amemiya"`: Amemiya (1971) suggests using the LSDV residuals instead of the OLS residuals.
- `"swar"`: Swamy and Arora (1972) suggest running a "within" regression and a between regression in order to get estimates for the variance components, σ_α^2 and σ_ϵ^2, from the corresponding mean square errors of the two regressions. It can be shown that $\hat{\beta}_{GLS}$ is the weighted average of the $\hat{\beta}_{within}$ and $\hat{\beta}_{between}$ estimators.
- `"nerlove"`: Nerlove (1971) suggests estimating σ_α^2 as $\sum_{i=1}^{n} \left(\hat{\alpha}_i - \overline{\hat{\alpha}}\right)^2 / (n-1)$, where $\hat{\alpha}_i$ are the dummy coefficients estimated by LSDV. The σ^2 are estimated from the "within" residual sum of squares divided by N.

8.2 Estimation of the Random-Effects Model

To estimate a random-effects model, we can use the `plm()` function with argument `model` set to `"random"`. As with the fixed-effects estimator, argument `effect` can be used to specify whether the estimation should include individual, time, or two-ways (random) effects. The following command uses the investment data (`Grunfeld`) to estimate the investment equation with the two-ways random-effects estimator:

```
invRE2 <- plm( inv ~ value + capital, data=Grunfeld,
  effect="twoways", model="random" )
```

By default, `plm()` estimates random-effects models by applying the procedure suggested by Swamy and Arora (1972). This procedure, however, can give a negative value for the estimate of the variance of the time effect. If this is the case, `plm()` sets the variance of the time effect to zero (as in the previous estimation).

We can use argument `random.method` to choose a different procedure for estimating the random-effects model, e.g., the procedure of Amemiya (1971):

```
invRE2a <- plm( inv ~ value + capital, data=Grunfeld,
  effect="twoways", model="random",
  random.method="amemiya" ).
```

Although earlier versions of the *plm* package were not able to estimate two-ways random-effects models with unbalanced panel data sets, it is now possible with the latest version of this package (1.6–6):

```
emplRE2 <- plm( emp ~ wage + capital, data=EmplUK,
  effect="twoways", model="random" ).
```

8.3 Estimates of the Variance of the Error Components

To get the variance of the error components of a random-effects model, we can use function `ercomp()`:

```
ercomp( invRE2a)
##                     var  std.dev   share
## idiosyncratic   2644.13    51.42   0.256
## individual      7452.02    86.33   0.721
## time             243.78    15.61   0.024
## theta: 0.868 (id) 0.2787 (time) 0.2776 (Total)
```

8.4 Testing the Assumptions of the Random-Effects Model

The assumption of the random-effects estimator is that the invariant effects are uncorrelated with the covariates. If this condition is fulfilled, the random-effects estimator is preferred because the estimates are more efficient. The Durbin-Wu-Hausman test examines the difference between estimates from a fixed-effects model and a random-effects model. Because the FE estimators are consistent if the invariant effects are correlated with the covariates, but the random-effects estimators are not, a statistically significant difference is interpreted as a rejection of the random-effects estimator.

```
phtest( invFE2, invRE2a )
##
##  Hausman Test
##
## data: inv ~ value + capital
## chisq = 8.9626, df = 2, p-value = 0.01132
## alternative hypothesis: one model is inconsistent
```

The same test can be conducted by the command:

```
phtest( inv ~ value + capital, effect="twoway",
  random.method="amemiya", data=Grunfeld )
##
##  Hausman Test
##
## data: inv ~ value + capital
## chisq = 8.9626, df = 2, p-value = 0.01132
## alternative hypothesis: one model is inconsistent
```

The following command uses the auxiliary-regression based version of this test that was suggested by Wooldridge (2010, Sec. 10.7.3.):

```
phtest( inv ~ value + capital, effect="twoway",
  data=Grunfeld, method="aux" )
##
##  Regression-based Hausman test
##
## data: inv ~ value + capital
## chisq = 13.117, df = 2, p-value = 0.001418
## alternative hypothesis: one model is inconsistent
```

This test can be conducted with robust standard errors:

```
phtest( inv ~ value + capital, effect="twoway",
  data=Grunfeld, method="aux",
  vcov=function(x) vcovHC( x, method="white2",
    type="HC3" ) )
##
##  Regression-based Hausman test, vcov: function(x)
##  vcovHC(x, method = "white2", type = "HC3")
##
## data: inv ~ value + capital
## chisq = 11.164, df = 2, p-value = 0.003765
## alternative hypothesis: one model is inconsistent
```

9 Tests for the Error Structure in Panel Data Models

As we have seen before, serial and/or cross-sectional correlation affecting the error terms of the same individual and/or time period are inherent to panel data sets. The idiosyncratic error term, however, also can be affected by serial or cross-sectional correlation, in which case the random- or fixed-effects estimators won't help.

This section presents some of the most important tests of the error structure that should be run on every panel data estimation model in order to find irregularities from the standard matrix (Eq. 10). The difficulty in detecting serial correlation in the idiosyncratic error term is to separate the serial correlation in the invariant effects from the serial correlation in the idiosyncratic error term. Simple marginal tests for one direction of departure from the hypothesis of spherical errors often are substantially biased; joint tests have power against both directions, but do not return any information about which error term causes the problem; conditional tests that actually return this information have power only against the alternative of interest. Although they are the most powerful tests, they depend strongly on the normality and homoscedasticity of the error terms (see Croissant & Millo, 2015, for further discussions on this subject).

9.1 Tests for Serial Correlation

9.1.1 *Unobserved-Effects Test*

The unobserved-effects test is a semiparametric test for the H_0: $\sigma_\alpha^2 = 0$. It is robust toward nonnormality and heteroscedasticity. The test does not differentiate between time-invariant unobserved effects and serial correlation in the idiosyncratic error term. Therefore, rejection of the H_0 does not necessarily imply that time-invariant effects are present.

```
pwtest(inv ~ value + capital, data = Grunfeld)
##
##  Wooldridge's test for unobserved individual effects
##
## data: formula
## z = 1.4922, p-value = 0.1356
## alternative hypothesis: unobserved effect
```

9.1.2 *Locally Robust Tests for Serial Correlation and Random Effects*

Function `pbsytest()` conducts a joint LM test that simultaneously tests random effects and serial correlation in the idiosyncratic error term. It assumes normality and homoscedasticity of the idiosyncratic error. Rejection of the H_0, however, does not give any information about the direction of the deviation.

```
pbsytest( inv ~ value + capital, data=Grunfeld,
  test="j" )
##
##  Baltagi and Li AR-RE joint test - balanced panel
##
## data: formula
## chisq = 808.47, df = 2, p-value < 2.2e-16
## alternative hypothesis: AR(1) errors or random effects
```

In another specification, function `pbsytest()` can test either for random effects:

```
pbsytest( inv ~ value + capital, data = Grunfeld,
  test = "re" )
##
##  Bera, Sosa-Escudero and Yoon locally robust test
##  (one-sided) - balanced panel
##
## data: formula
## z = 25.787, p-value < 2.2e-16
## alternative hypothesis: random effects sub AR(1) errors
```

or AR(1) serial correlation in the idiosyncratic error term:

```
pbsytest(inv ~ value + capital, data=Grunfeld,
  test="ar" )
##
##  Bera, Sosa-Escudero and Yoon locally robust test -
##  balanced panel
##
## data: formula
## chisq = 10.31, df = 1, p-value = 0.001323
## alternative hypothesis: AR(1) errors sub random effects
```

Either test for one effect (random effects or serial correlation) is robust against local (i.e., moderate) departures from zero of the other effect (serial correlation or, respectively, random effects). Both tests are inferior to more specific tests for random effects or serial correlation (e.g., Baltagi-Li test), but can indicate the right direction of departure from the H_0 of no serial correlation and no random effects.

9.1.3 *Conditional Tests for AR(1) and MA(1) Errors Under Random Effects*

Baltagi and Li (1995)'s LM test for the detection of serial correlation under random effects has the null hypothesis that there is no serial correlation of the idiosyncratic error term. The test can be one-sided (only positive correlation) or two-sided (default):

```
pbltest( inv ~ value + capital, data = Grunfeld )
##
##  Baltagi and Li two-sided LM test
##
## data: inv ~ value + capital
## chisq = 69.532, df = 1, p-value < 2.2e-16
## alternative hypothesis: AR(1)/MA(1) errors in RE panel
## model
```

9.1.4 General Serial Correlation Tests

The Breusch-Godfrey test and Durbin-Watson test for panel data uses the residuals of a demeaned (fixed-effects) or quasidemeaned (random-effects) model, under the H_0 assumption that, under these conditions, the remaining idiosyncratic errors are serially uncorrelated. Unlike most other serial correlation tests for panel data, the Breusch-Godfrey test allows to test for higher-order serial correlation.

```
pbgtest( invFE2, order = 2 )
##
##  Breusch-Godfrey/Wooldridge test for serial
##  correlation in panel models
##
## data: inv ~ value + capital
## chisq = 53.093, df = 2, p-value = 2.959e-12
## alternative hypothesis: serial correlation in
## idiosyncratic errors
 pbgtest( invRE2a, order = 2 )
##
##  Breusch-Godfrey/Wooldridge test for serial
##  correlation in panel models
##
## data: inv ~ value + capital
## chisq = 53.909, df = 2, p-value = 1.967e-12
## alternative hypothesis: serial correlation in
## idiosyncratic errors
```

Likewise, one can apply the Durbin-Watson test on the demeaned data.

```
pdwtest( invFE2 )
##
##  Durbin-Watson test for serial correlation in panel
##  models
##
## data: inv ~ value + capital
## DW = 0.96869, p-value = 1.209e-13
```

```
## alternative hypothesis: serial correlation in
## idiosyncratic errors
pdwtest( invRE2a )
##
##  Durbin-Watson test for serial correlation in panel
##  models
##
## data: inv ~ value + capital
## DW = 0.96267, p-value = 4.631e-14
## alternative hypothesis: serial correlation in
## idiosyncratic errors
```

The Breusch-Godfrey test does not perform well on fixed-effects models with short T. In fact, for finite T, if the errors of the original model were spherical, those of the demeaned model are serially correlated with a coefficient inversely proportional to T: $-1/(T-1)$. This issue becomes negligible in long panels, but in short ones the test is severely biased toward rejection. Wooldridge (2010), therefore, suggests a test for fixed-effects models with short T that is implemented in function `pwartest()` and that does not rely on large T asymptotics and, therefore, has good properties in short panels.

```
pwartest(log(emp) ~ log(wage) + log(capital), data = EmplUK)
##
##  Wooldridge's test for serial correlation in FE
##  panels
##
## data: plm.model
## F = 312.3, df1 = 1, df2 = 889, p-value < 2.2e-16
## alternative hypothesis: serial correlation
```

9.1.5 First-Difference Based Tests

The `pwfdtest()` is a serial correlation test that also works as a specification test to choose the most efficient estimator between the "within" estimator and the first-difference estimator. The starting point is the assumption that if the errors in the model in levels are not serially correlated, then the errors of the first-difference estimator will be serially correlated with −0.5, while any invariant effect is wiped out in the differencing. So basically, for a given model:

$$\hat{u}_{it} = \delta \hat{u}_{it-1} + v_{it} \tag{40}$$

the test examines whether $\delta = -0.5$, corresponding to the H_0 of no serial correlation in the first-difference estimation. If the differenced errors $\hat{u}_{it} - \hat{u}_{it-1}$ turn out to be serially uncorrelated, however, then it follows that u_{it} is a random walk. In this case, the first-difference estimator is the most efficient one, otherwise the fixed-effects estimator is preferred.

We can use the `pwfdtest()` command to test for serial correlation in the first-difference estimator:

```
pwfdtest( log( emp ) ~ log( wage ) +log( capital ),
  data=EmplUK )
##
##  Wooldridge's first-difference test for serial
##  correlation in panels
##
## data:  plm.model
## F = 1.5251, df1 = 1, df2 = 749, p-value = 0.2172
## alternative hypothesis: serial correlation in differenced
## errors
```

The following command conducts a test for serial correlation in the idiosyncratic errors of the fixed-effects model:

```
pwfdtest( log( emp ) ~ log( wage ) +log( capital ),
  data=EmplUK, h0="fe" )
##
##  Wooldridge's first-difference test for serial
##  correlation in panels
##
## data:  plm.model
## F = 131.55, df1 = 1, df2 = 749, p-value < 2.2e-16
## alternative hypothesis: serial correlation in original
## errors
```

9.2 Tests for Cross-Sectional Dependence

The problem of cross-sectional dependence arises if the n individuals in our sample are no longer independently drawn observations but affect each other's outcomes. For example, this can result from the fact that we look at a set of neighboring countries, which are usually highly interconnected.

To test for cross-sectional dependence in the model residuals, we can use the Pesaran CD test, which is based on a scaled average of the pairwise correlation coefficients between the residuals of each individual unit:

```
pcdtest( invFEi, test="cd" )
##
##  Pesaran CD test for cross-sectional dependence in
##  panels
##
## data:  inv ~ value + capital
## z = 4.6612, p-value = 3.144e-06
## alternative hypothesis: cross-sectional dependence
```

Rejection means that the residuals are cross-sectionally dependent.

10 How to Handle Serial Correlation

After we've established that we have serial correlation or cross-sectional dependence in the idiosyncratic error term, we need to handle this problem somehow. There are basically two approaches: We can use parameter tests with robust covariance matrices for panel data models or we can exploit the characteristics of the feasible GLS estimator.

10.1 Parameter Tests with Robust Covariance Matrices

Error correlation per se does not cause inconsistency of the OLS estimators for the parameters, but of the classical OLS standard errors. By using robust covariance matrices in the parameter tests, we can overcome serial correlation, cross-sectional dependence, and heteroscedasticity across groups or time, a third problem we haven't touched yet.

There are three generic functions which can be used to derive robust tests on panel data with serial correlation or cross-sectional dependence:

- `coeftest()`: Can be used to conduct z-tests and (quasi)t-tests on estimated coefficients. `coeftest()` works in particular for objects that were created by `lm()` and `glm()` but it also can be applied easily to objects that were created by `plm()`.
- `waldtest()`: A generic function for the comparison of models using a Wald test.
- `linearHypothesis()`: Another generic function for testing linear hypotheses with a flexible interface for specifying the linear hypotheses.

In all three functions, one can replace the nonrobust covariance matrix from the model by a robust covariance matrix using the argument `vcov`.

The most common function for robust covariance matrices is `vcovHC()` from the *sandwich* package. The *plm* package includes a specialized panel data method for the `vcovHC()` generic function, which can apply three different methods to calculate White's heteroscedasticity-consistent covariance matrix. All three methods, however, are not robust toward cross-sectional dependence. Although all three methods are robust against group-wise heteroscedasticity, only method `"arellano"` is fully robust against serial correlation.

```
coeftest( invFEi, vcovHC( invFEi, method="arellano",
  type="HC3" ) )
##
## t-test of coefficients:
##
##           Estimate  Std. Error  t value    Pr(>|t|)
## value     0.110124    0.016312   6.7509  1.774e-10 ***
## capital   0.310065    0.062248   4.9811  1.427e-06 ***
## ---
## Signif. codes:
## 0 '***' 0.001 '**' 0.01 '*' 0.05 '.' 0.1 ' '1
```

Other robust covariance estimators for panel data models are:

- `vcovBK()`: An unconditional estimator for robust covariance matrices developed by Beck and Katz (1995). If observations are clustered by "group", the estimator will account for time-wise heteroscedasticity and serial correlation. If observations are clustered by "time", the estimator will account for group-wise heteroscedasticity and cross-sectional dependence.
- `vcovDC()`: An estimator for robust covariance matrices for error structures that cluster along both dimensions, in other words, for models with two-ways effects.
- `vcovNW()`: A nonparametric estimator for robust covariance matrices for panel data models with serial correlation, which is a special case of `vcovSCC()` assuming no cross-sectional correlation.
- `vcovSCC()`: A nonparametric estimator for robust covariance matrices for panel data models with serial correlation and cross-sectional dependence.

Function `linearHypothesis()` that is provided by the R package *car* can be used to perform Wald tests of linear parameter restrictions—both with and without using a robust covariance matrix. As an example, we will test the (null) hypothesis $\beta_1 + \beta_2 = 0.4$:

```
linearHypothesis( invFE2, "value + capital = 0.4" )
## Linear hypothesis test
##
## Hypothesis:
## value + capital = 0.4
##
## Model 1: restricted model
## Model 2: inv ~ value + capital
##
##   Res.Df Df Chisq Pr(>Chisq)
## 1    170
## 2    169 1 10.881 0.0009715 ***
## ---
## Signif. codes:
## 0 '***' 0.001 '**' 0.01 '*' 0.05 '.' 0.1 ' ' 1
```

The following command repeats this test with robust standard errors:

```
linearHypothesis( invFE2, "value + capital=0.4",
  vcov. = vcovHC )
## Linear hypothesis test
##
## Hypothesis:
## value+capital=0.4
##
```

```
## Model 1: restricted model
## Model 2: inv ~ value + capital
##
## Note: Coefficient covariance matrix supplied.
##
##   Res.Df Df Chisq Pr(>Chisq)
## 1    170
## 2    169  1 2.3586     0.1246

linearHypothesis( invFE2, "value + capital=0.4",
  vcov. = vcovHC( invFE2, method = "arellano",
    type = "HC3" ) )
## Linear hypothesis test
##
## Hypothesis:
## value + capital = 0.4
##
## Model 1: restricted model
## Model 2: inv ~ value + capital
##
## Note: Coefficient covariance matrix supplied.
##
##   Res.Df Df  Chisq Pr(>Chisq)
## 1    170
## 2    169  1  1.2124     0.2709
```

Argument `vcov.` can be either a function that returns the (robust) covariance matrix or the covariance matrix itself.

10.2 FGLS Estimator

The FGLS estimator is based on a two-step procedure. First, an OLS (pooling), fixed-effects ("within"), or first-difference model is estimated, and then the residuals, $\hat{u}_{it}$ are used to estimate the covariance matrix of the error term:

$$\hat{\Omega} = \sum_{i=1}^{n} \frac{\hat{u}_{it}\hat{u}'_{it}}{n} \tag{41}$$

which is the used as a correcting factor in the second step GLS estimator:

$$\hat{\beta}_{FGLS} = \left(\mathbf{x}'_{it}\Omega^{-1}\mathbf{x}_{it}\right)\mathbf{x}'_{it}\Omega^{-1}y_{it} \tag{42}$$

By using the covariance matrix of the error term as weighting factor, the covariance structure within a group (for effect `"individual"`) or time period (for effect `"time"`) becomes fully unrestricted and, therefore, will be robust against group-wise serial correlation and heteroscedasticity. It is important to note, however, that this correction of the covariance matrix is identical across groups, which makes the FGLS estimator inefficient in cases of group-wise heteroscedasticity. Also, the FGLS estimator with individual effects cannot handle cross-sectional dependence. If looking at time effects, however, the FGLS can handle cross-sectional dependence, under the condition that the effect is constant across all time periods.

The FGLS estimator can be estimated using function `pggls()` with either pooled (`"pooling"`), fixed-effects (`"within"`), random-effects (`"random"`), or first-difference (`"fd"`) and with individual or time effects, e.g.:

```
emplFGLSr <- pggls( log( emp ) ~ log( wage ) +log( capital ),
  data = EmplUK, model = "pooling" )

emplFGLSf <- pggls( log( emp ) ~ log( wage ) +log( capital ),
  data = EmplUK, model = "within" )
```

11 Simple Instrumental Variable Estimators

In the following section, we will estimate the (static) investment equation by instrumental-variable estimators for panel data. In these estimations, we instrument the firms' current value by its lagged value in order to take into account that the firm's current value might be influenced by the same unobserved variables as its current investments.

11.1 Fixed-Effects Estimation

Because the use of a lagged variable implies that observations from the first year in the data set cannot be used in the estimation, we start by estimating a standard fixed-effects model without observations from the first year in the data set so that it uses the same observations as the instrumental-variable fixed-effects estimation:

```
invFEt1<- plm( inv ~ value + capital,
  data=Grunfeld[ Grunfeld$year !=1935, ] )

invFEIV <- plm(inv ~ value + capital |
  lag(value)+capital, data=Grunfeld)
```

In this instrumental-variable estimation, a complete list of all instruments is specified as the second part of a two-part formula. Alternatively, the instrumental variables can be specified as a modification of the list of explanatory variables:

```
invFEIV2<- plm( inv ~ value + capital |
   . - value + lag( value ), data=Grunfeld )
all.equal( coef( invFEIV2 ), coef( invFEIV ) )
## [1] TRUE
```

By default, plm() estimates instrumental-variable models by the procedure suggested by Balestra and Varadharajan-Krishnakumar (1987). Argument inst.method can be used to select the procedure suggested by Baltagi (1981). When using fixed-effect estimators, both procedures give the same estimates:

```
invFEIVB <- plm( inv ~ value + capital |
    lag( value )+capital,
  inst.method="baltagi", data=Grunfeld )
all.equal( coef( invFEIVB ), coef( invFEIV ) )
## [1] TRUE
```

11.2 Random-Effects Estimation

When estimating random-effects instrumental-variable models, the procedures suggested by Balestra and Varadharajan-Krishnakumar (1987) and Baltagi (1981) give different estimates:

```
invREt1<- plm( inv ~ value + capital, model="random",
  data=Grunfeld[ Grunfeld$year !=1935, ] )

invREIV <- plm( inv ~ value + capital |
    lag( value )+capital, model="random",
  data=Grunfeld )

invREIVB <- plm( inv ~ value + capital |
    lag( value )+capital, model="random",
  inst.method="baltagi", data=Grunfeld )
```

11.3 Hausman Test

The following command conducts a Hausman test of the null hypothesis that the OLS estimates of the fixed-effects model are consistent against the alternative hypothesis that these estimates are inconsistent, while the instrumental variable estimates of the same model are still consistent:

```
phtest( invFEt1, invFEIV )
##
##  Hausman Test
##
## data: inv ~ value + capital
## chisq = 4.8306, df = 2, p-value = 0.08934
## alternative hypothesis: one model is inconsistent
```

The null hypotheses cannot be rejected at 5% significance level, which could be used to justify estimation of the fixed-effects model by OLS, because if the OLS estimates are consistent, they are more efficient than the instrumental-variables estimates.

The following commands apply the same Hausman test to the random-effects models:

```
phtest( invREtl, invREIV )
##
##  Hausman Test
##
## data: inv ~ value + capital
## chisq = 5.5093, df = 2, p-value = 0.06363
## alternative hypothesis: one model is inconsistent
phtest( invREtl, invREIVB )
##
##  Hausman Test
##
## data: inv ~ value + capital
## chisq = 0.90909, df = 2, p-value = 0.6347
## alternative hypothesis: one model is inconsistent
```

12 Panel Time Series Models

In the context of long panels, also called "panel time series," in which the time dimension is sufficient for estimating separate regressions for each individual, Pesaran and Smith (1995) popularized a heterogeneous estimator called "mean groups" (MG) based on averaging the individual coefficients. Notably, the individual OLS regressions will provide consistent estimates also for dynamic models, a property that carries on to the averaged coefficients. Function `pmg()` in the *plm* package can estimate such models:

```
invMG <- pmg( inv ~ value + capital, data=Grunfeld )
```

Panel data can be subject to pervasive cross-sectional dependence, whereby all units in the same cross-section are correlated. This is usually attributed to the effect of some unobserved common factors, common to all units and affecting each of them, although possibly in different ways. Examples are technological evolution, world prices, such as oil prices, or risk-free interest rates. If the common factors, which are omitted from the model, are correlated with the regressors, which is usually the case, both the standard homogeneous estimators for panel data (FE, RE, or FD) and the heterogeneous MG estimator are inconsistent. In this case, Pesaran (2006) suggested to approximate the unobserved common factors by cross-sectional averages of the regressand and regressors, augmenting the model with the latter to obtain unbiased estimates. This kind of augmentation, known as "common correlated effects" (CCE), is implemented in the `pmg()` function by setting the `model` argument to `"cmg"`:

```
invCMG <- pmg( inv ~ value + capital, data=Grunfeld, model="cmg" )
```

Standard errors for these estimators are computed based on the sample variance of the individual coefficients.

13 Unit Root Tests for Panel Data

A popular procedure for testing panel time series for unit roots, suggested by Im, Pesaran, and Shin (2003), is to extend the well-known ADF test to the panel context, averaging the results of the relevant t-tests.

These tests (known as first-generation unit root tests), however, do not take into account cross-sectional dependence, which can occur in panel data (see, e.g., Section 9.2). Pesaran (2007) suggested to employ a CCE procedure to robustify the panel ADF procedure against unobserved common factors. This last goes under the name of CIPS test, for cross-sectionally augmented IPS.

To apply the unit-root tests that are provided by the *plm* package, one must use a panel data set that has been returned by `pdata.frame()`. Therefore, we use the data set `GrunfeldPdata` in this section.

The following code tests the (null) hypothesis of a unit root in the investment variable (`inv`) by applying the procedure suggested by Im et al. (2003):

```
cipstest( GrunfeldPdata$inv, type = "trend", lags = 4,
  model = "mg" )

## Warning in cipstest( GrunfeldPdata$inv, type = "trend",
##    lags = 4, model = "mg" ): p-value greater than printed
##    p-value
##
##   Pesaran's CIPS test for unit roots
##
## data: GrunfeldPdata$inv
## CIPS test = -1.2031, lag order = 4, p-value = 0.1
## alternative hypothesis: Stationarity
```

This test does not reject the null hypothesis that the investment variable (`inv`) has a unit root.

The following code conducts the CCE-augmented variant of the test by Pesaran (2007) and is robust against cross-sectional dependence:

```
cipstest( GrunfeldPdata$inv )
## Warning in cipstest(GrunfeldPdata$inv): p-value greater
##    than printed p-value
##
##   Pesaran's CIPS test for unit roots
##
## data: GrunfeldPdata$inv
## CIPS test = -1.397, lag order = 2, p-value = 0.1
## alternative hypothesis: Stationarity
```

The `model` argument is left at the default value of `"cmg"`. According to this test, we still cannot reject the null hypothesis (at the 10% or at an even greater significance level, see the `warning`) that the investment variable (`inv`) has a unit root.

14 Dynamic Panel Data Models

In cases in which we want to estimate dynamic models with panel data, the usual approaches such as fixed-effects or random-effects models won't work. For the random-effects estimator, it can be shown that a dynamic panel data model does not fulfill the exogeneity condition $E(\alpha_i x_{it}) = 0$. Therefore, by default, this rules out the usage of the RE estimator. The "within" transformation can be applied in principle, however, one can show that the resulting estimates will be severely biased for the autoregressive parameter $\rho > 0$. The closer ρ gets to zero and the larger T is, however, the smaller also the bias; a larger n, on the other hand, has no effect.

Instead, we can use the IV estimator by Andersson and Hsiao or the Arellano Bond GMM estimator. Both estimators use the first-difference transformation to get rid of the time invariant effects. This comes at a price, however, that we generate a correlation between the differenced lagged dependent variable, $\Delta y_{i,t-1} = y_{i,t-1} - y_{i,t-2}$, and the differenced error term, $\Delta_{it} = \varepsilon_{it} - \varepsilon_{i,t-1}$, because $y_{i,t-1}$ is correlated with $\epsilon_{i,t-1}$. Therefore, Andersson and Hsiao propose to use the second lag as an IV for the first lagged variable. Likewise, Arellano and Bond (AB) propose to use all available IVs, defined by the dimensionality of T. Both estimators return consistent results, but only the AB GMM estimator exploits all available orthogonality conditions.

The underlying assumptions of both estimators are stationarity of the time-series ($\rho < 1$) and an i.i.d. distribution of the original (nondifferenced) idiosyncratic error term, i.e., no serial correlation in the original errors.

We should be aware that, because of the lag structure, gaps in unbalanced panels will widen, because a missing link in the time series will lead to two missing differences, and so on. Also, for panels with large T, the number of IVs in the GMM estimator might become too large because the number of moment conditions grows exponentially with T. For example, for $T = 4$ we get 6 valid moment conditions, however, for $T = 9$ the number of moment conditions becomes 36. Therefore, for a long panel, especially if n is comparatively small, an unrestricted inclusion of lagged IVs risks reducing the efficiency of the GMM estimates. In fact, Monte Carlo studies show that for panels with large T (> 30) and small n, the asymptotic properties of the GMM estimator no longer hold. Results still are inconclusive to some degree, but it seems that as long as $T/N \rightarrow 0$, the GMM estimator is consistent even for large T. It is advisable, however, to reduce the number of lags to around 2–5. One should bear in mind that because of the autoregressive structure of the model, the first-differencing to get rid of the time invariant effects, and the lag structure of the IV, the AB GMM estimator reduces T by at least 2 time periods (Table 1).

For an example of $T = 4$ and a simple autoregressive model:

$$y_{it} = \rho\, y_{it-1} + \alpha_i + \epsilon_{it} \tag{43}$$

TABLE 1 Losses in *T* by Using the A-B GMM Estimator

t	y_{it}	$y_{it}-1$	Δy_{it}	$\Delta y_{it}-1$
0	Yes	No	No	No
1	Yes	Yes	Yes	No
2	Yes	Yes	Yes	Yes

we get the following IVs and moment conditions:

$$\begin{aligned}
t=2 &: E[\Delta\epsilon_{i2}\, y_{i0}]=0 \\
t=3 &: E[\Delta\epsilon_{i3}\, y_{i0}]=0 \\
&\quad E[\Delta\epsilon_{i3}\, y_{i1}]=0 \\
t=4 &: E[\Delta\epsilon_{i4}\, y_{i0}]=0 \\
&\quad E[\Delta\epsilon_{i4}\, y_{i1}]=0 \\
&\quad E[\Delta\epsilon_{i4}\, y_{i2}]=0
\end{aligned}$$

where the instrumental variables are y_{i0}, y_{i1}, and y_{i2}.

So far, two types of panel GMM estimators are implemented in *plm*:

- Difference GMM, which is the classical Arellano-Bond estimator that uses only differenced variables as IVs. For the previous example, instead of using y_{i0}, y_{i1}, and y_{i2}, the estimator uses Δy_{i1} and Δy_{i2} as IVs, which unfortunately means that we lose yet another time period, i.e., we start at $t=3$.
- System GMM (Blundel-Bond), which additionally adds the corresponding levels as IVs. Simulations show that the System GMM estimator often is more efficient and, in some cases, even more consistent than the Difference GMM. Especially if the instruments of the Difference GMM are weak, applying the System GMM often leads to dramatic improvements of the GMM estimator.

In the R function `pgmm()`, the Difference GMM estimator is the default estimator. If we wish to apply the System GMM estimator, we need to set option `transformation="ld"`.

When using the R function `pgmm()`, we also have the possibility to use a one-step or two-step approach to compute the weighting matrix of the moments. In the one-step approach, the weighting matrix is calculated based on the covariate matrix and a known weighting matrix (see Croissant & Millo, 2015, for details). The two-step approach uses the residuals of the one-step model to calculate the weighting matrix. The two-step approach usually results in more asymptotically efficient estimates, because the two-step approach uses the consistent covariance matrix from one-step GMM and it is more robust toward heteroscedasticity and other disturbances. In older textbooks or articles, the two-step approach often is described as suboptimal because it produces biased estimates. This point no longer applies, because modern applications use the Windmejer correction procedure, which alleviates this problem.

In function `pgmm()`, we set option `model = "twosteps"` if we want to overrule the default one-step setting. Furthermore, we can choose option `effect = "individual"` if we want to estimate the classical AB GMM estimator where we get rid of the time invariant effects through first-differencing or option `effect = "twoways"` (the default) if we want to additionally capture time effects by adding time dummies.

We use the employment data set (`EmplUK`) to estimate specification (b) of the employment equation of Arellano and Bond (1991):

$$\begin{aligned}\log(emp_{it}) =& \rho_1 \log\left(emp_{i(t-1)}\right) + \rho_2 \log\left(emp_{i(t-2)}\right)\\ &+\beta_1 \log(wage_{it}) + \beta_2 \log\left(wage_{i(t-1)}\right) + \beta_3 \log(capital_{it}).\\ &+\beta_4 \log(output_{it}) + \beta_5 \log\left(output_{i(t-1)}\right) + \alpha_i + \gamma_t + u_{it}\end{aligned} \quad (44)$$

The following code[5] reproduces the results of model (b) in Table 4 of Arellano and Bond (1991):

```
emplGMM <- pgmm( log(emp) ~ lag(log(emp), 1:2)+
     lag(log(wage), 0:1)+log(capital)+
     lag(log(output), 0:1) | lag(log(emp), 2:99),
   data=EmplUK, effect="twoways", model="twosteps" )
summary( emplGMM, robust = FALSE )
```

The part of the formula behind the vertical line (|) specifies that all available lags beyond lag 1 of the dependent variable, i.e., log($emp_{i(t-j)}$); $j \geq 2$, should be used as GMM instruments; all other explanatory variables, i.e., log($wage_{it}$), log($wage_{i(t-1)}$), log($capital_{it}$), log($output_{it}$), and log($output_{i(t-1)}$), are used as normal instruments. If we choose to use lagged variables of the other covariates as instrument variables, the number of instrument variables increases accordingly:

```
emplGMM2<- pgmm( log(emp) ~ lag(log(emp), 1)+
     lag(log(wage), 0:1)+lag(log(capital), 0:1) |
     lag(log(emp), 2:99)+lag(log(wage), 2:99)+
     lag(log(capital), 2:99), data=EmplUK,
   effect="twoways", model="onestep",
   transformation="ld" )
```

5. This code was taken from or inspired by Croissant and Millo (2008, p. 18), Kleiber and Zeileis (2008, p. 87–89), Croissant and Millo (2015, p. 23–24), and Kleiber and Zeileis (2015, p. 3).

14.1 Tests for Panel GMM

Given that we use lagged variables as IVs in the panel data GMM estimator, we need to be extra careful about AR(t) processes in the idiosyncratic error term. Because the basic assumption of GMM are i.i.d. idiosyncratic errors, theoretically, we shouldn't worry about much more than the usual AR(1) process generated through the first-difference transformation. This is not necessarily fulfilled in reality, however, so we also should check higher order processes in the error term. By default the `summary()` command tests AR(1) and AR(2) processes, however, we can use the Arellano-Bond test for serial correlation, `mtest()`, to test higher order processes:

```
mtest( emplGMM, order=3 ).
##
##  Autocorrelation test of degree 3
##
## data: log(emp) ~ lag(log(emp), 1:2)+
##    lag(log(wage), 0:1)+log(capital)+...
## normal=0.18874, p-value=0.8503
```

Also, by default `summary()` returns the results from the Hansen-Sargan test on the overidentifying restrictions. The hypothesis being tested with the Hansen-Sargan test is that the instrumental variables are uncorrelated to some set of residuals, and therefore they are acceptable, healthy instruments. If the null hypothesis is confirmed statistically (that is, not rejected), the instruments pass the test; they are valid by this criterion.

The test can be accessed through

```
sargan( emplGMM, weights="twosteps" )
##
##  Sargan test
##
## data: log(emp) ~ lag(log(emp), 1:2) +
##    lag(log(wage), 0:1)+log(capital)+...
## chisq = 30.112, df = 25, p-value = 0.2201
```

15 Systems of Linear Equations

In this section, we use the *systemfit* package (Henningsen & Hamann, 2007) and the investment data set (`Grunfeld`) to estimate the investment model as system of equations. In contrast to recent versions of the *plm* package, the current version of the *systemfit* package does not recognize the panel data structure unless the data set has been created by `pdata.frame()`. Therefore, we will use the data set `GrunfeldPdata`, which we created with `pdata.frame()` in Section 5.5.

The specification of a panel data model as a system of equations is basically the same as the specification of the variable coefficients model with individual-specific coefficients (Eq. 12). The only difference is that the variable coefficients model ignores contemporaneous correlation of the error term, while the estimation as system of equations can account for contemporaneous correlation of the error term, i.e., $E[\epsilon_{it}\epsilon_{js}] = 0 \; \forall \; t \neq s$ and $E[\epsilon_{it}\epsilon_{jt}] = \sigma_{ij}$.

The estimation of a system of equations by the OLS method ignores contemporaneous correlation of the error term and, therefore, gives the same estimates as the variable coefficients model with individual-specific coefficients:

```
library( "systemfit" )
invSysOLS <- systemfit( inv ~ value + capital,
  method="OLS", data=GrunfeldPdata )
all.equal( coef( invSysOLS )[c(1:3,7:30,4:6)],
  c( t( coef( invVCMi ) ) ), check.attributes=FALSE )
## [1] TRUE
```

In contrast, the estimation of a system of equations by the seemingly unrelated regression (SUR) method (a FGLS method) takes contemporaneous correlation of the error term into account[6]:

```
invSysSUR <- systemfit( inv ~ value + capital,
  method="SUR", data=GrunfeldPdata )
```

We can use a likelihood-ratio test to compare the fit of the OLS model with the fit of the SUR model and, therefore, test whether the off-diagonal elements of the residual covariance are jointly zero, i.e., $\sigma_{ij} = 0 \; \forall \; i \neq j$, and the diagonal elements of the residual covariance are all equal, i.e., $\sigma_{ii} = \sigma \; \forall \; i$:

```
lrtest( invSysOLS, invSysSUR )
## Likelihood ratio test
##
## Model 1: invSysOLS
## Model 2: invSysSUR
##   #Df  LogLik Df Chisq Pr(>Chisq)
## 1  31 -738.54
## 2  85 -728.60 54 19.877          1
```

This test indicates that there is no significant contemporaneous correlation of the error term in this model so we can estimate the model by OLS, making it unnecessary to use the SUR method.

---

6. The SUR/FGLS estimator also can be iterated, but the iterated SUR estimation of this model does not converge.

Argument pooled of systemfit() can be used to restrict the coefficients to be equal across all firms. If this model is estimated by the OLS method, which ignores contemporaneous correlation of the error term, the estimated coefficients are equal to those of the pooled model that we estimated in Sections 4.1 and 6.3:

```
invSysPoolOLS <- systemfit( inv ~ value + capital,
  method="OLS", pooled=TRUE, data=GrunfeldPdata )
all.equal( coef( invSysPoolOLS )[1:3], coef( invPool ),
  check.attributes=FALSE )
## [1] TRUE
```

In the following, we estimate the system of equations by the seemingly unrelated regression (SUR) method that considers contemporaneous correlation of the error term:

```
invSysPoolSUR <- systemfit( inv ~ value + capital,
  method="SUR", pooled=TRUE, data=GrunfeldPdata )
```

In case of the pooled estimation, the test also indicates that there is no significant contemporaneous correlation of the error term so we can estimate the model by OLS, making it unnecessary to use the SUR method:

```
lrtest( invSysPoolOLS, invSysPoolSUR )

## Likelihood ratio test
##
## Model 1: invSysPoolOLS
## Model 2: invSysPoolSUR
##   #Df LogLik Df Chisq Pr(>Chisq)
## 1   4 -881.1
## 2  58 -877.7 54 6.7985          1
```

Further likelihood-ratio tests confirm our results from Section 6.4 and clearly indicate that the coefficients significantly differ across firms:

```
lrtest( invSysPoolOLS, invSysOLS )

## Likelihood ratio test
##
## Model 1: invSysPoolOLS
## Model 2: invSysOLS
##   #Df  LogLik Df  Chisq Pr(>Chisq)
## 1   4 -881.10
## 2  31 -738.54 27 285.11  <2.2e-16 ***
## ---
## Signif. codes: 0 '***'0.001 '**'0.01 '*'0.05 '.'0.1 ' ' 1
lrtest( invSysPoolSUR, invSysSUR )
## Likelihood ratio test
##
```

```
## Model 1: invSysPoolSUR
## Model 2: invSysSUR
##   #Df LogLik Df  Chisq Pr(>Chisq)
## 1  58 -877.7
## 2  85 -728.6 27 298.19  <2.2e-16 ***
## ---
## Signif. codes:
## 0 '***'0.001 '**'0.01 '*'0.05 '.'0.1 ' '1
```

16 Conclusion

This chapter has demonstrated the use of the statistical software R (R Core Team, 2018) to explore and prepare panel data, to analyze these data with several frequently used panel data estimators, and to conduct various statistical tests for panel data and panel data estimators. Further and more detailed information can be found in various sources, e.g., Henningsen and Hamann (2007), Croissant and Millo (2008), or Croissant and Millo (2018).

Acknowledgments

We thank the authors of the *plm* package, Yves Croissant, Giovanni Millo, and Kevin Tappe, for assistance with the software and helpful discussions.

References

Amemiya, T., 1971. The estimation of the variances in a variance-components model. International Economic Review 12 (1), 13.

Arellano, M., Bond, S., 1991. Some tests of specification for panel data: Monte Carlo evidence and an application to employment equations. Review of Economic Studies 58, 277–297.

Balestra, P., Nerlove, M., 1966. Pooling cross section and time series data in the estimation of a dynamic model: the demand for natural gas. Econometrica 34 (3), 585–612.

Balestra, P., Varadharajan-Krishnakumar, J., 1987. Full information estimations of a system of simultaneous equations with error component structure. Econometric Theory 3 (2), 223–246.

Baltagi, B.H., 1981. Simultaneous equations with error components. Journal of Econometrics 17 (2), 189–200.

Baltagi, B.H., 2008. Econometric analysis of panel data, 4th ed. Wiley.

Baltagi, B.H., Li, Q., 1995. Testing AR(1) against MA(1) disturbances in an error component model. Journal of Econometrics 68 (1), 133–151.

Beck, N., Katz, J.N., 1995. What to do (and not to do) with time-series cross-section data. American Political Science Review 89 (3), 634–647.

Breusch, T., Ward, M.B., Nguyen, H.T.M., Kompas, T., 2011a. Fevd: Just iv or just mistaken? Political Analysis 19 (2), 165–169.

Breusch, T., Ward, M.B., Nguyen, H.T.M., Kompas, T., 2011b. On the fixed-effects vector decomposition. Political Analysis 19, 123–134.

Croissant, Y., Millo, G., 2008. Panel data econometrics in R: the plm package. Journal of Statistical Software 27 (2), 1–43.

Croissant, Y., Millo, G., 2015. Panel data econometrics in R: The plm package. Vignette to version 1.5-12 of the R package "plm".
Croissant, Y., Millo, G., 2018. Panel data econometrics with R. John Wiley & Sons Ltd.
Greene, W., 2011. Fixed effects vector decomposition: a magical solution to the problem of time-invariant variables in fixed effects models? Political Analysis 19, 135–146.
Grunfeld, Y., 1958. The determinants of corporate investment. PhD thesisUniversity of Chicago.
Henningsen, A., Hamann, J.D., 2007. Systemfit: a package for estimating systems of simultaneous equations in R. Journal of Statistical Software 23 (4), 1–40.
Hsiao, C., 2007. Panel data analysis–advantages and challenges. TEST 16 (1), 1–22.
Im, K.S., Pesaran, H.M., Shin, Y., 2003. Testing for unit roots in heterogeneous panels. Journal of Econometrics 115 (1), 53–74.
Kleiber, C., Zeileis, A., 2008. Applied econometrics with R. Springer, New York.
Kleiber, C., Zeileis, A., 2010. The Grunfeld data at 50. The German Economic Review 11 (4), 404–417.
Kleiber, C., Zeileis, A., 2015. Applied econometrics with R: Package vignette and errata. Vignette to version 1.2–4 of the R package "AER".
Nerlove, M., 1971. Further evidence on the estimation of dynamic economic relations from a time-series of cross-sections. Econometrica 39, 359–382.
Pesaran, M.H., 2006. Estimation and inference in large heterogeneous panels with a multifactor error structure. Econometrica 74 (4), 967–1012.
Pesaran, M.H., 2007. A simple panel unit root test in the presence of cross-section dependence. Journal of Applied Econometrics 22 (2), 265–312.
Pesaran, M.H., Smith, R., 1995. Estimating long-run relationships from dynamic heterogeneous panels. Journal of Econometrics 68 (1), 79–113.
Plümper, T., Troeger, V., 2011. Fixed-effects vector decomposition: properties, reliability, and instruments. Political Analysis 19, 147–164.
R Core Team, 2018. R: A language and environment for statistical computing. R Foundation for Statistical Computing, Vienna, Austria.
Swamy, P.A.V.B., Arora, S.S., 1972. The exact finite sample properties of the estimators of coefficients in the error components regression models. Econometrica 40, 261–275.
Wallace, T.D., Hussain, A., 1969. The use of error components models in combining cross-section and time-series data. Econometrica 37, 55–72.
Wooldridge, J.M., 2010. Econometric analysis of cross section and panel data, 2nd ed. MIT Press.

Index

Note: Page numbers followed by *t* indicate tables, and *np* indicate footnotes.

D

E

Q

R

V

W

Printed in the United States
By Bookmasters